Music and Poetry
in the Early Tudor Court

Music & Poetry
in the Early Tudor Court

JOHN STEVENS

*Fellow of Magdalene College, Cambridge
and University Lecturer in English*

UNIVERSITY OF NEBRASKA PRESS · Lincoln

Publishers on the Plains

UNP

Copyright © by John Stevens 1961

Library of Congress Catalog Number 63-8426

No part of this book in excess of 250 words
may be reproduced in any form without permission
in writing from the publisher

TO MY FAMILY

especially the younger members of it
without whose help
this book would have been
finished much sooner

Foreword

JOHN STEVENS's *Music and Poetry in the Early Tudor Court* will introduce the reader to a subject less known than it should be, will stimulate him to study the subject further, and will provide the complete bibliographical material and much of the textual material needed for such study. The book can well be used in conjunction with the author's *Music at the Court of Henry VIII*, No. XVIII in the series *Musica Brittannica,* a complete musical edition of the manuscript which Stevens calls "Henry VIII's." The musically trained reader can then make his own judgment on the pieces discussed in the present work and, most interestingly, can compare his own experience of them with the experience of the author as recorded in the epilogue, "The Song-books Revisited."

While only the musically trained can absorb the full value of this book, there is much that can be understood and reflected upon by the student of poetry who has no more than a general acquaintance with music. By intelligent use of the work he can make himself at home with a body of lyric poetry that has been grossly neglected in comparison with the definitely medieval poetry preceeding it and the later Elizabethan poetry which follows and admittedly excels it. Appendix A presents the verbal texts of some 113 lyrics, many previously available only in learned periodicals, a collection that would be a valuable book in itself. Appendix B indexes and locates more than 375 songs of the period 1480 to 1550, and provides a better bibliography of the subject than has been presented before. Two other appendixes, a list of manuscript and early printed sources, and a comprehensive list of related books and articles, complete the armory which the book provides for the serious student.

Some readers may be surprised to learn how many of all the early Tudor songs which survive are contained in the three manuscripts, the "Ritson," the "Fayrfax," and "Henry VIII's," which form the basis of the author's exposition in the main part of the book. Had these three been caught in the draught of destruction of manuscripts, it would have been hard indeed to write the history of the lyric in this period. Even with these three substantial collections available, the student will find some aspects of the subject for which the evidence is limited to one or two pieces, for instance, the tournament as a theme in the fine carol "My soverayne lorde" or the adaptation of the old holly-and-ivy motif, usually associated with Christmas, to the uses of love poetry in the carol attributed to the King himself, "As the holy grouth grene." That such songs were unique in their own time is highly unlikely, for one of the most characteristic features of this song-poetry is its adherence to convention and lack of concern for great originality. In fact, as Mr. Stevens points out in an important part of his exposition, the whole conception of poetry as expressive of personal emotion is one that is hardly to be found at this time and place.

Unlike the poetry of some later periods which is an utterance—an outgoing of the poet's thought or dream toward any who choose to read or hear most of these songs are directed at a particular audience, and there is more concern in them for this relationship than for their relationship to their authors and composers. That so many are anonymous is one sign of this. Even the love songs appear to be written to be overheard by an audience at the same time as they are heard by the lady to whom they are addressed. They are written from a pose, an assumption of character by the poet, which is as perennial as its products tend to be ephemeral. It is the pose which persists from the time of medieval courtly love to eighteenth- and nineteenth-century *vers de société*, a perpetual gallantry which exaggerates both the joy found in a welcoming response by the lady and the sighs and pains of an unrequited passion. Mr. Stevens aptly connects this pose with "the game of love," that set of observances which formalizes and makes public the expression of amorous or at least flirtatious preferences and which underlies not merely the song of this volume but dancing, masking, playing at dice or cards, putting and solving verbal puzzles and riddles, and sometimes going a-hunting or a-maying, not altogether in earnest.

This pose, maintained charmingly in some pieces and clumsily in others, is one of the reflections of the occasional character of early Tudor lyric verse which Dr. Stevens convincingly shows and contrasts with the expressive quality of later poetry. There are two principal kinds of occasional verse: that *for* an occasion and that *on* an occasion. Romantic and twentieth-century poetry has been highly productive of the latter type but has tended to scorn the work produced for performance as part of a scheduled event. There was no such scorn in the early sixteenth century: a social gathering, especially a banquet or dinner, was then a worthy occasion for poetry and song which noticed the setting in its text. The late medieval carol for Christmas or for a specific saint's day is a conspicuous example.

There are more than a few pieces of verse in this book which clearly imply performance in a special social setting, even though we cannot always define it exactly. The song with the burden

> From stormy wyndis and grevous wethir,
> Good Lord, preserve the Estrige Fether!

is obviously prepared for some setting-forth of a Prince of Wales; it is less obvious what we are to picture as the "rude play" of the piece assigned to Henry VIII which begins "Lusti yough shuld us ensue" and ends:

> Now unto God thys prayer we make,
> That this rude play may well be take,
> And that we may ower fauttes amend
> An blysse opteyne at ower last end.

or the game of finding partners implied in

> Who shall have my fayre lady?
> Who but I, who but I, who but I
> Undir the levys grene?

Most of the love songs, even the slightest, carry the implication of a refined audience made up of both sexes and familiar with the idiom of courtly love. If we remember that Chaucer's audience was of this kind and undoubtedly heard his fabliaux as well as the *Knight's Tale* and *Troilus,* we are the less surprised at finding pieces as hearty and free as "Manerly Margery, milk and ale," probably by Skelton, or

> And I war a maydyn
> As many one ys,
> For all the golde in England
> I wold not do amysse,

or the *pastourelle*-like

> Hey troly loly lo!
> Mayde, whether go you?
> I go to the medowe to mylke my cow.

The presence of such themes reminds us that while much courtly song may have been unknown to simple country people without education, every courtier, like every cleric, would have known, probably from childhood, many of the songs current among such people and, unless hopelessly affected, would have continued to relish them. All too few of such popular songs are preserved, but it cannot be doubted that a very great number circulated without being written down or printed. Their music as well as their words was influential, and Dr. Stevens treats of these relations in his chapters "Popular Songs" and "Music and the Early Tudor Lyric II."

What may be called the "practical" questions of musicology are boldly faced and given answers as positive as a careful and conservative interpretation of the evidence will justify. The status, the activities, and the rewards of music-makers are examined. Though the chapter "Professional Musicians" is not the comprehensive work on minstrels that is needed, it does make more clear than many writings have done the essential character of medieval minstrels as instrumentalists, socially quite separate from the singing men and choir boys who were called upon for vocal entertainment as well as for vocal worship. It also notes the

Foreword

change in the application of the word that comes at about 1500, so that "minstrel" comes to mean a vagabond performer rather than a retainer of a court or noble household as in older days. There are many illuminating citations from contemporary documents, some well known, others little used.

The critical reader will be pleased with Dr. Stevens's concern for the nature of the evidence which he cites and with his policy of not straining that evidence in an attempt to make it prove more than it should, though he is far from deficient in imagination or originality. This is a book that throws a steady light upon a segment of English musical and poetical history which has not before been fully illuminated.

RICHARD LEIGHTON GREENE

Wesleyan University
Middletown, Connecticut

Contents

Contents

Acknowledgments

I wish to thank – the Royal Musical Association and Stainer and Bell Ltd for permission to quote from my edition of BM Add. MS 31922 (*Henry VIII's MS*) which will appear shortly as *Music at the Court of Henry VIII*, Musica Britannica, vol. xviii; the Royal Musical Association also for permission to reprint in chapter 11 some material published in 'Carols and Court-songs of the Early Tudor Period', *Proceedings of the Royal Musical Association*, vol. lxxvii (1951); Mme Nanie Bridgman, and Professor Rossell Hope Robbins for giving me copies of their unpublished dissertations; Dr Arthur Brown, Dr A. W. Byler, Dr David Lumsden, and Mrs Catharine K. Miller for allowing me to use and quote from their unpublished dissertations; the Trustees of the British Museum for permission to publish in full the words of three early Tudor song-books, BM Add. MSS 5465, 5665 and 31922, and to reproduce as frontispiece f.27 of Add. MS 5465.

From among many who have kindly read this book in whole or in part I single out a few who have earned my special gratitude: Mr Thurston Dart greatly helped me, particularly in the early stages, with many musical problems; Dr Macdonald Emslie and Mrs H. M. Shire have regularly allowed me to discuss words-and-music with them over many years; Mr Arthur Sale kindly undertook to read the whole book in typescript and offered many comments on substance and on detail; Professor Bruce Dickins advised me about the Literary Text and its notes; Mr A. Bonvalot, Mr Thurston Dart, Rev. A. J. Denney, Dr A. I. Doyle, Dr Macdonald Emslie, Mr P. J. Frankis, Dr R. L. Greene, Dr F. Ll. Harrison, Dr D. Lumsden, Professor R. H. Robbins, Mrs H. M. Shire and Mr Denis Stevens helped me with contributions or corrections to Appendix B, Index of Selected Songs; Miss Carolyn de Sainte Croix, Mr John Daw and the Revd Michael Waters rendered invaluable help in the correction of proofs.

Finally, a particular debt to Mr H. A. Mason will be obvious to anyone who has read his book, *Humanism and Poetry in the Early Tudor Period*, 1959. But my sense of indebtedness is of much longer standing than this, for it was under the stimulus of his encouragement and scepticism that I first began to see the problems of music and poetry in a proper social context.

Author's Note

The letter H or F or R in brackets followed by a number, e.g. [H50], refers the reader to Appendix A, Literary Text, where he will find the texts of all the poems in the three main song-books together with information about musical settings, related poems, etc. Small numbers in the text refer to the Notes at the end of each chapter.

The word 'Song' followed by a number, refers the reader to Appendix B, Index of Selected Songs, where he will find a note about the source of the song and its musical setting (if any), and other references.

Works cited more than once are described throughout the footnotes either by abbreviation, or by author's name, or by name and short title. The Reference List (Appendix D) provides an alphabetical key and gives fuller details. Thus, 'Huizinga, 56' refers to J. Huizinga, *The Waning of the Middle Ages* (Eng. edn, 1924), p. 56; GGB no. 60 refers to *A Compendious Book of Godly and Spiritual Songs, commonly known as 'The Gude and Godlie Ballatis'*, ed. Mitchell, A. F., Scottish Text Society, 1897, no. 60.

Throughout the quotations in this book I have standardized the old spellings and orthography in accordance with the principles described on p. 337, second paragraph.

ERRATA

p. 11: example 2, bar 2, stave 3, G: insert dot after this minim.

p. 40: bar 43, B: editorial natural required.

p. 48: bar 6, stave 2, F: insert dot after this crotchet.

p. 99: bar 11, stave 1, B: editorial flat required; stave 2, flat: should be on third line.

p. 126: example 1, treble clefs: emend to modern tenor clefs.

The Song-books

There is something deeply fascinating and stirring to the imagination in handling an old book or manuscript. Like any household stuff, a book is the thing itself. This cover was held, these pages were turned, these lines were read by people long dead who have left perhaps scarcely a name behind them. At moments like these we feel the closeness of the living past, its solid physical presence. And yet, this sense of 'the warm reality' quickly and inevitably gives way to a sense of bafflement. What fascinated us by its closeness now fascinates by its mystery. How little we know, how little we can ever know, of those who wrote and read and owned the very books that lie in front of us. We should like to see – or, better, hear – them reading to themselves or one another, observe their gestures, accent and intonation, enter into their world of feeling and thought, into their certainties and doubts. But, because we cannot now challenge *them*, their familiar and well-loved 'objects' present a perpetual challenge to *us*. We are enticed so warmly, possession seems so near; and then a veil descends.

Those who are interested in early Tudor music and poetry can, if they go to the British Museum, have in front of them at one time three manuscripts which must for them exercise this peculiar kind of fascination to a marked degree. They are the three song-books which contain virtually all that is known of early Tudor song. They are not big; the largest is only $12'' \times 8\frac{1}{4}''$. The original binding of one is still preserved. It would be worth a great deal to have seen even one of them in use – to have seen the singers or instrumentalists, to have sensed the spirit of the occasion, the style of the performance and its reception. Unfortunately, the books can only stimulate, they cannot satisfy our imaginations.

The stimulus towards the exercise of historical imagination is powerfully, if crudely, aroused by a fairly typical song in the latest of the three song-books, the one which I shall refer to as *Henry VIII's MS*. Alongside the verses of a carol, 'Whilles lyve or breth is in my brest' [H50],[1] are faintly scribbled the words – 'henr[y?] henr[y?]'. The following two verses will give the tone of the poem:

> My soverayne lorde for my poure sake
> Six coursys at the ryng dyd make,
> Of which four tymes he dyd it take;
> Wherfor my hart I hym beqwest,
> And of all other for to love best
> My soverayne lorde.

> My soverayne lord of pusant pure
> As the chefteyne of a waryowere,
> With spere and swerd at the barryoure
> As hardy with the hardyest,
> He provith hymselfe that I sey best,
> My soverayne lorde. [H50]

The song clearly reflects the 'correct' chivalric attitude for a woman to adopt whose knight is jousting for her at a tournament. The 'soverayne lord', verse 3 makes clear, must be Henry VIII himself; the composer of the music was William Cornish; the author of the words is unknown.

A host of questions spring to mind: were the words written by a lady of the court? If not, by whom? Was her love part of real life? or was it a courtly game, fitting for a season of jousts and tournaments? Why was Cornish chosen to set the poem to music? And why did he, or the author, choose carol-form? Why is no music provided for the verses (only the burden – that is, the external refrain – is set)? What singers and instrumentalists performed it? On what occasions? Ceremonially, during a tournament, or privately, for the king's pleasure? Finally, who scribbled 'henr', and what, if anything, does it signify? This list does not by any means exhaust the interesting questions that might be asked; it does not include all the questions, for instance, about the relationship between the words and the music. But it shows, I hope, the extent, the many-sidedness and the fascination of the problems involved in an understanding of early Tudor music and poetry. This book was written to provide some aids towards an understanding. It must start, where its author's enquiry started, with an examination of the song-books themselves.

The Song-books

I

The easiest of the three surviving song-books to describe is the one known as *The Fayrfax Manuscript,* or *The Fayrfax Book.*[2] It is well written in a professional hand on vellum, the only paper pages having been inserted to fill in gaps where vellum pages have been lost. The Fayrfax of the title is the celebrated composer, Dr Robert Fayrfax, organist of St Albans and Gentleman of the Chapel Royal. Whether the skilled hand was Fayrfax's own, remains an open question. His arms, however, are on the title-page [f.1]; and in 1618 the book was in the possession of the Fairfax family – Charles Fairfax was then its owner.[3] So there must have been some special connection between the book and the composer. Further than this one cannot go. The connection is marked again, on the title-page, by a list of the songs ascribed to Fayrfax in the volume. No other composer is honoured in this way.

Turning over three blank pages, we come to one [f.1v] faced on the other side by some keyboard music [f.2]. This appears to be a fragment of a two-part piece for organ, copied out sometime in the middle of the six-teenth century. 'There is no traceable plain-song basis: the music seems to be a free fantasia or voluntary, and no immediate comparison with any contemporary keyboard work is suggested by it.'[4] The English songs follow consecutively, starting with: C[*antus*]*i:*

> The farther I go, the more behynde;
> The more behynde, the nere my wayes ende; [ff.2v–3]

and ending with *C.li,* an incomplete song:

> *Burden:* In a slumbir late as I was . . .
> *Verse:* 'Beholde', he saide, 'my creature'. [ff.122v–124]

There is no manuscript index and therefore no means of knowing what has been lost at the end of the book. But from the manuscript numbers we can tell that only two out of the fifty-one songs are altogether lost. Seven, unfortunately, are incomplete.

The composers are chiefly those of Henry VII's court and include Newark, who was Master of the Children of the Chapel Royal from 1493 to 1509, and his predecessor, Gilbert Banastir (d. 1487). The 'Browne' of this manuscript is usually identified with John Browne of the Eton Choirbook, although the Christian name is not given here.[4a] Fayrfax himself, 'William Cornish Junior', and Richard Davy lived well

3

into the next reign but figure prominently in the manuscript. A younger generation of court-composers, however, is not represented – Lloyd ('Flude'), Farthing, Cooper, Pygott. Topical songs refer to the union of the two houses of Lancaster and York, and to the welfare of Prince Arthur, Henry VII's eldest son who died in 1502. The natural conclusion is that the song-book was written about the year 1500 or earlier, and reflects the taste of the court under the first Tudor king. The songs, which are all in English, are of three kinds: two- and three-part songs on themes of courtly love; others, designed on a larger scale, treating of the Passion and Christ's Pleading with Man; lastly, topical, satirical and humorous songs.

The next song-book, *Henry VIII's MS*,[5] forms, as it were, a sequel to *The Fayrfax MS*. It is a manuscript of about the same size, beautifully written on vellum, with some initial letters decorated in blue, red and gold. It was, it seems, intimately connected with the life of the court. The convenient title must not be allowed to beg the question of its original ownership; it is meant chiefly to acknowledge the fact that thirty-one pieces in the manuscript bear the superscription, 'the kynge h.viij'. Numerically speaking, Henry VIII (with thirty-four compositions) is by far the most important composer of the book; the others, mostly musicians of his chapel, contributed as follows: Cornish, twelve pieces; Farthing, seven; Lloyd and Dr Cooper, three each; Fayrfax, two; and so on. One in every three pieces is anonymous.

Most of the items are English part-songs on courtly and chivalric themes, such as 'Adew, adew, my hartis lust' [H16] and 'Departure is my chef payne' [H56]. There are also, as in *The Fayrfax MS*, songs on topical and political themes: 'Englond, be glad' [H96] probably refers to Henry VIII's 'personal' invasion of France, in 1513, complete with the Chapel Royal and many members of the Household; 'Adew, adew, le company' [H68] must have been written for the festivities which celebrated the birth of a prince on New Year's Day, 1511. A likely dating for the manuscript on these and other grounds is *c.* 1515.

Henry VIII's MS differs from *The Fayrfax MS* in containing various other items besides English part-songs: foreign songs, instrumental pieces, musical puzzles, and rounds. The foreign songs include compositions by Hayne von Ghizeghem (*fl.* 1470), Agricola (*fl.* 1480) and Isaak (*fl.* 1480), as well as such 'international song-hits' as *En frolyk weson* [H4] and *Fors solemant* [H99]. One group of pieces without words is generally thought to be for instruments, probably recorders or mixed instruments, since consorts of viols were, apparently, not fashionable in the English court until after about 1525. Another group of pieces without words consists of puzzle-canons: usually all the parts of the piece are written out except one which has to be reconstructed from a Latin riddle ('canon', here, simply means 'rule'). The rounds, lastly, are among the earliest, as well as the most complicated, English examples of the form; all except one are for three voices – perhaps, as the following verse suggests, for three soloists:

> Now let us syng this rownd all thre;
> Sent George, graunt hym the victory! [H97]

This manuscript differs again from *The Fayrfax MS* in having no religious songs. The moving Lullaby carol, *Quid petis, o fily* [H105], is the single exception.

Both *The Fayrfax* and *Henry VIII's MSS* belong indisputably to the court circle. They contain music by the principal composers of the royal chapel; the words of the songs point to a courtly audience. In some way, yet to be defined, they had their place in the life of the early Tudor court. However, the third principal source of secular songs is of a rather different kind: it has little obvious connection with the court; it was compiled over a number of years by a number of different scribes; its composers are either anonymous, or, if named, difficult to trace; and it contains, besides secular songs, forty-four carols, four Latin masses, many Latin motets and an English canticle. It is usually called *Ritson's MS* after its nineteenth-century owner.[6]

Ritson's MS comes from the West Country. As a book it is less tidy than the other two; at least eight different hands have been traced in it. The principal composer of the carols, all written in the traditional style of the medieval carol, was Richard Smert, rector for thirty years of the village of Plymtree (near Exeter), with which his name is linked in the manuscript itself. A fair-sized choir of skilled men and boys is required by the music; and the presence of ceremonial carols suggests elaborate ritual. Perhaps Exeter Cathedral was its place of origin. At a first glance, therefore, it might seem that the manuscript had changed hands before the secular songs were entered in it. There are two groups of these: some love-songs in the style of the Burgundian chanson of the fifteenth century, and a later group of songs similar to various English songs of *The Fayrfax* and *Henry VIII's MSS*. But a varied repertoire does not necessarily imply varied ownership. Every large ecclesiastical establishment had its social responsibilities, such as entertaining princes and bishops, as well as its own internal needs. The convent of Glastonbury, for example, retained a harper, an 'idiot', and a 'French poet'.[7] *Ritson's MS* contains just the items one would expect in the general-purpose song-book of a provincial establishment – songs suitable for many kinds of civil and religious occasions. The book may have been augmented, revised and kept in use over a period of fifty years (1470–1520?). Perhaps it passed at the end of this period into private hands, for there are signs in the last pieces of less professional composers and scribes at work.

The comparative intricacy of musical notation even in the early sixteenth century makes it possible to detect amateurishness with some certainty. Compared with contemporary church-music or with the secular songs of fifty years earlier, the songs of these three Tudor books are elementary. But they are certainly the work of professionals. There are signs (not only in puzzle-canons) that notation was still not, and was not intended to be, a means of easy communication. The three song-books show considerable variety. *Henry VIII's MS*, the latest, is also the simplest, because the songs are mostly in duple time; the carols of *Ritson's MS*, by contrast, written in black and red full notes, employ the standard devices of late medieval notation, designed for writing music in triple time – 'coloration', 'ligatures', 'alteration', 'imperfection', and so forth. *The Fayrfax MS* occupies a midway position.

The carols of *Ritson's MS* are also set out in a different way from the other songs. They are presented in what seems to us the natural way of presenting part-music – that is, in score. The voices are one above the other – *triplex* (treble), *medius* and *tenor* – though the chording, the vertical alignment, is very rough-and-ready. One traditional feature of this style of writing is that only the bottom part, the tenor, has the words. The arrangement of the other two books is that known as 'choir-book' arrangement. Each part is presented separately, not in separate books, as later became the fashion, but all on a single 'opening' of the manuscript. If the song is a long one, all the performers turn the page together. The large church manuscripts of this period and of this design meet the needs of a group of singers standing together at a lectern. Hence, the name 'choir-book'. *The Fayrfax* and *Henry VIII's MSS* copy the prevailing mode but are only large enough for a small group of singers.

Many poems of the period are known only from these musical manuscripts, and reconstruction of the original text is not always easy. Songs written in score present the words once only; so also do rounds. But they at least spare an editor the trouble and difficulty of deciding between different readings in the different voices of a part-song.

These three song-books contain between them almost the whole repertory of early Tudor songs – that is, of poems set to music. There exist a few complete songs besides, such as those at Ripon and Wells; and a few fragments, mostly in Oxford and Cambridge libraries. Two more substantial books contain only single parts of songs. The printed *Twenty Songs* (1530), of which the bass only survives, is useless from the musical point of view. A manuscript from the Royal collection at the British Museum, which has tenor and counter-tenor parts to various songs, has at least some good 'tunes' (tenors) in it, such as the famous 'Westron wynde'. There is a further bass-part in the Public Record Office, but of slightly later date.[8]

Other musical manuscripts survive, of course, from the early Tudor period, and some of them have a direct bearing on this study. But they are of a different kind and do not contain vernacular songs. Among them are the huge ecclesiastical 'choir-books' just referred to, such as the *Caius Choirbook*, which stands a yard high; anthologies of keyboard pieces, mostly for organ but some having secular titles, like 'Fortune unkynde' [Song 95];[9] and musical treatises containing puzzles in musical notation. No English lute-music can be dated earlier than 1540; and there are no instrumental tutors or books of that sort. The great majority of surviving musical manuscripts and printed books are liturgical service-books and contain only plain-song to Latin words.[10]

The surviving English songs, then, are few. But poems (verses without music) can be numbered in their hundreds. The three main song-books contain only a small fraction of the total corpus of early Tudor verse. 'Literary' manuscripts are far more numerous than 'musical' ones. This is not a peculiarity of the early Tudor period. It applies throughout the fourteenth and fifteenth centuries. Perhaps the most striking fact about the native sources of English medieval music is their paucity: important manuscripts, except of plain-song, can be numbered on the fingers. But nearly a hundred Middle English poems survive in ten or more versions: *Piers Plowman, The Canterbury Tales* and *Confessio Amantis* are each represented by fifty or more; and Richard Rolle's celebrated poem, *The Prick of Conscience*, has over a hundred sources.[11] Allowing for the greater difficulty of writing music, these figures nevertheless prove that the public for verse was incomparably larger than that for written music. Nor has poetry been exceptionally favoured by the ravages of time.

Treatises on alchemy, grammar, medicine, theology, cooking, outdoor sports, etc., quite clutter the pages of late medieval manuscripts.[12] Music was in this respect the Cinderella of the arts and sciences. There are several reasons for this scarcity – among them, the vandalism of the Reformers. (A minor vandal has even scarred the carols of St Thomas of Canterbury in *Ritson's MS*.[13]) But one very likely explanation is that musical manuscripts were never numerous. Written part-music, I hope to show later, was until Elizabethan times a luxury only to be afforded by the few.[14]

The 'literary' sources of the early Tudor lyric are a fascinating study in themselves. Lyrics are found in many unexpected places, such as the work-books of lawyers, students and priests, in household account-books and on the backs of legal documents. But the two richest sources are commonplace-books, of private individuals or of communities, and poetical anthologies of various kinds. The best-known example of the first is perhaps the book owned by Richard Hill, servant to Mr Wyngar, an alderman of London – it contains, besides poetry, treatises on good behaviour, puzzles, riddles and recipes.[15] The second, poetical anthologies, are of many kinds – from collections of minstrels' songs to the courtly anthologies of noble families.[16] The total number of surviving poems must run into thousands, compared with the mere 200 or so found with music. Nevertheless, although only a small proportion of the whole, the poems of our three chief song-books, *The Fayrfax, Henry VIII's* and *Ritson's MSS*, illustrate most kinds of lyric which survive. There is no great dissimilarity, in fact, between the 'literary' lyrics and those with musical settings. A description, therefore, of the poems in the three song-books will serve as a synopsis of the extant 'secular' lyric as a whole, though it will have a bias towards the courtly.

II

There is really no such a genre as early Tudor lyric – for two reasons. First, because the description 'early Tudor' applied to poetry is scarcely a term of distinction at all. At least, in the absence of the known writings of courtiers ten or twenty years senior to Wyatt, it seems so. To take a few examples, the heyday of the medieval carol was the late fifteenth and early sixteenth century; the carol died, not at the accession of Henry VII but at the Reformation. Again, the Lydgate tradition in poetry flourishes still unchecked in Hawes's *Pastime of Pleasure* and in Barclay's *Eclogues*. To describe the categories of early Tudor lyric is to find oneself describing the medieval lyric. The second reason is the misleading nature of the word 'lyric'. If the period 'early Tudor' is not an entity, so neither is the genre 'lyric', defined as it usually has been defined. The Romantic conception of a lyric as the record of an intimate personal experience ('a lyric is simply a perception') has no validity in this period; and the term itself is an anachronism.[17]

A conventional survey of early Tudor lyrics, based on the customary classification by subject-matter, does not ultimately prove of much use for understanding them. The songs, as later chapters will show, were much more closely bound up with the life of their times than the purely 'literary' lyrics of later ages. But as a preliminary it will be helpful to say briefly what they are about, what styles they are written in, and with what music they are generally found.

There are three main groups of poems. The first is on religious and moral subjects, including most of the carols from *Ritson's MS*, the very different carols of *The Fayrfax MS*, and one song from *Henry VIII's MS* [H105]. From a literary, as well as from a musical point of view, *Ritson's MS* stands at the end of a tradition – the tradition of the medieval carol. In origin a popular song with a strong didactic flavour, the carol, even in the late fifteenth century, still retained its basic form of alternating burden and verse, its qualities of vigour and directness and its traditional subjects.[18] These subjects are summarized by the Latin rubrics of *Ritson's MS* – *de Maria, in die nativitatis, de innocentibus, de Johanne*, and so on. A typical carol is

> Nowell, nowell, nowell, nowell,
> Tydynges gode Y thyngke to telle.

> 1. The borys hede that we bryng here
> Betokeneth a Prince withowte pere
> Ys born this day to bye us dere;
> Nowell, nowelle. [*MC*, 79]

Among the others are one or two poems which had been in circulation for years, as, for example, 'Pray for us, thou prince of pesse' [*MC*, 13, 106, 115].

By contrast, the religious verse of *The Fayrfax MS* deals almost entirely with the Passion; a typical poem is Lydgate's 'Uppon the cross nailid I was for the', in which Christ pleads with man.

Uppon the cross nailid I was for the,
 Suffyrd deth to pay thi rawnsum;
Forsake thi syn, man, for the love of me;
 Be repentant; make playne confession.
 To contryte hartes I do remission;
Be not dispayryd, for I am not vengeable;
 Gayne gostly enmys thynk on my passion;
 Whi art thou froward, syth I am mercyable? [F34]

There are two points of similarity between *Ritson's MS* and *The Fayrfax MS* in their religious verse. Composers of both manuscripts chose to set either old poems (Lydgate died about 1450) or, at least, poems in a traditional style; and they preferred to have them in carol-form – the composer Sheryngham, or someone else, has added a burden to the poem quoted above and thus made it into a carol:

 'A, gentill Jhesu!'
 Who is that that dothe me call?
 'I, a synner that offt doth fall' . . . [F34]

Despite the identity of form, no two traditional styles could be more unlike. The 'popular' carol, rough and direct, combines a warmth of human feeling with a matter-of-factness and a sense of wonder; the 'clerical' carol, complex and often ornate, dwells with dramatic intensity on the physical and spiritual anguish of the Passion. The one didactic but gay; the other solemnly devotional.

This marked contrast in tone and treatment is found also in the music of the two kinds of carol. A certain style of rhythm and melody is what makes the traditional 'popular' carol a natural whole, a unity, and distinguishes it from other music of the time. The carols are all in triple metre with a strong 'punch' to it; this punch is accentuated by the werds. As each phrase progresses there is an increase of rhythmical activity – the top part, especially, becomes florid, with many syncopations and cross-rhythms, but it is still full of energy and life. The melodies are 'paradoxically both smooth and angular'.[19] If the 'directness' of these carols is conveyed by the rhythms, their 'warmth' lies in the simple harmonies – major thirds and sixths, for the most part, moving in parallel, the medieval equivalent of modern 'close-harmony'.

To call this kind of carol 'popular', as I have, is perhaps to court misunderstanding. The *words* belong to the popular tradition; but the music,

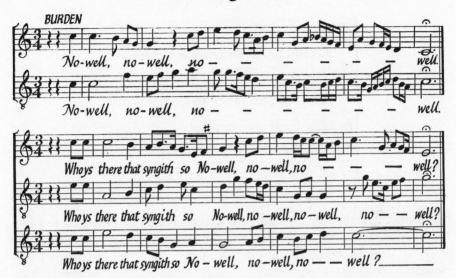

though based perhaps on an earlier style of song intended for the 'lewd' and unlettered, shows that sophisticated composers have been at work. These carols were written by professional composers for professional musicians.

A few bars from 'Woffully araid' [F33], a spacious and solemn carol of the Passion from *The Fayrfax MS*, will show the composer in a quite different world.

Whereas the music of the popular carol was 'objective', extroverted, full of vigorous patterns, the music of this clerical carol is inward-turning, flexible and dramatic. The composer of the first seemed to use the words as percussive counters with little regard for their sense or individual sound; the composer of the second concentrates closely on illustrating the poem in

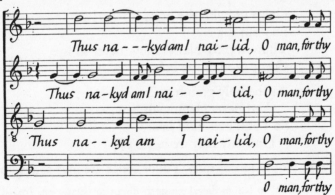

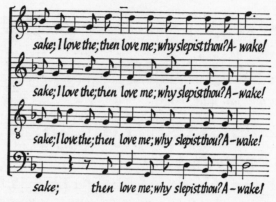

sake; I love the; then love me; why slepist thou? A-wake!

sake; I love the; then love me; why slepist thou? A-wake!

sake; I love the; then love me; why slepist thou? A-wake!

sake;   then love me; why slepist thou? A-wake!

his music. The rhythms, against a background of duple metre, are flexible and varied, according to the needs of the text; an extremely rare melodic leap is used to point the word 'nailid' in bar 4; the harmonies are sonorous (e.g. bar 5 onwards) or bleak (bars 1–2) as required. The music, like the poetry, is distinguished by the dramatic imitation of natural detail.*

The medieval English carol, granted its strict form, can be a song on any subject from the fear of death to the unpredictability of women. The use of carol-form is confined in *The Fayrfax MS* to the devotional songs just described, and in *Ritson's MS* to 'Christmas carols' and a few songs giving moral counsel:

> In every state, in every degree
> The mene ys the beste, as semeth me. [*MC*, 85]

But in *Henry VIII's MS* we also find love-songs cast into the mould of the carol:

> Grene growith the holy,
> So doth the ive,
> Thow wynter blastys blow never so hye,
> Grene growth the holy.

> 1. As the holy grouth grene
>   And never chaungyth hew,
> So I am, ever hath bene,
>   Unto my lady trew. [H33]

The greater proportion of early Tudor songs are love-songs, 'balads of

* 'Naturalism' in late medieval music is discussed below, pp. 102–4.

fervent amyte', though only a handful are in carol-form. To the general reader, approaching backwards from the sixteenth century, some of the verse may seem fresh and genuine compared with the stylized poetic conceits of the Elizabethans. But this freshness is largely an illusion; most of the poems are narrow and ridden with convention. They elaborate the time-honoured chivalric themes of absence, desertion, 'departure', service. 'Absens of you causeth me to sygh and complayne' is the tone of dozens. The lover goes through all the stages recommended by the 'rules' of courtly love 'from wo to wele, and aftir out of joie'.

There are two main styles of love-lyric – one found chiefly in *The Fayrfax MS*, the other in *Henry VIII's MS*. *The Fayrfax MS* opens with more than two dozen lyrics in the traditional post-Chaucerian style. Many of them are in the rhyme-royal stanza (*ababbcc*) introduced, we suppose, into England from France by Chaucer, who used it in *Troilus and Criseyde* and elsewhere. It is one of the 'consecrated' forms of courtly verse:

> Alas, it is I that wote nott what to say,
> For why I stond as he that is abusyd;
> Ther as I trusted I was late cast away,
> And no cause gevyn to be so refusyd;
> But pite it is that trust shulde be mysusyd
> Other by colour or by fals semblaunce;
> Wher that is usyd can be no surance. [F14]

Often found in association with this stanza is the ornate style usually called 'aureate'. The concept of style as ornament, which they learnt from treatises on rhetoric, encouraged poets to cultivate an elaborately verbose and heavily patterned Latinate style. They have a lot to answer for. Their *splendida verborum venustas* makes uncommonly dull reading. The worst excesses, however, were avoided by the poets of *The Fayrfax MS*; the song just quoted is entirely free from 'inkhorn' terms. But phrases in other songs like 'Most clere of colour and rote of stedfastness' [F20] betray their origin. 'Aureate' language is not confined, of course, to serious amorous verse. Many religious poems have been decked out in it. And it is sometimes used with satirical intent, as in 'Jhoone is sike' [F40]:

> Her contynaunce with her lynyacion,
> To hym that wolde of such recreacion
> That God hath ordent in his first formacion,
> Myght wel be calde an conjuracion.

13

The Song-books

Henry VIII's MS contains love-lyrics of a different kind. They are written within the same great tradition – courtly love; but they are much lighter in tone:

> Adew, adew, my hartis lust!
> Adew, my joy and my solace!
> Wyth dowbyl sorow complayn I must
> Untyl I dye, alas, alas! [H16]

This and similar lyrics are written in 'common measure' – that is, in four-line stanzas with 3 or 4 stresses to each line. The style is one which Caxton would have called 'plain', rather than 'curious' on the one hand, or 'rude' on the other. This plain style, from which rhythmic conciseness has pruned most traces of 'rhetoric and colour crafty', is still courtly. Wyatt's slighter lyrics, his 'balets', as we can conveniently call them, are written in this style:

> Now must I lerne to lyve at rest
> And weyne me of my wyll,
> For I repent where I was prest
> My fansy to fullfyll.[20]

Most balets not in 'common metre' are written in stanzas of short lines like the following poem.

> Margaret meke
> Whom I now seke
> Ther is non lyke
> I dare well say,
> So manerly
> So curtesly
> So prately
> She delis allway. [F39]

The two kinds are often closely related: this example, for instance, could be written out in 'common measure' with internal rhyme. It is not easy to decide what made such verse-forms so popular – whether the influence of popular song, or of French *lai* and *descort*, or of medieval treatises on rhetoric with their elaborate expositions of stanzaic pattern. Probably any single explanation would be misleading.

Although the medieval Latin element is generally strong, the metre of a piece like 'My love sche morneth for me' must owe much to popular tradition. Like several love-songs in all three song-books, it is clearly an adaptation of a popular song, in words and in music:

> My love sche morneth
> For me, for me,
> My love sche morneth for me.
> Alas, pour hart,
> Sen we depart
> Morne ye no more for me for me.
>
> In lovys daunce
> Syth that oure chaunce
> Of absence nedes must be,
> My love, I say,
> Your love do way
> And morne no more for me. [H25]

'Grene growith the holy' [H33], quoted above, is certainly another courtly version of a popular song. In the second half of *The Fayrfax MS*, after the carols of the Passion, are several songs of a similar kind, though more elaborately worked out. Here is the burden of 'Jhoone is sike':

> Jhoone is sike and ill at ease;
> I am full sory for Jhoon's disease.
> Alak, good Jhoane, what may you please?
> I shal bere the cost, be swete Sent Denys! [F40]

Finally, the love-lyrics of *Henry VIII's MS* have these special characteristics: they include a number of poems of chivalric doctrine:

> Whoso that wyll for grace sew,
> Hys entent must nedys be trew, [H79]

and some hunting poems with an erotic meaning, spoken in the person of the 'foster', with inevitable play on words and phrases – 'dere', 'hart', 'make a sute', and so on.

This distinction between two main kinds of love-lyric has been made chiefly on grounds of literary style. Those written in the vernacular 'high' style, as the rhetoricians would have called it, tend also to use stately seven- and eight-line stanzas. Those written in the 'middle' style fall, as a rule, into 'common measures' of four lines, or into long, complicated stanzas composed mostly of short lines. There is one other important difference between them, purely as poems – in rhythm.

It used to be common form among critics to describe fifteenth-century ornate verse as 'blundering' or 'broken-backed', because it cannot be made to scan as the verse of Spenser or Keats will scan. The reasons they gave were the unsettled state of the language, competing dialects and changing pronunciation, and an inability on the part of poets to grasp the secret of the iambic line. In the last few years opinion has changed.[21] It was, surely, absurd to imagine that courtly versifiers lacked even the elementary craft shown in popular 'metrical' poetry like the carol. Wyatt's balets scan quite effortlessly; the different rhythms encountered in his translated sonnets and psalms cannot, then, be the result of incompetence. Mere common sense suggests that courtly writers in the 'high' Chaucerian style were not trying to write iambics. Their line, whether one calls it 'the fifteenth-century heroic', or the 'pausing', or the 'balanced' line, is modelled rather on the old alliterative poetry. Their *un*-alliterative metre with the same rhythms, or rather 'balanced stresses', is the staple of 'serious' poetry during the early Tudor period. It is certainly the staple metre of *The Fayrfax MS*:

> Yowre counturfetyng   With doubyll delyng
> Avaylyth nothyng;   And wote ye why?
> For ye with your faynyng   Hath such a demyng
> To make a belevyng: Nay, nay, hardely! [F18]

Often the pause in the middle of the line, essential to correct reading, is marked in literary manuscripts by a short stroke, the *virga*. The difference between the movement of this verse and the movement of lighter courtly and of popular verse needs no comment.

It is not fanciful, I think, to see the artistic ideals of the two types of love-poetry reflected in the musical settings. The conception of style as ornament dominates the settings of *The Fayrfax MS*; the mock-simplicity of the courtly balet has its counterpart in the musical trifles of *Henry VIII's MS*. The ornate musical settings are best studied first in the two-part love-songs which open *The Fayrfax MS*. 'My wofull hart' by Sheryngham [F5] is a straightforward example. Each phrase of the words is introduced with a point of musical 'imitation', one syllable to a note. When all the syllables have been used, the music becomes more lively; shorter, quicker notes, often in triplets, dance the phrase along until a cadence is reached. Then the process begins again with the next phrase. The phrases cor-

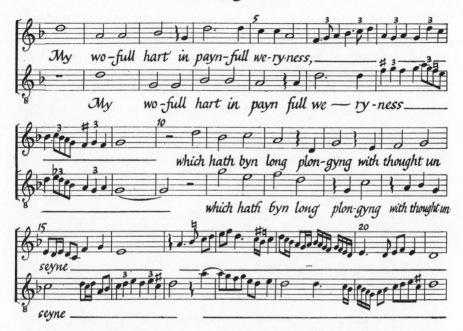

respond closely to the balanced units, the half-lines, described above. The long wordless roulades are chiefly ornamental. This is the counterpart in music to the ornate 'figures', the 'rethoryke' and 'termes eloquent' of courtly verse, and perhaps also to visual decorations, the 'garnishing' of a jousting-house with 'six dozen silk roses' or of a banqueting-hall with piles of otiose gold plate. In the early Tudor court, where everything was 'garnished', music was clearly no exception.

The three-part songs which follow in *The Fayrfax MS* develop the same style, which seems, incidentally, to be a purely English invention. In them, moreover, poetic form is treated in the same stereotyped way. Nothing illustrates better than this the continuance into the early Tudor period of the typically medieval, 'abstract' approach to the setting of words to music. The songs are in two sections. Each section may end with the same roulade making musical 'rhyme'. The break invariably comes after the fourth line of the words, irrespective of the sense. 'So fer I trow from remedy' [F4] is typical. The meaning runs on,

> So mekyll dred, so lytyll trust
> Cannot be well for to be wisht:

but in the song as set by Newark there is a roulade twelve bars long, and the most important cadence of the piece, between the words 'trust' and 'cannot'.

The slightness of the love-songs in *Henry VIII's MS* is in striking contrast. A charming trifle is the king's own setting of 'Wherto shuld I expresse?' [H47]. The main voice, perhaps older than the setting (there is no way of telling), is the tenor (Voice II), though in effect the top part seems to bear the 'tune'; the phrases are balanced; the harmonies simple and 'progressive'; the musical metre overrides the rhythm of the words. The song takes its shape entirely from the shape of the poem – there are no extensive roulades, no repetition of words, no counterpoint between melodies.

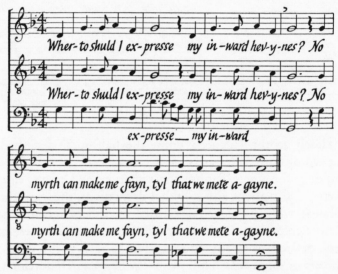

The main technical difference between this sort of song and the elaborate love-songs of *The Fayrfax MS* is between a chordal and a contrapuntal style; the one is 'vertically', the other 'horizontally', conceived; the one is, in essence, a harmonized tune, the other, an interweaving of extended melodies. Described in terms of their likely effect on the listener, the songs of *Henry VIII's MS* are pointed and concise and calculated to make an immediate impression; the songs of *The Fayrfax MS* have their own brilliance, but it is the brilliance of elaboration. The first are musical epigrams with a gay or pompous or sometimes a melancholy twist; the second are more like short formal tales where artificial pattern is all-important.

To make clear the basic differences between the two main types of religious song and the two main types of love-song, it has been necessary to over-simplify the issues, to choose examples of music and verse fitting neatly into the fixed categories, and to analyse only those features of them which were of central importance. But no living art can be pigeon-holed so neatly. To illustrate a third and last category of early Tudor lyric, political and topical songs, I choose an example which is less convenient to handle and more true to life:

> This day day dawes,
> This gentill day day dawes,
> This gentill day dawes,
> > And I must home gone.

1. In a glorius garden grene
   Sawe I syttyng a comly quene
   Among the flouris that fressh byn.
   She gaderd a floure and set betwene;
   > The lyly-whighte rose methought I sawe,
   > The lyly-whighte rose methought I sawe,
   > > And ever she sang:

> This day day dawes ... [F45]

Songs written like this one for obvious social occasions are very varied. There are some in both court song-books. *Henry VIII's MS* contains trivia, such as 'Adew, adew, le company' [H68], which scarcely even rhymes or scans, and rather more substantial songs like the near-carol, 'Englond, be glad' [H96]. *The Fayrfax MS* has, as usual, the most ambitious and weighty examples of the genre. 'This day dawes', written perhaps in honour of the white rose, Queen Elizabeth of York, the wife of Henry VII, combines many traditions into an attractive whole. On the literary side, it inherits the favourite poetic form of the fifteenth century – the carol; it interweaves the central symbols of courtly love (lovely lady sits in rose-garden) with a popular *aubade* 'This day day dawes' [F45] (known from numerous references), and makes the whole serve a political purpose. On the musical side, what must surely be the original popular tune is used for the burden, in free counterpoint; this tune is freely 'coloured' with varied rhythms, some at cross-purposes with the metre, some reminiscent of more popular carols (bass 2–3); the burden ends with a long, formal roulade, but the roulades of the verse (tripping triplet passages) are fitted, unusually, with words; finally, imitative and chordal elements are skilfully balanced, and the texture skilfully varied.

To sum up, the songs of these music-books can be divided into three main groups. The first consists mainly of the carols in *Ritson's MS*: the 'rude' popular verses receive vigorous metrical setting in highly stylized music built up from an old-fashioned popular mode. The second group includes the traditional amorous and political songs and long Passion carols from *The Fayrfax MS*: here, ornate, 'rhetorical' verse is set to contrapuntal music, sometimes elaborately patterned, sometimes dramatic and expressive, in the 'English' manner; passages in which natural accent is treated with some respect merge into florid, ornamental roulades. The third group is made up of the chordal songs of *Henry VIII's* and *Ritson's MSS*: courtly 'balets', some of the slightest kind, are set in a concise and balanced chordal style.

III

The fear of over-simplification is not the only thing which has made these paragraphs of description difficult to write. There is another and particular reason that makes it less easy to talk about a song by Cornish or Fayrfax than about a song by Schubert or Benjamin Britten. A work by any nine-teenth- or twentieth-century composer is a comparatively fixed thing: there is little doubt what the symbols stand for in terms of sound, and how the song should be performed. No recent composer would countenance a performer who introduced radical alterations into his finished work. Songs of the Middle Ages and Renaissance were never crystallized in this fashion. The performer had more rights and duties, the composer fewer; and musical notation was both more complicated and less explicit than it is today.

To begin with, no medieval composition had what might be called an 'authentic shape'; a song was what musicians could make of it when they needed it. Chansons from *Henry VIII's MS* like *De tous bien plane* [H36] and *Jay pryse amours* [H37] survive in innumerable different versions, having one, two, or more voices in common as the case may be. The king's own (so-called) composition, *Gentil prince de renom* [H45], was published abroad when he was only a boy; the third voice alone is Henry's contribution. Two songs in *The Fayrfax MS* bear the direction *bassus ad placitum* – we should say, *ad lib.* [F18, F26]. And in all three song-books there are songs from which parts could be omitted if the occasion demanded: that quoted on p. 18 is one.

Apart from the choice between written variations, there were other ways in which performers could show their individual taste and suit their individual needs – in the choice of ornaments, in the choice of instruments, and in the fitting of the words to the notes. At a time when the very essence of composition was to decorate one melody with another, im-provised ornaments simply carried the process further. It is admittedly hard to imagine additions to the *cantus florizatus* of many songs in *The Fayrfax MS*. Ingenuity could go no further (see the example on p. 17). But some of the ostensibly plain 'balets' of *Henry VIII's MS* may well have received 'tuppence-coloured' performance. The instrumental pieces of the manuscript suggest the sort of thing:

[H66]

The use of instruments is, in accordance with tradition, never specified in the three song-books. The presence or absence of words is a most un-reliable guide in deciding what should be sung and what played. The musical style is equally misleading; what seems 'instrumental' to us may have seemed thoroughly 'vocal' to medieval singers. In choosing instru-ments and deciding when they are to double, replace or accompany the voices it is important to realize afresh the anachronism of searching for the one 'authentic' version of a song. A 'broken consort' of mixed instruments seems to accord with medieval practice.

Lastly, the freedom which marks the use of ornaments and the choice of instruments applies also to the fitting of the words to the notes. In this period we have to distinguish all the time between what is actually written down and what was intended. This applies, as we have seen, to per-formance in general; but particularly to the problem of the text. Not all scribes were equally careless, not all musical styles allow equal ambiguity. But, generally speaking, the words of a song were underlaid in an in-creasingly ambiguous fashion throughout the fifteenth century. The problem is a difficult one. It is from a theorist of the mid-sixteenth century that the clearest explanation comes. Adriaan Petit Coclicus writes that his master, the great Josquin des Pres, went on to the next step in musical training, 'if he saw that his pupils were as far advanced as possible in singing . . . and knew how to fit the text to the music'.[22] It was, beyond doubt, the singer's task to fit the words to the notes, and not the scribe's.

To examine this aspect of the songs is to see again at first hand the fascination of music as a craft, and its complete and assured independence. To analyse poetry in the rhetorical tradition is to have similar reflections – poets are extremely conscious of the techniques at their command, and ingenious in using them. This is interesting; but, if it were all, it would not prevent most of us from shutting up our books in boredom. We need to see more in the arts of a past age than merely 'interesting' examples of this or that technique. These early Tudor songs are, I think, more. They are at least a living part of social history. When we are in a position to answer some of the questions raised in this Introduction about one song only, we shall have a livelier sense of what it felt like to live in the English court around the year 1500. We shall find, I hope, that we 'understand' the songs better. (At this stage I have been able to do little more than to take them to pieces as if they were puzzles.) The slight attempts so far made at critical judgment – 'trivial', 'ornamental', 'pompous', and the rest – will then have to stand to the test; and terms of praise or blame will begin to have some more precise meaning. Conversely, if knowledge of court-life enables us to interpret the songs, the songs surely will help us to interpret that life. For they are living history – documents that can almost be made to live and breathe again. And if some of the songs are found also to transcend the actualities of history and to have a virtue which strikes home to us as, say, some of Chaucer's poems or the Passion plays of the York Cycle do, we shall be doubly rewarded.

NOTES TO INTRODUCTION

1. [H50] invites the reader to turn to App. A, 'Literary Text' (p. 405), where he will find as item 50 in *Henry VIII's MS* the words of the song in full, information about the musical setting(s), and a note of concordances, if any.
2. BM Add. MS 5465; further described, App. A, p. 351 below.
3. Dom Anselm Hughes, 'An Introduction to Fayrfax', *Musica Disciplina*, vi (1952); and *DNB*, vi. 1002.
4. Denis Stevens, *Commentary*, 13.
4a. A 'William Browne' was a Gentleman of the Chapel Royal at the same time as Fayrfax and Cornish. The problem is discussed by F. Ll. Harrison, ed. *The Eton Choirbook: I*, Musica Britannica, x (1956), pp. xvi–xvii.
5. BM Add. MS 31922; described at length in *Music at the Court of Henry VIII*, Musica Britannica, xviii (1961), 'Introduction', and in App. A, p. 386 below. The entire musical contents of the MS are there printed. (The edition is hereinafter referred to as *MCH8*.)
6. BM Add. MS 5665; further described, App. A, p. 338. The carols of the MS are printed in *Mediaeval Carols*, Musica Britannica, iv (2nd edn, 1958), hereinafter referred to as *MC*.

7. *L&P*, iii, pt 1, no. 1285, 'Accounts of the Duke of Buckingham', 30 April, 2 May, 1508. See also C. E. Woodruff's article on the Priory of Christchurch, Canterbury, in *Archaeologia Cantiana*, liii (1941).

8. For details of these secondary sources see App. C, 'List of Sources'. The royal manuscript is BM Roy. MSS, App. 58 (App. C, 72); the PRO bass-part is SP 1/246 (ibid., 68).

9. [Song 95] refers to App. B, 'Index of Selected Songs', no. 95, where further details are given.

10. 'Choir-books': Gonville and Caius MS 667. Keyboard collections: Roy. MSS, App. 56 (App. C, 71); Add. MS 30513, *The Mulliner Book* (ibid., 7). Notational exercises: Cambridge, Trinity College MS O.38. Earliest English lute-pieces: Roy. MSS, App. 58 (ibid., 72); Stowe 389 (ibid., 84); Folger 448. 16 (ibid., 46).

11. See *Index MEV*, App. V, 'Preservation of Texts'.

12. See, especially, H. S. Bennett, 'Science and Information in English Writings of the 15th Century', *MLR*, xxxix (1944).

13. See *MC*, nos 96, 109.

14. See ch. 12, pp. 283-7 below.

15. Oxford, Balliol MS 354 (see App. C, 18).

16. e.g. Cambridge, St John's MS S.54 and BM Add. MS 17942, *The Devonshire MS* (App. C, 5).

17. The earliest uses recorded in the *OED* are 1581, Sidney; 1586, W. Webbe; and 1589 (probably written earlier), Puttenham. On the use of the new word, see p. 70 below.

18. R. L. Greene, *The Early English Carols* (1935), p. xxiii, defines the late medieval carol as 'a song on any subject, composed of uniform stanzas, and provided with a burden'.

19. Bukofzer, *Studies*, 168.

20. *Wyatt* (ed. Muir), no. 129.

21. See especially D. W. Harding, 'The Rhythmical Intention in Wyatt's Poetry', *Scrutiny*, xiv (1946-7); C. S. Lewis, 'Heroic Line'.

22. Quoted by A. Smijers, 'Josquin des Pres', *PRMA*, liii (1926/7), 105, from *Compendium Musices* (Nuremberg, 1552).

PART ONE

Music and Poetry

CHAPTER I

The Problem – Assumptions and Distinctions

One of the persistent problems confronting the reader of an early English lyric is, simply, this: was this poem intended to be sung? and, if so, how did music affect the writing, and how should it affect the reading, of the poem? In this and the following chapters I shall try to answer these questions – by questioning the notion of a traditional artistic union; by assessing the importance of an indubitable union in popular song; by examining late medieval ideas about music and about poetry, and the impact of the Reformation upon them; and, lastly, by using the social information about music and musicians, fully set out in Part Three, to interpret the evidence of the songbooks themselves.

I

It may be useful, first, to assemble some previous critical opinions on the subject of words-for-music and to discuss the possible reasons for their contradictions and confusions. Thus, J. M. Gibbon described the pre-Elizabethan lyric as 'amphibious – living half in words and half in music'; John Erskine, on the other hand, characterized Wyatt's most typical work as 'songs meant to be enjoyed without music, as opposed to the practical song'.[1] The weight of recent critical opinion has fallen on the former side of the scale. To take the case of Wyatt alone, Sir Edmund Chambers has given his authority to the following statement: 'music . . . lent its aid; and the simpler patterns of melody devised by the lutenists made a suitable background for lyrical utterance'.[2] So also Miss A. K. Foxwell: 'a large proportion of Wyatt's songs have refrains. His musical ear and his skill on the lute account for this partiality'.[3] Or Wyatt's latest editor, Professor Kenneth Muir: 'Many of Wyatt's poems mention the accompanying lute . . . and many others were clearly written to be sung'.[4]

Music and Poetry

Here Professor Muir is at variance with Professor C. S. Lewis, the former holding that 'Wyatt's songs, though written to be sung, need no such assistance', the latter, that in early Tudor lyric 'richness and deliciousness would be supplied by the air and the lute and are therefore not wanted in the words'.[5] Finally I quote Dr Bruce Pattison, who has recently contributed the only serious modern study of words and music in the sixteenth century: 'the lyrics of Henry VIII and his contemporaries were intended for performance in the Court circle'; 'the incentive to lyrical composition was primarily the prospect of musical performance'.[6]

Some of the opinions I have quoted rest on a widespread but mistaken notion about the nature of the problem. A very simple answer is sometimes given to such questions as I have raised. It is that we have only to look at a poem to see whether the poet intended it for music or not. A series of verse-tests is invoked and 'evidence' is produced (or assumed) that the words were from the beginning intended for music. 'Melody is latent in the flowing movement of [the verse]', says one writer; 'Has anything been written in English more singable . . . ?' asks another.[7] In the context of the surviving songs of the late Middle Ages such remarks are strictly non-sense. Where tunes alone are concerned these verse-tests can be useful; but about the possibility of a setting in parts they tell us practically nothing.

The recurrence of fixed forms is sometimes regarded as a good test. Certainly it is true that the composer liked a shape (a carol or a rhyme-royal stanza) round which to build his composition; but it does not follow that the presence in the song repertory of such shapes implies the expectation of musical setting on the poet's part. After all, the musician is not demanding something that the poet can himself do without. Poets also need forms.

Simplicity of mood, also, is often named as a *sine qua non* of musical setting, and therefore as presumptive 'evidence' of musical intentions. The poems in the song-books have, indeed, simplicity of mood. But so has the early Tudor lyric as a whole. The complexity of even the most ornate and 'literary' lyrics is more apparent than real, and on analysis resolves itself into a trick of gorgeous vocabulary, a playing with words not thoughts. Special musical circumstances cannot be pleaded to account for the almost universal absence of subtle sequences of thought or feeling. Moreover, with the songs of *The Fayrfax MS* before us, it is impossible to hold that mere elaboration of diction was a deterrent to musicians. Richard Davy's treatment of the text, 'Nowe the lawe is led be clere conciens'

The Problem – Assumptions and Distinctions

[F10], quoted on p. 356, suggests that composers were sympathetic even to far-fetched rhetorical devices; his setting points the double meaning of the poem.

Other internal tests, thought to indicate poetry intended for musical treatment, are: strophic construction, the presence of refrains, and rhythmic lilt. As for the first, the apparently careless handling of the text of the carols in *Ritson's MS* and, equally, the carefully written-out second and third verses with music in *The Fayrfax MS* show that in the more elaborate musical styles the singer could easily make the necessary small adjustments if the words did not exactly fit. With regard to the chordal settings of *Henry VIII's MS* the point admittedly has some force: violent irregularities in a light balet would make it unsuitable for strophic setting. The test is, otherwise, fruitless.

The presence of refrains is an even more dubious clue, for neither the early Tudor composer, nor his Elizabethan successor, regarded the literary text as sacrosanct, and if he required a refrain, he would invent it. Furthermore, he was quite capable of introducing a purely musical refrain without any warrant for it in the text.

There remains the rhythmic 'lilt', sometimes said to be a special mark of words-for-music. Again, the song-books show that 'lilt', by which is generally meant a balanced iambic metre, was not a quality which the musicians of the time either demanded, or, if they met it, gave much attention to. There are one or two exceptions in *Henry VIII's MS*, as for example, 'My love sche morneth' [H25] and 'Trolly lolly' [H39], but the lilt of similar metres elsewhere is not reflected at all in the music.

II

Verse-tests, then, in relation to musical settings are at worst thoroughly misleading, and at best inconclusive. No valid opinions about medieval lyric can rest upon them. Other authoritative opinions quoted earlier are based on a hazy and, I think, uncritical picture of the state of music in early Tudor times, for which musical historians are largely to blame. J. M. Gibbon is only voicing a commonplace when he says, 'the English in Tudor days were undoubtedly a musical race';[8] Dr Pfatteicher, in his more detailed appraisement, also has general support: 'the musicianship of Redford's ecclesiastical superiors is not as surprising as it might otherwise be, when one bears in mind *the widespreadness of musical culture* in Redford's day. Even the king . . . occupied himself with music.'[9] I would

29

feel some presumption in challenging such long-standing beliefs, were it not a necessary stage in the inquiry.

By way of clearing the ground I propose to list some assumptions which are commonly made when people talk about words-and-music in the sixteenth century, and to suggest appropriate new distinctions which might replace them.

A prolific source of error arises, I am sure, from a failure to distinguish between the musical culture of the Elizabethan period and that of the reigns of Henry VII and VIII. Gibbon's generalization about 'the English in Tudor times' is one of dozens which have done duty for the 120 years between the battle of Bosworth and the death of Elizabeth. It is necessary, rather, to accord the early Tudor period separate treatment, and to allow, at any rate until the opposite has been proved, that the practice of music may have been less widespread and perhaps of a different character. When does the 'Elizabethan' in music begin?

Another source of confusion has been the uncritical grouping of different social classes together. Is it true that 'music made by the King's Musicians was a natural part of the domestic life of the people'?[10] Or, that city merchants and country squires formed for the lyric a musical public of the same calibre as the gentlemen and ladies of the court? Moreover, a further distinction has to be made between the music and poetry of amateurs and that of professionals; another, between what an amateur was trying to do then and what he tries to do today; another, between the social standing of a courtier-poet and that of a royal singing-man.

The third assumption is one, of course, that in its crudest form no intelligent person could ever have adopted – namely, that all early Tudor art-music is of one kind. Nevertheless, the almost exclusive attention given by some critics to one particular branch of music, usually solo-song with lute-accompaniment, does reflect not only our scanty knowledge of the music of the time, but also a readiness to believe that the picture is simpler than it is. Music in the late Middle Ages was immensely diverse, and its secular manifestations ranged from elaborate concerted music, in which many instruments and voices took part, to solo pieces for virginals and organ.

A closely related misunderstanding concerns the actual musical treatment a poem could receive. Lute-song has ousted other instrumental and vocal settings from the imagination of critics: 'lutenists were encouraged to come from Italy, and with the lute flowers the lyric'.[11] The song-books themselves show how important, numerous and varied other settings might

The Problem – Assumptions and Distinctions

be. And, above all, one must discriminate between every kind of *art-setting*, written music in parts, and the mere addition of a single vocal line, a *tune*. It is hardly an exaggeration to say that it is the absence of this fundamental distinction which renders most generalizations about music and poetry in this period to some degree misleading. A setting must be the work of a trained musician; but anyone could learn a popular tune by rote. Moreover, a setting is generally added *after* the event, whereas a tune often exists *before* words are written to go with it. The two operations are as different as can be.*

Hasty assumptions about 'singable' poems and about the state of music in the courts of Henry VII and VIII account for a great deal of what seems to me mistaken talk on the subject of music and the lyric. But other long-standing assumptions have also nurtured error. For instance, the historical belief in a traditional, changeless union of the two arts, music and poetry, from the troubadours up to the Elizabethans; and the 'philosophical' assumption that there is something essentially natural, right and true about the conception we have inherited of an 'expressive' relationship between words and music.

In these pages I have made free, but I hope not unfair, use of selected generalizations from many previous writers. This somewhat ungracious act will have justified itself, if the reader has by this stage conceded the necessity of questioning the premises on which their generalizations are founded. We may turn now to a more constructive and rewarding part of the task.

NOTES TO CHAPTER I

1. Gibbon, introd., p. viii; J. Erskine, *The Elizabethan Lyric* (1903), 73.
2. Chambers, *Wyatt*, 99.
3. Foxwell, *Study*, 105.
4. *Wyatt* (ed. Muir), introd., p. xxix.
5. *Wyatt* (ed. Muir), p. xxvii; Lewis, *Sixteenth Century*, 222.
6. Pattison, 33, 34.
7. Moore, 105; R. Preston, 'Chaucer and the *Ballades Notées* of Guillaume de Machaut', *Speculum*, xxvi (1951), 620.

* This statement has eventually to be qualified (p. 132 below), but not until the basic distinction has been thoroughly enforced.

31

8. Gibbon, 25.
9. C. Pfatteicher, *John Redford* (1934), 12 (my italics).
10. Hayes, 10.
11. Gibbon, 25. See also *Wyatt*, introd., pp. xxvi–xxvii, where Professor Muir says of two vocal part-songs by Henry VIII and Cornish, that they 'require the accompaniment of the lute for their full effect'. They are not lute-music.

CHAPTER 2

The Tradition and the Divorce

What is the so-called 'traditional' union between music and poetry? Many people think of this union, as of other things of art, almost exclusively in terms of evolution. Time marches on; and, as it marches, the baby-talk between the two arts becomes the devoted friendship of medieval times. This in turn ripens into the perfect marriage of Elizabethan song. This analogy is misleading in the extreme. The relationship between words and notes underwent a series of changes, it is clear, during the last centuries of the Middle Ages; but the changes do not reflect a steady development.

I

A natural, unsophisticated, unselfconscious union between music and poetry occurs only in folk-song: the singer, it is well known, cannot remember his words without the tune, or his tune without the words. Other early relationships are, for the most part, utilitarian; they have some practical purpose. The origin of the *sequence* illustrates perfectly the marriage of convenience: words were introduced to help the singers memorize the long melodies on the last *a* of *alleluia*.[1] On the other hand, in the recitation of long poems the music was there to help the words to carry, as it is in the intoning of church prayers. In early songs for one voice the words may merely help to 'articulate' the music – that is, help to separate the notes. This is said to be true of the songs of St Godric, an illiterate hermit who lived in a cave in the north of England.[2]

Sometimes, in the twelfth and thirteenth centuries, the words have an even more important practical function in song. They do not merely articulate the music, or make it easy to memorize; they measure out the lengths of the notes. 'Modal rhythm', as it is called, was a system of making music mensural by means of words, at a time when musicians had no mensural symbols of their own. A dactyl, for instance, $— \cup \cup$, stood for ♩. ♪♪ . So, if the poem was in dactyls, the music had to follow this pattern and no other. Only slight variations were allowed. Monsieur Aubry's phrase is both accurate and memorable: 'the music of the troubadours is prosodised music'.[3]

Before the invention of proper symbols for long and short notes, words were a principal means of establishing the metre of a piece of music. This metrical relationship survived, a sort of musical coccyx, long after the physical need for it had ceased. We still find it in the robust rhythms of the fifteenth-century carol.[4] When the same old rhythmic patterns are used and the words fit these patterns, the *effect* is the same. The difference is that earlier the words establish the metre, but in later music they merely emphasize it. The main point is this: the music was in no way designed to mirror or express the meaning of the text. Quite otherwise; in this early period music needs words to make itself articulate, metre to give it rhythmical pattern, and a form to give it shape.

The thirteenth century was the last in which music and poetry and the dance, because they had grown up together and were still useful to each other, were naturally one and the same art.

> And after that they wenten in compas,
> Daunsynge aboute this flour an esy pas,
> And songen, as it were in carole-wyse,
> This balade, which that I shal yow devyse.[5]

From this time onward music is increasingly able to stand alone, as the popularity of such independent musical creations as the motet shows. Nothing illustrates better than the medieval motet the unemotional, detached way in which the union of words and notes was approached in the later Middle Ages. It was not that the words did not matter. The words, if religious, were a creative contribution to the great corpus of sacred texts. It was simply that, to judge from the music which survives, neither composer nor author was interested in an emotional connection between words and music. Intelligibility, let alone expressiveness, was quite a secondary concern, for the work was offered to God rather than directed at the congregation.

The most obvious symptom of this lack of interest is the widespread practice of combining different sets of words together in the same motet. Different texts are sung simultaneously throughout the piece. Thus, in one typical example: the tenor (the principal voice) sings the plain-song melody *Regnum mundi*, while the *motetus* ('word-voice') sings *Ad te, virgo, clamitans venio*, and the *triplum* ('treble' or 'third voice') sings *A vous, vierge*

The Tradition and the Divorce

de douçour.[6] In origin the polytextual motet, to use the technical word, is simply an application in polyphony of the time-honoured principle of troping, the insertion of material into the liturgy by way of commentary and interpretation.

The lack of emotional *connection* does not mean, of course, that there was no emotional *correspondence* between words and music. *Angelus ad virginem* is certainly different in tone from 'Worldes blis ne last no throwe', although it is easy for us to read more joy or gloom into the music than was perhaps intended.[7] The correspondence, however, was of the vaguest possible. Plain-song will be our safest measuring-rod, as it was surely their unconscious model. In early English songs, as in plain-song, author and composer are connected 'in parallel'; if the music expresses the text, it is because musician and poet are contemplating the same thing or taking part in the same action.

II

In the fourteenth century the natural and necessary union of music and poetry finally broke up. Poetry had become a branch of *ars rhetorica*; that is, it was concerned with style and stylistic devices to the exclusion of almost everything else. Music, too, was entering upon a phase of unparalleled complexity, in which abstruse systems of notation played a leading part.[8] It follows that the talented amateur, who in the troubadour period could set his own poems, was outreached. At this moment in the story of music and poetry it becomes vital to distinguish between musical settings in parts and mere melodies. Amateurs probably went on writing tunes throughout the fourteenth and fifteenth centuries. But a high degree of special skill was now required for the composition and notation of part-music. Looked at from the social angle, the distinction is also one between a tradition of art-music,* composed by professional choirmen for Church and Court, and a tradition of popular songs and dances in the hands of minstrels and amateurs unable for the most part either to write or to read music. Finally, from the point of view of words-and-music, the statement, 'this lyric was written for music', can from now on mean, equally well, two distinct things: either, 'this lyric was written to fit a tune already in

* The awkward but unavoidable terms, 'art-music', 'art-song', 'art-setting', are generally used in this book to denote the written musical compositions of professionals and trained amateurs. It is occasionally necessary to widen the term 'art-music' to include the highly skilled, craftsmanlike, but unwritten, contributions of the minstrels (professional instrumentalists). I hope the context will always make the meaning clear.

35

existence'; or, 'this lyric was written so as to be suitable for setting, later, to music in parts'.

The widening of the rift between polyphony and melody, between professional and amateur accomplishment, helps us to understand Chaucer's position better.[9] His references to music are general and untechnical; he shows little acquaintance with it either as a science or a craft. Music to him was, primarily, popular music. He saw it, in any case, as one of the interesting things that interesting people did, a personal qualification: the Squire, for instance, was not merely a good horseman, fencer and dancer; 'he koude songes make and wel endite'. Chaucer himself, as a writer of lyrics, belongs fairly clearly to the generation of Deschamps, for whom poetry (*musique naturele*) was superior to music (*musique artificiele*), though the two might still with advantage be combined. In brief, he was essentially, if not only, an artist with words for the words' sake.*

Despite the ever-increasing rift between the two courtly arts, throughout the Middle Ages musicians never ceased looking to poetry to provide them with the *forms* of their secular compositions. The important medieval fixed forms – *ballade, virelai, rondeau*, carol and the rest – were all poetic as well as musical forms. (In the fifteenth century, however, composers showed their growing independence even in this respect by elaborating and modifying poetical forms to suit their musical fancy.) Moreover, from the late fourteenth century onwards a new though tenuous link appears between the two arts. Musicians began again to exercise their minds on detailed connections between the words and the music: these connections were not, as previously, purely utilitarian, but took the form of attempts to represent natural detail in various ways, such as the following. There is, first, the stylized reproduction of natural sounds. In the Italian *caccia* ('chase'), noises of the hunt, the street and the market were imitated in sound. Secondly, the imitation in music of human speech produced 'natural accent' in a few fifteenth-century compositions, such as Dunstable's *Quam pulchra es?*, and in some of Ockeghem's songs. When the speech was passionate (for example, the phrase *O morte, O morte* in an Italian madrigal, *c.* 1400), then the musical effect was of strong declamation.[10] And, lastly, towards the end of the fifteenth century musicians started using the technique generally known as word-painting. Instead of merely imitating sounds in a stylized manner the composer makes his music symbolically representative of ideas or images in the text. Two kinds

* Moore, 107–, makes the useful additional points, that Chaucer is never described as a musician, and that no contemporary or fifteenth-century settings of his lyrics survive.

have to be distinguished: visual effects in the notation, intended for the eye of the learned performer; and truly musical effects appealing to the listener. Sometimes both are combined in one. Thus, in one song, on the word 'strained' (referring to Christ on the cross) long notes with pauses are introduced in every voice: the performer *sees* an elongated shape on the page in front of him; the listener *hears* a note stretched out.[11]

While the borrowing of poetical forms was very common in fourteenth- and fifteenth-century music, attempts at naturalism were not. But were there, it may be asked, no other links between music and poetry than these? Certainly the method of continuous emotional commentary on the sense and feeling of the words was very rare indeed, even abroad, before the sixteenth century. But although composers did not draw their music out of the text in this manner, as did the Elizabethans, they could not altogether disregard the words they set. On the contrary, they sometimes achieved an effect best described, perhaps, as 'musical paraphrase' – the music envelops the poetry like a cloud and seems to transmit the general mood of the words.

There are, of course, many different kinds of fifteenth-century music and different styles of word-setting to suit the different kinds. To speak only of English music, in the simpler pieces such as the carol, the words are fitted to the music in a strict, 'metrical' fashion; that is, the words are strait-jacketed into the metre of the music.[12] On the other hand, in long and elaborate compositions such as settings of the Mass, the words may be set in a very florid and free manner (sometimes the singers will vocalize on one syllable for minutes on end).[13] But whatever the style of word-setting, and whether or not the pervasive mood of the music mirrors that of the words, certain things are sure and predictable: little care will be given to the natural accent of the words; verbal phrases will not be repeated as in the later madrigal or the Handelian aria; and the detailed emotional con-notations of the words will be largely, or entirely, disregarded.

As often happens, the composers' frame of mind is faithfully reflected in the actual way the manuscripts are set out. In this period their negli-gence about the detail of the poems they set expressed itself in scribal care-lessness about the underlay; a general correspondence between phrase and phrase is all that can be expected. The exact underlay was by tradition the duty of the singer, one of his elementary 'skills'.[14] Furthermore, not only the underlay but also, it seems, the expressiveness was the singer's con-cern. One reason, perhaps, why so many medieval songs seem emotionally detached from the poems is that it was for the performer to be lively or lugubrious as the case might be.

To approach the early Tudor song-books from this background will be to see in them what they have – typical songs of their period with many up-to-date features. They will only appear as 'primitive madrigals' to those who insist that a close, 'expressive', mutually responsive link between words and music is a mark of all good songs. Nothing in the history of the changing relationship of music and poetry up to about the year 1500 suggests that composers or poets idealized the union of music and poetry. The early marriage of convenience was followed by the inevitable divorce. There are only slight signs in the fifteenth century that the alliance is being patched up again.

Meanwhile, on another level the union of music and poetry continued, as it had throughout the Middle Ages, comparatively undisturbed. In the realm of popular song the phrase 'words for music' has some meaning. But it is, we shall see, a very different kind of meaning; the realm has its own laws.

NOTES TO CHAPTER 2

1. Reese, *MMA*, 187–.
2. J. B. Trend, 'The First English Songs', *M&L*, ix (1928); Reese, 241; *HAM*, i, no. 23a.
3. P. Aubry, *Trouvères and Troubadours*, trs. Aveling (1914), especially ch. 1. More recently the rhythmic modes have been described by Reese, *MMA*, 206–, 272–; by W. Waite, *The Rhythm of Twelfth Century Polyphony* (1954); and by C. Parrish, *The Notation of Medieval Music* (1957). See also Apel, *Notation*, 228–.
4. See *MC*, especially the earlier ones in the collection.
5. Chaucer, Prologue (G) to *LGW*, line 199–.
6. ed. G. de Van, *Les Monuments de l'Ars Nova* (L'Oiseau Lyre, 1938).
7. *Angelus ad virginem*: ed. H. Gleason, *Examples of Music before 1400* (1946), 51; and see p. 40 below. 'Worldes blis': *HAM*, i, no. 23b.
8. See, for instance, the pieces ed. W. Apel, *French Secular Music of the Late 14th Century* (1950).
9. The most thorough discussion is by C. C. Olson, 'Chaucer and the Music of the Fourteenth Century', *Speculum*, xvi (1941), 64.

10. *Caccia*: see Reese, *MMA*, 364–. Dunstable's *Quam pulcra*: pr. *Cappella: Meisterwerke mittelalterlicher Musik*, ed. Besseler (1950–), i. 5. 'O morte': see musical supplement to F. Ghisi, 'Italian Ars-Nova Music', *Journal of Renaissance and Baroque Music*, i (1946), nos 3, 4. See also p. 102 below for 'natural accent' in early Tudor songs.

11. F35, 'Woffully araid'; contrast the setting of the same passage in F33. See also Lang, 190: Christ's family tree executed in notation.

12. See *MC*, *passim*, especially the earlier carols.

13. See, for example, the Mass, *O Quam Suavis*, ed. H. B. Collins, PMMS (1927).

14. See Introduction, p. 22 above.

CHAPTER 3

Popular Songs

One of the most delightful of all popular songs is that which 'hende Nicholas' sang in *The Miller's Tale*, 'so swetely that all the chambre rong', *Angelus ad Virginem*:[1]

1. Th'an-gel to the ver-gyn said, En-treng in-to her bou — re for drede of
3. Th'an-gel went the la-de fro; This wo-mons wombe with we — le __ Hit wax
5. Make joy, mo-dir of our Lord, that Cryst con-ceivedest cle — ne __ An-gels,

qua-kyng of this mayd, He said 'Hail', with gret ho-nou — r(e). 'Hail!' be thou
gret as o-der do, This bles-sid burth of he — le He was __
men and all this world, God pes and rest us lea — ne. Mar — y, thy

quene of mai-dyns mo, Lord of he-ven and erth al-so, Con — sayve thou
in her wome I wene The nom-bur ful of moneth is nine Heut he out
Son thou for us pray As ye beth ful of mer-cy ay And send us

schalt, and bere with-al __ the Lord of myght __ Hele of al __ mon-kyn. He will
yed ba-te-lis bed-to al __ the flok, Beryng on his shul-deris bloo The __
to, and so to do __ a-way our syn. And gef us helpe of the, He-ven

make the gate of he-ven bryght Mede-syne of all our syn.'
ho — ly cros that kene a knock Un-to our ded-ly foe.
blis we may __ dwel __ in Aff — tur thys out-law-ry.

Popular Songs

It is songs of this sort which show the need for a 'third estate' when we are talking of medieval music. *Angelus ad Virginem* is clearly neither folk-song nor art-song, but something in-between. The difference is easy to sense, not so easy to define. Among the relevant questions to ask must be the following: did the song exist in oral or written form? what was its origin? for what purpose, and for whom, was it made? was the subject a topical one? is the style of the words direct? has the tune an obvious catchiness?

I

The word 'popular', in relation to art, is a difficult one. It can be used to mean 'made *by* the people' – that is, popular in origin – or 'made *for* the people' – that is, adapted to their tastes, popular in aim.[1a] Or it can be simply a synonym for 'well-known' or 'well-liked'. In this chapter I shall use the term 'popular music' in a combination of the second and third senses, to mean 'music composed or adapted to meet the people's taste, and current amongst them'. 'People' in the present context means 'the nation at large', not merely 'the court circle'. This definition excludes, first, 'failed' popular songs: James Ryman, the Franciscan, wrote many songs, carols and hymns apparently to edify layfolk, but, perhaps because they were dull, they never caught on.[2] The definition also excludes part-songs such as 'Benedicite! Whate dremyd I?' [F12], well known at court but not, probably, outside it; and lastly folk-songs which, however they may have originated, are the common creative possession of many minds and are not consciously adapted to popular taste. The distinction between folk-song and popular song is an important one. Above all else, folk-song has qualities of music and poetry which seem quite unaffected by changing fashions in the two arts. It has, in short, timelessness.

> I leand my back unto an aik,
>   I thought it was a trusty tree;
> But first it bowd, and syne it brak,
>   Sae my true-love did lightly me.
>
> O waly, waly! but love be bony
>   A little time, while it is new;
> But when 'tis auld, it waxeth cauld,
>   And fades away like morning dew. . .

41

Music and Poetry

> But had I wist, before I kissed,
>   That love had been sae ill to win,
> I'd lockd my heart in a case of gold,
>   And pin'd it with a silver pin.[3]

Compared with these verses from 'Waly, waly', 'And I war a maydyn' [H101] has a limited and dated air. It is a popular song adapted in this version especially to courtly taste. The popular singer always has his eye on the audience.

> And I war a maydyn
>   As many one ys,
> For all the golde in England
>   I wold not do amysse.

> When I was a wanton wench
>   Of twelve yere of age,
> Thes cowrtyers with ther amorus
>   They kyndyld my corage.

> When I was come to
>   The age of fifteen yere,
> In all this lond, nowther fre nor bond,
>   Methought I had no pere.

Many popular songs have topical themes, besides a topical manner. 'Lilli-Burlero' was written as an anti-papist song in the late seventeenth century; and in Elizabethan times dozens of broadside ballads were published on political and religious matters. The abrupt, elliptical manner and the impersonal atmosphere of the folk-ballad give place in these broadsides to crude moralizing, foul abuse and sickly sentiment.

On the musical side the distinction is equally marked. With the melodic catchiness, or tunefulness, of *Angelus ad Virginem* may be compared the strange angularity of this melody for the folk-ballad, 'Edward':

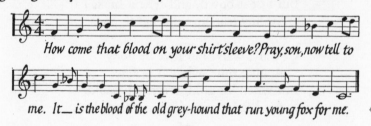

How come that blood on your shirt sleeve? Pray, son, now tell to

me. It is the blood of the old grey-hound that run young fox for me. [4]

Popular Songs

When art-music abandoned the modes and popular music followed suit, folk-singers clung still to the old style and preserved their 'unharmonic' melodies through the centuries. Their tunes are distinguished also by the use of certain rhythmical formulae, gapped scales, and formal variety.

Another characteristic of popular songs is that they are handed down partly in oral, partly in written tradition. This is true, for instance, of American dance-tunes today. Most people learn to sing them through hearing them. In the late Middle Ages *written* music played a very small part in musical life. The polyphonic songs which have survived in such elaborately written manuscripts as *Henry VIII's MS* and *The Fayrfax MS* were sung chiefly by professionals on courtly occasions; travelling minstrels and amateur musicians were reared in a different tradition. Skilled as many of them became in playing or singing, they did not necessarily *read* music, but improvised songs and dances on the tunes they already knew. *Votre trey dowce* [R17] appears to be that rare thing, a piece of written-out improvisation. It suggests the style of a whole lost world of improvised music.[5]

Angelus ad Virginem opened, and it can also sum up, these paragraphs of definition. The tune, not necessarily composed by a trained musician, though certainly written down by one, has a wonderful lilt and a fresh, major quality. It is unlike most folk-melodies and yet it is not art-music – or, rather, one should say, not *merely* art-music, because although the tune was used more than once as the basis of a setting in parts, it also existed in its own right. It was widely current: no less than three English and four foreign versions survive. *The Miller's Tale* shows that it was not confined to court circles. There are, besides, two Middle English translations of it. One appears as an alternative 'ditty' to a polyphonic version; the other, printed above and previously unnoticed, occurs in the attractive collection of carols and poems by the blind monk, John Audelay. This latter version has no music but fits the known tune and must have been written for it.[6] Can *Angelus ad Virginem* also be described as topical and 'popular in aim'? I think so. It belongs to the tradition of the English popular carol: it is one of many songs written on that favourite theme of medieval clerks, the Annunciation of the Blessed Virgin, and surely, like the carols, had the aim of teaching through delight.

II

During the fourteenth century, as has already been said, a vital change came over the relationship of words and music. The two arts, whose early association was utilitarian, inevitably began to develop separate and highly specialized techniques. Their usefulness to each other diminished, and with it their mutual interest. The problems of composing and notating polyphony absorbed musicians; the application of 'rhetoric' to the mother tongue absorbed poets.

What happened in the meantime to popular song? The answer is, very little. There was no revolution here. Music was still invented, though rarely written down, for the singing of poems; poems were still made to the patterns of existing tunes. An account of words-and-music in popular song at the turn of the fifteenth century need do little more than show how rich and ramifying these processes could be. Unfortunately, even this is not an easy task. For obvious reasons the surviving remains of early Tudor popular songs are tantalizingly small. They are also often difficult to interpret; the melody, for instance, of 'And I war a maydyn' [H101] has to be deduced from the five-part setting in *Henry VIII's MS*. In fact, apart from a few manuscript jottings, our knowledge of popular tunes is mainly derived from the use or abuse of them by courtly and clerical composers.

How is it known, then, that there *was* a large repertory of popular songs? Chiefly, from references to well-known songs in contemporary literature (e.g. *The Colkelbie Sow*) and in plays (e.g. *The Longer Thou Livest*, by Wager); from lists of titles (e.g. in *The Complaint of Scotland*) and from courtly or moral versions of the original poems (e.g. *The Gude and Godlie Ballatis*).[7] Popular songs were not only abundant but disseminated throughout all classes of society, including the court itself. Henry VIII and Sir Peter Carew are described as singing 'certeyne songes they called *fremen* songs, as namely "By the bancke as I lay", and "As I walked the wode so wylde"'. At the other end of the social scale there were those who 'had levere syttyn at the ale, iij mens songys to syngyn lowde, thanne toward the chyrche for to crowde'.[8]

Popular tunes were not always composed by different men from those who wrote poems or art-songs; nor is all the music which survives dressed up in a sophisticated garb. As an example of a manuscript jotting, one scribe has written before a carol:

Thys is the tewyn for the songe foloyng; yf so be that ye wyll have another tewyn, it may be at yowre plesur, for I have set alle the songe.[9]

Popular Songs

The last phrase suggests that the writer has composed a new tune for the carol, 'Nowell nowell: Tydyngis trew' [Song 220], which he offers rather diffidently in place of those which might have been chosen. Certainly the writing of mere melodies was not beneath the dignity of a trained composer. In popular song, it is true, new words are as often fitted to an old tune as to a new tune specially composed. Nevertheless, one air from a late fifteenth-century manuscript, *Nova nova* [Song 217], may have been composed directly, like 'Tidings true', for the words. Songs like these are the only written records of popular music in what may be called its original state. Not all monophonic fragments, it must be added, are necessarily popular songs. Sometimes a single line of music, as for example *Salve sancta parens* [Song 275] or *Psallimus cantantes* [Song 267], may be a treble or a tenor part taken out of a part-song.[10]

It is no accident that, in picking up the story of popular song in the late Middle Ages, we have immediately become involved with the carol. As popular song the carol seems to have reached the peak of success in the early years of the sixteenth century. John Dorne, the Oxford bookseller, was probably only one of many who made a good thing out of selling penny and twopenny printed sheets. Dozens of entries in his registers of sales refer to 'Kesmes coralles' and the like.[11] The carol followed two main lines of development in the fifteenth century, distinguishable more on social and musical than on literary grounds. The first is the tradition of ceremonial song composed for liturgical or courtly occasions by professional musicians. A late example of this kind is the litany-like carol, *Jhesu, fili virginis*:

> *Jhesu, fili virginis,*
> *Miserere nobis.*

> 1. Jhesu, of a mayde thow woldest be born,
>   To save mankynde, that was forlorn,
>   And all for owre mysse.
>   *Miserere nobis.*[12]

The other carol tradition shows its continuous growth as popular song, both in pious use ('Nowell nowell: Tydyngis trew' [Song 220]) and in profane ('Thei Y synge and murthus make' [Song 319]). This tradition, rich as it must have been, is only known through a handful of tunes, mere scraps and orts of song. However, of sixteen melodies of the period no less than ten are carols; two others are Latin songs connected with the carol; and two are English songs of the same kind.[13] The carol, quite apart from its development as polyphony, was clearly popular verse intended for singing. Perhaps the most delightful of these jottings is the carol, *Nova nova Ave fit ex Eva* [Song 217]:

No-va, no-va, A-VE fit ex E-VA. 1.Ga-bri-el of hye de-gre, He— came doun from Tri-ni-te, from Na-za-reth to Ga-li-le : [No-va, no-va.]

Of the two songs left over out of the total of sixteen, one occurs on the same page as a carol and is in a popular metre:

> Nowe well and nowe woo,
> Now frend and nowe foo,
>   Thus goth this worlde i-wysse;
> But sen that it is so,
> Lat itt passe and goo,
>   And take itt as it ysse [Song 227].

This is in essence the pattern of *The Nutbrown Maid* and many other balets; the popular wisdom of 'Nowe well' has a metre to match. The other song, however, 'My herte ys so plungit' [Song 205], is not in the slightest degree popular; it consists of one stanza of *ottava rima* with an ornate melody.[14]

III

A tune is a tune, however roughly it may be jotted down; and its relevance is scarcely ever in doubt. The 'literary' evidence that certain poems were popular songs or were sung to their tunes is much more difficult to assess. Only one sort is incontrovertible – a marginal note in a contemporary hand, saying: 'to the tune of . . .' The procedure of naming tunes is, of course, an old one. Several Latin lyrics in *The Red Book of Ossory* are marked with vernacular tags, obviously from popular song: 'Do do nightyngale synges ful myrie', 'Mayde yn the moore lay', and so on.[15] Unfortunately, tunes are rarely named for the fifteenth-century carols, and if named, even more rarely known. Two carols in a manuscript at

Gonville and Caius College are tantalizing: one bears the legend 'Bryd on brere' but does not fit the fourteenth-century melody which has these words [Song 56]; the other is headed with a scrap of notation and 'le bon l. don' [Song 171]. These other tunes are named for fifteenth-century carols: 'Alone I live alone' [cf. Song 34], 'Now must I syng', and 'And I were a mayd' [cf. H101]. It is possible to make something at any rate of the last of these. The carol, 'Swet Jhesus | Is cum to us | This good tym of Crystmas', has a specific manuscript heading: 'A song in the tune of | and I were a mayd &c.'[16] I have already referred to the fortunate survival in *Henry VIII's MS* of a part-song, 'And I war a maydyn' [H101]. The tenor, usually the first part to be written, is probably the popular tune. The words of this song were quoted earlier. It is not surprising that in the interlude of *Thersites* the main character uses them for sardonic comment on a young woman in distress; they hardly fit the mood of this carol. A reconstructed version of the carol might run:

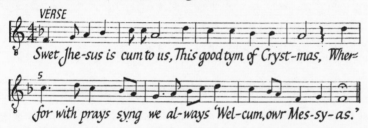

for with prays syng we al-ways 'Wel-cum, owr Mes-sy-as.'

The last collection of 'medieval' carols appeared in the mid-sixteenth century (it is the only printed set to survive), Richard Kele's *Christmas Carolles newely Inprynted.*[17] It contains a variety of traditional carols and a number of other pieces belonging to the same world but not in the same form (like the macaronic *Psallimus cantantes* [Song 267]). It is puzzling to find, again, no tunes named. Is it that there was a large corpus of popular tunes, all fitting the carol metre, on which people drew according to taste? This may be, but the basic metre of popular song, as of folk-ballad, is $\overset{abab}{4343}$, while the carol stanza normally runs $\overset{aaab}{4444}$. Or, is it that something in the text of the carol itself was supposed to give the cue? This was often the procedure in the case of the French *noël*. An amorous carol in the 'Findern' MS has the burden, 'Up, son, and mery wether | Somer draweth nere'.[18] It seems much more likely that this burden indicates the tune than anything else. But in this it can be too easy to jump to conclusions. The carol, 'Swet Jhesus', for example, has for burden, 'Hey now now'. If we did not know the carol had to be sung to 'And I were a mayd', we might well have thought – and wrongly – that the burden gave the cue.

Sometimes the opening words are more distinctive than 'Hey now now', which is a veritable cliché of Tudor song. Thus, in the manuscript compiled by the Franciscan friar, James Ryman, two carols are evidently based on one of the most widely circulating songs of the fifteenth century, the Latin carol *Ecce quod natura | Mutat sua jura* [Song 83]. It is the only carol in English or Latin to survive with music in three separate manuscripts. This makes it almost certain that Ryman had the tune in mind. This tune is of the catchy sort and fits the English words quite well. It bears, incidentally, no resemblance either to plain-song or to folk-song, but has all the qualities of popular song as I attempted to define it above – 'tunefulness', obvious rhythmic balance and major tonality.

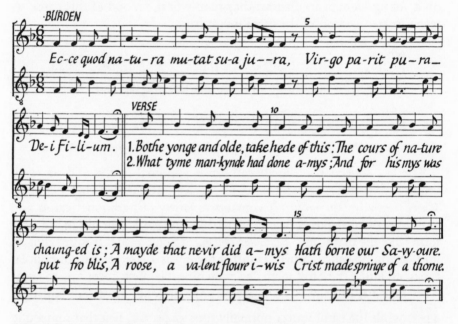

This kind of 'inside pointer' was not, of course, confined to the carol, though the carol provides the best examples of it.[19]

We must not overlook another great repertory and source of tunes for poems – plain-chant. Some carol-burdens, in particular, suggest plain-song melodies. The whole history of the carol, quite apart from any direct evidence, would lead one to expect this. When Ryman uses *Sancta Maria, ora pro nobis* for the burden of no less than seven carols, one naturally wonders whether the music of the litany was implied.[20] A cursory glance through Ryman's poems, with plain-song in mind, is enough to whet the inquiring appetite. Litanies, hymns, the *Te Deum*, psalms, the four antiphons to the Virgin, the *Laetabundus* prose – these are some of the things which immediately catch the eye. Which, if any, are relevant to an inquiry about the singing of poetry?

Ryman's poems as a whole were certainly meant to be sung. In Ryman's manuscript we have, to be brief, several tunes in musical notation of a rough kind; one tune named (perhaps); and one well-known Latin song twice paraphrased in the original metre.[21] If we add to this the association of Ryman with the missionary work of the Franciscans and with the popular carol, the case is reasonably strong for assuming that his poems were songs. In fact, short of a complete set of notated or named tunes, it is hard to see what other evidence one could wish. The manuscript must be a song-book. One of the most interesting series of songs in it consists of eight translated hymns all relating, except one, to the season from Advent to Epiphany. Ryman's method as a translator can be shown from the hymn, *A solis ortus cardine* (sung on Christmas Day at Lauds). The translation is as far as possible line by line:

Beatus auctor saeculi	This blessed Lord that this worlde did make
Servile corpus induit,	A subjecte body on hym hath take
Ut carne carnem liberans	In our manhode making man free;
Ne perderet quos condidit.	That he had wrought, not lese wold he.

Ryman was making a song, where some other translators were writing meditations or devotional exercises.[22]

The second portion of Sedulius' alphabetical hymn, from the letter H onwards, *Hostis Herodes impie*, with its colourful stanzas about King Herod and the Magi, was more popular than the first. On the next page I give Ryman's translation with the melody of the Sarum Use.

Another, a rough and vigorous translation, occurs in an important fifteenth-century collection of popular songs and carols:

> Enmy Herowde thu wokkyd kyng
> Qwy dredes thu the of Christ's comyng?
> He desyrt here non erthely thing
> That heven hat at his geving.[24]

This manuscript has sometimes been described as a minstrel's song-book. It certainly contains the sort of songs minstrels sang. It is, therefore, most interesting to find in it this translation of a Christmas, liturgical hymn, designed to fit the plain-song tune. This suggests that at any rate some plain-song hymns had currency as popular songs.*

The full implications of this can hardly be worked out here. Let it suffice to say that the repertory of plain-song provided a background of melodies. Several of these could be called popular – melodies which had an immediate appeal (though their 'catchiness' does not necessarily catch

1. Wik-ked——— He-rode thou mor—tall foo,
2. The king————is went theire way all three
3. That heven———ly lamb so myelde & good
4. A new——— mer-vaile is done in dede

That Criste shulde come, why dredst thou soo?
Su — yng the sterre, which they did see:
Took the bap-tyme of Jor-dan flood:
The wa — ter clere wax—ed full red

He claymth no-thing ter-res-tri-all
With light they sought Criste, that lyght, than,
The synnes that he with hym not brought
And com —maund-ed by grace dy-vyne

That gev'th king— domes ce-les-ti-all.
With gyftes know— leg- ing God and man.
He toke from us that we had wrought.
Chaun-gyd his na- ture in—to wyne.

23

us at first) and which were widely current.[25] In particular, certain hymns provided tunes for the singing of English verses. One may go further and say that these verses were, probably, not always translations of the hymns themselves but other words which happened to fit the tunes. Thus, some

* I base the assertion that they were current on the number of translations into English and the places in which they are found, not on the mistaken notion that liturgical hymns were a part of congregational worship.

carols of the Christmas season, using, as most carols do, the hymn metre of four lines, each with four stresses, may have been sung to the Christmas hymn-tunes. For instance,

> *Salvator mundi, Domine*
> Father of Hevene, blyssid thou be;
> Thou gretyst a mayde with on AVE
> *Que vocatur Maria.*[26]

This first verse comes from the same 'minstrel' collection as 'Enmy Herowde', mentioned above, a manuscript which, however it came to be compiled, indisputably contains *songs*. The verses of the carol are not a translation of the hymn; but each verse starts with the first line of the parallel Latin verse in the correct order. The burden consists largely of the word *Alleluia*, for which it cannot have been difficult to find another plain-song melody. I give here the verses only, to the hymn melody *Salvator mundi, Domine*:

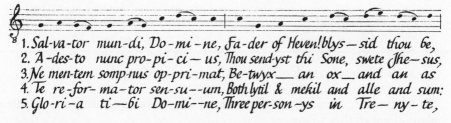

1. Sal-va-tor mun-di, Do-mi-ne, Fa-der of Heven! blys-sid thou be,
2. A-des-to nunc pro-pi-ci-us, Thou send-yst thi Sone, swete Jhe-sus,
3. Ne men-tem somp-nus op-pri-mat, Be-twyx __ an ox __ and an as
4. Te re-for-ma-tor sen-su--um, Both lytil & mekil and alle and sum:
5. Glo-ri-a ti-bi Do-mi--ne, Three per-son-ys in Tre—ny-te,

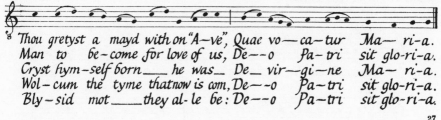

Thou gretyst a mayd with on "A-ve", Quae vo—ca-tur Ma—ri-a.
Man to be-come for love of us, De--o Pa-tri sit glo-ri-a.
Cryst hym-self born __ he was __ De __ vir—gi-ne Ma— ri-a.
Wol-cum the tyme that now is com, De--o Pa-tri sit glo-ri-a.
Bly-sid mot __ they al-le be: De--o Pa-tri sit glo-ri-a.

27

There were whole tracts of the vast plain-song repertory of the later Middle Ages which ordinary layfolk would never have heard. But, besides hymns, there were other kinds of plain-song which they must have known. Prominent amongst these are the litanies. It is now some seventeen years since Miss Margit Sahlin elaborated, on social and historical as well as on philological grounds, a case for deriving the words *carol* and *carole* not from the Greek *choros* and related words but from the expression *kyrie-eleison*.[28] She argued that this phrase, familiar to everyone before the Reformation from its use in the Mass and in the litanies, was a popular acclamation (like the English 'Lawk-a-mercy') and widely used as a refrain in popular poetry. In support of her case Miss Sahlin gave reasons for regarding many medieval English carols as, in effect, 'popular litanies for use in ecclesiastical processions'. They have, as she observed, the literary form of litanies – petition with choral response. Plain-song litanies are quite unlike hymns. Whereas the hymns are balanced, often almost metrical, strophic melodies, the litanies are among the 'recitation tones' and can be expanded or contracted at will as the words require. Like the psalms, the litanies consist of balancing phrases, *A* against *B*, repeated over and over again.

Ryman, who never did anything by halves, has whole sets of carols with a marked litanic pattern. One carol has for burden *Pater de celis deus, miserere nobis.* The four verses of the carol correspond to the first four versicles of the Litany of St Joseph:

Pater de celis Deus . . .	O highe Fader of heven blys . . .
Fili Redemptor mundi Deus . . .	O Sone of God namyd Jhesus . . .
Spiritus Sancte Deus . . .	O Holy Gost, thatt doist procede . . .
Sancta Trinitas unus Deus . . .	O iii and i, of myghtys most . . .[29]

To what music could the carol more suitably have been sung than to the plain-chant of this Litany?*

[30]

* An objection to this reconstruction is that in the Litany each versicle is immediately followed by its response, whereas in the carol three versicles must, presumably, precede each one response. However, litanies have sometimes been shortened thus in actual liturgical practice.

Popular Songs

IV

In the foregoing argument I have spoken, for simplicity's sake, as if plain-song and popular song were always simply tune – melody unadorned with any sort of harmony. But this is an over-simplification. In an age when everything was 'garnished', music was no exception. A very common way of singing the simple chants of the litany, for instance, was with fa-burden: in 1535

> was a great procession at London by ye kyngis commandement: fyrst went ye wayts of ye citie all vj, and nexte folowynge ye children of ye gramer scoll of sente Thomas of Acres . . . next came ye blake fryars with theyr crosse and every fryar a cope, *syngynge ye letany with faburdyn*: . . . Aftar them cam Powles quere, every priste and clerke had a cope with all theyr residentaris in copes, *syngynge the letany with faburden*. . . .[31]

It is a reasonable conjecture, though only a conjecture, that some popular songs were sung with fa-burden, that is, with improvised parts in parallel harmony, according to the method described later (p. 64). The method made no great demands on the musical skill of the singers; they did not necessarily even have to be able to read music, since fa-burden could be supplied simply by ear.

It would also be an over-simplification to give the impression, as perhaps I have, that poets adopted one unchanging attitude to the words of popular songs – namely, to disregard them and substitute their own. On the contrary, there were all kinds of permutations. Both moral versions, ('moralizations') and courtly versions were commonly made of current songs. 'My love sche morneth' [H25], for instance, appears dressed as a courtly balet in *Henry VIII's MS* and as a godly song in *Twenty Songs*. Later, in 1567, another moralization of the same song was published without music in *The Gude and Godlie Ballatis*. 'My love she morneth' illustrates admirably the general allegorizing frame of mind, the determination to interpret everything in every possible way – whether Latin grammar, or the steps of the basse-danse, or the stories of the Old Testament, or the latest popular song.[32] It would not be surprising to find that the song had been used for political purposes also. This happened, for example, with 'By a bancke' [Song 60]. This song, which Henry VIII and Sir Peter Carew sang together, is listed among Captain Cox's ballads and books and mentioned by the Fool in *The Longer Thou Livest*; one of three musical settings is found in manuscript at the back of the printed *Twenty Songs* and is a political version praising Henry VIII.[33]

Just as learned composers were not bound to use the complete tunes connected with the words they set, so poets often used only the first words of a song. In fact, the words 'By a bancke as I lay' may be little more than an opening cliché, comparable to the conventional tags and 'padding' lines – 'which grieves me passing sore', 'whiles my life doth dure'; and to refrains – 'hey nonny nonny', 'trolly lolly'. Such lines are connected neither to each other nor to any particular song.

The relationship between popular song and court-song was a complicated and fruitful one. Poets could adapt a popular song as a channel or 'mask' for their own thought, amorous, moral or political; or they could borrow part of a song and turn it into a burden or refrain; or they could use a few words as an opening gambit, perhaps indicating in this way the tune for singing the poem. Musicians, on their side, might write counterpoints to the entire tune or only part of it; or they might use it, so to speak, thematically, a phrase here and a phrase there. Furthermore, poets and musicians acted independently. It is most unlikely that the original 'Come over the burne, Besse' [cf. R16] was expanded *pari passu* as a moralization and as a musical composition. The moralization was current, probably to the original tune, before and after being set to part-music. 'Besse' of the poem was everything, in the course of time – a country sweetheart, sinful Mankind, even, later, 'the quenes majestie'.

However, although it may sometimes be difficult to sort out the popular from the courtly, and the names of tunes from literary clichés, one thing at least is clear: dozens of popular songs were known within the court circle and formed a staple of both literary and musical composition. As a result, the connection between words and *tune* was ever present in people's minds; 'metrical' words were still naturally connected with melody. The wide currency of popular song in courtly circles meant that a natural, unsophisticated relationship between words and melody was never lost sight of. Later I shall try to show that these popular tunes were the music, if any, which the 'courtly makers' had in mind when they were writing their balets.[34]

Meanwhile, let us return to the problem of art-music and art-poetry and approach it from a different angle. What light can the history of ideas and feelings throw upon it?

Popular Songs

1. *Angelus ad Virginem*. This popular song of the thirteenth and fourteenth centuries survives in three English MSS: (i) BM Arundel 248: anon (1 voc); (ii) BM Cotton MSS, App. xxix: anon (2 voc); (iii) Cambridge UL Add. MS 710: anon (3 voc). Facsimiles of (i) and (iii) are in *EEH*, i, plates 34, 46–7. These versions are listed in *EEH*, ii. 71, together with four foreign sources, all for one voice. There are two translations into Middle English: (i) 'Gabriel, fram evene-king' (Carleton Brown, *XIII*, no. 44); (ii) previously unnoticed, 'The angel to the vergyn said', ed. E. K. Whiting, *The Poems of John Audelay*, EETS, clxxxiv (1931), no. 21 (no music). This version by Audelay is here published with the well-known tune for the first time.

1a. For this useful distinction, see Greene, p. xciii.

2. Ryman's carols and hymns are in his autograph MS: Cambridge UL Ee.i.12 (see note 21 below).

3. F. J. Child, ed., *The English and Scottish Popular Ballads* (one-vol. edn ed. Sargent and Kittredge, 1904), 667, in the note to no. 204.

4. C. J. Sharp and Maud Karpeles, eds, *English Folk-Songs from the Southern Appalachians* (1932), i. 46, no. 8a.

5. Cf. the style of the polyphonic basse-danse (Bukofzer, *Studies*, ch. 6).

6. See note 1 above.

7. See Reference List under 'Colkelbie', Wager, *GGB* and *Complaint*. The other principal sources of information are: *Captain Cox*; Skelton's poems; the ballad entries in the Stationers' Registers (analysed by H. E. Rollins in *Broadside Index*); the carols in Greene; and the popular songs in Robbins, *Secular Lyrics*.

8. *Carew*, 113; *Castell of Perseverance*, line 2435 (ed. F. J. Furnivall and A. W. Pollard, *Macro Plays*, EETS, 1904).

9. See *MC*, no. 4A and note.

10. See p. 310 below for further discussion.

11. See Reference List under Dorne. Wynkyn de Worde and Copland also printed cheap collections of carols; see Greene, 349–50; and E. B. Reed, who gives facsimiles of all three printers' work.

12. Greene, no. 91B, burden and verse 1; *MC*, no. 98. In *MC* introd., and in *Grove* (5), 'Carol', I argue in detail the case for describing the carol as *processional* song with due acknowledgment to Miss Margit Sahlin and Mrs C. K. Miller. The view is supported, too,

by Robbins, 'Carols as Processional Hymns'. Harrison, however (*Music in Medieval Britain,* 416–18), puts forward the alternative theory that the sacred polyphonic carol succeeded the *conductus* as a festal substitute for the *Benedicamus* at the end of the Office. The term 'ceremonial' is intended to cover these and other possible (courtly and civic) uses.

13. These songs are listed in App. B, nos 56, 134, 137, 171, 184, 205, 217, 220, 222, 227, 232, 237, 256, 267, 275, 278.

14. See transcription, p. 124 below.

15. See Greene, p. cxviii, who gives three examples, and St J. D. Seymour, *Anglo-Irish Literature 1200–1582* (1929). *The Red Book* was begun in 1316 by the Franciscan, Richard de Ledrede, Bishop of Ossory. An edition by R. L. Greene is in preparation.

16. Greene, no. 93; from Bodl. MS Eng. poet. e.1 (see App. C, no. 42), which contains many carols and popular songs but only scraps of music.

17. Reproduced in facsimile by E. B. Reed, *Christmas Carols.*

18. Greene, no. 469. The 'Findern MS' is the title given by Robbins to Cambridge UL Ff.i.6; see his article in *PMLA,* lxix (1954), 610.

19. See ch. 7 below, p. 124–, for court-songs with 'inside pointers'.

20. Greene, nos 220–6.

21. *Ryman's MS* is Cambridge UL Ee.i.12 (see App. C, no. 78): it has an interesting colophon (f.80) establishing his 'authorship' (see Greene, pp. cxxv, 393). Musical notation occurs on f.1, 'Synge we now' [Song 278]; f.1v, 'I hard a maydyn' [Song 137]; f.46v, 'Of thy mercy' [Song 237]; f.81, many dots on 4-line staves, hard to decipher but containing amongst other melodies a version of the Sarum hymn, *Salvator mundi,* with rough fa-burden beneath, no words. The possible name of a tune is 'anthonys songe' (f.24) in margin of a carol to the BVM. The well-known song is *Ecce quod* [Song 83].

22. BM Add. MS 34193 contains a hymnal *de tempore* (pr. F. A. Patterson, *Medieval Studies in Memory of G. S. Loomis* (Paris, 1927), 443–: the source of another translation (f.111v).

23. Melody from *Sarum Hymnary,* 23. In the Middle Ages the different sections of Sedulius's hymn were sung to different melodies. In current Roman use *Crudelis Herodes* (words slightly altered) is sung to the *A solis* melody (*Liber Usualis,* 464).

24. BM Sloane MS 2593 f.32v; pr. Carleton Brown, *XV,* no. 90. The

MS is described by Greene, 330. There are two other translations of the hymn *Hostis Herodes* in M.E.: one is by the Franciscan, William Herebert (d. 1333), most of whose poems are pr. Carleton Brown, *XIV*, 15–; the other is in the ornate 'hymnal' (see note 22 above). Neither of these translations fits the music (though other translations by Herebert do).

25. Other hymns that could be used to support the case are, for example: *Ave maris stella* (six M.E. translations or paraphrases) and *Christe qui lux* (eight versions: see Robbins in *Harvard Theological Review*, xlvii (1954), 55). These tunes were not, admittedly, popular in the sense of being 'consciously adapted to popular taste'; but they certainly met it.

26. Greene, no. 86A, from BM Sloane MS 2593. He prints two other versions of the carol: one from Bodl. MS Eng. poet. e.1, a popular collection, the other from Bodl. MS Ashmole 189 (contains also an 'Englishing' of the *Laetabundus* prose).

27. *Sarum Hymnary*, 10.

28. Margit Sahlin, *Étude sur la carole médiévale* (Uppsala, 1940).

29. Greene, no. 305; see also nos 220–6, all using the response, *Sancta Maria, ora pro nobis*.

30. *Liber Usualis*, 1879.

31. Stow, *Two London Chronicles*, ed. C. L. Kingsford (1910), 11–; the chronicler says with pride that 718 copes were worn in this procession.

32. See p. 61 below, ch. 4, Ideas and Theories.

33. Further concerning moralizations, especially of court-songs, see p. 125 below.

34. See ch. 7, Music and the Early Tudor Lyric, II.

CHAPTER 4

Ideas and Theories, Medieval and Humanist

In Chapter 1 I tried to sketch a history of the relationship between music and poetry up to about 1500. The approach chosen may be called the 'technical' one, for it was concerned almost exclusively with what can be learnt from looking at the way words and notes come together in song. Their relationship was described as being at various stages 'natural', 'utilitarian' and 'abstract'. 'But', the reader may object, 'you are surely going beyond your evidence in suggesting that because the relationship had these qualities, it *therefore* had no others? Could it not be that medieval composers also thought of the relationship as emotionally expressive? Because a wife does the housework, it doesn't necessarily follow that marriage has no other meaning.'

I want now to try another approach – it may be called the 'aesthetic', for it is concerned with feeling. We can try to discover whether in the Middle Ages music could ever have been felt to have the 'emotional meanings' which we now take for granted in the art of the song-writer. What is the place of 'emotional expressiveness' in the art-music of the period? What attitude did theorists and composers take to their art? By importing back into this early period the mentality of a later age we have, I think, misconceived the relationship between music and poetry. The idea of pre-Reformation musicians deliberately 'expressing' the emotions aroused by the words they set, is anachronistic and misleading. And yet the assumption that they did, underlies many pronouncements about the medieval lyric:

> It would be very easy for him [the author] to consider his verse as merely the complement of the music, and to rely upon the aid of the music, from outside his work as poetry proper, to supply the emotional transport necessary to its success.[1]

But composers did not look at music in this way. Their attitudes were highly speculative, metaphysical, on the one hand; and severely practical, craftsman-like, on the other. It was never the first duty of music to express emotion.

I

In Richard Pace's *De Fructu*, 1517, the science of music is defended in a speech showing, it seems, remarkable erudition.[2] His citation of classical philosophers and others turns out, however, to be common stock. Every writer felt obliged to draw on Plato, Aristotle, Quintilian, Cicero, on ancient myth and epic poem, on the Bible and the writings of the early Fathers, and lastly on the mediators of Greek musical science, Boethius and Cassiodorus. The surprising thing to us is that in the early sixteenth century these ancient writings were culled not merely for information or for illustration but for *authority*. It is not merely the fact that they were used but the way they were used which makes them in an important sense contemporary documents. For the ideas and attitudes described in this chapter, Quintilian is as good an authority as Erasmus or John Bale.

It is common knowledge that much medieval speculation about music took as its starting-point the treatise *De Institutione Musica* by Boethius (executed in A.D. 525). This book, which purports to be about Greek music, formed the staple of subsequent writing and teaching for centuries.[3] Nearly a thousand years after Boethius wrote, the famous Flemish theorist, Tinctoris, thought it necessary to say that he did not want to differ *irrationabiliter* ('without good reason') from the master.[4] Boethius's view is essentially the philosophical-mathematical one. He defines a musician as one who thinks about music *beneficio speculationis* ('for the thinking's sake'). This definition in itself shows how highly the speculative side of music was regarded. It was repeated from generation to generation and was still commonplace in the fifteenth century.[5] Significantly, the difference between a musician and a mere performer was thought to be the same as between a *theologus* and a *recitator* (lesson-reader). It is not a surprise to find that *summus ille musicus* (the supreme musician) is Christ himself.[6]

Why was the philosophical side so strongly emphasized? Simply, because music was a *speculum*, a mirror of the Universal Order, and to contemplate it was to contemplate 'a hieroglyphical and shadowed lesson of the whole world'. Boethius distinguished three kinds of music: *mundana, humana* and *in instrumentis constituta*; that is, first, the music caused by the motions of the spheres; secondly, the music of man's personality or

59

of the body politic; and thirdly, the music played or sung by voices or instruments. As early as 1300 it became common to doubt the practical truth of *musica mundana*. People said that they could not in fact hear the planetary music – to which the correct retort was that we do not hear the sounds because they are always ringing in our ears. But as a symbol the music of the spheres retained its hold on men's imagination for centuries. 'It is proportion that beautifies everything,' wrote Orlando Gibbons; 'this whole Universe consists of it, and Musicke is measured by it.' [7]

It follows from this that actual music did not exist in its own right but 'borrowed its meaning from the *musica mundana*',[8] that is, from the music of the universe. Music played or sung was the reflection on earth of God's arithmetic in heaven and a symbol of His order. Saint Augustine went further and saw in music not merely a passive but an active reflection of God the Creator:

> For Augustine, creation was not a finite event, but a continual process. Music, creating order from chaos, the new from nothingness, continues the process. . . . Thus the power of music is such that it must address itself to the most sublime task of which human activity is capable: the restoration of the harmony of the universe, shattered in the first great fall of the angels from grace.[9]

Surely, in this view, the very last thing music would be thought of as doing is 'expressing human emotion'? At least this must be true of the philosopher-sage-musician. In a famous passage of the *Confessions* Saint Augustine writes:

> How did I weep, in Thy hymns and canticles, touched to the quick by the voices of Thy sweet-attuned Church! The voices flowed into mine ears and the Truth distilled into my heart.

The passage, it has been pointed out, 'recalls the idea, expounded in numerous instances elsewhere in Augustine, that music communicates a knowledge about God, indeed, the very knowing of God'.[10] This is very different from the Romantic conception of music as the very sublimity of human self-expression.

In this argument a good deal turns on the use of the words 'express' and 'expressive'. In present-day usage the literal meanings of the words have been lost and the metaphorical meanings severely limited. The verb 'express' has two prevailing meanings: (i) to represent in language ('The Princess expressed her surprise that people in a famine did not eat buns');

and (ii) to reveal feelings, especially, or personal qualities by means of external tokens ('Never did tone express indifference plainer'). The earlier, more intellectual meanings have been crowded out. We can no longer say with Udall, 'Man expresseth God . . . as the child doeth resemble hys father or mother'; nor with Coverdale that Christians should 'expresse a life worthie of their profession'.[11] It is easy to take the word wrongly even in Elizabethan writings. When Thomas Morley, the theorist and composer, talks about 'dittying' (setting words to music), he uses 'express' with several different shades of meaning.[12] Not many medieval uses of the modern senses of the word are recorded in the dictionary. But, in any case, it seems certain that medieval music must be conceived as 'expression' in the older senses. It would be safer perhaps for us to use the obsolete noun, 'express'. Jeremy Taylor uses it when, addressing God, he says 'making all Thy creatures to be expresses of Thy power'.[11] Music was thought of, fundamentally, as an 'express' of God's order.

Under the basic idea, unquestioned so far as I know throughout the Middle Ages, of music as symbolic, lie various lesser symbolisms. The Universal Music consists of rhythm (measure of time) and of harmony (measure of concordance). To take the latter only, Stephen Hawes, in *The Pastime of Pleasure*, invokes the musical scale to harmonize all knowledge.[13] And Sir Thomas Elyot in *The Boke of the Governour* commends music 'for the better attaynynge the knowlege of a publike weale'; music will give the young prince an insight into the laws which govern the universe and thereby into the method of good government.[14]

What is difficult to discover is, of course, to what extent either these lesser symbolisms or the greater idea behind them, of music as a mirror of eternity, affected ordinary listeners and players and composers. How many really *felt* in music 'an hieroglyphical and shadowed lesson'? and how many were merely creatures of the habit which invented, but did not necessarily feel, connections everywhere? Sir Thomas Elyot's speculations often seem to be of this second kind. Thus, in chapter xxii, defending dancing, he argues that the first move in the dance (the 'reverence') denotes honour to God; the 'braule' stands for celerity and slowness; the 'singles' for providence and industry, and so on.[15] This is scarcely removed in spirit from *Donatus moralisatus*, a much-used theological interpretation of the Latin grammar ('the noun-substantive is the man, the pronoun means that he is a sinner', and so on).[16]

Number, arithmetic, is the basis of the symbolic view of music as it was held in the Middle Ages. So one way of testing the truth of the symbol for ordinary music-making is to see whether numbers do, or do not, play a part in the composition of medieval music. In Chapter 2 I mentioned one of the classic forms of medieval music, the motet, and said that the way the words were set did not encourage one to think that either their meaning, their mood, or their natural accent mattered to the composer. The simultaneous singing of two or three different texts emphasized this 'abstract' approach. The corollary of this is that number mattered greatly; 'it is proportion that beautifies everything'. Among the numerical features of the typical motet three are outstanding: the use of triple metre; the mathematical division of the tenor; and the observance of basic concords.[17] Triple metre, first, was almost universally used for church-music in the Middle Ages, a fact explained by contemporary writers as a similitude of the divine nature. The tenor, secondly, was the structural voice on which the whole motet was built; the original plain-song melody was cut up and reproduced in complex, repeated rhythmic patterns for which the only justification was a deep-set belief in 'the close relation of rhythm to numbers'. Finally, the strict observance, on important beats, of concords such as fifth and octave has as its speculative basis the knowledge that 'the same numerical proportions by which different tones sound together in consonance also determine . . . the harmony of the universe'.[18]

The merest nodding acquaintance with medieval ways of thought is sufficient to confirm one in the idea that these symbolisms of number were not incidental but essential to their way of musical thought. They were the chief means, surely, for the conveyance into sound of that abstract, truly philosophical music which governs the universe.

Whether speculations about number had any great effect during the early Tudor period upon the music that was written, is another and difficult question. There are certainly no compositions like the 'isorhythmic' motets which I have been describing, whose very design was largely a matter of mathematical calculation.* But there are plenty of musical riddles and puzzles, such as those in the grandly designed Mass, O Quam Suavis, c. 1500, to show that the connection between music and mathematics was not a dead one.[19] The secular songs of the time are conditioned, naturally, more by social needs than by a priori calculations about the philosophy of music and the universe. But this does not, I think, affect the main argument, which is that during the Middle Ages neither poets nor musicians would have thought of music as having the capacity or the duty to

---

* The recent discovery of an isorhythmic song, O potores exquisiti [Song 250], in a mid-fifteenth-century English manuscript shows the pertinacity of the technique.

express the feelings aroused by the words in a poem. The early Tudor songs were written for the most part in this medieval tradition.

It should be worth while now examining some typical theoretical writings about both music and poetry for any additional light they may shed on the relationship between the two arts.

II

Musical theory in early Tudor England was of two main kinds: 'international' Latin scholarship, much of it highly philosophical, of foreign theorists; and more practical, vernacular treatises on improvised discant. These were, to invoke the old distinction once again, respectively the provinces of *musici* (the thinkers) and of *cantores* (the performers). To both sorts of author and student practical music was in varying degrees a craft, a 'mystery'. The highly developed special techniques, belonging respectively to notation, composition and performance, were to the scholar the terrestrial workings of the celestial arithmetic, and to the choirman the jealously guarded secrets of his trade.

Notation was a most complicated science, and the theorists seemed to delight in making it appear even more complicated than it was. Every topic that could be was elaborated beyond all practical use. In the early sixteenth century the system of 'proportions' (a significant term) was a favourite subject for mathematical speculation; the theorists described such utterly impracticable ratios as *proportio subdupla supertripartiente quartas*, i.e. the ratio $4:11$.[20] The complicated sets of time-values represented by ligatures invited similar study. The second subject of practical interest in theoretical treatises, namely composition, needs little elucidation. The approach is melodic: *ars contrapuncti* is the art of writing one melody against another, of handling concords and discords, and so on.[21] But the third subject, performance, requires definition. Their treatment of it does not include many of the matters which would now be of supreme interest – directions for speed, mood, style of singing, fitting of text, choice of instruments and their use.* Only two matters are fully considered, and these occur in treatise after treatise: methods of improvising discant and the technique of solmization.

Improvised harmony was not, according to the theorists, a matter of

---

* It is not quite accurate to say that speed was never discussed. Speed was governed by the *tactus*, a fixed beat of about one second, to which in this period the semibreve was held equivalent.

singing by ear, but by what was technically known as 'sight' (*perfectio ocularis*).[22] Thus in one system the tenor alone, the middle part, was written down; the other singers 'imagined' their parts from the tenor. The treatises describe how this was to be done. As the improvisation was normally based on a plain-song melody, the only ability required from the discanter, once he had found his first note, was the ability to read a familiar melody.

Solmization (the modern sol-fa system descends from it) was part of the elementary instruction of any musician.[23] He had to know his 'gamut', or scale, in which the notes were grouped not by octaves but by sixes (hexachords). The naming of notes and the introduction of accidentals were two practical matters inextricably bound up with the hexachord system. It seems, also, that singers used the hexachord names (as sol-fa can be used today) to learn to judge their intervals. Even in Elizabethan times the hexachords, and how to change ('mutate') from one to the other, were among the first subjects taught by Morley's 'master' to his 'pupil', Polymathes.[24]

The most noticeable fact about the musical theory of the fifteenth and early sixteenth centuries is the complete absence of the very thing we are looking for – an account of music as an expressive agent, as speaking the 'language of the heart'. This is not to say that the medieval theorist saw no connection between music and human feelings. On the contrary, he knew that music affected people powerfully in a way that might be good and might be bad. The *Complexus Effectuum Musices* of Tinctoris contains twenty points, of which no less than sixteen pronounce on religious and ethical issues: it starts, *Musica Deum delectat*, and ends, *musica animas beatificat*.[25] In a later chapter we shall see what use contemporary dramatists made of the inevitable association between 'loose' music and loose morals. The wrong sort of music sends people straight to the 'stews' – to sex and the Devil. So it cannot be maintained that medieval theorists were indifferent to the emotional effects of the music they had in mind. The crux of the matter is, I think, that up to the sixteenth century, good moral results and devotional stirrings were regarded as the natural by-product of good music. A polyphonic mass or a motet was not written to make you feel good; but if it was written in accordance with the God-given rules, it could not fail of the right effect. Music, Saint Augustine said, was the art of *bene modulandi* – that is, probably, 'of right proportioning'. If the composer's proportions were aesthetically (which meant metaphysically) right, then it followed as a matter of course that the moral results would be good. The music would put the 'little world of man' in tune again with the Infinite. Hence the absorption of the theorists in mathematical detail; and hence also their apparent indifference to ethical results.

In any case, concern with emotional *effects* is a quite separate thing from concern with emotional *expression*. To establish a firm connection between the two was a new thought, perhaps, in the sixteenth century. Sir Thomas More, contrasting the music of Utopia with the music of early Tudor England, made the connection explicit (I quote Robinson's translation):

> [Utopian music] dothe so resemble and expresse naturall affections . . . the fassion of the melodye [i.e. music] dothe so represent the meaning of the thing, that it doth wonderfullye move, stirre, pearce, and enflame the hearers myndes.[26]

The new music of the Elizabethan age will be music which does just this: it will move the heart *by representing* to it (in Hooker's words)

> the very standing, rising, and falling, the very steps and inflections every way, the turns and varieties of all passions whereunto the mind is subject.[27]

A sign of their lack of concern with what has been regarded for centuries since as the very soul of music, its 'expressiveness', is the indifference of the musical theorists to the problem of words-and-music. For them there is no problem. They are scarcely interested in the relationship between the two arts. Gafori, it is true, in his *Practica Musicae*, 1496, treats of poetic metres, but only to show that mensuration in music is equivalent to metre in poetry.[28] Ornithoparcus is more practical and shows, I think, in what shape the problem presented itself to the ordinary singer:

> Let every singer conforme his voyce to the words, that as much as he can he make the concent sad when the words are sad, and merry when they are merry. . . .[29]

Just as it is the singer's duty to fit the words to the music, so it is *his* responsibility rather than the composer's to 'express' the text. Rules for 'dittying', such as Morley and Butler give, are not found in medieval, even late medieval, treatises.

Music and Poetry

III

If musicians were indifferent to the relationship between words and music, except in one or two limited instances, literary theorists in the medieval tradition were no better. Their main concern was with the art of rhetoric. As with music, an unbroken tradition runs back to post-classical and patristic writers. The pseudo-Ciceronian treatise *Ad Herennium* contains a list of the *exornationes* of formal speech. These were greatly expanded by later writers, particularly the medieval rhetoricians, Matthew of Vendôme, Geoffrey de Vinsauf, John de Garland and others. The writings of Chaucer's French contemporary, Deschamps, and others, contributed to the revival in the fifteenth century of the rhetorical attitude to poetry. The poet's art, as a rhetorician, was to 'embellish, ornate and make fair' our English. *The Pastime of Pleasure* by Stephen Hawes, groom of the chamber to Henry VII, contains a long panegyric of Dame Rhetoric; the poem conveys in somewhat vague terms both the theory and the practice of rhetorical poetry.[30] And, even as late as 1551, Thomas Wilson can recommend rhetoric for using

> gaie painted sentences, and [setting] forthe those matters with freshe colours and goodly ornaments, and that at large.[31]

The ingenuity of the rhetoricians was lavished on two aspects of poetry – stylistic ornament and formal pattern.

Just as musicians had their *cantus florizatus* and were much given to 'colouring' and 'figuring' their melodies, so poets had the 'colours' and 'figures' of rhetoric. John de Garland compiled, like every other writer, a long list of the colours, in which he names *annominatio, traductio, exclamatio, repetitio*, and many others.[32] As Stephen Hawes said, 'under a colour a truth may arise'. These ornaments of style were usually divided into difficult and easy. Other important matters were methods of beginning and ending a poem, methods of 'amplification' and 'abbreviation', and the choice of a style suitable to the writer, his theme, and his audience.

The interest in formal pattern, 'proportion', is an extension of the same habit of mind; elaborate patterns seem usually to have been devised, not to convey elaborate arguments, but simply as another means of stylistic decoration. Rhymes, for example, could be *orbiculati (abba), equicomi (aabb aabb), serpentini (aabb ccbb)*, and so on. Every kind of metre had its name – even blank-verse (*rithmus decasillabus iambicus*).[33] Late medieval poetry was pervasively influenced by such theorizing. Musicians showed no less

66

ingenuity; the late fifteenth-century carols are constructed with great subtlety. And, in music generally, canons and puzzle-canons mirror literary palindromes and verses *qui directe laudant, retrograde vituperant*. Both poets and musicians were fascinated by the medium in which they worked.

This fascination grew rather than declined during the Tudor period. Wyatt's 'conscious and sometimes graceful' use of the art of rhetoric 'offers vernacular illustration of practically every important figure which was authorized by rhetorics of the time'.[34] This stanza quoted by the Elizabethan rhetorician, George Puttenham, from Tottel's *Songs and Sonets* shows one sort of interest that Wyatt's contemporaries, too, must have taken in his poetry.

> The restlesse state renuer of my smart,
> The labours salve increasing my sorrow:
> The bodies ease and troubles of my hart,
> Quietour of mynde, mine unquiet foe:
> Forgetter of paine, remembrer of my woe,
> The place of sleepe wherein I do but wake:
> Besprent with teares, my bed, I thee forsake.[35]

This illustrates, Puttenham says, the figure of rhetoric called *irmus* or 'the long loose'. It is a 'maner of speach drawen out at length and going all after one tenure and with an inperfit sence till you come to the last word or verse [line]'.[36] The stanza embodies various other figures as well: for example, *parison* (the use of parallel phrases) and *traductio* (repetition of a word in different forms: quietour, unquiet).

The proper relationship between poetry and music does not enter into rhetorical theory. If the very fact of 'the second rhetoric' were not enough to establish the complete separation of the two courtly arts, this omission would clinch the matter. Music, certainly, is mentioned, and in two connections: firstly, it is the larger whole which embraces *musica instrumentalis* and its subdivisions *melica, metrica et rithmica*; secondly, it helps elocution (*pronuntiatio*, as the theorists called it).[37] Perhaps William Horman (d. 1535), the celebrated grammarian, was thinking both of philosophy and of elocution when he said, 'No one can be a grammarian without a knowledge of music'.[38] But the lack of vital connection between music and poetry could not be disguised. It was left to the Reformers of the sixteenth century to assert the supremacy of words over music, and to the humanists to base their attitude to the two arts on the conviction that they were, or could be made, the *same* art. And it is to these two great movements – the Reformation and humanism – that we shall have to turn to find an explanation for the idealized union of 'artistic' music and poetry in the later sixteenth century.

IV

Humanism, in music, has been described and discussed by several previous writers.[39] I do not wish to deny its importance in a study of words and music. However, I hope to show in the next chapter that it was not humanism but the Reformation which brought about a revolution in the way English people thought about song. So, giving humanism rather less than its due, I shall briefly summarize in the last few pages of this chapter the musical causes for which the humanists stood.

In music and in the other arts the worship of antiquity had been, throughout the Middle Ages, constantly present, though with various degrees of intensity. But it was a misdirected because a misinformed worship. This was doubly so in the case of music, for the remnants of Greek music were not only scarce but indecipherable. The first task facing the humanists, in their renewed enthusiasm for antiquity, was to discover what had been the character of ancient music. Richard Pace, whilst in Rome, consulted books in the Vatican library for this very purpose. Similarly, the Italian polymath, Hieronymo Cardano, says in his autobiography:

> in music I discovered new notes, new combinations – or, rather, I brought back into use, from the writings of Ptolemy and Aristoxenus, those already discovered.[40]

After consulting the writings of antiquity the humanists judged contemporary music in the light of their findings. Pace, in a tone of superior knowledge, complained that everything done by modern musicians was trivial:

> you can scarcely find a single one who understands what music is – and they are always singing it.[41]

This amounts to little more than the time-honoured observation that very few practical musicians are philosophers, *musici*. Sir Thomas More's reflections, in a passage already quoted, are brief but more valuable:

> [Utopian vocal and instrumental] music doth so *resemble and expresse*

naturall affections, the sound and tune is so applied and made agreeable to the thing, that whether it bee a prayer, or els a dytty of gladnes, of patience, of trouble, of mournynge, of anger, the fassion of the melody dothe *so represente the meaning* of the thing, that it doth wonderfullye move, stirre, pearce, and enflame the hearers myndes.[42]

More introduces this description by saying, 'in one thinge doubtless they goo exceding farre beyonde us', so it is quite in order to regard it as a critique of contemporary music. Music could be a part of *boni mores*, if the text were handled with sufficient dexterity and imagination.

The connection between music and the good life was, we have already seen, a sanction for music in the medieval scheme of things. But the humanists of the sixteenth century were not content, like earlier moralists, simply to state on ancient authority, *musica voluntatem malam revocat*, or the opposite, that it was an incitement to 'likerous lusts'. They set out to discover what it was in Greek music which had produced the marvellous ethical effects they read of. Amongst other things they experimented with the modes; Glareanus, friend of Erasmus, with his new theory of the modes, 'flattered himself with the hope of restoring that very practice of music to which such wonderful effects had been ascribed'.[43] But, at an early stage it became clear to the humanists that a close relationship between music and poetry was of the essence of antique theory.

The ideal resolved itself into three: vivid expression of the sense of words, careful accentuation, and audibility. In the middle of the sixteenth century the name *musica reservata* was given by Adriaan Coclicus to the music of Josquin and his contemporaries, in which the quality of vivid emotional expressiveness is first apparent. This puzzling term has since been widely adopted. Whichever of the many interpretations of the word *reservata* is correct, a characteristic of the music itself is its power of producing an emotional commentary on the chosen text.[44] A distinction already made may be recalled here: this *expressiveness*, called out by the inmost meaning of the words, must not be confused with the *naturalism* of certain late medieval composers, consisting of a purely intellectual or pictorial illustration of the text. In the Elizabethan madrigal both naïve pictorialism and subtle nuances of expression are to be found; in early Tudor songs the first is rare and the second practically unknown.

To suggest that the wonderful achievements of sixteenth-century composers were directly due to humanistic teaching would be absurd. Many thorough-going humanists, in fact, despised polyphony, and others wanted to reform it radically. The wonders were, rather, achieved under the cloak of humanism with the spur of new musical needs. Where the endeavours of the humanists bore most practical fruit was in the field of careful accentuation.

This, again, has to be distinguished from a wider idea with roots in late medieval practice. The natural imitation of speech was aimed at and achieved by Ockeghem and others on the Continent, and, as we shall see, by the composers of *The Fayrfax MS* in England. A continuous tradition of speech-consciousness can, in fact, be traced from the declamations of the late *ars nova* to those of Dowland and the early Italian opera. The humanist ideal, on the other hand, was often purely metrical. This was so particularly in France, where the *Académie de Musique et de Poésie* (1571) experimented with classical metres.[45] French poems were set to music which admitted only two time-values, for the long and the short respectively. This *vers mesuré* was an extension to the vernacular of a practice which had been observed in setting Latin verse since the beginning of the century. 'As early as 1507 Petrus Tritonius . . . set to music the odes of Horace *secundum naturas et tempora syllabarum et pedum.*'[46]

These quantitative settings were choral, since counterpoint, by obscuring the words, was felt to deprive music of its ethical power. Audibility was a *sine qua non* of morality. Another alternative to music 'bated with fugue' was the solo-song with instrumental accompaniment. The Greek lyric, so the neo-classicists argued, was sung to the lyre; therefore the lute-song, the later 'air', had a peculiarly antique virtue.[47]

The more advanced ideas of the humanists were not current even in France and Italy until the second half of the sixteenth century. Apart from the passage of Thomas More already quoted, there are few signs that English humanists were considering the problem of music and words, even in its most elementary aspects. Church reformers were more active (see p. 79–). George Puttenham was perhaps one of the first to speak of 'Lirique Poets'; he described them as men who 'delighted to write songs or ballads of pleasure, to be song with the voice, and to the harpe, lute or citheron . . .'[48] Humanism, it seems, did not affect the arts in England until Elizabeth's reign. Before that the humanist ideal can hardly have been a positive stimulus to the practice of music and poetry as a single art, either in the early Tudor court, or, if not in court, anywhere else.

Ideas and Theories, Medieval and Humanist

1. G. Kane, *Middle English Literature* (1951), 167.
2. Pp. 27– deal with music; there is no modern edition of *De Fructu*. Pace says that it was William Latimer who suggested this 'musical' reading to him. (I thank H. A. Mason for bringing the passage to my notice. He discusses *De Fructu* in *Humanism and Poetry*, 33–35.)
3. Boethius's treatise was printed at Venice in 1491, 1492, 1497, etc.; see Pattison, 125, note. The Oxford Bachelor of Music was licensed to teach Boethius until the mid-nineteenth century. The whole subject of late classical, patristic and medieval speculation is admirably summarized in Reese, *MMA*, 52–53, 57–67, 117–19, 125–7. See also Lang, 55–61; and Dent, 'Social Aspects of Music in the Middle Ages'. Text of *De Musica* pr. in Migne, *Patrologiae* (*Lat*), lxiii. 1167. The digest in Abdy Williams, *A Short Historical Account of the Degrees in Music at Oxford and Cambridge* (1893), 22–, is not altogether reliable.
4. Coussemaker, iv. 79.
5. See Tinctoris, *Diffinitorium: MUSICUS est qui perpensa ratione beneficio speculationis, non operis servitio, canendi officium assumit . . . . Musicorum et cantorum magna est differentia:* | *Illi sciunt, ii dicunt quae componit musica.* | *Et qui dicit quod non sapit diffinitur bestia* (Coussemaker, iv. 186). See also the proverb: *Sicut judex ad praeconem, sic musicus ad cantorem* (Coussemaker, iv. 344).
6. Tinctoris, *Proportionale* (Coussemaker, iv. 154); Christ is described elsewhere as *doctor in arte citharisandi* (Reese, *MR*, 145, footnote).
7. Gibbons, dedication of *The First Set of Madrigals and Mottets*, 1612 (ed. Fellowes, *EMS*, vol. v).
8. Bukofzer, 'Speculative Thinking in Medieval Music', *Speculum*, xvii (1942), 165.
9. Perl, 'Augustine and Music', 501.
10. Perl, 506–7.
11. See *OED* s.v. 'Express' for these quotations.
12. Morley, *Plain and Easy*, 290–.
13. *Pastime of Pleasure*, 62.
14. *The Governour*, i. 43: this well-known quotation is often misinterpreted.
15. *The Governour*, i. 238–; 'Howe daunsing may be an introduction unto the firste morall vertue, called prudence.'

16. Huizinga, 190; he also quotes from *Le Parement et Triumphe des Dames of Olivier de la Marche*, 'in which each article of female costume symbolizes a virtue'. Shoes stand for care and diligence; the garter for resolution. See also Hawkins, ii. 238, 241, for the fifteenth-century theorist, Wylde, who attempted 'to prove the resemblance of Leah and Rachel to the tone and semitone'; and for the tract, *Distinctio inter Colores musicales et Armorum Heroum*, establishing analogies between music and heraldry.

17. Bukofzer (in art. cited, note 8 above) develops these three points.

18. Bukofzer, 174, from M. Gerbert, *Scriptores ecclesiastici de musica* (3 vols, 1784), i. 172.

19. ed. H. B. Collins, PMMS (1927), with elaborate and informative introduction.

20. See W. Apel, *The Notation of Polyphonic Music* (3rd edn, 1945), 145–.

21. See, for example, Tinctoris, *Liber de arte contrapuncti* (Coussemaker, iv. 76–).

22. The scholarly literature on the subject of discant, 'English' discant, *bourdon, faux-bourdon,* fa-burden, etc., is now vast. A useful summary of controversy, with a new interpretation of the concept 'faburden', is to be found in Dr B. L. Trowell's recent article in *Musica Disciplina*, xiii (1959).

23. *HDM* s.v. 'Hexachord'.

24. Morley, *Plain and Easy*, 15–.

25. Coussemaker, iv. 191–.

26. More, *Utopia*, 182–3: Latin text, 420.

27. Hooker, *Ecclesiastical Polity*, bk 5, sect. xxxviii.

28. See Hawkins, ii. 307–.

29. See Hawkins, ii. 405–, quoting Dowland's translation; also, Boyd, 243.

30. There are dozens of accounts of rhetoric. The two I have found most interesting are: E. R. Curtius, *European Literature and the Latin Middle Ages*, trs. Trask (U.S.A., 1953); and Rosamond Tuve, *Elizabethan and Metaphysical Imagery* (U.S.A., 1947).

31. Quoted, D. L. Clark, *Rhetoric and Poetry in the Renaissance* (1922), 57, from *Rule of Reason* (1551).

32. Garland's *Art of Poetry* is pr. by G. Mari, *I trattati medievali* (Milan, 1899), treatise no. v.

33. Described by Garland as *iste modus rithmi authenticus ab antiquo tempore.*

34. V. L. Rubel, *Poetic Diction in the English Renaissance* (1941), 50–51.

35. Puttenham, 176; *Wyatt* (ed. Muir), no. 115, presents a rather different text.

36. Puttenham, 176.

37. A. F. Leach, *Educational Charters and Documents* (1911), 513, quotes from the 1560 statutes of Westminster School: 'As a knowledge of singing is found to be of the greatest use for a clear and distinct elocution . . .'

38. Quoted by Foster Watson, *The English Grammar Schools* (1908), 142.

39. I have been helped, especially, by D. P. Walker's series of arts in *MR*, ii–iii (1941–2); and Macdonald Emslie, 'The Relationship between Words and Music in the English Secular Song: 1622–1700', unpubl. diss. for Ph.D. (Cambridge, 1957). Walker's chief contribution is, I think, to make it clear that the central concept of humanism in music is an ethical one. See also Pattison, 125: summary of the Camerata's views. Many of the Italian texts are trans. in O. Strunk, *Source Readings in Music History* (1952).

40. Cardano, *De Vita Propria,* in *Opera Omnia,* i. 39 (1663). (I thank H. A. Mason for this reference.)

41. Pace, *De Fructu* (see note 2 above).

42. See note 26 above.

43. Quoted by Hawkins, ii. 424.

44. See *HDM* s.v. 'Musica reservata', where various explanations are given.

45. Examples of *vers mesuré* in *HAM*, i. no. 138, and in Besseler, *Musik des Mittelalters und der Renaissance* (1931), 303. See also: Frances B. Yates, *The French Academies of the 16th Century* (1947); and Pattison, chs 4 and 7.

46. Lang, 198. See also A. Pirro, *Histoire de la Musique (1400–1600)* (1940), 160.

47. See Pattison, 118–. It will be noticed that I differ from Dr Pattison chiefly in the important point of doubting the existence of a continuous tradition of courtly and artistic lute-songs.

48. Puttenham, 25.

CHAPTER 5

The Reformation

In the preceding chapter two questions were asked. (1) Had 'emotional expressiveness' any place in medieval music or musical theory? The answer to this was, I suggested, 'Little or none.' And (2) Have we not radically misconceived the relationship between music and poetry by importing back into this early period our own preconceptions? To this second question I should answer with a decided 'Yes'; the idea of medieval musicians deliberately 'expressing' emotions aroused by the words they set is anachronistic and misleading. Additional force is lent, I think, to these arguments by the indisputable fact that during the course of the sixteenth century a great change came over musicians' attitude to words. By reflecting on the nature of this change we shall be able to re-capture more vividly what it felt like to write poems and to write songs under the first Tudor kings, before the change occurred.

Two important things happened, I have said, during the course of the century, neither having much effect on the arts until after 1540. The first was the Reformation; the second, humanism, the rediscovery and idealization of ancient culture. The Reformation has a chapter to itself because it was, as I conceive it, the most important single influence, and because it has been somewhat neglected in previous studies of words-and-music.[1]

I

The history of words-and-music in the sixteenth century is inseparably bound up with the history of the greatest religious, political and social up-heaval this country had known for centuries. The Reformation has been described as primarily and necessarily 'a revolt of clerics against clerics'. But this ecclesiastical storm was one that affected the lives of the millions. The upheaval was far from being a professional squabble.

During Edward [VI]'s reign the fact that England's religion was really a different kind of thing was brought home unmistakably to everyone, when changes so concrete were made as the substitution of the Communion Service for the Mass, and the abolition of all penalties against clerical marriage.[2]

The profound social changes which accompanied the theological Reformation can only be compared in their far-reachingness to the vast reorganization of society which takes place in a modern war – 'evacuation', universal conscription, rationing, and so on. The musical profession was disrupted more than most.* Thomas Tallis, head of the singing-men at Waltham Abbey, was perhaps lucky: after a short interval at Canterbury, he went to a post in the Chapel Royal. Hundreds of other singers were simply thrown out of work by the dissolution of the monasteries. Taverner and Merbecke were two amongst a crowd of musicians whose lives were completely disrupted by work as propagandists or agents.[3]

The Reformation in England was many things – an ecclesiastical schism, a piece of economic nationalism, an act of wilful rebellion on Henry's part, the expression of widespread moral dissatisfaction. It was also – and here lies its importance for the present inquiry – part of an intellectual revolution, manifested in *an intense concern with words*, and above all, with God's words as revealed in Holy Scripture. For centuries the Bible had been a closed book, closed not only to the laity but in effect to many of the clergy through their ignorance of Latin.[4] The people acquired their knowledge of the Faith from hearing sermons, watching miracle-plays, looking at paintings and carvings, not from reading the Bible. Most of them could not have read it in any case, even if it had been translated. And, generally speaking, its translation into the vernacular was not only discouraged but forbidden during the later Middle Ages.[5] The rediscovery of the Bible and its enthronement as an authority above that of the voice of the living Church completely reversed the medieval position. The people 'found, tho' late, That what they thought the *Priest's* was *Their Estate*'. This reversal was not confined to those who accepted the Lutheran or Calvinist theologies. Fr Hughes writes of the English Church in 1540: 'The bishops have, indeed, all abandoned the principle that the authority of the teaching Church is the first source of a Christian's knowledge.' In their councils 'the measure of orthodoxy' is now 'their own scriptural and patristic learning'.[6] Between the Anglican bishops and the extreme Puritans was a great

---

* E. Walker, *A History of Music in England* (rev. ed. J. A. Westrup, 1952), 50, minimizes 'the actual artistic upheaval'. This is, of course, another matter. But this chapter is concerned to show that, although the superficial upheaval may have been exaggerated, the underlying aesthetic revolution needs more attention than it has so far attracted.

gulf. The latter made the Word of God, plainly interpreted, the touch-stone of *all* their doings and cared nothing for patristic learning:

> . . . whatsoever is added to this word by man's device, seem it never so good, holy or beautiful, yet before our God . . . it is evil, wicked, and abominable.[7]

Yet both parties have this in common, that in place of the traditional wisdom of the Church they have put their own reading of words, and especially of God's Word.

II

One of the most striking effects of the intellectual revolution (of which the Reformation in the Church was part cause, part effect) was to enhance the status not merely of the Bible but of language as such: 'The reformers believed in literacy, in the importance of words in reading, and in preaching; and they disbelieved in drama, in acting, and in symbols.'[8] In York Minster, Scripture sentences were to be painted up where the images stood.[9] This is itself a symbol of the way things were going. In place of the knowledge of ear and eye, of movement and gesture, the preachers put words – the words of the preacher, of the Bible-lesson, of the homilies. These things were 'the prior means conditioning all other means of grace'.[10]

The same forces which enhanced the status of language as opposed to symbol also enhanced the status of the vernacular as against the learned, 'dead' language of the medieval Church. What the growing nationalism of the century would have achieved in its own good time was achieved almost overnight in the name of religious truth. When the services of a national Church were conducted by command of the sovereign, even on the most august occasions, in the English tongue, no stigma of inferiority and little fear of impermanency could attach to its use elsewhere.*

The prospect of more people being able to read was also encouraging. The educational zeal of the Reformers was a natural outcome of their beliefs. The Word was truth. And the Word was now in a public book, open to all. So all must learn to read it. Illiteracy was a peril to the soul;

---

* Furthermore, the establishment of a national liturgy, backed by the power of an authorized press, by the dictates of religious zeal, and by political conviction, was strong guarantee that English itself would soon shake off the variety of dialects that bewildered Caxton. English would for practical purposes become standard; and the author would be able to count on a wider public among his own countrymen than ever before.

it meant that all knowledge of God's Word and of His Will for men would be at second hand. Cheap-jack printers were quick to take advantage of the new literacy.* When the Great Bible went through seven editions between 1539 and 1541, publishers must have realized what a shining prospect they had. The spate of broadside ballads in the early years of Elizabeth's reign is a sign of the times.[11] The importance of the English Bible, the Book of Common Prayer and the new metrical psalms in the educational movements of Elizabeth's reign is hard to estimate exactly. (Grammar-school education was still based on a thorough study of the Latin language; grammar *was* Latin.) But it will not easily be over-estimated: God's Word was the incentive, the means, and the reward. Indirectly, also, the new teaching-through-words of the greatest knowledge of all, the Bible, gave a stimulus to popular didactic work in every field: English could unlock the secrets, which Latin had hidden, of law, history, mathematics – even, eventually, of music.

The Reformation also brought, or encouraged, a new *attitude* to words. Words have not merely become of greater moment; what they say in plain, literal sense matters more. Those who followed Luther in returning to *unum simplicem, germanum et certum sensum literalem* in Biblical interpretation were reacting against a three-fold or even four-fold method which had prevailed since the time of Origen.[12] 'Plainness' was now in the ascendant. An incidental result of this shifting emphasis was certainly to strengthen the authority of 'meer English', the plain vernacular idiom, as against the subtle elaboration and refinement of 'humanist' English.[13] Dogmatic insistence on 'the very pure Word of God' (a favourite phrase of the Reformers) seemed to demand plain sense and a plain style:

> I framed my pen, not to any affected phrase, but to a meane and popular stile.[14]

III

'A meane and popular stile' is a criterion above all for the *music* of the Reformation. The medium is a different one; but the requisites are basically the same. During the later Middle Ages church-music, according to the Reformers, had become as 'dark and dumb' as the ceremonies of which it was an ornament. It must be purified with the rest of the stable. The Reformers did not, of course, *invent* a dislike of elaborate church-

---

* This is to be compared, perhaps, with the success of the national newspapers in exploiting the move towards universal literacy during the last eighty or so years.

music. Ever since the earliest Christian days men had been worried about
the hold music had over the affections of sinful men. During the Middle
Ages St Augustine was remembered for having been piously stirred by
music:

> . . . the voices flowed into mine ears, and the Truth distilled into my
> heart, whence the agitation of my piety overflowed and my tears ran
> over, and blessed was I therein.[15]

But writers also recalled that the saint gravely mistrusted the passions
aroused by self-abandonment even to hymns and canticles. The problem
was not confined to music in church. Music in general could only be
sanctioned if it put men in touch with the divine or with the good life.
Church-music simply raised the issues in the most acute form, and reformers of every age and of every persuasion agreed that here Mansoul must
be carefully guarded. Behind their attacks can perhaps be sensed a fear of
music's emotional associations, of 'lascivious harmony and delectable
music'. Openly, the chief points of attack in the later Middle Ages were
'vain' singing, the use of instruments, and the obscuration of the sacred
text. Wyclif voiced the complaints of many:

> . . . and of schort tyme thanne weren more veyn japis founden; des-
> chaunt, countre note and orgon and smale brekynge, that stirith veyn
> men to daunsynge more than to mornynge . . . oure fleschly peple hath
> more lykynge in here bodely eris in sich knackynge and taterynge than
> in herynge of goddis lawe . . . whanne ther ben fourty or fyfty in a
> queer thre or foure proude and lecherous lorellis schullen knacke the
> most devout servyce that no man schal here the sentence, and alle othere
> schullen be doumbe and loken on hem as foolis. And thanne strum-
> patis and thevys preisen sire Jacke or Hobbe and Williem the proude
> clerk, hou smale thei knacken here notis.[16]

In the period of the Reformation the tone and manner of complaint
varies considerably. On the one hand there is the irritation of Erasmus with
English church-music:

> Modern church-music is so constructed that the congregation cannot
> hear one distinct word. The choristers themselves do not understand
> what they are singing, yet according to priests and monks it consti-
> tutes the whole of religion. . . . In college or monastery it is still the
> same: music, nothing but music. There was no music in St Paul's

time. Words were then pronounced plainly. Words nowadays mean nothing. . . . If they want music, let them sing psalms like rational beings, and not too many of these.[17]

Against this can be set the wild ravings of the Protestant bishop, an ex-Carmelite, John Bale:

Neither shall the sweet organs, containing the melodious noise of all manner of instruments and birds, be played upon, nor the great bells be rung after that, nor yet the fresh descant, pricksong, counterpoint, and fa-burden be called for in thee, which art the very synagogue of Satan.[18]

But, whatever the manner of complaint, the points of attack remain constant: the central point is always that church-song, as they know it and have known it all their lives, is *un-spiritual*. 'Yea, let them hear,' writes Thomas Becon, 'whose office it is to sing in the church, that they must sing to God, not in the voice but in the heart.' [19] A hundred years later *The Westminster Directory* (1644) emphasizes the same idea:

In singing of Psalms the voice is to be tunably and gravely ordered, but the chief care must be to sing with understanding, and with grace in the heart, making melody unto the Lord.[20]

By 'singing in the heart' the Reformers clearly mean one of *two* things: either, not singing at all except metaphorically (Becon) – this need not concern us; or, knowing and feeling what the words are about whilst singing them (*The Westminster Directory*). In any case *the words must be supreme*. In the barbaric ages just passing, church-song was un-spiritual because the words meant nothing. Morley could find nothing good to say about his great predecessor, John Dunstable, in this respect. Dunstable treated words like a dunce (it is Morley's pun), committing one of the greatest absurdities Morley had seen in the 'dittying' of music.[21] In the Middle Ages words were fitted to music; but now music is to be fitted to words.

It would be a grave mistake, however, to think of music as in the centre of events or of people's thoughts. The ideals of the Reformers as they affected church-song are all of a piece with their general programme – or, rather, programme*s* – of liturgical reform. And they have their basis in theology, just as the other reforms had. The Word was in the centre, and everything else was made to revolve round it. To the ordinary layman the greatest change in the liturgy must have been visual. God's Word did not warrant the use of candles, of the marriage-ring, kneeling at the Holy

Communion, the use of holy water, the blessing of candles and palms, the sprinkling of ashes, the sign of the Cross. On February 21st, 1548, 'it was ordered that *all* religious statues and pictures should be removed from the churches and destroyed'.[22] Visual deprivation must have been the first sensation, the wholesale loss of devotions in colour, gesture and movement – in a word, of 'popish ceremonies':

> Christ's Gospel is not a ceremonial Law . . . but it is a Religion to serve God, not in the bondage of the Figure or Shadow, but in the freedom of the Spirit, being content only with those Ceremonies which do serve to a decent Order and godly Discipline.[23]

In place of the Mass, the Holy Communion; in place of the consecrated altar with its candles, 'an honest table decently covered'; instead of the priest's cope and alb, a plain white surplice. The extravagances of the old order were removed, the 'dark and dumb' ceremonies of the complicated medieval rites, to reveal the purity of God's Word.

Whether or not 'a doctrinal revolution' was intended, was indeed already taking place, does not concern us. That a *liturgical* revolution was under way was now the everyday experience of thousands. Music, throughout the period of the Reformation, is treated as one facet of the great problem of liturgy. Except by musicians it is rarely treated at length. And compared, say, with the great controversy over vestments early in Elizabeth's reign, it is of minor importance, though worth its mention amongst all the other gifts of God needing rescue from the perversions of papistry:

> Alas, gossip, what shall we now do at church, since all the saints are taken away, since all the goodly sights we were wont to have are gone, since we cannot hear the like piping, singing, chanting, and playing upon the organs that we could before?[24]

In considering the effects of the Reformation on religious 'song' (I use the word to cover every type of vocal music), and through that on the changing relationship of music and poetry in sixteenth-century England, it is as well to start with the twin pillars of the Continental Reformation, Luther and Calvin. Despite their theological divisions they had much in common: they agreed, for instance, in attacking late medieval teaching about the Mass, current conceptions of priesthood, false honouring of the Saints. They agreed in their desire to restore the worship of the primitive Church, with a simple Communion Service in which the laity should not be merely spectators.

With this generous measure of agreement, why are the liturgies of Luther and Calvin so different? The answer, in Horton Davies's words, is this:

> Luther will have what is not specifically condemned by the Scriptures; whilst Calvin will have only what is ordained by God in the Scriptures.[25]

Provided that Scripture was not flouted, Luther was prepared to allow and to encourage considerable freedom of choice. Variety of worship, reflected still in Lutheranism today, was, he thought, a condition of 'inwardness' in worship and a part of Christian freedom:

> I desire that all arts, particularly music, be employed in the service of Him who has given and created them.[26]

Luther's demands of church-song were that it should be predominantly (but not exclusively) congregational, vernacular and scriptural, 'so that through the medium of song the Word of God may remain among the people'.[27] Unlike Calvin, Luther had no objection either to the traditional Catholic chant or to contemporary part-music. Having decided that the Scriptures warranted music, he would have the best.[28] And in this determination to use the best to the glory of God, the divines and composers of the 'Anglican' persuasion agreed with him.

Calvinistic worship is less rich in ceremonial, for ceremony is an impertinency in the circumstances; God's imperfect, corrupt creature must rather wait in obedience to the declared Will for the gracious intercession of the Holy Spirit.* Church-song must be limited to the songs actually appointed by God in his Word, the Psalms and Canticles; they should be sung by the congregation as an integral part of the Church service, without accompaniment and, above all, 'with understanding':

> As for public prayers, there are two kinds. The ones with the word alone: the others with singing. . . . Care must always be taken that the music (*le chant*) be neither light nor frivolous: but that it have weight and majesty . . . there is a great difference between the music which

---

* Horton Davies, 23–, describes Calvinistic worship as differing from the Lutheran in four main points: it is more objective, because concerned less with the worshipper's feelings than with God's Will for man; it is more Biblical, because the Bible alone declares that Will; it stresses obedience, 'reverential abasement before the Living God', rather than gratitude; and it is less rich in ceremonial.

one makes to entertain men at table and in their houses, and the Psalms which are sung in the Church in the presence of God and His angels.[29]

Church-music to Calvin is a species of congregational prayer; its supreme expression, the vernacular psalm.

IV

Luther and Calvin typify two important Reforming attitudes. (Needless to say, neither of them was as consistent in his views as this little summary has suggested.)[30] The two attitudes are roughly those adopted in England by the 'Anglican' and 'Puritan' parties respectively. But, as we must realize, this was not solely a party matter. Everyone wanted change – of some sort. (The Council of Trent is as much a part of the Reformation in its widest sense as John Knox's Genevan Service Book.) The changes advocated ranged over the whole field of church-music and differed widely. But everyone wanted at least one or two of the following: the setting of Biblical texts in the vernacular with a strong bias towards the Psalms; more congregational and unison, less choral and polyphonic singing; the banishment of instruments, including the organ, from the services, and sometimes from the church itself; a syllabic treatment in music of the words set; 'sober', 'modest' and 'distinct' performance without the distraction of vain ornamentation; and a restrained style of musical composition, which should yet 'wonderfullye move, stirre, pearce and enflame the hearers myndes'.[31]

The introduction of the vernacular was of prime importance to all except Catholics. In a well-known and often-quoted letter to Henry VIII, Cranmer speaks first about 'certain processions'; the letter then goes on:

> Concerning the *Salve festa dies*, the Latin note, as I think, is sober and distinct enough; wherefore I have travailed to make the verses in English, and have put the Latin note unto the same. Nevertheless they that be cunning in singing can make a much more solemn note thereto. I made them only for a proof, to see how English would do in song.[32]

This is clearly one way of meeting the demand that church-song shall be in the vernacular – to take the traditional music of the chant and fit English words to it. This method commended itself not only to the Reformers but also, for different reasons, to those who opposed reformation. The

The Reformation

Edwardian rite lent itself to camouflage, and the Protestants soon complained that

> . . . in the churches they always chant the *hours* and other hymns relating to the Lord's Supper, but in our own language. And that popery may not be lost, the mass-priests, although they are compelled to discontinue the use of the Latin language, yet most carefully observe the same tone and manner of chanting to which they were heretofore accustomed in the papacy.[33]

An important earlier attempt to adapt the traditional chant was Cranmer's Litany of 1544, part of a projected Processional; it was a setting of the Litany to the traditional chant but in a 'reformed' translation.[34]

The chant of the Litany was only slightly modified to fit the 'reformed' text. But this pointed the way clearly to the next and obvious step in producing a vernacular liturgy. John Merbecke was the first to modify the plain-chant on a large scale and to publish his attempt, *The boke of Common praier noted*, 1550 – 'In this booke is conteyned so much of the Order of Common Prayer as is to be song in Churches'.[35] Many of Merbecke's melodies are derived from plain-song; but they differ from the originals in two important ways: his settings are entirely syllabic, word for note, and they stress the effective words by setting them to high notes. Here is a transcription into modern notation of part of Merbecke's second post-Communion, which illustrates tricks of verbal emphasis foreign to plain-song:[36]

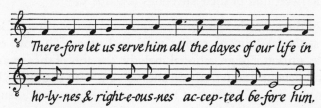

There-fore let us serve him all the dayes of our life in ho-ly-nes & right-e-ous-nes ac-cep-ted be-fore him.

Another way of introducing the vernacular without upsetting things too much was to fit English words to polyphony written for a Latin text. The result is not usually a great success. Luther had felt the same difficulty – the life goes out of the music when another language steps in. A good way of testing this for oneself is to take parallel phrases from the two versions of Taverner's Mass, *Sine Nomine*, and to observe the now-flaccid, now-strained quality of the English setting.[37]

The modification of the simpler Gregorian melodies for use in English must have been common, though it has not left many records. The modification of Latin polyphony was, in the nature of things, both less common and less successful. It soon became clear that the only really satisfactory way of providing music for the new liturgy with its idealization of the Word, and of words in general, was to write it. This, composers set about doing.

V

In the history of Reformed 'song' there are two chief trends to be observed. First, there is the urge towards a simplification of music. This takes, in extremes, the form of a return to *melody*, the single, unadorned line of sound, in the simplest of rhythms. One sure way of achieving a clear hearing for the Word was to abolish the superstitious practice of singing in parts. It is almost as if by an intuitive piece of musical history the Reformers divined that the primitive Church knew no harmony. At any rate, this return to melody (not merely to a melodic conception of music, for the Middle Ages had that) bore rich fruit. Many fine tunes still enrich the Protestant worship of England and Germany today.

Secondly, by way of reaction against this over-simplification, other composers developed quite deliberately the representative and emotive resources of music, adding to words (like King David)

> melodie both vocall and instrumentall for the raysing up of mens harts, and the sweetning of their affections towards God.[38]

The first of these trends was the 'Puritan' one, derived from Calvin; the second was the 'Anglican', owing more to Luther. The aim of the first was simple, unison, congregational melody; the aim of the second, 'sober, discrete and devout singing, music and playing with organs'.* These are, I must emphasize, only trends. Once again, there was never such a neat division into parties as the terms suggest. We cannot, and need not, here examine the numerous shades of liturgical theory and practice, reflecting a multitude of sects and zealots, from Anabaptists to Catholic recusants. I shall continue to use the words 'Anglican' and 'Puritan' in quotation marks as a reminder of the simplifications they conceal.

The 'Puritans' found that the metrical psalm was the only kind of church-song that really satisfied all their demands. Let us take for an

---

* These two trends correspond to two found in contemporary humanist theory. On the one hand there were those who wanted to abolish counterpoint altogether; on the other, those who sought by its proper employment to achieve the splendid ethical effects of Greek music.

example Psalm 23, in the version by Whittingham, to the tune of the Anglo-Genevan Psalter, 1556:

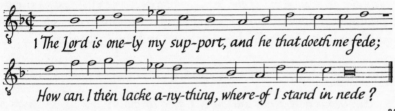

1 The Lord is one-ly my sup-port, and he that doeth me fede;

How can I then lacke a-ny-thing, where-of I stand in nede?

39

Here we have the strictest Reformation principles: one syllable to one note; one line of melody only; a vigorous interaction between the natural accent of the words and the natural phrasing of the music; great economy of rhythmic means – only two note-values are used; and a restricted range, ideal for congregational singing. The effect, though strong, is not wooden; it is not even set-square. In their easy and flexible combination of groups of two and groups of three the metrical psalm tunes owe something, surely, to a live plain-song tradition.

Not by any means all the multifarious literary, musical, devotional, and social activity which centred in the psalms at this period can be attributed to the vogue of the *metrical* psalm of 'Puritan' worship. The psalms of Wyatt, for instance, belong to a medieval tradition of translation from the Seven Penitential Psalms; those of Sidney and his sister owe more to the courtly French versions of Clement Marot than to the English tradition; and so on.[40] Many learned poets worked the psalms because they were 'a divine poem' justifying, against all attack, the use of metre and of figurative speech.[41] 'Holy David' had much to offer to those who were interested in the 'defense of poesie'.

The Reformers, moreover, were not innovating when they elevated the psalms to a position of importance in Christian worship and in Christian devotion. This place the psalms had occupied from time immemorial. They were the very blood and bone of the medieval rite, especially of the services of the Hours. What the Reformers (in particular, the 'Puritans') did, was to recover for the psalms their popularity as *congregational* songs, by translating them into the vernacular, setting them in metre (mostly the ballad metre), giving them tunes that appealed, and making the people sing them.*

* A similar impulse lies behind the present popular Catholic revival of psalm-singing, inspired by the versions of Fr Joseph Gelineau.

Music and Poetry

The earliest metrical version of the psalms for congregational use was that of Miles Coverdale, the translator of the Bible: *Goostly psalmes & spirituall Songes drawen out of the holy Scripture* [*c.* 1543]. Most of the songs and psalms are translated from German and the German tunes are retained. The well-known 'Oure God is a defence and towre' begins:

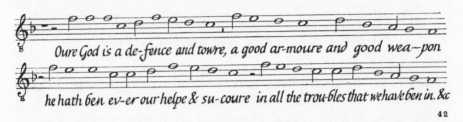

Oure God is a de-fence and towre, a good ar-moure and good wea—pon

he hath ben ev-er our helpe & su-coure in all the trou-bles that we have ben in. &c

42

The book was suppressed and burnt by Henry VIII as Lutheran heresy, and many 'Puritans' welcomed the suppression because the singing meant 'conjoint voices', 'conjoint voices' meant a premeditated 'set form' of praise, and 'set form' meant spiritual death. There were always certain extremists who held that God's Word only warranted extempore *solo* singing, as and when the Spirit moved it. Others had scruples about metre – was it not a tampering with the literal truth of the Word to make rhyme and verse of it?[43] But the great body of 'Puritan' opinion came to accept unison singing (which is all that is meant by 'conjoint') as sufficiently Scriptural, otherwise the metrical psalms could hardly have caught on as they did.

The astounding popularity of the 'Old Version' could not have come about unless the tunes had been good and strong. This they were. But, at the same time, the tunes were only one factor. Much is due to the fact that they were in regular and approved liturgical use. 'The metrical Psalms', it has been said, 'were the people's part in the worship of the Reformed Church'; they were, moreover, 'an integral part of these services, not mere punctuations [of them]'.[44] Thanksgiving, praise and adoration were largely absent from the rest of the service that they might be present on the people's lips in the metrical psalms. But this is not the whole story, for the metrical psalm was taken up by 'Anglicans' as early as 1559. Strype tells us the custom was introduced at St Paul's, 'as was used among the Protestants of Geneva, all men, women, and young folks singing together'.[45] In the 'Anglican' rite the metrical psalms did not take the place of the office psalms, which continued to be read or sung in the prose version of the Great Bible, but might allowably be sung 'in the beginning or end of common prayers'.[46]

The Reformation

The metrical psalms (among which 'Sternhold and Hopkins' versions were pre-eminent*) presented to the people – whether they were always aware of it or not – the very type of Reformed church-song after the Calvinist model. To the 'Puritans' this was 'godly song', and nothing else could meet with the same approval. But the metrical psalm is also interesting, to us, for what it leaves out. It is 'a playn and distincte note' – but no more. It makes no attempt at musical refinements such as 'just accent', word-painting, or other expressive and dramatic techniques. It is, so to speak, simply *purified medieval* song. Even if this were all that could be shown by way of change, the Reformation would warrant an important place in any historical account of words-and-music. The new emphasis on clarity and intelligibility, the reversal of the ancient roles of music and poetry, the general simplification of music for worship – these were bound to have a radical effect upon the spirit in which composers worked. But there is more. It is the other trend, which I am calling for convenience the 'Anglican', which invites our principal attention. The 'Anglican' composers (I include those who still occasionally composed for the Roman rite), rebelling against the liturgical and musical asceticism of the 'Puritans', were forced to develop a way of setting words to music which satisfied the demands of Reform and yet did not deny God's good gift of the 'sweetness' of melody.

VI

Just as it would be wrong to distinguish too sharply between a Lutheran and a Calvinistic view, between an 'Anglican' and a 'Puritan' party, in doctrine or church government, so in music. The two trends of Reformation song are a necessary simplification for the purposes of discussion. There are several shades of compromise which must perforce be passed over. A convenient half-way house, for instance, between 'plain tune' and polyphonic setting was the chordal harmonization of a melody. Only a few years after the first printing, in Geneva, of the 'church tunes' to 'Sternhold and Hopkins', John Day published in London *The whole psalms in foure parts*, 1563, a sort of 'musical companion' to, or 'music edition' of, the metrical psalms. Even more interesting, though less influential, are the note-against-note settings by Thomas Tallis of Archbishop Parker's

* 'Sternhold and Hopkins' achieved roughly 300 editions by the end of the seventeenth century.

metrical psalms. Tallis clearly aimed in this book (it was printed but never published) to catch the attention of more than one 'party':

> The Tenor of these partes be for the people when they will syng alone, the other parts, put for greater queers, or to suche as will syng or play them privatelye.[47]

(That is to say, these are good congregational songs and choral anthems, besides being suitable for domestic devotion.)

However, leaving such compromises aside for the moment, we must, I think, emphasize the basic distinction between the 'Puritan' and the 'Anglican' trend in church-music. Whereas the 'Puritans' cared merely to *present* the words, holding that all 'artificial' music was a mere distraction, the 'Anglican' ideal was to *represent* the words by making music 'serve to the very kinde and degree of those impressions' which the words conveyed.

Even in this over-simplified form the difference is not absolute. The 'Anglican' ideal does, to some extent, embrace the 'Puritan'; 'Anglicans', too, take care to present, as well as to represent, the text clearly. Their composers do this, even in contrapuntal pieces, by making the imitative points short and pithy; by defining clearly the ranges of the voices; by keeping fairly closely to the principle of a syllable to a note; by interspersing the counterpoint with passages of straightforward chordal writing. Indeed, in this matter of presentation the skilled composer of music for the Anglican rite improved in some respects on the metrical psalm of the 'Puritan'. The 'Anglican' was not content merely to put the same number of notes as there were syllables; he tried to follow in his music the accentuation of the words. We can see this by comparing the way Sternhold's version of Psalm 6 fits to the church tune with the way William Byrd set the same words in *Psalms, Sonnets and Songs*, 1588.[48] Morley, organist of St Paul's, was insistent in the *Plain and Easy Introduction* that composers should not commit the 'barbarism' of having long notes with short syllables, and vice versa.[49]

There was yet another way of presenting the words intelligibly to the listener, and that was by repeating them. We must turn for an explicit statement to a later writer. Charles Butler did not publish *The Principles of Musik* until 1636. But it was then old-fashioned; so the practice which he rationalizes is 'artificial' church-music in the second half of the sixteenth century. He writes:

> Reports require Repeats: that if the Points Ditty be not apprehended at the first; yet, in the iterating thereof, it may. Such Repeats should be

Emphatical, importing some special matter: and which, in Divine uses, may help both to excite and to express due zeal and Devotion.[50]

To repeat a verbal phrase two or three times in each part has, then, its justification, if not its essential motive, in Reformation theory.

However, the characteristic 'Anglican' concern, as already observed, is not merely to present but to *represent* the words, and by representing 'to move and to moderate all affections'. The evidence of this is in the music itself, in the well-known anthems and canticles. The ways in which it was attempted are multifarious: the two most obvious are word-painting and the expression of mood. Word-painting is a sort of musical simile. As Morley puts it:

> you must have a care that when your matter signifieth 'ascending', 'high', 'heaven', and such like you make your music ascend; and by the contrary where your ditty speaketh of 'descending', 'lowness', 'depth', 'hell', and others such you must make your music descend; for as it will be thought a great absurdity to talk of heaven and point down-wards to the earth, so will it be counted great incongruity if a musician upon the words 'he ascended into heaven' should cause his music to descend, or by the contrary upon the descension should cause his music to ascend.[51]

It is clear from the example Morley uses here, and others elsewhere, that he has church-music in mind as much as madrigals. Word-painting, of course, is not merely a matter of melodic direction. It affects every aspect of composition, as Morley later shows. Word-painting and 'expression of mood' are not separate issues. They are different aspects of the same thing. Word-painting should be a mere symptom of a concern with the deeper kind of expression which, by representing the words, serves 'to move and to moderate all affections' (i.e. to excite and to control all emotions).

The Anglican divines who, like Richard Hooker, accepted the Elizabethan Settlement, inherited a medieval attitude towards church-music: music is an echo, or mirror, of heaven; it will put us

> in remembrance of the heavenly triumphant church, where is everlasting joy with continuall laud and praise to God.[51a]

This recalls the commonplaces of medieval thinkers: *Musica Deum delectat*; *Musica ecclesiam militantem triumphanti assimilat*. To experience music is to join the cosmic harmony. Luther, in a similar vein, likens the cavorting of the voices in polyphony around the plain-song to 'a kind of divine dance'.[52] And throughout the century it was customary to defend religious music on this philosophical ground. But divines were not slow to develop and adapt this attitude to the needs of the times. The sentence just quoted (from a *Book of Ceremonies* prepared by a group of conservative Bishops in 1540–3) begins:

> The sober, discrete and devout singing, music and playing with organs used in the church for the service of God are ordained to move, and stir the people to the sweetness of God's word the which is there sung, and by that sweet armony both *to excite them to prayers and devotion* and also to put them in remembrance. . . .[53]

This sets out a Reformed ideal: music will only have good effects if it is 'sober', i.e. restrained, free from showy ornament; 'discrete', i.e. distinct, each note separated from its fellows; and 'devout', sung in the heart and 'with the understanding'. Furthermore, the prominence given to the devotional effect of the music (always very much a secondary concern in the Middle Ages) and the telling phrase, 'the sweetness of God's word,' reveal, on the part of these anti-Lutherans, a Lutheran concern with feelings very much in keeping with the times.

The connection between music and behaviour is now, by the Elizabethan period, rarely left in the air. The good Reformer of the more moderate persuasion defended church-music against the austerities of Puritanism on these very grounds that it would 'excite' the congregation 'to prayers and devotion'. The classic defence is that of Richard Hooker in the fifth Book of *The Ecclesiastical Polity*: he describes 'musicall harmonie' as

> a thing which delighteth all ages and beseemeth all states; a thing as seasonable in griefe as in joy; as decent being added unto actions of greatest weight and solemnitie, as being used when men most sequester themselves from action. The reason hereof is an admirable facilitie which musique hath to expresse and represent to the mind more inwardly than any other sensible meane the very standing, rising and falling, the very steps and inflections every way, the turnes and varieties of all passions whereunto the minde is subject.[54]

Music is an art of Imitation. By 'Imitating' virtue and vice, music brings the mind of the listener to share in those 'passions' (emotions). Nothing, therefore, is more 'pestilential' than bad music; nothing more saving than good.

What is new here is not the observation that music is a moral agent; it had scarcely escaped the notice of the Middle Ages that men are affected by what they hear. The novelty consists in making a logical connection between 'expression' and 'emotion'. (This is the same connection as Sir Thomas More made in reference to the music of Utopia.)[55] The worshipper will be moved to exultation because the composer *expresses* exultation; to sadness because the composer *expresses* sadness. The composer has to write the music of a 'spiritual religion'.

VII

'Opposed to the more universal-objective nature of the Gregorian conception,' writes Professor Lang, 'which elevates man to higher regions by grades of perfection through a long continued process, the Protestant conception rests on a personal and immediate faith, experienced once for all. . . . *It was this principle of spiritual religion as opposed to sacramental religion which dominated musical thought.*' [56] The truth of this for England has been shown, I hope, in the paragraphs above. Morley wrote late in the century, when the issues had become clear, the lines of defence strong and well-manned. (This is not to say that Morley is entirely free from confusion himself.) Morley's defence of church-music clearly rests on 'experience', on 'spiritual religion': the composer must 'possess himself' of the experience carried in the words; he must convey both the words and the experience behind them into his music; the listener will hear the words and share the experience, and his 'affections' towards God will be 'sweetened'. Morley's approach to the madrigal is similar: 'in this kind you must possess yourself of an amorous humour (for in no composition shall you prove admirable except you put on and possess yourself wholly with that vein wherein you compose)'. The new, subjective, 'spiritual' conception is henceforward to dominate even those kinds of music which are 'made upon songs and sonnets'. And – this is the important retrospective point – it is a *new* conception of song-writing. The love-songs of the early Tudor court songbooks were written under the old régime and according to the old conception.

The antithesis, 'sacramental/spiritual', serves very well to indicate the fundamental change which was coming over people's attitude to music. Another antithesis will further illuminate the changing relationship of music to words. If, for the Middle Ages, *symbolic* is the word to describe the musical order that we enter and experience, for the Elizabethan period, *symptomatic* is perhaps appropriate. A symptom can be defined as 'a phenomenon . . . accompanying some condition, process, feeling . . . *and serving as evidence of it*'. Post-Reformation music is often a phenomenon in sound accompanying some mood or sequence of moods and serving as evidence of it. The crucial test is to take the words away from a motet or anthem and to see what the music conveys. Some pieces of Reformed church-music and some madrigals would, I think, stand this test. We must not, of course, expect a complete answer from a single symptom, any more than we should expect a doctor confidently to diagnose measles simply from a few spots. The definition requires evidence, not complete evidence.

This 'invention', or finding out, of a direct and detailed emotional connection between words and music is a revolutionary change – deeply revolutionary, because the previous relationship has been turned up-side-down: the former mistress (music) has become the servant, the servant (words) now reigns supreme. To put it another way, medieval music was dominated by Number; now, because of The Word, music is to be dominated by Word. This revolution has coloured our views on music and poetry and their 'proper' relationship to this day; but it coloured first of all the theory and practice of madrigal and lutenist composers in Elizabethan England. It was a prime factor in the artificial reunion of music and poetry in the later sixteenth century.

NOTES TO CHAPTER 5

1. The Reformation is scarcely mentioned even in Pattison's comprehensive and standard book.
2. Hughes, *Reformation*, ii. 4.
3. Biographical information about Tallis, Taverner and Merbecke can be obtained from *Grove (5)*.
4. Margaret Deanesly, *The Lollard Bible* (1920), *passim*. Even Sir Thomas More seems to accept the traditional view that Bible-reading should be the licensed privilege of the few.
5. Deanesly, ch. 1, sect. 3: the Oxford constitutions of 1408 (aimed at the Lollards?) were generally interpreted as banning all translation.
6. Hughes, ii. 3.
7. Preface to the 'Waldegrave Prayer Book', *c.* 1585, from P. Hall, *Reliquiae Liturgicae* (1847), i. 115. See also Horton Davies, *The Worship of the English Puritans* (1948), ch. 9, 'Puritan Prayer Books'. I am much indebted to Davies' book in this chapter.

8. Morison, *English Prayer Books*, 61, writing *à propos* the Great Bible of 1539 and the preachers.
9. Frere, *Visitation Articles and Injunctions*, ii. 'Archbp Holgate's Injunctions for York Minster (1552)', art. 22, p. 320.
10. Morison, 61.
11. *Broadside Index* is the best analytical survey of broadside literature. It was far from being all secular; many religious broadsides are highly scurrilous in character – e.g. 'A Lamentation from Rome', by a fly that lay in the Pope's nose; pr. Chappell (1859), i. 113.
12. See B. Willey, *Seventeenth Century Background* (1946), ch. iv, 'On Scriptural Interpretation'.
13. It might also be argued that the Reformation helped to change the traditional *sounds* of language, especially in poetry. The 'balanced' line of late medieval courtly and clerical verse was replaced between about 1540 and 1560 by the evenly flowing iambic line with five regular stresses. This extraordinary change in taste has never, I think, been satisfactorily explained. It is tempting to see it as reflecting, in part, a great movement of popularization. This – a mighty popularizing force – the Reformation in some of its aspects certainly was. The Reformers wanted everything 'plain', in its two related senses of 'openly intelligible to all' and 'free from all adornment'. One way of achieving open intelligibility was, they thought, to use proven popular modes, and amongst these the metres and rhythms of popular song ranked high. The metrical psalms are a good example of this kind of popularizing. One collection of Scriptural poems in English (that known as 'Sternhold and Hopkins') was authorized for liturgical use by all ecclesiastical parties. It was so well received that it went through an average of two editions a year for one hundred and fifty years. But would even such a success have had a decisive influence on 'the English ear'? We may be dubious. The 'stateliness' (to use Tottel's word) of Surrey's verse, and of Wyatt's, in the revised versions of the *Songs and Sonets*, was a quality admired by 'the learned', by such men as Puttenham and Ascham; and they gave their approval precisely because the verse was '*removed from* the rude skill of common ears'. Courtly verse underwent a rhythmic simplification which brought it closer to the popular style; but the simplification itself cannot be explained merely as an attempt to accommodate the courtly mode to a popular ideal. The change of taste remains mysterious.

14. L. B. Wright, *Middle-Class Culture in Elizabethan England* (1935), 350.

15. Quoted, Reese, *MMA*, 64 (I have amended the trans. as suggested by Perl, 506–7; see p. 60 above).

16. Wyclif, *English Works*, ed. F. D. Matthew, EETS (1880), 191–. (I thank Hans Käsmann for this reference and for another to Cambridge, Trinity College MS B.v.25 [Lollard version of Rolle's Psalter], f.108v, where 'curious singing' and 'highe rorying' of motets are referred to as despicable.)

17. Quoted P. Scholes, *The Puritans and Music* (1934), 216.

18. John Bale, *Select Works*, ed. H. Christmas, Parker Soc. (1849), 536, from 'The Image of both the Churches'.

19. Thomas Becon, *Works*, ed. J. Ayre, Parker Soc. (1843), i. 134, from 'The Pathway unto Prayer', ch. 5. Becon was one of Cranmer's chaplains under Edward VI.

20. G. W. Sprott and T. Leishman, *The Book of Common Order, etc.* (1868), 322. See also Horton Davies, 127–. The Directory was the official Puritan prayer-book passed by Parliament during the Commonwealth.

21. Morley, *Plain and Easy*, 291: Dunstable divided the word *angelo—rum* with a musical rest.

22. Hughes, *Reformation*, ii. 101. I have been much helped by Fr Hughes' exposition of the ecclesiastical changes.

23. *Book of Common Prayer*, 'Of Ceremonies, why some be Abolished and some retained'.

24. Boyd, 19, from *Certain Sermons or Homilies*, SPCK (1864).

25. Horton Davies, ch. 2, 'The Theology of Reformed Worship'. Their agreements had their roots in three basic doctrines which they shared: that the Bible was the prime source of revealed truth; that men are justified by Faith and not by Works; and that the sole mediator between man and God is Christ. Mr Davies further comments that 'the Lutheran service tends to become the expression of the experience that the Word engenders. Its atmosphere is one of glad thankfulness for God's gracious forgiveness' (p. 23).

26. Quoted, W. E. Buszin, 'Luther on Music', *MQ*, xxxii (1946), 88, from preface to *Geistliches Gesangbüchlein* (1524).

27. Quoted, Buszin, 87, from a letter.

28. '. . . Next to the Word of God, only music deserves being extolled as the mistress and governess of the feelings of the human heart. . . .

Even the Holy Spirit honours music as a tool of his work' (Buszin, 81, translating from *Praefatio D. M. Lutheris in Harmonias de Passione Christi*, OPERA LATINA, vii. 551–4).

29. Calvin's Preface to the *Psalter* (Geneva, 1542). Original French text in O. Douen, *Clément Marot et Le Psautier Huguenot*, 2 vols (Paris, 1878–), i. 348–; translation above from Garside, 'Calvin's Preface', *MQ*, xxxvii (1951), 568 (I have altered his translation of *chant* as 'song' to 'music'; cf. Middle Eng. 'song').

30. H. A. Mason has drawn my attention, for instance, to Calvin, *Institutiones*, lib. iv, cap. x: its spirit is summed up in the phrases: *sed quid noceat vel aedificet, caritas optime judicabit, quam si moderatricem esse patiemur, salva erunt omnia.*

31. More, *Utopia*, 183, in another context (see ch. 4, note 26 above).

32. Cranmer, *Miscellaneous Writings and Letters*, ed. J. E. Cox, Parker Soc. (1846), 412. The probable date is 7 October 1544. See also E. H. Fellowes, *English Cathedral Music* (1941), 25–26.

33. Hughes, *Reformation*, ii. 110, from *Original Letters relative to the English Reformation*, Parker Soc. (1846–7), i. 72.

34. Cranmer's Litany is printed by J. E. Hunt, *Cranmer's First Litany, 1544, and Merbecke's Book of Common Prayer, 1550* (1939). The chant was to be 'sayde or songe of the priest with an audible voyce'; the choir, not the people, were to answer 'sobrely and devoutely'; the people were to listen and 'read' (if they could), devoutly praying the while.

35. London, Richard Grafton, 1550; reproduced in facsimile by Hunt; articles by R. R. Terry in *PRMA*, xlv (1919), 75, and by R. Stevenson in *MQ*, xxxvii (1951), 220, on musical characteristics and sources. See also Morison, 79: 'Merbecke's intention was to provide the basis for musical uniformity side by side with the liturgical uniformity as authorized'. With slight exceptions 'there is no authentic plain-song throughout the book' (Terry, 82).

36. Transcribed from Hunt, 226. As Stevenson observes (p. 228), 'Lengthy notes, high notes and notes preceded and followed by a skip' are now 'associated with emphatic words in the text'. Merbecke's noted book has achieved wide popularity in recent years, not only amongst Anglicans. The interesting thing is that it did not catch on at all at the time when it was written. Indeed, the revision of the *Book of Common Prayer* in 1552 must have made his efforts seem quite papistical. And to judge from his later utterances, at the end of a

long life devoted to polemical theology, he could scarcely have approved of it himself:

'What shall we say of chauntinge, which onyle feedeth the eares with a vaine sounde . . . I say it [music] is not onely an unadvised zeale, but also a wicked stubbornesse' (quoted, Stevenson, 224).

Probably the book was too closely associated with the insufficiently Protestant *Book of Common Prayer* of 1549.

37. e.g. *Domine deus* from the *Gloria*: Latin, *TCM*, i. 52; English, iii. 145. In the so-called Wanley MSS (see Fellowes, *Cathedral Music*, 8) three out of the ten settings of the Mass in English, *c.* 1546–7, are adaptations of Latin Masses; two of the three are by Taverner (pr. *TCM*, vol. iii).

38. Hooker, *Ecclesiastical Polity*, bk v, sect. xxxviii (2).

39. Frost, no. 41. See also Boyd, 41. I have altered the clef from treble to modern tenor and added the words to Frost's version.

40. Wyatt's psalms are pr. by Muir, 203–; Sidney's (completed by his sister, Countess of Pembroke) by A. Feuillerat, *Complete Works,* iii (1923). See also J. Holland, *Psalmists of Britain,* 2 vols (1843). On Wyatt's psalms and their source see H. A. Mason in *TLS*, 27 Feb., 6 Mar. (1953).

41. See Sidney's *Apologie* (Gregory Smith, i. 154); Hallett Smith, 'English Metrical Psalms . . . and their Literary Significance', *HLQ*, ix (1946), 249–.

42. Ps. 46 (Frost, no. 277) from Klug's *Gesangbuch* (1529). (Coverdale uses the old numbering of the Pss.)

43. Horton Davies, 168–70.

44. W. D. Maxwell, *John Knox's Genevan Service Book* (1931), 61–.

45. Quoted, Maxwell, 62.

46. Queen Elizabeth's Injunction is pr. in H. Gee and W. J. Hardy, *Documents illustrative of English Church History* (1896), 417–; it covers more music than the metrical psalms, of course, allowing 'the best sort of melody and music that may be conveniently devised'.

47. On the Parker–Tallis psalter, see Frost, 374 (with tunes); Fellowes, *Cathedral Music*, 59; Boyd, 45 (with tunes); and Ellinwood, 'Tallis' Tunes and Tudor Psalmody' in *Musica Disciplina*, ii, fasc. 3–4 (1948), 189 (with tunes). A curious feature is a set of rhymed tags, describing 'the nature' of the tunes.

48. Frost, no. 21, from *Anglo-Genevan Psalter*; Byrd (ed. E. H. Fellowes,

EMS, vol. xiv), no. 9, 'Lord in thy wrath'. It seems to have escaped notice that two of Byrd's psalms are settings of 'Sternhold and Hopkins' versions.

49. See p. 70 above; Morley, *Plain and Easy*, 291.
50. Charles Butler, *The Principles of Musik* (1636), 97. (I have modernized his eccentric orthography, retaining only his capital letters.)
51. Morley, 291.
51a. See note 53.
52. Buszin, 81.
53. C. S. Cobb, ed., *The Rationale of Ceremonial: 1540–43* (1910), 14: the book, which was never published, contains explanations (e.g. of vestments) in plain language for laymen. (My italics.)
54. Hooker, bk v, sect. xxxviii (1).
55. See p. 65 above.
56. Lang, 212.

CHAPTER 6

Music and the Early Tudor Lyric: I

SONG-BOOKS AND MUSICAL SETTINGS

The purpose of introducing a chapter on the Reformation out of chronological order was to show, I hope decisively, from what point in history, and from what seminal ideas, many of our present notions about words-and-music derive.[1] The early Tudor song-books stand on the other side of 'the great divide'. They were written at a time before it became axiomatic that the prime duty of music was to 'express' the moods of men's minds as signalized in the words of a song. There is, however, danger of over-simplification in the neat antithesis with which the last chapter ended, between a medieval number-dominated music and a post-Reformation word-dominated music. The composer of such a song as *Madame d'amours* [H67] clearly did not think of himself simply as a mathematician in sound; there is always a sense in which music must 'express' the mind of its maker. In the present chapter we turn again to the songs and poems of the period, 1480 to 1530, and try first to answer this question: When a composer took a poem and set it to music in the sophisticated style of the part-songs in the court song-books, what did he think he was doing? How did he conceive his responsibility in the joint venture of making a song?

I

Any useful inquiry into this problem will begin with the songs themselves. This has not always been easy in the past because of the inaccessibility of the material. But there is no substitute for the evidence of the words and notes.

We may begin with a quotation (ideally it should be a quotation in *sound*). It shows the first section and the opening bars of the second section of a typical three-part song from *The Fayrfax MS.*

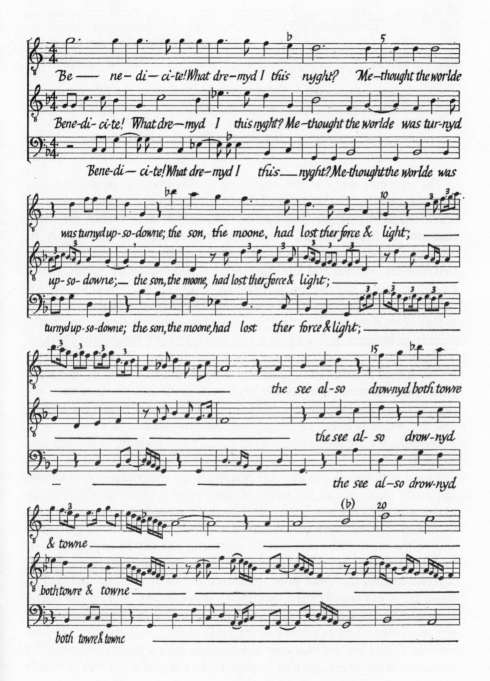

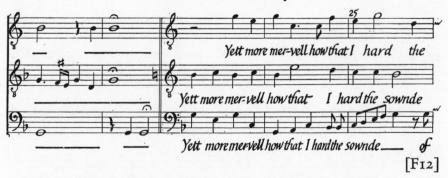

Yett more mer-vell how that I hard the

Yett more mer-vell how that I hard the sownde

Yett more mervell how that I hard the sownde___ of

[F12]

The two-part songs at the beginning of this manuscript illustrate the *genre* most clearly. Each phrase of the words is introduced with a point of imitation, at the octave, unison, or fifth, which may extend for some measures in strict canon. When the verbal phrase, treated largely in minims and crotchets, comes to an end, the music merges without break into quicker rhythms and introduces triplets and sequential figures. In the three-part songs, like the one just chosen for quotation, imitation may involve all three voices or any two of them. The rhythmic clashes met with in the two-part songs – for example, four-against-three – are still common: there is an instance in bar 29, just after our quotation breaks off. Passages of chordal writing occur in some songs; but this way of varying the style is only hinted at here (bar 23). There is no particular feeling of harmonic progression; in modern terms, the key hovers around G minor most of the time, occasionally verging towards C or D. The interest, rather, is melodic, and the music is linear in conception. We must listen to it, as it were, *horizontally*, for the subtle interplay of melody and melody, of rhythm and metre.

This description shows that it is possible to say many of the obvious and important things about the music of these songs without much reference to the words. In discussing, say, an Elizabethan madrigal, this would not be so easy. But this must not obscure one important fact: the song owes its *form* to the poem. The rhyme-royal stanza, as one would expect from its high literary standing, was a favourite amongst musicians. As a fixed form it ranks second, though a poor second, to the carol. The normal way of handling it has already been described (Introduction, p. 17): the poetic form, *ababbcc*, is set with a break between the fourth and fifth lines, irrespective of whether there is a break in the sense or not.[2] In 'Benedicite! Whate dremyd I?' the break fortunately corresponds with a turning-point in the argument of the poem. As if to emphasize the cut-and-dried way in which

the musical form is derived from the poem, each section commonly ends
with the same long melisma.

In one fundamental respect, then, the words and notes of the early Tudor
songs cannot be separately considered – the forms (carol, refrain-song,
strophic song, rhyme-royal stanza, *ottava rima*, etc.) are 'musico-poetical'
forms. It would be unthinkable even in the early sixteenth century for a
composer to set a carol except *as* a carol. Nevertheless, the hegemony of
fixed poetical forms is being broken up in several unmistakable ways. The
impatience of composers under the strict yoke of poetical form shows itself
in musical elaborations of two sorts: the construction of formal patterns
unconnected with the words; and the insertion of purely musical material.
The first, ever-increasing formal elaboration, is seen in the continental
rondeau and in the English carol. Even mid-fifteenth-century carol composers experimented freely with musical rhyme between burden and refrain, with links of various kinds between the two burdens, and so on.[3]
The composers of *The Fayrfax MS* went further, varying or repeating the
music of burden and verse as it pleased them.[4] As for the insertion of ex-
traneous musical material, the rhyme-royal songs provide the best English
example of this with their long and lively melismatic passages.

Around the year 1500, we can say, composers *used* but no longer strictly
required poetical forms. They were in a position, if they wanted, to treat
each poem in the musical style most appropriate to its other features. A
composer like William Cornish, capable of writing in four styles so diverse
as those he used for *Fa la sol* [H6], *Adew mes amours* [H8], 'Woffully
araid' [F33], and 'A the syghes' [H27], to say nothing of his church-
music, had the means to be independent.[5] He chose, on the whole, to observe the traditional decorum of forms. Why should he not? Nevertheless,
in the songs of this period there are hints that the words are beginning to
matter to the detail of the music. To this detail we must now turn.

We may disregard here the music of the carols and chansons in *Ritson's
MS*. Word-setting in them follows the traditional medieval, 'abstract'
pattern already described. The words are a physical presence in the music;
they contribute to the rhythm and to the colour of the melodic line, but
the musician seems to have made no allowance for their individual meaning, 'accent' or savour. Regard for detail, as more than a spasmodic touch,
first occurs in English song at the end of the fifteenth century, the period
represented by *The Fayrfax MS*. We can observe its characteristic working
in 'Benedicite! Whate dremyd I?' [F12] (p. 99). The main feature is the
syllabic treatment of the text – one syllable, one note. This is found in very

nearly all the typical 'English' counterpoint of *The Fayrfax* and *Ritson's MSS*. The opening measure of any section, it must be admitted, is often stiff and formal; there is a trace of this in the upper voice of our example. But after that the phrases are more flexible, even though the tendency is for the syllable to change as often as the beat. Flexibility is achieved partly through the judicious mixture of (speaking in modern values) dotted crotchets, crotchets and quavers, with an occasional minim or triplet figure; and partly through the grading of the melodic curve to bring out the natural accentuation of the words. (The first five bars of Voice II illustrate this.)

This care for natural accentuation, 'just note and accent', is, I have said, a new thing. At first sight it seems to anticipate in a striking manner some of the characteristic effects of Elizabethan song. Yet I believe its motive force to be radically different. Here is no humanist desire to achieve the ideal union, known to the ancients, between words and music; nor Reformation zeal for the mere supremacy of the words (the swirling *vocalizes* belie this).[6] We have, instead, that passion for natural detail which is a general characteristic of late medieval art in the north of Europe. To speak only of music, Paul Lang has written of Ockeghem and his school that they

> applied it [naturalism] to the smallest details, observing human speech, noting where the natural accents lie, their quality and quantity, and how they are influenced by different moods. They copied all these and transferred them into music.[7]

The oddity is to find this naturalism grafted on to a conception of song so abstract and 'numerical'.

The fine distinction between this attitude and that of later 'reformers' (whether ecclesiastical or would-be Greek) is chiefly a distinction of motive. The results in each case are somewhat similar. Not only is the ordinary duration of the syllables in speech copied, but even the intonation of speech in the musical melody. The music is normal speech *stylized*. It is a small step from this to the declamatory style based on impassioned utterance. There is a hint of such declamation in this line of melody from 'Benedicite!' [F12]:

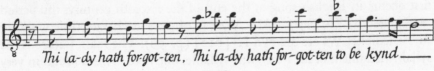

Thi la-dy hath for-got-ten, Thi la-dy hath for-got-ten to be kynd___

One of the best examples comes in a religious carol from the same manuscript, 'A, gentill Jhesu!' [F34]:

However, passionate declamations of this sort are decidedly rare.

The preoccupation with natural detail occasionally leads composers in this style to the naïve pictorialism, or 'word-painting', already mentioned (p. 36). It is a familiar feature of the later madrigal. We meet one of the rare earlier instances of it in 'Benedicite! Whate dremyd I?', where the 'worlde' is 'turnyd up so downe' in the melody of two of the parts (bars 5–7). The continuation of the sentence, 'The son, the moone, had lost ther force and light', is set to a long descending scale; this may be another 'musical simile'.

Where natural presentation ends and 'expressiveness' begins is a difficult question to answer. The difference between the two is somewhat like the difference between simile and metaphor in language. Naturalism (musical simile) appeals first to the intellect, often through the eye;[8] the composer says, as it were, 'the world was turned up-side-down, *like this*'. 'Expressiveness', on the other hand (musical metaphor), works more directly on the feelings, in the widest sense of the word; we are involved not in an intellectual comparison but in a musical *experience*; we are affected with the same directness as affects us in such an image as Lady Macbeth's 'the blanket of the dark'. If, in 'Woffully araid' [F35], the phrase 'so strained' is not intended to be naturalistic representation (see p. 36 above), then it must be taken as emotional emphasis, a means of 'expressing' the text.

Other examples show an equal ambiguity of intention. For instance, in both settings of 'Woffully araid' [F33, 35], the words 'O, man, for thy sake' are set in a striking way, apparently emphasizing the central issue of the poem, Christ's Pleading. This may be an early instance of the direct 'expression' of emotion; it may, on the other hand, take the form it does simply because the composer tried to *present* objectively in his music an impassioned cry, a *symptom* of agony rather than the agonized feeling itself. The first setting of 'Woffully araid' contains a remarkable passage [F33, bar 75] just before 'O man': the words 'Thus nakyd am I nailid' introduce the rare progression of a diminished fourth, F to C sharp, emphasizing the brutal act of the tormentors who nailed Christ to the cross. But does the emphasis lie primarily in the sound, or in the visual transition from F natural, in the notation, to C sharp,* symbolizing the cruelty of the nails in the soft flesh? One last example of particular interest is the passage in 'Jhesu, mercy' [F31, bars 80–83], 'wayling, ye, sownyng for wo'. Besides the naturalism of 'wailing' with its long notes, there is an unusual modulation to an A flat chord. An A flat is something of a sensation in this music; and it is hard to explain it in this passage, except in terms of 'expressiveness'.

After the metrical and dispassionate treatment of words in the fifteenth-century carol the novelty of the naturalistic, presentational techniques just described is striking. But they must be seen in proportion. These methods are still rare, except in so far as they apply to the careful accentuation of the text. (The accentuation of *The Fayrfax MS* songs is, by the way, based entirely on natural stress and pitch, and not at all on ideas of classical quantity.) It is no accident that almost all the more 'advanced' passages occur in the big three- and four-part carols of the Passion. Isolated instances of word-painting, declamation and expressiveness (if they are such) can be found elsewhere, especially in *The Fayrfax MS*, but they are not frequent.

Furthermore, granted that the existence of such songs is important in a study of music and poetry, two things must be borne in mind. Firstly, even in the most 'advanced' songs there are still long melismas, which were probably sung, as in the church-music of the period.[9] The style has none of the homogeneity of the madrigal style. And, secondly, the poems chosen by musicians for their most ambitious effects are not the latest productions of court poets but rather the opposite: 'Woffully araid', for example, had been a literary favourite for a generation and is written in the traditional, 'high' religious vein. This means there can have been little expectation on the *poet's* part to hear such rare flights of musical fancy implementing his work. What he might sometimes expect to hear was a rough

* The music is printed on p. 11 above. In the notation the sharp (as we now call it) is represented by the sign which distinguishes *B durum* from *B molle*.

reflection in the music of the general mood of the words. The rumbustious cross-rhythms of 'Hoyda hoyda' [F43] produce quite a different kind of atmosphere from that implicit in the stately four-square 'Enforce yourselfe as Goddis knyght' [F47]. This 'diffused' kind of expressiveness, familiar in other medieval songs and in plain-song,[10] raises curious problems in more than one style of word-setting. In the two songs just mentioned there is what may seem to us a general appropriateness in the music. The expressiveness is detached from the details but reflects the overall tone of the poem. But what is to be said about 'And I war a maydyn' [H101]? The unusual five-part setting with its full harmony and passing-notes (including a dominant seventh at the cadence) is certainly expressive, but not of the frivolous words. If this is not a musical joke of a kind without parallel in English songs of the period, it strikingly confirms the lack of connection possible between the emotion of the words and the emotion of the music.

The style of setting represented by 'Benedicite! Whate dremyd I?' is the most interesting of the early Tudor repertory. But, if *Henry VIII's MS* is a reliable index to court-music, a poet of his court was likely to find his words set in a much lighter style. 'Iff I had wytt' [H29] is fairly typical:

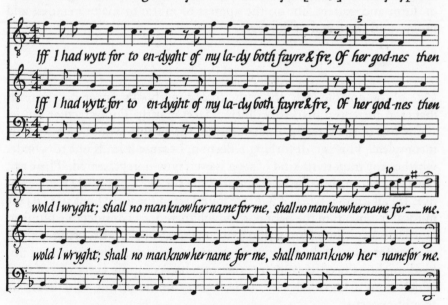

This setting is, again, syllabic; but the musical rhythm is only moderately sensitive to natural accent (one cannot help noticing the long thud on the word 'to' in the first line), and the last line of words is repeated, not as part of a declamatory effect, but purely for formal reasons. This song, like so many others in the same style, has several verses, which is one reason why the composer responded less sensitively to the words. Other musical features are far more important in the total effect than the detailed relationship between words and notes. They are concise rhythms, balanced phrases, an increased sense of tonality, a strong 'harmonic' bass, duple time (with occasional triplet sections), and the predominance of one voice – usually, in effect, the top, even if the song is built round a tenor-melody.

This chordal manner of word-setting, whether free or strict, is used extensively in England for the first time in the early Tudor song-books. But it is not a new thing; it is anticipated in a few fifteenth-century songs,[11] and to some extent in the carol. The syllabic, 'naturalistic' style of 'Benedicite!', on the other hand, if not new in itself, contains many new features. It contains, in fact, the seeds of a new relationship between words and notes. This, surely, is why the two approaches, which for convenience we may label 'naturalism' and 'expressiveness', are in analysis so difficult to distinguish. The 'natural representations' of the composers of *The Fayrfax MS* inevitably open the way to a relationship in song based not on form and pattern but on the aptness of music to make manifest and meaningful the detail of the text.

II

One of the notable facts about the three song-books under discussion is that each presents a markedly different facet of early Tudor secular music. If any one of the three had not survived, the picture would be essentially incomplete. This is a disturbing reflection, because it leads one to wonder whether any important kind of song is even now unrepresented. There are, however, fair reasons for believing that the surviving songs *are* representative: (i) all known types of lyric are found set in the three books;[12] (ii) the musical fragments of the period, of which there are a considerable number, raise little suspicion of lost styles;* (iii) the song-books seem between them to cater for most of the obvious occasions on which written music of this kind might be needed; and (iv) the song-books supply every sort of song which from a knowledge of contemporary music on the Continent we should expect.[13]

* The fragment, 'Awake, synner, out of thi slepe' [Song 45], is the only one known to me that suggests a style otherwise unrepresented among the surviving songs.

Music and the Early Tudor Lyric: I

Of the Elizabethan madrigal style, it should be added, there are only a few scattered hints in the early Tudor court song-books. The madrigal differs from early polyphonic songs in these respects: each phrase of the text is given an appropriate melodic figure which is developed by imitation, and during the course of which *the words may be repeated*; the musical sections (that is, the verbal phrases) overlap each other instead of being divided by cadences; harmonic suspensions play a large part in expressing the text; naturalistic effects on words like 'sighs', 'hover', 'aloft', are so common as to be trite. The matter-of-course repetition of the words is most important. Repetition is found also in the early Tudor books, but with a different meaning: it has an effect of climax, it is part of declamation. The song which comes nearest of all to introducing the madrigal style in its completeness is the carol by Pygott, *Quid petis?* [H105]. In both burden and verse 1 there are consistent imitation, repetitions of the text, and overlapping of sections; but verses 2 and 3, surprisingly, revert to the old syllabic style.

One thing at least becomes clear from the wide variety of musical styles and poetical styles chosen for setting – the almost complete independence and absolute technical assurance of the early Tudor song-composers. They were masters of a complicated craft, and in the exercise of this craft, choice of words mattered very little. They could just as easily set a complex, 'rhetorical' poem of double meaning [F10][14] as they could set a balet in a light, popular style [H16]. Some lyrics (those in 'short-line' metres, for example) could be set in several styles. It is nonsense, therefore, in this period, to speak of the *needs* of musicians. They could do what they liked with words, almost (one is tempted to say) with any words. *Any early Tudor lyric could be set to music in a traditional style.* The suitability of a particular musical style to a particular poem is not a matter of emotional fitness but of convention. And the conventional alliance between music and poetry of a certain kind (for example, in the carol) is largely dependent on the wider, social use of the song.

It is equally clear that the interesting developments in early Tudor song belong, as we can see from the words and notes alone, not to the history of literature but to the history of *music*.

It may be worth while at this point to emphasize a truism about songs. To find a poem set to music tells us nothing in itself about *the poet's* intention. Even in these musical sources there are many poems which had been in circulation, simply as poems, for some years. 'Woffully araid' [F33 and 35] is one of several examples. It was a favourite piece of devotional verse, and in one earlier text has the rubric: 'Ho-sum-ever saith this praier in the worship of the passion shall have C. yere of pardon'.[15] 'Deme the best of every dowt' is another [H74]: the couplet forms part of a verse written on a bronze jug of Richard II's time.[16] These facts make one wonder whether 'the demand of the musical establishment' for texts to set could possibly have been a live factor in the literary situation.[17] If a musician required a poem, he could go, as it were, to the library.

Paradoxically, the chief musical sources (the sources of polyphonic secular music, that is) leave us quite in the dark about what the writers of the words intended. The songs are often far, far removed from the fountain-head of 'literary' composition. Thus, to give one final example (this time, a courtly one), the song chosen to open *The Fayrfax MS* uses a poem written nearly a century before. The single stanza, 'The farther I go, the more behynde' [F1], was probably written in the early fifteenth century by one John Halsham; it was appropriated by Lydgate, who used it as the first stanza of his 'Tyed with a line'. But it continued to have a separate existence, though usually in conjunction with 'The world so wide th'aire so remuable'.

III

The 'technical' approach to words-and-music is bound, we can see, for many reasons, to be inconclusive. No amount of looking at the mere notes will ever bring us to the heart of the problem. The chief reason for this is that most statements about music and poetry are, in one way or another, statements about society. It is, therefore, not merely styles of song but modes of life that must be investigated.

A theory that words were written to be set to music in this period will probably rest on one of the following beliefs: the poet wrote words in a special way – either, because he was himself a creative musician and able to set them; or, because he worked in close collaboration with a composer and could be told what was needed; or, because the active music-making of his environment forced him to think imaginatively in terms of music. Our willingness to accept one or other of these suppositions depends very much on the sort of music and the sort of society we have in mind. It is here that we can, perhaps, 'apply' conclusions which will be fully argued later, in answer to such questions as the following: 'When and where was music made? Who were the active composers and performers? How close was the association between composers and poets? What was the place of music in daily life?' The account of music in courtly society* will have, I hope, an interest transcending the narrow use we are now going to make of it. It will have the interest of helping to establish the 'tone' of court-life in the early years of the sixteenth century, of providing a ground for a fuller understanding of the court song-books, of enabling us to see Art as part of the business of Life. To these wider issues we shall return later. For the present it equips us with certain facts and probabilities which we can use to unravel the limited problem in hand.

The functional, 'applied' nature of much late medieval music cannot be doubted; in all kinds of ceremonies and entertainments music helped to glorify the courtly way of life, though not itself receiving much honour in the process.[18] A tentative, 'Aristotelian' definition of the place of art-music in the early Tudor court might run: *art-music† (the music of trained musicians) was a social luxury, conducted largely by professionals and applied to courtly ends.*

This state of affairs was not new in England. In the early years of the sixteenth century court life, court entertainment and court-music were all of a piece with what had been going on for two centuries, if not longer. Conditions were, of course, changing. They always are. But the time of swiftest change was certainly not, as generalizations about 'the Tudor period' usually imply, around the year 1500 or earlier; it was, rather, about 1530 or 1540 that the old order began decisively to give place to a new. The mid-sixteenth century gets its character from the appearance of such 'newfangilnes' as the consort of viols, the pavane and galliard, the metrical psalm, the art-song for voice and lute, the new polyphonic style, semi-professional musicians as servants, popular instrumental tutors, and increased musical literacy. Some of these are what might be called 'Renaissance-Italian' by origin or importation (the court viol-consort, for example, came from Milan, Venice and Cremona). The influence of Italian culture, which culminated in the Elizabethan madrigal, superseded an 'international' French culture symbolized by the basse-danse, the disguising, the courts of love, chivalric ceremonies of all kinds, an esoteric 'professional' attitude to music, the popularity of the harp in courtly circles, widespread itinerancy amongst musicians, fixed forms for composition (*rondeau, virelai* and carol), and so on. To this older culture the early Tudor court, despite

---

* See Part Three, Music at Court.

† I include here under this term the skilled improvisations and traditional repertory of the minstrels. (See p. 313 below.) Perhaps the term 'craft-music' is really needed to supplement 'art-music'.

its 'new Latin' poets, its Italian secretaries, its Greek scholars, owed its chief allegiance. In fact, two words that one would choose to describe its atmosphere from 1480 to 1530 are 'medieval' and 'Burgundian'.

In the absence of a detailed survey of music in the court of Elizabeth, this conclusion must remain tentative. At the moment it is easier to be sure of the absence of certain Elizabethan features from the early sixteenth-century scene than of the opposite. It is certain, for example, that there was still much ceremonial music at court in Elizabeth's reign. Music-making, like the drama, may have retained many medieval features.

These reflections have an obvious bearing on the problems of music and poetry. They lead one, first, almost to *expect* amid the great social and artistic changes of the mid-sixteenth century a change in the relationship of the two arts. Some of the reasons for this change and some of its effects have already been described. In the early Tudor period, before the change took place, words and music were 'applied' *together* for a single purpose rather than *to each other*. Words and music must have been commissioned for many occasions, such as royal entries;[19] and, to judge from the verses which have survived, the poet, and doubtless the musician also, did his best to make an excellent contribution in his own art, without too much regard for his companion craftsman. This is very different from the attitude of later musicians and poets whose end and aim, we know, was to achieve an ideal union, and the wonderful ethical effects that went with it.

Earlier, then, the chief collaboration between the arts was a matter of professional duty: poets and musicians worked together in the service of the court or noble household. The lowly social status of most professional musicians (even Gentlemen of the Chapel were not highly placed) means that opportunities of collaboration between choirmen, such as William Cornish, and courtly 'makers', such as Sir Thomas Wyatt, were limited and rarely sought after.[20] The song-books do not, except by their silence, provide evidence on this point; and it may, admittedly, be just an unfortunate accident that deprives us of musical settings of courtier poets, of the circle represented by *The Devonshire MS*, for example.[21] But I incline to believe that the settings never existed. At least we have to acknowledge that out of the one hundred and forty or so songs in the three principal song-books only one (excepting Henry VIII's own) has a courtier's name attachable to it: the song, 'A robyn, gentyl robyn' [H49], attributed to Wyatt, was set by Cornish in canonic style. Another and longer version of the poem is found in Egerton MS 2711, Wyatt's autograph manuscript, without music. The words in the song-book are:

Music and the Early Tudor Lyric: I

> A Robyn, gentyl Robyn,
> Tel me how thy lemman doth,
> And thow shalt know of myne.

> 1. My lady is unkynde I wis.
>   Alac, why is she so?
>   She lovyth another better than me
>   And yet she will say no.

> 2. I cannot thynk such doubylnes
>   For I fynd women trew;
>   In faith my lady lovith me well;
>   She will change for no new. [H49]

There is nothing specifically in Wyatt's manner here; and the opening lines certainly reflect an older tradition (Wyatt nowhere else uses the word 'leman'). The four verses added in the other manuscript are a little more characteristic, especially the ending,

> Lerne this lessen of me;
> At othre fires thy self to warme,
> And let theim warme with the.[22]

Wyatt, born in 1503, was only in his early 'teens, when most of the songs in *Henry VIII's MS* were (I conjecture) composed (1510–15).[23] It is not impossible that he wrote the trifle which Cornish set. (Cornish lived until 1523.) But another explanation which fits the facts is that Wyatt's poem is a later handling and amplification of a popular song already known at court. It was possibly sung to the original tune, which Cornish's version may incorporate.

That courtier poets or their friends could have composed musical settings for poems seems unlikely, since few amateurs (if any) were as talented as Henry VIII. Most of their music, at court and elsewhere, was probably semi-literate.[24] Much of it was, it seems, improvised round popular tunes, and sung, or strummed on an instrument. Melody, in fact, was more important than harmony or counterpoint. If courtiers wrote, in any sense, 'for music', they are more likely to have written poems to popular tunes than for complicated settings in parts.

The king was, we must allow, an exception. There are thirty-four pieces in the song-book I have called *Henry VIII's MS*, which bear the inscription (invariably as a heading, not postscript): 'the kynge H.viij'. One of these, 'Pastyme with good companye' [H7], is found also in *Ritson's MS*, entitled 'the Kynges Balade'; it also survives in roughly written lute-tablature elsewhere. Only one other composition ascribed to the king survives: *Quam pulcra es* [Song 270], a motet for three men's voices, in a much later manuscript.[25] This motet is an ambitious work, competently carried out. The songs and instrumental pieces in the court song-book, on the other hand, are slight and exhibit a level of professional skill rather less distinguished. It is not merely that the king only seems to have one or two 'tunes' – 'Though sum saith that yough rulyth me' [H66] is uncommonly like 'Pastyme' – ; it is a certain blundering about in the inner parts that betrays him. Here is a cadence from 'Adew madam et ma mastres' [H9]:

The alto voice, presumably added last, makes awkward musical grammar with the rest. The song, 'Helas madam' [H10], following in the manuscript, confirms the suspicion. It also entitles us to wonder how much of the king's composing was of his own invention. 'Helas madam' borrows some material from a continental chanson of the same title; the piece is listed as a basse-danse by Antonius de Arena (1536). It looks as if Henry has added Voice III to an original three-part setting. This is certainly what he has done in 'Gentil prince' [H45]: the first, second and fourth voices were printed in the famous song-book, *Harmonice Musices Odhecaton A* (Venice, 1501), when Henry was only ten years old. Voice III, his added part, reveals again a certain poverty of invention. There may be among the other royal compositions similar cases undetected. Not that there is anything unusual, let alone reprehensible, in this kind of 'borrowing'. Medieval and later music is full of it. But it puts a limit on our estimate of even the king's capabilities as a setter of songs.

To the best of our knowledge Henry VIII is the only noble person who could lay claim to be considered a latter-day troubadour, poet and musician in one. But there were, of course, a number of professional musicians – Banastir, Cornish, Barclay, Redford, Heywood, Rhodes – capable of composition in both arts. When a song was required for a particular occasion, a man like William Cornish, author of a *Treatise bitwene Trowth and Enformacion* and other works, probably wrote the words which he also set to music.[26] There is nothing to show, however, that he wrote the words in any special manner. He did not, so far as we know, think of himself as the appointed agent either of a natural or of an idealized union between music and poetry. A natural union between music and poetry exists only in folk- and popular song; Cornish and his contemporaries were composers of the highest sophistication. On the other hand, an idealized conception of the mutual responsiveness of the two arts was to wait for a later generation and later needs.

Current attitudes to music confirm the drift of these suggestions. A generally philosophical and quasi-mathematical conception still discouraged, if it did not entirely debar, the centrally 'human' approach which characterizes the reunion of music and poetry in Elizabethan times. This omission is not merely the pose of an intellectual coterie. It also seems to distinguish the responses, so far as we can gauge them, of those who were less articulate, less conscious of the issues. When medieval people listened to music, they do not seem to have described their reactions in terms of 'expressiveness', the suitability of the music to the emotion (in song, the words) with which it was connected. Their terms of praise tended to be either vague – 'sweetness' and 'light' are favourite images; or quasi-theological – an echo of paradise, of another world; or social – 'a fine triumph and very pompous'; or technical – 'many a sweet refreet'.[27] They never seem to feel of a song that it is 'framed to the life of the words'.

So far, then, from music and poetry being bound together 'by tradition and social circumstance',[28] it is probably truer to say that the two arts, as *arts*, were separate in the early Tudor period, unless drawn together for a social occasion under the light yoke of practical necessity.

NOTES TO CHAPTER 6

1. The 'expressive' view of music has recently been called in question, on philosophical grounds. See, for example, Suzanne Langer, *Philosophy in a New Key* (3rd ed. 1957).

2. See p. 17 above concerning F4.
3. These variations are analysed in *MC*, 126–.
4. See F31–F35 for some of the formal permutations. A brief formal analysis of each song in R, F and H is given in the notes of Appendix A.
5. See *MCH8, passim*. Some of Cornish's polyphonic church-music is now available in F. Ll. Harrison's edition of *The Eton Choirbook*, Musica Britannica (1956–).
6. See pp. 68–, 84– above, where the tenets of humanists and 'Reformed' musicians are discussed.
7. Lang, 190. He uses the term 'realism' to describe the phenomenon.
8. See 'The Lekingfelde Proverbs', ed. Flügel, *Anglia*, xiv (1892), 479, st. 24: 'The margent silver and the notis sabyll | Shulde move us to remembrance of the joyes intermynabill'.
9. See Harrison's remarks, *The Eton Choirbook: I*, introd., pp. xxii–xxiii; the question is whether in court-song the melismas may also have been played *as well as* sung.
10. See ch. 1 above, pp. 35, 37.
11. e.g. 'Tappster, dryngker' [Song 291]. These songs and carols belong to the style of medieval song known as *conductus*.
12. See Introduction, p. 10 above.
13. Particularly, it would be suspicious if either polyphonic or chordal styles were completely absent. There are two trends in European song at this time. On the one hand the chanson of the late fifteenth century is being gradually transformed: voice-parts are now of more equal importance; their ranges are more clearly defined; the texture is clear and varied; the words are set more syllabically; and, above all, contrapuntal imitation with its repeated phrases imposes a unity of style in place of the old formal unity (*rondeau, virelai*, etc.). On the other hand, with the *frottola, lied* and *villançico* (see examples in *HAM*, i, nos 93–98), all having popular roots, a chordal style asserts itself in art-music. Its characteristics are concise rhythms, balanced phrases, a growing tonal sense – exactly the features of the song, 'Iff I had wytt', from *Henry VIII's MS*, described above. In the middle of the sixteenth century the fully-fledged madrigal style brought into being an equilibrium between the two.
14. See p. 29 above.
15. Carleton Brown, *XV*, 156.

16. Joan Evans, *English Art: 1307–1461* (1949), 90. The verse begins 'He that wyll not spare . . .'
17. Pattison, 34.
18. See pp. 235– below.
19. See pp. 241– below.
20. See pp. 320– below.
21. See pp. 118, 205 below.
22. *Wyatt*, no. 55.
23. See *MCH8*, Introduction (description of *Henry VIII's MS*).
24. See pp. 285– below.
25. BM Roy. Lib. RM 24.d.2, ff.166v–167; see App. C, no. 17.
26. Cornish's treatise is pr. Flügel, *Anglia*, xiv (1892), 466. See p. 251 below concerning his interlude, *Troilus and Pandar*.
27. Some suggestive remarks on this difficult topic can be found in Dent, 'Social Aspects', and in K. E. Gilbert and H. Kuhn, *History of Aesthetics* (rev. edn 1956), ch. 5.
28. Pattison, 36.

CHAPTER 7

Music and the Early Tudor Lyric: II

THE 'LITERARY' LYRIC AND ITS TUNES

At the beginning of the last chapter the question was posed: What was the musician's attitude to song-writing? The unromantic answer was – poems were convenient pegs on which to hang his compositions. Convenient, but no longer necessary. Every kind of lyric of the fifteenth and early sixteenth centuries is found set to music in an appropriate style. And by 'appropriate' is meant, simply, 'traditionally appropriate', for there are very few signs in the song-books that composers were interested in anything but the poetic shape and, occasionally, the physical qualities of the words.

These conclusions were essentially one-sided. So was the evidence on which they were based. We were considering solely the evidence of the song-books and of the artistic musical settings contained in them. These settings, interesting though they are as musical history, tell us nothing about poetic intention. Moreover, we have to remind ourselves of the fact that only a very small proportion of late medieval lyrics is found in music-books. In the period from Chaucer to Wyatt, musical manuscripts and books are extremely scarce. The four major carol-books excepted, no sizeable collection of vernacular songs survives from the fourteenth or fifteenth centuries. (A Cambridge manuscript, containing eighteen English, French and Latin songs, is easily the largest.[1]) The early Tudor song-books are the earliest surviving court song-books in English. They cannot *in fact* have been the earliest song-books. But the almost total disappearance of their predecessors suggests, as at least a possible explanation, that they were never numerous. Written part-music was a luxury afforded only by the few.[2]

We turn now to what, for want of a handier term, I shall call the 'literary' lyric – that is, the lyric found without music in the manuscript or printed book that has ensured its survival. What evidence is there that it was intended for singing?

Music and the Early Tudor Lyric: II

I

Hundreds of 'literary' lyrics survive from the fifteenth and early sixteenth centuries. By no means all of them are found in books of poems or songs. A typical commonplace-book now in the library of Trinity College, Cambridge, contains

> miscellaneous verses in English and Latin, e.g. *hi quattuor magni fuerant . . .* , 'Farewell this world, I take my leve for ever' (found in three manuscripts), a moralized version of 'Come over the burne, Besse' [see R16]; indentures mentioning Bromley and Wimbledon; an account of Prince Arthur's christening; a list of diseases; an alphabetical set of Latin proverbs; political and historical matter, e.g. *de homagio regum Scocie regibus Anglie*; a letter asking for school books; verses on purchasing; English prayers and a dispensation by Cardinal Wolsey about Lent; instructions how to set a harp; instances of St Edmund's charity, and many other writings.[3]

The manuscript – this one thing is clear – was a repository over many years for every kind of miscellaneous jotting.

As a commonplace-book it is slightly unusual in one respect: it contains neither romances nor 'courtesy-books'. Both of these items were exceedingly popular in the fifteenth and early sixteenth centuries. The well-known commonplace-book of Richard Hill, 'servant with Mr Wyngar, alderman of London', has been mentioned earlier; it includes two romances and four tracts on 'courtesy', besides numerous lyrics, puzzles, riddles, and so forth. Hill's book (*c.* 1505–35) differs from the other also in being written almost entirely by one man, and bearing, thus, the stamp of an individual taste. His taste ran more in the direction of popular song than of courtly lyric, whether ornate or plain.[4]

In the commonplace-books, to come across musical notation is unusual; a poem set to music in parts is a rarity. This should not surprise us. Nor should it surprise us to find ourselves reminded at every turn that the lyric, to us traditionally the most intimate form of poetic expression, was often, at the end of the Middle Ages, of an 'eminently practical nature'; verses were copied, as they were composed, to preserve in memorable form useful information or wise sayings. Poems about alchemy are found stained with chemicals, devotional verses were certainly used in private prayer.[5] To seize this point is to understand at any rate one kind of poetic 'intention'.

To the other main type of source for early Tudor lyrics I have given the rather anachronistic label 'poetical anthologies'. The word suggests a higher degree of discrimination and taste than went to the compilation of most of them, suggests indeed the wrong sort of interest. For instance, various 'anthologies' of popular poems and carols look more like minstrels' song-books. There is one at St John's College, Cambridge.[6] Amongst the carols in it are the obviously popular 'War yt, war yt: Stel is gud' and 'the carol of Jack Reckless'. Any word that suggests poetasting is wrong for this kind of book. Whether it was actually a minstrel's pocket-book, however, is not easy to decide. It measures six inches by four and is enclosed in a vellum wrapper. This is certainly suggestive. But were minstrels as proficient at Latin as the complicated (and accurate) Latin refrains of 'Nowell: This word is falce' imply?[7] The question remains open.

There are at least two other manuscripts of the same type.[8] All three do, indeed, form 'an index of popular taste'; they surely preserve minstrels' songs, as the mode of address ('lovely lordynges, ladys lyke') and appeals for money and drink suggest. But minstrels' songs were not necessarily written down by the minstrels themselves; Richard Hill, for instance, copied out several songs of this kind. These manuscripts were perhaps personal 'anthologies', in which many favourite items found a place. However this may be, they belong indisputably to the world of popular wisdom, popular story, and popular *music*. To say that music was part of the 'poetic intention' is to use too lofty a phrase. We have, simply, songs.

At the other end of the social scale are a number of courtly 'anthologies'. They are made up of poems current among, if not always written by, members of the court circle. *The Devonshire MS* is the 'anthology' which shows most clearly a group of courtly persons writing to, for and about each other. Besides sixty-eight poems presumably by Wyatt himself, there are forty others, some bearing the names or initials of Antony Lee (Wyatt's brother-in-law), Lord Thomas Howard (who married the king's niece, was imprisoned, and died in the Tower), Lady Margaret Howard (his wife), Mary Howard, and so on. The book is in several hands and probably belonged to some member of the Howard family.[9]

This 'anthology' seems to be a living document of social life at the court of Henry VIII; the poems are not merely written in courtly styles, they seem to refer, in stylized terms, to actual relationships. Not all the poems are original by any means; but this does not affect the argument about a social clique. In poetry, as in music, the skilful adaptation or translation was not merely admired; it was the very essence of composition. A poet and lover chose the conventional 'mask' best suited to what he had to say. In *The Devonshire MS* Lord Howard and his lady vow and sigh to each other straight out of Chaucer.[10] Other signs of the adaptation of courtly poetry to social needs are 'answering' poems, verse letters and the addition of lines to other people's verses.

It is easier to sense than it is to prove that a particular manuscript belonged to a closed circle and served not only 'literary' but social purposes. It is even more difficult to define what exactly 'social purposes' were – whether serious affairs of the heart, or a courtly game, or something like a literary club. To take an obvious example, a poem by Wyatt has these lines:

> Then in my boke wrote my maystresse;
> I am yowres, yow may well be sure,
> And shall be whyle my lyff dothe dure.[11]

Later in *The Devonshire MS* someone has written: 'I ama yowres An'. This can be taken to mean almost anything, from a treasonable affair between Wyatt and Anne Boleyn to a private joke.

In Part Two I try to account for the courtly lyric as, to put it crudely, a social phenomenon. The questions are fascinating; the answers elusive. Fortunately, the fact of some sort of social intercourse is sufficient for our immediate purpose. This makes the whole traffic of versifying seem, if not quite 'commercial', at least far removed from any world where poets gracefully chisel their little statuettes of sound simply for the pleasure of having them apparelled in music.

The evidence, then, of the sources, considered as documents of social history, reveals that the centre of interest in those short poems which we misleadingly lump together under the anachronistic title, 'lyric', might be very varied. A poem might be written, without much thought of literary quality, for information or for instruction, as an act of devotion or a part of entertainment. These practical attitudes strongly confirm that the prospect of musical *performance* in even the simplest 'art-setting' was far from the authors' minds. Lyrics written purely for 'pass-time', especially the popular 'hits' collected by Richard Hill and others who liked minstrelsy, not uncommonly bring us into touch with music. But it is never the music of the court. It is the music of the tavern, the highway and the market; it is *popular* melody. There is no call to repeat here the arguments of an earlier chapter. A vast repertory of popular songs and dances has been lost for ever; the few surviving fragments serve to keep us in mind of a kind of words-for-music which persisted unchanged for centuries, unaffected by the shifting fashions and ideals of art-song.

II

Tunes are practically non-existent for the courtly, as distinct from the popular, lyrics. So the evidence that they were sung is not simple. (If it were so, it could never have been misinterpreted.) As in the case of popular song, we have to piece together a multitude of scraps. We may begin with an outright statement by the Puritan moralist, William Baldwin, in the dedication of his *Canticles or Balades of Salomon* (1549):

> Would God that suche songes myght once drive out of office the baudy balades of lecherous love that commonly are indited and song of idle courtyers in princes and noblemens houses.[12]

This is a clear indication that a kind of courtly lyric – we must beware of speaking of *the* courtly lyric – was sung. Yet this does not entitle us to take all references to music, singing and the lute at their face value. There are two difficulties here: the first is a difficulty of terminology; the second, of poetic interpretation.

There is a bewildering array of terms to be sorted out: 'read', 'sing', 'song', 'balade', 'ditty', 'set', and so on. Baldwin, for instance, spoke of *singing* 'balades'; Bannatyne, on the other hand, follows a direction, 'To the *reidar*', with the comment, 'Heir haif ye luvaris ballattis at your will'.[13] The implication seems to be that these courtly poems in his book are to be *read*, not sung, though the ambiguity of the word 'read' must always be borne in mind. Furthermore, what gloss are we to put on Skelton's title, *Dyvers Balettys and Dyties solacyous*? To such a query there is no easy answer. These and similar terms were used in the early sixteenth century with patent inconsistency. Nevertheless, there seems to have been a tendency to use 'song' to mean any piece of music, with or without words; 'balet' to mean, as Dr Pattison has said, 'a courtly song of popular character'; and 'ditty' to mean the words, the *dictum*, of a lyric.[14] (The one word which is never found before the Elizabethan period is the word 'lyric', coined to express the new attitude of a new age.[15])

'Balet' continues, all the same, to be a puzzling term. The 'balet-book' that Fayrfax gave the king for a New Year's present must surely have contained part-songs; and yet, if his songs in *The Fayrfax MS* are anything to go by, the poems he would choose were not 'of popular character'.[16] The balet Stephen Hawes was paid ten shillings for making was, one would expect, an ornate piece of versification.[17] Certainly the word must sometimes have been used still in its older sense of a courtly poem ('a balade made by daun John Lidegate for a momyng') in the sophisticated style, if not the form, of the French *ballade*. But the process of popularization, leading to the broadside-ballad hawked and sung about the streets, was already at work. Baldwin, in the passage already quoted, confirms that the balet could be courtly *and* connected with music. The fact, however, that neither he nor any other moralizer gives or refers to part-music suggests that 'balets' of his kind were written 'to the tune of . . .', rather than for subsequent setting in parts.

The difficulty of words and their meanings is even more acute when the 'internal' evidence of the poems themselves is in question. To the problem of deciding the meaning of disputed terms is added a new problem – the separation of convention and fact. This is primarily a matter of poetic interpretation. References to music ('My lute, awake . . .') do not, it should hardly be necessary to say, always imply what at first sight they seem to.

The clearest and most natural of all are references to singing in the carol and in other forms of popular poetry. One is inclined to take them at their face value *because* of their naturalness: they seem to refer in concrete terms to an actual situation:

> Therfore every mon that ys here
> Synge a caroll on hys manere:
> Yf he con non we schall hym lere,
> So that we be mere allway.[18]

Even in the carol there are occasional references to reading; these were to be expected in the more devotional carols. But they are far outnumbered by the 'singing' references. (One interesting feature is that in scores of passages mentioning music and singing, the lute is never found as an accompanying instrument.)

Courtly verse in the ornate, 'high' style presents a very different picture. References to music are not uncommon in themselves, especially in Skelton's poetry. Many such references are technical, detailed and informative. Barclay quotes musicians of the court by name – 'the birde of Cornewalle, the Crane and the Kite'; Hawes has a courtly comment on the basse-danse, *Mamours* – 'the swete and the gentyll daunce';[19] Skelton names popular songs, talks about the teaching of music, methods of improvisation, dances, and so on.[20]

Other ornate lyrics are cast in dramatic form, so that when the poet refers to music it is quite clear that it is not his own singing and playing but that of one of his characters – King David, for example, in the psalms; Jopas in Wyatt's *Jopas Song*.[21] The problem arises when the poet (usually a lover) seems to refer to the poem as a musical part of the experience he is describing as his own:

> Before my deth this lay of sorow I sing
> With carefull melodye and entunyng.[22]

How literally are we supposed to take this? We are not dealing, we must remember, with a crude or primitive tradition but with one manifestation of the refined and elaborate 'world' of courtly love. Every love-lyric is to some extent a dramatization of the Courtly Lover, is a literary expression of a courtly ideal. Even at the height of the Elizabethan age, when the art-song for voice and lute was in great vogue, it is natural to take the sonnet openings, 'Whenas my lute is tuned to her voyce' and 'Strike up, my lute, and ease my heavie cares', as purely conventional and literary.[23] The traditional place of practical music in the etiquette of courtly love could easily account in poetry for dramatizations of the lover as musician. The clearest examples of this occur in ornate lyrics, since these are more circumstantial than the balets. I quote a stanza from a poem in William Thynne's *The workes of Geffray Chaucer* (1532):

> With fervent herte my brest hath brost on fire
> *Lardant espoir que mon cuer poynt est mort*
> *Davoir lamour de celle que je desire*
> I meane you swete most plesaunt of porte
> *Et je say bien que ceo nest pas mon tort*
> That for you synge, so as I may for mone,
> For your departyng *Alone I lyve alone*.[24]

At the moment of departure the lover, in the poet's imagination, is singing a love-song.

The courtly balet, the light quasi-popular courtly lyric, pictures the singing poet even more prominently. One begins his poem 'Mourning mourning | Thus may I sing'; another complains that singing does him 'mikell pine'.[25] And Wyatt:

> Me list no more to sing
> Of love nor of suche thing,

122

Howe sore that yt me wring;
For what I song or spake
Men dede my songis mistake.

My songes ware to defuse,
They made folke to muse;
Therfor, me to excuse,
Theye shall be song more plaine
Nothr of joye nor payne.[26]

Both extremes of courtly lyric, however, also refer dramatically to the act of poetical composition and to letter-writing:

'Yet for thy sake this lettre I do reherce . . .'

'My pen, take payn a lytyll space . . .'

'Crystes dere blessyng and myne
I sende yow yn grettyng of thys letter.' [27]

Of course, letter-writing may be a dramatic pose just as easily as singing or playing the lute. The musical and literary references (they sometimes occur in the same poem) do not merely contradict each other; they prove, I think conclusively, that the case for holding that the courtly balet, or any other poem, was meant to be sung cannot rest at all on *internal* evidence.

III

We are on surer ground when we find tunes, names of tunes, and other marginalia indicating singing. The evidence has already been anticipated in an earlier chapter, 'Popular Song'.[28] Popular poetry, such as the carol, was sung to popular tunes. Of this there can be no doubt. Furthermore, to repeat, 'dozens of popular songs were known with the *court* circle and formed a staple of both literary and musical composition',[29] their words being tricked out in courtly manner, their tunes being taken for use in part-song. 'The connection between words and tune was ever present in people's minds. . . . The wide currency of popular song in courtly circles meant that a natural, unsophisticated relationship between words and melody was never lost sight of.' [30]

Only one melody, out of sixteen which survive, is associated with a love-lyric in the traditional courtly style: 'My hert ys so plungit' [Song 205].

Music and Poetry

This unique song has never been published. It is given here in its entirety, with its curious heading:

vnres [?] ys ffulle of vertues mor þan wyll or rerson can exprese.

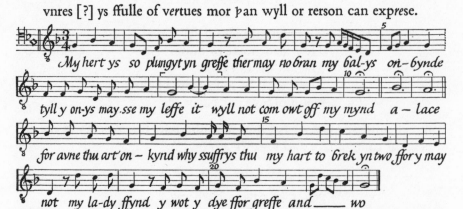

My hert ys so plungyt yn greffe thermay no bran my bal-ys on-bynde
tyll y on-ys may.sse my leffe it wyll not com owt off my mynd a – lace
for avne thu art on – kynd why ssuffrys thu my hart to brek yn two ffor y may
not my la-dy ffynd y wot y dye ffor greffe and___ wo

We have here a stanza of *ottava rima*, a favourite metre of ornate courtly poetry; and the melody found with it may perhaps be 'extracted' from an ornate polyphonic setting. It is accurately written in complicated notation (a characteristic group of two 'coloured' breves and two minims cuts across the 'perfect time'). Unless the part was only intended to be sung in consort, it shows that even ornate poetry in the 'high' style might be sung by a single voice. All other surviving tunes ('tenors' excepted) belong to carols and popular songs.

Named tunes are almost equally scarce for the courtly lyric. A shortened version of one of Wyatt's balets has the footnote in one manuscript: 'To Smithe of Camden'. I have not so far found a tune of this name; but as the same balet in another manuscript is glossed, 'Lerne but to syng yt', a tune seems likely.[31] It could hardly be a dedication. The marginal comment, 'the old Bettye to w. Bayslegh', against the poem 'Musing greatly' (not by Wyatt) in a third courtly anthology, takes more explaining.[32] In this case perhaps some personal allusion was intended.

When tunes are not separately named, the opening words or refrain may perhaps, as in popular song, provide the musical cue. A poem in a manuscript at Trinity College, Cambridge, recalls a popular song which Chauntecleer and Pertelote sang 'in swete accord': 'My lefe ys faren in a lond'.[33] The poem is introduced in the Trinity MS with the words, 'And for your love evermore wepyng I syng thys song'. Even if the musical settings with their suggestive melodies did not survive, it would be natural to conjecture that balets beginning 'My love sche morneth' [H25], 'A

Robyn, gentyl Robyn' [H49], and 'Grene growith the holy' [H33] were sung to the tunes of the songs whose words are re-worked in the verse.

Too much cannot be built on phrases like 'My woeful heart', 'Ah, my heart, ah', or 'Alone alone alone'. There are literary clichés as well as musical ones. However, one class of poems, based strongly upon popular songs, uses the first words in an unmistakable way both to point a moral and to point a tune. These are the moralized versions of courtly and of popular songs. The best known books containing 'moralizations' are *The Gude and Godlie Ballatis*, 1567, and John Hall's *Court of Vertue*, 1565.[34] These are late and of a strongly Puritan complexion. But what the authors, or editors, were doing was nothing new. 'My love sche morneth', which appears in *The Godlie Ballatis*, had been moralized nearly forty years before and published as a godly part-song in *Twenty Songs*, 1530 [see H25]. Among the moralizations in *The Godlie Ballatis* are: 'Grievous is my sorrow', 'Musing greatly in my mind', 'The hunt is up', 'Alone I weep in great distress', and 'All my heart ay'. There would have been little point in moralizing these unless they were current and in favour.

The moralizations, I must stress, include not only popular songs but courtly balets, since ladies and gentlemen of the court were to be reformed as well as children and servants at large. The 'lecherous ballades' of the *Court of Venus* were to be ousted by the spiritual songs of John Hall's *Court of Vertue*: Wyatt's 'My pen, take pain' is printed in the first; Hall's moralization 'My pen, obey my wyll awhyle' [Song 211] in the second.[35] No amorous 'complaints' in the melancholy, ornamental style of Lydgate and his followers are found moralized. The moralizers are, apparently, only concerned with popular songs and their use in and outside the court.

Sometimes tunes may have been themselves 'moralized'. Instead of ex- posing the to-be-reformed courtier, or citizen, to the pernicious and pro- fane associations of the original tune, certain reformers seem to have pro- vided their own. Some such procedure may explain the type of tune we find in *The Court of Vertue*. In the copies I have seen there are thirty melodies to poems and one setting for four voices ('All vertuous men').[36] The musical resources are simple: only two note-values are employed, semi- breve and minim, until the long which marks the end of the song. The printing – diamond-shaped notes on a single stave, by single impression – is cheap and smudgy. Both words and music show an affinity to the metrical psalm: musically, restricted rhythmical formulae, no regular metre, one syllable to a note, 'gathering' notes at the beginning of phrases, mixed angularity and movement-by-step in the melody;[37] from the literary point of view, limited vocabulary, stereotyped metres, strong rather than subtle rhythms, etc. It has been suggested that the readers composed accompaniments for instruments.[38] This is quite unacceptable: the book, like the psalm-books, appeals to a public barely literate, musically speaking. Here is a sample of Hall's work, 'In sommer time when flowrs gan spryng' [Song 148]:

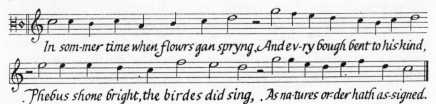

In som-mer time when flowrs gan spryng, And ev-ry bough bent to his kind, Phebus shone bright, the birdes did sing, As na-tures or-der hath as-signed.

Sometimes Hall cribs outright from the metrical psalm: 'The dauning day', for instance, borrows two phrases entire from the Old Hundredth. Quite what Hall hoped to achieve in relation to court-culture it is not easy to see. Did he really imagine that his books, *The Court of Vertue* and *The Proverbs of Salamon* [?1549], were going to stop the court from singing 'songes of love to the goddes of lechery'? However this may be, his sermonizing and his poetico-musical experiments strongly presuppose a background of courtly melody in the period of Wyatt.

The same background is implicit in another late and extremely dubious source of music for the courtly poetry collected and published by Richard Tottel. At some time, perhaps in Elizabeth's reign, someone (we do not know who) wrote in a copy of the *Songs and Sonets* (we do not know which edition) twelve tunes.[39] These were copied, with patent ignorance of the notation, by Dr G. F. Nott for his 1814 edition of Tottel's *Songs and Sonets*. The copy of Tottel used by Nott cannot now be traced; Nott's edition was burnt almost entire in a printer's fire. Only one surviving copy, at Arundel Castle, contains the tunes. I give two here to illustrate the difficulties of interpretation [Songs 150, 201]:

In win-ter's just re-turn

Mar-tial the things that do at-tain

Whatever this may be, it could never have been lute tablature. Nott's statement that they were 'airs for the lute' is probably no more than a wild guess, based on ignorance.

The best clue is provided in a note to one of the tunes, saying, 'and in any tune of the psalms in metre'. The poem in question is 'Phillida was a fair maid' [Song 260]. It would be rash to assume that all the 'Arundel' tunes are psalm-tunes – some of them have melodic idioms more appropriate to bass-parts or to flowing trebles. But the marginal gloss is significant in confirming a late date and in suggesting the sort of musical world the marginator was at home in. Until the original copy which belonged to Sir W. W. Wynne turns up, no firm conclusions at all can be drawn.

IV

The reasons so far given for thinking that the balet (the light, 'metrical' courtly lyric) was sung to current, often popular tunes can now be summed up: (i) Baldwin and other moralizers specifically state that a type of courtly lyric was sung; (ii) the courtly lyric is frequently found 'moralized' in the same books as is popular song; (iii) the scarcity of tunes and names of tunes is compensated for by an abundance of literary 'cues' pointing to the popular repertory. The strongest evidence, however, in support of the case lies in the court song-books themselves. In *Henry VIII's MS* we find, first, gaps left in musical settings which need to be filled with tunes; secondly, part-songs embodying known popular tunes; thirdly, part-songs of which the tenors are found separately elsewhere; and, lastly, part-songs having 'tuneful' tenors which although not found elsewhere may have had an independent existence.

'Grene growith the holy' [H33], 'Blow thi horne, hunter' [H35], 'Yow and I and Amyas' [H41] and 'Whilles lyve or breth' [H50] are all songs with gaps. That is to say, music is provided for the burden only. The verses follow in each case without music. With the possible exception of 'Blow thi horne', each song requires a different pattern of music for the verses. The music provided just cannot be made to do a double office. For instance, here is the tenor of 'Yow and I and Amyas', with the words of the burden:

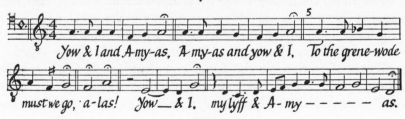

There is more than enough music here for two verses:

> The knyght knokett at the castell gate;
> The lady mervelyd who was therat.
>
> To call the porter he wold not blyn;
> The lady said he shuld not com in.

What is the explanation of these gaps? A reasonable explanation is that they were intentional and that they were to be filled with known, probably popular, tunes. They could hardly have been left accidentally in a manuscript so carefully produced.[40] About the probable relationship between the written music for the burden and the unwritten music for the verses one can only speculate. A late carol [Song 314] in a Royal MS of the period shows one way sophisticated musicians handled the problem. The dance-like tune of the verse goes in triple time as follows:

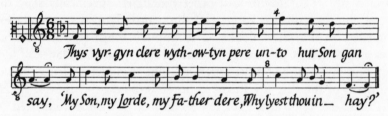

Thys vyr- gyn clere wyth-ow-tyn pere un-to hur Son gan say, 'My Son, my Lorde, my Fa-ther dere, Why lyest thou in— hay?'

In the burden of the carol the tune is put in the tenor *in four-four time*. This has the effect of disguising it. One can only wonder if some similar trick has hidden away popular tunes in the songs under discussion.

It is beyond dispute that many court-songs use known tunes ('known' is perhaps a less question-begging word than 'popular'). The simplest method was to make the tune, entire and complete, the basis of a part-song. (Plain-song was used for centuries in this way by church-composers.) Even in seemingly 'free' compositions like the fifteenth-century carol there may be more of this than we can diagnose: *Ecce quod natura* [Song 83] and 'Nowell nowell: Owt of your slepe' [Song 219] seem to be based on existing tunes. In the court song-books the tune is sometimes in the tenor, as for instance in 'Blow thi horne' [H35]; sometimes in the treble, as in 'I have bene a foster' [R1, H62]. Another song, certainly popular, was written up as a round, 'Alone, I leffe, alone', by Dr Cooper [H14]; the words and a semblance of the tune are also found as the burden of a carol (*c.* 1530). And in an earlier manuscript a completely different carol, 'Hos is to hoth at hom', is headed 'alone y lyve alone'; its burden may well have been sung to the same tune [see H14]. There is no end to the ingenuity displayed by court-composers: Cornish, in 'A Robyn' [H49], seems to have constructed his canon around a known tune. And again in 'My love sche morneth' [H25]. Here the two under-parts share the tune:

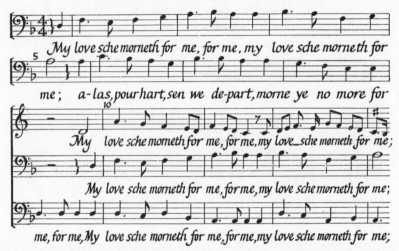

These are comparatively simple examples. But only comparatively. Even in these compositions it is difficult, or impossible, to tell how much of the popular song remains. It varies from perhaps a few notes in 'I have bene a foster' to what may be the complete tune in 'And I war a maydyn' [H101]. In some part-songs the existing song-melody, if used at all, is very heavily disguised or 'coloured': in 'Hoyda, hoyda' [F43] and in 'Come over the burne, Besse' [R16] it can perhaps just be glimpsed. The significant point is this: courtly balets are frequently found in the song-books associated with known, if not always in the full sense 'popular', tunes.

We may perhaps go further. The Royal MS (Appendix 58) previously mentioned is a source of court-songs.[41] These songs are single parts, not complete settings as in *Henry VIII's MS*. There are over two dozen such parts with English words, besides several single parts of motets, antiphons, and the like. There is also the full contra-tenor part of a Mass. The first page of the book bears the single word 'Tenor'. The manuscript is, naturally, assumed to have started its existence as a single (Tenor and/or Contra-tenor) part-book of a set. The format (it is a small oblong, octavo volume) is quite suitable; and some of the parts make very little sense without others to support them, because of their rests and awkward progressions. There are, however, other ways of explaining at least the tenor 'tunes' in the book. In Paris there is a *chansonnier* which contains tenors taken from part-music for use as independent melodies; in other continental manuscripts tenors were collected for use by improvisers.[42] A third possibility is that the tenors, or some of them, were known tunes that were later incorporated into settings. The first nine songs certainly bear this out. Three of them, 'A the syghes' and 'Iff I had wytt' and 'Blow thi horne', are found as the tenors of part-songs in *Henry VIII's MS* [H27, 29, 35]; a fourth, 'Downbery down', is found in both books as a round [H18]. Two others were well known as popular songs: 'Colle to me the rysshys grene' [Song 71] and 'Westron wynde' [Song 346].

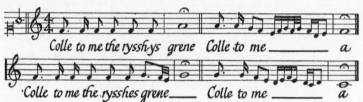

Colle to me the ryssh-ys grene Colle to me _____ a

'Colle to me the rysshes grene____ Colle to me ____ a

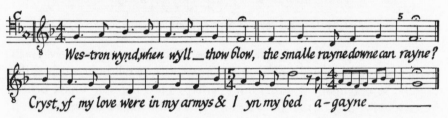

Wes-tron wynd, when wyll__ thow blow, the smalle rayne downe can rayne?

Cryst, yf my love were in my armys & I yn my bed a-gayne____

The other songs, also, are courtly-popular – that is, they are balets, not ornate lyrics. They are little known and I give two of them in full (Song 322 below and Song 363 on facing page).

Though that she can not re-dresse Nor helpe me off my smerte,

Yet sure hyt comyth of gen-tyl-nesse that py-ty-eth a mornyng hert.

[Song 322]

The presence, later in the manuscript, of solo-music for virginals and for lute lends colour to the idea that some, at least, of the secular songs were written out as *solo* songs.[43] This is no place for a detailed description of this complex and puzzling manuscript. But, on the face of it, it seems likely that it was or became a professional musician's commonplace-book, in which he, and others at court, entered music which might be useful in the course of duty. The obvious sort of person to name as owner would be a man like John Heywood – 'player at virginals', 'singer', wit and poet.[44] At any rate, some connection with the court is indisputable, and thus with the courtly lyric at its source.

Why soo un-kende? A-las, why soo un-kende to me? Syne the tyme I knew yow first Yow were my Joy and my trust__. Why soo un-kende ? A-las why so un-kende to me, Soo to be kende to me?

[Song 363]

The last stage of the argument follows naturally, if tentatively, from what has gone before. If it is asked whether any source exists of the tunes to which light courtly lyrics were sung, the answer might well be, 'the court song-books'; or, to be more precise, *Henry VIII's MS*. There are many tuneful tenors such as the following:

O my hart and O___ my hart, my hart it is so sore, sens I must nedys from my love de-part and know no cause where-fore.

[H15]

The 'self-sufficiency' of such a tune as this is in marked contrast to any part that could be extracted from the more contrapuntal court-songs of *The Fayrfax MS*. Known tunes may indeed lie behind the weaving polyphony of the latter. But *Henry VIII's MS* preserves the thing itself.

Concerning the discipline of writing words to a pre-existent tune little need be said. It is first and foremost a discipline in sound: the poet has to make words to a pattern and, in a strophic song with several verses, to go on repeating that pattern. The demands of a musical tune (allowing the courtly maker of this earlier period to have a less tender conscience about accent, intonation and quantity than, say, Campion) are not stringent.

The sort of music the court-poet wrote for presented a challenge which was simplicity itself compared with the complicated problems of *ars rhetorica*.[45]

This discussion needs only one postscript. We can see now that the distinction insisted on up to this point, between musical settings in parts and simple tunes, is not entirely a valid one. Could there not be court-songs so straightforward that words might be written to them? There are certainly some songs in *Henry VIII's MS* which fit this requirement – simple, chordal songs in three or four parts, with a 'metrical' tune in the tenor. A poet could easily substitute one set of words for another. This must have happened sometimes in the early Tudor period, though no actual examples survive among the part-songs we have. Later, of course, many examples can be found: Dowland's *The Frog Galliard* was printed with one set of words in his *First Booke of Ayres* and later used by Nicholas Breton for another poem.[46] It follows that a composition in parts could stand in the same relation to a poem as a mere melody. However, this additional distinction is not of basic importance. A straightforward chordal setting imposes exactly the same sort of simple discipline on the poet as a tune.* The discussion may be concluded with an example of such a setting. Whether the poet wrote to the tune (the tenor), or to an improvised two-part setting (the top voice 'discanting' in sixths above the tune, with occasional octaves), or to the full three-part chordal song, his problem was the same.

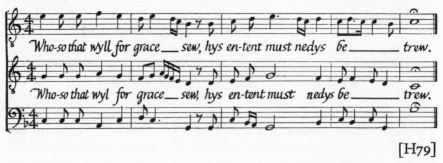

Who-so that wyll for grace__ sew, hys en-tent must nedys be__ trew.

Who-so that wyl for grace__ sew, hys en-tent must nedys be__ trew.

[H79]

V

Any interesting inquiry into the early Tudor lyric must encompass the poetry of Wyatt. I shall attempt now to draw the threads together in an answer to the straight questions: 'Did Wyatt write words-for-music?' 'Was

---

* This is the only kind of song which might cause us to modify the statement above (p. 107), that to find a poem set to part-music tells us nothing in itself about the poet's intention.

the prospect of musical performance his chief incentive to lyrical composition?'

One of the problems which faces any reader of Wyatt's poetry is to
reconcile the conventional picture of him as a 'maker of songs' with the
unanimous comment of his contemporaries that he was 'weighty' and
'depe-witted'. These two things are not of course incompatible. But why
is the emphasis in each case so widely different? Wyatt's latest editor has
written that his 'reputation rests, or should rest, on his lyrics or balets';[46a]
Surrey praised

> A hed where wisdom misteries did frame,
>   Whose hammers bet styll in that lively brayn
> As on a stithe, where that some work of fame
>   Was dayly wrought, to turne to Britaines gayn. . . .
>
> A hand that taught what might be sayd in ryme,
>   That reft Chaucer the glory of his wit;
> A mark the which (unparfited, for time)
>   Some may approche but never none shall hit.[47]

(It is a fine poem, not mere funereal chatter.)

Of Wyatt's learning, in the ordinary sense, there is no doubt: he translated Plutarch's *Quyete of Mynde* (1528), and French epigrams, besides
the Italian sonnets and satires for which he is chiefly remembered in
literary histories.[48] It used to be held that he was educated at St John's
College, Cambridge, but there is no evidence of this. His career as Esquire
of the Body and Gentleman of the Privy Chamber suggests the usual
courtier's education as page and then henchman in some noble household.[49] His father was Treasurer of the Chamber.

Learning is one thing, musicianship another. Was Wyatt a musician?
Courtly education would certainly have laid some stress on practical
music. But, in fact, outside the text of his lyrics, there is no evidence whatsoever that he had musical ability, as singer, lutenist or composer. It is
likely that Wyatt was put through the mill (he was taught to joust effi-
ciently) and learnt to sing a little and strum upon the lute. But, if he had
been proficient and taken great pleasure in music, surely some contemporary would have mentioned the fact, or he himself in the First Satire:

> This maketh me at hom to hounte and to hawke
> And in fowle weder at my booke to sitt.
> In frost and snowe then with my bowe to stawke,
> No man doeth marke where so I ride or goo.[50]

Music and Poetry

It is particularly significant that Leland, who considers every aspect of Wyatt's career in his *Naeniae in Mortem Thomae Viati Equitis* (1542), does not even hint at musical skill, when he is searching for talents to praise. Among the less high-flown of Leland's headings are *Delectus amicorum*, *Anglus par Italis* (i.e. Dante and Petrarch), *Viatus psaltes* (referring to the psalm translations). The literary tone is given by

> *Anglica lingua fuit rudis et sine nomine rhythmus*
> *Nunc limam agnoscit, docte Viate, tuam.*[51]

It might be objected that this is just the sort of tone a learned, royal antiquary would adopt. But Tottel's preface to the reader (*Songs and Sonets*, 1557) makes, with less reason (since he aims at a wider public), the same noteworthy omission:

> That to have wel written in verse, yea, and in small parcelles, deserveth great praise, the workes of divers Latines, Italians and other doe prove sufficiently. That our tong is able in that kynde to do as praiseworthely as the rest, the honorable stile of the noble earle of Surrey and the weightinesse of the depe witted sir Thomas Wyat the elders verse . . . doe show abundantly. It resteth now (gentle reder) that thou thinke it not evill doon, to publish to the honor of the Englishe tong and for profit of the studious of English eloquence, those workes which the ungentle horders up of such treasure have heretofore envied thee. . . . If parhappes some mislike the stateliness of stile removed from the rude skill of common eares, I aske help of the learned to defend their learned frendes the authors of this work. . . . And I exhort the unlearned, by reding to learne to be more skillful, and to purge that swinelike grossenesse that maketh the swete majerome not to smell to their delight.[52]

There are no references to music.

Wyatt's lack of interest in music is, on the whole, confirmed by his poetry. All his references to music are vague and conventional, even the most famous of them. He blames his lute, or not, as the fancy takes him, but never talks about it in the way of a man who really understands and cares for it. In this he stands in marked contrast to Skelton, who shows himself remarkably well acquainted with musical terms and musical practice. On the evidence of the poetry alone he appears much more knowledgeable than Wyatt about contemporary music; Wyatt could never have written 'Agaynst a comely coystrowne'.[53] Skelton may have acquired this knowledge in the process of co-operating in social tasks with court musicians, for he was of the class to do such work – occasional, 'applied' poetry in the narrowest sense. When the banqueting-house at Calais required 'florisshing' with 'histoires and convenient raisons', it was not Wyatt or Lord Vaux or Sir Anthony Lee who was summoned, but Alexander Barclay, a professional literary cleric of the same social standing, roughly, as Skelton and Cornish.[54] Wyatt would have had no call to collaborate with professional musicians in the course of duty; and it is at least doubtful whether he would have done so for pleasure in the normal round of social life.

Only one early musical setting of a poem in the Wyatt canon survives – 'A Robyn, gentyl Robyn' [H49]. When discussing it earlier, I gave reasons for thinking that Wyatt's longer poem in a later manuscript may have built on the shorter court-song, itself indebted to popular song. There is no evidence that Wyatt wrote the lyric for Cornish to set.[55]

All other music connected with Wyatt's poetry is later and its exact bearing on the question is difficult to assess. The settings are as follows:

(i) 'Blame not my lute' [Song 57]

> Folger Shakespeare Library MS 448.16, f.4v: anon; lute tablature, with inadequate rhythmical signs; no words except title. BM Sloane MS 3501 f.2v: listed as a title with other songs and dances. Hall's *Court of Vertue*, f.74v: moralized version, tune for one voice. There is no connection between the Folger version and Hall's version. The latter is a little less like a psalm-tune than usual. Hall's moralization is in the metre of Wyatt's poem (ed. Muir, no. 132); his tune has no known source.[56]

(ii) 'Heven and erth' [Song 105]

> BM Roy. MSS, App. 58, f.52 (concluded on f.55v): anon; lute tablature. Wyatt has a poem which begins 'Hevyn and erth and all that here me plain | Do well perceve what care doeth cause me cry' (complete text in Egerton MS 2711; last three verses in *The Devonshire MS*: ed. Muir, no. 73). The two items are presumed to be connected: the music will accommodate one four-line stanza of the poem. The music is found on the same leaf as tablatures of 'If care cause men to cry' and 'In winter's just return' (both poems in Tottel, and later issued as broadsides). Dr Byler describes the lute-music as having some relationship to the Italian ground, *romanesca*; the same music was published by Attaignant, in 1555, as Pavane d'Angleterre. The music became

extremely popular in the second half of the sixteenth century and is found in numerous English and Scottish sources.[57]

(iii) 'My lute awake, perfourme the last | Labor' [cf. Song 210]

> *Court of Vertue*, f.76v: anon; no music but headed 'Syng this as, My pen obey &c'; a moralization beginning 'My lute awake and prayse the Lord' in the same metre as Wyatt's poem (ed. Muir, no. 66). The poem also occurs in two of the *Court of Venus* fragments (ed. Fraser, p. 119).

(iv) 'My pen, take payn a lytyll space' [cf. Song 211]

> *Court of Vertue*, f.87v: anon; music for one voice; a moralization beginning 'My pen obey my wyll awhyle' in the same metre as Wyatt's poem (ed. Muir, no. 103). The poem also occurs in two of the *Court of Venus* fragments (ed. Fraser, 118).

(v) 'If ever man might him avaunt' [Song 121]

> Arundel Castle, *Songs and Sonets* (ed. Nott, 1814), no. 4: anon; music for one voice. *Tottel* (ed. Rollins), i. 58. *Wyatt* (ed. Muir), no. 183.

These are all the musical versions with which we need concern ourselves. An attempt has been made to include with these two lute-pieces of the late sixteenth century – 'No peace I find' and 'What vaileth' – but, rightly, abandoned.[58] One might as well expect John Attey's madrigal (1622) on Wyatt's 'Resound my voyse' to convey useful information about the early Tudor tradition. If even a contemporary setting tells us, by necessary logic, nothing about the poet's intentions, then music not committed to paper until a decade or two after the poem was written will be even less informative. We may indeed learn something about the later history of the poem, its place in popular favour, but this is a different matter.

It would be unnecessary to make such obvious warnings so emphatic, were it not that the lute tablatures dated about 1550 (or slightly later) have led scholars to describe Wyatt's lyrics indiscriminately in such phrases as 'words needing tunes, as stained glass needs the light'.[59] A more judicious approach is required.

So far as Wyatt's poetry is concerned, the problem is epitomized in 'Blame not my lute'. It seems, first, most unlikely that the prospect of 'musical performance' was an incentive to him to write it; part-music can safely be left out of the discussion. *Tune* is what we have to consider. Hall's moralization, late though it is, is good *prima facie* evidence that 'Blame not my lute' was current as a song in the 1560's. This is the tune which Hall supplied:

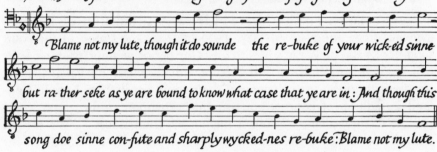

¶ A ditie named blame not my lute whiche under that title toucheth, replieth & rebuk-eth, the wycked state and enormities of most people in these present miserable dayes.

'Blame not my lute, though it do sounde the re-buke of your wick-ed sinne

but ra-ther seke as ye are bound to know what case that ye are in : And though this

song doe sinne con-fute and sharply wycked-nes re-buke : Blame not my lute.

60

The lute tablature in the Folger MS gives a completely different tune:*

bis

finis

This setting is based, like many lute-pieces of the early and later Elizabethan period, on a stereotyped sequence of bass-notes known as a 'ground' (in this case the *folia*). Dr Byler contends that 'the use of Italian ground-basses as a harmonic foundation for composition and improvisation was well established in England at least by the middle of the sixteenth century and continued in use to the end of the century'.[61] With this statement no

* Dr Byler suggests the poem was sung as follows: he repeats one phrase of the music, and one (other) line of the words, inserts rhythmical indications, and adds a fourth part to the harmony (Byler, p. 136-).

one could quarrel. But Dr Byler seems also to infer that *in the Wyatt period*

> ... English poetry was sung to the lute in a manner comparable to the Italian. ... While the singer could improvise melody appropriate to the text of the poem, the constantly recurring harmonic pattern of the accompaniment provided a unifying element.[62]

Whatever may have been achieved by Elizabethan times, there is but scant evidence from *earlier decades* (say, 1500 to 1540, the period of the court song-books and of Wyatt's life) to offset the pervasive impression we have of a French-Burgundian court culture, still distinctly un-Italianate. To repeat an argument used elsewhere, 'there could hardly have been in England a tradition of courtier-poets singing extempore to their lutes, comparable to the Italian, without it having left some traces'.[63] We are left with the possibility of yet another new development in the middle of the sixteenth century; and we may suppose that those who admired Wyatt's poems were not slow to take advantage of the new Italian techniques. It is significant that 'Hevyn and erth' is music not for the basse-danse but for the new Italian dance, the pavane.

To sum up, the evidence is insufficient to support any definite conclusion about Wyatt's *original* intention. 'Blame not my lute' later became, like 'Pastyme' [H7, R12] and a few other courtly songs, popular.[64] That is evident. But I suspect that musical intentions of any kind that could be called 'artistic' were far from Wyatt's mind when he wrote, and far, too, from the minds of his contemporaries. This observation holds, even if the lyric was written to be sung to a fashionable tune, as I believe it was (the tune of the Folger version seems the most likely). This type of poem may have had a special appeal for the poet's immediate society, besides having currency in a wider circle as 'a good song'. A courtier writing a poem to the pattern, and possibly on the theme, of a popular song (Wyatt's 'A robyn', for instance) would know that his sophisticated listeners or readers, his friends, would enjoy the use he made of the popular element. If the poem, with or without his consent, became current outside his own circle, that was another matter. It would become so on its more general appeal. What later readers or singers made of Wyatt's best balets is for our present inquiry irrelevant.

VI

The delicate problem of deciding whether a poem was written to be set to music, to be sung to a tune, or neither, cannot in the early Tudor period possibly be decided on the evidence of the poem or song alone. The problem of music and poetry is the problem not of 'words and notes' but of a whole mode of life; it is therefore by examining the difference between early and late sixteenth-century ways of making music – its occasions, its performers, its techniques and its purpose – that we shall most safely begin to judge the relationship between the two arts. The brief inquiry of Part Three into the state of music in the early Tudor court must determine how the evidence of the manuscripts and of the poems themselves should be interpreted. It will, I think, allow no doubt that courtly music and poetry were emphatically the 'provinces of experts in each art', who did not greatly care what the others were doing. The lyric is no exception to this. Unless they were working together for a common social purpose, the 'garnishing' of a noble occasion or of a courtly act, the only strong link between poets and composers was their mutual interest in popular song. Whatever the mainspring of the early Tudor courtly lyric, it was not, as I see it, music.

In Elizabethan England there was, I have suggested, an 'artificial reunion' between music and poetry; the experts then began to know and to care what the other experts were about. The reunion was certainly artificial in the sense that it was not the natural climax of co-operation between arts 'bound by tradition and social circumstance'; it was also artificial in the sense that it was encouraged by a small group of humanists under foreign influence. Whether the word 'artificial' should imply more than this, it is difficult to say. Was the reunion of written music and the written lyric superficial and restricted – an 'uneasy flirtation', it has been called[65] – or was it, while it lasted, deeply and widely felt throughout many classes of society? Until the social history of Elizabethan music has been fully written, this question cannot be answered with any great confidence.[66]

Meanwhile, we are left with a challenge. If music was not 'the chief incentive to lyrical composition', what was? In the next part of this book I endeavour to fill the gap which I have been at pains to open in our study of the subject.

NOTES TO CHAPTER 7

1. Cambridge UL, Add. MS 5943 (see App. C, no. 22).
2. See pp. 284– below.
3. Cambridge, Trinity College MS O.2.53 (M. R. James, *Catalogue of the Western MSS*, iii. 169–, lists contents).

4. Oxford, Balliol College MS 354 (see App. C, no. 18).

5. These observations I owe to Professor R. H. Robbins. See his introductions to *Index MEV* and to *Secular Lyrics*.

6. Cambridge, St John's College MS. S.54; described and edited by M. R. James and G. C. Macaulay, 'Fifteenth Century Carols and other Pieces', *MLR*, viii (1913), 68–.

7. Greene, no. 366.

8. BM Sloane MS 2593 (see Greene, 330) and Oxford, Bodl. MS. Eng. poet. e.1 (see App. C, no. 42). Robbins, *Secular Lyrics*, p. xxvi, is the most recent writer to use the term 'Minstrel Collections'; Moore, 157, and E. K. Chambers, *English Literature at the Close of the Middle Ages* (1945), 90, have been cautious about, or even opposed to, it.

9. BM Add. MS 17942, *The Devonshire MS*, see p. 205 below.

10. See p. 213 below.

11. *Wyatt* (ed. Muir), no. 114 and introd., p. xi. Chambers, *Wyatt*, 131–, discusses the personal problem in detail.

12. *The Canticles or Balades of Salomon phraselyke declared in Englysh Metres*, by William Baldwin (1549). Dedicated to Edward VI. No modern edition.

13. *The Bannatyne MS* (see App. C, no. 19) was 'written in time of pest, 1568', but contains many older poems. The quotation in the text is from Ritchie's edition, iii. 241. There is no music in the MS.

14. Pattison, 161–2. The most comprehensive treatment of the terminology is in Baskervill, 28–31. I use the spelling 'balet' (following Chambers) rather than 'ballad' in order to avoid confusion with the folk- or broadside ballad, and to distinguish the courtly nature of the lyrics so described.

15. The earliest usages recorded in the *OED* belong to the 1580's (see p. 24 above, note 17).

16. For Fayrfax's gift see p. 283 below.

17. Baskervill, 90, note 3, suggests that the 'balet' for which 10*s*. was paid (see *DNB* s.v. 'Hawes') may have been 'in the nature of song drama for court performance'. This introduces a further complication in terminology.

18. Greene, no. 10, st. 3. See also no. 382, and no. 420 (minstrel's song or comic 'patter'?).

19. Barclay: see p. 288 below. Hawes: *Pastime of Pleasure*, 63: 'She comaunded her mynstrelles ryght anone to play | Mamours, the

swete and the gentyll daunce'. Michel Toulouze, *L'Art et Instruction de bien Dancer* [before 1496], lists *Mamours* and gives its music.

20. Skelton mentions the titles of at least 15 songs in his works. His knowledge of the teaching (and the teachers) of music can be deduced from 'Agaynste a comely coystrowne' (Dyce, i. 15). See also, especially, 'Phyllyp Sparowe'(Dyce, i. 51); 'Colyn Cloute', line 491– (Dyce, i. 330); 'Magnyfycence', line 138– (Dyce, i. 230). There are many other references in his works to contemporary music both popular and professional.

21. *Wyatt*, no. 101, line 34, 'To busy work for my pore harp'.

22. Oxford, Bodl. Selden MS b. 24, f.217 (I thank P. J. Frankis for this reference).

23. Quoted J. Erskine, *The Elizabethan Lyric* (U.S.A., 1903), 147, 150.

24. 'Alone I leffe alone': see H14, note. The poem 'I have non English convenient . . .' is pr. Skeat, vii. 281–4.

25. *EEL*, nos xxxviii and cxxvi.

26, *Wyatt*, no. 138.

27. The quotations are, respectively, from: Skeat, vii. 282; *Wyatt*, no. 103; Robbins, *Secular Lyrics*, no. 129.

28. See pp. 44– above.

29. See p. 54 above.

30. See p. 54 above.

31. 'Now all of chaunge | Must be my songe' (*Wyatt*, no. 158). See also Foxwell, *Poems*, i. 339.

32. 'Musing greatly in my mind', BM Add. MS 18752, f.88v (ed. Reed, no. 17). See also *GGB*, 165, 178.

33. 'My lefe ys faren in a lond': Cambridge, Trinity College MS R.3.19, f.154 (words only); pr. Robbins, *Secular Lyrics*, no. 160. It is presumably the song referred to in *The Nonne Preestes Tale*, vii. 2879 (ed. Robinson, 200). Whether the Trinity text is the original song or a courtly version is not clear. The first is quite possible since, a few lines earlier in the Tale, Chaucer appears to quote from the song 'She hath the herte in hold' – line 5 of the Trinity text.

34. John Hall's *Court of Vertue* is unpublished; the songs are listed in App. B and indexed in App. C, no. 51. *The Gude and Godlie Ballatis* was edited for the STS by A. F. Mitchell (1897).

35. *Court of Venus* (ed. Fraser), 118, no. 1; *Court of Vertue*, f.87v.

36. At the British Museum and at the Bodleian Library.

37. The metrical psalm is described above, pp. 85–.

38. Russell A. Fraser, 'An Amateur Elizabethan Composer', *M&L*, xxxiii (1952).

39. The songs of this book are listed in App. B, below, and indexed in App. C, no. 12, q.v. for further information.

40. For apparent exceptions to the careful production, see notes to H68, H92, and *MCH8*, nos 68, 92.

41. BM Roy. MSS, App. 58: see App. C, no. 72 below.

42. *The Tournai chansonnier*: Paris, Bibl. Nat. n.a.fr.4379. The whole question of monophonic *chansonniers* is discussed by Reese, *MR*, 205.

43. Amongst the music for virginals is Aston's *Hornepype*. Amongst the pieces for lute are transcriptions of 'Pastyme' [H7, R12] and of 'Ough warder mount' [H42].

44. See ch. 12, p. 267 below, and note 10.

45. A comparison of the analyses by Pattison (Wyatt's strophic technique) and by Rubel (Wyatt's rhetorical diction) will quickly confirm the point.

46. Pattison, 172, with musical illustrations.

46a. *Wyatt* (ed. Muir), introd., p. xxiii.

47. Quoted, *Wyatt* (ed. Muir), introd., p. xxxiv.

48. C. R. Baskervill has edited a facsimile of Wyatt's translation from Plutarch (U.S.A. 1931).

49. Wyatt's life: see Foxwell, *Poems*, i, p. xiii–; Chambers, *Wyatt*, 100–. They both state he was educated at St John's; Cooper, *Athenae Cantabrigienses*, iii (1913), 124, disproves.

50. Wyatt's jousting is recorded by Halle, *Chronicle* (ed. Whibley), ii. 21–; Christmas, 1525. Wyatt's *First Satire* is pr. *Wyatt*, no. 196.

51. Leland's *Naeniae* is pr. Foxwell, *Poems*, ii. 231 (App. B).

52. Richard Tottel, *Songs and Sonets*, 1557, 'To the Reader'.

53. See p. 314, note 110 above. 'Agaynste a comely coystrowne' (Dyce, i. 15) is sufficient on its own to establish the point.

54. *L&P*, iii, pt 1, no. 737 (10 Apr. 1520): Sir Nicholas Vaux to Wolsey.

55. See p. 110 above.

56. Byler, 58. Hall's *Court of Vertue*: see p. 125 above.

57. Byler, 49.

58. Ivy L. Mumford in *M&L*, xxxix (1958), 262–.

59. ibid. Dr Byler dates the tablatures of Roy. MSS, App. 58, and of the Folger MS in the 1550's; Dr D. J. Lumsden, 'The Sources of

English Lute Music', dates RA58 ('undoubtedly the earliest source') *c.* 1550.

60. *Court of Vertue*, f.74v.
61. Byler, 111.
62. Byler, 123.
63. See p. 282.
64. 'Pastyme' [H7, R12] and 'I love unloved' [H108] were both mentioned in a sermon preached by the King's Almoner in 1521; the first appears with music 4 times in 3 MSS of the period and again 100 years later in a Scottish song-book. Fayrfax's 'Sumwhat musyng' [F24, H107] is its only rival. The three-part 'Pastyme' must of course be distinguished from a possible 'Pastyme' *tune*, extracted from, or even antecedent to, the King's composition. Another court-song which may have been well known in a limited circle is 'Benedicite! Whate dremyd I?' (F12): it is found among Sir Thomas More's Latin epigrams (see App. A, F12, note).
65. F. Kermode, reviewing Pattison in *RES*, xxv (1949), 266. I pursue this point further in 'The Elizabethan Madrigal', *E&S*, ed. B. Willey (1958), 17–37.
66. Professor Woodfill's book has done much to fill the gap: *Musicians in English Society from Elizabeth to Charles I* (U.S.A., 1953).

PART TWO

Courtly Love and the Courtly Lyric

CHAPTER 8

Introductory: 'A New Company of Courtly Makers'?

George Puttenham, writing his *Arte of English Poesie* in Elizabeth's reign, described in words which have often been quoted, one aspect of the poetic scene under Henry VIII:

In the latter end of the same kings raigne sprong up a new company of courtly makers, of whom *Sir Thomas Wyat* th'elder and *Henry* Earle of Surrey were the two chieftaines, who having travailed into Italie, and there tasted the sweete and stately measures and stile of the Italian Poesie ... they greatly pollished our rude and homely maner of vulgar Poesie, from that it had bene before, and for that cause may justly be sayd the first reformers of our English meetre and stile.[1]

This 'new company' has usually been taken, with Puttenham's apparent support, to constitute 'a decisive novelty in the history of our literature'.[2] Two issues may easily become confused here: the novelty of their achievement, and the novelty of their existence as a 'company'. Their achievement in Puttenham's eyes was to have introduced into English Italian 'measures' (such as the sonnet) and the mellifluous rhythms of Italian verse.

Whatever the novelty of their achievement (and it has often been exaggerated) there is little reason for regarding the *existence* of a 'company' of 'courtly makers' as a decisive novelty. What exactly Puttenham means by 'new company' in his context is not clear. But he has just surmised that Chaucer and Gower, the last courtly poets mentioned, were 'Knights'; and he will shortly speak of 'an other crew of Courtly makers Noble men and Gentlemen of her Maiesties owne servauntes'. Thus it is not likely that he thought the 'courtly makers' a new phenomenon. And, indeed, they were not, although the scarcity of records gives them a seeming isolation. It will be my chief aim in this part of the book to describe the

147

tradition of courtly 'making' to which Wyatt's balets belong. It is a
tradition that can be traced back fairly easily to Chaucer, if not farther.

The phrase 'Wyatt's *balets*' was used deliberately, for it is this side only
of Wyatt's art with which we are here concerned – the art which produced

> And wylt thow leve me thus?
> Say nay, say nay, for shame,
> To save the from the blame
> Of all my greffe and grame:
> And wylt thow leve me thus?
>   Say nay, Say nay!
>
> And wylt thow leve me thus,
> That hathe lovyd the so long,
> In welthe and woo among?
> And ys thy hart so strong
> As for to leve me thus?
>   Say nay, Say nay! . . .[3]

and a host of lesser poems in the same vein. This is not the Wyatt whom
Leland, the king's antiquary, remembered, in a set of published elegies
dedicated to Surrey, as a glory of English letters and learning. Neither is it
the Wyatt whom Surrey himself commemorated in a fine elegy:

> Wyatt resteth here, that quick could never rest,
>   Whose heavenly giftes encreased by disdayn,
> And vertue sank the deper in his brest –
> Such profit he by envy could obtain.
>
> A hed where wisdom misteries did frame,
>   Whose hammers bet styll in that lively brayn
> As on a stithe, where that some work of fame
>   Was dayly wrought, to turne to Britaines gayn . . .[4]

My first reason for making Wyatt's balets the centre of this inquiry is
that the great bulk of his poems are written in this particular courtly vein,
which must therefore have had some special meaning for him. I do not
think they have ever been described for what they are. Moreover, it is they,
and not the translated sonnets, psalms and satires, that have sustained
Wyatt's reputation through the last hundred years.

This view of Wyatt as memorable for his amorous verses, either with a
light touch ('Wyatt could at times be exquisite in the lyric measures of

which he was a master'), or with a fire of personal intensity ('Wyatt's real affinities, if with any, are with John Donne'), is of comparatively recent growth.[5] It was not held by his contemporaries: Tottel speaks of 'the weightinesse of the depe-witted sir Thomas Wyat the elders verse'. Nor was it held by the eighteenth-century historians (when they read him): Thomas Warton considered his genius to be of the 'moral and didactic species'; nor by his first scholarly editor, G. F. Nott, who described his satires as 'unquestionably his happiest and most finished productions'.[5] The valuing of Wyatt's balets above his translated epistles and psalms is nineteenth-century in origin. It was nourished and encouraged by the current 'lyrical' view of poetry: poetry was considered at its 'purest' when it was most lyrical, nearest to the condition of music; lyric was at its most moving when its 'music' reflected an exquisite moment of personal experience. Of recent years this valuation has been modified and refined. In accordance with our present preferences for 'moral-social' verse it has been argued that the lyrics are more than they seem: they reflect the complex stresses of a complex court-society ('the convention of the love-lament offered indirect expression to a range of feeling'); or they are at least 'dramatic' ('he used emotions he had experienced: but he made them serve the purposes of his art').[6] Still more recently, however, the nineteenth-century view of Wyatt has been called entirely in question, notably by Mr H. A. Mason and Professor Hallett Smith, both of whom see the essential and worthwhile Wyatt in the translated poems, especially in certain sonnets and epistles, and not at all, or only occasionally, in the balets.[7]

Barrenness, monotony, superficiality – these are the terms that will come to the minds of most of those who have read Wyatt's balets *in extenso*, however greatly they admire his craftsmanship. Professor C. S. Lewis gives a much-needed warning when he writes of the following lines,

> My days decaies, my grefe doeth gro
> The cause thereof is in this place,

This was not intended to be read. It has little meaning until it is sung in a room with many ladies present. . . . The poet did not write for those who would sit down to *The Poetical Works of Wyatt*. We are having a little music after supper. . . .[8]

The poetic plainness is, for Professor Lewis, partly explained by the fact that these are songs: 'richness and deliciousness would be supplied by the air and the lute and are therefore not wanted in the words'.[9] In so far as

Courtly Love and the Courtly Lyric

Professor Lewis suggests a social setting for Wyatt's balets, he is providing an essential clue. But if we are invited to see the setting as a *musical* evening, then we are, I think, being misled. The logical end of such a process of reasoning is Professor Pattison's statement, already quoted, that 'the incentive to lyrical composition was primarily the prospect of musical performance'.[10] I have argued in Part One that this view rests on mistaken assumptions about the place of music in social life, about the relationship between words and music in the late Middle Ages, and about the nature of the surviving songs. The time has now come to make that negative stand positive by an analysis of what is shallow and lacking in Wyatt's balets. In the following chapters I shall attempt to supply a lost dimension of the courtly lyric.

To me the most suggestive phrase in the imaginary description quoted above is 'a room with many ladies present'. Wyatt's balets were written for occasions when the presence of ladies was more important than the presence of music. The balets belong to a tradition of *vers de société* which can be traced back at least a hundred and fifty years. This tradition is inseparably bound up with courtly love. The 'courtly makers' were the 'courtly-love makers' before they were anything else. Perhaps also the 'courtly love-makers', though this does not necessarily follow. We shall not, I think, understand what the courtly love-lyric meant in the fifteenth century to those who wrote it and to those for whom it was written, without trying to feel the meaning of the whole code of courtly love. (Its meaning, needless to say, is not the same thing as its supposed historical origins, about which we may be sure the medieval courtier knew far less even than the modern scholar.)

One basic false assumption has vitiated much critical comment on the literature of courtly love in the later Middle Ages; it is the idea that courtly love was either 'literary' or 'actual'. The conclusion reached is that as it was, manifestly, seldom 'actual', a matter of historical fact, it must therefore have been purely 'literary'. One senses, moreover, behind such comment as 'throughout the fifteenth century the letter-form was growing in popularity', and such a phrase as 'community of artistic interests', a concept of literature inapplicable to the period. Due weight must be given, of course, to the tradition of rhetoric, of translation from foreign models, and of imitation of the masters; the fifteenth-century poets were never tired of acknowledging their debt to Chaucer, 'fader and founder of ornate eloquence'. The point is that literature was not only literature but very much more. What appears to be a 'community of artistic interests' may in fact be only a symptom of a far deeper community of interest. In short, much of what we today call the 'literature' of medieval England, is a *symptom* of a certain kind of social activity. Of no 'literature' is this more true than of the literature of courtly love. But the observation holds, of course, for the mass of devotional verse and prose. As Professor Robbins has observed, Middle English religious poetry is 'eminently practical' in its nature.[11] No one would think now of explaining the resemblances between certain versified prayers, hymns, 'commandments', and so forth, as 'literary' resemblances. The verses are alike because they reflect the religious activity of a community.

Once anachronistic ideas of 'literature' have been discarded it is of course easy to see that devotional poetry is a symptom. This is because the religious activity which nourished it and gave it meaning expressed itself in many other ways – in the liturgy, in the religious drama, in the architecture of our cathedrals. The liturgy survives, but the 'ritual' of courtly living has largely perished. It is this ritual which we have to reconstruct in imagination, if we are to understand the courtly lyric which it nourished and which adorned it.

'Ritual' is a possible word with which to describe the 'middle space' of courtly love, a space of attitude and behaviour, words and actions, included neither under actual *amours* nor under literature. But the word I prefer and shall use is 'game' – a good Middle English term with a wealth of association: fun; a diversion; amorous play; a contest; an intrigue; the chase; the quarry. All these related meanings are apt when we are trying to reconstruct the social fiction which was courtly love in action.

Courtly love provided the aristocracy not only with a philosophy and a psychology of love but also with a code of social behaviour. It was a school of manners, of 'politeness', of 'chere of court'. In this code – social philosophy, one might call it – the sexual attraction between man and woman was the central motif, or (to change the metaphor) the 'ground' on which everything stood. Even if you were not a lover, you must – at least in mixed company – *act the lover*. Professor Huizinga's comments on French court-life are profoundly true for England also:

> In no other epoch did the ideal of civilization amalgamate to such a degree with that of love . . . The theory of courtly love . . . tends to embrace all that appertains to the noble life.[12]

With courtly love is linked, of course, another ideal – that of chivalry, which claimed to teach men, but in a manner more reconcilable with

Courtly Love and the Courtly Lyric

Christian doctrine than the code of courtly love, how to behave to one another, to their king, and before their God. Honour is the central motif of this code, and 'public service' (as we should call it today) its proper field of endeavour. The high ideal of Christian knighthood is little to our present purpose. But the ideal had its lighter side in the 'play' of jousts and tourneys. This 'play' belongs essentially to the world of courtly love, to the manly display of social virtues where women can admire them. We shall therefore be concerned with the Squire (who could '*juste* and eke daunce, and well purtreye and write | . . . In hope to stonden in his lady grace'), but hardly with the Knight ('At mortal batailles hadde he been fiftene, | And foughten for oure feith at Tramyssene'), though knightly exploit could, as the Dame of La Tour Landry reminds us, easily become a means for men 'for to enhaunce themself and for to drawe unto them the grace and vayne glory of the world'.[13]

The social philosophy which courtly love, in its widest sense, provided for the court circle, expressed itself in word and in act, sometimes together, sometimes apart. These words and acts I shall refer to as the 'game of love'.[14] In this 'game' (part imaginary, part real) people acted out their aspirations to a leisured and gracious life, where Lady Courtesy led the dance and Beauty, Simplesse, Swete-Lokyng, Fraunchise, Mirth and Gladness danced with her.[15]

NOTES TO CHAPTER 8

1. Puttenham, 60.
2. Lewis, *Sixteenth Century*, 222.
3. *Wyatt*, no. 113.
4. cit. *Wyatt*, p. xxxiv (among Critical Comments selected by Muir).
5. The quotations, with their authors and sources, can be found in Muir's edition, pp. xlv (Tillyard), xlviii (E. K. Chambers), xxxv (Tottel), xxxvii (Warton), xxxix (Nott).
6. D. W. Harding, 'The Poetry of Wyatt', in B. Ford, ed., *The Age of Chaucer* (1954), 206; and Muir's introduction, p. xxviii.
7. Hallett Smith, 'The Art of Sir Thomas Wyatt', HLQ, ix (1946), 323–; Mason, *Scrutiny*, xvii (1950), 72, reviewing Muir's edition; and, principally, Mason's book, *Humanism and Poetry in the Early Tudor Period* (1959).

8. Lewis, *Sixteenth Century*, 230.
9. idem., 222.
10. See p. 28 above.
11. See p. 235 below.
12. Huizinga, 96.
13. *La Tour Landry*, 172.
14. My use of the phrase, the 'game of love', may recall the title of Dr D. L. Stevenson's *The Love-Game Comedy* (Columbia, 1946), which sets Shakespeare's comedies of courtship in an historical perspective. Despite the suggestive similarity of title, Dr Stevenson's views of the love-literature of the fifteenth and sixteenth centuries have little in common with those here outlined. Dr Stevenson accepts, in particular, two notions which I cannot: (i) that there is 'a rather sharp break in English literature between Chaucer as literary representative of the Middle Ages and Sir Thomas Wyatt as herald of the Renaissance' (p. 69); and (ii) that in the sixteenth century men made for the first time an attempt 'to actualize theories of courtly love' (ch. vii), i.e. to experience them in real life. Nevertheless, Elizabethan courtly comedy clearly stands in a relation to the social fiction here described
15. The first impulse to attempt this inquiry came from conversations with H. A. Mason and from reading his account, then unpublished, of the tradition to which Wyatt's balets belong. I gratefully acknowledge to him the fundamental observation that 'the study of these poems belongs to sociology rather than to literature' (*Humanism and Poetry*, 171), and many other hints and thoughts. I am also greatly indebted to Professor Huizinga's two books, *The Waning of the Middle Ages* (English edn 1924) and *Homo Ludens* (1949). The first contains chapters on courtly love, 'The Dream of Heroism and of Love', 'Love Formalized' and 'The Conventions of Love', which I have known and pondered over for a long time. The second came to my notice only after these chapters had been written, and my sense of indebtedness to it is of another kind: it provides a perfect frame of reference and background to the 'game of love' idea.

CHAPTER 9

The 'Game of Love'

This chapter does not aim at being a rounded piece of historical writing. It is not so much concerned with reconciling facts as with reconstructing a *fiction*. I am trying to isolate one strand only from the complicated web which was the culture of the court – the strand of courtly love. Only the 'courtly love' meaning of the various activities described will matter to us in the present context. For instance, when thinking of the elaborate disguisings in which courtiers and their ladies acted the allegories of love, we shall have to disregard all economic considerations (how the shows were paid for), all political (they were often put on to impress foreign visitors), and many others (their relation to popular culture, to changing fashions of dress, music, *décor*; their concessions to the new 'Renaissance' mythologies). It is only their 'courtliness' that matters.[1]

To say we are concerned with a fiction is not to make a special case of the period in question.[1a] All social life is in some sense a fiction, a 'game'. We act many parts; and we try to act consistently, not mixing our roles. We play one role in our families, another at our work, yet another (or others) to our friends. One fiction is appropriate to a sherry-party – that of being naturally gay, conversational and 'interested in people'; another to a business meeting – the man prudent, far-sighted and discreet. These fictions, which are all simplifications, are necessary; they allow social life (and business) to be carried on. Nor should it be thought that they are always a burden to those who have to adopt them. Far from it. They may provide us with a refuge and release from our more complicated selves; they may give us an outlet, a channel, a form, for certain emotions and desires; and lastly, if they are habitual, they will permanently simplify our responses. But, though the need for social fictions is not confined to the social life of any one age or country, we may feel bound to ask why the court circles of Chaucer's and a later day preserved a fiction so extravagant and remote as the fiction of the courtly lover. It is not enough to answer that by this time it was a hallowed and traditional pattern in all European courts. It must have retained an appropriateness or it would have been dropped more quickly.

The especial appropriateness of the fiction of courtly love was that it showed how life in 'middeleard', which orthodox theology taught men to despise, could be made a beautiful and worshipful thing. It gave the urge to make beautiful objects, the artistic and creative urge, a legitimate field of expression outside the Church. The Bible did not tell a man whether he might pare his nails at table, kiss a lady when he met her, or write a love-song. It told him of his salvation, of his duties and responsibilities, of the spirit in which he should work and pray. Courtly love, on the other hand, was a gospel of leisure and pleasure. It taught you how to behave to your peers when you all had time on your hands; not how to do them good, but how to make yourself desirable; how to 'commune', especially in mixed company, and how to please.

'Thou shalt please' – this is the great commandment in the courtly code. And it has remained a central concept in the idea of the Gentleman. Newman's description of the Gentleman in one of his University discourses is the classic statement; the passage begins, 'Hence it is that it is almost a definition of a gentleman to say he is one who never inflicts pain . . .'[2] The gentleman is concerned, at all costs, to avoid unpleasantness; he wants social life to be a good show – appearances must be preserved. Moreover, he knows that appearances cannot be preserved without realities, and he cultivates virtues which will sustain the appearances.

The courtly situation presented a similar difficulty. The 'pley' and 'disport' of courtly life required that men and women alike should be 'mery', 'debonair', full of 'fraunchise' and 'fredom' – in short, as I have said, that they should please. But how could this gallant and high-hearted atmosphere be supported? The answer was – through Love. The experience of 'falling in love' would confer on you the inestimable benefit of a 'goodly manere': Troilus

> . . . bicom the frendlieste wight,
> The gentilest, and ek the mooste fre,
> The thriftiest and oon the beste knyght,
> That in his tyme was or myghte be.[3]

And the discipline of being in love, of wooing, would confirm and strengthen you in your new life, free of 'japes' and 'cruelte', a life, whether you won or lost, of faithful service.

The logic of love proceeds, then, like this. It starts from the observed and fundamental truth that 'falling in love' makes a man pleasing to others – 'all the world loves a lover'. The first deduction from this is that, if you want to please, you must allow yourself to fall in love and remain in love. The second is that, if you want to please, and you are not in love, you must *act the Lover*. This is why the art of living approximates to the art of loving; and why the great first psychology of love, the *Romance of the Rose*, is also the source and pattern of 'curtesy' books.

Yet another simplification will be necessary. I shall treat the period 1370 to 1530 as more or less static, disregarding the obviously unstable elements in the situation – dynastic upsets and courtly upheavals, increased and changing foreign contacts, a shifting economy, to say nothing of personalities. I shall concentrate, instead, on the continuity of the courtly world, on the ways in which Chaucer and Wyatt, Charles of Orleans and Henry VIII can be said to have been playing the same game and obeying the same rules. It may be that by the time of Wyatt's death the tradition was in a state of rapid disintegration. But *Henry VIII's MS* and *The Devonshire MS*, to name no others, assure us that it was still a force – alive, if not kicking – in the early sixteenth century.

The 'game of love' has never, I believe, been reconstructed for the England of Chaucer to Wyatt. I shall attempt to do this under four main heads: reading of love; talking of love; acting (including games in the modern sense); and *mores* (manners and behaviour). Much of the evidence I shall use is literary, but we must be constantly on guard against thinking that literature was more important in the 'game' than it really was.[3a] Moreover, this evidence varies greatly in kind: different poems bear different relations to the 'game' – some may have had actual part in the proceedings, others are perhaps stylized records or imaginary descriptions, others works of pure fancy.

I

Among the pleasures of his youth at Windsor which Surrey recalled in a poem written during his imprisonment, are (my italics)

> The statelye sales: the ladyes bright of ewe;
> The daunces short; *long tales of great delight*.[4]

The reading of 'long tales' was a favourite courtly pastime for centuries before Surrey. What we think of now as a solitary pursuit was, in the days before printing, a social recreation. A well-known manuscript of Chaucer's

The 'Game of Love'

Troilus and Criseyde shows the poet reading from a sort of pulpit to a courtly gathering which consists mostly, though not entirely, of ladies.[5] Occasions of this sort must have been frequent and of varied kinds. Perhaps the illumination just referred to shows a 'command performance'. Court-servants other than Chaucer were called upon to show their prowess by reading in public. Hawes is said to have had a reputation for being able to recite long passages from the early English poets, particularly Lydgate, by heart.[6] Skelton's *Garland of Laurel*, too, seems to reflect a society of which the Countess of Surrey was the hub: its members are bent to 'work' him a 'chaplet'; in return he is devising a 'goodly conceit'. Froissart, while in Orthez, had to read each night after supper to Gaston de Foix from a book of love-poems.[7]

More informal occasions are suggested by the passage in *Troilus and Criseyde* where Pandarus goes to call on Criseyde,

> And fond two other ladys sete, and she,
> Withinne a paved parlour, and they thre
> Herden a mayden reden hem the geste
> Of the siege of Thebes, whil hem leste;[8]

Gower's Lover, too, pleading 'not guilty' to the sin of Somnolence, points out that he is always ready

> . . . on the Dees to caste chaunce
> Or axe of love som demande
> Or elles that hir list comaunde
> To *rede and here of Troilus*.[9]

These two passages are interesting not so much as evidence (of which there is plenty) that reading was a social rather than a solitary activity, as because they both show that such an activity could be part of the 'game' of courtly love. The Lover, in Gower, does not think of *Troilus* as literature; he associates it with such things as 'questions of love' and dice-play with amorous stakes. Pandarus, too, has one idea in his head:

> 'But I am sory that I have yow let
> To herken of youre book ye preysen thus.
> For Goddes love, what seith it? telle it us;
> Is it of love? O, some good ye me leere!'
> 'Uncle,' quod she, 'youre maistresse is nat here.'[10]

Romance-reading upon the book was a fine opportunity for 'dalliance'.

Courtly Love and the Courtly Lyric

'Dalliance' is a word which has lost some of its meaning. There is little or no flirtatious undertone to the word as used of the conversation between Sir Gawayne and the Lady of the Castle: – 'her dere dalyaunce of her derne wordez'.[11] The word describes the by-play of courtly conversation, though it is easy to see how the purely amorous implications developed (the talk was private, 'derne'). Reading of love in the right company gives the courtier an opportunity to display the finesse of his approach to the opposite sex and the delicacy of his understanding.

There was perhaps a general expectation of 'dalliance' before, after, and perhaps even during, a reading of a love-poem (the illumination already mentioned shows one couple 'commoning' as Chaucer reads). It is one of the subtleties of Chaucer's poetic art that he so nicely conveys this atmosphere and uses it. Whatever else its implications, *The Parlement of Foules* has this atmosphere. The closing lines, which have often been taken as an appeal for royal favour, are surely a gambit in the 'game' of love – what one might call a 'dally':

> I hope, ywis, to rede so som day
> That I shal mete som thing for to fare
> The bet, and thus to rede I nyl nat spare.[12]

This perfectly rounds off a poem which began with a playful twisting of the age-old aphorism, *Ars longa vita brevis* – 'Al this mene I by Love . . .' [declare in respect of] – and with an equally playful claim, 'I knowe nat Love in dede'. It may be that Chaucer's favourite dramatic pose of himself as an unsuccessful, or inexperienced, lover, one who serves the servants of Love (as he says in *Troilus*) but is not quite 'up to it' himself, is a deferential recognition of the comparatively lowly place he himself occupied in the high society of Richard's court. However this may be, that Chaucer 'dallies' in his more courtly poems with the 'gentils' of his audience is undeniable. The Prologue to *The Legend of Good Women* is a long semi-flirtation, a piece of gallantry, directed at the ladies of the Court. And to describe the subtlety of his dramatization of himself as the poet of Love in *Troilus and Criseyde* would require a whole essay. Chaucer plays to his gallery of lovers. Other poets did the same, though with less subtlety.[13] It was partly the expectation of this play which gave a spice to the reading of books of love and made such occasions as much social as literary.

The 'Game of Love'

II

'To rede and here of Troilus' did not merely give a spur to 'dalliance'; it was also a lesson in it, a sentimental education. (It was a lover's duty to become acquainted with the 'canon' of historic love-affairs.) This education had many facets. Courtly 'conversation', or 'commoning', was a diverse craft and one that took long to learn. But one facet of it could be studied particularly well by reading tales of love, and that was the art of *talking*.

The importance of talk in the aristocratic, ideal world of courtly living can hardly be exaggerated. When the Lord of the Castle and his court realize they have Gawayne as their guest:

> Uch segge ful softly sayde to his fere,
> 'Now schal we semlych se sleghtez of thewez
> And the teccheles termes of talkyng noble;
> Wich spede is in speche, unspurd may we lerne,
> Syn we haf fonged that fyne fader of nurture;
> God hatz geven us his grace godly forsothe,
> That such a gest as Gawan grauntez us to have,
> When burnez blythe of his burthe schal sitte
> > And synge.
> > In menyng of manerez mere
> > This burne now schal us bryng,
> > I hope that may hym here
> > Schal lerne of luf-talkyng.[14]

It is 'luf-talkyng' that is going to bring them 'in menyng of manerez mere' [into a proper understanding of the noble life]. Such a fine enthusiasm for elegant discourse was not confined to the borders of Wales. It is writ large over the courtly literature of England. One of Criseyde's first questions to Pandarus comes rather as a surprise to the modern reader:

> 'Kan he wel speke of love,' quod she, 'I preye?
> Tel me, for I the bet me shal purveye.'[15]

Troilus can, and frequently does.[16]

In *The Knight's Tale* reference is made to a festive occasion on which there was rivalry, 'who moost felyngly speketh of love'.[17] And Charles of Orleans borrows and amplifies the tag of Ovid about the three 'scolis' of wooing. You can win the love of a peasant woman simply by knocking

Courtly Love and the Courtly Lyric

her down, and of a merchant's daughter by larding her with presents; but

> . . . to nobles longith sewte of curteys speche
> As he fynt tyme bi mouth or writyng seche.

'Gentille must be wonne with gentiles', and 'goodly speche' should be the chief weapon in your armoury. Conversely, a successful love-affair will increase your command of the language of lovers:

> The speche of love so fresshely depaynt is
> With plesere where love sett is hertily. . . .[18]

The lover must 'take measure' in his talking and not be 'outrageous'; he must observe decorum.

So much of 'literature' in this period is stylized or idealized talk that we can catch, surely, in many poems the very tone and accent of their 'courteous carp':

> 'A question wolde Y axe of yow, lady.'

> 'Of me?' quod she. 'Now, good, what thing is that?'
> 'It is not smalle, madame, Y yow ensewre.
> I put a case: if so myn hert it sat
> To yow in love above eche creature,
> Told Y it yow, wold ye it so diskever
> And make of it a skoffe or yet a play?
> In which, percas, my lijf so myght it way.'

> 'God helpe me, nay! Why, wat erthely wight
> That lovyd me unto myn honour evyr,
> Sothely me-thynke, Y did him gret unright. . . .[19]

This passage from Charles of Orleans has an authentic note. In Gower's verse, too, the accent of 'polite and easy society' is particularly marked.[19a] A slightly more trenchant style is exemplified by some of the speeches in *La Belle Dame*, in Sir Richard Ros's translation.[20]

I shall often use the argument that 'literature' in this period presents us with stylized talk, idealized talk. The reader may, therefore, be helped if I explain in a short digression why and in what senses the argument can be held a sound one. There is, first, the argument from the discipline of rhetoric, in which, traditionally, little distinction was made between the spoken and the written word. They both obeyed the same basic rules, and served the same basic ends – to 'praise' and to 'persuade'. Then, supporting this, there is the open and 'diffuse' style of most medieval poetry, whether in a Chaucerian or in an alliterative vein. Nothing could be more unlike the packed, richly metaphorical style of the Elizabethan dramatists, for instance. Lastly, and most importantly, one cannot but be impressed by the closeness of literary to spoken forms: the epigram is a stylized derivative from the spoken joke; the epistle derives from familiar conversation; the oration from the formal speech; encomium from compliment; elegy from condolence; satire, so-called, from abuse; and so on. This closeness of formal connection did not, of course, drop out at the end of the Middle Ages. There is still vitality in it in the period of Dryden and Pope. But today it is almost dead. To what *form* of talk do *The Four Quartets* or *The Pisan Cantos* belong? In the Middle Ages, by contrast, the formal as well as stylistic connections were almost universal. Even a long poem like Gower's *Confessio Amantis* is based on interchange of the spoken word in love's confessional. And there are very few poems which the narrator does not introduce in the dramatized first person.

'Luf-talkyng' could take many different forms. A good talker could coin maxims and aphorisms, devise riddles and jokes, develop 'themes', formulate 'questions' concerning love, start a debate or a 'contention', take part in talking-games, and so on. Such talk is nearly always *dramatic*. The word is ambiguous: I mean, not that there is bound to be an element of impersonation, but simply that there will be tension, if not conflict, between different speakers. This is seen even in so simple and favourite a medieval 'ploy' as the riddle. The tension between questioner and answerer is not resolved until the solution has been given. An interesting little riddle occurs at the end of an 'amerous balade by Lydegate made at the departyng of Thomas Chaucer on the kynges ambassade into Fraunce'. The biographical truth of the rubric is disputed; it is, in any case, clearly a poem made for a lord to 'use' on his lady.

Devynayle par Pycard:

> Take the seventeth in ordre sette
>   Lyneal of the ABC,
> First and last to-geder knette
>   Middes e-joyned with an E,
>   And ther ye may beholde and se
> Hooly to-gidre al entiere
>   Hir that is, wher-so she be,
> Myn owen soverayne lady dere.

Courtly Love and the Courtly Lyric

The 'devynayle' was, I suppose, devised as a playful coda to Lydgate's poem, in partial concealment, partial revelation, of the lady's name. This may have been A-L-E-Z, i.e. Alice.[21]

If the word- and letter-play of the riddle is developed, it may turn into anagrams and acrostics and rebuses, all of which pandered to the love of intrigue, secrecy and reserve, which is a central motif in the 'game of love'. They were probably used even more widely than the plentiful evidence suggests.[22] Analogous to the riddle, on this side, is the *double entendre*. I do not mean, particularly, the 'dirty joke' hidden behind the apparently harmless riddle, of which there were certainly plenty,[23] but the speech or poem of syntactical double meaning:*

> In women is rest peas and pacience
> No season | for-soth outht of charite
> Bothe by nyght and day | thei have confidence
> All wey of treasone | Owt of blame thei be
> No tyme as men say | Mutabilite
> They have without nay | but stedfastnes
> In theym may ye never fynde Y gesse | Cruelte
> Suche condicons they have more and lesse.[24]

The relevance of such contradictory and double-edged moods to the 'game' of love is discussed later.

On a more elevated plane the riddle merges into the love-problem, *demande d'amour*, of which *The Wife of Bath's Tale* gives us a sample:

> I grante thee lyf, if thou kanst tellen me
> What thyng is it that wommen moost desiren.[25]

A secondary 'problem' in *The Knight's Tale* is posed directly by its narrator to his 'audience':

> Yow loveres axe I now this questioun:
> Who hath the worse, Arcite or Palamoun?
> That oon may seen his lady by day,
> But in prison he moot dwelle alway;
> That oother wher him list may ride or go
> But seen his lady shal he nevere mo.[26]

The main 'problem' of *The Knight's Tale*, as to which of two young

* Two such poems, it is interesting to note, are found set to music [Songs 151, 226], which shows that the effect was not thought to rest on *visual* comprehension. Doubtless, the essential double-edged effect could be achieved just as easily in a light-hearted talking-game as in song.

courtly lovers deserves to have the lady, is also touched on in the Duke of
Suffolk's 'Parlement':

> If tweyn love one, this thapoyntment:
> Loke who can best deserve to stande in grace,
> But hyndre not to forther his entent . . .[27]

The discussion of 'problems' of this kind, like reading tales of love,
provided a pleasant entertainment in which subtlety of discourse and
elegance of manner could be displayed.

The love-problem tended, on the one hand, towards mere casuistry.
Huizinga quotes a game, 'Castle of Love', which consisted of 'a series of
allegorical riddles'.[28] One wonders whether something of the same kind
was recalled by the chronicler, Edward Halle:

> the kyng [Henry VIII] the same night made to the Ambassadors a
> sumpteous banket with many ridelles and muche pastyme.[29]

On the other hand, the genius of Chaucer could lift a 'question' of
potential triviality, 'Which was the mooste fre, as thynketh yow?' to a
level at which the real relevance of doctrines of love to human behaviour
could be seen.[30] More practical considerations enter into the fictional
debate between the Knight of La Tour Landry and his wife over the love-
problem; whether 'a lady or damoyselle myght love peramours [passion-
ately] in certayne caas'.[31]

The riddle or love-problem, as was suggested earlier, contains the germs
of 'dramatic talk'. Dramatic talk took various forms and gave varied scope
to the 'game of love'. There was straight debate, and its companion, the
contention or 'flyting'; and there was the Court of Love. In *La Belle Dame
Sans Mercy* the debate is between L'Amant, who presses his suit, and La
Belle Dame, who mercilessly refuses; it is pure courtly talk, a very model
of 'talking noble'.[32] Both *Sir Gawayne* and *Troilus* have, of course, long
passages of love-debate. Finally, in John Heywood's *Play of Love*, what
may have been an improvised talking-game is cast into stage-form: the
characters are The Lover Loved, The Lover Not Beloved, Neither Lover
nor Loved, and the Woman Beloved not Loving.[33]

A favourite way of diversifying the debate was by introducing birds as
the protagonists. The *locus classicus* in this period is *The Parlement of Foules*;
but there are many other examples. In *The Cuckoo and the Nightingale*,
of the Chaucerian apocrypha, the nightingale defends love, listing its
statutes and the benefits conferred by 'worshipful desyr', while the cuckoo

dispraises it as a cause of 'rage' in young folk, 'dotage' in old. The poet eventually throws a stone at the cuckoo and earns the nightingale's thanks.[34] The use of birds as symbols for lovers permeates the whole of the literature of love and will be mentioned again later. It would be extremely interesting to know whether this symbolism ever found its way into actual games of love.

III

The presentation of courtly talk in the setting of a 'parlement' or court of some sort, raises one of the most interesting issues we have to consider – the 'Court of Love'. The symbolism of lovers serving in a court has three principal meanings. There is first, and most obviously, the idea of the social court, governed by a queen, in which the lover is at school and receives instruction in polite behaviour and the doctrine of love. Related to this, in fiction as in historical fact, is the idea of a court of law, with its statutes, presided over by a judge: here lovers present their 'bills', advocates plead causes, judgements are given, and penalties and prizes dispensed. (Somewhere between these two, perhaps, is the idea of the court presided over by the Muses, a 'rhetorical chamber', where lovers compete in their artistic skills – in fact, a 'puy'.) And there is, thirdly, the image of the feudal court, in which the subject pays homage to a sovereign who is God's vice-gerent on earth. A fourth image is obviously related to these: the court is seen as a congregation of the faithful, presided over by a God of Love; love is a religion; lovers must worship, go to confession, pray for each other, and accept 'in gree' whatever falls to their lot. These ideas, naturally, overlap. In the middle of the *Kingis Quhair*, for instance, one finds a curious mixture of the courtly company, the suppliants at law, and the 'confessors and martyrs' of love. But for purpose of analysis it will be convenient to treat them separately.

In some contexts the word 'court' simply means a company. When the Lover in *Confessio Amantis* sees his rival in a group round his lady he refers to them as the 'court of Cupid'.[35] But in general, more is made in social contexts of the fact that the court centres on the person of a sovereign, generally a queen. This sovereign has courtiers who are referred to as 'servants': Chaucer says he is one who serves the servants of the God of Love; Charles of Orleans is admitted as 'oure servant'; Lydgate writes a ballade for 'a squire that served in love's court'.[36] Such servants, like the servants of the real court, swear fealty, are assigned 'the fayrist pencioun' their services deserve, are exiled or advanced, and allowed to leave the service through old age or incapacity. They can also present pleas and register complaints of service unrewarded. Charles of Orleans carries the fiction further and gives a 'jubilee' banquet.[37] (A 'jubilee' is an entertainment given on retirement.)

When the legal side of the court is stressed, lovers present 'bills' or 'complaints'; they employ advocates or argue with those of Venus; and they are expected to observe statutes.[38] The court may be summoned for a particular day by special announcement in public, or by a 'clark' sent for the purpose; it may also be adjourned if a decision is not reached. Suffolk's *Parlement* (one of many which blend the legal with the royal) is summoned in the poem of that name for the 22nd February at *Secret Pense* and adjourned until *Vivre-en-Joye* on 29th April.[39] The judge may be Cupid or Venus, or a council of the Gods, or a company of women.

It is not a very big step from the court to the church of love – temple it is more usually called –, from the judge to the God, from the advocate to the priest, from the appellant to the worshipper in prayer. In *The Court of Love* a thousand lovers are kneeling in the 'temple bright' of Venus, uttering a prayer which is strongly reminiscent of Troilus's hymn to Venus:

> Venus, redresse of all division,
> Goddes etern, thy name y-heried is!
> By loves bond is knit all thing, y-wis,
> Best unto best, the erth to water wan,
> Bird unto bird, and woman unto man;[40]

Troilus and Criseyde opens with a great bidding prayer; Charles of Orleans asks lovers to pray for his soul;[41] the poet of the *Kingis Quhair* says his beads 'with humble hert entere';[42] and the envoy of Suffolk's *Parlement* is another exhortation – 'O ye peple, that lovers yow pretende, | Prayeth hertly to Venus'.[43] Lovers dedicate themselves with vows; retail the Ten Commandments; make their humble confessions; say funeral rites in the church of love.[44] These things scarcely need illustration, and yet this abundance of available illustration drives home to us how thoroughly religious images permeate the 'literature' and, I suggest, the 'game' of love.

The well-authenticated fact of debates on 'questions' of love is of itself almost sufficient to establish 'Courts of Love' as an aristocratic pastime. But there is no need to rest the case simply on this. W. A. Neilson gives an account of the *Cour Amoureuse* which was founded at the French Court in 1400. Huizinga relates it to the controversy over the two conceptions of love found in the *Romance of the Rose*:

> The cause of chivalry triumphed in the form of a literary salon. The court was founded on the virtues of humility and of fidelity, 'to the honour, praise and commendation and service of all noble ladies.' The members were provided with illustrious titles. The two founders and the king were called the Grands Conservatours . . . A certain Pierre d'Hauteville, from Hainault, was Prince of Love; there were also ministers, auditors, knights of honour, knights treasurers, councillors, grand-masters of the chase, squires of love . . . The business of the court much resembled that of a 'rhetorical chamber'. Refrains [? themes, proverbs of love] were set to be worked up into . . . songs . . . There were debates 'in the form of amorous law-suits to defend different opinions.' The ladies distributed the prizes . . .[45]

The existence of something on such a grand and pompous scale as this presupposes smaller institutions. But perhaps 'institutions' is not the right word. The *Cour Amoureuse* has the nature of a permanent game, a game kept perpetually alive. I have in mind something much more informal, like the occasion described in Boccaccio's *Filocolo*, when Fiametta is chosen to be queen and arbitress in a love debate and crowned with a garland.[46] Or, in the *Book of the Courtier*: 'Then were they governed as the dutchesse thought best, which many times gave this charge unto the Ladye Emilia.'[47]

I have found no direct evidence of the Court of Love as a pastime in English courtly life. But the circumstantial evidence is strong. Such 'courts' existed abroad in the courtly cultures which most influenced our own. Moreover, there *is* evidence that royal judgment on a point of honour involving love for a lady could be acted as part of the courtly 'game'. The following account is taken from a contemporary description of Princess Margaret's royal progress to Scotland in 1503 for her marriage to King James. The general situation is not unlike that in *The Knight's Tale*, where Theseus comes across Palamon and Arcite fighting.

> Halfe a Mylle ny to that within a Medewe, was a Pavillon, whereof cam owt a Knyght on Horsbak, armed at all Peces, havyng his Lady Paramour that barre his Horne. And by Avantur ther cam another also armed, that cam to hym, and robbed from hym hys sayd Lady, and at the absenting blew the said Horne, whereby the said Knyght under-

stude hym, and tourned after hym, and said to hym, wherfor has thou this doon? He answerd hym, what will you say therto? – I say, that I will pryve apon thee, that thou has doon Owtrage to me. The tother demaunded hym if he was armed? He said ye, wel then said th'other, preve the a Man, and doo thy Devoir. [*They fight with* 'Sperys' *and then with* 'Swerdes' *and make* 'a varey fayr Torney' – *the* 'caller' *knocks the* 'defender's' *sword out of his hand, gives it back, and they fight again*] and they did well ther Devor, tyll that the Kynge cam hymselfe, the Qwene behynd him, crying Paix, and caused them for to be departed. After this the King called them before hym, and demaunded them the Cause of ther Difference [*they explain, and are told*] brynge youre Frends, and ye schall be appoynted a Day for to agre you.[48]

The intention of this carefully staged 'incident' was doubtless to lead up to the formal joust promised in the last sentence. But the judicial element in the tournament game is parallel to a similar element in games of 'luf-talkyng'.

Lacking direct evidence, we are more likely to be convinced that the Court of Love was not merely a literary fiction but also a formula for courtly 'pleyinge', if we are convinced that such 'pleyinge' was an important and extensive manifestation of courtly love. It is, therefore, to games of love in the more restricted sense – games, that is, involving movement, apparatus, impersonation, perhaps competition, and played to rules – that we shall now turn.

IV

Important as reading and talking and debating about love were in the 'game' of courtly life, they were not all-important. In this leisured and luxurious, yet hectic and unpredictable world, 'the slipper top of court's estate', the urge to find meaning and shape, to express and so to control manifold desires and emotions, took other forms than mere words. Among these forms were dancing, formal and informal games, and sports.

Dancing was the very embodiment of the courtly way of life – 'curtesy' in action.[49] Some idea of its importance as a representation of the way courtly persons should behave to one another can be got elsewhere in the narrative just quoted, *The Fyancells of Margaret*:

The Kynge flyinge as the Bird that syks hyr Pray, tuke other Waye and cam prively to the said Castell, and entred within the Chammer

with a small Company, wher he found the Qwene playinge at the
Cardes. At the Entrynge, the Qwene avaunced hyr toward hym in
receyving hym varey gladly, and of Good Wyll kyssyng hym, and
after he gaffe Salut to the Ladyes and Company presente.
In Commonynge togeder, cam the sam Lordes here abouffe named,
to whom the Kynge did Reverence, his Bonnett in hys Haund, in
specyall to the Arch Byschop of York . . . After som Wordes
rehersed betwyx them, the Mynstrells begonne to play a basse Daunce,
the wich was daunced by the said Qwene and the Countesse of Surrey.
After thys doon, thay playde a Rownde, the wich was daunced by the
Lorde Gray ledynge the said Qwene acompayned of many Lordes,
Ladyes and Gentylwoemen. After was brought Wyn and Bred to the
Kynge the wiche tuke the Bred, and thereof served the said Qwene.
Lykwys the Coupp of wich he fyrst servyd hyr. And after all the
Company presente draunke also.⁵⁰

I have quoted at some length because it shows that to the narrator basse-
danses and 'rounds' were courtly disports which it was not ignoble to
mention in the same breath as ceremonious 'salutes' and other evidences
of the highest good-breeding. It shows not only that dances were used but
also *how* they were used. The courtly signification of the dance is apparent
in nine out of every ten literary contexts:

> I sawgh hyr *daunce so comlily,*
> *Carole* and synge *so swetely,*
> Laughe and pleye so womanly,
> And loke so debonairly,
> So goodly speke and so frendly . . .⁵¹

'The figure of very nobilite' is set out and expressed in the dance. But there
is a nobility proper to each sex, and in the dance a man shows his man-
liness and a woman her womanliness in 'gentyl behavyng', the one to the
other. It was the perfect symbol then, as in all ages, of male-and-female, of
sex – even if not always signifying 'matrimonie'.⁵² The dance also
'betokeneth concorde', social solidarity, and youthful gaiety. The strength
with which these 'meanings' were felt, if it were not immediately apparent
in the context of courtly narrative (poetry or prose, 'Chauceriana' or the
chronicles), could be gathered from the extensive use of the dance as a
symbol in the writings of the age. Love itself is often spoken of as a dance:
'loves daunce', 'the old daunce', 'the dance of lufe' – the image became a

cliché of the language of love.[53] The idea of a dance is not a simple symbol; it is, rather, a cluster of symbols. They are all present in the dance of the *Romance of the Rose* – youth, sexual desire, gaiety, social enjoyment and 'curtesy'. Moreover, these associations are what gives the use of the same symbol in the Dance of Death its macabre relevance and potency: death is everything that love is not – the extinction of all 'kindly' impulses and social joys. The special association, too, of the dance with the highest expressions of 'curtesy' makes its use in connection with the 'great leveller' even more poignant. The same might be said of the contrast between the idealized courtly virtues and the gross reality of vice in the Dance of the Seven Deadly Sins.

A courtly dance was normally the centre-piece of the elaborate formal entertainments which characterized festive occasions such as Christmas, early May, or the 'birth of a prince'. From one point of view the 'disguising' was an elaborate device for giving additional significance and glamour to the moment when the courtly persons descended from their 'pageant' and danced. But this would be an over-simplification. These 'disguisings' were also games of love, in the narrower sense of the word. Perhaps the title 'entertainment' which I give them in a later chapter is a little misleading.[54] It may too much suggest that, like a modern revue or musical comedy, 'the Golldyn Arber in the Arche-yerd of Plesyer' was publicly performed to an 'audience'. Performed it was, certainly; but the performance would not have lost its courtly significance, even if no one had seen it. The element of communication was not paramount. The courtly ritual, whether 'in ernest or in game', existed chiefly for the benefit of those who conducted it. In these formal games the king and the court *performed* the allegory of love.

Allegory is perhaps more at home in periods like the Middle Ages when the line between art and life was less decisively drawn than it is today. However this may be, the symbols most frequently used in medieval allegories do not belong to an exclusively 'literary' tradition but are drawn from the objects and activities of the everyday world – the Garden, the Court, the Pilgrimage, the Battle, the Dance, the Game of Chess. In *The Book of the Duchess* a lover is represented as playing chess with Fortune, because chess was a favourite pastime; the courtly virtues and graces are described as dancing a 'carole' in the *Romance of the Rose*, because dancing was universal. All this is perhaps too obvious. What is more important is to realize that these very same patterns of action which the allegorists used for their own purposes – the young man going through a hedge into a garden to pick a rose, the messenger with bad news interrupting a courtly dance, the warrior assaulting a castle – these patterns could be *acted* as well as described in words. Thus, to take a non-courtly example, the Dance of Death exists not only in literary and pictorial form, but, in the earliest morality plays, also as drama (e.g. *Pride of Life, Everyman*). In this case the acted allegory 'meant' the same, roughly, as the written. But this did not necessarily follow. The function of allegory proper is, of course, to define, more exactly or meaningfully than direct description can do, certain mental and moral qualities, in their growth and in their relations with one another. But the function of most courtly acted allegories was, by means of an 'approved' plot with the right kind of associations, to put the actors, the courtly personalities, into graceful attitudes, to enable them to play their part in the 'game' of courtly love, to display and enhance *their personalities*. This attitude of mind has seeped, too, into many of the minor allegorical poems of the period. Professor Lewis has remarked that the authoress of the *Assembly of Ladies* 'is moved, by a purely naturalistic impulse, to present the detail of everyday life' at court.[55] That is to say, she was far more interested in the courtly 'game' than its allegorical meanings. This must surely also have been true of the courtiers and their ladies as they played at their favourite allegories of the Garden and the Castle.

'The Golldyn Arber in the Arche-yerd [i.e. "orchard", garden] of Plesyer' is not the only title of the period to suggest the enchanted rose-garden of romance. In 1517 we meet 'the Gardyn of Esperans', that the accounts describe as a garden railed with banks of artificial flowers, representing probably the hedge or wall round the Rose. Another 'pageant' was entitled the 'ryche mount' (punning presumably on 'Richmond') and may have belonged rather to the Garden than to the Castle genre. 'Castle' disguisings include 'Dangerus Fortress' (1512); 'the Pavyllon un the Plas Parlos' (1515); the castle of timber (1516) connected with Cornish's 'story of Troylous and Pandor'; and 'the Schatew Vert' (1522).[56] The castle may represent the Lady's heart and love, recalling the scene familiar in medieval ivories, 'a castle defended by ladies with showers of roses against their lovers'.[57] In this case the defending party of knights will recall the defenders of the Rose. Or, alternatively, the castle may represent a danger or captivity from which the Lady has to be rescued. In this case the motif is 'The hero who serves for love'. This motif has been described by Huizinga as 'a sensuality transformed into the craving for self-sacrifice'.[58] One might add that in the game-form the psychological motive of self-immolation is dwarfed by another which was always present, the desire for self-display: the joust, tourney or 'barriers' is a rippling of the biceps on a gigantic scale.

The line between chivalric 'disguising', incorporating an 'assault' of some kind, and a tourney cast in dramatic form is very fine-drawn. It was not enough simply to have blood (real blood) and bravery (in every sense). The imagination was better satisfied if the scene were cast into dramatic form. Thus, for a Joust of Honour in February 1511, 'a forest was constructed within the house of Black Friars, Ludgate, 26 ft. long, 16 ft. broad, 9 ft. high', with artificial trees of eight kinds, and beasts and birds 'embossed of sundry fashion'.[59] There were four men-at-arms riding in the forest; and six dozen silk roses were needed for the garland which was delivered to the Queen when the joust began.

V

When they met on her 'progress' to Scotland, Margaret and James did other things besides dance basse-dances, play their musical instruments and take bread and wine together. We read of the company on one occasion that 'they past the Tyme at Games, and in commonyng'.[60] Unfortunately neither chroniclers nor poets normally tell us what the games, 'disports', 'pleyinge', 'pastimes' consisted of; or if they do, they mention only bare titles and leave the rest to the reader's imagination. I shall use an episode from Froissart's *Chronicle* to introduce such scanty hints about games as I have gathered, because for once we are made to feel vividly both the detail and the 'style' of the thing:

> So he called for chess, and the lady had it brought in. Then the King asked the lady to play with him, and she consented gladly, for she wished to entertain him as well as she might. And that was her duty, for the King had done her good service in raising the siege of the Scots before the castle, and he was her right and natural lord in fealty and homage.
>
> At the beginning of the game of chess, the King, who wished that the lady might win something of his, laughingly challenged her and said, 'Madam, what will your stake be at the game?'
>
> And she answered, 'And yours, sir?'
>
> Then the King set down on the board a beautiful ring with a large ruby that he wore.

Then said the Countess, 'Sir, sir, I have no ring so rich as yours is.'

'Madam,' said the King, 'set down what you have, and do not be so concerned over its value.'

Then the Countess, to please the King, drew from her finger a light ring of gold of no great value. And they played chess together, the lady with all the wit and skill she could, that the King might not think her too simple and ignorant. The King, however, deliberately played poorly, and would not play as well as he knew how. There was hardly a pause between the moves, but the King looked so hard at the lady that she was very much embarrassed, and made mistakes in her play. When the King saw that she had lost a rook or a knight or some other piece, he would lose also, to restore the lady's game.

They played on till at last the King lost, and was checkmate with a bishop. Then the lady rose and called for the wine and comfits, for the King seemed about to leave. She took her ring and put it on her finger, and wanted the King to take his back also. She gave it to him, saying, 'Sir, it is not appropriate that in my house I should take anything of yours, but instead, you should take something of mine.'

'No, madam,' said the King, 'but the game has made it so. You may be sure that if I had won, I should have carried away something of yours.'

The Countess would not urge the King further, but going to one of her damsels, gave her the ring and said, 'When you see that the King has gone out and has taken leave of me, and is about to mount his horse, go up to him and courteously give him his ring again, and say that I will certainly not keep it, for it is not mine.' And the damsel answered that she would do so.

At this, the wine and comfits were brought in. The King would not take of them before the lady, nor the lady before him, and there was a great debate all in mirth between them. Finally it was agreed, to make it short, that they should partake together, one as soon as the other. After this, and when the King's knights had all drunk, the King took leave of the lady and said to her aloud, so that no one should comment upon it, 'Madam, you remain in your house, and I will go to follow my enemies.' At these words the lady courtesied low before the King, and the King freely took her by the hand and pressed it a little, for his pleasure, in sign of love. And he watched until the knights and damsels were busy taking leave of one another. Then he came forward again to say two words alone: 'My dear lady, to God I commend you till I return again . . . and I hope you will feel otherwise than you have said to me.'

'My dear lord,' answered the lady, 'God the Father glorious be your guide, and put you out of all base and dishonorable thoughts, for I am and ever shall be ready to serve you to your honour and mine.'

Then the King went out of the room, and the Countess also, and she conducted him to the hall where his palfrey was. Then the King said that he would not mount while the lady was there; so, to make it short, the Countess took her full and final leave of the King and his knights, and returned to her bower with her maidens.

When the King was about to mount, the damsel whom the Countess had instructed came to the King and knelt; and when the King saw her, he raised her up quickly, and thought she would have spoken of another matter than she did. Then she said, 'My lord, here is the ring which my lady returns to you, and prays you not to consider it as discourtesy, for she does not wish to have it remaining with her. You have done so much for her in other ways that she is bound, she says, to be your servant always.'

When the King heard the damsel and saw that she had his ring, and was told of the wish and the excuse of the Countess, he was amazed. Nevertheless, he made up his mind quickly; and in order that the ring might remain in that house as he had intended, he answered briefly . . . 'Mistress, since your lady does not like the little gain that she won from me, let it remain in your possession.'

Then he mounted quickly and rode out of the castle to the lawn where his knights were. . . . Then they all set out together. . . . And the damsel returned and told the King's answer, and gave back the ring that the King had lost at chess. But the Countess would not have it, and claimed no right to it. The King had given it to the damsel; let her take it and welcome. So the King's ring was left with the damsel.[61]

This may be thought an extreme example of a game pressed into the service of *the* 'game'. But it shows what we ought to be looking for on a less serious level. Some lines of Gower quoted earlier will help to establish a lighter tone:

> And whanne it falleth othergate
> So that hire liketh noght to daunce
> Or on the *Dees to caste chaunce*

> Or axe of love som demande
> Or elles that hir list comaunde
> To rede and here of Troilus. [62]

Here playing at dice is mentioned with dancing, talking and reading of love; and, as the editor rightly comments, 'This casting with the dice would not be for ordinary gambling, but for divining characters and telling fortunes in matters of love.' [62]

Two of the well-known manuscripts of Chauceriana contain a poem, *On the Chaunce of the Dyse*, in which a divination is given for each possible throw of three dice: for example, the throw of six, four and ace produces a 'character' who is

> . . . The lorde of vertu and al vices cure,
> Perfit beaute grounded without envye,
> Assured trust withoute gelousye. [63]

Divination can be either by chance (dice-play), by blind choice (cards, *Ragman Roll, Blind Man's Buff*) or by skill (chess, shuttlecock). It is an accident of literary survival that enables us to be sure that dice were used to tell fortunes in love. No such happy accident describes the use of cards in this way. But it seems at least possible that number-cards could be picked out, or cut, just as dice could be thrown; [64] and, in addition, that the picture-cards (the King of Columbines, the Ace of Roses, etc.), in conjunction with the symbolism of colours, flowers and heraldic emblems, could be used for divination. *Ragman Roll* is another game with *written* divinations, and so we know more about it than about others which have left no records. *Ragman* is described as 'a game of chance, apparently played with a written roll having strings attached to the various items contained in it, one of which the player selected or "drew" at random'. [65] Two copies of the roll (perhaps one should say *a* roll) used in this game survive in the same two 'Chaucer' manuscripts already mentioned. The roll opens:

> My ladyes and my maistresses echone,
> Lyke hit unto your humbible wommanhede,
> Resave in gre of my sympill persone
> This rolle, which, withouten any drede,
> Kynge Ragman me bad sowe in brede,
> And cristyned yt the merour of your chaunce;
> Drawith a strynge, and that shal streight yow leyde
> Unto the verry path of your governaunce. [65]

The 'Game of Love'

I suggested above that divination from cards may have made use of flower and colour symbols, and so forth. Despite the lack of direct evidence it is tempting to think that chess, also, a favourite courtly pastime, may particularly have lent itself to love-allegory.[66] Everything about it – names of pieces, names of games, symbolic use in poems – suggests that this was so. The pieces (*miles, domina, armiger, generosa,* etc.) could be used on a variety of boards to play such games as 'The knight's game', 'The ladies' game', 'Fair and small', 'The chace of the queen and the knight', 'The messengers', 'The ladies and the damsels'. Poetical references to the game at chess are numerous. The lover plays at chess with 'Danger' or with Fortune:

> At the ches with me she gan to pleye
> With hir false draughtes dyvers
> She staal on me, and tok my fers . . .[67]

(That is to say, Fortune stole his Queen, his lady.) Or, with his mistress herself:

> . . . I will have your ferse.
> And when your ferse is had
> And all your warre is done,
> Then shall your selfe be glad
> To ende that you begon.
>
> For yf by chance I winne
> Your person in the feeld,
> To late then come you in
> Your self to me to yeld . . .[68]

Here the queen-piece symbolizes the lady's person (the usual puns on 'check' and 'mate' follow).

The subject of games of divination must not be pursued too enthusiastically since the evidence is extremely scanty; but there is one further kind of divination which must be mentioned. The Middle Ages were saturated in astrological lore. Perhaps, then, horoscopy of a light-hearted sort offered all the opportunities which chess and cards, 'the chaunces of the dyse' and *Ragman* offered in their different ways. Chaucer's *Complaint of Mars*, a St Valentine's Day poem, gives some corroboration to this view. In the poem, an astrological situation is given an allegorical meaning in terms of courtly love.

Thus be they knyt, and regnen as in hevene
Be lokyng moost; til hyt fil, on a tyde,
That by her bothe assent was set a stevene,
That Mars shal entre, as fast as he may glyde,
Into hir nexte paleys . . .[69]

and so on. It does not take much imagination to see how courtly persons born under different planets, with certain 'characters' and 'fortunes' attaching to them, could make delightful play with speculations about their future relationships, the whole discussion being complicated, naturally, according as it took place on Venus's day or Saturn's or Mars's.

To 'make delightful play' – this was, surely, the motive behind the games I have tried to describe. We can, if we like, see behind the games of chance and their evident popularity the same psychology that drew people to the image of Fortune, the blind goddess, imperturbably, indifferently, turning her wheel – and, indeed, to romantic love itself in all its inexplicable ups-and-downs, its evanescent beauty, its inevitable 'lak of stedfastnes'. But it is more realistic (unless we are reading a poem of high seriousness like *Troilus and Criseyde*) to see in these games simply an opening for correct, polite and joyous 'dalliance' – 'And thus thou shalt the tyme wel begyle'. In particular, games of chance provided the amusement of seeing the company's lightly amorous expectations fulfilled or thwarted, as in modern games with Christmas-cracker mottoes and paper hats. They must have created exactly the right teasing and flirtatious atmosphere.

These games, and others like 'tables' (backgammon), could, of course, be made to yield a different sort of spice to social intercourse. If 'divination' sets up one sort of exploitable tension, then clearly games of forfeit, with prizes or stakes, set up another. Froissart's story of Edward III and the Countess of Salisbury, transposed into a lighter vein, suggests what could be done.[70] The point need not be elaborated. But the following passage from *Sir Gawayne* is particularly illuminating:

And sythen riche forth runnen to reche honde-selle,
Yeied yeres giftes on high, yelde hem bi hond,
Debated busyly aboute tho giftes;
Ladies laghed ful loude, thogh thay lost haden,
And he that wan watz not wrothe, that may ye wel trawe.
Alle this mirthe thay maden to the mete tyme;
When thay had waschen worthyly, thay wenten to sete . . .[71]

The 'Game of Love'

What exactly this game at the giving of New Year's Gifts was, is not known. It may perhaps have been a variety of Handy-Dandy. But the 'crying' of the gifts, the debating about them, the possibility of winning or losing, all suggest a courtly variety of the bran-tub, the 'lucky dip'. It is characteristic of the poets as it is of the chroniclers to give little detail and yet to convey the atmosphere of the game or ceremony they are describing. The lack of detail need not worry us unduly, for their beautiful idealization of the forms of social life is the very thing that we are trying to fix and grasp.

VI

Almost all the informal games so far described might be called sitting-and-thinking games. But there were many others of a more active kind. I am not thinking merely of sports, though sports must have had some importance in the 'game' of love. Hunting and hawking, in particular, were mixed pastimes, and emphatically noble. They have left traces of their language in the language of love-poetry ('reclaymed to the lure', etc.)[72] and they gave scope for plenty of *double entendre,* for moods of cynicism and coarseness. The occasions for 'dalliance' were, however, perhaps incidental rather than central to the sport. (The Lover, in Gower's poem, always liked to lift his mistress on to her horse.)

I am thinking rather of the sort of company-game described in the following passage of Charles of Orleans:

> And homward thus as Y gan me repayre,
> I fond a company, some yong some olde,
> That gan eche othir fast in armys hold,
> For at the *post and piler* did thei play;
> And alle were gentil folkis, dar Y say

[among the knights and ladies he suddenly catches sight of the one he is destined to love]

> Now was ther on had knowen me to-fore,
> That me aspide; and Y not how,
> And in his corse he fel, and had fortore
> His hose, at which fulle many of hem lough.
> 'Now laughe', seide he, 'for some han pleid y-nough.'
> Which to me spake, 'Y thank yow, frend, my fal,
> For nad ye be, Y had hit not at al.

But nevyrtheles, ye ar welcome, parde!
So now, gef rome! take here a pleyer in!
For he shal pley his pagaunt now for me' . . .

Bi hond he hent me so, and to the place,
He drew me in, 'Is ther noon othir bote?'
Seide Y. 'Noo, no, ye get no bettir grace.'
Quod Y, 'Then must Y to that nedis mote.'
And so to renne Y gan to make a-foot;
And wel Y wot Y ran not long a-bowt
Or that Y on had towchid of the rowt.

And as the corse thus drove me here and there,
Unto my lady newe so streight Y went
With gastful hert that quoke for verry fere,
How me were best to uttir myn entent;
Yet at the last, on this poore posse y-bent,
When that there stood no mo but she and Y –
'A questioun wold Y axe of yow, lady.'

'Of me?' quod she, 'Now, good, what thing is that?'
'It is not smalle, madame, Y yow ensewre.
I put a case: if so myn hert it sat
To yow in love above eche creature,
Told Y it yow, wold ye it so diskever
And make of it a skoffe, or yet a play?
In which, percas, my lijf so myght it way.'

'God helpe me nay! . . .'

[the lady says she would never scoff at honourable love – Charles then declares his love and asks her to take him as her 'gostly child' and be his 'fayre shrift-fader dere' – at this point the lady apparently shows signs of emotion]

'Allass! be war! yowre coloure gynnys faynt.
Pynne up yowre kercher! kepe yowre face covert!
Ye mow say how the sonne hit doth yow smert.'
Bi my good soth, Y holde yow nyse', quod she;
And did right so, and syns seide to me.

[she then makes her reply to his declaration][73]

The 'Game of Love'

It is hard to be sure in matters of this sort, but I think we have here a scene which bears a recognizable, if simplified, relation to the reality of a courtly game. Perhaps a parallel in our own times would be the love-stories of the women's magazines, at once naturalistic and highly conventionalized. (Both not only reflect but mould feeling.) The game, *Post and Pillar*, seems to have resembled *Prisoner's Base* – that is, it was a company chasing-game. Perhaps it was played over a wide area, or in a garden where there was cover, since it clearly gave scope for a *tête-à-tête*. To this piece of 'dalliance' we shall return later.

Another game (if that is the word) which allowed the same sort of 'communing', and may have been taken up expressly for the purpose, provides the setting for the *Assembly of Ladies*:

> It happed thus, that, in an after-noon
> My felawship and I, by oon assent,
> Whan al our other besinesse was doon,
> To passe our tyme, into this *mase* we went,
> And toke our wayes, eche after our entent;
> Some went inward, and wend they had gon out,
> Some stode amid, and loked al about.
>
> And, sooth to say, some were ful fer behind,
> And right anon as ferforth as the best;
> Other there were, so mased in her mind,
> Al wayes were good for hem, bothe eest and west.
> Thus went they forth, and had but litel rest;
> And some, her corage did hem sore assayle,
> For very wrath, they did step over the rayle.[74]

The passage quoted is really the-setting-within-the-setting: in her tale the lady quickly succeeds in reaching the 'herber, fair and grene' and 'closed wel', in the centre of the maze. In the *poem* she is telling this tale to a knight whom she had met while again wandering in the same maze:

> [there were ladies and gentlewomen]
> Disporting hem, everiche after her gyse,
> In crosse-aleys walking, by two and two,
> And some alone, after her fantasyes.
> Thus occupied we were in dyvers wyse;
> And yet, in trouthe, we were not al alone;
> There were knightes and squyers many one.

179

'Whereof I served?' oon of hem asked me;
I sayde ayein, as it fel in my thought,
'To walke about the mase, in certaynte,
As a woman that [of] nothing rought.'
He asked me ayein – 'whom that I sought,
And of my colour why I was so pale?'
'Forsothe,' quod I, 'and thereby lyth a tale.'[75]

Game is not perhaps too inaccurate a word, since there was competition
to reach the centre of the maze. But it was also 'game', 'disport'; and the
losers, too, had their reward. If the naturalistic bias of the authoress is
admitted beneath a slight idealistic haze,[76] then there are several interesting hints, suggestions for 'dallies'. The conversation between the lady and
the knight is, it is agreed, not a 'wooing'. But, unless I am reading too
curiously, it is more than 'ordinary'. The question, 'Who are you looking
for?', is perhaps harmless enough; but the first question, 'Whereof do you
serve?' is certainly reminiscent of the phraseology used of the games played
by 'companies' – that of the Flower and the Leaf is the best known. It
seems to mean, 'What is your allegiance?' 'Whose side are *you* on?' The
lady declines the gambit (perhaps this was the proper thing to do); she
has no particular errand to party or person. But the question remains a
significant one. The reader will recall the well-known passages in *The
Legend of Good Women* in which Chaucer refers to the 'companies' of the
Flower and the Leaf:

> Ye lovers that kan make of sentement;
> In this cas oghte ye be diligent
> To forthren me somwhat in my labour,
> Whethir ye ben with the leef or with the flour
>
> . . . ne wene nat that I make
> In preysing of the flour agayn the leef,
> No more than of the corn agayn the sheef;
> For, as to me, nys lever noon ne lother,
> I nam withholden yit with never nother;
> Ne I not who serveth leef, ne who the flour.
> Wel browken they her service or labour.[77]

Professor Robinson's useful note on this topic is:

Court society in both England and France was apparently divided into two parties or amorous orders devoted respectively to the Flower and to the Leaf . . . In England Philippa of Lancaster was the great patroness of the Flower.[78]

But we must be careful not to take the 'orders' of love too solemnly. It was clearly more than a mere 'literary' convention; but no high degree of organization need be assumed. Indeed, it may be that a pretence of secrecy obtained: the Knight asks the Lady what her allegiance is; Chaucer says he does not know who belongs to the two parties. Perhaps they were not the only alternatives, for in Gower's 'company led by youth',

> Some of the lef, some of the flour
> And some of the grete Perles were;
> The newe guise of Beawme there,
> With sondry thinges wel devised.[79]

Some play at secrecy fits in well with the general spirit of the 'game of love'. But other references do not, admittedly, very strongly support it. According to Charles of Orleans allegiance was decided by lot:

> The joly tyme the first fresshe day of May
> Mi fortune fille to be in compane
> The which that were, a verry trougthe to say,
> Repleet of grace and passyng gret bounte;
> For which, forto expelle alle thought heve,
> That we shuld chese ordeynyd to us was,
> Right *as that fortune lust agide the caas,*
> The leef so fresshe and fulle of gret verdure
> Or ellis the flowre so fayre and soot to smelle:
> I took the leaf to me alle yere to dwelle
> As that tyme was myn hap and aventure.[80]

Charles later comments that 'rightwisly the choyse was falyn' of the Leaf, because his lady was the 'flowre of alle bewte' and now she is dead. This passage is of interest because it shows that the game of choosing your order was a seasonal one, part of the May ceremonies; that your allegiance lasted for a year; and, most of all, because it conveys the atmosphere of 'jolitee', 'bountee' and 'fresshe' gaiety proper to the occasion.

It is in this spirit, surely, that the poem *The Flower and the Leaf* is to be read. The authoress

> wanders into a forest where she witnesses the revels of two parties of

mysterious beings, who are distinguished as the company of the Leaf and the company of the Flower. The latter are afflicted by excessive heat and violent showers, while the former remain in comfort under the shade of a 'fair laurer'. When the storm is over, the servants of the Leaf, cool, dry, and comfortable, offer hospitality to the wet and blistered followers of the Flower, and prescribe 'plesaunt salades' . . . Finally an unnamed lady . . . explains to the authoress the meaning of the vision. The Queen of the Leaf was Diana, and the Queen of the Flower, Flora. Their two companies consisted entirely of ghosts – the ghosts of virgins, true lovers, and valiant knights following Diana, while Flora's retinue consisted of those who had loved idleness and found no better occupation than 'for to hunt and hawke and pley in medes'.[81]

Professor Lewis, whose description of the poem I gratefully borrow, remarks about it that 'the antithesis [between the two companies] is purely moral, and the morality is that of modern life'; and that it is 'a little psychomachia of Virtue and Vice . . . in fact, a hybrid – a moral allegory wearing the dress of the Rose tradition. . . . Hence, though she deals with the moral choice, her treatment of it "turns all to favour and to prettiness"'.[81] Why, one must ask, did she write the poem at all? Precisely, I think, *in order to* turn all to 'prettiness'. The poem makes sense if we see it, not so much as an exercise in a fashionable mode as a deliberate attempt to enlist this fashionable mode on her side in the 'game'. The allegory is used not for its own sake, nor for the sake of the 'story' (which is trivial), but in playful championship of the company of the Leaf, to which the authoress pretends allegiance. This is allegory used for fun.[82]

To choose, deliberately or by lot, either the Flower or the Leaf may have been part of the 'observaunce' (to use a favourite word) done in May. When Emily does hers, she 'gadereth floures, party white and rede'; when Arcite his, he makes 'a gerland of the greves, | Were it of wodebynde or hawethorne leves'.[83] But the May game certainly involved more than this. Here we leave games proper and come to consider what are better termed seasonal 'revels': Christmas; St Valentine's Day; the May festival.

VII

I have only scattered hints to offer about the possible adaptation of Christmas festivities to the 'game of love'. There is a little song by Henry VIII

[H33] which shows for instance how the traditional strife of Holly and Ivy could be pressed into courtly service:

> Grene growith the holy,
> So doth the ive,
> Thow wynter blastys blow never so hye,
> Grene growth the holy.

> 1. As the holy grouth grene
>   And never chaungyth hew,
>   So I am, ever hath bene,
>   Unto my lady trew.

> 2. As the holy grouth grene
>   With ive all alone
>   When flowerys cannot be sene,
>   And grenewode levys be gone. . . .

And the records of the entertainments at Court show that Twelfth Night, the culmination of the 'short' Christmas season, was often marked by a big disguising, as often as not on a theme of courtly love or chivalry. Sir Edmund Chambers writes that 'a succession of gaieties filled the Twelve nights from the Nativity to the Epiphany, or even the wider space from St Thomas's day to Candlemas'.[84]

Prominent among seasonal gaieties, to judge from the number of poems and references which survive, was the exchange of gifts at New Year. It was a prime occasion for courtiers and court-servants to pay a tribute to their lord and for him to acknowledge the tribute graciously in kind: a musician might offer a 'ballat'; a scholar, his latest treatise.[85] Dunbar offers a poem:

> My prince in God gif the guid grace,
> Joy, glaidnes, confort, and solace,
> Play, pleasance, myrth, and mirrie cheir,
> In hansill of this guid new yeir.[86]

New Year was also an occasion for lovers. Two gift-poems for the season are quoted in the next chapter.[87] A third is attributed to Lydgate:

> In honour of this heghe fest, of custume yere by yere,
> Is first for to remembre me upon my lady dere.

1. For nowe upon this first day I wil my choys renuwe
All the whyles that I lyve to hir to be truwe,
　　Both to serve and love hir best with al myn hert entier.

. . . .

15. I have nothing to gyven hir at this gladde time
But myn hert undeparted, nowe this first pryme,
　　The which this day I sende hir al hooly and entier.[88]

Here, for want of information, the matter must be left. Christmas revels at least remind us that the culture of the court in the two centuries before the Reformation was not the simple, one-stranded affair which the present chapter is describing, but a complicated web having many nodes, many focal points.

The great festival for lovers was early May. But several weeks before this they were encouraged by St Valentine's Day (14 February) to settle their thoughts on their hopes for the spring. Chaucer, we know, writes for or refers to the day, in *The Parlement of Foules*, in *The Legend of Good Women* and in *The Complaint of Mars*. A lesser known instruction is that in *The Flour of Curtesye*, attributed to Lydgate:

> The same tyme, I herde a larke singe
> Ful lustely, agayn the morowe gray –
> 'Awake, ye lovers, out of your slombringe,
> This gladde morowe, in al the haste ye may;
> Some observaunce doth unto this day,
> Your choise ayen of herte to renewe
> In confirming, for ever to be trewe!
>
> And ye that be, of chesing, at your large,
> This lusty day, by custome of nature,
> Take upon you the blisful holy charge
> To serve love, whyl your lyf may dure . . . '[89]

The 'observaunce' of St Valentine's Day has three features: the assembly or 'parlement', the symbolism of birds, and the choosing of mates. Perhaps here, as so often in the May ritual, we have to discriminate between popular custom and belief and the courtly 'play' based on them. When Dame Elizabeth Brews writes to John Paston, her daughter's intended, in the following terms:

And, cosyn, uppon Fryday is Sent Volentynes Day, and every

brydde chesyth hym a make; and yf it lyke yowe to come one Thursday
at nyght . . . I trusty to God, that ye schall so speke to myn husband;
and I schall prey that we schall bryng the mater to a conclusyon . . .[90]

it is difficult to be sure what she believed. But it seems to be something
more naïvely superstitious than the audience of *The Parlement of Foules*
could have believed. And her beliefs are more likely to have their roots in
popular lore than in the aristocratic transmutation of them. If courtly love
is in many respects a glorified rationale of natural instincts, then it is not
surprising to find that the great spring festival of courtly lovers draws life
and strength from popular festival. This is eminently true of the May-game,
but also true of St Valentine's Day and its lore.

The choosing of a mate is the central motif. In the courtly ritual this is
no simple and sudden affair ('ech of hem gan other in wynges take') but
requires 'gret avysement'. This calls for a 'parlement' (such as the one of
lovers, pictured by the Duke of Suffolk as meeting at *Secret Pense* on 22
February,[91] or the one of birds, which in Chaucer's poem meets on St
Valentine's Day itself), for there are delicate questions of precedence and
procedure to be debated. The place of 'luf-talkyng' and 'questions' of love
has already been described at some length (pp. 159– above) and need not be
re-examined here. There is only one feature of the Valentine debates that
calls for special comment, and that is the fiction that they are conducted by
birds. This fiction also extends to the 'observaunces' of May.

This symbolism has often been noted, less often shown to be meaningful.
Primarily, it is a way of relating man's strongest natural instinct to the
forces of 'great creating Nature'; the goddess of 'Kynde', in medieval
terminology, is usually prominent when there is a parliament of birds. But
the birds do not merely represent the force of Love; they represent lovers of
all classes of society. The hierarchical idea is especially strong because of
the associations of hawking and, perhaps, heraldry. And then, also, it is
particularly apt to think of a *courtly* lover as a bird, for a bird is not only
a lover, he is also a talker, a singer, a worshipper. As a courtly talker, the
bird will arrange a parlement;[92] as a singer he pours forth secret and
joyous praises of his lady.[93] And often his singing is represented as part of
a service of worship. The most extended example of this charming fancy
occurs at the end of *The Court of Love*:

> On May-day, whan the lark began to ryse,
> To matens went the lusty nightingale
> Within a temple shapen hawthorn-wise;

He might not slepe in all the nightertale,
But 'Domine, labia' gan he crye and gale,
'My lippes open, Lord of Love, I crye,
And let my mouth thy preising now bewrye.'

The eagle sang 'Venite, bodies all,
And let us joye to love that is our helth' . . .[94]

To summarize, the proper courtly 'disport' for St Valentine's Day was clearly a 'parlement', a debate about love. But whether dramatic, 'impersonating' use was ever made of the symbolism of birds, so apt to the occasion and so widespread in the 'literature' belonging to the day, remains an open question.[95]

Sir Edmund Chambers has described the popular May-game at length, noting towards the end of his chapter how 'the village festival found its way to court, and became a sumptuous pageant under the splendour-loving Tudors'.[96] One of these pageants (of 1515) is described in a later chapter.[97] In 1515 the underlying motif, 'going to fetch in May', was somewhat obscured by a Robin Hood game, shooting-matches, a banquet in a carefully prepared bower, and a triumphal procession in which those favourite figures of literary allegory, Lady May and Lady Flora, were prominent. (Robin Hood was, of course, by this time mixed up in the May-game of popular tradition also.) We have nothing much new to learn about the 'game of love' from this exercise in pomposity. Like some of the tournaments and disguisings it was rather too much of a state occasion. More revealing is Halle's account of how in 1510, Henry and his courtiers dressed up as Robin Hood and his men and

> came sodainly in a mornyng, into the Quenes Chambre, all appareled in shorte cotes, of Kentishe Kendal, with hodes on their heddes, and hosen of the same, every one of theim, his bowe and arrowes, and a sworde and bucklar, like out lawes, or Robyn Hodes men, wherof the Quene, the ladies and al other there, were abashed, as well for the straunge sight, as also for their sodain commyng, and after certayn daunces, and pastime made, thei departed.[98]

This incident certainly belongs to the 'game of love' and shows how people dramatized their courtly attitudes. The queen was, it seems, genuinely surprised. And – a real pointer to the tone of the occasion – Robin Hood's men then proceeded to perform courtly dances before departing.

The 'Game of Love'

What one would most like to know is what 'going to fetch in May' really meant in courtly circles of the fifteenth century. The literature of romance is full of idealized pictures: lovers are always getting up early without 'slogardy' and wandering out into the dewy fields to 'don hir observaunce'. Perhaps Malory makes it seem most plausible in his imaginary description of Queen Guinevere's ill-fated Maying, when she was captured by Sir Meliagraunce:

> So hit befelle in the moneth of May, quene Gwenyver called unto her ten knyghtes of the Table Rounde, and she gaff them warnynge that early uppon the morn she wolde ryde on maynge into woodis and fyldis besydes Westemynster:
>
> 'And I warne you that there be none of you but he be well horsed, and that ye all be clothed all in gryne, othir in sylke othir in clothe. And I shall brynge with me ten ladyes, and every knyght shall have a lady be hym. And every knyght shall have a squyar and two yomen, and I woll that all be well horsed.'
>
> So they made hem redy in the freysshyst maner, and thes were the namys of the knyghtes . . .
>
> And so uppon the morne or hit were day, in a May mornygne, they toke their horsys wyth the quene and rode on mayinge in wodis and medowis as hit pleased hem, in grete joy and delytes.
>
> So as [the quene] was oute on mayynge wyth all her knyghtes whych were bedaysshed wyth erbis, mossis, and floures in the freysshyste maner, ryght so there cam oute of a wood sir Mellyagaunte.[99]

A courtly maying, this account suggests, was above all a *social* occasion. It enabled you to dress extravagantly; to ride out on horseback – one of the prime courtly exercises; to enjoy 'dalliance' with a lady. It was a hallowed 'gaderyng', rich in romantic associations, to be enjoyed in the company of your peers. It emphasizes what is, perhaps, one of the central paradoxes in the 'game of love' – that the desired fruit of personal experience of love is joyous social activity. The 'game' is private but it is played in public.

VIII

This is a long preamble of a tale, and we come now to the darkest part of it. At the beginning I said that the task was to describe the 'middle space' of courtly love, a whole range of social activity and expression which was neither 'pure literature' nor 'real life' in the most limiting sense of those phrases. We started on the literary border and saw how 'romantic' literature could cater for the social needs of a courtly company: 'To rede and here of Troilus' became an occasion of dalliance and a spur to 'luf-talking', a sentimental education. We approach now to the other border which marks off the 'game of love' from the actuality of everyday life. To what extent did the ethos of courtly love affect the attitudes of men and women towards one another? The question needs phrasing rather delicately. I am not attempting to describe, or even to discover, how men *in fact* treated their sweethearts or their wives, but how they pretended to feel about them. We are still concerned not with 'reality' but with a fiction.

In the last few pages of this chapter I shall try to describe some of the ways in which this fiction, or 'act', sustained itself, when there was no formal or informal game in progress to sustain it. Most of these ways can be subsumed as aspects of a complicated craft of wooing, of courtship; but the 'act' was so treasured, and (we must assume) was felt to supply so fully a need which nothing else could supply, that its ways of thought and feeling were borrowed for the sake of their power to refine other relationships also. The rules of courtship became the rules of, in a wider sense, 'paying court'.

IX

It is from literature [wrote Professor Huizinga] that we gather the forms of erotic thought belonging to a period but we should try to picture them functioning as elements of social life. A whole system of amatory conceptions and usages was current in aristocratic 'conversation' of those times. What signs and figures of love which later ages have dropped![100]

English literature is not deficient in the sort of hints we are looking for. Charles of Orleans speaks of the 'craft' of love as one that will not be learnt quickly, though 'fervent love kan cause it to be doon'.[101] The craft taught how to express nuances of sentiment, not only through 'sewte of curteys speche', but through clothes, in the symbolism of odours, jewels and flowers, in the choice of 'devices', 'posies', embroideries, mottoes, 'words', sleeves, tokens, 'trewloves', 'herts', rings, garlands, and crowns. The evidence is fragmentary and assorted. I shall not attempt, and doubt the possibility of, a complete exposition. One or two examples will suffice to show the openings which this apparatus provided for amorous 'conversation'. We have to remember, too, that the system was not a closed one but lent itself to novel elaboration. 'Be jolif, fresh and fete, *with thinges newe*', advises Statute XVIII of *The Court of Love*;[102] and Gower's Confessor tells his penitent about a model lover who

> . . . stant desguised.
> Mor jolif than the brid in Maii
> He makth him evere freissh and gay
> And doth al his array desguise,
> So that of him the newe guise
> Of lusti folk alle othre take.[103]

The basic symbolism of colour is well known: blue for constancy; green for novelty, or 'newfangelnes'; black for melancholy. L'Amant in *La Belle Dame* wore 'all blak . . . and no devyce but playn'.[104] Some hints towards a more subtle use of colour can be got from Charles of Orleans:

> Of *gold* on hir ther lith an ymage clere
> With *safyr blew* y-sett so inrichely,
> For hit is write and seide how the safere
> Doth token trouthe, and gold to ben happy.[105]

(The introduction of the jewel clinches the point: 'The good Saphir, mos mekest in moode, | Nat variable ne movyng, but knyt al in oone . . . a stidefast stone'.[105a]) Or again:

> A trouthe, ye say me soth, so sett me wel,
> For as for *blew* Y clothe therin myn hert;
> And alletha *rosett* is y-entirmelle,
> I kepe therin my pouer thought covert –
> Alle suche as esy arne, not suche as smert –
> For in *tawny* Y leie alle them aside
> And to my deth in *blak* mysilf Y bide.[106]

The mantle of Dame Fortune is appropriately described:

> Of which the coloure blak nor grene it nas
> But most lijk to a raynbow hewe it was,
> Forwhi the silkis were so verry straunge
> That ay from *blew* to *reed* or *grene* thei chaunge.[107]

No doubt the subtlety of the 'sentimental' gambit consisted in combining or varying your different signs of love, signs of mood. A courtier's 'array' probably resembled nothing so much as the riddles and enigmas that they enthusiastically set and solved. It was not his intention to be plain and open, but to be 'covert' and 'secree', to dissimulate. The message should presumably be decipherable only by the person who held the key. Unfortunately, most of the rules of the 'game' are lost and the tradition abandoned. One can only guess what a world of sophistication and sentiment, to take another instance, was bound up with the enjoyment of flowers and plants and trees. (No one at the court of Richard II or of Henry VIII could ever, surely, have spoken of a *simple* primrose?) The laurel, the woodbind, the *agnus castus*, the 'margarette' or daisy, the 'ne-m'oublie-mies', the 'sovenez' or 'remember-me', the 'povre pensées', rue, the 'trew-love', the rose itself: the very names alone are enough to make the point.[108]

Nothing much would be gained by building an edifice of detail, which must be partly conjectural, from the innumerable scattered hints in fourteenth- and fifteenth-century literature. We may close our partial reconstruction of the apparatus of courtship with one reflection: the world of courtly love did not exist merely in the head; it was a world in which actual physical objects had a place. When, therefore, a medieval writer used a word like 'hert' or 'trewlove', it is often possible and sometimes certain that he was thinking of a *thing*, an emblem or a device.[109]

Not only the lover's 'apparatus' but the technique of wooing in its wider aspects are described in the so-called 'Statutes of Love'. These 'statutes', a feature of the literature of courtly love, occur in their fullest English form in the early Tudor poem, *The Court of Love*.[110] They make up a curious rag-bag of advice, information and command. Statute XIII deals with the 'apparatus' of gift-giving; Statute XI deals with another branch of technique: the language of hand and eye:

> . . . Thy signes for to con
> With ÿ and finger, and with smyles soft,
> And low to cough, and alway for to shon,
> For dred of spyes, for to winken oft:
> But secretly to bring a sign a-loft,
> And eke beware of over-moch resort;
> For that, paraventure, spilleth al thy sport.[111]

This language of love is less susceptible to change and we are better placed to understand it. There is, however, one respect in which the atmosphere, the style, of such amorous play may be hard for us to grasp; that is, in its persistent emphasis on secrecy, dissimulation, reserve. I do not mean that the motif of secrecy itself, which had formed a part of courtly love from its very beginnings (*Qui non celat, amare non potest*), is difficult to understand. This 'rule' is far from being a mere convention. It has its *raison d'être* in one of the strongest psychological urges of romantic love, and is still with us today in the love-stories of popular magazines ('theirs was a secret love . . .'). The difficulty arises from the fact that it was regarded not merely as natural but also as the very height of good breeding to 'ben secree'. With the exception of his Friend (every lover is allowed one confidant), no one must know where the lover's heart is set. 'Secretly to kepe counsel of love' is high among the lover's moral and *social* obligations. It is his duty not only to his lady but also to himself and to his peers.

On the level of the 'game' it is easy to see that this restriction was necessary. Once drop the pretence that everyone was a lover, that everyone nursed an eternal attachment which was refining his sensibilities and infusing grace into his everyday life, and the whole gossamer fabric would collapse. It was, of course, a pretence, a fiction, a 'game'. In brute fact it was common knowledge that Lady A—— had had three lovers and that Lord B—— was 'not interested in women'. But such brute facts do not help in the least to sustain the delicate play of social relations in a comparatively closed, leisured and idealistic society. The situation must have been complex. There was the added complication that at any moment the 'game' might turn into 'ernest'. Not all love was 'honourable love', as the Dame of La Tour Landry well knew; not every courtier was prepared to wait 'to saye to his lady that he loveth her tyll the tyme of seven years and a half be passyd and gone'. This game, of all games, as the moralists observed, has a way of playing the players. The Dame forbids kissing, except when 'they kysse them before all, to th'ende that they lose not theyr valour'.[112]

I do not think, however, that either the romantic psychological need, or the need to preserve the social fiction which supported their code of politeness, entirely explains the emphasis on and urge towards intrigue. We have been told by many social historians of the desperate lack of privacy and the omnipresence of the spy in court society. One feels this even in such small things as the insistence that all arbours had a

> . . . hegge as thik as a castle-wal,
> That, who that list without to stond or go,
> Thought he wold alday pryen to and fro,
> He shuld not see if there were any wight
> Within or no; . . .[113]

Courtly Love and the Courtly Lyric

This side of the 'game of love' may, in fact, be to some extent symptomatic of a widespread need to keep one's individuality intact, to have some privacies, some safe counsels, and some secrets. But I do not wish to press this point too far. It is a serious mistake to see the whole 'game' as symbolic of deeper interests and graver concerns.

I have dealt at some length with the admired quality of 'secretnesse' partly because it is easily misunderstood, but more because it will later help to explain much that is at first sight puzzling in the courtly lyrics. It is obvious that the necessity of concealing and revealing at the same time will have special effects on poems about personal relationships. Here are two further, and diverse, quotations to foreshadow the essential point. The first is from the *Ten Commandments of Love* (addressed to a woman):

> Secretly behave you in your werkes,
> In shewing countenance or meving of yur iye;
> Though soche behavor to some folke be darke,
> He that hath loved woll it sone aspie,
> Thus yur-selfe yur counseyle may descrye; . . .[114]

The second quotation is from Castiglione:

> . . . the maner of the gentlemen in the house was immediately after supper to assemble together where the Dutchesse was. Where among other recreations, musicke and dauncing, which they used continually, sometime they propounded feate questions, otherwile *they invented certayne wittye sportes and pastimes* at the device sometime of one sometime of another, *in the which under sundry coverts oftentimes the standers by opened subtilly their immaginations* [disclosed their thoughts figuratively] unto whome they thought best.[115]

The occasions on which you could 'act the lover' (the ambiguity in the word 'act' is apt here) included all the obvious ones. It was a pose, or a pursuit, for the chamber, the hall, the garden, the arbour. (A pilgrimage gave even more extended opportunities.) The Lover in *Confessio Amantis* is elated, if he may have the occasion to dance with his lady 'in chambre':

> For whanne I mai hire hand beclippe
> With such gladnesse I daunce and skippe
> Methenkth I touche noght the flor; . . .[116]

The 'Game of Love'

Other lovers made of the dance what it was in the Garden of the *Romance of the Rose*

> . . . they daunced queyntely,
> That oon wolde come all pryvyly
> Agayn that other, and whan they were
> Togidre almost, they threwe yfere
> Her mouthis so, that thorough her play
> It semed as they kiste alway.
> To dauncen well koude they the gise;[117]

As the narrator of *The Squire's Tale* says, not without irony,

> Who koude telle yow the forme of daunces
> So unkouthe, and so fresshe contenaunces,
> Swich subtil lookyng and dissymulynges
> For drede of jalouse mennes aperceyvynges?
> No man but Launcelot, and he is deed.[118]

What is more surprising is to find the Lover's style appropriate to church-going:

> . . . whan sche goth to hiere masse
> That time schal noght overpasse,
> That I naproche hir ladihede,
> In aunter if I mai hire lede
> Unto the chapelle and ayein.[119]

And not merely to church-going but to actual devotions within the church. The Lover says he has no inclination to steal the vestments, but

> . . . I wold stele, if that I mihte
> A glad word or a goodly syhte;
> And evere mi service I profre,
> And namly whan sche wol gan offre,
> For thanne I lede hire, if I may,
> For somwhat wold I stele away.
> Whan I beclippe hire on the wast,
> Yit ate leste I stele a tast
> And otherwhile 'grant mercy'
> Sche seith, and so winne I therby
> A lusti touch, a good word eke.[120]

Courtly Love and the Courtly Lyric

Finally, then, what was to be learnt from playing the 'game of love'? What were the qualities of the admired lord and lady? What was the 'flour of curtesy'? There is a revealing couplet in the *Romance of the Rose*. It is said of Vilenye, that 'he litel coude of nurture | *To worship any creature*'. This is what the 'game of love' taught, or (to put it another way) what the 'game' was a vehicle for. It was a machinery for 'worshipping' – that is, 'honouring' other people. There is a possibility of misunderstanding here. This attitude was a social rather than a moral one. It must not be confused with a respect for personality. It is rather a respect for *personages*. The 'game of love' was a way of behaving in a way befitting your own and others' dignity, and it inculcated not so much an attitude to others as a *manner* towards them. That is why the key-words to describe the quality and degree of anyone's courtliness are words like 'manere', 'chere', 'port', 'fassoun', 'countenance'. Despite his vaunted humility towards his lady, the courtly lover is full of self-respect; he is a model of good breeding, and knows it. He is one who knows how to conduct himself not only to ladies but to his social inferiors, to old people, to his acquaintances. He knows how to greet, and how to say farewell; he is a master not only of the simple knife and fork but of the complicated etiquettes of carving and serving. He even has some hints on how to behave in prison (a situation which suited the courtly lover, psychologically, very well). Above all, he is (or likes to think he is) never 'deignous', 'dangerous', 'straunge' or 'soleyn'. He is the perfect gentleman.

It may be well to recall, in conclusion, that the narrower purpose of this inquiry is to recover a fuller meaning for Wyatt's balets and the love-songs in the Tudor books. They belong, I hope to show in the next chapter, to the limited and artificial environment here isolated and described under the title of the 'game of love'. This 'game' was more far-reaching and consequential than has usually been allowed. A proper understanding of it will, I think, illuminate the 'Chaucer tradition' as a whole, not merely its decadence in the early sixteenth century. But, to repeat, it was not, of course, the whole of life. The question we have attempted was simply: in what kinds of reading, talk, pastime and seasonal celebration, in what relationships and on what occasions did this rarefied and civilizing 'dream of love' find expression? There is a more difficult and ultimately more interesting question which perhaps only Chaucer's poetry can answer for us: what part had courtly love in the fullness of life in courtly circles of the late Middle Ages?

The 'Game of Love'

1. In this chapter I have deliberately confined myself to the English court, making only the most casual reference to Scotland and Scottish court-culture. Mrs H. M. Shire's forthcoming study on Festival Song and Poetry in Sixteenth-Century Scotland (*Aberdeen University Studies Series*) will reconstruct the Scottish scene much more fully than I could do.

1a. It is quite beyond the modest scope of this inquiry to consider the place, in different cultures and at different periods, of the idea of 'dramatic fictions', of 'games', of play. The necessity for attempting it is, in any case, removed by a book of outstanding range and stimulus – Professor Huizinga's *Homo Ludens: A Study of the Play-Element in Culture*, English edition 1949.

2. *The Idea of a University* (Longmans, 1912), Discourse viii, 208.

3. *Troilus and Criseyde*, i. 1079.

3a. It will be apparent to anyone with a knowledge of the period that a wealth of relevant evidence could be assembled from the *visual* arts also – illuminations, tapestries, ivories, etc. The interpretation of such evidence would be a delicate matter even for one deeply acquainted with late medieval art; I hope I shall not be censured for refusing to rush in where experts might fear to tread. The subject is, of course, one for a whole book.

It will also be apparent that even the *literary* evidence here presented represents only a fraction of that which diligent scholarship could assemble. The case could be *enlarged* by the use of material such as that presented, for instance, by A. K. Moore, 'Some Implications of the Middle English *Craft of Lovers*', in *Neophilologus*, xxxv (1951); I do not think it would be substantially altered. Veritable storehouses of material and of references can be found in: Hammond, *English Verse between Chaucer and Surrey*; Utley, *Crooked Rib*; Moore, *Secular Lyric in Middle English*; Robbins' anthology, *Secular Lyrics*, as well as in his numerous contributions to periodicals; and, above all, in the monumental *Index of Middle English Verse*, ed. Carleton Brown and R. H. Robbins, 1943.

4. *Surrey*, no. 31; *Tottel*, no. 15 (*reading* seats *for* sales).

5. Chaucer illumination: Cambridge, Corpus Christi College MS 61; reproduced and described at length by Brusendorff, 19–.

6. Hawes: see *Pastime of Pleasure*, introd., p. xiv.

7. Skelton: Dyce, i. 361–; Froissart: *Chronicle*, 329.

8. *Troilus and Criseyde*, ii. 81–.

9. *Confessio Amantis*, iv. 2792; my italics.

10. *Troilus and Criseyde*, ii. 94.

11. *Gawayne and the Green Knight*, line 1012 (her = *their*).

12. *Parliament of Fowls*, line 697.

13. e.g. *Kingis Quhair*, st. 184; MacCracken, 'Suffolk', no. 20; Sir Richard Ros, trans. *La Belle Dame* (Skeat's supplementary volume to *Chaucer's Works*, vii. 299). See also Chaucer's *The Complaint of Mars* and p. 175 below.

14. *Gawayne and the Green Knight*, line 915.

15. *Troilus and Criseyde*, ii. 503 (Robinson, 407, punctuates differently).

16. e.g. *Troilus and Criseyde*, iii. 1796, 'so wel koude he devyse | Of sentement' (*Of sentement*: perhaps, 'as a result of his personal feelings, his experience').

17. *Knight's Tale*, line A.2203.

18. *Charles of Orleans* (ed. Steele), lines 145, 3093.

19. *Charles of Orleans,* line 5246 (here and on p. 177– I have freely introduced modern capitals and punctuation to help the reader).

19*a*. e.g. *Confessio Amantis*, v. 7107–. The excesses of 'sugred eloquence' seem to be the hall-mark not of the courtier (Chaucer, Wyatt) but of the professional hack (Lydgate, Hawes, Skelton).

20. e.g. *La Belle Dame*, line 789– (Skeat, vii. 324). The poem survives in four MSS and in one printed edition. An aphoristic style in 'luf-talkyng' was much admired, if we can judge from the many reported lovers' speeches in the longer poems of courtly life. Pandarus is an acknowledged master of this sort of thing: 'Wo worth the faire gemme vertules', 'Love for love is skilful guerdonynge', 'Elde daunteth daunger at the last'. There is no good reason for thinking that any of these were original mintings by Chaucer. Some of the proverbs of love are recognizably from popular, some from Scriptural, sources. Here are some non-Chaucerian ones: 'A faithful herte ever is acceptable' (*A Goodly Balade*); 'Love is exyler ay of vice and sin' (*Court of Love*); 'Worse it is to breke than bowe, certayn, | And better bowe than fal to sodaynly' (*La Belle Dame*). (See Skeat, vii. 406; 425; 314.)

Some of these aphorisms represent what must have been the

great talking-points in 'trweluf craftes', capable of varied development – 'themes' for straightforward display and illustration; 'questions' to be argued out; 'laws' to be obeyed. These different applications of the lore of love are not always easily distinguished. In short poems we tend to find *one* theme developed ('I love unloved' [H108], 'Myn hert ys set, and all myn hole entent' (MacCracken, 'Suffolk'), no. 19, 'Fresshe lusty beaute joyned with gentylnesse' (Robbins, *Secular Lyrics*, no. 131). These represent the *one* speech of courtly talk. But talk is nearly always dramatic. And so it is in longer poems that we can most nearly perceive what 'luf-talking', bandied from one person to another, must have been like.

21. *Lydgate* (ed. MacCracken), ii. 424 (and see i, p. xxii); editor's gloss is 'R, first and last, joined with E, will show her'; but this does not make sense. The riddle accounts for A ('first') and Z ('last') and E ('middes ejoyned'). I cannot get L out of 'seventeth' unless the seventh true consonant is meant, BCDFGKL.

22. Acrostics are found, for example, in 'Envoy to Alison' (Skeat, vii. 359); *Charles of Orleans*, 221, 'Anne Moulins' (perhaps by Suffolk). Rebuses: musical rebus is in R, f.135 (see R10).

23. 'Dirty jokes': see More's epigrams; the riddle poems in Robbins, 'Religious Lyrics', ii. 520, e.g. 'the Fairest Lady in the Land'; and some of the 'popular' poems in Robbins, *Secular Lyrics*. We should not too hastily conclude that they were 'for men only'; see pp. 222– below.

24. Double-meaning: Robbins, *Secular Lyrics*, no. 112. This is one of the two set to music [Song 151; Robbins does not list this text]. The other song is 'Nowe the lawe is led' [F10].

25. *Wife of Bath's Tale*, line D.904.

26. *Knight's Tale*, line A.1347.

27. MacCracken, 'Suffolk', no. 20. With English love-problems compare the *dubbi*, *questioni* and *giochi* of Italian court-life: see Neilson, 246, from Boccaccio's *Filocolo*; and Castiglione, *Il Cortegiano* ('englished' as *The Boke of the Courtier*), *passim*.

28. 'Castle of Love': see Huizinga, 108.

29. Halle (ed. Ellis), 592. Perhaps the riddles were in the confectionery.

30. *Franklin's Tale*, line F.1622.

31. *La Tour Landry*, 171.

32. *La Belle Dame:* Skeat, vii. 299.

33. Pr. Brandl, 159; Chambers, *Medieval Stage*, ii. 144.

34. *Cuckoo and Nightingale*: Skeat, vii. 347. Its alternative title is *The Book of Cupid, God of Love*; it opens with a reminiscence from *The Knight's Tale* (line 1785) and is attributed to Sir Thomas Clanvowe, friend of Henry of Monmouth. Other bird, or 'mixed', debates (of this period) are: Dunbar, no. 63, 'The Merle & the Nychtingaill'; and the poems pr. Robbins, *Secular Lyrics*, nos 179, 180.

35. *Confessio Amantis*, ii, line 39.

36. *Troilus and Criseyde*, i. 15; *Charles of Orleans*, line 7 (the prologue to his poems is a 'letters-patent' admitting him to court service); Lydgate: see *Lydgate* (ed. MacCracken), ii. 379.

37. *Charles of Orleans*, line 3104.

38. See, for instance, images in Shingleton's (?) prologue to *The Court of Venus* (ed. Russell Fraser), in *The Court of Love* (Skeat, vii. 409), in *Kingis Quhair* (ed. Mackenzie). Henryson's 'court' in *The Testament of Cresseid* belongs, however bizarrely, to the tradition, whose conventions it utterly transcends; it formed part of the Chaucer apocrypha.

39. MacCracken, 'Suffolk', no. 20: *Parlement*, lines 6 and 102; the allegory 'means' that the secret thoughts of St Valentine's Day will come to fruition at the beginning of May.

40. Line 591 (Skeat, vii. 425).

41. *Charles of Orleans*, line 3105.

42. *Kingis Quhair*, st. 62.

43. Suffolk's *Parlement*, line 113.

44. See Robbins, *Secular Lyrics*, no. 135 (based on religious lyric); no. 177 (commandments for a woman in this case); *Charles of Orleans*, line 2297 (funeral rites).

45. *Cour Amoureuse*: Neilson, ch. 8; Huizinga, 103. Neilson states that the title, Court of Love, was not given to the supposed 'institution' (i.e. to the pastime) until after 1400. Before that it referred simply to the literary allegory.

46. cit. Neilson, 246.

47. *The Courtier*, 22.

48. Leland, iv. 288.

49. Dancing: see p. 244–.

50. Leland, iv. 284.

51. *The Book of the Duchess*, line 848. See also *Gawayne and the Green*

Knight, line 1885 ('he mace hym as mery among the fre ladyes |
With comlych caroles and alle kynnes joye').

52. Even Sir Thomas Elyot has to give the sexual, though christianized,
meaning of the dance pride of place (*The Governour*, ch. xxi:
'Wherefore in the good ordre of daunsinge a man and a woman
daunseth together') before adumbrating his 'moralization' of the
dance as an introduction to the virtue of Prudence.

53. 'Loves daunce': Besides the references in Chaucer (for which see
Skeat, vi, 'Glossary'), the image is found – to pick a few
random examples – in *Kingis Quhair*, st. 45, 185; in *The Court
of Love*, line 586 (Skeat, vii. 425); and in *Wyatt*, no. 8, line
25.

54. See p. 244 below.

55. Lewis, *Allegory*, 249. Following the line of thought developed in this
paragraph, it is tempting to see some of the 'Chauceriana' of the
fifteenth century not only as reminiscences of courtly pastimes such
as 'parlements' of love, but as actual prologues or introductions to
such pastimes.

56. For these disguisings, see: 'Revels Accounts' (details in Reference
List) under the dates given in the text; and p. 247– below.

57. Steele's introduction to *The English Poems of Charles of Orleans*,
p. xxxix. See also Neilson, 137.

58. Huizinga, 67, and chs v and vi, *passim*.

59. Joust of Honour: 'Revels Accounts', under date.

60. Leland, iv. 286.

61. Froissart's *Chronicle*: quoted from Edith Rickert, *Chaucer's World*,
ed. Olson and Crow (1948), 229, from Berners' translation.

62. *Confessio Amantis*, iv, line 2790 (G. C. Macaulay's note is in vol. i,
510).

63. See *Index MEV* 803. This 'character' is quoted by Macaulay, *Confessio Amantis*, vol. i, p. 511; the whole poem is pr. by Miss E. P.
Hammond, *Eng. Stud.*, lix (1925), 5–16.

64. Another way of allotting numbers was in the game of battledore or
shuttlecock. See A. B. Gomme, *The Traditional Games of England,
Scotland and Ireland* (1894) s.v. 'Shuttlefeather'; it is ancient, adult
and divinatory (ii. 192–).

65. See *OED* s.v. 'Ragman² ' and 'Ragman's Roll' for several references:
Gower, Douglas and others mention the game. The opening of
the 'roll' is quoted, Gomme (ii. 104–) s.v. 'Ragman', from

Wright, *Anecdota Literaria* (1844); see *Index MEV* 2251, for editions of the 'roll'.

66. Games of chess: see Strutt, 312–. He translates the titles given from BM Roy. MS 13.A.xviii. It is interesting to note that the ecclesiastical intruder into chess – the bishop – did not exist under this title in medieval chess. The piece was called the 'affin' or 'alphin' (see *OED*), i.e. elephant, and associated with Fr. *fol*, fool, because of his limited moves. This is a more appropriate role in present context.

67. With 'Danger' (*Charles of Orleans*, Ballade 61); with Fortune (*Book of the Duchess*, line 652).

68. *Surrey*, no. 12.

69. *Complaint of Mars*, line 50. At the end Chaucer addresses in turn 'yow, hardy knyghtes', 'ye, my ladyes', and 'ye lovers al in-fere'.

70. Froissart's story, see p. 171– above.

71. *Gawayne and the Green Knight*, line 66: 'Handy-dandy' is Gollancz's suggestion (97 of his edn. ʒeʒed).

72. See also, for example, the quotation on p. 167 above: 'The Kynge flyinge as the Bird that syks hyr Pray. . . .'

73. *Charles of Orleans*, line 5200 (see note 19).

74. *Assembly of Ladies*, line 29 (Skeat, vii. 381).

75. Line 8 (Skeat, vii. 380).

76. See Lewis, *Allegory*, 249: 'What the writer really wants to describe is . . . the stir and bustle of an actual court. She is moved by a purely naturalistic impulse to present the detail of everyday life.'

77. *Legend of Good Women*, lines F.69, F.188.

78. Robinson's note is on p. 841.

79. *Confessio Amantis*, viii, line 2468 (Beawme = *Bohemia*).

80. *Charles of Orleans*, line 2226. See also G. L. Marsh's article in *Modern Philology*, iv (1906–7), 121–, 281–.

81. *The Flower and the Leaf* (Skeat, vii. 361): description and comments taken from Lewis, *Allegory*, 247–8.

82. The end of the poem is, admittedly, 'literary' in tone; it is possible that we have here a revised version of a poem originally intended to be oral and 'social'.

83. *Knight's Tale*, line A.1053.

84. Chambers, *Medieval Stage*, i. 391; and see Strutt, 339–.

85. See Utley, no. 127, *The ymage of love*, pr. Wynkyn de Worde (n.d.; 1525).

86. *Dunbar*, no. 26, p. 51.
87. See p. 209–.
88. *Lydgate*, ii. 424.
89. *Flour of Curtesye*, line 8. The poem is pr. in Skeat, vii. 266.
90. *The Paston Letters*, v. 266 (no. 896); Feb. 1477.
91. *Secret Pense*: see p. 165 above and note 39.
92. e.g. at the end of *The Cuckoo and the Nightingale* (Skeat, vii. 358); the speech begins line 266.
93. e.g. *Troilus and Criseyde*, ii. 918; *Legend of Good Women*, line F.139.
94. *Court of Love*, line 1352 (Skeat, vii. 445).
95. For the use of bird imagery to address noble persons, see 'Unto the rial egles excellence . . .' (presentation verses addressed to the Duke of Bedford), *Index MEV* 3831; and see 3604.
96. Chambers, *Medieval Stage*, i. 179 (and ch. viii, *passim*).
97. The 1515 'Maying': see p. 243 below.
98. Robin Hood and his men: Halle (ed. Whibley), i. 15.
99. Malory, bk xix, sects 1–2.
100. Huizinga, 107 (the quotation marks round 'conversation' are mine).
101. *Charles of Orleans*, line 4375.
102. Skeat, vii. 422.
103. *Confessio Amantis*, bk i, line 2702 (ed. Macaulay, i. 109).
104. *La Belle Dame*, line 130 (Skeat, vii. 303).
105. *Charles of Orleans*, line 2308.
105a. *Charles of Orleans*, vol. ii, note to line 2309.
106. Line 4806.
107. Line 4998.
108. See especially *The Flower and the Leaf*, line 158–; *Assembly of Ladies*, line 57–; Bodl. MS Rawl. C.813 f.61 (ed. Padelford, no. 44); *Charles of Orleans*, line 5019. Flowers also played an important part in the courtly game called 'Sales of Love' (see Huizinga, 108: 'the lady mentions a flower; the young man has to answer with a compliment').
109. See p. 209– below for a further comment and examples.
110. *Court of Love*: pr. Skeat, vii. 409–. See pp. 164–7 above.
111. Line 379– (Skeat, vii. 419).
112. *La Tour Landry*, 185.
113. *The Flower and the Leaf*, line 66– (Skeat, vii. 363–).
114. Robbins, *Secular Lyrics*, no. 177.
115. *The Courtier*, 21 (my italics).

116. *Confessio Amantis*, bk iv, line 2783 (ed. Macaulay, i. 376).
117. *Romance of the Rose* (Chaucer's trans.) Frag. A, line 783.
118. *Squire's Tale*, line F.283.
119. *Confessio Amantis*, bk iv, line 1133 (ed. Macaulay, i. 332).
120. Bk v, line 7137. The church was as good a place as any for 'paying court' in every sense; but courtly moralists cavil at the lax amorous encounters of 'common lovers'.

CHAPTER 10

The Courtly Makers from Chaucer to Wyatt

T he relation between literature and life is rarely a simple one. Apart from students of literature, most people who read books are more conscious of their own present need than of anything else. They may want to be informed (*The Water Rat and his Habitat*), or to be amused (*Three Men in a Boat*), or simply relieved from consciousness (*Murder with Flowers*). They seldom want the strenuous exercise of entering into possession of a complicated whole, a unique thing-in-itself – still less of realizing its contribution to the ever-changing, because ever-growing, pattern of past writing which we call 'literature'. The concept of a 'literature' is perhaps mainly necessary, even now, to those whose job it is rather to classify books by seeing them in relation to one another than to understand them in their unique relation to life. This is not to say that the concept of a 'literature' is merely part of an academic game. If it was shared by the *writer*, it becomes a necessary part of understanding. This 'sharing' may only be a matter of borrowing from some past work; or it may take the form of re-statement, re-creation, 'imitation' – like Chaucer's use of Boccaccio, Pope's use of Horace, Arnold's use of classical epic.

In the Middle Ages the relation between literature and life was, it would seem, not less but more complex than it has since become. With the full range of this relationship, from the *Divine Comedy* to 'Hey nonny nonny', we are not concerned. I wish to consider only the courtly lyric, and whether the 'literary' approach to it can ever be a rewarding one. The usual view of the medieval lyric can, I think, fairly be called 'literary'; it consists in the adoption and application to the lyric of a whole set of assumptions which have accrued chiefly from a study of later literature. One may even doubt whether the corpus of 'lyrics' (that is, of short poems) itself forms a homogeneous whole, a whole which can be understood by internal classification – e.g. as 'complaint', satire, *aubade*, *chanson d'aventure*, and all the other familiar terms. If our chief aim is to discover what is interesting, memorable, valuable in the courtly lyric, we shall not, I think, find it by distinguishing seventeen varieties of amorous 'complaint', or by discussing whether the love-epistle was, or was not, growing in popularity. It may not help even to be asking whether a 'community of artistic interest' bound together certain poets and 'distinguished their work from others'. At the risk of seeming to deny altogether the usefulness of the idea of a 'literature', I shall, after a few preliminaries, start at the other end and consider the lyric as 'life'.

This discussion of 'courtly making' must be prefaced with the same warnings of deliberate limitation as were necessary in the previous chapter: I shall treat the period 1370 to 1530 as static, ignoring change and variation; and I shall look all the time for principles of continuity in courtly 'pastime'. There are other complications, too, which we may set aside for the time being, or pretend not to notice: the dissemination of court culture, for instance, to a wider circle. It is obvious that there was both a 'below-stairs' and a provincial, courtly literature. The aping of courtly attitudes by those who were not really 'in the swim', and the attempts of men like John Shirley, the London bookseller, to commercialize courtliness, are at the moment irrelevant. For present purposes a sharp distinction must be made between the poet's original intention and the eventual fortune of his work. Richard Tottel's publishing venture, for example, tells us nothing about what Wyatt had in mind. Original intention and immediate use are our concern.

We must also ignore, for now, the dependence of the Court upon a living popular culture. It can be no part of our present purpose to decide, for instance, whether the meaning of the May festival as a folk celebration infiltrated into courtly life or not.

When describing the 'game of love' I precipitated an impossibly pure essence from the blended and mixed stream of courtly life. This 'essence', unadulterated by the grossness of other realities – political, social, and moral – I shall be using as the basis for what I now have to say about the 'literature' of courtly love.

I

To consider the lyric as 'life' is not as absurd as it sounds. We are accustomed to find religious verse with actual functions – crude, practical applications, as rubrics in the manuscripts show. We are also accustomed to the functions of medieval music – 'blowing to supper', etc. Some verses (if they are verses) in the *Paston Letters* show 'literature' also in the closest relation to life. Margery Brews writes to John Paston, in 1477:

> And yf ye command me to kepe me true wherever I go,
> I wis I will do all my might you to love and never no mo,
>   And if my friends say that I do amiss
> They shall not me let so for to do
>   Mine heart me bids evermore to love you
> Truly over all earthly thing . . .[1]

Another example of the practical love-lyric occurs in *The Devonshire MS*, a courtly anthology of the Wyatt period which belonged to a member of the Howard family.[2] Some of the poems in it clearly refer to an actual affair of the heart between Lord Thomas Howard and Lady Margaret Douglas. For marrying her (she was the king's niece), Lord Thomas was thrown into the Tower and died a prisoner. Poems which they sent to each other at this critical time are extant; including one written by her after his death. Lord Thomas writes:

> . . . My love truly shal not decay
> For thretnyng nor for punyshment;
> For let them thynke and let them say . . .

and,

> My lytle wych ys good and stronge
> That I am yours and yow ar myne . . .
> Now fayre ye well, myn one swete wyfe,
>   Trustyng that shortely I shall here
> From yow the stay off all my lyfe.[3]

In these and similar verses they express (or struggle to express) their feelings for each other, using the age-old clichés of courtly love.

But here we may begin to doubt. Margery Brews is a well-attested lover; so are the Howards. But there are hundreds of love-lyrics. What 'affairs of the heart' can be produced to explain them? Is not this emphasis on 'life', on biographical truth, simply the old nineteenth-century critical fallacy rearing its buried head? The biographers have in this way made nonsense of Elizabethan sonnets, particularly Shakespeare's. This is admitted. Nevertheless, when by way of reaction we are encouraged to read everything as 'poetry', we are in danger of missing some significant points which the older, biographical approach was likely to reveal.

Courtly Love and the Courtly Lyric

It may help our understanding to think, in turn, of at least three kinds of 'literature' of courtly love. This is only a basic classification: the shades are infinite. The first kind we have already considered: a class of poetry, very small in dimension, in which the Lover is unmistakably and demonstrably a Lover. The love he parades is an actual love. His language may not be adequate to his needs and his feelings, but it is an instrument of a real purpose, of an emotion which matters.

The second kind includes those poems and songs which belong to what I have called the 'game of love'. The Lover here poses as Poet. He writes poems and songs because they are part of the technique of courtly love. They are less ends in themselves than *means*. Not means of the urgent and actual kind which genuine lovers use; but means, nevertheless. The poems and songs are intended as contributions to social life and, especially, to the delicate fiction of courtly love which helped to sustain the life and interest of social relations. There is two-way traffic here. The poem (or song) is not merely a communication from a poet to his readers (or audience) but a part, even if only a small part, of a mutual 'playing' with ideas and sensations of love. It is *inter*communication. Such a poem belongs to a favoured group and has its full meaning only when they respond to it. The Lover as Poet may, moreover, borrow his songs, his feathers, from elsewhere. The extensive 'use' of Chaucer and the Chaucerian apocrypha in fifteenth-century writing proves only how useful Chaucer was, not how widely spread the enjoyment of literature had become. Chaucer was the greatest exponent they knew of the 'art of love', the most accomplished guide that the 'game of love' had ever had. As it was chiefly the social *use* of poetry that mattered, it was comparatively unimportant whether the courtier got his song out of a book, wrote it himself, or employed some professional (such as Lydgate) to write it for him. Love-songs were a part of his contribution to the social life of the court, a 'grace' (like music, dancing, jousting, games, and witty talk) of his fictional, adopted personality as Lover.

In the third category of 'courtly making', a man who is a Poet, one who delights in words, dramatizes himself as a Lover in order to make his proper contribution to the 'game of love'. His entering the 'game', as it were from outside, is at least partly for the sake of his poetry, whereas in the former case the Lover simply *used* poetry as one way of displaying his skills in the art of love. Between the Lover-as-Poet and the Poet-as-Lover the shades are various. The eventual distinction, however, is decisive. It is the distinction between a game which all share and a performance which one gives; between a broadly functional and a more nearly artistic view of courtly poetry; between art for use and art for delight. The Poet-as-Lover presents a dramatized excerpt from the 'game of love'. Here the element of communication, not of mutual give-and-take, is paramount. We are near to regarding him as an Entertainer, and doubtless this was one of his important functions. It is to this sphere that 'festival poems' of courtly love belong. The 'professional' poet like Lydgate here proved his use to the courtly society by producing a set-piece – for St Valentine's Day, or for May Day. The high-placed amateur, like Chaucer, was also called upon for contributions. These could be either of a 'festival' nature – *The Parlement of Foules* – or 'occasional', in a looser, or lost, sense – *Troilus and Criseyde* and *The Legend of Good Women*. (In both of these Chaucer dramatizes himself as the courtly lover, now unsuccessful, now cynical, now admiring.) Also to this sphere belong, I believe, those balets of courtly love which were commissioned by royalty and aristocracy from their 'professional' poets: 'Loo here begynnethe a balade | whiche that Lydegate wrote at the request of a squyer that served in loves court.' [4]

With the more ambitious productions of the courtly makers – the festival poems, the high romances, the poems which come nearest to making a 'literature' – we cannot here be concerned. Our business is with verse of lighter weight. The lyric of courtly love, the most ephemeral of courtly poems, belongs to neither extreme. It helps to occupy the middle space between 'life' and 'literature'; it belongs to my second category almost entirely, and is for the most part, I suggest, a mere tool in the 'game of love'.

It may seem that I am naïvely suggesting that the medieval poet would have been dissatisfied with the idea of producing, simply, love-*poetry*, mere 'literature', which was to be no more than a faithful and arid replica of similar 'literature' in different European languages through the centuries. There remains, nevertheless, a problem of motive. We cannot shoulder all the responsibility off on to Dame Rhetoric. *Why* were such hackneyed, trite, flavourless trifles so popular? *Why* were they produced in their hundreds? The answer, I think, may lie in the fact that a farewell-poem, an *aubade*, a debate, a confession – all the other familiar 'type' poems of courtly love – were like any other of the forms of social intercourse – sports, pastimes and games – mere *formulae* for the personalities of the players to occupy and give life to. No one complains that chess is a dull game because the moves are always the same. Chess, or any other game, is dull only if you go on playing it with the same opponent. And so it was, surely, with the courtly love-lyric? The lyrics of Chaucer and Charles of Orleans and Wyatt are on the whole dull – it is no use pretending otherwise. But if we could enter their world and see their lyrics as gambits in a 'game of love', half-mocking, half-serious, we might then be less puzzled by them. The smooth impersonality of the courtly lyric may easily deceive us. The shades and nuances of meaning – everything, in fact, that might distinguish the individual from the type – arose from situation, not from words. The spice and piquancy of debate, the saucy-solemn atmosphere of 'problems of love' may have given the love-lyric the individuality it so conspicuously lacks when regarded as 'words on the page'.

The existence of a social 'world' behind the courtly lyric is confirmed by the 'entitulyng' which Shirley (not only bookseller but book-circulator, as well) gave to the Chauceriana which he put in his 'anthologies';[5] by the dramatization of the society of lovers which forms the frame for Charles of Orleans's 'artistic' assemblage of courtly-love poems;[6] and by the fact that an early, lost, printed miscellany of courtly lyrics had as one of its titles *The Court of Venus* and as its preface a 'court of love' poem in which all the social images traditionally connected with the 'game of love' are hinted at.[7] Author and publisher alike simulate as a setting for their pieces the *society* which alone could make the poems interesting and meaningful:

> And here foloweth, wherin you may rede,
> To the court of Venus a greate nomber;
> Their harts they say be as heavy as lead.
> Their sorowful wo, I am sure you wil tender,
> For if that I were mayden uncumber
> And had such myght as she hath mone,
> Out of their payne they should be lettin gone.[8]

(This prologue, like many courtly poems, is addressed, fictionally at least, to the ladies in semi-flirtatious banter.)

II

A paradox of courtly love, as we saw earlier, is that an idealized personal relationship was made the ground for an elaborate code of social behaviour. The discipline and delight of being a Lover, whether 'in ernest or in game', would teach you how to behave – especially in mixed company. Love, despite its privateness, would make you able to 'commune' (or 'common') gracefully, keep 'mesure' in your talking, display your social skills and make you 'acqueyntable'. This paradox also lies at the heart of the 'literature' of courtly love – of what one might call the *written symptoms* of the 'game of love'. I want now to amplify the suggestion, made above, that the courtly love-lyric is, perhaps before all else, a tool in the game. Poems purporting to be about the intimacies of joy and grief encountered in the Lady's service are made the occasion for social play, for social *display* and ultimately for social entertainment. The idea of display is the simplest, and we may take it first.

In Thomas Usk's *Testament of Love*, the God of Love says:

> whan any of my servauntes ben alone in solitary place, I have yet ever besied me to be with hem . . . and taughte hem *to make songes of playnte and of blisse*, and *to endyten letters of rethoryke* in queynt understondinges, and to bethinke hem in what wyse they myght best their ladies in good service plese; and also *to lerne maner in countenance, in wordes and in bering,* and to ben meke and lowly to every wight . . . and *to yeve gret yeftes and large, that his renomè may springen.*[9]

In this short view of the Lover's character, Usk makes it clear, as dozens of other writers also do, that poetry and music are part of 'the technique of courtly love'. This notion goes back in English at least to the translation of the *Romance of the Rose* – and perhaps much further. The capacity to write love-songs, 'complaints', 'praises', rhetorical letters, is only a small part of the Lover's total equipment. But it is fairly important – especially if you happen to have a talent for it. Like having a good seat on a horse, appearing in 'fresh array', and knowing the ins and outs of courtly etiquette, courtly 'making' has uses both social ('good loos and pris') and personal ('to sette my purpos alofte').

Sometimes the Lover's verses were subsidiary to another expression of his 'good chere', his determination to please in the art of love. Thus a poem could, and often did, accompany the giving of a present – a heart, a token, a 'trewlove', a flower. This point needs no lengthy illustration: the world of courtly love was not merely a world of ideas; it embraced actual physical objects. When, to repeat an observation made earlier, the courtly maker uses a word like 'hert' or 'trew-love', he may well be thinking of a *thing*, a physical emblem or device. Out of several examples I choose a poem by Wyatt:

> To seke echewhere, where man doeth lyve,
> The See, the land, the Rocke, the clyve,
> Fraunce, Spayne and Ind and everywhere

Courtly Love and the Courtly Lyric

Is none a greater gift to gyve,
    Lesse sett by oft and is so lyeff and dere,
    Dare I well say, than what I gyve to yere.

I cannot gyve browches nor Ringes,
    Thes goldsmythes work and goodly thinges,
    Piery nor perle oryente and clere;
But for all that is no man bringes
    Leffer juell unto his lady dere,
    Dare I well say then that I gyve to yere.

     .   .   .   .   .

To the, therefore, the same retain,
The like of the to have again;
    Fraunce would I gyve if myn it were.
Is non alyve in whom doeth rayne
Lesser disdaine. Frely, therefore, lo here
    Dare I well gyve, I say, my hert to yere.[10]

This is a New Year's gift poem on a traditional model; it may be compared with another some years older:

Juellis pricious cane Y none fynde to sell
    To sende you, my Sovereign, this newe yeres morowe,
Wherfor, for lucke and good hansell,
    My hert Y sende you, and Seynt John to borowe,
    That an hundred yeres withouton adverssite and sorowe
    Ye mowe live . . .[11]

In neither case can it be *proved* that an emblem in the shape of a heart accompanied the poem to the lady. And each poet declares himself unable to give precious jewels. But 'heart' often has this physical and concrete meaning, as for instance the 'Statutes of Love' make clear: 'Som thing devise . . . And send it her . . . Some hert, or ring, or lettre, or device | Or precious stone.'[12] To send a jewelled heart with the message of love would be more courtly – and more witty.

    The idea of display does not, it will be clear, depend on an actual, present and admiring audience. Love, in Usk's *Testament*, taught the servants of love how to display through 'songs and complaynts' and through 'letters of rhetoric'. There must have been much *written* exchange as well as oral – paperwork as well as talking and singing. Anelida, Chaucer tells us, was 'so ferforth yeven' to please Arcite that

> There nas to her no maner lettre sent
> That touched love, from any maner wyght,
> That she ne shewed hit him, er it was brent;
> So pleyn she was, and dide her fulle myght
> That she nyl hiden nothing from her knyght.[13]

Charles of Orleans's poems, in which the 'game of love' is dramatized for us, refer to exchanges of missives between lover and lady:

> Most goodly yong, o plesaunt debonayre,
> Yowre sendying which me gaf comaundement
> A balad for to make, ye speke so fayre
> That with glad hert Y shew here myn entent.[14]

This is one of many which end with the 'Go, little bill' formula:

> Go rewdisshe bel, complayne my ponysshement.

The man who invented letter-writing is praised:

> For when to speke they [lovers] nave tyme nor metyng
> To say ther ladies of ther adversite
> Yet doth it them a gret tranquyllite
> Forto endite and send as in writyng.[15]

It is clear, I hope, that, whatever else it may have been, the 'balet' of love was one of the means adopted by the Courtly Lover to display his personal qualities to social advantage. There was one quality above all which the 'balet', whether 'complaynt' or 'praise', enabled him to develop and display – his articulateness, his mastery of words, the art of courteous speech. 'Courtly making' is an extension of courtly discourse; the love-poem is 'luf-talkyng' raised, formalized and crystallized.

> For to nobles longith sewte of curteys speche
> As he fynt tyme by mouth or writyng seche.[16]

Evidence of improvised versifying, though sparse, is not entirely lacking: Huizinga tells of a courtly game, played abroad, *Sales of Love*, in which compliments had to be versified on the spur of the moment.[17] And, indeed, there was a vast stock of tags and rhymes ready for use – 'my woful hert', 'whether I wake or sleep', 'sew/trew', 'refrayn/disdayn', and so on. Extemporization cannot have been too difficult in these circumstances. The Lover must have had *some* ready-made style for his 'courteous carp'. Whether or not the 'language of love' had an existence outside the 'literature' of love must, however, remain for the moment in abeyance. The main point is not affected: the Lover was able to display his talents, if he 'koude songes make and wel endite'. If he could sing them as well as reciting them, that was an added grace.

III

The idea of the love-lyric having a use in social *display* is simple enough. The idea of its contributing to social *play* is more elusive. It will, I hope, at least be agreed for a start that to postulate a social 'world' behind the courtly lyric may be in itself a help towards understanding. The idea will encourage us to look for a balance between a too-biographical and a too-'literary' view of the lyric. It will prevent us from taking the declarations of unrequited love either too seriously or not seriously enough. It will give the lyric the possibility of another dimension. Can we, perhaps, go further than this? I shall argue that the social 'world' explains several features of courtly verse which are otherwise puzzling and unsatisfactory: the stilted lifelessness of its language; its frequent air of dissimulation and obliqueness; and its seeming incompatibilities of mood.

Nothing strikes a reader who is making his first acquaintance with the courtly lyric so forcibly as its drab lifelessness. (I speak of the great bulk of lyrics, not of a few anthology pieces.) The writers have what amounts to a genius for the stilted and colourless. Why is this? It is not merely that they are third-rate. They are third-rate in a special way. The courtly balet of this period seems to talk a recognized language of love. The 'makers' have and use, it is obvious, a huge stock of phrases hallowed by use. I take a few at random from a *virelai* by the Earl of Warwick: 'my woful hert', 'with bisy thought and grevous peyne', 'I yow ensure', 'changed for no nuwe', 'whyles that I have lyves space', 'for euermore whyles that I lyve'. This poem was written sometime after 1422.[18] A century later we find the same sort of phrases – sometimes, indeed, the very same phrases – in *The Devonshire MS* (of Wyatt's circle): 'Wyth sorowful syghes and wondes smet', 'My hart ys set nat to remove', 'Enduryng payne in hope of pyttye', 'As hart can thyncke or tong expresse'.[19] 'Can we doubt', Mr Mason asks,

The Courtly Makers from Chaucer to Wyatt

'that if we had *all* the songs sung at court between Chaucer and Wyatt, we should be able to shew that every word and phrase used by Wyatt was a commonplace . . . ?' [20]

It is no accident, and certainly no anomaly, that *The Devonshire MS* includes several 'poems' which are simply excerpts from Chaucer – from *Troilus and Criseyde* and *Anelida and Arcite*. The lovers are so satisfied with (or bound by) the traditional language of love that they utter their hearts to one another in the very words of the great poet of love, who had a word for everything they felt – Chaucer. Who can doubt that to this group of courtiers and their ladies Chaucer was, above all, the Articulate Lover, the 'well of eloquence', the master of the language of the heart? To read *The Knight's Tale* or *Anelida and Arcite* was a sentimental education. And when the Lover exhorted his Lady in the words which Saint Troilus had taught him:

> Wo worthe the faire gemme vertulesse,

what need she reply but with Criseyde:

> For love ys yet the mooste stormy lyfe . . . ?[21]

It did not always happen that the courtly 'maker' *lifted* his poems out of Chaucer. But with very few exceptions it can be said that he *wrote* them out of Chaucer. In particular he wrote them out of *Troilus and Criseyde*, the great poem in which he could study and find how 'most felingly' to speak of love. In the course of the poem Chaucer ranges the whole gamut of 'luf-talkyng' both naturalistic (dramatized speech) and 'literary' (stylized, poeticized speech). In fact, the best way of suggesting the debt of the courtly makers to Chaucer is, I think, simply to quote a stanza from the *Litera Troili*, Troilus' letter to Criseyde:

> Right fresshe flour, whos I ben have and shal,
> Withouten part of elleswhere servyse,
> With herte, body, lif, lust, thought and al,
> I, woful wyght, in everich humble wise
> That tonge telle or heste may devyse,
> As ofte as matere occupieth space,
> Me recomaunde unto youre noble grace.[22]

With one obvious exception it would be easy to parallel every phrase used here with one from the courtly makers of the next 150 years. The stanza is, like most courtly lyric, courtly epistle, a mere tissue of clichés. – Or is this unfair? Is it simply that later courtiers made them clichés, and that we should read Chaucer's verse more freshly? My opinion is that Chaucer is here exploiting a recognized 'language of love': the stale weariness and flatness of the poetry is appropriate, dramatically, to this stage of the poem. This view is confirmed by the fact that elsewhere in the poem the stylized laments, 'complaynts' and praises, are not cliché-ridden, and we get quite a different impression from them:

> O cruel day, accusour of the joie
> That nyght and love han stole and faste i-wryen
> Acorsed be thi comyng into Troye
> For every boor hath oon of thi brighte yën!
> Envyous day, what list the so to spien?
> What hastow lost, why sekestow this place
> Ther God thi light so quenche, for his grace?[23]

A 'language of love' which had an identity of its own, and oral as well as 'literary' uses, cannot, of course, have been as simple as the letter of Troilus suggests. It must have been at least as complicated as the 'game of love' in which it had such a large part to play. It must, that is, have found words not only for the happy idealisms of courtly love but also for its idealistic discontents, for its flirtatious banter, its naturalness, its streaks of common sense and its occasional 'nasty-mindedness'. The 'language of love' even in its purest, most essential form – in minor Chaucer, in Charles of Orleans, in the poets of *Henry VIII's MS* and of *The Devonshire MS* – is crossed with the more natural love-language of popular lyric and romance ('My love is to the grenewode gone, Now after wyll I go'), with the cynical common sense of proverb ('turn up hyr haltur and let hyr go') and with the *double entendre*, tending to raise a snigger ('Foster wyl I be no more; No lenger shote I may'). Moreover, this language was subject to modification as the living language changed, and as individual talkers and writers gave it new shades, new idioms. For although we are concentrating for the moment on the unchanging *continuum*, the love-language of Wyatt must, of course, have been in some respects different from that of Chaucer.

There is a further difficulty. For the purpose of description it has been necessary to isolate the ethos, the mode of thinking, feeling and behaving, called courtly love. But this is a mere historical convenience. Nothing so simple, so securely insulated from the world around, ever existed. Similarly the concept of a 'language of love' is a necessary simplification. It could never have had an absolute identity any more than sherry-party talk or schoolboy language has absolute identity today. However, with these limitations, the notion of a 'language of love' can be a useful one. It suggests that the courtly love-lyric belonged not so much to a 'literature' as to a society, and that its words (like the words of many medieval religious plays) rarely pretended to artistic sufficiency – they were mere *formulae*.

The objection may be put forward that the courtly balet was sometimes sung. But even when it was sung, this would not necessarily transfer interest away from the social to the musical. Song could be merely a superior kind of ornamented speech, a more distinguished delivery, heightened recitation. If the courtly maker sang his balets informally, it must have been, as I have already tried to show, to popular tunes or others like them, easily memorable, easily singable. The complicated 'professional' art-song would have been altogether unsuitable for his purposes of 'dalliance'. The connection with *talk* is the important one; to make a good 'dally' he had *to be understood*. One of the marks of most secular polyphonic styles is the obscuration of the text: the words tend to be lost in the web of counterpoint and of ever-winding, melismatic melody. The words, to repeat, had to be understood, for the poem made the 'play'. In order to achieve this it was not necessary that it should be individual, distinctive utterance. As suggested earlier, the words could be as traditional, as impersonal as a 'How do you do?' or 'Not a very bright morning, is it?' The personalities of the players gave them meaning; the words were in most cases mere forms to set the players in action. The courtly maker did not aim at distinctive speech.

The impersonality of the courtly love-lyric has, then, some partial explanations. The poems were written in a traditional 'language of love', drawing on a huge stock of hallowed terms and phrases. This language, dependent as it was on social usages, never pretended to self-sufficiency; it was never intended to be mere words on a page; it was part of a social 'drama'. However, these are only partial explanations. There must also be taken into account certain features of the 'game of love'. The impersonality was perhaps to some extent also policy.

IV

There are one or two passages in the 'literature' of courtly love which, fortunately, tell us quite plainly what sort of 'play' the love-lyric set out to stimulate or direct. One of these is in *The Franklin's Tale*. Arveragus has gone away leaving his wife mourning at home; while he is gone a 'lusty squier' falls in love with her:

> But nevere dorste he tellen hire his grevaunce.
> Withouten coppe he drank al his penaunce.
> He was despeyred; no thyng dorste he seye,
> *Save in his songes somwhat wolde he wreye*
> *His wo, as in a general compleynyng;*
> *He seyde he lovede, and was biloved no thyng.*
> Of swich matere made he manye layes,
> Songes, compleintes, roundels, virelayes
> How that he dorste nat his sorwe telle . . .
> In oother manere than ye heere me seye,
> Ne dorste he nat to hire his wo biwreye,
> Save that, paraventure, somtyme at daunces,
> Ther yonge folk kepen hir observaunces,
> It may wel be he looked on hir face
> In swich a wise as man that asketh grace . . .[24]

The courtly love-lyric is, perhaps in essence, an enigma – a riddling, or dark, way of conveying your thoughts to someone who is, or pretends to be, your lover. Or, since most love-lyrics are 'compleyntes' (in every sense), to someone you want, or pretend to want, to be your lover. The courtly lover must 'wreye' his feelings: if he has been accepted, because her identity must remain a secret ('Shal no man know her name for me'); if unaccepted, like Aurelius, because he fears to declare his love. The balet of love was not peculiar in this respect. It was simply one tool in the complicated equipment of hearts, jewels, flowers, tokens, emblems, colours, sleeves, garlands and crowns. No doubt the subtlety of the 'sentimental' gambit consisted in combining or varying your signs of amorous inclination. A courtier's array, I suggested earlier, was a sartorial enigma: it was not his intention to be plain and open, but to be 'covert' and 'secree' – in a word, to 'dissimulate'. The lyric, although intended to be read or sung in society, to a present and observing audience, was another gambit of dissimulation. It was a public utterance which had, *or pretended to have*, a private meaning. Or, looked at from the audience's point of view, the love-lyric was a confidence which they were intended to overhear, a loud whisper. 'Covert communication' (or the pretence of it, for we are still partly in the land of make-believe) explains the oblique tone of many courtly love-lyrics. Wyatt's in particular have it, and one soon recognizes it as characteristic:

> Deme as ye list! Uppon goode cause
> I maze and think of this or that;
> But what or whye my self best knowes,
> Whereby I thinck and fere not.[25]

Or

> I shall *assay by secret sute*
> *To show the mynd of myn entent,*
> And my desertes shall gyve suche frute
> As with my hart my wordes be ment.[26]

On another occasion Wyatt seems to be regretting that he has overdone it:

> My songes ware to defuse
> Theye made folke to muse . . .[27]

But this is not, of course, a serious regret — any more than his bitterness, mocking tone, irony or cynicism are serious. He still goes on playing the same game, and the poem ends:

> Yf this be undre miste,
> And not well playnlye wyste,
> Undrestonde me who lyste;
> For I reke not a bene,
> I wott what I doo meane.

Examples need not be multiplied tediously. Explicit references to 'covert communication' are found more frequently in Wyatt's poetry than elsewhere. But the atmosphere of it is ubiquitous in the lyric of courtly love (see, for example, H29). The lyric, in sum, gives ample opportunity for putting one of the 'commaundements' of love into action:

> Secretly behave you in your werkes,
>   In shewing countenance, or mevyng of yur iye;
> Though soche behavor to some folke be darke,
>   He that hath loved woll it sone aspie.
>   Thus yur-selfe yur counseyle may descrye . . .[28]

A *caveat* ought perhaps to be added here. I do not mean to suggest that every courtly lyric had, originally, a direct relation to the social relationships of the poet, however lightly pretended. We must remind ourselves that between the Lover-as-Poet, to whom words are a mere tool in the 'game', and the Poet-as-Lover, to whom the 'game' is an excuse for making poems, the emphasis shifts subtly but markedly. Chaucer writing 'many a hymn for loves halydays', Charles of Orleans hoping that in his book is something 'to fede' other lovers on, Wyatt dramatizing the woman's point of view – all these are perhaps as often providing fuel for others' fires as stoking their own. Moreover, it is tempting to see in the large number of absence, farewell and unrequited-love poems a sign of the need to adopt the conventional pose as Lover, while at the same time avoiding even the lightest actual entanglement. 'Absens it is that wolde me wrong' was a sufficient concession to the pressure of the convention. Then, again, in the 'court of love' atmosphere, any general contribution to 'Love's philosophy' would be sure of an audience. *Henry VIII's MS* contains many songs, we recall, of courtly manners. Love is the great civilizer, love is a natural good:

> Whoso that wyll all feattes optayne,
> In love he must be withowt dysdayne,
>
> For love enforcyth all nobyle kynd,
> And dysdayne dyscorages all gentyl mynd. [H34]

The hearers could make of the doctrine whatever personal use they liked. The lyric, like other courtly poems, could be made to serve any purpose – the lightest dalliance, a flirtatious intrigue, a solemn courtship.

The idea of the lyric as 'covert communication', although central, is not, of course, all-embracing. The play of ideas and sensations could be maintained in a more open manner, too: through 'answering' poems, poems debating set themes, through dialogues, riddles, jests and conceits. These are obvious categories and need little illustration. Wyatt's 'Patience' poems will show some of the possibilities. Patience is a good 'theme' for lovers and is enjoined among the Commandments of Love. Wyatt assays the 'theme' four times in *The Devonshire MS*.[29] Two of the poems hang together. Wyatt opens with

> Patience, though I have not
> The thing that I require,
> I must of force, god wot,
> Forbere my moost desire;
> For no ways can I fynde
> To saile against the wynde.[30]

The Courtly Makers from Chaucer to Wyatt

(All four poems, by the way, are in the same metre. This suggests a common tune.) The poem which goes with this one has a marginal note which, I think, exactly confirms the 'game of love' atmosphere:

> Patiens tho I had not etc. To her that saide this patiens was not for her, but that the contrarye of myne was most metiste for her porposse.

The poem opens,

> Patiens for my devise
> Impaciens for your part;
> Of contraries the gyse
> Is ever the overthwart.
> Paciens, for I ame true,
> The contrary for yew.[31]

(The word 'devise' suggests the wearing of some visual emblem.)

The microcosm of courtly love could find a place not only for set themes but also for a variety of musings on moral and philosophical issues. We frequently find, for instance, Boethius transposed into a soft Lydian air, especially the 'complaynt' against Lady Fortune, the blind goddess:

> For she hath turned to her whele,
> That I, unhappy man,
> May waile the time that I did fele
> Wherwith she fedde me than;
> For broken now are her behestes
> And plesant lokes she gave;
> And therfore now all my requestes
> From perill cannot save.[32]

It was perhaps the easy amorous analogy that contributed to the popularity of the poem 'Sumwhat musyng | And more morenying'. The words are ascribed to Antony Woodville, Lord Rivers, who is said to have written them during his imprisonment at Pontefract. But they apply, by analogy, to Any Lover:

> Sumwhat musyng
> And more morenyng
> In remembryng
> The unstedfastness,

Courtly Love and the Courtly Lyric

This worlde beyng
Of such welyng
Me contraryyng;
What may I gess? [F24, H107]

V

On an earlier page I said that there were three features of the courtly love-lyric which the background of the 'game of love' might help to clarify: its stereotyped phraseology; its oblique and dissimulating tone; and its strange contradictions of mood and manner. 'But', the reader may object, 'these contradictions scarcely exist: the most striking feature of the courtly lyric is its tedium, its endless and boring repetitiveness.' And indeed the lyrics from which I have quoted are all much of a muchness – mere pegs (and very uniform pegs) on which to hang the garment of social and amorous sensation, mere formulae. But the objection arises, I think, from a greatly over-simplified view of the courtly mode.

It has been pointed out more than once that the code and 'literature' of courtly love could embrace a good deal of internal criticism, that satire against love was an integral part of the whole 'system'.[33] The intense idealisms of courtly love were bound to produce, we may add, intense disillusions; the unearthly and rare ecstasies of the Garden of the Rose could be transformed in a moment by the bitter knowledge that in another and earlier Garden the first Woman revealed the essential frailty of her sex. As desirable as the Rose, as weak as Eve, as inaccessible as the Blessed Virgin – this was the paradox of Woman.

In one of the few balets in which Wyatt rises above the common 'social' mode, we feel the disillusion as serious and genuine:

> It was no dreme: I lay brode waking.
>   But all is torned thorough my gentilnes
> Into a straunge fasshion of forsaking;
>   And I have leve to goo of her goodenes,
>   And she also to use newfangilnes.
> But syns that I so kyndely ame served
> I would fain knowe what she hath deserved.[34]

But this is exceptional. In place of personally felt disillusion we more often find attitudes, poses, stereotyped though diverse, and eminently suited to their *social* purpose of lending additional spice to the 'game of love'. Unlike

The Courtly Makers from Chaucer to Wyatt

the idealisms of love, the cynicisms allowed a great deal of playful variety –
more variety, perhaps, than my account of the 'game of love' has so far
suggested. The criticism could, and did, range from the most delicate
pricking of the romantic bubble to violent and foul-mouthed abuse of the
female sex.

No one called the idealisms of courtly love more lightly and delicately
into question than Chaucer: the poem, *To Rosemounde*, which begins,

> Madame, ye ben of al beaute shryne
> As fer as cercled is the mapemounde,
> For as the cristal glorious ye shyne,
> And lyke ruby ben your chekes rounde . . .

also contains the well-known lines,

> Nas never pyk walwed in galauntyne
> As I in love am walwed and y-wounde,
> For which ful ofte I of myself devyne
> That I am trewe Tristam the secounde.[35]

Any doubts we might have about the intention of the indecorous image
of the pike are surely settled by the mock-pomposity, the assumed prophetic
afflatus, of 'I of myself devyne | That I am trewe Tristam'. This irony de-
pends for its effect on our catching the slight absurdity, the whimsical
hyperbole; the main tone of the balade is unexceptionably courtly. The
bantering, teasing, is wholly delightful.

It goes without saying that verses of this sort could have appealed fully
only to those who knew the courtly world and the proper expression of
romantic sentiment. The next step takes us further out of the charmed
circle of courtly romance. There are many poems of mocking or of abuse
which, while still using courtly forms or modes, are violently coarse in
tone. One writer parodies the 'catalogue of charms':

> Youre camusyd nose, with nose-thrylls brode,
> Unto the chyrch a noble instrument
> To quenche tapers brennyng afore the roode,
> Ys best apropred at myne avysement;
> Your leud likyng, doble of entent,
> Wyth courtly loke al of saferon hew,
> That never wol fayle – the colour is so trew![36]

Wyatt uses the rondel form, associated with Charles of Orleans's amorous
trifles, for a poem against a lady who will not grow old gracefully:

Courtly Love and the Courtly Lyric

> Ye old mule, that thinck yourself so fayre,
> Leve of with craft your beautie to repaire,
>   For it is time withoute any fable:
>   No man setteth now by riding in your saddell;
> To muche travaill so do your train apaire.
>   Ye old mule![37]

Mr Utley has well said that,

> When Chaucer makes fun of women or of courtly love he is attempting neither to abolish a code nor to transform a sex. He is merely participating in a very courtly game.[38]

The danger is that we may think that only light parody, of the bantering and teasing sort, was acceptable in courtly circles. But this would not, I think, be true. The 'courtly mode' could embrace more violent extremes than this. There is no reason to think that Wyatt's, or Skelton's even foulermouthed, poems against women were mere private exasperations. They were just as appropriate, we may hazard, to certain moods, certain groups perhaps, of the aristocratic social world. Among the balets of *Henry VIII's MS* are, moreover, some 'forester' poems.* They belong, apparently, to the same world as the rest of the courtly poems of the manuscript. But their tone is hardly up to drawing-room expectations:

> I have bene a foster
> Long and many a day;
>
> .   .   .   .   .
>
> Every bowe for me ys to bygge;
>   Myne arow ny worne ys;
> The glew ys slypt frome the nyk;
>   When I shuld shoote I myse;
>   Yet have [I bene a foster.]
>
> Lady Venus hath commaundyd me
>   Owt of her courte to go;
> Ryght playnly she shewith me
>   That beawtye ys my foo;
>   Yet have I b[ene a foster.] [H62]

---

* Forester-songs with an erotic double-meaning are a feature also of German literature of this period.

The erotic undercurrent can hardly be missed. But were such songs 'for men only'? We have no reason to think so.

The juxtaposition even in popular religious drama of feelings of tender compassion, cheap jibes at matrimonial upsets, grotesque parody, and violent cruelty, should put us on our guard against expecting the courtly mode to be a simple, uncomplicated thing. Alongside the delicate and playful scepticism of 'Merciles Beaute', the abusive parody of 'Ye olde mule', and the sophisticated *double entendre*, we can expect to find, as part of the play of the 'game' of love, some common-sense criticism ('Let them enjoye the gayn, | That thynkes yt worthe the payn'); some pastoral idealization of a more fulfilled, natural and idyllic love ('Who shall have my fayre lady. . . . Undir the levys grene' [F42]); some hints of *esprit gaulois* ('Now yn this medow fayer and grene | We may us sport and not be sene' [H109]); and some traditional satire (*Bicorne and Chichevache*).

It appeared, earlier, that in describing the 'game of love' and the courtly making which arises out of it, I should not be able to avoid presenting 'an impossibly pure essence from the blended and mixed stream of courtly life'. The 'essence' however has not turned out quite so 'impossibly pure' as Charles of Orleans's.* One of the delights of the 'fiction' consisted precisely, perhaps, in feeling it tremble in the balance as it was injected with carefully measured doses of 'reality'; another, in reacting against it with every possible coarseness and vulgarity. This is psychologically likely and apt. But it must be stressed that it all belongs essentially to the 'game'. We do not, I think, find anywhere in the courtly love-lyric any serious attempt to come to terms with life.[39] It is all a matter of action and reaction, statement and counter-statement, idealisms and cynicisms. We may seem to be at liberty, but we are still, in fact, prisoners within the closed and enchanted Garden of the Rose where the 'game of love' was played. The *Romance* itself, we remember, had *two* sides. In the lyric these two sides are symbolized, as well as presented, by such ambiguities as the poem already quoted [Song 151]:

> In women is rest peas and patience
> No season for-soth outht of charite. . . .[40]

---

* It may seem strange that Charles of Orleans's poems do not figure in the quotations above. This has a ready explanation. In his 'cycles' of love-lyrics Charles dramatizes and *idealizes* the 'game of love' for us. We get from him the essential spirit unadulterated by any of these other views of love.

or in Chaunticleer's immortal words,

> *Mulier est hominis confusio,* –
> Madam the sentence of this Latin is,
> 'Womman is mannes joy and all his blis'.[41]

VI

To sum up, the lyric of courtly love from Chaucer to Wyatt is in its most characteristic form a mere gambit in the 'game of love' – deliberately stylized in language, oblique in purport, idealistic, bantering and abusive by turns. Its full, indeed its essential, significance can never be recovered, only guessed at: its study 'belongs to sociology rather than literature'.[42]

These generalizations will not, of course, cover the whole corpus of surviving love-songs. The verses of Humfrey Newton, the verses of the Rawlinson MS C.813, the compilations of John Shirley – all these suggest deliberate borrowing of the courtly mode by those outside the charmed circle. The courtly ideal is there rehearsed by those who have learnt the idiom of the language of love but somehow seem to be missing the meaning. Even here, two separate trends are probably to be distinguished: the 'provincial' and the 'below-stairs' respectively.*

However, leaving aside entirely the question of the dissemination of the courtly ideal among the provincial aristocracy, and 'below-stairs' at court and in city, the account I have given of the lyric as part of the 'game of love' is intended chiefly as a corrective to the conventional account; it does not pretend to explain everything, to put everything in a correct proportion. Above all, it minimizes what to us must be perhaps the most important and interesting feature – the gradual struggle by which the poet lifts his art out of the social milieu which gave it birth and sustained it. 'Lifts out' is slightly misleading. 'Extends out' might be a better phrase. Even Chaucer's roots remain deep set in the aristocratic world. The thing that distinguishes his greatest poetry is not the dismissal of the society felt so vividly behind his early work, but the transcendent quality of the art which can now compass so much more than that society demands.

---

* Humfrey Newton's book and the 'Findern MS' seem to be the first, with Newton slightly further from the fountainhead of cultural sweetness. Shirley and the Rawlinson MS, on the other hand, may be respectively the products of bourgeois (the butcher and the baker) and servant aspiration (the butler and the housemaid). These conjectures are obviously too neat and superficial but suggest perhaps the scope, difficulty and interest of the problem.

The Courtly Makers from Chaucer to Wyatt

The courtly maker of lyrics rarely achieves even a partial disengagement from the courtly milieu. A short poem, for one thing, does not give him much time to take flight. But we can trace some of the steps by which he begins to achieve it. The Poet-as-Lover will write poems for others, as rubrics to poems by Skelton and Lydgate show;[43] he will also write poems on general themes that appeal to all. He will become, in a word, the Entertainer.

But he has a loftier office than this to undertake. He will produce poems for festivals, for the high-days and holidays in love's calendar, whether seasonal (St Valentine) or occasional (birth, marriage and death). He has the office of Spokesman; he puts into words what all feel (or wish to feel) at impressive moments. And here we are reminded that the forms and feelings, the tone and vocabulary, of courtly love had an appropriateness and a function beyond the mere celebration of courtship. The rules of courtship became, it was said above, the rules of paying court in the widest sense. Just as the lovers' code taught men and women how to behave, how to be pleasing companions in the leisurely society of their peers, so the 'language of love' provided words not only for informal dalliance but also for ceremony and celebration. *The Book of the Duchess* is the supreme example of public elegy in the style of courtly love:

> Therto she koude so wel pleye,
> Whan that hir lyste, that I dar seye,
> That she was lyk to torche bryght
> That every man may take of lyght
> Ynogh, and hyt hath never the lesse.
> Of maner and of comlynesse
> Ryght so ferde my lady dere;
> For every wight of hir manere
> Myght cacche ynogh, yif that he wolde,
> Yif he had eyen hir to beholde.
> For I dar swere wel, yif that she
> Had among ten thousand be,
> She wolde have be, at the leste,
> A chef myrour of al the feste.[44]

This is only one of many poems (whether any of them can be called 'lyrics' scarcely matters) in which the 'language of love' is used by the courtly maker for a wider and deeper concern – the celebration of a public event.

Courtly Love and the Courtly Lyric

A curious minor example of 'celebration' occurs in *The Devonshire MS*: the 'testament' of Lady Margaret Howard:

> Now that ye be assembled here,
>   All ye my freynds at my request,
> Specyally you my ffather dere,
>   That off my blud ar the nerest
>   Thys unto you ys my request
> That ye wol pacyently hyre
>   By thys my last words exprest
> My testament yntyer.[45]

She asks her father to bear her death with patience and to pardon her offence,

> Syth yt prosedeth off lovers fervence
> And off my harts constancy
> Let me nat from the sweet presence
> Of hym that I have caseyt to dy.

(Seven years later, having recovered from her grief, she married the Earl of Lennox and became the mother of Lord Darnley.) Quite on what sort of occasion and to what sort of company and in what sort of style this poem was to be read, it is impossible to say. But the poem is hardly to be explained as 'literature', even though the 'testament' is a well-known genre of medieval poetry. It must, surely, belong to ceremony, formal or semi-formal. Occasions of personal grief or joy or decision were less private then than now, as witness the publicity of the marriage-bed. The courtly-love attitudes spilled over into and gave style to the publishing of them.

Thus, finally, with the poet as Entertainer, Spokesman and Celebrator for his society, we move towards a more familiar conception of the relationship between literature and society. The Poet-as-Poet replaces the Lover-as-Lover. He conceives his poetry as 'literature'. Whatever the origins of the genre he is using, his art has risen above the sustaining context of social life. It may superficially treat the same themes, play the same 'game', but its real interest and life is on another plane. The poet sees his work in its relation to the great works of the past. In the later Middle Ages he will be a craftsman in the great rhetorical tradition. And, according to taste and nationality, he will be a 'disciple' of Petrarch or Boccaccio, Machaut or Deschamps, Chaucer or Lydgate.

We are now as far removed as possible from the 'real life' poems of the

Pastons and Howards; we have reached a level at which writing is no longer enmeshed in the life of a particular social group. But this 'literature' is, paradoxically, a literature which takes in far more of life than the hybrid, fictional productions of the 'game of love', where the Lover plays at being a Poet, the Poet at being a Lover. It is a literature which takes as one of its main tasks the reconciliation of the courtly way of life with wider and deeper, older and newer, ways, and which attempts the radical evaluation of the courtly ideal.

NOTES TO CHAPTER 10

1. *Paston Letters*, no. 783; see *Index MEV* 303. See also Letter no. 866: in five rhyme-royal stanzas, from John Pympe to Sir John Paston.
2. See p. 118. The non-Wyatt poems of *The Devonshire MS* are transcribed and pr. by Muir (see Reference List). A list of ascriptions missed by Muir is given by Miss Ethel Seaton in *RES*, n.s. vii (1956), 55. The relation of Wyatt's 'Devonshire' poems to 'popular' and 'courtly' traditions is the subject of Mason, *Humanism*, 143–78.
3. Muir, *'Devonshire MS'*, no. 9. See further, Mason, 166–7.
4. See p. 164.
5. Shirley: e.g. 'Balade made by Chaucer At the reverence of a lady that loved a knyght' (Brusendorff, 261).
6. The social 'frame' can be seen at a glance in Steele's edition, p. ix, 'Contents'; Mason, 164, describes the poems as 'part of a courtly ceremonial – unfortunately they, the only surviving part, are the deadest part of the ceremonial'.
7. *Court of Venus*, 115–: 'the generic title for three different fragments of a xvi-century poetical miscellany' (see Russell Fraser's recent elaborate edn, vii); the Prologue, by Robert Shyngleton, once chaplain to Anne Boleyn, is in typically 'high', though degenerate, 'Troilus' verse.
8. *Court of Venus*, 118: the stanza quoted ends the Prologue (tender = receive graciously).
9. Skeat, vii. 12.
10. *Wyatt*, no. 85.

11. *Political, Religious, and Love Poems*, ed. F. J. Furnivall, EETS (repr. 1903), 66.

12. *Court of Love*, line 396, i.e. 'the thirteenth statut' (Skeat, vii. 420). See also: *Wyatt*, nos 48 and 109, for other 'hearts'; *Lydgate* (ed. MacCracken), ii (*Secular Poems*), 424, 'Lovers' New Year's Gift', espec. st. 16; Bodl. Rawl. MS c. 813 (ed. Padelford, no. 44) for the 'trewlove' flower ('trewlove' can also be a knot); *Tottel*, no. 203, a ring; *Index MEV* 768, sending a token (Humfrey Newton). Mrs H. M. Shire has drawn my attention to similar poems by Montgomerie and Alexander Scott, as well as to tapestries which show the Lover handing a heart to his Lady.

13. *Anelida*, line 113.

14. *Charles of Orleans*, line 762 (Ballade 19).

15. idem, line 828 (Ballade 21).

16. idem, line 145.

17. Huizinga, 108.

18. MacCracken, H. N., 'The Earl of Warwick's Virelai' in *PMLA*, xxii (1907), 597–. See also the clichés and sets of rhymes given by Mason, 160; 170–1.

19. See Muir, '*Devonshire MS*', *passim*.

20. Mason, 171.

21. *Troilus and Criseyde*, ii. 344; ii. 778.

22. idem, v. 1317.

23. idem, iii.' 1450.

24. *Franklin's Tale*, line F.941. I thank H. A. Mason for first drawing my attention to this passage (which he uses, 158–9, for a different purpose) and for the idea of the 'overheard confidence'.

25. *Wyatt*, no. 166 (Muir reads 'maye').

26. idem, no. 126. See also no. 167.

27. idem, no. 138.

28. Robbins, *Secular Lyrics*, no. 177.

29. *Wyatt*, nos 39, 40, 118, 162.

30. No. 39.

31. No. 40.

32. No. 183.

33. In particular, though with different emphases, by C. S. Lewis, *The Allegory of Love*, and by F. L. Utley, *The Crooked Rib*, to both of which I am indebted. Utley observes that the integral connection between satire on women and courtly love is firmly established in

the realm of 'courtly festivity by its [satire's] intrusion into the fortune-game, the riddle and the holly-ivy carol' (p. 28).

34. *Wyatt*, no. 37.
35. *Chaucer*, 533.
36. Robbins, *Secular Lyrics*, no. 209, from Bodl. MS Rawl. poet. 36. The verse would, of course, bear a slightly different interpretation if written, as it were, 'below-stairs' (see p. 224).
37. *Wyatt*, no. 35.
38. Utley, 30.
39. One or two of Wyatt's excepted.
40. Robbins, *Secular Lyrics*, no. 112; and see p. 162 above and note.
41. *The Nun's Priest's Tale*, line B².4354.
42. Mason, 171.
43. Skelton's 'Go, piteous heart, rased with deadly wo' was written *At the instance of a nobyll lady* (Dyce, i. 27). Lydgate's 'Fresshe lusty beaute, joyned with gentylnesse' was written . . . *at the request of a squyer that served in loves court* (*Lydgate*, ii. 379).
44. *The Book of the Duchess*, line 961.
45. Muir, 'Devonshire MS', no. 42.

PART THREE

Music at Court

CHAPTER 11

Music in Ceremonies, Entertainments
and Plays

A song is a complex thing. It has words and an author who wrote them; music and a composer who made it; and a relationship between them. We have so far considered two of these: I have tried to display the relationship between words and music in a historical perspective, and tried to reconstruct a social world of courtly versifying. The third element, music, is equally important, if not more so, for it is music that makes a song. I do not intend, however, to pursue in the following chapters the line of technical analysis. In so far as the technique of song-making can help us, it has already done so, in the Introduction and in Chapter 6. I return in the Epilogue to the musical *experience* of the songs – a very different matter. Meanwhile, I intend a short *excursus* into the social history of music. Knowledge of *ars contrapuncti* will not greatly help us to understand the songs; knowledge of music-making may.

There are two further reasons why the study of these early Tudor song-books, as distinct from the song-books of other periods, should go hand in hand with a study of music in society. The first is that the sources of late medieval music, the actual surviving pieces, are quite unrepresentative of the music we know existed. There is, for instance, an enormous gap in our knowledge, covering almost the whole repertory of professional secular music, the music of minstrels. How, then, can we be sure that the songs which survive really represent the songs which were sung? The second reason why the background must be studied is that medieval people themselves always thought of Art as having a Purpose. Since they related their music and songs to the business of living, it is the least we can do to discover how and why.

It will be necessary to restrict the inquiry largely to the state of affairs in the court circle, for several reasons. It would in any case be natural to begin there, for not only do the actual sources of music point strongly in that direction, but also almost every named composer or musician or patron,

almost everyone who had pretensions to being someone or doing something, spent part of his life there. At court, if anywhere, the cream of the
nation's talent was assembled around the person of the king:*

> My soverayne lorde in every thyng
> Above all other as a kyng,
> In that he doth no comparyng
> But of a trewth he worthyest
> To have the prayse of all the best;
> My soverayne lorde. [H50]

The focus of court life in the first decade of Henry VIII's reign was the
small group of intimates who hunted, jousted and gambled with him –
Bryan, Brandon, Norris and Carew, to name no others. They were
'Esquyers of the Body', the king's own bodyguard, his 'minions'; and it is
they who were somewhat ignominiously removed from the scene in 1519.
But by 'the court circle' I mean a far wider group than this. It includes all
those nobles and prelates who may be presumed to have modelled their
way of life upon the royal pattern, who were in the habit of seeking their
entertainment at Westminster or Windsor, and who themselves entertained the king in their own establishments. It also, for our purpose, includes the professional purveyors of entertainment, household musicians,
poets 'laureate', devisers of masks and interludes and pageants.

Those who wrote primarily for this exclusive 'upper class' were sometimes its members and sometimes its servants; they include figures as diverse
as John Skelton (Henry's former tutor), Sir Thomas Wyatt (son of a Privy
Councillor), William Cornish (Master of the Children of the Chapel
Royal), John Heywood (virginalist, singer, epigrammatist and son-in-law
to Sir Thomas More), and, a little later, Henry Howard, Earl of Surrey,
one of the highest born in the land. Of these, and of innumerable lesser
men, the same question must be asked: what was the place of music in
their daily lives?

In Chapter 6, I said that most statements about music and poetry were,
in one way or another, statements about society and argued that it was not
merely styles of song but modes of life that had to be investigated. It was
this conviction, and the curiosity aroused by it, which first led me to seek
answers to the obvious questions about the occasions, performers and
'means' of music. I hope that the conclusions here reached will give

* This is not to deny the richness and vigour of the *City's* musical life, so ably demonstrated by Dr Hugh Baillie in his recent studies of London music and musicians.

substance to my previous generalizations about words-and-music. Nevertheless, the subject has, I think, an interest transcending the particular end to which it has been applied; and so, for the sake of readers whose main interest is in the social history of music, I have made the following account of Music at Court as much of an entity as possible.

I

One of the most important historical facts about the public music of the late Middle Ages is that it was functional rather than expressive. I do not mean for a moment to suggest that its first hearers never felt the 'lift upwards and divine' that later ages have felt. On the contrary, commentators are lavish with such phrases as 'the marveiles swett armone of the sayd ynstermentes . . . soundes to be a thinge of another world';[1] and, in fact, we can with difficulty imagine how violent an emotional impact music may have made on minds less battered with sensations than our own. But the certainty remains that it was rarely, if ever, the *first* duty of music to express emotion for its own sake. It should rather be regarded as part of worship, part of ceremony, part of an allegorical entertainment or a moral play.

This point, obvious but seldom made, is quite in accord with what we know of the place of the other arts in society. 'The Middle Ages', in the words of Professor Huizinga, 'knew only applied art. They wanted works of art only to make them subservient to some practical use.'[2] Portraits and effigies are clear examples of this. Similarly, Professor Robbins has stressed the 'eminently practical nature' of Middle English verse, quoting the lyrics written for banquets and mummings and the devotional poems written to stir up the wills of faithful people.[3] Rhetoric, moreover, was an art which taught men how to speak and write persuasively, that is, how to achieve actual results. Even the abstruse science of astronomy was pursued partly for the purpose of fixing the dates in the ecclesiastical year.

How then was music 'applied' in the life of the court? The present chapter will, I hope, answer this question. It is based largely on historical accounts of events taken from chronicles, dispatches, household books, and the like. Although the detailed descriptions of ceremonies and entertainments leave much unsaid about the music, there is no dearth of material. First and foremost, music was widely used in ceremonies of all kinds. It is not difficult to find records of music being played on the field of battle, at the changing hands of an important town, or on board ship.[4] The pompous diplomatic meetings of heads of states called for music. On these occasions the first moment of personal contact between the potentates was acclaimed by an outburst of minstrelsy on each side – 'suddenly the trumpets and other instruments sounded, so that never was heard such joy'.[5] At the Field of the Cloth of Gold, the scene of a great ceremonial meeting between Henry VIII and Francis I of France,

> then up blewe the Trumpettes, Sagbuttes, Clarions, and all other Minstrelles on bothe sides, and the kynges descended doune towarde the bottome of the valey of Andern . . . and embrassed the twoo kynges eache other.[6]

In general, all meetings between noble persons or their representatives, all important receptions, processions and journeys, were supported by music. For instance, when Henry VII dispatched his daughter, Margaret, to Scotland in 1503 for her marriage with James IV,

> among the sayd Lords and the Qwene, was in Order Johannes and his companye, the Menstrelles of Musick, the Trompetts in disployed Banneres, in all the Departyngs of the Townes, and in the Intryng of that sam, playing on their Instruments to the Tym that she was past owt.[7]

Any ambassador was entitled to trumpets, and the *King's Book of Payments* abounds in payments on a generous scale to trumpeters going overseas.[8]

Even if there were nothing to be said about the way music was made, its sheer bulk would be impressive. Whereas today ceremony and therefore ceremonial music play a negligible part in our lives, in early Tudor times they were inescapable, particularly in court circles. Royal entries, tournaments and 'running at the ring', funerals and executions, banquets, weddings, coronations – these were the occasions on which a courtier from his youth up would hear music.

There is no easy distinction to be made between religious and state ceremonial, any more than between a 'sacred' and a 'secular' song. There was no domain of life into which religion did not enter, no activity which was not thought of as part of God's purpose. Latin grammar, the steps of the basse-danse, a lady's garter, were all thought capable of divine significance. The chief distinction the Middle Ages would have understood was between 'godly' and 'profane', 'good' and 'bad'. This means that, on the one hand, worldly songs could be used in the divine service and, on the other, plain-song canticles could be sung at royal entries without any sense of incongruity. Thus, three early Tudor composers used the love-song,

'Westron wynde' [Song 346], as the main theme for a setting of the Mass;[9] and Henry V, God's vice-gerent on earth, was welcomed back into the City after Agincourt with *Benedictus qui venit*.[10] In ceremony there are some curious mixtures (anomalies only to *our* way of thinking): a state banquet would be conducted with ritual dignity; the service of the Mass could serve a political purpose, and could be tricked out with mechanical devices. When Cardinal Wolsey celebrated High Mass at the Field of the Cloth of Gold,

> after the Elevation, the Eucharist was seen in the air floating over the tilt yard, no one perceiving whence it issued nor who propelled it, to the height of a tall tower, and even beyond, for it travelled half a mile, *to the surprise of those who did not know how it was done*.[11]

Royal entries were the shows put on by towns and cities as an expression of loyal welcome to their distinguished visitors. Endless care, ingenuity and expense were lavished upon them (often the city's income was mortgaged for years); and as the king or prince went in procession through the main streets he was confronted at each important stage with a 'sight', an allegorical tableau, mounted on a 'pageant' or scaffold.

Music formed a part of these shows from the very earliest days. When Richard II rode through the City in 1392 there was a young man at St Paul's 'enthroned amongst a triple circle of singing angels'.[12] And so it continued. At Coventry in 1498, for Prince Arthur's visit, '. . . the crosse in the croschepyng was garnysshed and wyne ther rennyng and angels sensyng and syngyng with Orgayns and other melody'.[13] Later on in this progress a balet entitled *Vivat le prynce Arthur* was sung:

> Ryall prince Arthur,
> Welcome, newe tresur,
> With all our hole cur
> To this yor cite.

All sorts of instruments were used in the shows. When Prince Arthur married Katherine of Aragon in 1501, a water-pageant conducted the court down the Thames to Greenwich

> with the moost goodly and plesaunt mirthe of trumpetts, clarions, shalmewes, tabers, recorders and other dyvyrs instruments, to whoes noyse uppon the water hathe not been hard the like.[14]

At a royal entry at Coventry in 1474, the young Prince Edward was

Music at Court

welcomed 'with mynstrallcy of the Wayts of the Citie', 'with mynstralcy of harpe and Dowsemeris', 'with mynstralcy of harpe and lute', by the 'Childer of Issarell syngyng', by 'ij knyghts armed with mynstralsy of smal pypis', and 'mynstralcy of Orgonpleyinge'.[15]

Tournaments and jousts were other occasions of dignity. The chronicler, Edward Halle, conveys something of the social 'meaning' of these occasions in his elaborate description of a Joust of Honour, May 1516:

> The kyng . . . and his company were appareiled horse and al in purple velvet, set ful of leaves of clothe of gold, engrailed with fyne flat golde of dammaske, embroudered like to Rose leves, and . . . on the kyng wayted v. lordes, xiiii. knightes in frockes of yelow velvet, garded and bound with riche clothe of gold, and . . . xl. officers in yelow satyn edged with clothe of gold: thus with great triumphe thei entred the fielde.[16]

These martial festivities were inevitably accompanied by instruments able to express in loud or confused noise the dignity of the occasion they were marking. The phrase 'great Triumphe' must refer to the 'trompettes, dronslades and other mynstrelsey' mentioned in this same passage. There were fourteen trumpeters and all were provided with blue sarcenet coats.[17]

Musical effects at tournaments cannot have been very varied. Banquets, on the other hand, when on a grand scale, were always graced with two sorts of music: first, the loud ceremonial music which marked the 'honourable service' of each gargantuan course. Edward Halle describes the coronation banquet of Henry VIII:

> . . . at the bryngyng of the first course, the trumpettes blew up. And in came the Duke of Buckyngham, mounted upon a greate courser, richely trapped and embroudered, and the lorde Stewarde, in likewise on an horse, trapped in clothe of golde, ridyng before the service, whiche was sumpteous, with many subtleties, straunge devyses, with severall poses, and many deintie dishes.[18]

Secondly, there was incidental music, played while the course was being eaten:

> The feast then commenced, and lasted more than three hours . . . In the centre of the hall there was a stage on which were some boys, some of whom sang, and others played the flute, rebeck and harpsichord.[19]

The Braunche brass at King's Lynn, Norfolk, shows both kinds very clearly: on the extreme right of the feast, where a peacock is being served in all its plumage, two trumpets and a shawm are playing; on the left a rebec and a cittern are performing softer music.[20] Even this softer music had, of course, its social significance: 'many thynges', wrote a thirteenth-century author, 'bene necessarye and worshyppe the supper . . . the viij is myrthe of songe and of instrumentes of Musike'.[21] In more modern terms, an expensive luxury like music was part of the vast apparatus of 'conspicuous consumption' necessary to the royal or noble estate. However, incidental music (often vocal) was comparatively emancipated; it was an art less closely bound up with movement and event than ceremonial music for the 'honourable service'.

Music, then, was widely used in ceremony. But it occupied a markedly subordinate position. Everything was, naturally, subordinate to the deep feeling for order, correct precedence and all the minutest decencies of etiquette; but, more than that, music did not rank very high as a ceremonial agent. A reading of the chronicles and household orders leaves one in little doubt about this; the prime grace of noble ceremonies was the display of costly clothing and jewellery. Thus, when Henry VIII met the Emperor Maximilian in Picardy,

> The noble men of the kynges campe were gorgeously apparalled . . . but in especial the Duke of Buckingham, he was in purple satten, his apparel and his barde full of Antelopes and swannes of fyne gold bullion and full of spangyls . . . of gold mervelous costly and pleasaunt to behold.[22]

One foreigner writes of an important reception that 'all bore such massive gold chains that some might have served for fetters on a felon's ankles'.[23]

Other things essential to the 'noble game' with its elaborate ritual were, at banquets, expensive food and plate and, at all times, expensive servants. The decorations of the banqueting-hall were of prime importance. In 1527 the Milanese ambassador reported home that Henry was having two large halls built 'with triumphal arches about them, and other most sumptuous preparations, including four great repositories, full of gold vessels'.[24] The social significance of displaying gold plate is evident from the fact that the ambassador thinks it worth mentioning. The 'garnishing of the cupboards with plate' for the meeting between Henry and Charles V in 1520 was a duty sufficiently important to be assigned to a Privy Councillor, Sir Henry Wyatt (father of the poet). Expensive servants, vicariously consuming time and money, were a perpetual subject of comment. The author of the *Italian Relation* was only one of many who noticed that a large retinue 'is a thing the English delight in beyond measure'. On public occasions, to use Halle's words, 'all men maie conjecture that nothyng was omitted that might be bought for golde'.[25] To put the extreme case, then, music was there to draw attention to something worth *seeing*, as for example royal meetings, or the appearance of a course of a hundred dishes, or 'the Godhead sitting full gloriously' on the top of a 'pageant'. To do this adequately it had to be, in Bacon's phrase, 'sharp and loud and well placed';[26] that is, it had to be in itself a gaudy noise. Thus, loud instruments, trumpets, clarions, sackbuts, drums, bells, organs and choirs, were very much in evidence. As one writer put it, 'then sounded guns and other instruments'. He may, certainly, have meant instruments of war rather than of music. But this scarcely affects the issue. As the history of the word 'noise' seems to show, the musical and the martial were not clearly distinguished. Out of doors, especially, noise was required, whether of guns, drums, trumpets or bells. All these are in fact mentioned as having a part to play, for example, in the water-pageant for Anne Boleyn's coronation. The procession down the Thames was led by a 'foist' full of ordnance, with a great dragon casting fire and 'terrible monstrous wild men' making hideous noises; the Mayor's barge carried 'shalmes, shagbushes [sackbuts] and divers other instruments'; and so on. There were fifty barges in all, 'every company havyng melodye in his barge by himself'.[27]

Besides drawing attention to something worth seeing, music itself had also, in order to dignify the ceremony, to speak to the eye. It is difficult for us, whom wireless and gramophone have increasingly removed from our music-makers, to recapture the frame of mind of earlier listeners, who always connected hearing music with *seeing* it. Musicians not only appeared in elaborate stage settings but they had to fit the setting and to draw out its allegorical meaning. In ecclesiastical settings the singers often represented 'the circute enumerable angells singing' around the Godhead; in more scholastic or humanistic 'pageants' they might be disguised as the Muses playing instruments beneath the throne of Apollo. At Coventry in 1474 the only mention of harps and dulcimers is in connection with an Old Testament scene of three Patriarchs and Jacob's twelve sons.[28] Moreover, the musicians were often elaborately dressed, in order to reflect credit on their noble patrons: minstrels, like actors, were expressly exempted from the Acts of Apparel which forbade people to wear clothes above their station.[29] And lastly, their instruments were decked out with banners and sometimes even with jewels. A common entry in the account books is 'warrant . . . for fifteen banners, with tassels, for the King's trumpets'; less common, though not rare, are descriptions of other instruments, such as the 'very beautiful silver organ, with gold ornaments' which adorned Henry's chapel at the Field of the Cloth of Gold.[30]

When considering the particular place of vocal, as distinct from instrumental, music in court ceremonies, we find, naturally, that its importance varies. Songs had, perhaps, little part to play in tournaments or 'running at the ring'. But *Henry VIII's MS* contains one which needs such a setting, the carol quoted in the Introduction, 'Whilles lyve or breth is in my brest' [H50]:

> My soverayne lorde for my poure sake
> Six coursys at the ryng dyd make,
> Of which four tymes he dyd it take;
> Wherfor my hart I hym beqwest,
> And of all other for to love best
> My soverayne lorde.

The next verse refers to her lord's prowess 'with spere and swerd at the barryoure'. The following verses make it pretty clear that the song must have been sung on behalf of Queen Katherine when Henry VIII had had a successful day.* Singing formed a substantial part of the music in many royal entries; Henry V was welcomed back into the city after the victory at Agincourt not only by the 'heavenly host' singing the *Benedictus* but by 'patriarchs syngyng *Cantate Domino*', by '12 apostles syngyng', by 'angels syngyng Nowell, nowell', and by 'a chorus of beautiful virgins singing in English "Welcome, Henry the fifte, Kynge of Englond and of Fraunce"'.[31] It is not easy to decide exactly what the musical effects were, but we may suppose that at this entry the various choruses sang their Latin canticles to plain-chant and their English songs to popular tunes, both perhaps with discant. On the other hand, when Anne Boleyn was welcomed into London for her coronation (1533), the 'qwyre of syngyng men and children', which 'sange newe balads made in prayse of her grace' from the roof of St Martin's, would probably have sung part-music.[32]

The song-books are not altogether deficient in suitable 'entry' songs. The clearest example is the carol, 'Enforce yourselfe as Goddis knyght | To strenkyth your comyns in ther ryght' [F47]. It follows the tradition of

---

* H22 may also fit a tournament setting.

direct address which is a feature of street pageantry on royal occasions. The petitioners point out to the King:

> God hath gyff you of his goodness
> Wisdome with strenkyth and soveraynte. [F47]

It is his royal duty to use these gifts to redress the 'hurtis of thi commynalte'. A royal entry is also the most likely *mise-en-scène* for several carols of a slightly earlier date. The famous Agincourt Song, for instance, *Deo gracias, Anglia* [MC, 8], must belong, with its intricate though forceful counterpoint, not to the battlefield but to the victorious Henry V's triumphal return to England.*

Choral singing was, then, a feature of royal entries, and it was clearly 'applied' music in all the various senses already noted. Like the carefully prepared orations and posies, the songs would be appropriate to the matter in hand. Moreover, the 'sight', the tableau, was still the most important thing, and the singers had to act their part in it: the patriarchs, for instance, sent a flight of sparrows and other birds fluttering round the king as he passed; and the angels were boys wearing feathers and flinging down gold coins and boughs of laurel.[33]

There were other ceremonies, too, in which songs were performed. Some articles ordained by Henry VII in 1494 require that on Twelfth Night

> the chappell to stand on the one side of the hall, and when the steward cometh in at the hall doore with the wassell, he must crie three tymes, Wassell, wassell, wassell; and then the chappell to answere with a good songe.[34]

The 'good song' may have been an Epiphany carol, such as *Gaudeamus pariter* [MC, 72]. It is less easy to surmise what songs were sung on the following occasion. It is an account of 'the Maner of Makynge Knyghtes . . . of the Bathe':

> . . . othar yonge esquiers of the howsolde with mynstrells syngynge and daunsynge shall go before the chamberleyn . . . unto the tyme that they come unto the chambre door.

Later,

> ye knyght shall be ledd unto his chambre with greate meltytwde of

* See also the Latin carol, *Anglia, tibi turbidas* [MC, 56]; and the English carol, 'From stormy wyndis and grevous wethir' [F44], referring to the Prince of Wales, which is a song for a ceremonial departure, like 'Englond, be glad!' [H96].

knyghtes, squires, and mynstrells yonge syngynge and dawnsynge into ye entre of his chambre.[35]

Lastly, a ceremony graced with many songs was the royal May-game of 1515. This 'Maying' was a sophisticated version of the popular country pastime (Herrick's poem *On Corinna's Going A-Maying* gives an idealized picture of a country 'maying'). Scores of courtiers and court servants were given special clothing to take part in it. The roles included Robin Hood, Friar Tuck and Maid Marian, Lady May 'and her four ladies', and various others. After a banquet in a bower, at which music and songs were performed, the king's procession started homewards, escorting a 'triumphal car full of singers and musicians and drawn by griffins with human faces'; it was met by a chariot bearing Lady May and her four ladies on horseback, who 'saluted the kyng with divers goodly songes and so brought hym to Grenewyche'.[36] *Henry VIII's MS* contains 'divers goodly songs' which may have been sung at 'Mayings', such as the round, 'In May, that lusty sesoun' [H20] and the part-song, 'Trolly lolly loly lo . . . My love is to the grenewode gone' [H39].*

The chronicler Halle's conventional phrase ('saluted the kyng') is significant. The songs, whenever introduced, were to salute the noble action of the King and his court in 'going to fetch in May'. To compare three different accounts of this festivity is most instructive.[36a] Halle, of course, gets the intended chivalric spirit of the thing: 'at this Maiyng was a greate number of people to beholde to their great solace and confort'. Sagudino, the Venetian ambassador, is more realistic and observant: 'in this wood were certain bowers filled purposely with singing birds' – 'singers and musicians . . . played on an organ and lute and flutes'. Finally, Richard Gibson the accountant takes us behind the scenes: 'hawthorn leaves made by the Queen's embroiderer'; 'for costs done on the five maidens, 12d'; 'six ladies' garments from the King's old store, for six children of the chapel,' etc. Henry's chivalric gestures required a huge off-stage organization for their support – and music was one of the things which was organized.[37]

The 'Maying' was a success. The Venetian ambassador described it in his dispatch as 'an extremely fine triumph and very pompous'. Pomp was an essential factor in all these ceremonies. That is why small consorts of singers are not very frequently found in open-air shows. The six children playing on the regals and singing goodly songs at Edward VI's coronation

* Cf. H41, burden: 'Yow and I and Amyas'.

entry are exceptional.[38] Massed music, whether of voices or instruments, was more appropriate; nothing delighted the chroniclers more than 'heavenly noyes on every side of the street'.

II

The royal May-game of 1515 makes it clear that any distinction between ceremonies and entertainments must, so far as the early Tudor court is concerned, be more or less arbitrary. Spectacle, the thing seen, is the key to both; but, what is more important, the entertainments as a whole were conducted with the same passionate decorum as the ceremonies. Courtly entertainments, of course, had their riotous moments, their 'wildmen' or 'woodwos', their conies let loose in the Hall; but they were, in essence, like the ceremonies, another channel for the 'aspiration to realize a dream of beauty in the forms of social life'.[39] The generic name for the entertainments at court was 'the revels'. This name conveys rather well their almost barbaric undercurrents – it often happened that 'the rude people ranne to the pagent' and 'rent, tare and spoyled it' and stripped the king, gentlemen and ladies of their rich clothes. But it does not convey at all their ceremonial splendour, their magnificent 'politeness'.

A typical evening of revels in February, 1511, included an interlude, performed by the Gentlemen of the Chapel Royal 'with divers fresh songes'; the conferring of a knighthood on an Irish lord; a general, informal dance; a disguising called 'The Golldyn Arber in the Archeyerde of Plesyer'; a formal dance, by couples; 'a great banket'; and, perhaps, later, more general dancing with a pause for a 'void' (light refreshment).[40] The banquet itself was often the setting for the evening's various activities. Wolsey's biographer, Cavendish, describes the entertainment of the French ambassadors in 1518:

> In the myddes of this bankett ther was tornyng at the barriers (evyn in the Chamber) with lusty gentilmen in gorgious complett harnoys on foote. Than was there the lyke on horssebake | And after all this there was the most goodlyest disguysyng or enterlude made in Latten and Frenche.[41]

Dancing was probably unrivalled as an indoor pastime for a courtier. It is possible that more musicians were regularly occupied in providing dance-music than for any other purpose. There seems to have been, firstly, a considerable amount of professional dancing at court. There are two extravagant payments in Henry VII's accounts to 'a litelle mayden that daunceth'; and Mark Smeton was described as 'one of the deftest dancers in the land'.[42] These professionals may have been as much acrobats as dancers, like the young Italian 'who played before the King on a Corde'.[43] But most dancing seems to have been done by the gentlemen and ladies of the court. Their dances were of two kinds – formal and informal.

The general evening's dancing in any season of 'revels' must have been informal. The records say that at a ball in 1514 the King, the Duke of Buckingham and other lords spent 'almost the whole night in dancing with the damsels'; Henry was 'in his shirt and without shoes [*senza scarpe*]'.[44] The Milanese ambassador reported on this occasion that in dancing 'he does wonders and leaps like a stag'.[45] Sometimes dancing was even more informal and private. The *Spanish Chronicle* tells how Anne Boleyn sent for Mark Smeton to play one morning, whilst she lay in bed, and ordered her ladies to dance. On another occasion she danced with him herself.[46]

Whether or not different music was used for the formal dances, they were clearly danced in a different style. At this important ceremonial, for example, after the usual salutes and greetings,

> the mynstrells begonne to play a basse daunce, the wich was daunced by the said Qwene and the Countess of Surrey. After thys doon, they playde a Rownde, the wich was daunced by the Lorde Gray ledynge the said Qwene, acompayned of many Lordes, Ladyes and Gentyl-woemen.[47]

The basse-danse is a stately couple-dance about which much is known, and for which there is music extant. Robert Copland's little print of 1521, *The manner to dance bace dances*, translated from the French of Michel Toulouze, testifies to the importance of the basse-danse in English social life. Moreover, *Henry VIII's MS* contains one or two pieces which were, or were related to, basse-danses: *Helas madam* [H10] and [*E*]*n vray amoure* [H81], for example. The round must be, as its name implies, a circular dance – little is known about it, although a keyboard version of one round survives.[48] Other English dances of the period are the morris, frequently mentioned as a kind of antimasque, the brawl and the hornpipe.[49]

Many combinations of instruments were used for dancing. On the occasion mentioned, when Henry VIII and the Duke of Buckingham were dancing in their doublets, music was provided by shawm, rebec, small pipe (and tabor?) and lute (or gittern). On another occasion 'dancing commenced to the sound of the tabour, pipe and viol [rebec?]'. A favourite indoor band in England seems to have consisted of lute (or harp), rebec and pipe-and-tabor. The *Northumberland Household Book* allows for just this: 'Item, Mynstralls in Houshold iij, *viz.* a taberett, a luyte and a rebecc.' Out of doors two shawms and a sackbut, much louder instruments, were usual. But other combinations were possible both in and out of doors. One commentator suggests that the Italian fashion was to dance to fifes and sackbuts; another describes a 'disguising' in Wolsey's house during which 'old men' and 'nymphs' danced 'to the sound of trumpets'.[50]

A formal dance was the centrepiece, as we shall see, of any mask or disguising. The contemporary terms, 'mumming', 'mask' and 'disguising', are used in a most confusing way; 'mask', introduced as a new term early in Henry VIII's reign, eventually ousted the others. For simplicity's sake I shall use 'mumming' to describe the visit of a band of masked and silent dice-players to another person's house or chamber; 'mask', to describe the formal entry into the Hall of one or two groups of disguised persons, who first alone and then together performed special dances; and 'disguising', to describe a mechanized mask – that is, one in which the courtly dancers were wheeled into the Hall on a moving stage or 'pageant'.[51]

Mummings, based on popular custom, varied greatly: Richard II in 1377 had been visited by 'one hundred and thirty citizens, disguised and well-horsed'; Henry VIII's style is exemplified by his visit to Wolsey at Christmas 1536 with a band of courtiers, all disguised as shepherds.[51a] The mumming involved, it seems, no music at all; but it was often the prelude to the ceremonial entry of the maskers, which was dignified by music. In October 1518, for instance, Cardinal Wolsey entertained the French ambassadors:

> And when the banket was done, in came vj mynstrels, richely disguysed, and after them folowed iij gentelmen in wyde and long gounes of Crymosyn sattyn, every one havyng a cup of golde in their handes, the first cup was ful of Angels and royals, the second had diverse bales of dyce, and the iij had certayn payres of Cardes. These gentelmen offered to playe at monchaunce, and when they had played ye length of the first boorde, then the mynstrels blew up, and then entred into the chambre xij ladyes disguysed . . .[52]

The entry of the maskers was the important moment, and music was held in reserve for that. The minstrels, on all such occasions, direct attention to the maskers with their instruments, just as the torchbearers illuminate them with torches.

It is significant that the instruments most often named are those with military and ceremonial associations – drum and fife. When Henry, dressed as a shepherd, took his mumming to Wolsey, there were, said Cavendish, 'suche a nomber of dromes and fyves as I have seldome seen together at oon tyme in any maske'. A simpler mumming on Shrove Sunday, 1510, came in with 'a drumme and a fife appareiled in white damaske and grene bonettes'. Drum and fife continued to be used for mumming and masking.[53]

A new Italian element was said to have been introduced into the mask in 1513. Halle calls the entertainment in question 'a maske, a thyng not seen afore in England'. The exact nature of the innovation has been disputed.[54] It certainly did not involve fundamental change. If it was the wearing of special clothes or a show of gallantry and intrigue, it did not affect the music. If, on the other hand, the maskers immediately chose ladies from the audience for their partners, then the formal dance may have been omitted and different music used.

The entry of the dancers was, as already said, an impressive moment in the mask. The chief purpose of the fully developed disguising was to make it even more solemn and striking. There is perhaps no better guide to the 'tone' of disguisings in this period than contemporary accounts of court entertainments. Edward Halle's *Chronicle* is by far the most revealing source of information, if we want to understand the social 'meaning' of these bizarre and often tasteless shows: his attitude is characterized by a blend of the materialistic and the idealistic; he conveys at once the chivalrous aspiration that inspired, and the vulgar extravagance that supported the disguising. The following characteristic description is abbreviated from his *Chronicle*:

In the middle of the general dancing the king slipped away unobserved; 'within a littell whyle . . . the trompettes at thende of the Hall began to blowe'. A pageant trundled in, 'out of the whiche pageaunt issued out a gentleman rychely appareiled, that shewed, how in a garden of pleasure there was an arber of golde, wherin were lordes and ladies, muche desirous to shew pleasure and pastime to the Quene and ladies'. The Queen gave her encouragement and the cloth which hid the pageant was removed; '. . . it was solempne and ryche, for every post or piller therof, was covered with fryse golde, therein were trees of

Hathorne, Eglantines, Rosiers, Vines and other plesaunt floures of divers colours ... made of Satyn, damaske, silke silver and gold'. In the arbour were six ladies; in the garden, the king and five gentlemen, gorgeously dressed, 'and every garment ful of poysees, made of letters of fine golde in bullion as thicke as they might be, and every persone had his name in like letters of massy gold'. The names were chivalric: *Cuer loyall, Bone voloyre, Bone Espoier, Valyaunt Desyre*, etc. Apart from their posies, every person's dress was embroidered with the letters H and K in gold. 'When time was come ... then discended a lorde and a lady by coples, and then the mynstrels, which were disguised, also daunced, and the lorde and ladies daunced, that it was a pleasure to beholde.'[55]

Halle, as usual, concentrates on the visual aspect of the entertainment – on the appearance of the pageant itself and the costumes of the disguisers, with special reference to their worth in money. Moreover, in doing this he surely reflects the tastes of the courtly audience. There should be no need to emphasize that the same elements of display are present here, and for the same reasons, as in ceremony; nor that these disguisings are the reflection in English court-life of an 'international' pastime.[56]

Disguisings were more complicated than masks from every point of view, including the musical. The approach of the pageant was signalled, as we have seen, by loud music, a fanfare. The actual descent of the courtly maskers from the pageant to perform their dance was another ceremonial moment. But before this the pageant had to be escorted down the hall. At Epiphany in 1517, 'The Gardyn de Esperans' trundled in to 'the noise of minstrels'.[57] On an earlier occasion a castle, representing the Mount of Love, was brought in with song,

> ... all the fowre Children singing most sweetly and hermoniously in all the comming the length of the hall till they came before the Kinges majestie.

The king in this case was Henry VII, and he was celebrating the marriage of his elder son, Prince Arthur, to Katherine of Aragon. The occasion evoked a whole festival of disguisings. In the last one the pageant was drawn by three wild men, and on either side were

> homely mermaides, one of them a man mermaide, the other a woman; the man in harness from the waist upwardes; and in every of the said

248

mermaides a Childe of the Chapell singing right sweetly and with quaint harmony.[58]

Gibson also notes that 'two garments like shipmen's' were provided 'for two gentlemen of the chapel who sang in the play'.

There are numerous items in the court song-books which could have been sung 'in the play' on such an occasion. Given a dramatic situation involving lovers, at once dozens of lyrics become apt. But there is one song in particular that should be mentioned here because it is a clear example of an 'exit' song for a pageant. It certainly belongs to that later festival of tournaments and disguisings which celebrated the birth of Henry VIII's first-born son, in the New Year of 1511:

> Adew, adew, le company,
> I trust we shall mete oftener.
> Vive le Katerine et noble Henry!
> Vive le prince, le infant rosary! [H68]

It is a fairly complex song, compared with others in *Henry VIII's MS*, and, unusually, has passages without words. There is no proof, but I think a strong likelihood, that these were played on instruments (vocalized as well, perhaps). The 'Revels Accounts' give some relevant extra details about the pageant 'The Golldyn Arber in the Archeyerd of Plesyer', described on page 247:

> ... and without un the syds were viii mynstrells with strange instre-ments, and befoor un the steps stood dyvers persoons dysgysyd, as Master Sub Deen, Master Kornyche, Master K[r]aan and other, and un the top wer the chylldyrn of the chappell syngyng so that oon thys pagent was xxx persons, weche was marvelus wyghty to remevf and karry, as yt dyd bothe up and down the hall and turnyd round.[59]

On another occasion there were six foresters 'sitting and going' on top of the pageant:

> When the pageaunt rested before the Quene the forenamed forsters blew their hornes, then the devise or pageant opened on all sydes, and out issued the foresaied foure knyghtes.[60]

These various 'passengers' were probably not purely decorative, but made music when the pageant was in motion. Amongst the songs they could have performed are the 'forester' songs of *Henry VIII's MS*, with their erotic double-meanings. Such a professional song is 'I have bene a foster' [H62]; another, the rollicking 'I am a joly foster' [H65]. Instruments mentioned in the records are sackbuts, shawms, viols (rebecs?), trumpets, tabors and drums.[61]

In the most elaborate disguisings, then, three groups of musicians were required: the trumpets who 'blew up' when the pageant entered; the tabors and rebecs who played for the dancing; and the minstrels or singers who escorted the pageant into the presence. The music of the escort would be less ceremonial than that of the trumpets; but it must surely have been fairly robust to compete with the rumbling of heavy pageants, the squeaking of wheels, however well oiled, and the strenuous efforts of the wild men or lions or antelopes that drew them. Moreover, the moment of entry was not one for subtle musical effects of any sort – if only for the reason that it was at this juncture that the costly spectacle first appeared before the eyes it was intended to delight.

It is in this light that the 'musical' disguising of Prince Arthur's wedding celebrations must be considered. One evening in Westminster Hall:

'two merveylous mountes or mountaines right cunningly practized were brought into view. The first was coloured green and 'planted full of fresh trees' and herbs, flowers and fruits; the second was 'like' unto a Rocke scorched and brent', and metals (gold, silver, lead, copper, etc.) 'grewe and eboyled' out of it. The two mountains were linked with a massive chain of gold, and were drawn on wheels 'prively and unperceived'. 'There were sitting uppon certaine steppes and benches on the sides of the first mountaine . . . xiij fresh Lordes Knightes and men of honor most seemely and straunge disguised making great and sweet melody with instrumentes musicall and of much harmony as with Tabors and Taborens lutes harpes and Recorders.' On the other mountain were twelve ladies, 'and one in the Toppe', sitting on 'the small hilles', 'all theise fresh apparelled Ladyes and women of honor having like Instrumentes of musicke as Claricordes dusymers Claricimballs and such other; every each of them as well Lordes . . . as Ladyes . . . used and occupied and played uppon the Instrumentes all the waye comming from the lower end of Westminster Hall, till they came before the King and the Queenes Highnes and Majestie, so sweetly and with such noyse that in my mynde it was the first such pleasant myrth and property that ever was heard in England of longe season.' On arrival the lords and ladies descended and danced together in the usual way, while the two mountains were wheeled away.[62]

This event has sometimes been described in terms of a modern concert: 'at a pageant given in Westminster Hall in 1502 a ladies' orchestra of twelve performers "made music on clarycordis, dusymers, clarysymballs and such other".'[63] The lords and ladies doubtless 'used and occupied and played upon the Instrumentes'; but it seems most unlikely that the performance was artistic in effect or in intent. The whole thing was, so to speak, a theatrical stunt. This fits in well with the striving after novelty and sensation already remarked on as a feature of court-life: this disguising, like the 'strange instruments' in others, was a musical *spectacle*.[64] In it the courtly spectators were delighted by seeing their peers striking an attitude recommended by all writers on courtly love: they acted the lover-as-musician.

Nevertheless, there were occasional genuinely musical interludes during disguisings. On Twelfth Night, 1516, seven minstrels 'un the walls and towrys [of a pageant] played a melodyus song'.[65] And, at an entertainment for the French ambassadors in 1518, the pageant returned in front of the king 'and the music of lutes and other instruments played beautifully'.[66] This incidental music was clearly played for entertainment and heard for its own sake.

The greater importance of this sort of music in disguisings (as distinct from other entertainments and ceremonies) is faintly reflected in the choice of instruments and in the presentation of vocal music. The soft, 'bas', instruments, which require close attention, figure more; trumpets and drums, except for specific ceremonial purposes and dancing, less. On several occasions groups of about three or four singers performed. But it might be as well to end these comments on the court entertainments with a reminder to ourselves of the comparatively lowly status of music and musicians in them. We should not know from Edward Halle's detailed account of disguisings and masks that such a person as William Cornish existed, even though he was certainly a principal deviser, writer, actor, singer and probably composer. But we become acquainted with many of the courtiers who danced and jousted on these occasions. It is solely from the account-books that we learn, for instance, of the 'melodyus song' played on Twelfth Night, 1516, and that Cornish wrote an interlude called *Troylous and Pandour* and played a prominent part in the whole proceedings. Halle's more typical comment is: 'this nyght the Cupboard in the hall was of xii Stages all of plate of golde *and no gilt plate*'.[67]

The Gentlemen of the Chapel Royal, when they took part in court entertainments, were both actors and singers. An 'interlude' was a customary part of an evening's revels. The various forms of entertainment were constantly encroaching upon each other. The 'story of Troylous and Pandor' preceded the military disguising of Twelfth Night in 1516; and the interlude devised by Sir Harry Guilford, Master of the Revels, for Christmas, 1514, contained a 'moresque' of six persons and two ladies.[68] Nevertheless, to the entertainments already described can now be added a distinct category – the drama of the spoken word.

Court plays were, roughly speaking, of two kinds. Plays produced by the *household* required a large cast, elaborate staging, and were often, as we have seen, merely a part of a larger scheme of entertainment; plays brought in by *outside companies* of players were less occasional in their appeal and could be staged more simply. A few surviving plays seem to be of the first type; but most are of the second. This is why they are so completely different in tone from the masks and disguisings. They were not intended to mirror the courtly world; with their strong moral and didactic strain they spoke to every Christian soul. After the courtly idealisms of 'the Golldyn Arber in the Archeyerd of Plesyer' even the crudity of *Thersites* is refreshing.

Popular drama, like popular music, found its way into court circles. So, to discuss music in court plays is, in fact, to discuss music in the early Tudor drama as a whole. Perhaps the most striking single feature of the use of music in the interludes is the way it is made to point a moral lesson.[69] This should not be a surprise. A didactic purpose openly avowed, though in an allegorical dress, is of the interludes' very essence.* Their subject is Everyman's salvation. Music and dancing are, as a matter of course, associated with the sinful part of man, or at least with the dangerous occasions of sin. In *The Four Elements*, for example, the musical references only begin with the entry of Sensual Appetite, who comes in crying:

> Make room, sirs, and let us be merry,
> With huffa gallant sing, tirl on the berry,
> And let the wide world wind!
> Sing, frisky jolly, with hey troly lolly.[70]

* I follow Dr T. W. Craik, *The Tudor Interlude*, p. 1, in his wide definition of the term 'interlude', accepting his emphasis on the didactic and allegorical qualities.

Music in Ceremonies, Entertainments and Plays

Many of the interludes portray the struggle between heaven and hell for the soul of man, usually a young man. *Lusty Juventus, Nice Wanton, Youth,* are all plays which deal with his temptation; and in all of them the musical characters have names like Pride, Riot, Hypocrisy, Fellowship and Abhominable Living.

Sex is the passion particularly represented by music. Ralph Roister Doister is addicted to love-melancholy:

> With every woman is he in some loves pang,
> Then up to our lute at midnight, twangledome twang,
> Then twang with our sonets, and twang with our dumps,
> And heyhough from our heart, as heavie as lead lumpes.[71]

In *Calisto and Meliboea* the young and immoral knight is addicted to music, and the bawd, Celestina, recommends it with joust and tourney as part of the 'loves' business'.[72] On the lowest level music is the highway to the bawdy-house. In Skelton's *Magnificence,* Folly says:

> So in their ear I sing them a song
> And make them so long to muse
> That some of them runneth straight to the stews.[73]

The connection between music and sex is an old one. The medieval romances often celebrate it; the moralists as often denounce it.

Even without this particular connotation music is suspect, for it is part of the vicious round of pleasure to which the rich and well-born were inevitably exposed. When the foolish Gentlewoman of Heywood's *The Weather* was asked by Mery Reporte how she spent the night, she replied, 'in daunsynge and syngynge'.

> *Mery Reporte*: Why, swete herte, by your false fayth, can ye syng?
> *Gentlewoman*: Nay, nay but I love yt above all thynge ...
> Ones in a nyght I longe for such a fyt
> For longe tyme have I ben brought up in yt.[74]

However, in at least one play, Redford's *Wyt and Science*, an attempt is made to make pastime legitimate. Honest Recreation and Idleness debate the matter:

> *Idleness*: Under the name of Honest Recreacion,
> She, lo! bryngth in her abhominacion!
> Mark her dawnsyng, her maskyng, and mummyng –

253

Where more concupyscence then ther cummyng? . . .
As for her syngyng, pypyng and fydlyng,
What unthryftynes therin is twydlyng!

Honest Recreacion: . . . Honest Recreacion is present never
But where honest pastymes be well usyd ever.
But in-deede Idlenes, she is cawse
Of all such abuses . . .[75]

The problem of 'honest mirth' – 'honest music' – was a perennial one, and the orthodox would only allow music a place as refreshment after toil.

A propensity towards music, as the general tenor of the interludes must show, was thought, if not in itself sinful, at least to indicate a weakness, an irresolution of character, which might lead its possessor into concupiscence and 'abhomination'. Music was preponderantly of the devil's party.

There are, naturally, a number of occasions, mostly religious, when music can appear in a more favourable light. In the Miracle Plays music traditionally symbolized God's order, heaven, the forces of right.[76] It is with similar effect that in Bale's *God's Promises*, 1538, each of the seven acts ends with one of the pre-Christmas antiphons; the directions are of this kind:

> then with sonorous voice, on bended knees, he begins the antiphon *O sapientia*, which the chorus should take up, accompanied by the organs . . . alternatively he can sing the same melody and in the same manner but with English words.

By 'organs' is suggested something more like today's piano-accordion than a church-organ. There is no evidence that the play was acted in church. Dr Craik suggests that 'chorus' simply means the rest of the cast.[77] Medwall's *Nature* provides another example of religious music; it is here again used to conclude the play: 'Let us by one accord togeder syng and pray . . .'[78]

Granted that music was more often used to symbolize evil impulses than good, still the element of entertainment is never entirely absent. The musicianship of Abhominable Living is not merely reprehensible, it is one of the most amusing features of the play, *Lusty Juventus*. There are many musical episodes, moreover, whose value as entertainment is of paramount importance. Exits and entrances, in particular, seemed favourable opportunities for music, though here the ceremonial element is not altogether lacking; at an entertainment in May 1527:

> first of all there entered the hall eight singers singing certain English songs; in their centre was a very handsome youth alone, clad in sky-blue taffety; . . . having presented themselves before the king, the singers then withdrew in the same order.

These singers were introducing a courtly kind of play – a debate (many interludes were little more) between Cupid and Plutus. This 'debate' was, in fact, the story of the 'disguising' which followed. It was resolved by a tourney and followed by a formal dance.[79] This was a musical entrance; *exeunt cantando* (they go out singing) was a favourite device also.

Sometimes songs are introduced during the action of the play merely to beguile the time and, presumably, to please the audience. In *Roister Doister*, Tibet Talk-apace, Madge Mumblecrust and another maid sing over their needlework.[80] And in *Wyt and Science*, Fame, Favor, Ryches and Woorshyp baldly say:

> Then let us not stay here muet and mum
> But tast we thes instrumentes tyll she cum.

They sing 'Excedynge mesure' and play their viols at the same time – not an easy feat.[81]

The question whether music was introduced to make a dramatic point, or in the summary fashion just described, is interesting and important. But what kind of music was it, and how did it differ from that heard at ceremonies and on more formal occasions? This musical repertory had, above all, a strong popular flavour. Admittedly one cannot build much on the numerous characters who sing 'hey trolly lolly', 'derry derry', and similar catch-phrases. But in two plays fools sing a miscellany of popular nonsense obviously quoting popular songs (probably with bits of tunes): 'Jack boy, is thy bow i-broke?', 'the wriguldy wrag', and so on.[82] In *King Johan* Dissimulacyon sings 'Wassayle, wassayle out of the mylke payle', and in *Roister Doister* actors sing and play 'I mun be maried a Sunday'.[83] Examples are numerous. These excerpts from the popular repertory are sung by one singer and are practically all unaccompanied; the songs would elicit a quick and easy response from the courtly audience, for they could not by any stretch of the imagination be thought 'difficult' music.

This impression is on the whole reinforced by what is known of the general choice of singers and instruments. Predominantly the actors *were* singers. They could not afford, for one thing, to share their profits with regularly retained instrumental musicians. As singers they performed often in groups of three or four. It is doubtful whether a professional troupe in the early sixteenth century numbered many more. Several plays (*King Johan, Mankind, Nice Wanton* amongst others) include songs in dialogue. There are also songs for chorus and solo and some more complicated still.[84] Practically none of the music survives; it is the context or stage-direction that tells us that it was intended. The same applies to the use of instruments. They are chiefly mentioned and played in connection with dancing. Most dances demanded wind-instruments, though sometimes the characters danced to their own singing. In *The Four Elements* Sensual Appetite 'singeth this song and danceth withal, and evermore maketh countenance according to the matter; and all the others answer likewise'. The song begins 'Dance we, prance we'.[85] A dance to an instrument is required in the 'popular morality', *Mankind*:

> Ande how mynstrellys! pley the comyn trace!
> Ley on with thi ballys tyll his bely brest.

Probably the 'ballys' are the knobs on the end of their drumsticks and the 'bely' belongs to a drum.[86] Pipe and tabor were the standard accompaniment for popular dancing; both instruments could be played together. Medwall's *Fulgens and Lucres*, on the other hand, was designed to use the musical resources of a great household. Instruments are called out for a 'bace-daunce after the gyse of spayne'. But one of the minstrels is out of action:

> Mary, as for one of them his lippe is sore,
> I trow he may not pype, he is so syke.
> Spele up tamboryne, ik bide owe frelike.

(Presumably the tabor-player was Flemish.)[87]

In the interludes I have examined, neither lute, harp nor gittern was, for certain, played on the stage. This may be an accident. In *Calisto and Meliboea*, Calisto calls for his lute:

> Give me my lute, and thou shalt see
> How I shall sing mine unhappiness.

But he does not perform. The lute is out of tune – which gives him a happy opening for philosophical reflection.[88] The gittern is mentioned in

Roister Doister as a 'thrumpledum, thrumpledum thrum'. He also has at home a 'toodleloodle poope', a recorder.[89] Neither are played on. In sum, instrumental music was subordinate to vocal music in the drama, though this varies both with the type of play and the date. There were no elaborate mixed consorts such as often garnished the rich and fanciful court disguisings. The chief instrument was the human voice.

Even two human voices, we know from the song-books, can be combined in elaborate musical patterns. What, then, were the songs in plays like? William Chappell, writing of part-singing 'in the moralities and earliest plays', stated that 'it was generally in canon'. He quoted in support of his statement these two phrases – 'let every man | *Follow after in order* as well as he can', and 'whoso that list *sing after me*'.[90] Other phrases, not quoted by him, are less convincing: 'Begyne thyself then, and we shall lepe in amonge'; 'Shall I begin?' | 'Yes, but take not too high.' It is obvious that someone must lead – choose the song, set the pitch, give the time. In *Youth*, the 'rector of the choir' is told to start first; the others will pick it up as best they can:

> *Pride:* Riot, we tarry very long.
> *Riot:* We will go even now with a lusty song.
> *Pride:* In faith, I will be rector of the choir.
> *Youth:* Go to it then hardily, and let us be agate.

Later in the play Riot talks again about going hence 'with a merry song'; Pride replies, perhaps with a hint of reproof: 'Let us begin all at once.'[91] Phrases like 'sing after me' may mean no more than 'sing in accord with me'. The other singers, if they are not in unison, may be descanting on the melody. There is a definite hint of this in *Hickscorner*: 'now Hey trolly lolly! Let us se who can descaunt on this same.'[92] A curious passage in the *Foure PP* also seems to refer to improvised singing:

> *Potycary:* I pray you, tell me, can you synge?
> *Pedler:* Syr, I have some syght in syngynge.
> *Potycary:* But is your brest anythynge swete?
> *Pedler:* What-ever my breste be, my voyce is mete.
> *Potycary:* That answer sheweth you a ryght syngynge man.[93]

For more than a century in England there had been a system of improvised singing to plain-song melodies in parallel thirds and sixths. 'Syght' is a technical term referring to this. Even the written art-music of the period had not broken free from this tradition. How natural, then, to suppose that some such method of improvisation held its ground in popular practice. Rounds and catches cannot be excluded altogether; but there are insufficient grounds for thinking that they were general. Other part-songs may have been learnt by heart from music-books; a few may even have been read from books on the stage, though I have found no evidence of this. When 'Welth' and 'Helth' open the interlude which bears their names, 'syngyng together a balet of two partes', we are not told that they were *reading* it, and it seems most unlikely that they were.[94]

The qualities we might expect in the songs, from the evidence of their popular flavour and their informal presentation, are brevity, simplicity and effectiveness; there is not much room in the drama for 'peevish, prick-eared song'.[95] The one surviving song with music, 'Tyme to pas with goodly sport' [Song 326], from *The Four Elements*, has the required characteristics. It is a three-part song, not merely after the style of the simpler chordal pieces of *Henry VIII's MS*, but actually adapted from one [H9]. It was clearly sung unaccompanied, for after it, Ignorance says:

> I can you thank; that is done well.
> It is a pity ye had not a minstrel
> For to augment your solace.[96]

A few notes of music are given in the text of Bale's *King Johan*: 'Pepe, I see ye! I am glad I have spyed ye' [Song 259]. It could be a fragment of a popular song.

It may be well to end with a warning against thinking that all Tudor interludes abounded in music, for they did not. If the surviving texts are indicative, Heywood's *Johan Johan* [1529?] and *The Pardoner and the Friar* [1529?], for example, seem to require no music; several plays had but one song. It may be that such plays were always given as part of a larger entertainment, or that music was inserted to taste, or, quite likely, that music was not regarded as part of a good moral disputation – many interludes are versified arguments. However, it must be admitted that moral problems of sin, temptation and honest mirth were well served by music in the interludes. Music owes its status to its dramatic usefulness as well as to its diverting qualities.

The music of ceremonies and entertainments was primarily, it is obvious, the hired music of professional musicians, whose livelihood it was to beautify courtly life and to bring honour to their employers.[97] The music of plays at court was slightly different; it was the province of semi-professionals, whose chief occupation was acting. Their inferior skill is shown in the prominence of vocal music, especially songs of a popular kind. A striking fact is that none of these occasions of music (except perhaps some 'royal entries') appears to leave room for music-making by amateurs. The next chapter tries to throw some light on the perplexing subject of amateur music in the court circle.

NOTES TO CHAPTER II

1. *L&P*, vi, no. 563 (31 May 1533): Coronation of Anne Boleyn.
2. Huizinga, 224.
3. Robbins, 'Religious Lyrics', i. 18; and *Index MEV*, p. xi.
4. See Thomas Elmham's account of the Battle of Agincourt in *Vita et Gesta Henrici Quinti*, ed. Hearne (1727). *L&P*, i, pt 2, no. 2173: 'For their field music they have a shawm, and a bagpiper [sack-pfeiffer], and certain of them have a trumpet.'
5. *L&P*, iii, pt 1, no. 869 (11 June 1520).
6. Halle (ed. Whibley), i. 199.
7. Leland, iv. 267.
8. See summary, *L&P*, ii, pt 2, pp. 1441–80; iii, pt 2, pp. 1533– (especially, May–July 1511, and April–May 1512).
9. Taverner, Tye, Shepherd: see Reese, *MR*, 778–.
10. See p. 241 below.
11. *L&P: Venice*, iii, no. 50, p. 29 (my italics).
12. Chambers, *Medieval Stage*, ii. 168. The English 'royal entry' is exhaustively treated in Withington, i, ch. 3, 'The Royal Entry, 1298–1558'. Kernodle, *From Art to Theatre* (1944), shows the international character of these shows and relates them to the history of art and of stage-design. More recently, Glynne Wickham, *Early English Stages*, vol. i (1959), has emphasized the importance in the English dramatic tradition of 'Pageant Theatres of the Streets'; and Hugh Baillie, 'London Churches', 175–, describes the musical contributions of the parish clerks.
13. Withington, i. 164. See *Index MEV* 2834.
14. From full account in *Antiquarian Repertory*, ii. 248–. See also Withington, i. 166.

15. *Coventry Leet Book*, ed. Mary D. Harris, EETS (1907), 390–. See also Withington, i. 153.

16. Halle (ed. Whibley), i. 151.

17. Halle (ed. Whibley), i. 151, and 'Revels Accounts' (see Reference List) under date, 19–20 May 1516.

18. Halle (ed. Whibley), i. 8. For a French example, see *L&P: Venice*, ii, no. 1134 (Jan. 1519). See, in general, W. E. Mead, *The English Medieval Feast* (1931), though the author betrays some lack of understanding in dismissing the ceremonies as 'juvenile', and his comments on the music are inadequate.

19. Rawdon Brown, ii. 102, translating an account by Sagudino, the Venetian secretary.

20. I have to thank John Page-Phillips for giving me a rubbing of this brass.

21. Dent, 'Social Aspects', 203.

22. Halle (ed. Whibley), i. 75. Further details from a German source in *L&P*, i, pt 2, no. 2173.

23. *L&P: Venice*, ii, no. 445 (12 July 1514): reception of papal envoy, Leonardo Spinelli.

24. *L&P: Milan*, no. 804 (10 May).

25. Sir Henry Wyatt: *L&P*, iii, pt 1, no. 804. *Italian Relation*, 39. Halle (ed. Ellis, 161) refers to an occasion *temp.* Henry VI.

26. Bacon's *Essays*, 'Of Masques and Triumphs'.

27. 'Noise' could mean a band of musicians, at least after 1558 (*v.* OED). The water-pageant: see Withington, i. 181, and Halle (ed. Whibley), ii. 230.

28. 'Circute enumerable': *Antiquarian Repertory*, ii. 248–. Apollo and the Muses: Withington, i. 182, note 5 (it is interesting to compare this 'mervelous connying pagyaunt made by the marchaunts of the Stylliard' with Holbein's design for the decoration of the Steelyard also produced in 1533, reproduced in H. Reinhardt's *Holbein*, trs. Montagu-Pollock (1938), p. 158, and see p. 27).

29. Collier, i. 65, note 1.

30. *L&P*, i, pt 1, nos 700, 1159, etc. *L&P: Venice*, iii, no. 83 (June 1520).

31. Chambers, *Medieval Stage*, ii. 168; Withington, i. 132–.

32. Withington, i. 184, note 3.

33. Chambers, *Medieval Stage*, ii. 168.

34. *Ordinances*, 121–.

35. This fifteenth-century account in Stow's handwriting is printed in *Three XV-Century Chronicles*, ed. J. Gairdner, Camden Soc. (1880), 106–.

36. The quotations are from note 36a (i).

36a. (i) Halle (ed. Whibley), i. 146–7; (ii) Rawdon Brown, i. 80, from *Sanuto*, xx, f.243; (iii) 'Revels Accounts' (see Reference List) for May 1515.

37. For popular May-games, see Chambers, *Medieval Stage*, i, ch. 8.

38. Leland, *Collectanea*, iv. 318. Cf. Stow, *Annals* (1592), 1044, choristers playing and singing, 1553; and *Dunbar* (ed. Mackenzie), 138, twenty-four maidens playing and singing.

39. Huizinga, 30.

40. Halle (ed. Whibley), i. 23–.

41. Cavendish, *Wolsey*, 73. The best example of an 'enterlude' prepared for a courtly feast is Medwall's *Fulgens and Lucres* (see Baskervill in *Modern Philology*, xxiv (1926), 438).

42. *Excerpta Historica*, 'Privy Purse Expenses of Henry VII', under dates 5 Aug. 1943 and 7 Jan. 1497. (In the first of the two entries she is called a 'young damoysell'.) The first payment is for £30 (more like £900 in modern money). A morris dance in the same accounts was worth £1. 13s. 4d. to £2. For Mark Smeton, supposedly one of Anne Boleyn's lovers, see *Chronicle of King Henry VIII of England*, trs. by M. A. S. Hume from Spanish of Marqués de Molins (1889), 55–; and the Appendix to *Wriothesley's Chronicle*, ed. W. D. Hamilton, Camden Soc. (1875).

43. Leland, *Collectanea*, iv. 297; the king was James IV of Scotland.

44. *L&P: Milan*, no. 654 (13 Sept. 1513). See also *L&P: Venice*, ii, no. 505 (30 Oct. 1514): betrothal of Princess Mary to the King of France.

45. *L&P: Milan*, no. 657 (18 Sept. 1513). See also, on Henry's dancing, jousting and playing instruments, no. 669 (11 Oct.).

46. *Spanish Chronicle*, 55 (see note 42 above).

47. Leland, iv. 283–4; Princess Margaret's journey to Scotland to marry James IV.

48. *My Lady Wynkfyld's rownde* (BM Roy. MSS, App. 58, f.54v), transcription pr. by F. Dawes, *Ten Pieces by Hugh Aston and others* (1951), 12–. For basse-danse, see Bukofzer, *Studies*, 190– (with bibliography), and *Mélanges Ernest Closson* (Paris, 1948).

49. Keyboard pieces based on dump and hornpipe are printed, from BM

Roy. MSS, App. 58, by F. Dawes. Concerning the dump, see Ward's article, ' "Dolfull Domps" '. M. Dolmetsch, *Dances of England and France* (1949), contains useful practical information for dancers but has been criticized on grounds of scholarship.

50. 'Dancing in their doublets': *L&P: Venice*, ii, no. 505 (30 Oct. 1514); the instruments are named in Italian as *piva, violetta, un certo pifaretto, cithara*. 'Dancing commenced': *L&P: Venice*, iii, no. 50, p. 23, from *Sanuto*, v. xxix, pp. 210–39. *Northumberland HHB*, 42, and see also Droz and Thibault, *Poètes et Musiciens du XVe Siècle* (Paris, 1924), illustration, 49. Out-of-doors music: see R. T. Dart, *The Interpretation of Music* (1954), 153, 157. The 'Italian fashion': *L&P: Venice*, iii, no. 50, p. 23. Wolsey: *L&P: Venice*, iv, no. 4 (4 Jan. 1527).

51. The terms are discussed by Chambers, i. 400; Welsford, 41; Withington, i. 105; Wickham, 191.

51a. Cavendish, 25–.

52. Halle (ed. Whibley), i. 170–1.

53. Cavendish, 25–. Halle (ed. Whibley), i. 16. Galpin, 155, discusses their use in military music. Reyher, 428 (and note 4), their later use in entertainment.

54. Welsford, 130–, summarizes the controversy.

55. Halle (ed. Whibley), i. 26.

56. J. Marix, *Histoire de la Musique et des Musiciens de la Cour de Bourgogne, 1420–67* (Strasbourg, 1939), ch. 3, describes music in Burgundian court entertainments. See also Huizinga, chs 5 and 9.

57. Epiphany, 1517: see Halle (ed. Whibley), i. 153; and 'Revels Accounts', under date.

58. Reyher, 500–, prints the contemporary account from BM Harl. MS 69.

59. 'Revels Accounts', under date 13 Feb. 1511.

60. Halle (ed. Whibley), i. 23.

61. The 'Revels Accounts' include mention of the following instruments or players: 13 Feb. 1511 – 8 minstrels with 'strange' instruments; 6 Jan. 1513 – 6 minstrels, 4 tambourines (i.e. tabors) and rebecs 'for the dance'; 25 Dec. 1514 – 4 minstrels, 4 drumslades; 6 Jan. 1515 – 6 or 7 minstrels 'with strange sounds, as sag[ebutts], shawms, viols &c', and 4 drumslades; 3 Feb. 1515 – 9 drumslades, and trumpeters; 6 Jan. 1516 – 7 minstrels who played 'a melodyus song' and 3 'tamboryns' or 'taborets'; 20 May 1516 – 14 trumpeters;

19 Feb. 1520 – drumslades and minstrels; 4 Mar. 1522 – 'vials and other instruments'. (The recurrence of the epithet 'strange' when the instruments mentioned are all, except perhaps the viol, perfectly familiar, leads one to suspect that they were 'strangely' decorated or 'garnished'.)

62. Reyher, 500–.

63. Galpin, 64.

64. Musical stunts of a different kind are recorded on the Continent: e.g. the famous musicians-in-a-pie, and animals playing instruments (Huizinga, 232). On a later occasion (1575) Queen Elizabeth was entertained by 'a melodious noiz' proceeding from six musicians concealed within a dolphin's belly (John Nichols, *Progresses* (1823), i. 457–8).

65. 'Revels Accounts', under date 6 Jan. 1516; Halle (ed. Whibley), i. 149.

66. *L&P: Venice*, ii, no. 1088 (9 Oct. 1518); the musicians were hidden on the pageant, probably inside the cave.

67. Halle (ed. Whibley), i. 149 (my italics). And see note 97.

68. *L&P*, i, pt 2, no. 2562 (6 Jan. 1514); Collier's account (*Annals*, i. 69) from an untraceable 'contemporaneous paper' may be a forgery.

69. I thank Dr Craik for some references in this section and for allowing me to use his dating of the plays. For other definitions of 'interlude' see Chambers, ii. 183; Rossiter, 104; Gayley, p. lvi.

70. Hazlitt's Dodsley, i. 20; composed 1517? (Craik, 140).

71. Gayley, 131; composed 1553? (Craik, 140).

72. Hazlitt's Dodsley, i. 74: composed 1527? (Craik, 140).

73. Dyce, i. 265: 1516? (Craik, 140).

74. Brandl, 242–: 1527? (Craik, 140).

75. Manly, i. 433; composed 1539? (Craik, 140).

76. This point is further discussed in my paper, 'Music in Medieval Drama'.

77. Hazlitt's Dodsley, i. 292: *tunc sonora voce, provolutis genibus, antiphonam incipit* O sapientia *quam prosequetur chorus cum organis . . . vel sub eodem tono poterit sic anglice cantare.*

78. Brandl, 158: composed 1495? (Craik, 140).

79. *Sanuto*, xlv, col. 265–.

80. Gayley, i. 119–. Some of their songs are discussed by Baskervill (see his index).

81. Adams, 335.

Music at Court

82. Ignorance in *The Four Elements* (Hazlitt's Dodsley, i. 49); Moros in
    L. Wager's *The Longer thou livest* [1564?] (Tudor Facsimile Texts,
    1910).
83. 'Wassayle': Manly, i. 597; composed 1535? (Craik, 140). 'I mun':
    Gayley, 148.
84. See further, Baskervill, 80.
85. Hazlitt's Dodsley, i. 47.
86. ed. F. J. Furnivall and A. W. Pollard, *Macro Plays*, 4.
87. ed. F. S. Boas and A. W. Reed (1926), pt ii, line 387.
88. Hazlitt's Dodsley, i. 57.
89. Gayley, 131.
90. Chappell (1893), i. 66, from *New Custome* (1570?) and from Hey-
    wood's *The Four PP* (1529?).
91. Hazlitt's Dodsley, ii. 24, 28; composed 1520? (Craik, 140).
92. Manly, i. 409; composed 1513? (Craik, 140); and see Baskervill, 84,
    quoting from *Tom Tyler* (1560?).
93. Manly, i. 493; composed 1529? (Craik, 140).
94. *Wealth and Health* (1554?), quoted Baskervill, 79.
95. The passage from *The Four Elements* (Hazlitt's Dodsley, i. 48–) is
    quoted and discussed in Baskervill, 29, and in Pattison, 162.
96. See note 92; the song is pr. in Reese, *MR*, 878.
97. I regret that Sidney Anglo's article, 'William Cornish in a Play,
    Pageants, Prison and Politics', *RES*, n.s. x (1959), 347, appeared
    too late for me to make use of it. It considerably amplifies our know-
    ledge of Cornish's early life at court and provides some fascinating
    new detail about court entertainments (see, especially, 'Cornish as
    St. George: Epiphany 1494").

CHAPTER 12

Domestic and Amateur Music

Music in the domestic life of the English people has often been a favourite subject for imaginative riot:

... our greatest national secular music is concerted music for voices or instruments that was to be performed, in the homes of an acutely musical people, for its own sake: music made by the King's Musicians was a natural part of the domestic life of the people.[1]

This writer envisages in the early Tudor period, as at other times, a musical culture at once widespread and deep-rooted – deep-rooted, that is, in the actual practice of music by amateurs and professionals of all classes. This is not the place, clearly, to question all the implications of this widely shared belief. We are concerned here only with the *courtly* practice of private music.

If one fact has emerged from the last chapter, it is, I hope, that on most of the occasions when it appeared at court, music was subordinate to something else – at banquets to the 'honourable service'; in disguisings to the gorgeous pageants; during the dance to the courtly dancers. Rarely, unless in the drama, was music performed for its own sake. I want now to consider what may be called the *musical* occasions of music. On these occasions people played and sang, not to draw attention to a moment or event of dignity, but because they wanted to play or others wanted to hear them.

I

The occasions of 'private music' were not all domestic in the strict sense of the word; nor were the performers always amateurs. Musical entertainment was often a professional business, and the virtuoso player was much in demand. When Fra Dionisius Memo, organist of St Mark's, Venice, arrived at court in 1516, bringing his own instrument, he was presented first to Wolsey:

> His lordship chose to hear him in the presence of many lords and virtuosi, who were as pleased as possible with him. . . .

He was then presented to the king:

> He played not merely to the satisfaction but to the incredible admiration and pleasure of everybody, and especially of his Majesty, who is extremely skilled in music . . . said Majesty has included him among his instrumental musicians, nay, has appointed him their chief, and says he will write to Rome to have him unfrocked out of his monastic weeds . . . and that he will make him his chaplain.[2]

It was Memo, now in high favour, who, in July 1517, gave a long recital (there is no more appropriate word) before a distinguished visitor.

> After dinner, his Majesty took this ambassador into the Queen's chamber . . . giving him amusements of every description, the chief of which . . . was the instrumental music of the reverend Master Dionysius Memo, his chaplain, which lasted during four consecutive hours.[3]

Another well-known foreign musician, Benedictus de Opitiis, 'player at organs', was appointed in March 1516 'to waite opon the king in his chambre', at 33s. 4d. a month. This Benedictus was previously organist at Antwerp. His motet, *Sub tuum presidium*, published there in 1515, is also found among the Royal MSS of the British Museum.[4] Not all foreign virtuosi were well received. One Zuan da Leze, a harpsichordist, was so disappointed with his reception that he hanged himself.[5]

The instruments most in demand for these formal and semi-formal occasions were the louder keyboard instruments, organ, harpsichord and virginals. But softer instruments, such as the lute, could be played in public. One evening in May 1517 the king made the court listen

> to a lad who played upon the lute, better than ever was heard, to the amazement of his Majesty, who never wearies of him, and since the coming of this lad, Zuan Piero is not in such favour as before.[6]

(The incident has a pleasant sequel. Dionisius Memo, it is related, had especially composed a part-song for his countryman, Zuan Piero, to *play* to the king. The king would be provided with the significant words: *Memor esto verbi tui Servo tuo perpetuo In quo mihi spem dedisti.*)[6a] In our modern nomenclature 'clavichord' refers to the softest of all keyboard instruments, but in the early sixteenth century it seems to stand for any keyboard instrument. 'The new player upon the clavicords', with whom, according to Pace, the king was having 'good pastime', may well have been a harpsichordist.[7]

The players so far mentioned were primarily soloists. Concerted music was played, of course, by professionals on many occasions as background music (during banquets, for example). It is less certain whether an instrumental consort was a common feature of 'concert-music'. Sagudino records that on a semi-formal occasion during the Maying of 1515, 'Peter the Luter' played a few items with him in the presence of 'the prelates and chief nobles'; the combination was lute and harpsichord. Afterwards two English professionals played an organ-duet,

> ... but very ill forsooth: they kept bad time, and their touch was feeble, neither was their execution good, so that my [Sagudino's] performance was deemed not much worse than theirs.[8]

There may have been many more such extempore concerts, in which the centre of interest was the display of virtuosity by two or three soloists in consort.

It is a curious feature of this court, where virtuosity of every kind was admired and rewarded, that there is no mention in the records for the early years of any distinguished solo-*singer* or performance. There are a few payments to singers in Henry VII's Household Book, such as 'to the women that songe before the King and the Quene . . . 6s 8d'.[9] But these, like the fiddlers from the same accounts, may have been itinerant minstrels, if not actual beggars. John Heywood is the first musician of the household (as distinct from the chapel) to whom the title 'singer' is given (1520).[10] The formation by the 1540's of a small troupe of 'gentlemen singers' or 'singers of the chamber' may perhaps point to a gradually increasing interest in solo-singing.[11] The secular needs of the court could always have been met, admittedly, by the Gentlemen of the Chapel Royal who must have sung solos in various pageants; the curious fact remains that not one of them, so far as can be seen, established a reputation by singing. Not only was there no Dowland attached to the court, there was no John Gostling in its chapel.[12]

I have stressed the virtuoso aspect of private music by professionals, because it is typical of the court. The royal account-books are full of 'sensations' of every kind – there are rewards to rope-dancers, bear-wards, donors of leopards, lions, etc. Among the expenses of the Princess Mary's household for Christmas, 1521–2, is a curious entry: 'paid to a man of Windsor, for killing of a calf before my Lady's grace behind a cloth'.[13] Such items recall the search for 'strangeness' and novelty, already noticed as a feature of disguisings and royal entries. Would musical activities, then, be free from a similar sense of strain? Besides the 'sensation' of admiring the brilliant performer, the attitude to foreign musicians and to child-musicians is worth noting. Whether or not it was due to their superior merit, a whole host of foreign instrumentalists were in the king's employ:

> Minstrels and singers be in the court likewise.
> And that of the best and of the French gise.[14]

Doubtless, English musicians were admired on the Continent for the same reasons. Richard Cromwell, in Rome with an embassy, arranged to have three-man songs sung to the Pope, presumably hoping that the novelty would please him.[15] The glamour of strangeness attached to foreign soloists then as always. As for children, besides the lad who amazed Henry VIII on the lute, there was a 'childe that playeth on the records', and at the Scottish court a 'chield [that] playit on the monocordis'.[16] These remarks are not made in a spirit of mere scepticism; there are good reasons for questioning the quality of the listening even on these 'musical' occasions. This is not to deny true musicianship amongst listeners, but merely to suppose it not universal.

True musicianship is better shown in practical music-making, and the rest of this chapter will be devoted to answering the following questions about it: On what private occasions was music performed by amateurs at court? What kind of music was it? And how many amateurs were able to sing, read music, play or compose?

II

Ceremonial and formal occasions may be excluded absolutely from the occasions of amateur music-making; the nobility never performed during banquets, tourneys or the like. Perhaps the most formal occasions of amateur music were those which demanded the civility of personal attendance and conversation. During the progress of Princess Margaret to Scotland (1503) she was visited by her future husband, James IV. On one visit, after a basse-danse and a round, a refreshment of wine and bread was brought in:

> Incountynent the Kynge begonne before hyr to play of the clarycordes, and after of the lute, wiche pleasyd hyr varey much, and she had great plaisur to here hym. | Apon the said clarycorde Sir Edward Stannely playd a ballade and sange therewith, wiche the Kynge commended right muche. And incountynent hee called a gentylman of hys that colde synge well, and mayd them synge togeder, the wiche accorded varey well. | Afterward the said Sir Edward Stannely and two of hys servaunts sange a ballade or two, wherof the Kynge gave hym good thaunke.[17]

On another day they

> drew them asyd for to commune, and after she playd upon the clari-cordys, and after of the lute, hee beinge apon his kne allwayes barr-heded.[18]

It is easy to underestimate the formality of these occasions. The chivalric nature of the meeting, the presence of many lords and ladies, and the formal dancing, all suggest that although the company was select the occasion could not be described as intimate. The music of James and Margaret, at least, is not to be looked upon as public performance; it was rather a form of good manners, a way of 'communing' together. Another instance, perhaps, of musical 'conversation' was the visit of the Venetian ambassadors to Richmond in May 1517, when 'in the evening they enjoyed hearing the king play and sing'.[19] If such an occasion can be called 'informal', it is perhaps informal in the calculated way that characterized the 'friendly' meeting of the Field of the Cloth of Gold.

On the whole, the relationship of performer and audience was reserved for professionals; but there seem to have been exceptions made for amateurs of outstanding ability. Sagudino, the Venetian ambassador's secretary, was asked to play on an occasion already mentioned, in May 1515:

> and I did so for a long while, both on the harpsichord and organs and really bore myself bravely, and was listened to with great attention.[20]

It is perhaps significant that this episode and those of Princess Margaret's royal progress should have found their way into the records. They had some social meaning. The completely informal 'secret recreation and pastime in chambers with company' which must have constituted the greater part of amateur music-making were passed over without comment.

III

Any account of amateur music in this period must be circumstantial, since so few notices of it survive. The chroniclers are busy with the public acts and shows, private letters are mostly concerned with practical matters, and diarists in the Pepysian manner do not exist. Household orders and other writings which indicate the place of music in courtly education have, therefore, a positive if limited value. Although they cannot tell us what was done, at least they reveal, like a school prospectus, what might be thought desirable.

The usual way a child of rank, a 'bele babee', received his education was not in grammar-school and University but in the household of some lord, temporal or spiritual. The Earl of Northumberland boarded henchmen and 'young gentlemen'; Cardinal Morton's household included the young Thomas More; and so on.[21] The henchmen were courtly 'midshipmen'. A certain number of young nobles were accepted in the royal household itself, which no doubt was taken as a pattern in this as in so many other things. There is abundant evidence that members of the royal family were taught music, from Prince Arthur in 1494, to the illegitimate Duke of Richmond in 1531.[22] This would be a good preliminary reason for thinking that all the henchmen learnt it too.

Music had an undisputed, though lowly, place in courtly and chivalric theory. In Dr Pattison's phrase, it was part of 'the technique of courtly love'.[23] Music and poetry are useful to the courtly lover, firstly, as a means of graceful self-display. *The Romaunt of the Rose* advises as follows:

> And if thy voice be faire and cler,
> Thou shalt maken no gret daunger
> Whanne to singe they goodly preye;
> It is thy worship for t'obeye.
> Also to you it longith ay
> To harpe and gitterne, daunce and play;
> For if he can wel foote and daunce,
> It may him greetly do avaunce.
> Among eke, for thy lady sake,
> Songes and complayntes that thou make,
> For that wol meven in hir herte,
> Whanne they reden of thy smerte.[24]

Domestic and Amateur Music

The courtly context of this is illuminating; Love has just advised the Lover about dress, manners and personal hygiene:

> Mayntene thysilf aftir thi rent,
> Of robe and eke of garnement
>
> . . . . . .
>
> Have hat of floures as fresh as May
> Chapelett of roses of Whitsonday . . .
> [keep your nails clean and don't use cosmetics, &c.]
> For men shulde, wheresoevere they be,
> Do thing that hem sittyng is,
> For therof cometh good loos and pris.
> [persevere in horsemanship & jousting until you win a
>   reputation].[25]

'Good loos and pris' are the end and aim of all the lover's courtly exercises; and music, along with sartorial elegance, good horsemanship and a pleasant manner, is one of the ways of attaining them.

The second use of music to the courtly lover is as an emotional stimulus. He is advised, like Shakespeare's Cloten, to ply his lady with music and poetry, 'for that wol meve hem in hir herte'. The erotic value of music is recognized in many medieval romances. Conrad, hero of *Guillaume de Dole*, experiences the emotional quickening of music and poetry, as well as of Nature's delights; and in the *Chatelain de Coucy* the courtly fêtes of dance and song create an atmosphere favourable to the hero's suit.[26] Music is part and parcel from the very beginning of the 'refined eroticism' which is the central motif of courtly love. In the so-called Courts of Love it was much in evidence.[27]

The sixteenth-century idea of a courtier – or rather the confused and contradictory bundle of ideas – is directly descended from this medieval idea of a perfect knight. The thirst for honour and glory which distinguishes the courtier is essentially the same as knightly striving after 'a sovereyn prys'; and conscious emulation of an ideal antiquity lies at the root of both systems. Caesar, the successful general, stood together with Lancelot for knighthood; the 'noblest and chiefest oratours' of Cicero's day helped form a pattern for the sixteenth-century courtier.[28] The position of music is not much changed. Castiglione, early in the sixteenth century, describes musical ability as a grace of the courtier's person, like dancing and jousting; but, unlike these intrinsically noble sports, music should not be practised in 'open sight':

271

And for all hee be skilfull and doth well understand it, yet will I have him to dissemble the studie and paines that a man must needes take in all thinges that are well done.[29]

The traditional association between music and making love continues. Music is particularly to be practised 'in the presence of women, because those sights sweeten the mindes of the hearers . . . and also they quicken the spirits of the very doers'.[30] Advice to old men is in the same strain; they should not sing to the lute in mixed company because such music is associated with love and 'in olde men love is a thing to be jested at'. The sentiment, like many of Castiglione's, can be traced to a classical source. This is Ovid's *Turpe senex miles, turpe senilis amor*.[31]

The proper role for an old man is as a connoisseur; he will 'much better and sooner discerne [music], and with much more pleasure judge of it, than other', because of the practical skill he is now obliged to forgo.[32] The idea of the courtly amateur as a knowledgeable critic rather than as a performer appealed to Sir Thomas Elyot, who thought a principal use of music to a nobleman was in 'hearynge the contention of noble musiciens, to gyve jugment in the excellencie of their counnynges'.[33] This is only a modification of the time-honoured medieval view that the real musician was a thinker, not a singer or player. In the hierarchy of music the philosopher stood at the top, the musical artisan at the bottom. Between, were ranked composers and, now, connoisseurs.

Both Castiglione and Sir Thomas Elyot are concerned, though in different ways, to reconcile actuality with medieval traditions and with humanist ideals. The reality of court-life at Urbino was, we know, a less rosy thing than *The Book of the Courtier* suggests. Sir Thomas, a more medieval figure in a more medieval court, dedicated *The Boke Named the Governour*, 1531, a treatise on how to educate a prince, to Henry VIII himself.[34] Naturally enough, it has to take into account actual princely behaviour. Elyot is an unenthusiastic apologist for chivalry; but the fact that he is obliged to defend the courtly pastimes of hunting, dancing and, to a lesser extent, music, testifies to the persistence of the chivalric ideal. He does not defend them on their own ground. Dancing is justified in a thoroughly casuistical way: the first move in the dance, the 'reverence', denotes honour to God; the 'braule' stands for celerity and slowness; the 'singles' for providence and industry; and so on.[35] Music, Elyot admits to be a harmless recreation if not taken too seriously – the orthodox moral view. Music to him is neither a mark of personal elegance nor a means towards the accomplishment of an amorous design.

If there was, in fact, fairly general agreement that music should form part of a courtly education, this was not because of what today would be called the 'educational value' of music, but because, as we have seen, music was a social qualification for knight and courtier. In the earlier Middle Ages the courtly exercises, including riding, music, knowledge of ranks, and carving, took precedence over academic studies. In *King Horn* Aylmar gives the following directions to his steward:

> Stiwarde, tak nu here
> Mi fundlyng for to lere
> Of thine mestere,
> Of wude and of rivere,
> And tech him to harpe
> With his nayles scharpe,
> Bivore me to kerve
> And of the cupe serve.[36]

This bias can still be seen in the *Liber Niger* of Edward IV. The master of the henchmen is directed,

> to shew the schooles of urbanitie and nourture of Englond, to lerne them to ryde clenely and surely, [*jousting, harness*, 'curtesy', 'rules of goynges and sittinges']. Moreover to teche them sondry languages, and othyr lerninges vertuous, to harping, to pype, sing, daunce . . . with remembraunce dayly of Goddes servyce accustumed.[37]

It may seem surprising that in the late fifteenth century the ideal remained so *un*academic, so chivalric. This impression is partly due to the fact that the *Liber Niger* was clearly a labour of love, of love of ceremony and the old ways – in fact, 'less an ordinance than an unfinished literary treatise by a household clerk'.[38] The writer did not wish to be more up to date than he had to be. Nevertheless, he must have found his justification in the atmosphere of the court under the Yorkist kings. A more prosaic set of 'Regulations for the Government of Prince Edward' (1474) lays down that

> the sonnes of nobles, lords and gentlemen, beinge in householde with our sayd sonne . . . be vertuously brought uppe; and taught in grammar, musicke, and other cunning, and exercises of humanyte, according to their byrthes.[39]

Grammar, by far the most important educational subject outside court circles, is simply Latin. At about this time young Richard Pace was being instructed in grammar and music in the household of Langton. Here the worlds of the courtier and the cleric meet.[40]

Despite the general agreement about the place of music in courtly education, there is some doubt whether the practice was as good as the theory. Pace describes the ideal which most people had in view:

> The 'done' thing for the sons of gentlemen is to be able to blow the horn properly, to hunt with skill, to handle a hawk and train it. . . .[41]

Moreover, the authors of fifteenth-century courtesy-books – *Stans Puer ad Mensam, Urbanitatis, The Babees Book*, and so on – do not generally include musical ability in the catalogue of good manners. But this can be partly explained by the fact that some of the treatises are not addressed to 'babees in householde that done duelle', but to children training to be servants. A good example of a servants' treatise is Hugh Rhodes' *Boke of Nurture* [1545?], explicitly addressed by its author, who was a Gentleman of the Chapel Royal, to 'Men, Servantes and Chyldren'.[42]

Household orders and other records tend to be somewhat vague about the actual course of musical study, but it seems to have been practical rather than theoretical. The Duke of Suffolk's children were to learn 'playing upon instrumentes'; young Gregory Cromwell was taught lute and virginals;[43] and most of the references in the royal accounts seem to be to instruments or teachers of instruments. Moreover, music is generally mentioned in the context of other practical, even chivalric, studies such as 'runnyng uppon a great horse'.

> The order of his studie, as the houres lymyted for the Frenche tongue, writinge, plaienge att weapons, castinge of accomptes, pastimes of instruments, and suche others, hath bene devised and directed by the prudent wisdome of Mr Southwell.[44]

Singing and dancing may, in noble households at least, be taken for granted. Grande Amour, the hero of Hawes' *Pastime of Pleasure*, laments that, being now in mourning, he 'maye not lute or yet daunce or synge'.[45] Dancing, the supreme courtly pastime, was formally taught to the royal henchmen; this we know from an entry: 'Hire of 17 dozen bells while the gentlemen learned to dance'.[46] Singing, to take only a single example, was one of the 'honest exercises apperteynynge to a gentleman' at which Sir Peter Carew excelled.[47]

Domestic and Amateur Music

The practical bias is, on the whole, confirmed by what is known about the teachers of music. Simon Burton, for instance, Princess Mary's teacher, eventually became an official 'player on the virginals' for Henry VIII; Arthur 'the luter', who in 1531 provided a lute for the Duke of Richmond and probably taught him, had already been twenty-two years in the king's employment.[48] The teachers were, it seems, professional musicians of the royal household, rather than of the chapel.

In the early Tudor court, to sum up, music was a recognized part of the courtly curriculum. Instruction in singing and playing instruments was the aim and sometimes the practice of the great households where the nobility received their training in 'urbanity' and the 'exercises of humanity'. Three comments must be made on this. First, musical composition and theory are never mentioned as fit subjects for amateur study; secondly, the comparative prominence of practical music in education does not in fact mean that everyone learnt to *read* music; and lastly, the attention given to music was no more bound to produce musical courtiers than Victorian piano-teaching to produce musical young ladies.

IV

Disguisings and royal entries, we saw earlier, were often chronicled with lavish wealth of detail. But private music of its very nature scarcely gets even the barest mention in the records. One way of supplementing the meagre evidence is to consider the presentation of music – what instruments and voices were used? Since we are only rarely told what music was performed, and seldom how it fitted into the social scene, we are obliged to deduce the musical *effects* from the means.

Solo-playing may be taken first. Without any doubt, it is Henry VIII himself of whom most is known. He was not at all loth to display his various talents in public: at a joust, for instance, in 1517, 'the king performed supernatural feats, changing his horses, and making them fly rather than leap'.[49] He probably exhibited his musical talents with equal enthusiasm, since there are many records of them. Apart from organ, lute and virginals, Henry also played on one occasion a freak instrument called the 'lute pipe' [*lira de' flauti*].[50] The Milanese ambassador wrote from Tournai, in 1513, that he had seen Henry 'play the virginals [*clavacimbolo*] and the recorders [*li flavuti*] in company most creditably, affording pleasure to all present'; it is difficult to decide whether he was playing solo or in a consort.[51] James IV of Scotland also, as we have seen, played solos on lute and keyboard; and so did his future queen. Lastly, Henry VIII's daughter Mary is known to have performed on her own, as when in 1520 she welcomed 'the French gentlemen' with 'pleasant pastime in playing at the virginals'.[52] One of the interesting points about the semi-formal music-making during Princess Margaret's journey to Scotland, already quoted, is that the instrumental items were played solo.

No hard-and-fast distinction can be made between solo and consort instruments. Nevertheless, there were then, as now, a few instruments better suited for one than for the other. The 'cornett', played by Henry VIII one evening in 1513, was an instrument of gentle tone, blending well 'with strings and with the human voice.'[53]

> The King of England, in the presence of the lady aforesaid, sang and played on the gitteron-pipe (*flauto de cythara*), and the lute-pipe (*lira de' flauti*) and on the 'cornet' (*corno*), and he danced.[54]

The freakish 'lute-pipe' has already been mentioned. The mystery of the 'gitteron-pipe' is increased rather than diminished by an entry in Henry VIII's inventory of instruments:

> Item: Twoo Gitteron pipes of Ivorie tipped with silver and gilte: they are called Cornettes.[55]

Perhaps the Venetian reporter got his instruments muddled. One would certainly have liked him to say whether Henry's performance was un-accompanied or in a consort. There is some other, but scanty, evidence that noble amateurs used consorts of instruments. Sir Thomas More's first wife was instructed 'in learning and in every kind of music'; his second wife was induced, in middle age, 'to learn to play upon the gittern, the lute, the clavichord and the recorders, and to give up every day a pre-scribed time to practise'.[56] More would perhaps not have been so insistent if private recreation were the only aim.

Some evidence of instrumental chamber-music is derived from the existence of a class of specially trained servants – semi-professionals. Among the Marquis of Exeter's servants in 1538 were the following:

> William Perpoynte, aged 20, unmarried, goodly stature, can play well upon sundry instruments, is the Lady Marquis' kinsman;
>
> Anne Browne, 22, not married, good with the needle, and can play well upon the virginals and lute;
>
> William Boothe, who can sing properly in three-man songs;

Hugh Browne, aged 33, can play somewhat on divers instruments and his knowledge is to teach men to do things in music which he himself cannot express nor utter, and yet he can perfectly teach it, wherefore he was master of the musicians;

Thomas Wright, 38, can play well with a harp, sing, juggle and other proper conceits and make 'pastetymes';

Thomas Harrys, 30, luteth and singeth well and playeth cunningly upon the viols and divers other instruments.[57]

Although such a team of musicians could have catered for dances, banquets and household plays, chamber-music was perhaps equally part of their duty, including chamber-music shared with their noble employers.

Sir Edward Stanley thirty-five years earlier – 1503 – had servants who could *sing* with him; but the playing of *instruments* by general servants, not professional musicians, may have been a comparatively new thing about 1540. The chief reason for suspecting that the Marquis of Exeter's establishment may not reflect the state of affairs at the turn of the century is that great changes of every kind can be traced to the last decade of Henry VIII's reign. It was then, perhaps, that the 'Elizabethan' tradition of household music began, epitomized later by Hengrave Hall, where Wilbye was the honoured servant of the Kytson family.[58] This period of the Reformation, and of fundamental social change, was marked by new styles in music and poetry; it was also marked by the rise to popularity of the viol, another symbol of the 'Elizabethan' in music.

In the early Tudor period the case for chamber-music among amateurs cannot rest on the assumption that every gentleman and gentleman's gentleman played the viol. Players upon the viol (the improved Italian instrument, as distinct from the English rebec, fiddle or kit) are scarcely mentioned, even as *professionals* in the royal household, before 1526: 'Viols' were used on a pageant in 1515, and in 1517 one 'Matther de Weldre', player upon lutes and 'veoldes', was getting monthly wages. After 1526 the position begins to change.[59] In the Scottish court viol-players were not permanently engaged before 1538, to judge from the Lord High Treasurer's Accounts.[60] Sir John Wallop's instructions in 1540 from Calais, where he was lieutenant, for his servant to be taught to play on the viols, are perhaps another sign of a new fashion.[61]

For different reasons the harp also can be excluded from consideration. It was admittedly a, perhaps *the*, favourite instrument of the English nobility, as of the Flemish, during the fifteenth century. Henry V and

Queen Katherine were harp-players, not, so far as is known, lutenists.[62]
The somewhat antiquarian *Liber Niger* of Edward IV still requires that the
henchmen should learn the harp.[63] But, by 1540, the instrument was
certainly out of favour; it is significant, for example, that the Marquis of
Exeter's servant who played it was obviously a popular entertainer, a
maker of 'pastimes'. The fallen social status of the harp is evident; it can
rarely have been used for instrumental chamber-music by amateurs in the
sixteenth century.

The harp was ousted by the lute, which had the musical advantages of
being a chromatic instrument. Lute, gittern, virginals, organ and recorders
are the chief instruments (known to have been played by amateurs) from
which the existence of chamber-music may be inferred. At his death,
Henry VIII had seventy-seven recorders alone; the recorder is an admirable
instrument for amateurs to play together, since its technique is fairly easily
mastered.[64] Nevertheless, the case for the performance of instrumental
chamber-music by amateurs rests, as yet, on very flimsy grounds. It is
natural that it should not find a large place in contemporary records, but the
sum total of evidence from all sources is disconcertingly small. Compared
with our knowledge of Elizabethan music-making, this knowledge is
meagre indeed.

One final point must be made. In an age when literacy was not general
even at the court, *musical* literacy, on which chamber-music of any
subtlety must depend, would inevitably be rarer.[65] Until the contrary is
proved, it will be safest to believe that the popular and the minstrel traditions of *extempore* playing on instruments also held sway to a very large
extent within the court circle.

V

Not instrumental but vocal chamber-music was the real *métier* of the noble
amateur. This we shall see later. First, the mixed art of accompanied song
must be considered. There is a widespread idea that the lute-song was as
much a feature of court-life under Henry VII and VIII as a hundred
years later. This idea may be checked by several questions: what accompanied songs survive? why was the lute popular? are accompanied songs
often referred to in the records? were such songs popular on the Continent?
and so on.

It can be said at once that no fifteenth- or early sixteenth-century songs
for voice and lute survive. That some lute-music was written down in the

fifteenth century cannot be disputed. On the back of an Irish ecclesiastical document a fifteenth-century musician has jotted down the music he possesses.[66] The list starts with 'nowellys v partes' (that is, presumably, carols for five voices – a thing not found in the surviving music);[67] all the other titles are of Latin liturgical texts, such as *Mirabile mysterium* and *Dum transisset sabbatum*, except one: 'all songys for the leute'. The writer heads his list: 'M[emo] that thys ys the so[n]gys that I hawe.' In Middle English 'song' means simply a piece of music – anything from a dance to a setting of the mass. His 'songys for the leute' does not, therefore, necessarily mean lute-songs in the modern sense; it means 'lute pieces'.

The two standard forms of accompanied song in the fifteenth century were the Burgundian *chanson* and the German 'tenor-song'. Both seem to have been intended for solo-voice and *melodic* instruments; and both are met with in English manuscripts. The earliest English lute-music (in BM Royal MSS, App. 58) consists of dances and arrangements for lute of part-songs.[68] 'The Duke of Somerset's Dump' is an example of the first; 'Pastime' is an example of the second. These transcriptions of vocal music – they are not earlier than 1540 – may have been made by the lutenist for use in a consort of voices and instruments, or as solo pieces, or for him to sing to his own accompaniment. None of them is likely to have been originally conceived as a lute-song. The arrangement of 'Pastyme with good company' [H7], 'the King's Ballad', is a very rough piece of work – the rhythmic signs are quite haphazard, and to judge by the flattened leading-notes the song was put into tablature without any thought of necessary 'accidentals'. Another lute-piece on the same page can be identified as *Ough war der mount* [H42]. This points more clearly towards true lute-song since only the two lowest parts are scored for lute, the upper presumably being supplied by the singer (or singers). Lute-music was, so to speak, a parasitic growth on the other products of the composer's art:[69] there are even transcriptions in lute tablature of motets and the like by Fayrfax, Taverner, Mundy and others.[70]

Despite the dearth of idiomatic music written especially for the instrument, the lute was popular. This popularity does not arise from a tradition of accompanied art-songs, but it can easily be explained. The lute, we have seen, was used both by professionals (Pietro Carmeliano) and amateurs (James IV) as a solo instrument. Furthermore, it was a satisfactory partner in a consort, having the advantage of being able to play more than one line at a time, if necessary. One consort, for instance, mounted on a triumphal car during the Maying of 1515, consisted of organ, lute and recorders.[71] The lute was also in demand for dance-music; when Skelton's 'comely coistrown', the upstart music-teacher, 'lumb'reth' on his lute, he is playing a basse-danse, *Roty bully joyse*.[72] The importance of the lute in the constitution of the early Tudor jazz-band has been mentioned earlier.[73]

One convincing proof that there was a courtly tradition of singing to the lute would be contemporary accounts of actual performances. These are very rare. Almost all early sixteenth-century references to accompanied songs specify some other instrument. Sir Edward Stanley on one occasion 'playd a ballade and sange therewith', the instrument being the virginals;[74] forty years later Princess (afterwards Queen) Elizabeth accompanied a chorister, who pleased her, at the virginals.[75] References to the lute in this capacity are surprisingly rare and mostly later: Mary Queen of Scots was described as having *la voix très douce et très bonne, car elle chantoit très bien, accordant sa voix avec le luth...*;[76] and Edward VI could be addressed by Dr Tye with the hope,

> That such good thinges your grace might move
> Your lute when ye assaye:
> In stade of songes of wanton love
> These stories then to playe.[77]

Slightly earlier, however, Anne Boleyn is known to have sung to her own accompaniment on the lute.[78] The passage recording this fact is very high-strung and high-sounding – she is a second Orpheus, the lions and wolves attend to her, she plays the harp better than King David; but the fact cannot be doubted. It is relevant to add, however, that in 1536 a Frenchman described her as being so accomplished you would never have thought she was English.[79] She was an 'advanced' young lady, educated in France.

So far as composed-songs for voice and lute are concerned, the state of affairs in England has a parallel on the Continent. The Spanish lute-books of Luis Milan (1536), Miguel de Fuenllana and Auriquez de Valderravano (*c.* 1550) contain the earliest examples of songs specifically written for voice with lute accompaniment.[80] In France, as in England, the earliest extant lute-music is transcribed for, not composed for, the lute. The titles of Attaignant's books of 1529 make this clear: *Dixhuit basse dances garnies de Recoupes at Tordions... le tout reduyt en la tabulature du Lutz*, Paris, 1529; and *Tres breve et familieure introduction pour entendre et apprendre par soy mesme a jouer toutes chansons reduictes en la tabulature du Lutz avec la manière daccorder le dict Lutz...* Paris, 1529.[81] Even in Italy the earliest lute-songs were, as the title implies, tablatures based on part-songs: *Tenori e contrabassi intabulati col sopran in cantu figurato* [i.e. measured music] *per cantar a sonar col lauto...* (1507).[82]

However, with the mention of Italy new complexities enter. When Bossinensis turned the *tenori* and *contrabassi* of *frottole* into lute tablature, he was in fact reconverting them to their original medium. The *frottola* was the written result of a long tradition of improvised songs-with-instrument. Serafino del'Aquila was perhaps the most famous of those who sang their own and others' poetry to the lute:

> This kind [of performance] Francis Petrarch was the first, so it is said, to institute amongst our [poets]. He sang to the lyre [?] his lofty songs. However, recently Serafino del'Aquila has been pre-eminent in restoring the tradition. He so emphasizes the melodious union of words and notes that nothing could be sweeter than his style of melody.[83]

But there were many other *improvisatori*, such as Benedetto Chariteo, Antonio Maria Terpandro, and Timoteo della Vite. The latter, with his 'lyra', *cantava all'improviso con grazia straordinaria*.[84] Some of the printed *frottole* by Cara and Tromboncino may be 'touched-up' versions of actual performances by the famous *improvisatori*. One of Serafino's colleagues in the art, Collo (known as 'Il Calmeta'), wrote his biography. But even if he had not, there would still be ample testimony to the existence of a 'school' of court-entertainers who made a living and won renown by singing their own verses and accompanying themselves on an instrument.[85] Although, from the musical point of view, many of their efforts were perhaps rudimentary, the tradition of singing lyrical poems with an instrument was unbroken from the time of the troubadours.

What can the English tradition offer to compare with this? First, there was the minstrel repertory of romances. Even in Elizabethan times, according to Puttenham, long poems were still recited to the harp:

> we ourselves . . . have written for pleasure a little brief *Romance* or historicall ditty in the English tong of the Isle of great *Britaine* in short and long meetres, and by breaches or divisions to be more commodiously song to the harpe in places of assembly, where the company shall be desirous to heare of old adventures and valiaunces of noble knights in times past. . . .[86]

Probably, 'blynde Dicke' and 'blynde More' of Henry VIII's establishment sang of 'old adventures' in this manner. More was chief harper under four sovereigns and died in 1564. When, in 1520, he paid a visit to Shrewsbury, the Corporation accounts mention wine, as well as a fee, and describe him as 'minstrel of our Lord king, the man who is blind and the principal harper in England'.[87]

Secondly, there was popular music for the lyric. In Chaucer, to take only one example, Absolon, the parish-clerk, sings a love-plaint 'ful wel acordaunt to his giterning'. To judge from the early Tudor records, this tradition of *popular* singing never, as in Italy, won high social honours. In 1495 Henry VII gave two shillings to 'a woman that singeth with a fidell', perhaps a wayfarer.[88] There may have been exceptions. If so, John Heywood is a likely man. Besides having a reputation for 'myrth and quicknesse' he was paid as virginalist *and singer*. Bale's catalogue of English writers describes him as *Orpheus alter, instrumentorum studiosus, musica et poeta*. Bale has a taste for panegyrical extravagance, a taste which the current vogue for clever epigrams did very little to discourage. However, he would not invent impossible qualities. Moreover, a manuscript containing some of Heywood's poems belonged to a musical circle centring on St Paul's. Later manuscripts preserve one or two of these lyrics set for voice and lute.[89]

To sum up, the evidence, heterogeneous though it is, is almost entirely negative; and negative evidence is never the most convincing. Nevertheless, there could hardly have been in England a tradition of courtier-poets singing extempore to their lutes, comparable to the Italian, without it having left some traces; and it is certain that the *composition* of songs specifically for solo voice and instrument was a new thing in the middle of the sixteenth century.

VI

One of the most striking single pieces of negative evidence about accompanied songs is derived from the works of Skelton. He has often been described as a poet who sang to the lute:

> Skelton exhibits . . . a wide acquaintance with musical terms, invariably used correctly. It is not hard to picture him singing to the lute.[90]

Skelton certainly was widely acquainted with music and musical life. Considering this, and his garrulity, it is all the more remarkable that he never mentions singing to the lute. A subject, however, which he often drags into his verse is part-singing. Riot, for example, a 'rusty gallant', could 'counter' the plain-song *O lux beata Trinitas* and frequently sang a song called 'In faith, deacon, thou crew'.[91] Vocal chamber-music, requiring a minimum of technical skill, was doubtless more practised than instrumental.

Part-singing 'by note', to use the contemporary phrase, was certainly not unknown. Among the New Year's gifts given by the king in 1519 is a reward to Dr Fayrfax for a 'balet boke limned'; this would probably be a manuscript song-book similar to those extant. This was the third year running that Fayrfax had given the king a musical present at the New Year.[92] Royal persons, then as now, tended to acquire presents which they could not possibly use. But Henry VIII could certainly read music at sight.[93] And the king cannot have been the only capable amateur. A certain amount must be allowed for royal example. Sagudino, the Venetian ambassador's secretary, was anxious to get compositions from Italy by Zuane Maria and 'a few new *frottole*' to exchange for English songs.[94] This at least proves interest, if not practical ability, among English courtiers. Some of Skelton's characters, moreover, aspire to being themselves practical musicians. Harry Hafter sighs:

> Wolde to God, it wolde please you some daye
> A balade boke before me for to laye,
> And lerne me to synge *Re-my-fa-sol!*
> And, whan I fayle, bobbe me on the noll.[95]

And Skelton's 'comely coistrown', that jumped-up fiddler, teaches 'prick-song' (i.e. written part-music in measured notes) as distinct from plain-song.[96] Another scrap of evidence is provided by an eighteenth-century manuscript copied by John Immyns, founder of the Madrigal Society, from a song-book dated 1551 (admittedly rather late) which belonged to a former Gentleman of the Bedchamber to Henry VIII.[97] A small circle close to the king must, it is safe to conclude, have been accustomed to sing part-music.

If, then, in the mixed social gatherings which formed such an important part of the courtly life, the courtier sang his verses, it cannot, nevertheless, have been to music as elaborate as that in *The Fayrfax MS*. For instance, the delightful little verse, 'Benedicite! Whate dremyd I this night?' [F12], turns out in its musical setting as something rather massive and ponderous and not at all easy to sing. The simpler songs in *Henry VIII's MS*, however, have several features which make them suitable for amateurs: they are notated very straightforwardly; they are composed for the most part in a chordal style (which means that the singers give each other support); they are short and repetitive and therefore quickly memorable. Songs like 'Iff I had wytt' [H29] or 'Hey troly loly loly' [H75] could, indeed, easily be learnt even by those who were not trained to *read* them.

How widely the circle of trained and literate amateurs extended is a matter for investigation. Negative evidence, it must be repeated, is always inconclusive. But the fact remains that the examination of several hundred wills and letters and some inventories has produced small result. It is quite an event to find a 'payre of claricordes' mentioned, while there are scores of bequests like 'my silver fork for the green ginger' or 'my best feather bed'. Prick-song books are rare indeed. In all the Paston correspondence only one song-book is mentioned.[98] However, a recent discovery amongst the *Cely Papers* has disclosed an interesting 'booklet recording some of George Cely's personal expenses in 1473–5': these include 'payments for instruction in playing a total of forty dances'; instruction in dance-steps; in harp- and lute-playing; and in seven songs, *O rosa bella* and 'Go, hert, hurt with adversite' amongst them. There may be some significance in the fact that all this took place at Calais, not in East Anglia. Equally suggestive is the entire absence of proof that even this middle-class enthusiast could *read* music: he never buys a song-book or pays a copyist; he gets 'Thomas Rede, harpar' to 'lerne' him what he wants to play. Nevertheless, if he played by ear, he must have had a most retentive memory.[99]

Another question – if there was a public, even a sizeable *élite*, eager to sing from music books, why are part-songs so rare in contemporary manuscripts, and why did the early printers not cater for the demand? These printers, as recent writers have shown, set out to meet demands that already existed. They had no need to create new markets; the public for printed books (of law, theology, chivalry) was the public for fifteenth-century manuscripts.[100] But printed part-music is even rarer than manuscript. The bass part of the expensively produced *Book of Twenty Songs*, 1530, is the only surviving song-book (three part-books of this set are missing).[101] So far as we know, the experiment was not repeated.

For the next fifty years music-printing was largely confined to music for the metrical psalm. These, the earliest examples of printed mensural music designed to reach a wide public, were commonly provided each with a 'short introduction into the science of musicke'.[102] If this was necessary as late as the 1560's (e.g. for the Sternhold and Hopkins psalter of 1561), what then can have been the state of musical literacy when Henry VIII came to the throne?

Far more common, however, than singing 'by note' must have been singing *all' improviso*. Improvised harmony (what we today call singing 'by ear') was at the end of the Middle Ages often provided with a visual aid; the best-known system was simply called 'sight'. There may, even in the thirteenth century, when the English predilection for singing in thirds becomes an observed fact, have been a system for devising 'gymel' (= twin-song), as there was later a system for devising the one or more additional voices of 'discant', fa-burden and *fauxbourdon*. 'Counter' has a strict meaning; it is the *ars contra-tenoris*, the art of fitting a free counter-tenor between the outer parts of a strict *fauxbourdon*. But as Skelton uses it, it probably means no more than the improvisation of any one part against another. Skelton talks, in one instance, of 'counteryng of carollis in meter and verse'; more carol music is in two than in three parts.[103] Other terms which may in the right context refer to improvisation are 'feigning' and 'figuration'. 'Figuration' is probably another broad term for ornamentation of a melody; Gavin Douglas uses the term in a passage of *Palice of Honour* where he seems to be lumping together quite indiscriminately all the musical terms he knows:

> In modulation hard I play and sing,
> Faburdoun, priksang, discant, countering,
> Cant organe, figuration, and gemmell.[104]

'Fayne' is a more difficult term. Skelton abuses his 'comely coistrown', again, by saying:

> For lordes and ladyes lerne at his scole.
> He techyth them so wysely to solf *and to fayne*,
> That neyther they synge wel pryck-songe nor playne.[105]

The word may stand for *fictus visus*, i.e. discant by 'sight'. Or it can mean 'sing in a falsetto voice' – e.g. 'Not . . . feynynge, but with a full brest and a hole voyce'. Perhaps a third meaning connects it with *musica falsa* or *ficta*, the technique of supplying accidentals, where needed, in part-singing. Which of these Skelton intended, it is difficult to say.[106]

How do these methods of improvisation, discussed in more detail elsewhere (p. 64), illuminate the subject of amateur part-singing at court? First, and most important, they show that there was an intermediate stage of musical literacy. The improvisation, by 'sight' or by ear, of extra parts to a known tune was, although it may not be immediately obvious, much easier than reading written polyphonic music. The problems of medieval music were very largely problems of *rhythm*, and a knowledge of 'alteration', 'imperfection', proportions, ligatures, etc., was essential for the fully literate musician. A singer 'discanting' on a plain-song, or 'countering' a popular tune, did not have to bother with these mysteries, for the rhythms were already in his head. Provided he could judge intervals with the help of solmization, he could sing in parts.

Another thing which a widespread practice of extempore part-singing would explain, if it required special explanation, is the wealth of popular tunes known in the court circle. The methods require a given melody, preferably a well-known one. The obvious sources for such melodies are plain-song and popular song. Tunes such as 'Alone I leffe alone' [H14] and 'And I war a maydyn' [H101] were quite probably used as the basis of compositions because they had already served for *improvised* part-music. There cannot be much doubt that there was a custom of improvisation *upon popular tunes*, and that this formed the staple of chamber-singing by amateurs at court. To quote again the words of Frewyll in *Hyckscorner*:

> . . . now 'Hey troly loly'
> Let us see who can descaunt on this same.[107]

Lastly, it is possible that the 'three-man song' had something to do with this kind of singing. Sir Peter Carew's biographer relates that he

> havinge a pleasaunte voyce, the Kynge woulde very often use hyme to synge with hime certeyne songes they called *fremen* songs as namely 'By the bancke as I lay' and 'As I walked the wode so wylde', &c.[108]

If a 'three-man song' consisted in the improvisation of two extra parts to a well-known tune, such as those named here, it explains how, later in the century, quite ordinary trades-people could be described as singing them.* Deloney is not exaggerating the standards of cobblers as much as might appear, when he makes them resolve to penalize

> what Journey-man so-ever he be hereafter, that cannot handle his Sword and Buckler . . . sound the Trumpet, or play upon the flute, and bear his part in a three-mans song. . . .[109]

Another possible interpretation of the term is as a round; and probably,

---

* There is the additional question, of course, – how did the king with *one* companion sing a *three*-part song, if 'fre-men' means 'three-man'?

like other technical terms of the same period, it was loosely used. Certainly the earliest literary references give the impression of a *popular* art, a style of singing which ordinary people could manage. In a morality play (*c.* 1425) people are reproved because they would rather 'syttyn at the ale, iij mens songys to syngyn lowde, thanne towarde the chyrche for to crowde'.[110] On the other hand, during Elizabeth's reign the title could certainly be used of written part-music bearing no resemblance to the improvised style I have described – for example, the 'three-man song', 'Come there any more knaves?'[111] Ravenscroft in the early seventeenth century uses the term variously of rounds and of simple chordal part-songs such as 'By a bancke' [Song 60].[112]

VII

It is impossible on the evidence so far available to answer all the important questions fully and decisively. But the information summarized above is sufficient, I think, to enable us to draw some conclusions about domestic and amateur music in the early Tudor court.

Contemporary generalizations have too often been taken uncritically, as for instance that of Erasmus, who, in *The Praise of Folly*, said:

> Upon this account it is that the English challenge the prerogative of having the most handsome women, of being the most accomplished in the skill of music, and of keeping the best tables.[113]

Erasmus does not elucidate. Did he refer to personal musical accomplishments? And if so, of what sort? Or did he have professional music in mind? Elsewhere he complains that English churches are full of music – the music of hired choirmen. At any rate, if the English held this opinion of themselves *as amateurs*, it was clearly not endorsed by a number of other writers. The author of *The Italian Relation* nowhere mentioned music in his report (after 1502) to the Venetian senate, although he commented on the extravagant use of dress, food and retainers. It is instructive, too, to compare Erasmus' well-known encomium of Henry VIII's court as 'a temple of the Muses' with this ambassador's report: 'few . . . excepting the clergy are addicted to the study of letters.' (Perhaps the filling of court appointments with Humanists – Greek and Latin scholars – did effect a decisive change.)[114] Even more powerful negative evidence against the view of a deep-rooted tradition of art-music at court among amateurs is provided by the later embassy from Venice (1515–19). Their despatches contain the most circumstantial and well-informed descriptions of musical occasions that survive. Yet they never say what a musical court they have come to, nor do they describe the musical activities of the nobility; they say only how musical the king is, and how proficient, or not, the professionals in his pay. It is surely significant that when Sagudino had shown his skill in the presence of many of the nobility, English *professionals*, not amateurs, made a rejoinder.[115] Sagudino's silence about amateur music might conceivably be accidental. But English writers give the same impression. The poet Barclay maintains in his Second Eclogue that at any rate the sense of hearing is pleased at court. Faced in his original with the phrase, *cantus sonosque musicorum*, he expands it to:

> All this may courtiers in court ofte times heare,
> And also songes oftimes swete and cleare.
> The birde of Cornewalle, the Crane and the Kite
> And mo other like to heare is great delite,
> Warbling their tunes at pleasour and at will,
> Though some be busy that therin have no skill.[116]

The professionals referred to are, of course, William Cornish and William Crane, successively Masters of the Children of the Chapel Royal, and John Kite, Sub-Dean of the Chapel until 1513, when he became Bishop of Armagh. Barclay was well acquainted with music and musicians, since, as *capellanus* in the College of Ottery St Mary, one of his duties was to instruct the choristers.[117]

To take the important questions in order – how many amateurs were able to compose, how many to play instruments, how many to read part-music? It can be stated fairly dogmatically that amateur compositon was scanty. Only the king and a few highly placed clerics are mentioned as composers; and only their compositions survive. Sir William Hawte, *miles*, is an exception. He was a Sheriff of Kent; and as the suffix 'knight' shows, he was not merely a clerical 'sir'. His compositions are found in two manuscripts.[118] John Heywood, mentioned above, is no exception since he was clearly, amongst other things, a professional musician and was paid as such. Dr Pattison's statement, then, 'compositions by others of the court circle rub shoulders in these manuscripts with the king's own works', should not be taken to mean that there are other known *amateur* compositions surviving.[119] There are not.

Although we know lamentably little about instrumental chamber-music amongst amateurs, it seems likely that in the period 1485–1530 much instrumental playing was done extempore. Nothing in the orders and treatises concerning musical education at court compels the belief that everyone learnt to read part-music. Probably many courtiers acquired technical dexterity on an instrument, who never took the trouble, or were unable, to master the problems of notation. Towards the end of Henry VIII's reign the apparently growing popularity of the viol and of servants trained to play domestic music may have changed the whole position.

Despite the example of the king and of other members of the royal family, it seems that there was probably not a great deal of art-music made among amateurs. The complete lack of evidence, for instance, that Wyatt was a musician has already been commented on.[120] Singers improvised in two or three parts from a known melody, usually a popular tune. This was not art-music in the proper meaning of the term; the effects were contrived quite simply, and a courtier need not have been at all acquainted with the intricacies of mensural notation to be able, in a true sense, to bear his part.

NOTES TO CHAPTER 12

1. Hayes, 10. For critical accounts centring on later periods, see J. A. Westrup, 'Domestic Music under the Stuarts' in *PRMA*, lxviii (1941–2), 19, and Woodfill, ch. ix.

2. Rawdon Brown, i. 296: ambassador's despatch, 30 Sept. 1516.

3. Rawdon Brown, ii. 97: 10 July 1517.

4. Nagel, 13; and 'King's Book of Payments' (see Reference List), under date, July 1516. See also Barclay Squire, 'Who was *Benedictus*?' in *SIMG* (1911–12), 264–; Reese, *MR*, 265; and articles in *MGG* and *Grove*. The motet is in Roy. MSS 11.E.xi, f.10v.

5. Hayes, 52, from Sanuto.

6. Rawdon Brown, ii. 75: letter of Sagudino, the Venetian ambassador's secretary. Concerning Zuan Piero (Carmeliano), see also Byler, 8.

6a. Rawdon Brown, ii. 75.

7. *L&P*, iii, pt 1, no. 1010 (4 Oct. 1520): letter from Pace to Wolsey; the same letter refers to a 'gentilman off Almayne' who performs well on the instrument he has brought with him.

8. Rawdon Brown, i. 78–: long letter of Sagudino, containing *inter alia*

accounts of the Chapel Royal's singing; of Henry VIII's musical talents; of the elaborate Maying of 1515; and of this musical interlude during it. Sagudino also asks for music to be sent to him in exchange for English compositions.

9. *PP Henry VII*, 2 Aug. 1495; and see 2 Nov. 1495.

10. For Heywood's career see A. W. Reed, ch. ii, correcting Wallace.

11. *L&P*, xxi, pt 1, no. 969; *L&P*, x, no. 908; Nagel, 21; Bridgman, 103, from Lafontaine, 8.

12. Pattison's statement, 50, is misleading: Cornish merely received in 1513 the traditional largess for his Children of the Chapel (cf. 'Kings Book of Payments' [see Reference List], Nov. 1510).

13. *L&P*, iii, pt 2, no. 2585.

14. Barclay, *Eclogues*, ii, line 326. For foreign musicians, se ealso p. 308 below.

15. *DNB*, v. 193 (col. 2).

16. Recorder player: *PP Henry VII*, 4 Mar. 1492. Clavichord (?) player: Dauney, 101. 'Child' could, of course, mean also 'young noble' at this time.

17. Leland, iv. 284: an unusually circumstantial account.

18. Leland, iv. 285.

19. Rawdon Brown, ii. 75.

20. Rawdon Brown, i. 80.

21. For courtly education, see *Babees Book*; also Bridgman, 14–; Harris (musical education outside court). For households, see *Northumberland HHB*; Roper's life of More; Cavendish, *Wolsey*; Pace, *De Fructu*. For henchmen, *Ordinances, passim*.

22. See *PP Henry VII*, 29 Nov. 1494 (Prince Arthur), 21 May 1501 (Princess Margaret), 1 Aug. 1505 (Princess Mary); *PP Henry VIII*, 2 May 1531 (Duke of Richmond, Henry VIII's illegitimate son). This list could easily be extended.

23. Pattison, 30.

24. Chaucer's translation, line 2317– (ed. Robinson, 587).

25. *The Romaunt of the Rose*, 2255– (ed. Robinson, 586). See also the portrait of the Squire, *Prologue to Canterbury Tales*, line 79– (ed. Robinson, 18).

26. Sarah F. Barrow, *Medieval Society Romances* (Columbia, 1924), 10, 53.

27. Marix, *Histoire de la Musique et des Musiciens*, ch. 4, 'Les Menestrels', sect. 1; Huizinga, 103 (a Parisian 'court'); and p. 164 above.

28. Huizinga, ch. 4, 'The Idea of Chivalry'.
29. *Courtier*, 100. Hoby's translation was first published in 1561.
30. *Courtier*, 101.
31. *Courtier*, 102; Ovid, *Amor*, I. ix. 41, see Vittorio Cian, *Il Cortegiano*, 3rd edn (Florence, 1929), 159, note.
32. *Courtier*, 102.
33. *Governour*, i. 42.
34. Croft's introduction lists similar treatises. The *Governour* was more popular than *Utopia*; eight editions were published by 1580 (Croft, p. lxx).
35. *Governour*, ch. xxii, 'How daunsing may be an introduction into the fyrst morall vertue, called Prudence.'
36. R. Morris, ed. *Specimens of Early English* (1885), pt 1, p. 244.
37. *Ordinances*, 45.
38. See Chambers, *Elizabethan Stage*, i. 29.
39. *Ordinances*, 29.
40. Pace, *De Fructu*, 27, says that Langton marked him out for better things when he found him excelling in music.
41. Pace, *De Fructu*, dedication, 15: *decet enim generosorum filios apte inflare cornu, perite venari, accipitrem pulchre gestare et educare*. Pace sets up *bonae literae* as his ideal. See p. 68 above.
42. Rhodes: see Reference List and pp. 309, 325.
43. Suffolk's children: Thomas Wilson, *Arte of Rhetorique*, ed. G. H. Mair (1909), 15; Richard Cromwell's son: H. Ellis, *Original Letters illustrative of English History*, ser. I, i (1824), 341–3.
44. Ellis, *Original Letters*, ser. I, i. 341–.
45. *Pastime*, 65: the poem presents an idealized account of courtly-cum-clerical education.
46. 'Revels Accounts', Jan. 1511: it was a morris-dance.
47. *Carew*, 106: 'for in singinge, vaultinge, and specially for rydinge, he was not inferior to anye in the courte'.
48. Burton: see Grattan Flood, 88 (there is nothing apparently to show that he was a *composer*). 'Arthur the Luter' (= Arthur Dewes?): see Nagel, 8–.
49. Rawdon Brown, ii. 102.
50. V. Denis, *De Muziekinstrumenten in de Nederlanden en in Italie* (1944), 236 (I thank Thurston Dart for this reference).
51. *L&P: Milan*, no. 669 (11 Oct. 1513).
52. *L&P*, iii, pt 1, 896 (2 July 1520).

53. *HDM*, s.v. 'Cornett'.

54. *L&P: Venice*, ii, no. 328 (7 Oct. 1513).

55. Galpin, 296.

56. *Epistles of Erasmus* (ed. Allen), iv, no. 999: I have altered the translation. The original names of instruments are *cithara, testudine, monochordo, tibiis* (ablative cases). *Cithara* might be 'cittern', instead.

57. *L&P*, xiii, pt 2, no. 754.

58. Wilbye: see E. H. Fellowes, *English Madrigal Composers* (1921), 209–, and references. Woodfill, 61, throws considerable doubt, however, on this 'tradition'.

59. Royal viol-players: Nagel, 16 (1526). 'Pageant': 'Revels Accounts', 6 Jan. 1515. 'Matther de Weldre': *L&P*, i, pt 3, pref. p. lxv, note 1.

60. Galpin, 89; *Accounts of The Lord High Treasurer of Scotland*, ed. T. Dickson and Sir J. B. Paul, 11 vols (1877–1916).

61. *L&P*, xv, no. 905 (23 July 1540).

62. Galpin, 18.

63. *Ordinances*, 45 (and see p. 273 above).

64. Henry VIII's list of instruments (1547) is printed in full from Harl. MS 1419 in Galpin, 292–. The collection included 78 cross-flutes (some of them military fifes?).

65. On literacy, see J. W. Adamson, *The Illiterate Anglo-Saxon* (1946), ch. 3.

66. On back of BM Add. MS 38163 (Record of the Acts of John Colton, Bishop of Armagh, on visitation of the see of Derry, 1397).

67. But see Church-Wardens' Accounts of St Mary-at-Hill in Littlehales, *Medieval Records of a City Church*, EETS (1905), 54: an inventory of 1553 containing the item 'v Caroll bokes'.

68. For BM Roy. MSS, App. 58, see App. C, no. 72.

69. This is confirmed by Alison Hanham, 'The Musical Studies of a Fifteenth-Century Wool Merchant', *RES*, n.s. viii (1957), 270–; George Cely learnt, on harp and lute, forty dances and seven songs. No specific lute-music was in his repertory.

70. BM Add. MSS 29246–7.

71. See p. 243 above.

72. *Roty bully* must have been widely known. Skelton twice refers to it: *Magnificence*, line 757 (Dyce, i. 249); *Comely Coistrown* (Dyce, i. 16). For the history of this dance/song, see Nan C. Carpenter, 'Skelton and Music: *Roty Bully Joys*', *RES*, vi (1955), 279.

Domestic and Amateur Music

73. See p. 246 above.

74. See p. 269 above.

75. E. Duncan, *The Story of Minstrelsy* (1907), 148, from Warton (1871), iii. 312. The account may not be authentic (see Hillebrand, 124, note).

76. cit. Dauney, 107, from Brantôme.

77. Christopher Tye, preface to *Acts of the Apostles* (1553), cit. Boyd, 69.

78. A. Strickland, *Lives of the Queens* (1842), iv. 168, from memoirs of Viscount Chateaubriant, courtier of Francis I.

79. *L&P*, x, no. 1036.

80. See *HAM*, no. 123: *Paseabase el rey*, by Fuenllana. The songs of Luis Milan are arrangements of popular and folk-song rather than original compositions.

81. From Apel, 64.

82. See Pirro, 165, with facsimile; he conjectures that the missing alto part was sung from the original *frottola* by another singer. Franciscus Bossinensis was the editor.

83. *Quod quidem genus primus apud nostros Franciscus Petracha instituisse dicitur, qui edita carmina caneret ad lembum. Nuper autem Seraphinus Aquilanus princeps eius generis renovandi fuit, a quo ita est verborum et cantuum conjunctio modulata nexa, quo nihil fieri posset modorum ratione dulcius* (Paolo Cortese, *De ¡Cardinal*, cit. Pattison, 119, from Tiraboschi, *Storia della Letteratura Italiana*, vi, pt 3, p. 1244: my translation).

84. Pirro, 167.

85. The most comprehensive account of the *improvisatori* is W. H. Rubsamen's *Literary Sources of Secular Music in Italy* (California, 1943), to which I am much indebted. See also Pirro, 166–7.

86. Puttenham, 42.

87. Chambers, *Medieval Stage*, ii. 252, from Corporation accounts. See also Nagel, 12–13, and Bridgman, 122.

88. *PP Henry VII*, 2 Nov. 1495.

89. Concerning Heywood, see A. W. Reed, ch. ii; Bale *Scriptorum*, ii. 110 (Wallace, 79, note, gives the full entry); Pattison, 52. Poems, ed. J. O. Halliwell, from Add. MS 15233, Shakesp. Soc. (1848); musical compositions in Add. MSS 4900 ('What harte can thincke') and 15117 ('All a green willow').

90. L. J. Lloyd, *John Skelton* (1938), 32.

91. *Bowge of Courte* (Dyce, i. 40–). 'Countering': see p. 285 below.

92. 'The King's Book of Payments', Jan. 1517, Jan. 1518, Jan. 1519.
93. Rawdon Brown, i. 86: Venetian ambassador's report.
94. Rawdon Brown, i. 81: letter of Sagudino.
95. *Bowge of Courte* (Dyce, i. 40), line 256–.
96. *Comely Coystrowne* (Dyce, i. 16–17) line 50–.
97. BM Add. MS 31406.
98. *Paston Letters*, vi, no. 1079, an inventory: contains 'j song boke pris . . . xxd'. See also H. S. Bennett, *The Pastons and their England* (1922), App. I, for a list of books owned by the family. Other collections searched: *Plumpton Correspondence*, ed. Stapleton (1839); *Cely Papers*, ed. Malden (1900); *Testamenta Cantiana*, extra vol., ed. L. L. Duncan (1906); the collections of wills publ. Surtees Soc. (1835, 1860) and Camden Soc. (1850); *Testamenta Eboracensia*, ed. Raine (1865). The question needs thorough investigation.
99. The discovery was made by Alison Hanham, *RES*, n.s. viii (1957).
100. H. S. Bennett, 'Caxton and his Public', *RES*, xix (1943), 113.
101. See App. C, no. 79.
102. See especially J. F. R. Stainer's informative article 'On Musical Introductions in Certain Metrical Psalters', *PRMA*, xxvii (1900–1), 1.
103. Dyce, i. 389; see also Bukofzer, *Geschichte*, 89–. Harris, 117, 119: choirboys taught to 'counter'.
104. cit. Dauney, 88; H. G. Farmer, 'Music in Medieval Scotland', *PRMA*, lvi (1929), 78.
105. Line 52– (Dyce, i. 17).
106. *OED*, s.v. 'feign' suggests the third of these meanings with another (well attested) 'to hum, sing softly'.
107. See above, p. 257.
108. *Carew*, 113.
109. cit. Pattison, 13, from Deloney's *Works* (ed. Mann), 89.
110. *OED*, from *Castle of Perseverance*, line 2335 (*Macro Plays*, ed. F. J. Furnivall and A. W. Pollard, EETS (1904), 147).
111. CUL, Add. MS 4250 (c. 1580). I thank Thurston Dart for lending me his transcription of this song.
112. Ravenscroft's music was not included by Fellowes in *EMS*. Available transcriptions are listed by Reese, *MR*, 833, note 68.
113. *Praise of Folly* (anon trans., London, 1887), 99.
114. *Italian Relation* (trs. Sneyd) (see Reference List), probably written

by Francesco Capello's secretary. Capello was the first Venetian ambassador to England, and this is the earliest Venetian 'relation' on record (Sneyd, introd., p. vii).

115. See especially Sagudino's letter of 1515, quoted at length on p. 267 above.
116. *Eclogues*, ed. B. White, EETS (1928), 60 (line 255).
117. Barclay's life: see B. White's introduction to *Eclogues*; W. Nelson in *RES*, xix (1943), 59; L. S. Colchester in *MLR*, xxxvii (1942), 198.
118. *Ritson's MS*, and Cambridge, Magdalene College, Pepys MS 1236.
119. Pattison, 49.
120. See p. 133 above. Even Leland, who aims at being exhaustive, found nothing to praise Wyatt for in this kind.

CHAPTER 13

Professional Musicians

The development of the musical profession during the reigns of the early Tudors remains an unwritten chapter in English musical history. But it is not for lack of material. Trying to answer the obvious questions about amateur music, in the last chapter, was like trying to put together a jigsaw puzzle of which most of the pieces were missing. The story of professional music is quite another matter. When the wealth of available material has been collected and analysed, there will be no doubt at all how the profession was organized, how the various branches were recruited and trained, what the chief qualifications were of singers and instrumentalists, how they were paid and what other rewards they were given. The present chapter, based on a fraction of the evidence, will provide, I hope, fairly conclusive answers to most of these elementary questions.[1] Its main purpose, however, is less easy to attain. Even when the musical profession has been systematically studied, it may not be possible to define exactly the status in society of different musicians. The question is difficult because it is wide – a status is not so much a way of life as what other people think of that way of life. But it is of paramount interest and importance to anyone who studies the place of music in the court circle.

I

Almost everyone with pretensions to rank or position employed musicians, from the king, who had dozens, down to a minor official like Wood, Treasurer of the Norfolk household, who had one minstrel in his pay and livery.[2] The widespread employment of musicians does not, however, prove an equally widespread regard for the art of music. A musician was another retainer. 'Another yl custume among the nobyllys ther ys', wrote Starkey, 'that every one of them wyl kepe a court lyke a prynce'.[3] As the author of the *Italian Relation* (*c.* 1503) remarked, 'a very great retinue in their houses' is 'a thing the English delight in beyond measure'.[4] The

moralists agreed that huge routs of retainers were parasitic and unproduc-
tive. But the habit continued, for when the resources of clothing and
jewellery, worn on the noble person, were exhausted, it was felt necessary
to have a retinue of servants conspicuously wasting time and money.
Musicians were, to put it crudely, a good social investment. Was it for
reasons of piety or to recover social standing that the sixth Earl of Northumberland hoped (after the pillaging of his late father's chapel by Wolsey)
'to be able ons to set up a Chapel off myne owne'?[5]

The number of musicians varied according to the employer's position in
the social scale; to be able to afford mass 'by note' was a mark of social distinction. It was typical of Wolsey's aspirations that he had at one time a
bigger and better chapel than the king's. Some letters which passed between Richard Pace, the king's secretary, and Wolsey, in 1518, show that
Henry did not altogether approve of this. Henry had pointed out to Cornish, the Master of the Children of the Chapel Royal (in effect, his
Director of Church-music), that Wolsey's choir could sight-read better
than his own. One practical consequence was that Richard Pygott, Wolsey's choir-master, was required to surrender one of his best trebles. This
he did – asking, however, that Cornish should treat 'young Robin'
decently ('otherwise than he doth his own').[6] To resume – a chapel on
the royal scale included about twenty singing-men (besides chaplains) and
a dozen or more boys. In 1509, for the funeral of Henry VII and the
coronation of his son, there were eighteen men and ten children. The Duke
of Norfolk, on the other hand, had sometimes as few as four boys.[7] To
judge from contemporary church-music, the smallest choir capable of
singing mass 'by note' (i.e. a polyphonic setting) would number ten or
twelve, and this was, in fact, the statutory minimum for the Papal Chapel
in the mid-sixteenth century for the singing of 'prick-song'.

'Chapel' was the accepted 'international' term for describing the ecclesiastical establishment of a prince or noble person. It included, of course,
far more than just the singers. The Chapel Royal was properly the 'chapel'
attached to the king's person, and in earlier times probably always travelled
with him. But the Eltham Ordinances of 1526 put a stop to this. When
the king was on a 'progress' only a 'riding household' accompanied him.
In this reduced court the chapel was represented by the Master of the
Children and six men, 'for which purpose no great carriage, either of
vestments or bookes, shall be required'.[8] The 'clerks' of the chapel did,
then, occasionally travel with the king. In addition, there was some slight
seasonal movement among lesser singers: in Wolsey's household there were

'dyvers reteynours of connyng syngyng men that came at dyvers sondrie pryncypall feastes';[9] and there was always some coming and going between London churches and the court as occasion called.

It has been a commonplace of musical historians that early Tudor England was rich in chapels such as these. The presence, too, in the royal household of an ever-increasing number of musicians, is a recognized fact. But the presence throughout the country of many small companies of instrumental musicians has been less remarked. Now that the word 'minstrel' has shaken off the heavy burden laid upon it by the Romantic poets, we can recognize the reality presented by chronicles and account-books: in the late fifteenth and early sixteenth centuries the minstrel was still an everyday figure in English life. At court, more perhaps than elsewhere, his chief function was to play a musical instrument.

Menestrallus, histrio, disour, lusor, are among the commonest terms used in the Middle Ages to describe the minstrel.[10] They seem to vary – though not at all consistently – according to what the minstrel did or was best at doing. The title 'minstrel' often seems to denote a general-purpose entertainer, a *Johannes-fac-totum,* the sort of man who could sing a bit, mimic, tell a story, chaff his audience, and strum a dance on the rebec. The following carol brings him and his 'patter' vividly before us:

> Be gladly, masters everychon;
> I am cum myself alone
> To appose you on by on;
> > Let se who dare say nay.
> > > Sir, what say ye?
> > > Syng on; lett us see.
> > > Now will it be
> > Thys or another day?
>
> Sir, what say ye with your fat face?
> Me thynkith ye shuld bere a very good bace
> To a pot of good ale or ipocras,
> > Truly as I you say.
> > > Hold up your hede;
> > > Ye loke lyke lede;
> > > Ye wast myche bred
> > Ever more from day to day.[11]

But minstrelsy also had its specialists. Some excelled in acting, some in acrobatics, some in tricks with animals, some in reciting tales and some in playing on musical instruments. Gower's description

> And every menstral hadde pleid,
> And every Disour hadde seid

seems to make a traditional distinction between two major functions of the higher minstrelsy – 'harping' and 'carping', music and speech.[12] The comment also shows that the special appropriation of the term 'minstrel' to the musical side of the profession was of long standing in early Tudor days. In certain contexts 'minstrel' could only mean 'instrumentalist' – in the royal account-books, for example, when applied to resident servants. In the mid-sixteenth century a further change of terminology came about. The word 'musician', 'musitien', came into common employment instead of 'minstrel', which now increasingly called to mind vagrants and beggars.[13]

How many minstrels were there, around the year 1500, on the roads and in the castles of England? It is hard to say. A cursory glance at the records reveals the existence of dozens of 'bands'. These were of two kinds: those bearing the livery of a particular lord; and those taking their name from a town or city. As example of the first, among the 'bands' which visited New Romney in Kent between 1480 and 1502 were those owning allegiance to the King, the Queen, the Duchess of York, the Prince, Lord Arundel, Lord Northumberland, the Duke of Bedford, Cardinal Morton, and the Lord Admiral. New Romney was also visited by the minstrels of Sandwich, one among the many townships which retained their own 'waits' and let them travel about to augment their wages.[14] Records of waits at Beverley, Cambridge, Canterbury, Coventry, Ipswich, Leicester and many other places go back to pre-Reformation times.[15]

The great increase in the number of instrumental musicians in the royal household is one of the impressive facts of the years 1470 to 1550. The permanent musicians in Edward IV's pay were two wind-minstrels, two string-minstrels (if the king thought fit), and the wait, a 'watchman-musician'. These numbers are established by the *Liber Niger*: the writer mentions thirteen minstrels and a wait, of whom nine minstrels came to the court only 'at five festes of the yere . . . and then they to avoyde the next day after the festes be don'.[16] Thus, only five were retained permanently. By the middle of the sixteenth century things were greatly changed. Edward VI in 1552 had sixty-five secular musicians, whose wages amounted to the equivalent of about £50,000 a year in present-day money.[17] But this increase was not matched elsewhere. At Henry VIII's accession he was served by sixteen trumpeters and roughly the same number of other players. But no one else had a permanent establishment even approaching this in size. Even Cardinal Wolsey, who prided himself on the number of his servants and of his servants' servants, was content with four minstrels (trumpeters and drummers excepted). Perhaps 'content' is too strong a word, since we find Wolsey in 1513 negotiating with Sir Richard Wingfield for the employment of two more 'drumslades'.[18]

In fact, outside the court, the actual size of a minstrels' band in livery of a great lord, or of a town, does *not* seem to vary much according to patron, nor to have increased during the period. The accounts of Shrewsbury Corporation in 1457 present roughly the same picture as those of Richard Cromwell eighty years later. The Bailiff's accounts of Shrewsbury show the following entries for 1457:

> Quatuor ministrallis domini ducis de Bukyngham . . . iiij ministrallis d'ni ducis de Eboraco [York] iv minstrellis d'ni ducis de Excestro.[19]

Eighty years later Richard Cromwell paid sums sufficient for three or four players, to: the king's minstrels (June 1538); the Lord Admiral's minstrels (September 1538); the prince's minstrels (January 1539).[20] What does vary is the number of bands attached to any one patron. Besides a troupe of actors and a band of minstrels, an earl or a duke was expected to have a band of trumpeters. The *Northumberland Household Book* has a section entitled, 'Al maner of rewardes customable usede yerly'. We can see from it that six was the appropriate number of trumpeters for an earl or duke.[21] The king's own household of musicians could easily break up into small units. In various account-books the following groups are named (they may not all be distinct): the king's trumpets, the king's minstrels, the king's shawms, the king's loud pipes, the king's flutes.[22] The problem arises, whether these groups were all from the household, or whether some simply wore the king's livery as a privilege without ever receiving regular wages. Thus, in 1520 there was an *inspeximus* of the charter of 1469 which made the royal minstrels a corporation with a marshal elected by themselves. The eight minstrels who benefited by this document nowhere appear in the household accounts as musicians.[23] A similar problem has to do with 'the Queen's minstrels'. In 1519, for example, 'the minstrels of the Queen's chamber' received a New Year's gift from the king. He also used to pay their quarterly wages. Their names were Baltazar (a taberet-player), Jaques ('Jaques the phipher', probably), Evans (rebec), 'and another'. The question is, whether this band was identical with the one that toured the country under the same name and is mentioned, rather earlier, in the Accounts of Shrewsbury Corporation.[24]

As will have been noticed, some entries suggest that small consorts of *similar* instruments toured around together, others that the typical minstrel band, whether at home or on the road, consisted of a small *mixed* consort. 'The Queen's minstrels' of 1519 are a possible case of the second – taberet, pipe and rebec. It is natural to wonder what this and similar bands were designed to do, what determined their special constitution. The answer must be – principally, to provide dance-music. There were, it seems, two standard combinations: for the basse-danse, two shawms and a sackbut; for less courtly dances, rebec, harp or lute, and pipe-and-tabor (not always, it seems, played by one man).[25] Another way in which these small bands of musicians were employed was in providing music for plays; New Romney, for instance, paid for the services of at least ten different bands between 1470 and 1500.[26] Perhaps, since they would try to meet every possible demand, the minstrels also acted plays themselves.[27]

However the various instruments consorted in actual performance, whether on tour or at court, musicians were grouped for payments and rewards according to the instruments they played. The principal divisions were three – trumpeters, minstrels and string-minstrels.

The employment of trumpeters was, from early medieval times, a jealously guarded civic or aristocratic privilege, since the trumpet was intimately connected with the ceremonies and rites which were the very life-blood of society. This exclusiveness early communicated itself to the trumpeters themselves, who 'were formed into a special corps, which afterwards became an exclusive guild'.[28] Henry VIII increased the number of royal trumpets from nine to fifteen or sixteen in 1509; and they were much employed, under their marshal, as in earlier reigns and in all countries, heralding royal personages, accompanying ambassadors abroad, assisting at jousts and ceremonies, and so on.[29] The musicians most necessary after the trumpeters for ceremonial display were the drummers, some of whom may have belonged to the same guild as the trumpeters: less select players on the drum can be classed with pipers, 'phiphers' and 'whistlers'.

The other principal wind-instrumentalists were players on sackbuts (trombones) and shawms (the oboe family). The royal account-books contain payments to both 'the old sagbutts' and 'the new sagbutts'. Thus, on New Year's Day, 1539, the king rewarded both groups.[30] By that time the 'new' sackbuts, whatever they were, were far from new, for on

9 November 1531 'Antony the Sagbut' was paid 53s. 4d. for 'his costes going to Southampton with the new sagbuttes'. There had been already ten sackbuts on the pay-roll in 1526, and these were perhaps divided into two companies.[31] The popularity of the shawm is demonstrated by the fact that the words 'shawm' and 'minstrel' were sometimes used synonymously: the 'mynstrelles' of Henry VII's funeral are the 'still shalms' of his son's coronation. With the 'still' (soft, indoor?) shawms should probably be contrasted 'lowd menstrales' and 'lowd pipes'.[32] Sackbuts and shawms, as already mentioned, were much in demand for dance-music. It was after playing for a dance that one of Wolsey's best minstrels ('he that played the shalme, an excellent man in that art') died in France – either of too much shawm-playing, or poisoned by a jealous rival – during Wolsey's embassy of 1526.[33]

String-players, although perhaps graded higher, were in a minority:

> For the most parte all maner mynstrelsy
> By wynde they delyver theyr sound chefly.[34]

Early in the reign there were two rebecs – perhaps these were the two string-minstrels regarded as optional by the *Liber Niger*; in 1526 there were three.[35] In this same year two viols appear for the first time, played by musicians with Netherlandish names, Hans Highorne and Hans Hossenet.[36] Although rebecs were still employed at court in the seventeenth century, the bowed instrument of greatest importance after about 1540, when the first Italian consort appeared, was the viol.[37] When Henry VIII died there were six Italian viol-players at court, besides English or Dutch players. The growing popularity of the lute is indicated by a slight increase in the number of lutenists on the pay-roll.[38] Quite outside these categories were the keyboard players: Dionisius Memo, Benedictus de Opitiis, John Heywood and others.

Professional musicians were, then, organized in two branches – the singers of chapels and colleges, and the instrumental players of noble households. These instrumentalists were only beginning at the end of the Middle Ages to exchange their itinerant and unsettled mode of life for the security of household employment. By the beginning of Henry VIII's reign regular quarterly payments in the account-books show that the musicians of the royal household, if of none other, had become resident. The increased frequency and magnificence of court entertainments doubtless m de it economical to keep musicians on the spot. This does not mean that they no longer had need or opportunity to accept engagements outside. Richard

Cromwell's accounts alone show a market for their skills. But it can only have been the lot of a handful of minstrels to enjoy a steady wage anywhere. The great majority trusted to a good 'livery', a good name, and the power of their 'trades-union'. They all had a vested interest in keeping impostors out of the way. The 'royal' as distinct from the 'royal *household*' minstrels headed the guild to which all players had to belong. They eagerly sought in 1520 to have their charter renewed, which protected them against illegal competition: their complaints induced the king to say that

> certain rude peasants and tradesmen of different crafts in our realm of England have pretended to be minstrels. Some of them have worn our livery, never granted them at all, and even pretended to be our own royal minstrels.[39]

It is, incidentally, an interesting comment on the skill of certain professional minstrels that illiterate peasants had to be legally restrained from impersonating them. However this may be, it was important for them, even in the early sixteenth century, to keep the homes and highways of England clear of rivals. The relative insecurity of the minstrel's life is the measure of his inferior status. This inferiority is noticeable at every point of comparison between the minstrel and the Gentleman of a chapel – training, education, pay, rewards, and privileges.

II

For many boys in the late Middle Ages formal education began, if anywhere, at the song-schools of cathedral, college or chantry. The only alternative at the primary stage was the A B C, later the 'petty', school.[40] Boys were needed in cathedrals and colleges to sing the services, and song-school education was, primarily, training for this purpose: they learnt to sing plain-song, to read the Latin psalter, and later, perhaps, their *Donat*, the Latin grammar. An intelligent boy, like, for example, Thomas Tusser, might be impressed from the song-school for service in a large chapel.

> Then for my voice, I must (no choice)
> Away of force, like posting horse,
> For sundry men had placards then
> Such child to take.[41]

The royal chapel-masters had considerable powers of compulsory recruitment. The earliest writ for the Chapel Royal seems to be that of 1420 to

John Pyamour to take up as many boys as he needed. That to John Mel-yonek in 1484 enabled him to impress men as well as boys.[42] All this does not mean that music was especially favoured. Royal impressment was used in every department of courtly life. Just as much trouble was taken to get suitable boys for the riding stable as for the chapel; masons were impressed as well as musicians.[43] An amusing light on the Falstaffian methods of the recruiting officers is shed by an entry in an account-book at Wells Cathe-dral: 'Given to the King's servants *not* to take away three choristers, 6s 8d.' Westminster Abbey had similar powers of impressment.[44]

But whatever song-school eventually claimed a boy, his syllabus of in-struction would be basically the same, though the quality of the teaching may have differed enormously. The Master of the Children of the Chapel Royal had 'to drawe these children, as well in the schoole of facett, as in songe, organes, or suche other vertuous thinges'. 'Facet' was short for *Facetus de Moribus*, 'used in schools as a book of instruction in behaviour'.[45] But we may suppose that the boys' instruction was rather for 'use' than for 'ornament'. The usual requirements for the master of a song-school seem to have been entirely musical. For example, the song-master at Lincoln in 1539 was

> duly and diligently to instruct chorister boys, both in the science of singing, viz. playn-songe, prykyd songe, fa-burdon, diskante, and counter, and also in playing the organs in the cathedral, especially two or three of them, whom he or his deputy shall find fit, docile and suit-able to be taught to play on the instruments called clavy-cordes. . . .

There is no mention of academic studies at all.[46] Merbecke's comment on his own education is illuminating: he says he 'in a maner never tasted the swetness of learned letters, but [was] altogether brought up in your High-nes college at Wyndesore in the study of musike and plaiying organs, wherin I consumed vainly the greatest part of my life'.[47] This is unmis-takable testimony to the vocational bias even of a royal song-school.

If the children, even of the Chapel Royal, were trained rather than edu-cated, their training was intellectually strenuous enough to fit them for the University. Failing a vacancy at court for a boy whose voice had broken, the king 'assigneth every suche child to a college of Oxenford or Cam-brige, of the King's foundation'.[48] The children's welfare was not left to chance, either while their voices were still good or after they had broken. Many children were boarded out and some instructed by senior members of the Chapel, such as Fayrfax and Cornish. Thus, in December 1510

Fayrfax was paid at the rate of 1s. a week for boarding William Alderton and Arthur Lovekyn, and 46s. 8d. 'for their learning' over the space of about a year.[49] This system continued after the child's singing days were over, if he was being retained at court; Cornish was paid in April 1517 for 'finding and teaching' William Saunders, 'late child of the Chapel'.[50]

A University career might lead to the Church. Richard Davy, for example, went up to Magdalen College, Oxford, in 1483, at about sixteen years of age; in 1490 he became master of the college choristers; in 1492 he left his job, perhaps to study; in 1497 he was ordained priest. The reward of his industry and ambition was the chaplaincy of the Boleyn family, which he held from 1506 until 1516 when he died.[51] By means of the Church even the lowest-born boy could rise to a position of wealth and power.

But, it seems, for the children of the Chapel Royal a University career was second-best. Preferment at court was put first, and even the University might only be a means of marking time, 'tyl the Kinge otherwise list to advaunce hym'.[52] The immediate preferment open to the 'late children' was to the position of yeomen of the Chapel, or 'pistellers' (i.e. epistle-readers), 'by the Deane his denomination, and for theire cunnyng and vertue'.[53] Later they might, like Robert Philip, become Gentlemen of the Chapel, the summit of a normal ambition, or 'gentlemen singers' of the chamber (this new class of appointment did not become important until the 1540's).[54]

The highest position open to the ordinary professional musician, who did not, like Davy, submerge his profession in a higher one, was that of 'master of the choristers'. But it seems that the status of a plain Gentleman of the Chapel Royal was thought equal or superior to that of a master elsewhere. In fact, there were probably *two* kinds of Gentlemen appointed: the active day-to-day singers, at whose head was the 'master of the children'; and musicians of especial repute like Fayrfax and Pygott, both of whom at some time had active appointments in other places – Fayrfax as organist of St Alban's, Pygott as Wolsey's chapel-master.[55] The distinction is analogous in some ways to that between a Fellow and an honorary Fellow of a College. But to be an 'honorary' Gentleman of the Chapel also brought with it additional income. This was perhaps by way of compensation, for surely the 'honorary' Gentlemen were not enrolled merely to do *them* honour; there must surely have been also an element of impressment – they were enrolled to do the *king* honour, and had to wait on his pleasure.

For boy-choristers who failed to win promotion in the senior branch of their profession there were still various openings as actors, as servants, as 'posture-masters', or as minstrels.[56] It has been suggested that minstrelsy in the widest sense, the entertainment profession, got recruits from song-schools. The point requires investigation. Since boys of most 'chapels' were called upon, probably, to act in plays and disguisings, acting was obviously a possible career. Whether jugglers, tumblers and acrobats were ex-choristers is more doubtful. Domestic service with the nobility may have claimed some boys. This is presumably what is meant by the *Liber Niger*'s promise of preferment at court; it also gives a particular motive for Hugh Rhodes' writing of *The Boke of Nurture* (Rhodes was a Gentleman of the Chapel Royal); and for training in 'facet' (curtesye) generally.[57] Finally, of course, there were the usual openings in trade. It was not too late, when a boy's voice broke, for him to become apprenticed in the usual way. Arthur Lovekin, mentioned above, may have become a tailor.[58]

Openings there were certainly for entry into the instrumental branch of the profession. The usual way of becoming a minstrel was, it appears, by *being* a minstrel. 'Education by employment' was a fundamental trait of medieval education: the young noble was a page and then a henchman in a great household; the 'children of the chapel' worked as singers. Only perhaps in the grammar-school was learning divorced from doing. Certainly the instrumental branch of the musical profession trained its recruits by employing them. A few children were virtuosi in their own right – Cuddy, 'the Inglis boy' lutenist at the Scottish court, perhaps; and the boy who ousted Pietro Carmeliano from the king's favour.[59] But most were clearly apprentices, serving, helping and learning from their masters, as in any other trade – 'the four shawms' had 'their four childer', for example.[60] In Scotland there were also 'scholar-minstrels',[61] and in the English court 'the young minstrels'. These minstrels were included among 'persons assigned to have lodging in the king's house when they repair to it', together with the six gentleman-waiters, the henchmen and their master (Sir Francis Bryan), the groom of the Privy Chamber, and the 'poticary'. It seems a fairly select company, but who the 'young minstrels' were, and what they had to do, I cannot determine.[62] A musical apprentice at court, apparently, on a lower level, was the 'groom wayte'.[63] Occasionally boys were sent away for instruction; John Lord Howard's (i.e. the *Norfolk*) *Household Book* contains the following entry:

Item the same daye my Lord made covenaunt with William Wastell of London, harper: he shall have the sone of John Colet of Colchester, harper, for a yere to teache hym how to harpe and to singe, for the which techynge my Lord shall geve hym 13s 4d and a gown, wherof my lord to hym in ernest 6s 8d.[64]

Far more common than this must have been the handing-down of musical craft from father to son – the names of More, van Welder, Bassano and, later, Lupo come to mind.[65]

Family tradition, however, and the normal apprenticeships seem not to have filled the vacancies at court, even in the reign of Henry VI, let alone under Henry VIII. In 1456 the king's minstrels were empowered to impress 'young men of comely appearance, trained in the art of minstrelsy'. The patent states that the king's minstrels are now ageing and will need assistance; they are to go and recruit young men wherever they may be found, whether in livery or out of it.[66] The minstrel had to be personable, for he might have to appear sitting on a pageant in the midst of a courtly disguising. Other minstrels were recruited from abroad.[67]

An industrious and talented minstrel might hope, in the early sixteenth century, to get himself permanently attached to the court or to some noble household or to a city corporation.[68] But something more than industry and talent was doubtless required in the highest and best rewarded post – musician 'of the pryvat chambre'. Besides the virtuosi, Memo and de Opitiis, there was room for a good all-round musician and administrator such as Philip van Wilder. A Peter van Wilder had been at court since 1519. Philip appears first in 1526 as a minstrel; but by 1530 he had already attained a position of importance, to judge from references in the *Privy Purse* expenses, not only to him but to his 'boy', 'the childe that waytes on Philip'. He seems to have been in charge of the music in the Privy Chamber; hence such entries as: 'paied to phillip of the pryvat chambre for ij sagbuttes ij tenor shalmes and two treble shalmesse £10. 10s.' He was later in general charge of the king's instruments, and was in addition a composer of repute. When he died someone wrote an elegy 'Of the death of Phillips' which Tottel thought worth including in *Songs and Sonets*, 1557; it ends:

> The stringe is broke, the lute is dispossest,
> The hand is colde, the bodye in the grounde.
> The lowring lute lamenteth now therfore
> Philips her frende that can her touche no more.[69]

Under Philip van Wilder, and in his charge during the 1530's, was a gallimaufry of musical entertainers – principally, 'the two Guillams' (one played the rebec), Mark Smeton (dancer and virginal-player), and Master Weston, the king's page (lutenist).[70] These, Weston excepted, may have risen from being minstrels. Their qualifications were, perhaps, chiefly social; their duties were to gamble with the king as well as to serenade him.

The foreigners of really outstanding ability were, of course, in no sense minstrels; some had risen from being singing-men. But there were in the early Tudor court a great number of foreign instrumentalists treated just like their English counterparts. Some were visitors, many were permanently engaged; their importance can hardly be overestimated. Among Henry VII's and Henry VIII's payments are sums given to German drumslades, a French organ-player, Dutch minstrels, the Queen of France's minstrels, the Prince of Castile's taberet – the list could easily be extended; at the Scottish court there were Italian trumpets, French 'whistlers' and minstrels of both nationalities.[71]

These facts call, in the present context, for two comments. First, minstrelsy was an international craft. This it always had been – witness the well-known gathering of minstrels from all corners of the earth at Pentecost, 1306, for the knighting of the future Edward II.[72] English instrumentalists must themselves have been 'trained', in the early sixteenth century as in earlier times, by travel, by contact with foreign players,[73] and by attendance at the 'schools' of minstrelsy commonly held during Lent. Secondly, if the supply of minstrels fell short, the Continent was a fruitful source of recruits. One account must suffice to illustrate the way in which many minstrels with names like John Droyt and John Blanche may have arrived at court:

> Chamberlain, court-master of the English merchants at Antwerp, writes to Paget, the first secretary of the court. He says that with the help of a local merchant he has found five musicians, of whom one can make all sorts of instruments. Four of them are young and would like to enter Paget's service; but they have no instruments of their own. The fifth, who owns the instruments, has with some difficulty been persuaded to go with them. They promise to stay in England until the New Year. Chamberlain has had to give them wages in advance and will pay their expenses. There are, he adds, also some Italians in the town, but they only play the viols 'and are no musicians'.[74]

The chief qualifications of a professional musician of either branch could simply be deduced from the sketch attempted here of their recruitment, training and scanty education. But the matter is sufficiently important to make it worth further exploration. What could the various professionals do in music? Could they all read it, copy and compose? Could they repair, as well as play, instruments? Who were the music-teachers? And so on.

III

The qualifications for a Gentleman of the Chapel are laid down in the *Liber Niger*. Both priests and singing-men are to be

> men of worshipp, endowed with vertuuse, moral, and speculatiff, as of theyre musike, shewing in descant clene voysed, well releesed and pronouncynge, eloquent in reding; sufficiaunt in organes pleyying, and modestiall in all other manner of behaving . . .[75]

A few singing-men – Banastir, Cornish, Hunnis, Rhodes, etc. – were men of letters, even if not distinguished. But, even so, it is doubtful whether much stress was laid on 'speculative virtue'. The probable level of their learning is indicated by Hugh Rhodes' *Boke of Nurture*, a treatise on etiquette for servants, and, later, Hunnis's metrical psalms and other verses.[76] The Master of the Children was, it is true, expected to teach elementary grammar; but, since the Master of Grammar himself very soon took the children over, the inference is that the musician only taught 'plainsong Latin'.[77] More practical sets of instructions than the *Liber Niger* appear to omit liberal attainments altogether; the new 'master' at the convent of Glastonbury, in 1534, had to be able to sing and play instruments at Christmas and other feasts, to teach six children prick-song and discant and two of them the organ.[78] A letter about Taverner's appointment as master of the choristers at Cardinal College, of Wolsey's foundation, specifies that he must have 'both his breste [? tenor or bass voice and falsetto voice] att will, the handling of an instrument, pleasure, cunning and exercise in teaching . . .'[79]

Singing-men were expected as a matter of course to be 'eloquent' in reading *music*, not only plain-song but 'prick-song'. They were probably the only musicians, outside the priesthood, who could do so; neither minstrels nor amateurs were ordinarily able to read music.[80] This means that many professional singers may have augmented their wages by music-copying. A payment by the Duke of Norfolk in February 1482 to a local chapel-master may have been for copying, rather than for composing, 'a song-booke and iiij amtemys'.[81] It has sometimes been said that the composer, Fayrfax, augmented his wages in this way; the books in question were, however, New Year presents to the king, who rewarded him with two payments of £20, a very considerable sum of money for those days and far more than the copying can have been worth commercially.[82] The duke's payment of 14s. 4d. seems more in the right scale.

Composing was a recommendation rarer than reading music or copying; but it was perhaps reasonably to be expected in several members of the Chapel Royal. That a firm distinction should be drawn between 'making' (composition) and 'setting' (arranging) seems most unlikely. Newark, for instance, was rewarded for making a song; Cornish for setting a carol.[83] One thing, at any rate, is clear: the principal composers of Henry VIII's reign were Gentlemen of His Majesty's most honourable Chapel. The principal exceptions were clerics – Richard Sampson (Dean of the Chapel Royal); Hacomplaynt; 'Sir' Thomas Pakke; 'Sir' Thomas Phillips; Richard Davy (ex-singing-man); Richard Smert (Rector of Plymtree), etc. As I have already emphasized, no *amateur* compositions are known to survive, except Henry VIII's and Sir William Hawte's.[84]

The highest 'paper-qualification' that a composer could acquire was a doctoral degree at one of the Universities;[85] and this several singing-men had – Fayrfax and Cooper, for instance. The earliest English musical degrees were awarded in the fifteenth century. The Bachelor's degree simply 'conferred the right of reading and lecturing' on the science of music (i.e. Boethius); no practical ability was required, but it could be a recommendation.[86] The doctorate, on the other hand, was usually conferred in the early sixteenth century on musicians of proven practical ability in the craft of composition. For example, John Gwynneth's final supplication was that

> whereas he had spent 20 years . . . in the practise and theory of music, and had published three Masses in five parts, and five Masses in four parts, and divers symphonies, and antiphons and songs for the use of the church, he might be admitted to proceed [in the faculty of music].[87]

At the end of the Middle Ages a composer was regarded as a clever craftsman, rather than as an individual gifted with supreme spiritual insight; so this practical bias does not of itself establish the high repute of the Mus.D. Rather the opposite – the real musician was still the philosopher. However, the first musical doctorates may have been conferred by royal prerogative – Saintwix (1463) was one of the king's chaplains. If so, the discrepancy between the doctor's gorgeous accoutrements and his humble academic status is partly accounted for. The degree, however acquired, was certainly an honourable one; but it ranked well below other doctorates. 'The title of doctor [of music] carried with it no rights such as were enjoyed in the case of other masters or doctors.'[88] He had, in fact, so far as the University was concerned, the show without the substance.

An unmistakable pointer towards the lower intellectual status of the creative art of composition, and therefore to the lower social status of the composer himself, is given by the position of musical theory. Speculative theory was the concern of the real musician (*musicus*), not of the performer (*cantor*).[89] The writers and compilers of learned musical treatises in England during the fourteenth and fifteenth centuries were not professional performers: Simon Tunstede, John Hothby, John Torkesey, Wylde and others, were clerics, Doctors of Theology rather than musical practitioners. The latter (among them Leonel Power) wrote only practical treatises, mostly in English, 'for hem that wil be syngers, or makers, or techers', about extempore discant. A talent for musical theorizing, however, on any level was clearly not a usual qualification for a singing man, and many of the 'discant' treatises were written by the learned.[90]

The principal qualifications were practical. A proportion of children were taught to play the clavichord and organ, so to be 'sufficiaunt in organes pleyyng' was clearly desirable. But it was not universal. In the Northumberland household the Master of the Children starts the weekly rota of organists, '*if* he be a player'. He is followed by 'A Countertenor that is a player'. And then by a tenor. From Henry VII's time onward there were organists at court – Arnold Jeffrey is named in 1498 – whose names do not appear in the chapel lists.[91] Their duties were probably not ecclesiastical at all. A chamber organ was a perfectly respectable instrument to use, for example, in a 'Maying' ceremony.[92] In Henry VIII's court Dionisius Memo and Benedictus de Opitiis had nothing, apparently, to do with the Chapel. Ability to play a keyboard instrument was for obvious reasons required of a 'Master of the Children'; ability to *teach* it to choristers seems to have been more in demand after 1535 than before.[93] Such accomplished musicians as the gentlemen of a noble chapel naturally played other instruments as well. A singing-man of the college of Rochester died possessed of a lute and a clavichord. On the other hand, no Gentleman of the Chapel Royal seems to have made a name for himself as an instrumentalist (though Cornish in his *Treatise bitwene Trowth and Enformacion* showed himself very knowledgeable about instruments[94]). The evidence on this point is entirely negative. No one says positively that the Gentlemen of the Chapel were *poor* lutenists or shawm-players. But to play on any instrument in public, other than keyboard, was probably beneath the dignity of a chapel-man. There was a hierarchy of instruments as well as of everything else in the Middle Ages; the chief 'instrument' was the human voice, its highest employment the service of God. The very idea of a singing-man playing, say, a shawm is ludicrous; it may in those days have seemed even offensive. Among 'artificial' instruments, organ and 'clavichord' (generic term in this period for virginals and the like) ranked very high, perhaps because they were played by the musically educated and used in church. The lute, or earlier the harp, might come next because courtly love had hallowed it. Then other strings, and lastly the numerous wind, wood and brass instruments.

Above all, a singing-man was a *singing*-man. It is impossible to say, as yet, what sort of tone and style was admired; but almost certainly a choir-singer had to be versatile enough to sing either in a true or a falsetto voice. The idea is sometimes put forward that Englishmen had a prerogative of 'natural', 'straightforward' singing, and that this singing 'displaced the old falsetto singing'.[95] Neither the music itself, nor the acid comments of the Reformers, nor the general tone of courtly life (with its tendency to 'garnish' everything) supports the idea. The popularity of the counter-tenor (presumably using a falsetto when necessary) has already been suggested. At one time Northumberland's chapel had six counter-tenors to two tenors and two basses.[96] Among other practical qualifications for a post as singer were the abilities to act as 'rector chori', to 'set the Queare', and to teach young choristers. The Northumberland regulations include: 'The Ordurynge for stonding Rector-chore at the Deske as to say at Mattyngis, Highe Masse and Evynsonge, oon on aither side'.[97] Some sort of conducting or directing must be meant. Perhaps 'Mr Lentall' of Cardinal College, Ipswich, was a 'rector chori':

> And but for Mr Lentall we cowde in a maner do nothing in oure quere. He taketh very great paynes and is alwaye present at Mattens and all Masses with evyn song, and settith the quere in good ordre fro tyme to tyme and fayleth not at eny tyme.

Lentall was, in addition, Master of the Children.[98]

The ordinary minstrel was in many ways less widely qualified than the professional singer; he was, first and last, an instrumental player. His office was often functional in the lowest sense. Trumpets and waits, in particular, 'blew to supper', piped the watch, announced revels, and so on. Although many minstrels must have been highly skilled on their instrument or instruments, it is most unlikely that many could read measured music, though some (especially if they came from a song-school) would be able to read plain-song and other unmeasured notation, e.g. basse-danse tunes.[99] It was remarked as a rare accomplishment that the oboes of Louis XII were able to play *res facta*, composed and written music.[100] There is little likelihood that English minstrels would be more skilled than their continental colleagues. Instrumentalists did, however, sometimes take part in complicated church-music; treble shawm and cornett, for instance, supporting the treble lines, bombard and sackbut the tenor. One of Wolsey's correspondents writes from France that at High Mass the Chapel of Francis I was accompanied by hautbois (shawms) and sackbuts.[101] In England at Canterbury, rather later (1549), 'two sackbutters and two cornetters were appointed, whose duty was "to support the melody on feast days and their vigils".'[102] Tinctoris, the Flemish theorist, approves of the use of reed and brass tone at least:

> for the lowest contratenor parts and often for any contratenor part, to the shawm players one adds brass players who play, very harmoniously, upon the kind of tuba which is called . . . *trompone* in Italy and *sacqueboute* in France.[103]

Instrumental accompaniment could have taken several forms: if the fundamental notes of the slowly-changing harmony were written out, they could have improvised round them; or they could have ornamented the melody, usually plain-song, on which many pieces were constructed; or perhaps, like many illiterates, they had extraordinary memories.

Many minstrels made a sideline of repairing instruments. The minstrels of 'my lord Dabney', for example, received 3*s*. 4*d*. in 1524 for 'setting and mending' an instrument belonging to Katharine, Countess of Devon. In the Norfolk household minstrels repaired a lute.[104] Instrument-*making*, as distinct from repairing, was a trade on its own, and not a normal skill for a musician in the late Middle Ages. Large organs excepted, many instruments must have been acquired from abroad: the Scottish king gave the 'scholar-minstrels' leave of absence 'to buy them instruments in Flanders'. On another occasion he sent a minstrel 'to go and buy a shawm in Edinburgh'.[105] At Oxford in 1452 a harp-maker called Robert was in business – and involved in litigation.[106] Although there are no records of a guild of instrument-makers in London, the City, like other cities, had its craftsmen. Some makers employed at court may have been City men. Among those retained in royal service were Anthony Basson, 'maker of divers instruments of music', John de John (a priest), William Lewes, William Betton, Gregory Estamproy.[107] The last name suggests foreign extraction at least. One foreign craftsman came with high recommendations – Michael Mercator. The Count of Buren wrote to Henry VIII thanking him for his generous reception of Mercator,

> whose skill in constructing musical instruments, and in other arts, deserves royal patronage. His dexterity is no less in public and private business, which the Count has made trial of in these disturbances in Lower Germany.[108]

This probably means he was also a good spy. The point will arise later.

That many instrumentalists were teachers goes without saying, since the profession trained its own members. The more talented and highly placed minstrels were able also to teach noble amateurs to play instruments. Henry VII's and Henry VIII's children were taught by the court lutenists.[109] Teaching was probably a step up for the ordinary minstrel, since Skelton refers in no mincing manner to the 'comely coistrown' as having been, in reverse order, 'a master, a mynstrell, a fydler, a farte'.

> Nay, jape not with hym, he is no small fole,
>   It is a solemnpne syre and a solayne;
> For lordes and ladyes lerne at his scole;
>   He techyth them so wysely to solf and to fayne,
>   That neyther they synge wel prycke songe nor playne:
> Thys doctor Devyas commensyd in a cart,
> A master, a mynstrell, a fydler, a farte.[110]

It is not easy to fish out the facts from the torrent of abuse, exhibitionism and sheer verbosity. Other references in the poem lead one to think that 'thys doctor Devyas' may have been a singing-man at some time. However this may be, most teachers of music were professional instrumentalists. Exceptions, apart from 'Masters of the Children', include Dr Abell, Katherine of Aragon's devoted chaplain who died in the Tower for opposing the divorce, and the Marquis of Exeter's servant Hugh Browne whose 'knowledge is to teach men to do things in music which he himself cannot express nor utter, and yet he can perfectly teach it'. He could, of course, 'play somewhat on divers instruments', but he was not a professional.[111]

Hugh Browne's name is a reminder that by about 1540 the tradition of household music was growing sufficiently strong for it to be worth an employer's while to have his servants trained to make music as an 'extra'. The opposite had been the rule for a long time: musicians of every branch were able, allowed, often encouraged and sometimes forced, to undertake other pursuits beside their music. For a minstrel like Alamire (Mr A-Below-Middle-C), who travelled widely, espionage was an ideal trade; Michael Mercator, mentioned above, probably had a good head for intrigue; and one of the king's minstrels, 'a fellow of Hans Nagel's', seems to have been a secret agent.[112] Trumpeters, moreover, were found useful as confidential messengers.[113]

A man of general competence such as Cornish was bound to be entrusted with administrative duties usually left to clerics; but surely he was not, as is sometimes said, responsible for items of general repair and maintenance about the court. The payment to

> Mr Cornisshe, paving, gutters of lead for urinals and other necessaries at Greenwich

must refer, like other entries in the accounts for June 1516, to the jousts and play done at Greenwich at Whitsuntide that year.[114] Cornish had general charge of organizing pageants and similar shows, but he was not quite the general factotum sometimes imagined. Other singing-men and a few minstrels were in business on their own account. It may be taken for granted that they dealt in musical instruments. One singer from St Paul's did a trade also in 'counterpoints', i.e. counterpanes, not music; and Noe de la Salle (minstrel or 'tabret') was an exporter of beer.[115] The musician, however, who was in business on the largest scale, was William Crane, successor to Cornish as Master of the Children. He was a water-bailiff, a wool-exporter and a wine-merchant; twice he was lent the enormous sum of, in modern money, about £30,000, presumably for a commercial purpose. His various businesses are conveniently summarized in an official description of him in the *Privy Seals*:

> Willelmum Crane de hospicio nostro Gentilman alias dictum Willelmum Crane unum Generosorum Capelle nostre alias dictum . . . de London Gent . . . de Parochia sancti Dunstan in le Est London Gent . . . contrarotulatorem parve custume nostre in portu nostro London . . . civem et pannarium London . . . de London Draper . . . de Haveryng at Bowre in Comitatu Essex Gent . . . Armigerum . . .[116]

He was also the 'furnisher or outfitter of three ships and three galleys to the King in 1528'.[117] No musical compositions by Crane survive; one wonders whether he can possibly have had time to write any.

In considering the general social position of musicians it is quite as important to know of these leisure occupations as of their professional duties. Other items of interest are their wages, rewards, titles, and privileges.

IV

One of the most difficult tasks is to estimate the value of cash-payments, grants of land, benefices and pensions. Crane is, admittedly, an exceptional case; but his official wage of perhaps £400 or £500 a year (in modern money) clearly does not signify greatly. The changing worth of money in a long reign, the value of board, lodging and service, a man's future prospects and the standard of life expected of him are a few of the factors which have to be taken into account. Nevertheless it is worth remarking that it was not the minstrels but the priests and chapel clerks whom the king 'avaunceth . . . by prebends, churches of his patrymony, or by his lettres recommendatory, free chappells, corrodies, hospitalles or pensions'.[118] Such rewards were presumably an addition to the singer's wage of $4\frac{1}{2}d$. a day, and not a mere accounting device. The comparison between this wage of $4\frac{1}{2}d$. and the chaplain's of $7d$. is probably a sound indication of their status, for clerks and chaplains lived and worked under similar conditions; but the fact that a trumpeter received $1s. 4d$., a minstrel in the navy $6d$., as against the singing-man's $4\frac{1}{2}d$., is in itself meaningless.[119] A safer guide to status, in a first survey, are the honours, titles, privileges and social contacts of each group of persons.

A convenient starting-point, in this attempt to summarize the status of different musicians in society, will be the orders of precedence compiled at the time. John Russell's *Boke of Nurture* contains one of many such lists. The fifth and last group consists of all those of squire's rank in order of merit, and runs as follows:

> Doctors of Law; ex-Mayors of London; Sergeants of Law; Masters of Chancery; Preachers of pardon; Masters of Arts, 'clerkes of connynge that han taken degre'; other religious orders, of poverty and chastity; Parsons and Vicars; Parish Priests; City Bailiffs; Yeomen of the Crown; Sergeants-of-arms; Heralds (beginning with the King's Herald), Merchants, Gentlemen and Gentlewomen.[120]

It is clear that no one below the rank of 'gentleman' could sit at a ceremonial banquet; the singers of the royal chapels were sufficiently honourable to have the lowest place. We know, for instance, from Leland (the king's antiquary), where the chapel-men sat at St George's Day feasts in Windsor. There were four tables: the king had a table to himself; at the right-hand table sat all the Knights of the Garter in their degree, with

> a littill byneith them ... on both Sides of the Table, the Dean, the Chanoignes [Canons] and the Por Knyghts of the College, in ther Mantells, and byneith theym the resideu of that Quere [i.e. the resident singing-men of Windsor] ...;

at the middle table sat various lords, 'and a lytill byneith theym satt the King's Chapell'.[121] The choirs took no part in the 'honourable service' of the feast, unless as Gentlemen. But they were called upon to sing. On one occasion 'the Song at this Fest songen' was a political carol:

> England now rejoysse, for joyous may thou bee,
> To see thy King so flowring in Dygnitie.[122]

It was at a Windsor feast, too, in the same year, that

> at the table in the Medell of the Hall sat the Deane and thoos of the Kings Chapell, whiche incontynently [i.e. immediately] after the Kings furst Course sange a Carall.[123]

Even allowing for the special connection between the royal choirs and Windsor, the fact still remains that *royal* singers, at least, were men of honour.

A Doctor's degree in music might qualify a musician to rank with 'clerkes of connynge that han taken degre', below Masters of Arts (according to Russell) but above the religious orders and the parish priests. Other degrees in music – Flude [H21, H26] is mysteriously described as *in armonia graduat[us]* – would have counted for less. Musicians of the professional class seem to have had no other academic degrees. Neither do any appear to have been knighted at any time. Fayrfax may have been the fourth son of a knight. But the highest 'rank' he attained was that of a 'poor knight of Windsor', a completely different thing: the status of a 'poor knight' was about that of a Canon. Crane and Heywood were *armigeri* – that is, entitled to wear a coat-of-arms.[124]

Another indication of rank was the style of dress appropriate to any particular person; no one was allowed to wear clothes above his station,

though, of course, everyone did. On particularly important occasions, like
the Field of the Cloth of Gold (1520), more than usual efforts were made
to enforce the Acts of Apparel. A 'memorial of the things necessary' for
this pompous meeting says that no man shall presume to wear apparel above
his degree. 'Minstrels, players in interludes, sights and revels' were eventually exempted from the Acts.[125] Numerous gowns were given to the
Gentlemen of the Chapel by the king, either as part of their 'finding' or as
special gifts; minstrels received them less frequently. Out of dozens of examples two must suffice: a Warrant of the Great Wardrobe to deliver
William Cornyshe, 'one of the Gentlemen of the Chapel', a gown 'which
we have given unto him by way of our reward'; and an interesting gift to
John Blak, 'our trompeter', of a gown of violet cloth with bonnet and hat
'to be taken of our gift against his marriage'.[126] These garments must have
been socially appropriate. But the exact significance of various types of
cloth – chamlet, tawny, velvet, etc. – is difficult to determine. And the
problem is complicated, also, because special clothes were worn for court
entertainments. But the principle of such grading is of the first importance.
In this court society everyone had his place, even if he did not keep it.

Another distinguishing mark was the 'service' allowed for each person.
The *Liber Niger* put the matter on a clear-cut arithmetical basis: each chaplain was to have 'one honest servant'; every two singing-men, one servant;
and thirteen minstrels shared two servants between them.[127] The relative
standing of professional singer and professional instrumentalist is epitomized here. The instrumentalist, even when he had permanent standing,
was of considerably lower rank. Many household books give wage-lists,
in which everyone occupies his proper station. The ecclesiastical singer
was the least among gentlemen; the instrumentalist was no higher than a
groom. The Northumberland household regulations present us with the
following list:

> Gentlemen Ushers and Gentlemen and young Gentlemen and Hench-
> men at their friends' finding; Officer of Arms; two Yeoman Ushers
> of the Chamber: then, Gentlemen of the Chapel [widely differing in
> wages]; Marshals of Hall; Yeomen of Chamber; Yeomen Officers of
> Household; Grooms and Groom Officers; Children for household
> offices; then, minstrels, followed by footmen, falconers, painters,
> joiners, gardeners and clerks.[128]

The service which above all others conferred honour, even if not permanent status, was waiting on the king in the privy chamber. Had Mark

Smeton not been of the chamber, he could hardly have been described as 'gentylman'.[129] On the other hand, John Heywood, who was never of the privy chamber, seems to have had a standing from the first. He is variously described as 'gentleman, recently of Hinxhill', and *generosus*; he owned estates in three counties, 'was a member of the Mercers' Company, and a measurer of linen cloths in the City of London'.[130] Heywood was clearly superior to the typical instrumentalist. It is probably significant that he was a keyboard player, for no minstrel proper seems to have played a keyboard instrument – this was a privilege reserved for singing-men, musicians of the privy chamber (Smeton was a virginalist), and foreign virtuosi.

It was a foreigner, Dionisius Memo, who of all musicians was closest to the king. The supreme token of his intimacy with the royal family was that in 1517, when the plague was ravaging the land and had even taken off some of the pages who slept in the king's bedchamber, the king retained by his side only three favourite gentlemen and Dionisius Memo out of the whole court. They accompanied the king and the queen 'through every peril'.[131]

The word 'intimacy' must be used with care. It has been suggested, for instance, that William Cornish was an 'intimate friend of Henry VIII and shared his innermost counsels'. Professor Wallace writes, romantically, of Cornish, Crane and Kite:

> These three good fellows the King found to be men after his own heart – educated, musical, full of the 'joy of life', and fond of its dramatic representation . . . There are no other such friendships in the life of Henry VIII.[132]

There is no real evidence that any professional musician, except Memo, was very close to the king. Gifts and rewards are not proofs of friendship. However, the musicians of the privy chamber must have been mixed up with the king's private life, though some of them on no very exalted level; they were perhaps not much more regarded than the rascally Domingo Lomelyn, or Patch the fool. Entries in the Privy Purse accounts show that Gentlemen of the Chapel Royal also shared the king's recreations; Crane and Browne played at archery for large sums of money:

> Item the same daye paied to William Browne for so moche money as he and other being matched with him wanne of the kinges grace and of his matche at the pryckes, and by bettes in Eltham parke divers and sundrye tymes as apperith by his bille subscribed with his hande the somme of . . . £132. 15s.[133]

We do not know how many persons had to share these huge winnings (something like £4,000 in present-day money); but the sum involved is large enough to make us wonder how non-royal losers paid their debts. At about the same time Crane won the more modest sum of £7 2s. 6d. (a mere £200 or so).[134]

How easily could professional musicians mix with courtiers? The very fact that society at court and elsewhere was so conscious of 'degree', believing it to be a reflection on earth of the Eternal Order, may have made for easier relationships. If you know, and everyone else knows, your place, you have additional freedom, since your freedom cannot be misconstrued. But, when all is said, it is very difficult indeed to get more than the haziest idea about the standing of any particular *individual* with the king or with other nobles. The evidence is scanty and liable to misinterpretation.

This does not mean, however, that the various *classes* of musician cannot be fairly precisely graded, for they can. Instrumentalists span a great part of the ladder of society. The itinerant minstrel was placed low – in *Cock Lorrel's Bote* he ranks with 'fruyters' and 'cheese-mongers';[135] the courtly minstrel, on the other hand, a skilled player attached more or less permanently to a great household, ranks among the waiting-servants of the household – he has the status of a groom. Besides them are two classes of players: chamber-musicians, rather like the itinerant minstrels in that they were entertainers, 'companions' as well as musicians – their status was an individual matter; and, secondly, virtuosi, many of them foreigners, who were more highly regarded, it seems, than any other musicians whatsoever.

Professional singing-men belonged to a different class (they were, incidentally, a closed, national class, including no foreigners). In the mass they inspired no great respect. Even Taverner was described as 'but a Musitian'; and Sir Thomas More, acting the common singing-man, drew forth exclamations of reproach from the Duke of Norfolk, 'God bodye, God bodye, my Lorde Chancellour, a parishe clarke, a parish clarke! You dishonour the Kinge and his office.'[136] But the Gentlemen of the Chapel Royal had some standing. They were, just, gentlemen. As such they doubtless cut a considerable figure *outside* the court circle. *In* it they were honourable servants – no more. Among the king's 'Esquires of the Body' and other attendants of noble birth a singing-man would not count for much. Above all, courtiers and musicians had no social activity in common. One cannot imagine even Cornish or Fayrfax descending from the pageant and dancing amongst the lords and ladies. The chronicler Halle never mentions the eminent musicians who are known to have been present on such occasions. This fact is much more impressive than negative evidence usually is. Halle mentions 'all the best people' by name; and his book, though shot through with traditional idealisms, is a good index to courtly fashion and high society.[137] The musicians did not dance or hunt.

On the other hand, several professional *cantors* from Abyngdon to Fayrfax were individuals of distinction and repute. Musicians, in general, do not find their way into epigrams; their prestige did not warrant it. But Abyngdon was twice remembered by More in this way – he was styled *nobilis*, a singer and an organist in a thousand.[138] Fayrfax and Cornish, too, were in their different ways men of outstanding ability, and this ability was recognized. But what degree of intimacy with the great lords of the land they may have won through their talents, is a question which may never be answered.

NOTES TO CHAPTER 13

1. The main sources used are: the *Letters and Papers* and *Household Books* (*HHB*) given in the Reference List; E. K. Chambers's volumes on the stage; Hillebrand; Wallace; Nagel; Pattison, ch. 3; Jusserand; Bridgman; Grattan Flood. Since this chapter was first sketched Woodfill's excellent conspectus of Elizabethan conditions has appeared. The unpublished researches of Baillie ('London Churches, their Music and Musicians') have also uncovered much new information about London musicians in this period. Finally, Harrison's recent *Music in Medieval Britain* gives much information about choirs and choir-men.
2. *Norfolk HHB*, p. xxi.
3. Starkey, *Dialogue*, 129.
4. *Italian Relation*, 39. See p. 287 above.
5. *Northumberland HHB*, 429.
6. For this fairly well-known interchange of letters, see *L&P*, ii, pt 2, nos 4024–5, 4043–4, 4053–5.
7. Convenient lists of the Chapel Royal at various dates can be found in Lafontaine; Rimbault, *Cheque Book*; Hillebrand, 'Chapel Royal' (printing a better version of the book used by Rimbault); and Bridgman. Other chapels: see Bridgman; Cavendish; Harrison; *Italian Relation*; *Surrey HHBs*; and scattered references in Davey, Collier, Grattan Flood, etc.

8. *Ordinances*, 160–.
9. Cavendish, 19.
10. There is no comprehensive study of the medieval minstrel; but see Chambers, *Medieval Stage*, ii (as dramatic figure), Jusserand (as itinerant). Many of the conclusions drawn by Woodfill (about Elizabethan musicians) apply also to the early Tudor period.
11. Greene, no. 420; see also Robbins, *Secular Lyrics*, nos 1, 4, 5, etc.
12. Gower, *Confessio Amantis*, vii. 2423. Chaucer, *House of Fame*, line 1197 (Robinson, 293), distinguishes 'gestiours' and 'menstrales'.
13. Woodfill, 57–58, discusses the debasement of the term 'minstrel' during the sixteenth century.
14. W. A. Scott Robertson, 'The Passion Play and Interludes at New Romney', *Archaeologia Cantiana*, xiii (1880), 224, note.
15. Woodfill, *passim*.
16. *Ordinances*, 48–.
17. Nagel, 23, gives details for 1552; the yearly sum involved was £1,728.
18. Wolsey's musicians: Cavendish, 20. 'Drumslades': *L&P*, i. pt 2, no. 1963 (4 June 1513).
19. Chambers, *Medieval Stage*, ii. 250 (App. E).
20. Cromwell's accounts (1537–9) are summarized *L&P*, xiv, pt 2, no. 782 (espec. p. 329–). The date, June 1538, shows a payment of 2s. 6d. to each of three minstrels. As most payments are 7s. 6d. or 10s., it seems reasonable to suppose that three or four players were usually involved.
21. *Northumberland HHB*, 331– (see, especially, 341).
22. Cromwell's accounts alone (see note 20) show payments to all these groups.
23. 1469 charter: Chambers, ii. 260. *Inspeximus: L&P*, iii, pt 1, no. 604. For lists of royal instrumental musicians see Nagel; Lafontaine; *Musical Antiquary*, i–iv (1909–13); and useful summaries in Woodfill, App. E, 296–9.
24. NY gifts: 'King's Book of Payments', 1 Jan. 1519. Names of minstrels: Nagel, 8–20 *passim*. Shrewsbury Corporation Accounts: summarized Chambers, *Medieval Stage*, ii, App. E, 250.
25. For instruments used in courtly dances, see p. 246 above.
26. See note 14, p. 299 above.
27. Musicians acted in *Wit and Science* (1539?); see p. 255 above. They are also known to have acted later in the century, despite the increasing tendency towards specialization.

28. Galpin, 199: no reference given.
29. See p. 236 above for use of trumpets in ceremony. Establishment of trumpeters: Nagel, 11; Campbell, *Materials*, ii. 142.
30. NY gifts: 'King's Book of Payments', 1 Jan. 1539.
31. 'Antony': *PP Henry VIII*, 174. The 1526 list: Nagel, 16.
32. Henry VII's funeral, etc.: *L&P*, i, pt 1, nos 20 (p. 18) and 82 (p. 42). 'Lowd' instruments: see Dauney, 356, App. III (LHT Accounts), under 1503; and Cromwell's accounts (note 20, p. 300 above), Sept. 1538.
33. Cavendish, 60.
34. Heywood's *Weather*, in Brandl, 234. See also Henry's list of instruments (1547), referred to above, p. 276, note 55.
35. Thomas Evans, John Severnacke, John Pyrot (Nagel, 12, 14, 16).
36. Nagel, 16; they were still serving in 1547.
37. Nagel, 20.
38. 1509, Master Giles; 1526, Giles, Arthur Dewes, Peter van Welder (Nagel, 8, 15, 23). Perhaps Philip van Welder should also be added (see Woodfill, App. E, note 13).
39. Translated from the Latin original, pr. Chambers, *Medieval Stage*, ii. 260.
40. D. G. T. Harris's most able and informative article, 'Musical Education in Tudor Times', does not perhaps sufficiently distinguish courtly and general education, the early and the later Tudor period, but it remains the best account.
41. *The Last Will and Testament of Thomas Tusser* [with] *his Metrical Autobiography* (ed. Charles Clark, 1846), verse 6 [no pagination].
42. Hillebrand, 'Chapel Royal', 236 (from *Patent Rolls*, 7 Henry V, memb. 11d, Jan. 14); and Collier, i. 41.
43. *PP Henry VIII*, 303; Hillebrand, 'Chapel Royal', 236.
44. Wells: *Calendar of MSS of Wells*, ii. 132, from accounts of Richard Pomeroy, keeper of the fabric. Westminster: Bridgman, 62, from *L&P*, viii, no. 291.
45. *Ordinances*, 51; and *OED*, 'facet' *sb*[1].
46. Harris, 119.
47. *TCM*, x. 159, from the dedicatory address to his *Concordance*.
48. *Ordinances*, 51. This happy state of affairs did not continue. Hence William Hunnis's petition to Elizabeth in 1583. (Hillebrand, 'Chapel Royal', 248.)
49. 'King's Book of Payments', under date. Similar entries for Fayrfax

in Dec. 1511 and Dec. 1513; for Cornish in Apr. 1514, and so on.

50. 'King's Book of Payments', under date.

51. Grattan Flood, 60–; authorities not quoted.

52. *Ordinances*, 51.

53. *Ordinances*, 50.

54. Robert Philip: as boy – 'King's Book of Payments', Apr. 1514; as Gentleman – *L&P*, iv, pt 1, no. 1939 (p. 870), 1526. Robert Pury is said to have achieved the same promotion (Bridgman, 82); he was certainly in Crane's care in 1530 (*PP Henry VIII*, 33 '(but this is *after* he appears in the lists as a Gentleman (*L&P*, iv, pt 1, no. 1939 [p. 870], 1526). 'Gentleman singers': see p. 267 above.

55. Grattan Flood, 37– (Fayrfax); 34– (Pygott). No authority is quoted for the statement that Pygott had also been a boy in Wolsey's chapel.

56. Foster-Watson, 145, from Warton, *History of English Poetry* (1871), iii. 310. The additional suggestion is Foster-Watson's also.

57. Child-actors: see Hillebrand, Wallace, Chambers, *Elizabethan Stage*, *passim*. There are, one must note, few records of child-actors outside the Chapel Royal before the mid-sixteenth century. *Liber Niger*: see *Ordinances*, 50. Rhodes: see p. 325 below.

58. I thank Dr Hugh Baillie for this information ('London Music', 284). The identification, he points out, rests on the name alone.

59. Cuddy: see Dauney, 357, App. III (under date 1503). The boy who ousted: see p. 266 above.

60. ibid. (1505).

61. ibid. (1512); these 'scholar-minstrels' went to Flanders to buy instruments.

62. *L&P*, iv, pt 1, no. 1939 (revision of Eltham ordinances); *L&P*, iii, pt 1, no. 577 (p. 198) (breakfasts in court).

63. *Ordinances*, 48.

64. cit. Collier, i. 38.

65. More: Robert, wait under Henry VI, and William the blind harper (see p. 281 above). Bassano: 17 members of family listed by Nagel (1538 onwards). Welder: Peter, Philip, Matthew and Henry; see Nagel; J. Pulver, *A Biographical Dictionary of Old English Music* (1927); Woodfill, App. E. Lupo: see Woodfill's index.

66. *De ministrallis propter solatium regis providendis* (1456), quoted Furnivall (Rhodes, *Boke of Nurture*), introd. p. viii, note 2.

67. See p. 308 above.

68. See Woodfill, ch. 2, 'The Waits of London' (authorities given for earlier history, 33, note); ch. 4, 'Waits' (i.e. in the provinces); this is the only comprehensive account available.

69. Philip van Welder: see Nagel (there are some mistakes in indexing the Welders); Pulver, *Dictionary*; *Grove* (5); *PP Henry VIII*. His compositions survive in English MSS and in foreign prints, 1544–97. He is frequently confused in MSS with Peter Philips (*floruit* 1580).

70. 'The two Guillams': see N. H. Nicolas's introduction to his edition, excellently indexed, of *PP Henry VIII*. Smeton: see p. 319 above. Weston: see *PP Henry VIII*, index.

71. See *PP Henry VII*; *PP Henry VIII*; 'King's Book of Payments'; and many other account-books, including (for Scotland) *LHT Accounts*.

72. List reprinted, Chambers, *Medieval Stage*, ii. 234.

73. Bridgman, 99, gives instances of English musicians travelling with their patrons, from *L&P*, xii, pt 2, no. 616; xiv, pt 2, app. 40. And see note 61, p. 306 above.

74. *L&P*, xx, pt 2, no. 1004 (p. 497); I owe this important reference to Bridgman, 98.

75. *Ordinances*, 50.

76. For BANASTIR's literary productions, see Wallace, 24–25; a *Miraculum S. Thome Martyris* (*Index MEV* 2296); a poem on Sismonda ('at the mocione off John Raynere'); perhaps an interlude of 1482; and perhaps the words of his songs in F. CORNISH's literary talents have often been described (see, especially, Wallace, who makes a great deal of them). RHODES's *Book of Nurture* [1545?] is a treatise on etiquette 'very necessary for all youth and children'; he was already a Gentleman of the Chapel in 1526 (list in Hillebrand, 245) – this fact was not known to Furnivall when he edited Rhodes's treatise. The pedestrian nature of TYE's verse is well known (extract from *Acts of the Apostles* in Boyd, 69–70). It is rivalled by HUNNIS's productions (an account of his activities is in Pattison, 56–57; q.v. also for EDWARDS, a Gentleman from 1552); Hunnis's psalms were published in 1549. MERBECKE, a member of the royal chapel at Windsor, also wrote – or rather, he became a writer when he ceased to be a singing-man. With the possible exception of Edwards, none of these were learned

men in any sense of the word. An attempt, finally, has been made (Edwards and Salter, in EETS, no. 233 (1956)) to trace a MS of Skelton's *Diodorus Siculus* to a Gentleman of the Chapel, Robert Pend. The identification seems to rest almost entirely on the name.

77. *Ordinances*, 50–51.

78. Harris, 110, from *L&P*, vii, 411.

79. *TCM*, i, p. xlviii.

80. Amateurs: see p. 284; minstrels: see p. 313.

81. *Norfolk HHB*, 161; to John Goram, 'Maister of the Children of Seint Anthony'.

82. 'King's Book of Payments', Jan. 1517, 1518, 1519. It is not unlikely that Fayrfax presented his own compositions, the best tribute for a king.

83. Newark: *PP Henry VII*, 6 Jan. 1493. Cornish: *PP Elizabeth of York*, 83; see also ibid., 2, Fayrfax for 'setting an anthem . . .'

84. See p. 288 above.

85. Rashdall, *Universities of Europe* (rev. ed. 1936); C. F. Abdy Williams (less balanced but very informative); Harris, 'Musical Education', 123–; N. C. Carpenter, *Music in Medieval and Renaissance Universities* (U.S.A., 1958).

86. Abdy Williams, 17–19; Harris, 126, 128.

87. See Harris, 125; Grattan Flood, 108; Abdy Williams, 68.

88. Rashdall, iii. 160; and see Abdy Williams, ch. 8, 'Academical Dress. – Degree Ceremonies, Feasts'.

89. See p. 59.

90. A convenient collection is in S. B. Meech, 'Three 15th-Century Musical Treatises', *Speculum*, x (1935), 235.

91. *PP Henry VII*, 20 July 1498.

92. See p. 243.

93. This needs further investigation; but see the scattered notices in Leach's volumes on medieval education and those given by Harris, 109–.

94. For Cornish's treatise, see Flügel, *Anglia*, xiv (1892), 466; he may also have written the musical part of the *Lekingfelde Proverbis*, see ibid., or ed. P. Wilson, *The Musicall Proverbis . . . [at] Lekingfelde* (1924).

95. Lang, 185, 272.

96. *Northumberland HHB*, 48, etc.

97. idem, 370.

98. H. Ellis, *Original Letters illustrative of English History*, first ser., vol. i (1824), 189.

99. Examples of this notation in Toulouze, *L'Art et Instruction*; controversial interpretations, see O. Gombosi, 'Dance Music', *MQ*, xxvii (1941), 289; Bukofzer, *Studies*, ch. 6; Reese, *MR*, 36–38.

100. Pirro, 146; his whole discussion is of great interest.

101. *L&P*, iii, pt 1, no. 843 (27 May 1520).

102. *Memorials of Canterbury Cathedral*, ed. Woodruff and Danks (1912), 447. Examples could be multiplied: see *L&P: Venice*, iii, no. 50 (p. 29) – trombones, cornetts and organs; Galpin, 192 – cornetts.

103. Tinctoris, *De Inventione*, trans. A. Baines (part only), *GSJ*, iii (1950), 20.

104. *L&P*, iv, pt 1, no. 771 (p. 340); *Norfolk HHB*, 218.

105. Dauney, 357, App. III, 30 Sept., 1503, from LHT; the shawms may, of course, have been imported.

106. Abdy Williams, 45.

107. Nagel, *passim*; the Scottish court had a 'Gillam, organist', maker of the king's organs (Dauney, App. III).

108. *L&P*, xiii, pt 2, no. 617 (15 Oct. 1538).

109. See p. 275 above.

110. Dyce, i. 16 (*Comely Coistrown*, line 50–).

111. *L&P*, xiii, pt 2, no. 755; see p. 277 above.

112. Alamire: see *Biographie Nationale de Belgique*; he was a music-copyist also. Mercator: see p. 314 above. 'Fellow of Hans Nagel's': *L&P*, ii, pt 1, no. 2136.

113. See Bridgman, 106–7.

114. 'King's Book of Payments', June 1516.

115. St Paul's singer: *Norfolk HHB*, 158. Noe de la Salle: Bridgman, 109–, from *L&P*, xii, pt 2, no. 881; and see Nagel, index.

116. Quoted, Wallace, 63, from *Privy Seals*, 8 Jan., 14 Henry VIII (1523). Wallace's account of Crane is the best yet published (Grattan Flood does not refer to it). See also Pulver, *Biographical Dictionary*, 124–.

117. Wallace, 630.

118. *Ordinances*, 50.

119. Various wages are listed and compared in *L&P*, i, pt 3, preface to the orig. ed. (by Brewer), p. lxiii–.

120. Russell, 71–; other lists are in Wynkyn de Worde, *Boke of Kervinge* (1513), and in Rhodes, *Boke of Nurture* (before 1554).

121. Leland, iv. 240.

122. idem, iv. 242; Dyce, ii. 387–8, prints a slightly different version (the lines were first attributed to Skelton by Ashmole). See also *Index MEV* 2526. The song seems to be a 'modified' carol.

123. Leland, iv. 237.

124. Fayrfax: see Introduction, note 3; and Grattan Flood, 39–. Crane: see note 116. Heywood: see p. 282, note 89.

125. See Collier, i. 65 (and note 1), concerning Acts of Apparel in 3rd and 4th years of Edward IV, and in 6th and 24th years of Henry VIII. Field of Cloth of Gold: see *L&P*, iii, pt 1, no. 704 (p. 238–).

126. *L&P*, i, pt 1, no. 490 (5 June 1510); *L&P*, i, pt 1, no. 1025 (14 Jan. 1512).

127. *Ordinances*, 48, 50.

128. Condensed from *Northumberland HHB*, 43–.

129. *Wriothesley's Chronicle*, appendix, p. 194: *Quendam Marcum Smeton, nuper de villa Westmonasterii in comitatu pradicto, gentylman ac unum grometorum dictae privatae camerae dicti domini regis.* And see p. 245.

130. Pattison, 52; and see pp. 282, 317 above.

131. Rawdon Brown, ii. 136.

132. Wallace, 36; see also Wallace, 58, suggesting that Cornish shared intimately in the king's political counsels.

133. *PP Henry VIII*, 227 (29 June 1532).

134. ibid., 227.

135. Pr. by Wynkyn de Worde (before 1509?); cit. Collier, i. 61.

136. Taverner, *TCM*, i. p. l. More: Roper's *Life*, ed. G. Sampson (with *Utopia*) (1910), 236.

137. See p. 251 above.

138. More's epigrams: see H. H. Hudson, *The Epigram in the English Renaissance* (U.S.A., 1947), ch. 2.

The Song-books Revisited

This inquiry into the music and poetry of the early Tudor court began with three song-books: *The Fayrfax MS*, associated with Henry VII's court; the manuscript called *Henry VIII's MS* because it contains his songs; and a third, *Ritson's MS*, which comes from the West Country but contains courtly songs including one of Henry VIII's own making. These song-books – in particular the first two – are documents of social activity at court, records of the noble life. As such, they both interpret and require interpretation. A historical document is in this respect rather like a letter from a friend, which not only tells you about the friend who sent it, but also cannot be fully understood unless you know him. The three main inquiries of this book have been directed towards making possible an interpretation of the court song-books: the inquiry into the historical relationship between words and music deters us from assuming too readily that an idealized relationship between the two arts was either a stimulus to song-writing or a conditioning factor of it; the inquiry into the social 'meaning' of the courtly lyric suggests the sort of traditions of speaking and writing, sport and 'game', that lie behind many of the songs; and the inquiry into the state of music as a social activity helps us to see the song-books from one aspect as a record of professional art-music 'applied' to courtly ends in ceremony and entertainment.

In this epilogue I shall not work out a detailed interpretation of the court song-books in the light of the analyses which have been made. Many of the songs have been referred to more than once and placed in a context. The reader will, at this stage, scarcely need informing that each song-book is a kind of palimpsest; and that the apparently uniform surface of *The Fayrfax* and *Henry VIII's MSS* contains hints of various half-concealed 'worlds' of social activity. Thus, a 'world' which lies very close to the surface in many songs is the world of chivalric ceremony ('Beholde the soveren sede of this rosis twayn'); another is that of dramatic festival and entertainment ('Adew, adew, le company'); a third is that of social 'play' of the lovers-in-company ('Who shall have my fair lady?'). Behind the songs of the court-books we know we can catch many fascinating glimpses of a way of life long lost and not easily recaptured. The insights need not be laboured.

Instead, then, of making detailed and obvious application of all that has already been said, I want in these last few pages to essay a more difficult task. The statement that the songs will interpret court-life for us (as well as being interpreted by it) is obvious enough. But by it I do not mean simply that the musical features of the songs will throw a light of confirmation on what we already know, or guess, from other sources – for example, that there was 'brilliant', professional music and easy, amateur music. I mean rather, that there is an experience in the songs themselves which may bring us to a closer understanding of the subtleties of feeling, to an actual sharing of the modes of feeling, of the early Tudor court.

It is hard even to begin describing the ways in which, one feels, something is conveyed in the court-songs when they are performed as songs, when they cease to be mere written symbols on a page and become sounds in the living air. Should not the music, we may ask, give us a ready insight into the 'meaning' of court life by conveying to a trained ear those delicacies and refinements of feeling which the words alone dismally fail to make felt? Would that this were an easy matter! It is not, as the discussion of a few songs will soon make clear. As soon as we try to come closer to the songs than the offer of a few external, social comments or internal, technical analyses, the mist gathers and we are left with an experience bafflingly difficult to talk about. So it is in a spirit, not of defeat, but of conscious inadequacy that I offer in the last pages of this book some reflections on the experience I have had in making the music of these songs. My choice of songs may seem a little arbitrary. I can only defend it on the grounds of experience: I shall speak only of the songs I really have 'experienced'. Lastly, the tone of the discussion may seem to some readers too personal. But this is inevitable – inseparable, indeed, from the attempt. I shall not be dealing with 'fixities and definites' but with personal impressions of an elusive and fleeting nature. To adopt a more authoritative pose would only be to mislead.*

---

* I am anxious that the general style of these analyses should not seem to contradict the arguments of earlier chapters. Issues of expressiveness and of the precise relationship between words and music need not now be in our minds at all. I try to speak of the songs almost as if they were instrumental music. But, in case of doubt, I ask the reader to recall the distinctions between effect and intention, between emotive *results* and deliberately expressive technique, and between general emotional correspondence and detailed emotional commentary. Music must

The Song-books Revisited

We may begin with one of the simplest court-songs, 'A the syghes that cum from my hart' [H27], by Cornish. I find this a pleasing trifle but no more. This is not merely on the score of brevity. The song seems to exude the essential languor of courtly love in its frequent drooping cadences. The first cadence [bar 2] may be deliberately old-fashioned. The fa-burden effect of thirds and sixths opening to octave and bare fifth is not in the most modern style of the court song-books; it suggests the nostalgia which the intense idealisms of romantic love are bound to generate. (This was not necessarily conscious in Cornish's mind when he wrote it.) The song is in four phrases, each of which is given a small impulse of energy which quickly dwindles away. The difficulty in singing it is to give it enough vitality to hold it together. It easily falls apart into a succession of 'sighs'. When the upper two parts have finished, the tenor has a separate 'sigh' of his own which arises out of his cadential ornament and eventually subsides into an octave with the part above. I have tried to be open-minded about this song, and I find that many singers accept it enthusiastically. But to me it conjures up too heavily, despite its slight texture, the easy melancholia with which the courtly lyric has made us all too familiar.

The king's setting of 'O my hart' [H15] is superficially similar to Cornish's 'A the syghes'. That is, it is short, proceeds quickly through four simple cadences, and has the same basically chordal style. But for some reason I feel in it more of the 'freshness' of the courtly world and less of the melancholy. This may be partly because a more static harmony obliges singers to take it rather faster than they take Cornish's song. 'O my hart' is more naïve in conception and craftsmanship (we note the progression in bar 2), and, partly for this reason, sturdier. Would contemporaries, one wonders, have acknowledged a difference? If indeed the difference is not purely imaginary, does it merely establish the king's failure to reach a professional level of musical craftsmanship? Or does it measure different shades of 'romantic' feeling?

'My wofull hert' [R2] is a chanson in the 'classic' style of Burgundian court-music: it is for one voice (of counter-tenor range and quality) and two accompanying instruments. To anyone who has heard such a song

stir the listener's feelings whether the composer wants it to or not. When the listener knows himself moved, his feelings must, surely, in some oblique way 'correspond' to the composer's own. Even though the composer's prime art may be to design patterns that will please the ear, to present us with 'proportions' (*ars bene modulandi*), the patterns that he makes seem to *refer* to something other than and outside themselves. A relationship of some kind between music and life as it is lived is a matter of common experience.

feelingly performed there is something which seems unquestionably fitting in the bodiless, detached, floating, 'frustrated' quality of the male alto voice. The sophistication of the melody, with its swooping and drooping, its turns and decorations, is fascinating but, here, ultimately enervating. There is something in the very continuousness of the winding polyphony, the avoidance of points of full close, that conveys, as it seems nothing else could convey, the longing, the endless service, the even and unbroken aspiration of a love fraught with true 'gentiless' and 'honour'. 'My wofull hert' illustrates the norm of courtly melancholy, the degree of spirituality which seems to have become, so to speak, standard.

With 'My wofull hert' might be usefully contrasted 'Go, hert, hurt with adversite' [Song 101]. This is not from one of the early Tudor court songbooks. It comes from a manuscript of the mid-fifteenth century to which no certain provenance can be set. In performance it turns out to be a jewel of its kind. Its kind is the same as that of 'My wofull hert'; and its success sets a limit on that of the other. 'Go, hert' is the shorter of the two and the simpler; it is, therefore, easier to take in as a whole and it forms a complete experience. 'My wofull hert' seems to drag on too long for what it has to say. 'Go, hert' comes to a satisfactory musical point of rest in the middle of the song; the purely formal pattern of the other song seems more arbitrary, less inherent in the material. If 'Go, hert' suggests a simplification of the courtly ideal (as compared, say, with O rosa bella), 'My wofull hert' suggests an unsuccessful struggle to enter into it.

The two-part songs at the beginning of The Fayrfax MS are among the most baffling of all. There is a cold, impersonal brilliance about 'A, a, my herte' [F2] which seems to reflect merely the 'good show' of courtly life, the external 'manere', 'fassion', 'countenance'. To me the song in performance is an experience which simply confirms the impression of professional heartlessness. This is not just because the harmonic feeling (of two voices only) is bleak, an effect which is accentuated by the frequency of rests in each part. The melodies (in which the chief interest of the song lies) are lacking, to me, in sensuous, in real *musical*, appeal; I feel the contrast between the syllabic, word-dictated passages and the swirling vocalizes to be too abrupt. The song impresses but it does not please. It has, of course, energy; it does not droop; there is a business-like vitality about it. But it is brittle and conveys merely the forms and graces of the courtly world.

This business-like vitality never, to my way of thinking, appears to better advantage than in the political, social and satirical songs of The Fayrfax MS. 'Jhoone is sike and ill at ease' [F40] and 'Ay besherewe yow'

[F41] have a brisk superficiality, a rattling energy which not only accords well with their general drift and mood as poems, but also vividly conveys the restive reaction of the courtly world against its own idealisms. 'Ay besherewe yow', compared with 'My wofull hert' or 'Go, hert', seems totally lacking in repose; it belongs to a world of lively common sense, not to the 'dream of fair women'. The heartless, detached quality, conveyed by busy triplets and other rhythmical ornamentations, seems more in place here than elsewhere.

A song in the same basic style as the two foregoing – 'A my herte' and Ay besherewe yow' – is 'Who shall have my fayre lady?' [F42]. The brilliance is still there, but the cold heartlessness is replaced by something gayer and kinder. It is difficult to say why one feels this. The music is certainly plainer – at any rate, to begin with: the solo-voice question of bars 1–2 is echoed, simply, in bars 3–4 by all three voices; and even the later vocalizations are comparatively restrained. A gentle delicacy is conveyed in the lilting triplets, in the interweaving voices (e.g. bars 8–9, 15–18), in the almost static harmony, in the 'major' quality of the whole song. Almost the same technical tricks are used as in other songs, but with a different effect. Even without the words one would recognize this as a light-hearted deviation from the high romantic ideal.

I shall reserve to the end the song *Madame d'amours* [H67], because it has, for me at least, the rare distinction of exceeding the bounds of expectation. This sense of added dimension must not be confused with mere scope. The scope, for instance, of 'This day day dawes' [F45] consists in a remarkable and sophisticated inclusiveness. The poem has already been briefly described: the white rose of York is also the Courtly Lady sitting in a 'garden grene'; in the garden are other flowers whose precise significance, if any, is lost; the burden consists of fragments of a popular *aubade*. The music reinforces the impression of complexity. What must surely be the original tune appears first in treble and then is picked up in the bass part. The curious feature of this presentation is that the tune is in triple time whereas the metre and movement of this polyphonic treatment are duple. Later in the burden the song lends its melodic germ to the dancing triplet figures. This musical analysis corresponds to some extent to what the composer must have had consciously in mind as he wrote the song and to what we can learn to *think* consciously as we hear it. But I do not know that it has very much to do with the 'experience' of the music. This experience has, nevertheless, an individual flavour. The effect of solid complexity characteristic of many songs in *The Fayrfax MS* is here lightened not only by the popular song but also by such touches as the lilting triplets to the words 'among the flowris that fressh ben' (first verse): treble and tenor are echoed by treble and bass.

'And I war a maydyn' [H101] may be recalled again here as a curiosity of the court repertory. The lightly bawdy words are set to music which seems to our musical experience utterly inappropriate. Five-part writing, though common enough in church-music, is elsewhere unknown in the secular music of early Tudor England. The effect of the full harmony and the moving, though not clogged, inner parts (especially Voice III) is to slow the whole song down well below the speed suggested by the 'tune' (presumably Tenor II – Voice IV). The harmonic movement and the 'dominant seventh' passing note of the penultimate bar set a speed at which sensuous pleasure can be felt from the changing chords. The song cannot be lightly skipped through. What does all this mean? Is the song intended as a musical joke? There are very few parallels in this period. Or should we take our puzzled response as a warning that our musical experience and theirs are worlds apart? I must admit to being charmed and yet completely puzzled by it.

Lastly, *Madame d'amours* [H67], which, as I have said, has for me a unique position in the secular music of the early Tudor court. Most of the other songs follow one or other of a number of stereotyped patterns; *Madame d'amours* has its own. Many of the other songs wear thin on frequent hearing; *Madame d'amours* keeps its richness and power to delight. One is struck from the first with its full, rich, continuous texture – the four voices produce, as they interweave within an effective range of only an octave and a third, a solid warmth of sound that is more reminiscent of the 'full' (*tutti*) passages in early Tudor church-music than of the other songs in *Henry VIII's MS*. (The composers of *Henry VIII's MS* seem on the whole to have deliberately unlearned the lessons in sonority which the writing of church-music in the high, pre-Reformation style had taught them.) An interesting feature is the almost continuous relation of treble to bass at the interval of a tenth. The principal melody, in effect, is in the top part; and it is beautifully balanced – the climax in bar 10 (in fact, the highest note) does not spoil the balance because of the climbing melodic figure (bar 14 to end) with the repeated words 'until I die, until I die, until I die'. The repetition of words, incidentally, does not anticipate the practice of madrigal composers; the effect here is more a matter of emphatic declamation – the melody stylizes the mounting emphasis of speech. The total effect of the song is not easy to describe. But, unless our modern way of feeling is wide of the mark, the 'major' harmony with its mounting inner parts counteracting the 'droop' of the cadences, does convey the warmth, security and happiness of love rather than its frustrations or its melancholy 'lak of stedfastnes'. In many of the other secular songs the composer almost appears to disdain his own resources; in this he rejoices in them.

There are other striking songs in the court song-books besides *Madame d'amours*; but none belonging to the courtly world so impresses one with the sense of a dimension of feeling beyond what one could expect. Something in the music seems to extend our way of thinking about, our understanding of, the courtly ideal. If small things may be compared with great, *Madame d'amours* may be compared with Chaucer's *Troilus and Criseyde*. Our insight into the 'noble life' would be the poorer without them. But the comparison with Chaucer's great poem, with its philosophical and religious overtones, reminds us finally and conclusively what a small world we enter when we open the song-books of the early Tudor court. The court-songs are not, even taken as a whole, comprehensive. Theirs is a world in which much that was most forward and alive in early sixteenth-century England has no place.

Literary Text and Notes

EDITORIAL NOTE

In editing the words of the songs my aim has been to present the poem which the composer had in front of him. The text of each song given below follows the words of Voice I (the highest voice). In the more complicated songs the gaps left in the text when Voice I is silent have been filled from the highest voice then singing. When Voice I has a palpably inferior reading I have corrected it from the other voices. Scribal errors have been corrected in the text. These and all other corrections and emendations are recorded in the notes, under the heading *Text*. It has not seemed worth while to record spelling or orthographical variants, repetitions and omissions made for purely musical reasons, or cues to the singers. In so far as the latter help to determine the form of the song (e.g. round or carol), they are, for *Henry VIII's MS*, fully recorded in the Commentary to *Music at the Court of Henry VIII*.

Throughout the English texts I have modernized capitals, punctuation, word-division and stanza arrangement. The letters *u, v, i, j, þ,* and *ȝ* have been replaced by their modern equivalents; *ff* is printed as *F* or *f*; roman numerals are spelt out. When a word in the MS ends in an ambiguous flourish, I have added or omitted the conjectural *e* to accord with present-day spelling. Manuscript contractions and abbreviations have been silently expanded. And in the Notes the expansions are only italicized where the reading might be affected. The purpose of these adjustments has been to make the poems (without falsification) as accessible as possible to the modern reader.

The words of the Anglo-French or French songs of H are here transcribed *literatim,* since they are obviously corrupt and resist normal editorial procedures. They are modernized in *MCH8*.

British Museum, Additional MS 5665, *Ritson's MS*, is described in *MC*, 125; by Greene, p. 331; by Harrison, *passim*; by Fehr, 262–; and it has been made the subject of a dissertation by Catherine K. Miller, 'A Fifteenth-Century Record of English Choir Repertory, BM Add. MS 5665', unpublished dissertation for Ph.D., Yale, 1948.* A complete photographic reproduction of the MS was published for the Modern Language Association, *Collection of Photographic Facsimiles*, xciv, 1927. The words were first transcribed by Fehr and published in 1901 (see Reference List).

Deeds and receipts in the MS are as follows: (i) receipt to the rector of Langtre, south-west of Torrington, near the west coast of Devon; (ii) banns for the church of Bycklegh, a few miles north of Exeter; (iii) power of attorney from the master of a chapel in East Tilbury, Essex, but dated at Pyworthy in Devon (just east of Bude, Cornwall). All three are dated *c.* 1510.

The composers named are Richard Smert; John Trouluffe; John Cornish; Henry Petyr; Sir Thomas Packe; Sir William Hawte, *miles*; Edmund Sturges (Turges?); T. B. (B. T.?); J. Norman; W. P.; and, by implication, Henry VIII (R12).

The songs, as distinct from the carols, of the MS are interspersed singly, or in groups, among the church-music. There are no poems without music.

R1   Y have ben a foster long and meney day;   [1
               My lockes ben hore.
               Y shall hong up my horne by the grenewode spray;
               Foster woll Y be no more.

               All the whiles that Y may my bowe bende   [2
               Shall Y wedde no wiffe;
               I shall bygge me a boure atte the wodes ende,
               Ther to lede my lyffe.

NOTE: f.53v: anon (1 voc survives). There are two parts without words on the other side of the opening; they appear to be fragments of another piece. R1 starts with the same melody as

---

* I am grateful to Mrs Miller for having allowed me to consult her work.

Ritson's MS

H62 but is considerably longer. Greene (no. 465, note) considers it to be the prototype of H62. Concerning 'forester' songs generally, see pp. 222, 249.

GLOSS: 1.1 foster: *forester* | 2.3 bygge: *build*
TEXT: 2.3 bygge: *MS* bygge*s*

R2   My wofull hert of all gladnesse baryeyne
    Enforsed me this complaynte for to make,
    Weche Y have songe with wepyng yën tweyne
    Full oghfte or this, Y shall undertake.
    Till gode tydinges com my sorwe to slake
    Y most obey fortuneys ordynaunce,
    For yet Y am all drowned in the lake
    Of sorfull joye and paynefull plesaunce.

    For sche weche ys of all godely the best
    To myn entent, and so sayeth mo then I,
    Ys full but late oute of hur kyndely rest
    Into gret sekenesse weche holdith hur grevowsly;
    Now Y pray God and that righth hertily
    That she be voyded owte of the grete grevaunce;
    For till she amende Y shall have noght truly
    But sorfull joy and paynefull plesaunce.

NOTE: ff.65v–66: anon (3 voc). Various other songs begin with the same words: e.g. F5; Bannatyne MS f.51, 'My wofull hairt me stoundis'; Cambridge, UL Ff.1.6 f.153, 'My whofull herte plonged yn hevynesse' (not in *Index MEV*; see Robbins, *Secular Lyrics*, no. 165, note); see also *Index* 2278–9. It was probably a purely literary cliché, like 'Ah, my heart'.

GLOSS: 1.1 baryeyne: *barren* | 1.4 oghfte or: *often ere* | 2.3 full: *fallen* | kyndely: *natural* | 2.6 voyded: *relieved*

R3   'Be pes, ye make me spille my ale!'   [1
    Now thyngke ye this ys a fayre ray?
    'Let go Y say, straw for yeur tale!'
    Leff werke a twenty-a-devell away!
    'Wene ye that everybody lest to play?'
    Abyde awhile! What have ye haste?
    Y trow for all youre gret afray
    Ye will not make to huge a waste.

    After asay then may ye wette;   [2
    Why blame ye me withoute offence?
    'Ywisse, wanton, ye shull not yette!

Appendix A

A, kan ye that? Nou, gode, go hens!
What do ye here within oure spence?
Recke ye not to make us shende?
Y wolde not yette for furty pence
My moder cam in, or that ye wende.'

Cum kys me! 'Nay!' Be God, ye shall!   [3
'Be Criste, Y nelle, what ses the man?
Ye herte my legge agenste the walle;
Ys this the gentery that ye can?'
Take to gev all, and be stille than!
'Now have ye leyde me un the flore,
But hadde Y wyste when ye bygan,
Be Criste, Y wolde have schytte the dore!'

NOTE: ff.66v–67: anon (3 voc). Although the 3 verses are strophic, it is difficult to see how the music will fit verses 2 and 3, not because the metre is irregular but because the pauses in the dialogue come in quite different places in the line.

GLOSS: This is a difficult, idiomatic text: neither the division of the dialogue nor its precise interpretation is certain. The Lady's remarks are within editorial quotation marks.
1.2 ray: *'array', state of affairs*; *i.e. Do you think this is a nice way to treat me?* | 1.3 straw: *i.e. I don't give two pins . . .* | 1.4 Twenty-a-devell: *intensifying away*; *i.e. let work go hang!* | 1.5 wene ye: *do you think?* | lest: *'list', has a mind to* | 1.6 What have ye . . . , *i.e. why are you in such a hurry?* | 1.7 afray: *alarm, fright*; *i.e. for all you're in a panic* | 1.8 to huge a waste: *obscure. Perhaps the waste is of his love, or of the amorous opportunity? For to (too), read so?* | 2.1 asay: *trial* | wette: *'wit', know* | 2.4 kan ye that: *Ah, is that what you're up to?* | gode: *for heaven's sake!* | 2.5 spence: *buttery* | 2.6 make us shende: *ruin us* | 2.8 or that ye wende: *before you're gone* | 3.2 nelle: *will not* | 3.4 gentery: *good breeding* | 3.5 Take to gev all: *take (upon yourself) to make a complete surrender (?)* |

TEXT: 1.4 away: *III* way | 2.3 yette: *MS* ȝette *could be modernized as* gette

R4   Absens of you causeth me to sygh and complayne
            For of my hert ye have the governaunce;
            And thogh Y wolde, Y koude me noght refrayne
            For yeu, dere hert, thoff Y suffere penaunce
            All for yeure sake, til God me so avaunce
            That Y fro yew may hyre sume gode tydyng,
            That myght my herte in more ese bryng.

NOTE: ff.67v–68: anon (3 voc). Musical form: *aab* (*a* 'rhyming' with *b*).
GLOSS: 3 refrayne: *i.e. give up loving* | 6 hyre: *hear*

R5   The hye desire that Y have for to se
The godely and wommanly bewte
Till that Y may in yeure presaunce
Prayng to yeure gracius pyte
That ye wilde fuchesaffe to have mercy on me
And only to be putte to yeure rememoraunce.

NOTE: ff.68v–69: anon (2 voc). Through-set in two sections with 'rhyming' melismas. The text of the words is obviously corrupt.

GLOSS: 5 wilde fuchesaffe: *would vouchsafe*

R6   O blessed lord, how may this be
That Y am thus in heviness?
And yet Y have do my besynesse
Ever to plese hym with all mygth,
Both erly, late, by day and by nyghth.

NOTE: ff.69v–70: anon (2 voc). Through-set in two sections with slight musical 'rhyme' between them.

R7   Thow man, envired with temptacion,
Unto Calvery caste thy mynde.
Remembre how feithefull, how treu, how kynde
This lyon and lambe was, causyng pyte;
And say after me, and be noght unkynde:
Paratus sum semper mori pro te.

NOTE: ff.70v–71: anon (3 voc). Through-set in two sections with long 'rhyming' melisma after each section.

GLOSS: 1 envired: *environed, surrounded with* | 6 Paratus sum . . . : *I am ever prepared to die for your sake*

TEXT: 1 envired *II* : *I* envred

R8   Now helpe, Fortune, of thy godenesse,
And onse withdrawe thy adversite
From thy servaund, the weche hathe plente
Of sorwe and all hevenesse.

NOTE: ff.71v–72: anon (3 voc). Through-set in two sections with long 'rhyming' melisma after each section.

TEXT: 3 plente: *I* plete

Appendix A

R9 Fayre and discrete, fresche wommanly figure,
That with yeure beute and fresche plesaunce pure
Arested hathe my herte in sodeyn wise,
Y recommaunde my symple service sure,
My lyves ladi and my hertis cure,
Unly to yeure swete grace a thousande sithe
Besechyng yeure excuse, ther Y supprise;
Sum love comaundes me this aventure,
Thorffe with yeur beute that Y most love and prise.

NOTE: ff.72v–73: anon (3 voc). Musical form: *aab*, with slight musical 'rhyme' between the two sections.

GLOSS: 1 discrete: *discerning, prudent* | 2 plesaunce: *pleasantness* | 6 sithe: *times* | 7 Besechyng . . .: *Beseeching you to excuse me when I do violence (to your feelings)* | 9 Thorffe: *penetrated*

R10 Alone, alone,   [1
Mornyng alone,
And all for one;
 Alas, why so?
My myrth ys gon
For on alone
Whych causyth my mone;
 Fortune ys my fo.

Sumtyme was I   [2
A lover trewly,
And now, fy, fy,
 Apon fals love!
Love I deny;
Hyt ys foly
To love vaynly;
 This do I prove.

Wheras I sought,   [3
And love dere bought
Settyth me at nought,
 This ys my chaunce;
Alas, with thought
My hert ys braught
Full low forfought
 Yn lovys daunce.

All lovers beware,   [4
For Y am bare
Of yoy, yn care
    To lede my lyf;
Takyn yn a snare
As carles doth ane hare,
Thus evyll Y fare,
    Lyving yn stryf;

Lyving yn payn,   [5
Lovyng yn vayne,
Hade yn dysdayn;
    What remedy?
Wher Y wold fayn,
Love doth refrayn,
Not lovyd agayn,
    Thus ever fynd I;

Thus ever y fynd   [6
My lover unkynd,
Turnyng as the wynd,
    No place to resorte.
I am put behynd,
As man that ys blynd,
Allmost owt of mynde;
    Alone ys no cumfort.

NOTE: ff.133v–135: ? T. B. (2 voc). Through-set, with long melisma and important cadence after verse 3.

GLOSS: 1.6 on: *one* | 3.5 thought: *anxiety* | 3.7 forfought: *wearied with struggling* | 4.6 carles: *countrymen*

TEXT: 4.3 yn: *II* and

At the bottom of f.135 occurs the following musical rebus: 'ye be **mi fa**-yr **la**-dye **fa**-yr be-**fa**-l yovre [?] grace [?]'. (The syllables in bold type are represented by musical notes.)

R11   My herte ys yn grete mournyng,   [1
                    My mynd also gretly waylyng;
                        Alas, alas, what remedy?
                        My lady hath forsakyn me.

343

The more sorow ys my payn [2
So onkyndly thus to be slayn;
    Alas, alas, what remedy?
    My lady hath forsakyn me.

Such a mastras I may calle [3
Dame Petyles yn every place over all;
    Alas, alas, [what remedy?
    My lady hath forsakyn me.]

I trow on me she wold rewe [4
Iff my sorow and woe she knew:
    Alas, alas, what remedy?
    [My lady hath forsakyn me.]

NOTE: ff.135v–136: anon (3 voc). Strophic setting. Two verses are underlaid to the notes. It
is possible that two six-line verses were intended, with musical form *aab*, but the way the
extra words are laid out suggests not.

TEXT: 1.2 gretly: *I* grete | 3: *MS* IIIius versus | 3.1 may: *MS* nay | 4: *MS* IIIIus versus

R12   Passetyme with good cumpanye [1
                I love and shall unto I dye;
                Grugge so woll, but noon denye;
                So God be plecyd, this lyve woll I;
                    For my pastaunce
                    Hunte, syng and daunce;
                    My hert ys sett
                    All godely sport
                    To my cumfort:
                    Who shall me lett?

                Yowth woll have nedes dalyaunce, [2
                Of good or yll some pastaunce;
                Company me thynckyth then best
                All thoftes and fantyses to dygest.
                    For idelnes
                    Ys cheff mastres
                    Of vices all;
                    Than who can say
                    But passe-the-day
                    Ys best of all?

Cumpany with honeste   [3
Ys vertu, and vyce to flee;
Cumpany ys gode or yll,
But every man hath hys frewyll.
    The best insew,
    The worst eschew,
    My mynde shall be;
    Vertu to use,
    Vyce to reffuse,
    Y shall use me.

NOTE: ff.136v–137 (first version), ff.141v–142 (second version): (3 voc). The first is anonymous; the second has the rubric, *The Kynges Balade* (cf. H7, The Kynge H. viij). Details of this popular strophic setting are given under H7.

GLOSS: 1.3 Grugge so woll . . .: *let grudge whosoever will, none shall refuse (it to me)* | 1.5 pastaunce: *pastime* | 2.4 fantyses: *caprices, extravagances* | dygest: *disperse*

TEXT: 1.2 unto: *II* untyll | 1.4 this lyve: *II* thus lyfe, *III* this lyfe | 1.5 pastaunce: *all* dystaunce | 2.3 then: *I* them, *III* hyt | 3.4 hys: *II omits*

The first version (ff.136v–137) is not printed here: it consists of verse 1 only and has no notable variants, except 1.5 pastaunce, which I have adopted.

R13   So put yn fere I dare not speke;   [1
            Thus under sylens I do endure,
            Unwetyng how myn hert to-breke
            To her which ys my yoyus plesure;
            Of my pore hert she may be sure,
            And so shall contynew tyll I dye,
            Abydyng your grace yn hope of mercy.

            The sterre of Venus which I call her yë,   [2
            Sharper than thorn, dyamond or steyll,
            So depe hath thrylled my hert ynwardly
            That wondyd soere myself Y fele,
            And no help but Fortunys whele,
            And only she which my wound begunne;
            Ther of right I apeyle hyr to be my surgyon.

            She hath me hurt; why shold she not hele,   [3
            And geve me salfe unto my sore?
            Or els yn feyth unkyndly she doth dele,
            For she hath that I hadde in store,

Myn hert and love; what wyll she more?
And all othyr for hyr sake to eschew,
And never to chaunge hyr for no new.

NOTE: ff.137v–140: anon (2 voc). Through-set in three sections.
GLOSS: 1.3 Unwetyng: *unheeding* | to-breke: *is shattered* | 2.1 yë: *eye* | 2.3 thrylled: *pierced* | 2.4 soere: *sore* | 2.7 Ther: *In that matter*
TEXT: 2.7 my: *I omits*

R14   Alone, alone,
Here Y am mysylf alone;
With a dulfull chere here I make my mone,
Pyteusly, my own sylf alone.

My blossum bright ys gone,
Takyn away from me bycause of hevynes;
With a dulfull chere [here I make my mone,
Pyteusly, my own sylf alone.]

NOTE: f.140v: anon (3 voc). Strophic setting with literary refrain; a rather amateurish composition.
GLOSS: 2.2 hevynes: *i.e. her illness (?)*

R15   In wyldernes   [1
Ther founde I Besse
Secret, alone,
In grete dystres,
Remedyles,
Makyng her moone.

'Alas,' she seyd,   [2
'Y was a mayde
As others be,
And at-a-brayde
Y was afrayde
Right pyteusly;

A wanton chyld   [3
Spake wordes myld
To me alone,
And me begylyd,
Goten with child
And now ys gone.

Now hit ys so,   [4
Lefe of my woe
With gode devyse,
And let hym goo,
With sorow allso,
And play the wyse.

Now may I wynd   [5
Withoute a frynd
With hert onfayn;
In ferre cuntre
Men wene I be
A mayde agayn.

This young men say   [6
Yn sport and play,
"Go wach a byrde!
Men tellyth yn town
When clothis be downe
The smocke ys hyd."

I cannot kepe   [7
But soore Y wepe
And all for oone;
So fro my hert
Shall he not stert,
Thof he be gon.

Alas, that he   [8
Has thus lefte me
Mysylf alone,
In wyldernes,
Remedyles,
Makyng my moon.'

NOTE: f.141: anon (3 voc). Strophic setting. Another version is BM Egerton 3002, f.2v: anon (3 voc); very roughly written, a fourth higher, and lacking the extra verses (the music of this version is not quite complete).

GLOSS: 1.1 wyldernes: *i.e. country, not town* | 2.4 at-a-brayde: *suddenly* | 3.1 chyld: *noble youth* | 4.3 With gode devyse: *with good counsel* | 4.6 play the wyse: *act the wise man* | 5.3 With hert onfayn: *'unfain', reluctant, sorry* | 5.4 ferre: *far* | 6.1 This: *these (used generically)* | 6.3–6 Go wach a byrde . . .: *obscure. Perhaps there is play on* byrde/burd [maiden]; *the point may be that when she is properly dressed, no-one will know her guilty secret* | 7.1 kepe: *attend; i.e. to what they say* | 7.5 stert: *start*

TEXT: 7.5 he: *MS* be

Appendix A

R16

Come over the burne, Besse,
Thou lytyll, prety Besse,
Come over the burne, Besse, to me!

The burne ys this worlde blynde　　　　　　　　　　　[1
And Besse ys mankynde;
So propyr I can none fynde as she;
She daunces and she lepys,
And Crist stondes and clepys;
Cum over the burne, Besse, to me!

NOTE: ff.143v–144: anon (3 voc). Apparently a modified carol: initial burden and verse-with-refrain. The song, in various forms, was widely current in the late xv and xvi centuries. Perhaps the earliest version is the long moralization in Cambridge, Trinity College MS O.2.53, f.55v– (12 verses), no music. An early xvi-century moralization is in Emmanuel College MS 263, f.i (flyleaf), no music. A secular version is in BM Harl. 2252, f.135 (a 'Speke Parotte' poem), no music. (These last two are given in Robbins, 'Religious Lyrics', ii, nos 418, 419.) Two verses without music are in Ashmole MS 176, f.100. *Broadside Index* 587 and 2377 lists *A Dyologe sett furthe bytwene the quenes majestie and Englonde* (1558–9), the same song turned to political purposes. A later musical setting is Cambridge, UL Dd.2.11, f.80v: (lute); apparently unrelated to R16.

GLOSS: 1.3 propyr: *pretty* | 1.5 clepys: *calls*

TEXT: 1.3 propyr: *III* prety | 1.4 she lepys: *I* lepys

R17　*Votre trey dowce.*

NOTE: ff.144v–145: anon (2 voc). Instrumental piece on tenor originally by Binchois. Skelton refers to the song in *Magnyfycence* (Dyce, i. 249).

TEXT consists of: *Voice I:* Votre | *Voice II:* Votre trey dowce regaunt plesaunt.

R18

Up Y arose *in verno tempore*　　　　　　　　　　　[1
And found a maydyn *sub quadam arbore,*
That dyd complayne *in suo pectore,*
Sayng, 'Y fele *puerum movere;*

Adew, plesers *antiquo tempore!*　　　　　　　　　　[2
Full oft with you *solebam ludere;*
But for my mysse *michi deridere;*
With right goed cause *incipeo flere.*

Now what shall Y say *meis parentibus*　　　　　　　[3
Bycause Y lay with *quidam clericus?*
They wyll me bete *cum virgis ac fustibus*
And me sore chast *coram omnibus.*

348

With the seid child, *quid faciam?* [4

Shall Y hyt kepe *vel interficiam?*

Yf Y sley hyt, *quo loco fugiam?*

I shall lose God *et vitam eternam.*'

NOTE: ff.145v–146: anon (3 voc). Strophic setting. The words of this song occur without music in Bodl. Ashmole 176, f.98v (no important variants).

The Latin half-lines may be translated: *. . . in the time of spring . . . under a certain tree . . . in her breast . . . a child moving . . . in time past . . . I was wont to play . . . laugh at me . . . I begin to weep . . . to my parents . . . a certain clerk . . . with rods and sticks (?) . . . in the presence of all . . . what shall I do? . . . or shall I kill (it)? . . . whither shall I fly? . . . and eternal life*

GLOSS: 2.3 mysse: *sin, fault* | 3.2 Bycause: *inasmuch as* | 3.4 chast: *chasten*

TEXT: 3.1 meis: MS *mei*.

R19   Hay how the mavys on a brere! [1

She satt and sang with notes clere;

I drew me nere

To se her chere

   The greves among.

When Y cam ther

She stode yn fere

And seyd, 'No nere!

What doyst thou here?

   Hyt ys grete wrong.'

I bade her abyde [2

And stop a tyde;

I shull her gyde

To a forest wyde

   .   .   .   .   .

She seyd me nay

And flo her way;

She wolde assay

To take her pray

   That she had lovyd so long.

Whan she was gone [3

And Y alone,

Makyng my mone

With sorowfull grone,

   This ys my song:

Appendix A

'Such on as she,
That away woll flee,
Yll must she the,
Wherever she be
Yn castell strong.'

NOTE: ff.146v–148: anon (3 voc). Through-set, with long melisma after verse 1 only.

GLOSS: 1.1 mavys: *song-thrush* | 1.3, 8 nere: *nearer* | 2.2 tyde: *time* | 2.8 pray: *prey* | 3.6 on: *one* | 3.8 Yll must she the: *ill betide her*

TEXT: 1.3 me: *II* here | 2.4 *I*, To a forest which was brode and wyde; *II*, To a forest which ys brode and wyde

There are a few small holes in the pages; but the gaps in one voice are always supplied by another.

R20   How shall Y plece a creature uncerteyne?

Your light grevans shall not me constrayne   [1
To avoyde your custumabyll disdayne;
That ye loth Y love—wrappe that yn your trayne!
How sholde Y [plece a creature uncerteyne?]

Your on-syttyng speche puttyth me to payne   [2
Withowt cause, Gode knowyth; Y do not fayne.
With hert Y wyll you plece and your love attayne:
How sholde Y plece a creature oncertayne?

When Y fynde you stedfast and certayne,   [3
Y am right glad, tristyng hit woll remanyne;
But light credens turnyth your love agayne:
How sholde Y plece a creature oncerteyne?

An olde seyde saw: hasty men sone slayne;   [4
Love me lytell and longe; hot love doth not reyne;
Speke or ye smyte, barke or ye byte; holde yowre hondes twane:
How sholde Y plece a creature oncertayne?

NOTE: ff.38v–39: anon (3 voc). Carol, not in Greene; pr. *MC*, no. 16A. It is evidently contemporary with the last group of songs, rather than with the 'medieval' carols and earlier songs of the manuscript; I have numbered it accordingly.

GLOSS: 1.3 wrappe that . . .: *i.e. 'put that in your pipe and smoke it!'* | 2.1 on-syttyng: *attacking, upbraiding* | 4.2 reyne: *prevail*

TEXT: *B* shall: *II* sholde

THE FAYRFAX MS

British Museum Additional MS 5465, *The Fayrfax MS.* 'Vellum (paper interleaved where parts of original are missing and ff. i, ii, 1), $11\frac{1}{2} \times 8$ in. ff.ii and 124' (Greene, 330). For the leaves missing after ff.9v, 10v, 11v, 19v, see the Literary Text. On the title-page (f. 1) are the arms of Robert Fayrfax, and the numbers of the songs ascribed to him: 'C.xii ad xv; xxii et C.xxiii; xxiiii et C.xxvi' (these numbers do not altogether agree with ascriptions over the songs themselves). On f.2 (f.1v is blank) is keyboard music of *c.* 1550(?). Songs F1–49 follow in consecutive order, each with manuscript number; only two songs are completely lacking: C.vii and C.xvii. F49, which bears the MS number C.li, may be incomplete. There is no MS index and therefore no means of telling the titles of the missing songs, or how many the MS originally had. The MS is written throughout by one hand in black and red full notation (except the keyboard piece); this type of notation had long been in disuse on the Continent but is found in several English church manuscripts of the period.

The dating of the MS depends partly on the composers who are found in it; they are, Cornish, Fayrfax, Davy, Banastir (d. 1587), Newark (d. 1509), Sheryngham, Tutor (Tuder), Turges, Browne, Sir Thomas Philipps. A younger generation (cf. H) does not appear. Fayrfax is not given the title of Doctor, which he acquired in 1504 at Cambridge.

A date of *c.* 1500 is borne out by the songs themselves; F8 – birth of 'sede' to the 'rosis twayn'; F27 – end of civil war; F44 – prayer for Prince Arthur (d. 1502); F45 – praise of Elizabeth (?), wife of Henry VII; F47 – prayer for strong government (admittedly not inappropriate later, also).

The MS has an interesting history: it was owned by the Fairfax family in 1618; by Ralph Thoresby in the 18th century; later by John White of Newgate Street. It was the only source of early Tudor song known to Burney (he was ignorant, also, of the church MSS); six of his transcriptions are in BM Add. 11583. Hawkins used it, and Stafford Smith, whose *Collection of English Songs,* 1779, remains the best printed edition (fourteen songs). The versions of PMMS 1891 and PMMS 1893 are not reliable. The MS has been described by: – Fehr, 48– (pr. *w* of most of the poems); Davey, 92; Greene, 330–1 (pr. most carols); *EEL,* 299; Reese,

Appendix A

MR, 768 (with exhaustive list of modern reprints in note 25); Hughes, Dom. A, 'An Introduction to Fayrfax' in *Musica Disciplina*, vi (1952), 83.

F1   The farther I go, the more behynde;
      The more behynde, the nere my wayes ende;
      The more I sech, the wers can I fynde;
      The lyghter leefe, the lother for to wende;
      The trewer I serve, the ferther out of mynde;
      Thoo I go lose, yet am I teyd with a lyne:
      Is it fortune or infortune this I fynde?

NOTE: ff.2v–3: William Newark (2 voc). Through-set in two sections, with slight 'rhyming' melisma. The poem has an interesting history. The single stanza was probably written in the early xv century by one John Halsham; it was appropriated by Lydgate, who used it as the first stanza of his 'Tyed with a line' (*Index MEV* 3436). But it continued to have a separate existence, though usually in conjunction with 'The world so wide th'aire so remuable' (*Index* 3504). See also Carleton Brown, *XV*, no. 171 and note.

GLOSS: 2 nere: *nearer* | 4 The lyghter leefe: *the easier it is to leave* | wende: *depart* | 6 lose: *loose* | 6–7: cf. Carleton Brown, *XV*, no. 171; *the order of these two lines is transposed and line 6 reads*, Is thys fortune, not I [*i.e. I know not*], or infortune? | 7: *i.e. is this lucky or unlucky?*

TEXT: 7 Is it: *MS* It is | *heading*: C.i [*i.e. Cantus no. 1*]

F2   A, a, my herte, I knowe yow well;
      Ye thynk for to discomfort me.
      Nay, nay, nay, nay, I warne the well,
      Thoo that all this yet in vayne be,
      Sum other grace may cum, perde;
      Or else I thynke to be content
      With my desyre tyll I be spent:
      Wherefor, my hart, lett be, lett be!

NOTE: ff.3v–4: anon, but possibly by Newark, like F1, 3, 4; (2 voc). Through-set in two sections. For the conventional opening words see F38; *Index MEV*; *Complaint*, p. lxxxiv; *GGB*, 139; *Wyatt*, no. 150; etc.

GLOSS: 6–7: *i.e. I'm content to love in misery till death*

TEXT: 3 the: *II* yow | *heading*: C.ii

F3   What causyth me wofull thoughtis to thynk
      Syn thoughtis byn cheff causers of my woo;
      For when nature wold oft that I shulde wynk,

Then be it they that doth me trobill so
That be won thought my rest from me doth go.
And yet mythynkyth hit grevith me moche more
That no thought can reless me of my sore.

NOTE: ff.4v–6: William Newark (2 voc). Through-set in two sections (1–4; 5–7) with break in sense between sections, and musical 'rhyme'. At the bottom of f.5v is a jotting on a four-line stave, apparently a piece of plain-song, without words.

GLOSS: 3 wynk: *close my eyes, sleep* | 5 be won: *by one*

TEXT: 7 me: *II omits* | *heading*: C.iii

F4 So fer I trow from remedy,
     And from all hope so fer banysshid
     Was nevir man saff only I;
     So mekyll dred, so lytyll trust
     Cannot be well for to be wisht:
     To thynk my sorows, well may I complayne;
     But them to tell cannott availe.

NOTE: ff.6v–7: William Newark (2 voc). Through-set in two sections (1–4; 5–7) with an awkward break in the sense between them.

GLOSS: 4 mekyll dred: *much fear* | 6: *i.e. thinking of my sorrows naturally leads me into 'com-playntes'*

TEXT: 6 complayne, *I, II: the rhyme-scheme demands a word to rhyme with* availe, *perhaps* bewayle | *heading*: C.iiii

F5 My wofull hart in paynfull weryness,
     Which hath byn long plongyng with thought unseyne,
     Full lyk to drowne in wavis of dystres,
     Saffe helpe and grace of my lord and soverayne,
     Is nowe be hym so comfortide agayne
     That I am bownde above all erthly thyng
     To love and dred hym as my lord and kyng.

NOTE: ff.7v–9: Sheryngam (2 voc). Through-set, with a break of the sense between the two sections (1–4; 5–7). For the opening, see R2.

GLOSS: 2 thought unseyne: *unforeseen anxiety* | 4 saffe: *save*

TEXT: 2 plongyng: *II* plungyng | 3 wavis: *I* waies, *II* wawis | 6 erthly, *II: I* ertly | *heading*: C.v

F6   Demyd wrongfully   [1
      In absent,
      And wote not why

Appendix A

Encrese of payne
To complayne
For with twayne
Demyd wrongfully.

Demyd wrongfully   [2
Withoute offens,
Assuryd am I;
Yet reson is
That I wis
Endure this
Demyd wrongfully.

Demyd wrongfully   [3
In your mynd
So unkyndly;
I undyrtake
It wolde me make
Plesure forsake
To be demyd wrongfully.

Demyd wrongfully   [4
Of one alone
That I must sett by;
For that to mone,
Remedy non
But everychone
Demyd wrongfully.

NOTE: f.9v: anon (2 voc). Incomplete; treble only. The syntax of this song is elliptical and the text almost certainly corrupt.

GLOSS: 1.6 *seems to imply some muddle with two mistresses* | 4.6 everychone: *by everyone (?)*

TEXT: 1.6 with twayne: MS w^t twayne (*without wayne (?), i.e. without advantage*); *Fehr emends to* with vayne | *heading*: C.vi

The leaf which, *recto*, contained the tenor of this two-part song is missing; its *verso* contained the top voice or voices of the song originally numbered C.vii and now totally lost. At least one other leaf is missing: it contained, *recto*, the bottom voice or voices of C.vii, and *verso*, the upper voice of C.viii (F7), verse 1. The MS continues with the tenor of C.viii (F7), verse 1.

F7   O my desyre, what eylyth the,
                      Whan that desert lakkyth remedy,
                      In willfullness so for to be,

354

The Fayrfax MS

Syn that it is playnly foly;
Thoo that ye wolde untill ye dye
Yet other grace can ye gett non
Butt yff hit be to wissh for one:
O my desyre, what eylyth the?

Treuth nor service nevir so playne
Cannot avayle, it shal be sayd;
Sum tyme is lost and all in vayne
Thynkyth my hart can be well payd
So for to se ye betrayd,
And all be folissh fantasy
In whom ther is no remedy;
O my desyre, what aylyth the?

NOTE: ff.10–10v: William Newark (2 voc). Through-set. The words are complete. For the phrase, 'what eylyth the?' cf. BM Add. MS 18752, f.91 (ed. Reed, no. 22); *Wyatt*, no. 150; etc. The music is incomplete; the tenor only of verse 1 (see F6) and the treble only of verse 2 (see below) survive.

GLOSS: 1.3 willfullness: *willing resolution (to love)* | 2.4 Thynkyth . . .; *does it seem (to you, my desire) that my heart can be well pleased to see you betrayed?* | 2.6 be: *by*

TEXT: 1.6 gett non: *MS* non gett | *heading*: C.viii

The leaf which contained, *recto*, the tenor of verse 2 above, and, *verso*, the treble of C.ix (F8) is missing.

F8   Lett serch your myndis yë of hie consideracion!
Beholde the soveren sede of this rosis twayn,
Renewde of God for owre consolacion
By dropys of grace that on them down doth rayn;
Through whose swete showris now sprong ther is ayen
A rose most riall with levis fressh of hew,
All myrthis to maynten, all sorous to subdewe.

NOTE: f.11: Hamshere (2 voc). Incomplete; tenor only (see F7). The words, however, are complete. 'The soveren sede' may have been Prince Arthur, Henry VII's first-born, or (though it is less likely) Henry, later VIII, his second-born.

GLOSS: 1 yë: *eye*

TEXT: *heading*: C.ix

F9   Love fayne wolde I;
Yff I coude spye
So prately
In Venus' trace

355

Appendix A

A lady fre,
I wolde bynde me
Her man to be
So long a space.

NOTE: f.11v: anon (2 voc). Incomplete: treble only.

GLOSS: 3 prately: *prettily* | 4 trace: *train* | 5 fre: *courteous*

TEXT: The leaf which contained, *recto*, the tenor and the MS number of this song is missing. The poem also seems incomplete. If so, further leaves are missing; the last of them must have contained, *verso*, the treble of C.xi (F10). If f.11v contained the complete treble-part of the song, one would expect the last note to be a long, possibly ornamented (cf. F1–8), not a breve. If on the other hand it contained only the first section, why is the usual note-guide, with the direction *verte folium*, omitted?

F10

Nowe the lawe is led be clere conciens
Full sylde covetise hath dominacion
In every place ryght hath residens
Nethir in towne ne fylde simulacion
Ther is trewly in every case consolacion
The pore pepull no tyme hath but ryght
Men may fynd day ne nyght adulacion
Now raynyth trewly in every mannys syght.

NOTE: f.12: Rycardus Davy (2 voc). Incomplete; tenor only (see F9). *Index MEV* 2364 lists four other versions of the same poem; Robbins, *Secular Lyrics*, no. 111, prints one of them. The words, which are complete, are underlaid to the notes, as in Song 151, so as to mark the double meaning as far as possible. No punctuation has been introduced into this poem because of the double meaning intended: it can also be arranged as a stanza of rhyme-royal with rhymes: sylde | place | fylde | case | hath [has?] | nyght | syght.

GLOSS: 2 sylde: *seldom* | 8 raynyth: *reigneth*

TEXT: *heading*: C.xi

F11

That was my woo is nowe my most gladness;
That was my payne is nowe my joyus chaunce;
That was my feere is nowe my sykyrness;
That was my grefe is now my alegeaunce.
Thus hath now grace enrychyd my plesaunce,
Wherfor I am and shal be tyll I dye
Your trewe servant with thought, hart and body.

NOTE: ff.12v–13: R. Fayrfax (2 voc). Through-set in two sections, with 'rhyming' melisma. Cf. F23, a poem expressing the opposite sentiment.

GLOSS: 3 sykyrness: *security*

TEXT: *heading*: C.xii

F12

Benedicite! Whate dremyd I this nyght?
Methought the worlde was turnyd up so downe,
The son, the moone, had lost ther force and light;
The see also drownyd both towre and towne:
Yett more mervell how that I hard the sownde
Of onys voice sayyng, 'Bere in thy mynd,
Thi lady hath forgoten to be kynd.'

NOTE: ff.13v-15: [Fayrfax] (3 voc). Through-set in two sections. The note on f.1 (see App. A, p. 351) attributes the song to Fayrfax. The song is of particular interest because Sir Thomas More translated it in a Latin epigram, *Dii melius* (see A. J. Sabol's article in *MLN*, lxiii (1948), 542).

TEXT: 2 the: *III* this | *heading*: C.xiii

F13

To complayne me, alas, why shulde I so?
For my complayntes it dyd me nevir good;
But be constraynt, now must I shew my woo
To her only which is myn yës fode,
Trustyng sumtyme that she will chaunge her mode
And lett me not allway be guerdonless,
Syth for my trouth she nedith no wittness.

NOTE: ff.15v-17: [Fayrfax] (3 voc). Through-set in two sections (1-4; 5-7) with 'rhyming' melisma and slight break in sense. The note on f.1 (see App. A, p. 351) attributes the song to Fayrfax.

GLOSS: 3 be constraynt: *of necessity* | 4 yës: *eyes*

TEXT: 3 constraynt: *MS* constraynd | 4 myn, *II, III*: *I* my | 5 chaunge: *III* chaunce | *heading*: C.xiiii

F14

Alas, it is I that wote nott what to say,
For why I stond as he that is abusyd;
Ther as I trusted I was late cast away,
And no cause gevyn to be so refusyd;
But pite it is that trust shulde be mysusyd
Other by colour or by fals semblaunce;
Wher that is usyd can be no surance.

NOTE: ff.17v-19: Turges [or Fayrfax] (3 voc). Through-set in two sections, with 'rhyming' melisma. The note on f.1 of the MS (see App. A, p. 351) attributes the song to Fayrfax; but 'Turges' is written after the bass in the song.

GLOSS: 2 For why: *for the reason that* | 6 Other by colour: *either by fair seeming, or . . .* | 7 surance: *confidence*

TEXT: *heading*: C.xv

Appendix A

F15
> I am he that hath you dayly servyd,
> Thow I be lytyll in your remembraunce;
> And mervell I have syth I not deservid
> To be put owte of your good governaunce . . .

NOTE: f.19v: Edmund Turges (3 voc). Incomplete: treble and part of bass only.

TEXT: *I* servyd: *II* omits

The leaf, f.19, which, *verso*, contains these words, has the treble and the beginning of the bass-part of a three-voice setting. Fehr pr. the words as part of F14. I think he is wrong in doing so, not because the words do not follow quite naturally, but because F14 is musically complete, ends with longs in all parts, and has no note-guides. In addition, there is illumination on f.19v, as customary at the beginning of a song. The MS number C.xvi, which would have decided the issue, is missing because it belonged to the right-hand page. This page was the *recto* of the first of a number of missing leaves which contained songs originally numbered: xvi [second half of bass, and tenor] (F15); xvii [totally lost]; xviii [upper voice(s)] (F16).

F16   .   .   .   .
> I pray daily ther paynys to asswage
> And sone to sende where they faynest wolde be,
> Withoute disease or adversyte.

NOTE: f.20: anon (3 voc). Incomplete: part of bass and tenor only (see F15).

GLOSS: 3 disease: *mental discomfort*

TEXT: no MS song-number; this suggests that the song covered at least two openings.

F17
> But why am I so abusyd?
> Syth worde and dede is take in vayne,
> And my service allway refusyd,
> Yet moreovyr a gretter payne,
> I wote nott where I may complayn;
> For where I shulde, they be mery,
> When that they knowe I am sory.

NOTE: ff.20v–22: William Newark (3 voc). Through-set in two sections, with a break in the sense and 'rhyming' melisma.

GLOSS: 6 shulde: *i.e. be merry*

TEXT: 6 mery: *III omits* | *heading*: C.xix

F18
> Yowre counturfetyng
> With doubyll delyng
> Avaylyth nothyng;
> And wote ye why?

For ye with your faynyng
Hath such a demyng
To make a belevyng:
Nay, nay, hardely!

Hit were to grete pite
That women truly
Hade so grete foly
That cowde nott tell,
When that ye do lye,
Then speke ye so swetely
And thynk the contrary:
Thus knowe we well.

NOTE: ff.22v–24: William Newark (3 voc; bass optional). Through-set in two sections, with 'rhyming' melisma.

GLOSS: 2.1 to: *too* (?)

TEXT: *II heading*: Bassus ad placitum | *heading*: C.xx

F19   Thus musyng in my mynd, gretly mervelyng
Houghevyr such dyversite in on person may be,
So goodly, so curtesly, so gentill in behavyng;
And so sodenly will chaunge in every degre;
As solen, as stately, as strange toward me,
As I of aquayntance had never byn afore;
Wherfore I hope to fynd a speciall remedy
To lett itt over pass, and thynk theron no more.

NOTE: ff.24v–26: William Newark (3 voc). Cambridge, Fitzwilliam Museum, unclassified MS fragment contains, *verso*, the last two staves of Voice III, anon. (The *recto* contains part of F24/H107, 'Sumwhat musyng'.) Drexel fragments no. 12: anon (portions of Voices II and III). The three versions, in so far as they can be compared, are almost identical. Through-set in two sections, with 'rhyming' melisma.

GLOSS: 2 on: *one* | 4 degre: *respect* | 5 solen: *strange, unsociable*

TEXT: *heading*: C.xxi

F20   Most clere of colour and rote of stedfastness,
With vertu connyng her maner is lede,
Which that passyth my mynde for to express
Of her bounte, beaute and womanhode;
The bryghtest myrrour and floure of goodlyhed,

Appendix A

Which that all men knowith, both more and less;
Thes vertues byn pryntyd in her doutless.

NOTE: ff.26v–28: Robard Fayrfax (3 voc). Through-set in two sections, with slight 'rhyme' in the melismas. After Fayrfax's name, a much later hand has written: '(whose armes is in the letter *M*)'. Fayrfax's arms are indeed in the initial letter of all voices, but penned in, it seems, by a later hand, who may well have copied them from the title-page.

GLOSS: 1 colour: *outward appearance* | rote: *root* | 2 connyng: *learned* | 4 bounte: *virtue*

TEXT: 4 womanhode, *all voices: read* womanhede *for the rhyme* ? | heading: C.xxii

F21   I love, loved, and loved wolde I be
In stedfast fayth and trouth with assuraunce;
Then bownden were I such on faythfully
To love, thowe I do fere to trace that dawnce,
Lest that mysaventure myght fall be chaunce;
Yet will I me trust to fortune applye;
Hough that evyr it will happ I wote nere I.

NOTE: ff.28v–30: Robard Fayrfax (3 voc). Through-set in two sections, with a break in the sense.

GLOSS: 3 on: *one* | 4 trace that dawnce: *take my part in the dance of love* | 6 me: *my (?)* – i.e. *I will leave the issue to Fortune*

TEXT: heading: C.xxiii

F22   Alas, for lak of her presens,
Whom I serve and shall as long,
Tyll deth my lyff departe from hens!
Absens it is that wolde me wrong;
And thus is the tyme of his song;
To gett mystrust is his entent
To send to her to make me shent.

NOTE: ff.30v–31: Robard Fayrfax (3 voc). Through-set in *one* section (this is unusual) with long melisma at end.

GLOSS: 3 departe: *separate* | 5 tyme: *i.e. the burden of his intent* | 6 gett mystrust: *i.e. cause (in me) lack of trust (in her)* | 7 shent: *confounded*

TEXT: heading: C.xxiiii

F23   That was my joy is now my woo and payne;
That was my bliss is now my displesaunce;
That was my trust is now my wanhope playne;

That was my wele is now my most grevaunce.
What causyth this but only yowre plesaunce
Onryghtfully shewyng me unkyndness,
That hath byn your fayre lady and mastress.

Nor nought cowde have, wolde I nevyr so fayne!
My hart is yours with gret assuraunce.
Wherfore of ryght ye shuld my greffe complayne,
And with pite have me in remembraunce
Much the rathir sith my suryd constaunce
Wolde in no wise for joy nor hevyness
Have but yourselfe, fayre lady and mastres.

NOTE: ff.31v–33: anon (3 voc). Through-set with no break between the two verses. The literary refrain is not reflected in the music. Cf. F11, a poem expressing the opposite sentiment.

GLOSS: 1.3 wanhope playne: *blank despair* | 1.5 plesaunce: *pleasure, wish* | 2.5 suryd constaunce: *sure fidelity*

The Lady speaks verse 1; the Lover replies with verse 2. But 2.3–4 would come more appropriately from her, and the beginning of verse 2 is abrupt. Perhaps the text is corrupt.

TEXT: 1.5 this: *III* thus | *heading*: C.xxv

F24   Sumwhat musyng   [1
                             And more morenyng
                             In remembryng
                             The unstedfastness,
                             This wordle beyng
                             Of such welyng
                             Me contraryyng;
                             What may I gess?

                             I fere doutless   [2
                             Remedyless
                             Is now to cess
                             My wofull chaunce;
                             For unkyndness
                             Withouten less
                             And no redress
                             Me doth avaunce

                             With displesaunce   [3
                             To my grevaunce

And no suraunce
Of remedy;
Lo, in this traunce,
Now in substaunce
Such is my daunce
Willyng to dye.

Methynkyth truly   [4
Bounden am I
And that gretly
To be content,
Sayng playnly,
Fortune doth wry
All contrary
For myn entent.

My lyff was lent   [5
To an entent;
It is ny spent;
Wellcum, fortune.
Yet I ne went
Thus to be shent;
But she it ment,
Such is her wone.

NOTE: ff.33v–35: Robard Fayrfax (3 voc). The song is also found (*a*) as H107: anon (3 voc),
q.v.; (*b*) as Cambridge, Fitzwilliam Museum, unnumbered MS fragment: anon (portions of
Voices I and II) (see also F19); (*c*) as Wells Cathedral, MS fragments: anon (portions of
all Voices with words from all verses); (*d*) as Drexel fragments, no. 9: anon (the first half of
Voice I). Cf. also Song 344. The words are ascribed to Antony Woodville, Lord Rivers,
who is said to have written them during his imprisonment at Pontefract (he was beheaded
in 1483); see J. M. Berdan, *Early Tudor Poetry*, 150, and E. Arber, *Dunbar Anthology*, 180.
The song is through-set. The five versions are substantially the same.

GLOSS: 1.6 welyng: *wheeling* | 2.3 cess: *cease* | 2.6 less: *lying; i.e. assuredly* | 3.5 traunce: *state
of dread* | 3.6 in substaunce: *in reality* | 4.6 wry: *twist* | 5.5 went: *thought* | 5.6 shent: *ruined* |
5.7: *i.e. but she had it in mind (the whole time)* | 5.8 wone: *wont*

TEXT: 3.2 my: *II, III*, my gret | 4.2: am: *III* were | For other variants see H107, note |
heading: C.xxvi

F25   Madam, defrayne!   [1
                           Ye me retayne
                           In every vayne
                           With wofulness;

362

The Fayrfax MS

I wolde full fayne
To you complayne,
That of my payne
Ye myght redress.

I thynk suerly   [2
Bounden were I
To you gretly
While I endure,
For to applye
With hart, body,
Tylle I dye;
I you ensure.

I have yow lent   [3
With good entent,
My hart is ment,
With thoughtis trew;
I am content
My lyffe to spente,
Thowe I be shent,
All other to esshewe.

NOTE: ff.35v–38: anon [? Fayrfax] (3 voc).

GLOSS: 1.2 retayne: *check* | 1.3: *i.e. in every 'nerve'* | 2.5 applye: *adhere* | 3.1 I have yow lent:
I have inclined towards you | 3.3 ment: *intended, destined* | 3.7 shent: *confounded*

TEXT: 1.7 that: *III omits* | *heading*: C.xxvii

In the top margin of f.37 are very lightly scribbled the letters *fay fa* (= Fayrfax?). However,
the letter *ff* for the gathering is written on the same leaf.

F26   O rote of trouth, o princess to my pay,
                  Endewid with vertu and goodly plesaunce,
                  In whom all vertu is knytt withouten varyaunce,
                  With welth and wordly joy long to endure,
                  I pray God hartely, withoutyn mysaventure.

NOTE: ff.38v–40: Tutor (3 voc; bass optional).

GLOSS: 1 to my pay: *to my liking* | 4–5 *i.e. I pray (you) will long endure* . . .

TEXT: *heading*: C.xxviii | *II heading*: Bassus ad Placitum

363

F27

'I love, I love, and whom love ye?'
'I love a floure of fressh beaute;'
'I love another as well as ye.'
   'Than shal be provid here anon
   Yff we three can agre in on.'

'I love a flour of swete odour'   [1
'Magerome, gentyll or lavendour,
Columbyne goldis of swete flavour?'
   'Nay, nay, let be;
   Is non of them that lykyth me.'

'Ther is a floure where so he be,   [2
And shall not yet be namyd for me;
Prymeros, violet, or fressh daysy,
   He pass them all in his degre;
   That best lykyth me.'

'On that I love most enterly.'   [3
'Gelofyr gentyll or rosemary,
Camamyll, borage, or savery?'
   'Nay certenly;
   Here is not he that plesyth me.'

'I chese a floure fresshist of face.'   [4
'What is his name that thou chosen has?
The rose, I suppose? Thyn hart unbrace!'
   'That same is he,
   In hart so fre, that best lykyth me.'

'Now have I lovyd, and whom love ye?'
'I love a floure of fressh beaute.'
'I love anothyr as well as ye.'
   'Than shall be provid here anon
   Yff we three can agre in oon.'

'The rose it is a ryall floure.'   [5
'The red or the white? Shewe his colour!'
'Both be full swete and of lyke savoure;
   All on they be;
   That day to se it lykyth well me.'

'I love the rose, both red and white.'   [6
'Is that your pure perfytt appetite?'
'To here talke of them is my delite.
   Joyed may we be
   Oure prince to se, and rosys thre.'

'Nowe have we lovyd, and love will we
This fayre fressh floure full of beaute;
Most worthy it is, as thynkyth me.
   Than may be provid here anon
   That we three be agrede in oon.'

NOTE: ff.40v–46: Syr Thomas Phelyppis (3 voc). Carol, strophically set. Greene, no. 433.
The music of the burden is slightly modified when repeated. Greene (note) suggests that 'this
gay and spirited carol celebrates the cessation of strife between the houses of York and Lancaster, the white and red roses'. In particular, as 6.5 shows, the birth of a royal child to
Henry VII and his queen, Elizabeth of York, seems to be celebrated.

GLOSS: B4 provid: *tried out* | 1.2 Magerome: *marjoram* | 1.3 goldis: *marigolds* | 3.1 on: *one* |
3.2 Gelofyr: *gillyflower* | 3.3 Camamyll . . .: *camomile, borage or savory* | 5.4 on: *one*

TEXT: 3.5 plesyth me: *III best lykyth me* | *heading*: C.xxix

Repetition of the burden is clearly indicated after each verse; and the modified burdens are
written out in full (as shown) after verses 4 and 6.

F28   Complayne I may wherevyr I go,
                Syth I have done my besy payne
                To love her best and no mo
                And she me takyth in gret disdayne:
                I-wiss yet will I not me complayne
                Tyll that I cum tyll her presens,
                Lest cause in me be fownd of offens.

NOTE: ff.46v–48: anon (3 voc; Voice II optional). A poem in Bodl. Rawl. C.813, f.46v,
begins with the same lines but deviates; it has three verses of rhyme royal.

GLOSS: 4 takyth in: *treats with*

TEXT: 1: *the first I is apparently erased and re-written in each Voice* | 5: *before II is written* Secunda
pars ad Placitum | 6 cum tyll: *II cum to* | *heading*: C.xxx

F29   Alone, alone, alone, alone,
                Here I sytt alone, alas, alone!

                As I me walkyd this endurs day   [1
                To the grenewode for to play
                And all hevyness to put away,
                     Myself alone;

Appendix A

As I walkyd undir the grenewode bowe   [2
I sawe a maide fayre inow;
A childe she hoppid; she song, she lough;
    That childe wepid alone.

'Son,' she sayd, 'I have the borne   [3
To save mankynd that was forlorne;
Therfor I pray the, son, no more,
    But be still alone.'

'Modyr, methynkyth it is ryght ill,   [4
That men sekyth for to spill,
For them to save, it is my will;
    Therfor I cum hyther alone.'

'Sone', she sayd, 'let it be in thy thought,   [5
For mannys gilt is not withstone,
For thou art he that hath all wrought,
    And I, thy modir, alone.'

NOTE: ff.48v–50: anon (3 voc). Modified carol (not in Greene): the verses are through-set, but with musical link between refrain and burden.

GLOSS: 1.1 this endurs: *the other* | 2.1 bowe: *bough* | 2.2 inow: *i.e. very* | 2.3 hoppid: *danced (transitive)* | lough: *laughed* | 3.3 *i.e. don't cry any more* | 3.4 still: *quiet* | 4.2 spill: *ruin (me)* | 4.4 cum: *came* | 5.2 not withstone: *notwithstanding*

TEXT: B2 alas: *only in III* | 5.3 hath all: *III all hath* | *heading: C.xxxi*

F30   'A, my dere, a, my dere Son,'
    Seyd Mary, 'A, my dere;
Kys thi moder, Jhesu,
    With a lawghyng chere.'

This endurs nyght   [1
I sawe a syght
    All in my slepe:
Mary, that may,
She sang lullay
    And sore did wepe.
To kepe she sought
Full fast abowte
    Her Son from colde;

366

Joseph seyd, 'Wiff,
My joy, my leff,
　　Say what ye wolde.'
'Nothyng, my spouse,
Is in this howse
　　Unto my pay;
My Sone, a Kyng
That made all thyng
　　Lyth in hay.'

'My moder dere,　　　　　　　　　　　　　　　　　　　　[2
Amend your chere,
　　And now be styll;
Thus for to ly,
It is sothely
　　My Fadir's will.
Derision,
Gret passion
　　Infynytly,
As it is fownde,
Many a wownd
　　Suffyr shall I.
On Calvery,
That is so hye,
　　Ther shall I be,
Man to restore,
Naylid full sore,
　　Uppon a tre.'

NOTE: ff.50v–53: anon (3 voc). Carol with strophic verses. *Index MEV* 3597; Greene, no. 146A. Another version of the poem (Harley 2380, f.70v, lacking burden) differs considerably from F30 but is recognizable as the same poem.

GLOSS: 1.4 may: *maid* | 1.8 fast: *firmly* | 1.15 pay: *liking*

TEXT: *heading*: C.xxxii

F31　　　　　Jhesu, mercy, how may this be,
　　　　　　　That God hymselfe for sole mankynd
　　　　　　　Wolde take on Hym humanite?
　　　　　　　My witt nor reson may hit well fynd:
　　　　　　　　　Jhesu, mercy, how may this be?

Appendix A

Crist, that was of infynyt myght,   [1
Egall to the Fathir in deite,
Inmortal, inpassible, the wordlis lyght,
And wolde so take mortalite!
  Jhesu, mercy, [how may this be?]

He that wrought this wordle of nought,   [2
That made both paynys and joy also,
And suffyr wolde payne as sorowfull thought,
With wepyng, wayling, ye, sownyng for wo.
  Jhesu, mercy, [how may this be?]

A Jhesu, whi suffyrd thou such entretyng,   [3
As betyng, bobbyng, ye, spettyng on thi face?
Drawne like a theffe, and for payne swetyng
Both water and blode, ye, crucified an hevy case?
  Jhesu, mercy, [how may this be?]

'Lo, man, for the that ware onkynd,   [4
Gladly suffyrd I all this.'
And why, good Lord? Express thi mynd!
'The to purchace both joy and bliss.'
  [Jhesu, mercy, how may this be?]

NOTE: ff.53v–58: Browne (4 voc). Carol; not in Greene because the verses are through-set.
The music of the burden is slightly modified on repetition.

GLOSS: 1.3 inpassible: *incapable of suffering* | 2.4 sownyng: *swooning* | 3.1 entretyng: *treatment* |
3.2 bobbyng: *buffeting* | 3.4 an hevy case: *in mournful plight (?)*

TEXT: 2.3 suffyr: *II* suffird | 3.1 suffyrd: *II* suffirst | 2.4 ye: *IV omits* | 3.4 ye, *I, II: IV omits* |
heading: C.xxxiii

F32   Affraid, alas, and whi so sodenli?
             Whi so dismaid?
             Whi shuld she hevy be?
             Or otherwise evyll apaide?

             Sith it concludid was in the Trinite   [1
             That the Son of God shulde make us fre,
             Though deth be bewaylid by waies of pite,
             Yet when oure Laidis Son was slayne
             Oure sowlis comfort cam agayne;
               Therfore, though deth be nevyr so sore,
               Now blessid Lady, wepe no more:
                 Affraide.

Methynkyth in my reson thou owfte to be gladd   [2
When Jewis with treson to deth thi son ladde;
They bet him for oure gilt, though he no syn hadd;
Thi son was doughti, the fende was adradde;
To joy of every wordlis wight,
So nowe is knowen thi sonnys myght:
  Therfor, thowe deth be never so sore,
  Now, blessid Lady, wepe [no more:
    Affraide.]

Well I remember his wowndis were full smert,   [3
The crowne on his hed, the spere at his hart,
They betyng they broysyng, or liff did depart;
All was on red blod withoute any shirt;
But blessid be that oure,
That he suffird that sharpe shoure!
  Therfore though deth be never so sore,
  Now, blessid Lady, wepe no more:
    [Affraide.]

Glorius Lady, of hevyn hie quene,   [4
Lay downe all thi wepyng, let no more be sene!
Remembir thi joys that joyfull aye byn!
Thi dere sone is past his trobill and his tene;
His deth was swete, hit did us goode;
He bought us with his precious blode:
  Therefore, though deth be nevir so sore,
  Now, blessid Lady, wepe no more:

NOTE: ff.58v–63: anon (4 voc). Modified carol; not in Greene, because the verses are through-set. The musical form is: B V1-R V2-R . . . V4-R B′ (B′ is modified B). *Index MEV* 3131.

GLOSS: B4 evyll apaide: *ill satisfied* | 1.3 waies: *i.e. in piteous wise (?)* | 3.3 broysyng: *bruising* | 3.4 shirt: *the garment worn next to the skin; i.e. he was utterly naked* | 3.6 shoure: *attack (of pain)* | 4.4 tene: *affliction*

TEXT: 1.2 us fre: *IV* us all fre | 1.3 bewaylid: *I* waylid | 2.2 to deth thi son: *II* thi son to deth | 2.4 was doughti: *III* was so dowty | 3.1 Well: *III* when | 3.3 did: *I* wolde | *second* they: *I* an | *heading*: C.xxxiii | The repetitions are clearly indicated whenever they occur.

F33   Woffully araid,
                    My blode, man,
                    For the ran,

It may not be naid;
My body bloo and wan,
Woffully araide.

Beholde me, I pray the, with all thi hole reson,　　　　　　　　[1
And be not hard-hartid, and for this encheson
Sith I for thi sowle sake was slayne in good seson,
Begylde and betraide by Judas' fals treson;
　　Unkyndly entretid,
　　With sharpe corde sore fretid,
　　The Jewis me thretid,
They mowid, they grynned, they scornyd me,
Condemp to deth, as thou maist se;
　　Woffully araid.

Thus nakyd am I nailid, O man, for thy sake;　　　　　　　　[2
I love the, then love me; why slepist thou? Awake!
Remembir my tendir hart-rote for the brake,
With paynys my vaynys constraynyd to crake;
　　Thus toggid to and fro,
　　Thus wrappid all in woo,
　　Whereas never man was so
Entretid, thus in most cruell wise
Was like a lombe offerd in sacrifice:
　　Woffully arayd.

Off sharpe thorne I have worne a crowne on my hede,　　[3
So paynyd, so straynyd, so rufull, so red;
Thus bobbid, thus robbid, thus for thi love ded;
Onfaynyd, not deynyd, my blode for to shede:
　　My fete and handis sore
　　The sturdy nailis bore;
　　What myght I suffir more
Than I have done, O man, for the?
Cum when thou lyst, welcum to me!
　　Woffully araide.

NOTE: ff.63v–67: William Cornyssh Junior (4 voc). Modified carol; not in Greene, because the verses are through-set. Musically, the last line of each verse is a refrain; nowhere is a return to the original burden indicated. The music of the refrain varies in each verse. *Index MEV* 497 lists three other versions of the text. Dyce (i. 141–3) prints a longer text; the *Index* does not attribute to Skelton, and the best texts represent a tradition too early for him. This is the clearest possible example of a poem being chosen for setting for non-musical qualities; it was a favourite piece of devotional verse (see Carleton Brown, *XV*, 156).

GLOSS: B4 naid: *denied* | 1.2 encheson: *reason* | 1.3 sowle: *soul's* | 1.3 in good seson: *at the proper time* | 1.5 Unkyndly entretid: *unnaturally treated* | 1.8 mowid: *grimaced* | 2.4 crake: *crack* | 2.8 entretid: *treated (N.B. music shows verbal grouping)* | 3.3 bobbid: *buffeted* | robbid: *robed* | 3.4 Onfaynyd, not deynyd: *unfeigned, and not in a haughty spirit (?)* | 3.6 sturdy: *harsh*

TEXT: 1.2 not hard-hartid: *III* not so hard-hartid | 2.7 Whereas: *II* as | *heading:* C.xxxv

F34   'A, gentill Jhesu!'
Who is that that dothe me call?
'I, a synner that offt doth fall.'
What woldist thou have?
'Mercy, Lord, of the I crave.'
Why, lovyst thou me?
'Ye, my maker I call the.'
Than leve thi syn, or I nyll the,
And thynk on this lesson that now I teche the.
     'A, I will, I will, gentyll Jhesu'.

Uppon the cross nailid I was for the,   [1
  Suffyrd deth to pay thi rawnsum;
Forsake thi syn, man, for the love of me;
  Be repentant; make playne confession.
  To contryte hartes I do remission;
Be not dispayryd, for I am not vengeable;
  Gayne gostly enmys thynk on my passion;
Whi art thou froward, syth I am mercyable?

My blody wowndes downe railyng be this tre,   [2
  Loke on them well, and have compassion;
The crowne of thorne, the spere, the nailis thre,
  Percide hand and fote of indignacion,
  My hert ryven for thi redempcion.
Lett now us twayne in this thyng be tretable:
  Love for love be just convencion;
Why art thou froward sith I am merciable?

I hade on Petur and Mawdlen pyte   [3
  For-thi contrite of thy contricion;
Saynt Tomas of Indes, in crudelite
  He put his handes depe in my syde adowne.

Role up this mater; grave it in thi reson:
Syth I am kynd, why are thou unstable?
My blode best triacle for thi transgression;
Be thou not froward syth I am merciable.

Thynk agayne, pride, on my humilite; [4
  Cum to scole; record well this lesson:
Gayne fals envy thynk on my charyte,
  My blode all spent by distillacion.
Whi did I this? To save the from prison.
Afore thi hart hang this litell table,
  Swetter than bawme gayne gostly poyson:
Be thou not affraide sith I am merciable.

Lord, on all synfull here knelyng on kne, [5
  Thy deth remembryng of humble afeccion,
O Jhesu, graunt of thi benignite
  That thi fyve wellis plentuus of fusion,
Callid thi fyve wondes by computacion,
May washe us all from surfettes reprovable.
  Now for thi moders meke mediacion,
At hir request be to us merciable.

NOTE: ff.67v–73: Sheryngam (4 voc). The verses are attributed to Lydgate (see *Index MEV* 3845; Greene, no. 263; MacCracken, ed., *Minor Poems of John Lydgate*, EETS (1911, pp. 252–4). The poem has been made into a carol (not found elsewhere) by the addition of a burden, presumably by the composer, Sheryngham. The only indication that the burden was repeated in full after each verse is one *ut supra* (Verse 4, Voice II, f.72); it may not always have been so repeated. The verses are strophic.

GLOSS: B8 or I nyll the: *ere I reject you (?)* | 1.6 vengeable: *revengeful* | 1.7 gayne: *against* | 2.1 downe railyng: *gushing down* | 2.6 tretable: *tractable* | 2.7 be just convencion: *by fair covenant* | 3.2 For-thi contrite . . .: *corrupt,* MacCracken's text gives For the grete constreynt of ther contricyoun | 3.3 in crudelite: *mistake for incredulite (?)* | 3.5 grave: *impress* | 3.7 triacle: *medicine* | 4.4 by distillacion: *drop by drop* | 4.6 table: *inscription* | 5.2 of: *out of, because of* | 5.4 plentuus of fusion: *plenteously flowing*

TEXT: 2.2 them: *II* hym | 3.6 syth: *II* syth that | 3.8 thou not: *II* not thou | 4.5 save: *I* have | 5.4 thi: *II, IV* the | 5.7 moders: *erased in all voices; in III replaced by* justys *in a later hand* | *heading*: C.xxxvi

F35   Woffully araid, | My blode, man, | For the ran . . .

NOTE: ff.73v–77: Browne (3 voc). Another setting of the carol text printed and described as F33; the verses are again through-set, and the initial burden is not repeated.

VARIANTS IN TEXT: 1.2 F33 hard-hartid: F35 *all so* hard hartid | 1.6 corde: *II, III,* cordes |

2.7 Whereas never man was so: *III* was never man so | 2.9 offerd in: *all* offerd up in |
3.4 deynyd: *II, III* deynd | *heading*: C.xxxvii

F36   My feerfull dreme nevyr forgete can I:
        Methought a maydynys childe causless shulde dye.

    To Calvery he bare his cross with doulfull payne,   [1
    And theruppon straynyd he was in every vayne;
    A crowne of thorne as nedill sharpe shyfft in his brayne;
    His modir dere tendirly wept and cowde not refrayne.
          Myn hart can yerne and mylt
          When I sawe hym so spilt,
          Alas, all for my gilt,
    Tho I wept and sore did complayne
      To se the sharpe swerde of sorow smert,
      Hough it thirlyd her thoroughoute the hart,
    So ripe and endles was her payne.

    His grevous deth and her morenyng grevid me sore;   [2
    With pale visage tremlyng she stode her child before,
    Beholdyng ther his lymmys all to-rent and tore,
    That with dispaire for feer and dred I was nere forlore.
          For myne offence, she said,
          Her Son was so betraide,
          With wondis sore araid,
    Me unto grace for to restore:
      'Yet thou are unkynd, which sleith myn hert,'
      Wherewith she fell downe with paynys so smert;
    Unneth on worde cowde she speke more.

    Saynt Jhon than said, 'Feere not, Mary; his paynys all   [3
    He willfully doth suffir for love speciall
    He hath to man, to make hym fre that now is thrall.'
    'O frend,' she said, 'I am sure he is inmortall.'
          'Why than so depe morne ye?'
          'Of moderly pete
          I must nedis wofull be,
    As a woman terrestriall
      Is by nature constraynyd to smert,
      And yet verely I know in myn hart
    From deth to lyff he aryse shall.'

Unto the cross, handes and feete, nailid he was;   [4
Full boistusly in the mortess he was downe cast;
His vaynys all and synowis to-raff and brast;
The erth quakyd, the son was dark, whos lyght was past,
  When he lamentable
  Cried, 'Hely, hely, hely!'
  His moder rufully
Wepyng and wrang her handes fast.
 Uppon her he cast his dedly loke,
 Wherwith sodenly anon I awoke,
And of my dreme was sore agast.

NOTE: ff.77v–82: Gilbert Banastir (3 voc). Carol, slightly modified; included in Greene (no. 165), not quite consistently because the burden is shortened for its repeat and the music of verses 3 and 4 slightly differs from that of verses 1 and 2. The words of the burden also occur as a round in Ravenscroft, *Pammelia* (1609), no. 2: anon (3 voc); there is no apparent musical link.

GLOSS: 1.3 shyfft: *'shoved', thrust* | 1.5 can: *did* | mylt: *melt* | 1.6 spilt: *ruined* | 1.10 thirlyd: *pierced* | 2.7 araid: *afflicted, disfigured* | 2.11 Unneth on: *hardly one* | 3.2 willfully: *willingly* | 4.2 boistusly: *savagely* | mortess: *i.e. the mortise, or socket, into which the cross was thrust* | 4.3 to-raff: *riven apart* | brast: *burst* | 4.4 son: *sun* | 4.6 Hely . . .: *Eli . . .* | 4.8 fast: *ceaselessly* | 4.9 dedly: *deathlike*

TEXT: *heading:* C.xxxviii

F37 A blessid Jhesu, hough fortunyd this?   [1
    My mode is changid in every wise,
    Nature of aquayntance ys turned to a gest,
    So shortly am I bydyn to a grevus fest,
    Whereas I am in ybid with bodily rest;
     Thus trobled am I yet I trust it shalbe for the best;
     Sicut domino placuit, ita factum est.

    Where art thou, Nature, that wont were me to store   [2
    To lusty plesure? Now lyyng in the flore,
    My tast disordyrd all reson far passyng,
    My face disfygurid, myn yës full daslyng;
    Thou, Nature, hast lefft me; by the fynd I no rest:
     Thus trobled am I [yet I trust it shalbe for the best;
     Sicut domino placuit, ita factum est.]

    My voice is so trobled, my seknes then feele I;   [3
    My slepis be so feerfull, I thynk then sure to dye;

My dreme is so mervelous, serpentis semyth me to tere;
Grete mowntens fallyng over me, thus slepe doth I yn feere:
So wakyng ne sleping fynd I no rest:
   Thus trobled am I [yet I trust it shalbe for the best;
   Sicut domino placuit, ita factum est.]

Now, mercyfull Jhesu, to the make I my mone;   [4
Nature hath forsakyn me, and lefft me thus alone.
'Remembir the, my creature, thou must nedis dye, I the ensure.'
Alas, to dye thou makyst me sure; yet then, good Lord, do thou
                               thi cure;
With all good sowlis to cause me lyve in rest.
   Thus trobled am I [yet I trust it shalbe for the best;
   Sicut domino placuit, ita factum est.]

NOTE: ff.82v–86: Richard Davy (3 voc). Drexel fragments, no. 1: anon (1 voc). Voice I to words of verse 1, lines 2–3. The verses are through-set.

GLOSS: 1.3 *Nature of aquayntance . . .*: *Nature (my natural powers of life) from being an acquaintance has turned into a stranger* (OED *guest*, 2) (?) | 1.4–5: *Thus, in the near future, I am called to a melancholy festivity, Where I am invited in with all physical comfort (i.e. when I am finally dead, not ill)* | 1.7: *As it pleased the Lord, so is it accomplished* | 2.1 *store: furnish with necessaries for* | 2.2 *in: on* | 2.4 *daslyng: dazzled*

TEXT: 2.5 fynd I: *III* I fynd | 3.2 My slepis be: *III* My slepe is | 3.3 semyth me: *II* semyng me, *III* me semyth | 3.5 ne: *II, III,* nor | *heading:* C.xxxix

F38   A, myn hert, remembir the well,
           And thynk on the paynys that byn in hell.

         A myn hart, remembir the well   [1
         Howgh gretly thou art bownd indede;
         Thou thynkyst on hym nevir a dele
         That helpis the ever at thi most nede.
         Alas, for sorow myne hart doth blede
         To thynk how grevusly I have offend:
         I crye God mercy, I will amend.

         With wepyng teris most lamentable   [2
         To God above I call and crye;
         I will axe grace while I am able,
         I have offendid so grevusly;
         Me to amend I will me hye

Fo all my lyff-daies I have myspend:
I crye God mercy, I will amend.

NOTE: ff.86v–89: Richard Davy (3 voc). Modified carol; the verses are through-set, the burden altered on repetition.

GLOSS: 1.2 bownd: *obliged (i.e. to Christ)* | 2.3 axe: *ask* | 2.5 me hye: *hasten*

TEXT: 1.6 offend, *III: I, II*, offendid | 2.5 will: *I*, did | *heading: C.xl*

F39

Margaret meke
Whom I now seke
Ther is non lyke
I dare well say,
So manerly
So curtesly
So prately
She delis allway.

That goodly las,   [1
When she me bas,
Alas, alas,
I wote not where
I go or stond;
I thynk me bond,
I se, in lond,
To comfort her:
    So manerly
    [So curtesly
    So prately
    She delis allway.]

Her lusty chere,   [2
Her yës most clere,
I know no pere
In her beaute;
Both Cate and Bes,
Mawde and Anes,
Sis is witness
Of hir fety:
    So manerly
    [So curtesly

So prately
She delis allway.]

My Margarit   [3
I cannot mete
In feeld ne strete;
Woffull am I.
'Leve, love, this chance,
Your chere avaunce,
And let us daunce
Herk, my lady!'
So manerly
[So curtesly
So prately
She delis allway.]

NOTE: ff.89v–93: Browne (3 voc). Modified carol; the verses are through-set, the burden shortened on repetition. Henderson, 37 note, suggests the poem may be by Skelton. There is no evidence for this. Rimbault, *Little Book*, 29, claims a private source for the same song.

GLOSS: 1.2 bas: *kisses* | 1.7: *In sea, on land* | 2.1 lusty chere: *pleasant demeanour* | 2.2 yës: *eyes* | 2.8 fety: *handsomeness (?)* | 3.5: *the Lady seems to speak here* | 3.6 chere avaunce: *cheer up!*

TEXT: *heading* C.xli

F40   Jhoone is sike and ill at ease;
           I am full sory for Jhoon's disease.
           Alak, good Jhoane, what may you please?
           I shal bere the cost, be swete Sent Denys!

           Hit is so praty in every degre;   [1
           Good Lord, who may a goodlyer be
           In favoure and in facion (lo, will ye se?)
           But it were an angell of the Trinite?
               Alak, good Jhoone, [what may you please?
               I shal bere the cost, be swete Sent Denys!]

           Her contynaunce with her lynyacion,   [2
           To hym that wolde of such recreacion
           That God hath ordent in his first formacion,
           Myght wel be calde an conjuracion.
               Alak, good [Jhoone, what may you please?
               I shal bere the cost, be swete Sent Denys!]

377

Appendix A

She is my lytell praty on;　　　　　　　　　　　　　[3
What shulde I say? My mynde is gone.
Yff she and I were together alone,
I-wis, she will not gyve me a bone:
　　Alak, good Jhoan, [what may you please?
　　I shal bere the cost, be swete Sent Denys!]

Alas, good Jhoan, shall all my mone　　　　　　　　[4
Be lost so sone? I am a fole:
Leve this array! Anothir day
We shall both play, when we ar sole:
　　Alak, good Jhoan, [what may you please?
　　I shal bere the cost, be swete Sent Denys!]

NOTE: ff.93v–96: Richard Davy (3 voc). Drexel fragments, no. 5: anon (1 voc). The greater part of the triplex (burden and verses 1–2) survives. Modified carol; the verses are through-set, the burden shortened on repetition. Rimbault, *Little Book*, 40, claims private source formerly belonging to John Heywood; this may conceivably have been Drexel.

GLOSS: 1.1 Hit: *it (i.e. she)* | 1.4 But: *unless* | 2.1 contynaunce: *'countenance'* | lynyacion: *'lines', figure* | 2.2 recreacion: *i.e. love-making* | 2.3 ordent: *ordained* | 3.2 mynde: *balance of mind?* | 3.4 bone: *'boon'* | 4.3 array: *i.e. stop behaving as you are now (perhaps spoken by the Lady) (?)*.

TEXT: 2.3 formacion: *I* firmacion | heading: C.lxii

F41　　　Ay, besherewe yow! Be my fay　　　　　　　[1
　　　　This wanton clarkis be nyse allway.
　　　　Avent, avent, my popagay!
　　　　What, will ye do nothing but play?
　　　　Tully, valy, strawe, let be I say!
　　　　　Gup, Cristian Clowte, gup, Jak of the Vale,
　　　　　With manerly Margery, milk and ale.

　　　　'Be Gad, ye be a prety pode,　　　　　　　　[2
　　　　And I love you an hole cart-lode.'
　　　　Strawe, Jamys foder, ye play the fode;
　　　　I am no hakney for your rode;
　　　　Go watch a bole, your bak is brode.
　　　　　Gup, Cristian Clowte, gup, Jak of the Vale,
　　　　　With manerly [Margery, milk and ale.]

　　　　I-wiss, ye dele uncurtesly;　　　　　　　　　[3
　　　　What, wolde ye frompill me now? fy, fy!
　　　　'What, and ye shal be my piggesnye?'

378

Be Crist, ye shal not! No, no, hardely!
I will not be japed bodely.
   Gup, Cristian Clowte, gup, Jak of the Vale,
   With manerly Margery, [milke and ale.]

'Walke forthe your way, ye cost me nought;   [4
Now have I fownd that I have sought,
The best chepe flessh that evyr I bought.'
Yet for his love that all hath wrought
Wed me or els I dye for thought!
   Gup, Cristian Clowte, your breth is stale,
   With manerly Margery, milke and ale;
   Gup, Cristian Clowte, gup, Jak of the Vale,
   With manerly Margery, [milke and ale.]

NOTE: ff.96v–99: William Cornyssh Junior (3 voc). Refrain-song; through-set, but with musical as well as literary refrain. The words of this song are probably by Skelton: see 'Garlande of Laurell', lines 1198–, 'Of manerly maistres Margery Mylke and Ale; | To her he wrote many maters of myrthe' (Dyce, i. 409).

GLOSS: This text is unusually difficult to interpret with any certainty; the Man speaks (it seems) the lines in editorial quotation marks.

1.1 besherewe yow: *curse on you* | fay: *faith* | 1.2 wanton: *wild* | nyse: *foolish* | 1.3 Avent: *'avaunt', be off!* | popagay: *parrot (i.e. vain fellow)* | 1.6 Cristian Clowte: *Dyce compares* Colyn Cloute *line* 881 | Jak of the Vale: *Dyce compares* Magnificence, *line* 260, 'some jangelynge Jacke of the vale' | 2.1 pode: *toad (?)* | 2.3 Jamys foder: *'fodder', james-weed, ragwort, i.e. useless stuff (?)* | fode: *'one who beguiles with fair words'* (OED) | 2.5 watch a bole: *meaning? – Dyce suggests 'bull'* | 3.2 frompill: *frumple* | 3.3 piggesnye: *sweetheart* | 3.5 japed bodely: *seduced* | 4.3 best chepe: *adj. lowest-priced* | 4.5 thought: *anxiety*

TEXT: 1.2 clarkis: *I* clars *above line* | 2.1 Gad: *I* erased | 3.5 japed bodely: *II erased but legible*; *I* Jamys foder *written over erasure* | 4.5 dye for thought: *II* shal be nought | *heading*: C.xliii

F42   Who shall have my fayre lady?
                Who but I, who but I, who but I,
                   Undir the levys grene?

                The fayrest man that best love can,
                Dandirly, dandirly, dandirly dan,
                   Undir the holy grene.

NOTE: ff.99v–101: anon (3 voc). Through-set, with a long melisma after each verse. Cf. *Twenty Songs*, no. 8: Jones (3 voc), 'Who shall have my fayr lady | who but I who but I', a moralization in carol-form using these lines as burden; no apparent musical connection. The interchange of the words 'levys' and 'holy' may have served a dramatic purpose.

GLOSS: 2.3 holy: *holly*

TEXT: 1.3 levys: *II* holy | 2.3 holy: *II* levis | *heading*: C.xliiii

Appendix A

F43   Hoyda, hoyda, joly rutterkin!
Like a rutterkin, hoyda!

Rutterkyn is com unto oure towne   [1
In a cloke withoute cote or gowne,
Save a raggid hode to kover his crowne,
    Like a rutter:

Rutterkyn can speke no Englissh;   [2
His tong rennyth all on buttyrd fyssh,
Besmerde with grece abowte his disshe,
    Like a rutter:

Rutterkyn shall bryng you all good luk;   [3
A stoupe of bere up at a pluk,
Till his brayne be as wise as a duk;
    Like a rutter:

When rutterkyn from borde will ryse   [4
He will piss a galon-pot full at twise
And the overplus undir the table of the newe gyse;
    Like a rutter:

NOTE: ff.101v–104: William Cornyssh Junior (3 voc). Carol with through-set verses, burden repeated in full. There is no particular reason for thinking the words are by Skelton. Courtly Abusion sings a snatch from them in *Magnyfycence* (Dyce, i. 249); but two other songs mentioned in the same passage are known not to be by Skelton. The passage merely indicates that there was a popular song of that title, or a cant phrase. Hawkins's suggestion that 'Hoyda hoyda' is a satire on the drunken Flemings who came to England with Anne of Cleves is certainly wrong; F43 must have been composed considerably earlier.

GLOSS: B1 *etc.* rutterkin, rutter: *swaggering gallant* | 2.2 rennyth: *runneth* | 4.2 at twise: *twice* | 4.3 of the newe gyse: *in the modern fashion*

TEXT: 3.3 brayne: *III* braynes | *heading*: C.xlv

F44   From stormy wyndis and grevous wethir,
Good Lord, preserve the Estrige Fether!

O blessed Lord of hevyn celestiall,   [1
  Which formyd hast of thi most speciall grace
Arthur oure prynce to us here terrestriall,
  In honor to rayne, Lord, graunt hym tyme and space,
    Which of aliaunce
    Oure prince of plesaunce

380

Be inerytaunce
Of Ynglond and Fraunce
  Ryght eyre for to be;
  Wherfore now syng we:

Wherfore, good Lord, syth of thi creacion   [2
  Is this noble prince of riall lynage,
In every case be his preservacion,
  With joy to rejose his dew enerytaunce,
    His ryght to optayne,
    In honor to rayne,
    This eyre of Brytayne,
    Of Castell and Spayne,
      Ryght eyre for to be;
      Wherefore now syng we:

Now, good Lady among thi sayntes all,   [3
  Pray to thi Son, the secund in Trinite,
For this yong prince, which is and daily shal
  Be thi servaunt with all his hart so fre.
    O celestiall
    Modir maternall,
    Emprise infernall,
    To the we crye and call,
      His savegard to be;
      Wherefore now syng we:

NOTE: ff.104v–108: Edmund Turges (3 voc). Carol; verses strophically set. Rimbault, *Little Book*, 21, claims private source. The song appears to be a ceremonial carol praying protection for Prince Arthur (d. 1502), elder brother of Henry VIII, as he sets out on a journey, perhaps on a sea voyage.

GLOSS: B2 Estrige Fether: *Ostrich Feather (heraldic badge of the Prince of Wales)* | 1.7 Be: *by* | 1.9 eyre: *heir* | 2.4 rejose . . . .: *make glad his future subjects* | 3.7 Emprise infernall: '*empress of hell*'

TEXT: 3.4 be: *II* be be | 3.8 To the: *I* now | 3.9 His savegard to be: *I* for to be, *III* ryght ayre for to be | *heading*: C.xlvi

F45   This day day dawes,
          This gentill day day dawes,
          This gentill day dawes,
          And I must home gone.

In a glorius garden grene   [1
Sawe I syttyng a comly quene
Among the flouris that fressh byn.
She gaderd a floure and set betwene;
    The lyly-whighte rose methought I sawe,
    The lyly-whighte rose methought I sawe,
        And ever she sang:

In that garden be flouris of hewe: [2
The gelofir gent, that she well knewe;
The floure-de-luce she did on rewe,
And said, 'The white rose is most trewe
    This garden to rule be ryghtwis lawe.'
    The lyly-whighte rose methought I sawe,
        And evyr she sang:

NOTE: ff.108v–112: anon (3 voc). Carol; verses strophically set, burden repeated almost entire. Written perhaps in honour of the white rose, Elizabeth of York, queen of Henry VII. The burden recalls a dance/song frequently mentioned in contemporary literature: (i) *Colkelbie Sow*, line 306; (ii) *Complaint*, p. lxxxvii, song 82; (iii) Dunbar, *Merchants of Edinburgh*, line 30; (iv) Gawin Douglas's 13th Prologue to *The Aeneid* (edn of 1533) f.358v; (v) *GGB*, 192, a moralized version. See also Greene, no. 432, and note.

GLOSS: B1 dawes: *dawns* | 1.4 set betwene: *sat amongst them* | 2.2 gelofir: *gillyflower* | 2.3 floure-de-luce: *fleur-de-lis* | 2.5 be ryghtwis: *by righteous*

TEXT: B4 I: *II, III*, we *and* I *variously* | 1.5 methought I: *II* methought that I | *heading:* C.xlvii

F46   Smale pathis to the grenewode,
            Will I love and shall I love,
            Will I love and shall I love
                No mo maydyns but one.

        Love is naturall to every wyght,   [1
            Indyfferent to every creature,
        Chaungyng his course, now hevy, now lyght,
            As fortune fallyth, I yow ensure;
            So rennyth the chaunce from one to one:

        One is good, but mo were bettyr   [2
            After my reason and jugement,
        Consideryng dyvers fayrer and fetter,
            Plesaunt, buxum, and ever obedient,
            Tyll sum of them begyn to grone:

But I will do as I saide furst,   [3
  So it is best, as thynkyth me,
To put in one my faithfull trust,
  Forever yff she will trew be,
  And love her only whereever she gone:

NOTE: ff.112v–115: anon (3 voc). Carol; verses strophically set, burden modified on repetition. The style of both words and music, especially bars 1–8, suggests an underlying popular song. See also Greene, 451.

GLOSS: B1 smale: *narrow* | 1.2 Indyfferent: *the same for*

TEXT: 1.5 chaunce: *II, III* chaunge | 2.4 ever: *I omits* | *heading*: C.xlviii

F47   Enforce yourselfe as Goddis knyght
         To strenkyth your comyns in ther ryght.

         Soverayn lorde, in erth most excellent,   [1
           Whom God hath chose oure gyde to be,
         With gyfftes grete and evydent
           Of marshiall power and also hye dygnite,
             Sith it is so, now let your labour be
               Enforcyng yourselfe with all your myght
               To strenkyth your comyns in ther ryght.

         God hath gyff you of his goodness   [2
           Wisdome with strenkyth and soveraynte
         All mysdone thynges to redress,
           And specially hurtis of thi commynalte,
             Which crye and call unto your Majeste.
               In your person all ther hope is pyght
               To have recover of ther unryght.

NOTE: ff.115v–118: Edmund Turges (3 voc). Carol; verses strophically set. Possibly early Henry VIII; but the vague generalities of the text could well refer to Henry VII.

GLOSS: B1 Enforce yourselfe: *exert yourself, strive* | B2 To strenkyth . . .: *strengthen your commons* | 2.6 pyght: *set*

TEXT: 1.6 with all your myght: *I* as godys knyght | *heading*: C.xlix

F48   Be hit knowyn to all that byn here
         And to all that here-afftir
         To me shal be leffe and dere,
         That I Jhesus off Nazareth

Appendix A

For thi love, man, have suffyrd deth
Uppon the crosse with woundis smert
In hed, in fete, in handis, in hart;
And for I wolde have thyne heritage agayne,
Therefore I suffird all this payne.

A, man, I have yevyn and made a graunt   [1
To the, and thou wilt be repentant;
Hevyn bliss thyn eritage withoute endyng
As long as I am Lord and Kyng,
Not covetyng more for all my smert
But a lovyng and a contrite hart,
And that thou be in charite;
Love thi neyboure as I love the!
This is that I axe of the,
That am the cheffe lorde of the fee.

If any man will say here agayne   [2
That I suffird not for the this payne,
[Rather then manne sholde be forlorne
Yet wold Y eft be all to-torne.]
Yet, man, that thou sholdest not be lorne,
In the awter I am offerd my Fader beforne;
Witness, the daye turnyd to nyghth,
Witness, the son that lost his lyghth,
Witness, the vale that then did ryve,
Witness, the bodies that rose from deth to lyve.

Witness, the erthe that did quake,   [3
Witness, stonys that all to-brake,
Witness, Mari, wittness, Seynt Jhon,
And othir wittness, many one;
Into witness of which thyng
Myn owne seale therto I hyng;
And, man, for the more sykyrnesse,
The wounde in my harte the seale it is,
Iyevyn upon the mownt of Calvary,
The grete daye of mannys mercy.

NOTE: ff.118v–122: anon (3 voc). Carol; verses through-set; burden slightly modified on repetition. This song represents the only known carol-version of the popular 'Short Charter' of Christ. See *Index MEV* 4184: seventeen sources are listed. I have replaced a missing couplet

The Fayrfax MS

from the version in Stowe MS 620, printed by M. C. Spalding, ed., *Middle English Charters of Christ* (Bryn Mawr, 1914).

GLOSS: B3 leffe: *dear* | B8 heritage: *your possessions – i.e. the Earth* | 1.2 and: *if* | 1.9 axe : *ask* | 1.10 fee: *estate, i.e. this world* | 2.6 awter: *altar* | 2.9 vale: *veil* | ryve: *split* | 2.10 lyve: *life* | 3.2 to-brake: *broke asunder* | 3.6 hyng: *hang* | 3.7 sykyrnesse: *assurance* | 3.9 Iyevyn: *given*

TEXT: 1.1 yevyn and: *III omits* | 2.1 man: *III omits* | 2.3 *see above* | 3.4 wittness: *I* witteness | heading: C.l

F49   In a slumbir late as I was,
      I harde a voice lowde call and crye
    'Amende the, man, of thi trespace,
      And aske forgeveness or evyr thou dye.'

    'Beholde', he saide, 'my creature,   [1
    Whome I did make so lyke unto me,
    What paynys I sofferd, I the ensure,
    Where thou were thrall, to make the free.
    Upon the cross with naylis thre
    Fast I was naylyd for thyne offence;
    Therfore remembir the or thou go hence.'

NOTE: ff.122v–124: anon (3 voc). Carol; the last piece in the MS and probably incomplete (all other carols of the same type have several verses). If the verses were through-set, then the music at least is complete.

GLOSS: B4 or evyr: *before ever* | 1.3 I the ensure: *'I can tell you'* | 1.6 Fast: *firmly*

TEXT: B4 evyr: *II, III omit variously* | heading: C.li

Vellum, 12 × 8¼ in., ff.129 (Greene, 333). Greene analyses the hands as follows: A ff.3v–21, 26; B ff.21v–25v, 27–124; C ff.124v–128. The distinction between hands A and B, however, seems to be more a matter of the words than of the music. Greene does not note that a fourth hand has added the instrumental piece, H85. The notation is in black void throughout, with occasional full notes for coloration. On f.1 an old hand has written: *henricus dei gracia res anglie*; ff.1v–2 are blank; ff.2v–3 contain a manuscript index of the songs with words, seventy entries in all (see notes to the songs printed in *MCH8*; its numbering and its entries disagree slightly with the contents of the MS); the songs then run continuously from f.3v to f.128, the last song (H109) being presumably a slightly later addition. Among scribbles on fly-leaves at the end are 'Sir John Leed in the parishe of Benyngden', 'Syr John Berde in the parishe of Benenden'.

The composers are: Henry VIII, Fayrfax, Cornish, Kemp, Rysbye, Farthing, Daggere, Dunstable, Pygott, Cooper, Floyd (Flude); there are also arrangements of foreign songs by Agricola, Hayne van Ghyseghem, Barbireau, etc. Twenty-six songs and eleven instrumental pieces are anonymous. Cooper is styled 'Doctor', which degree he acquired in 1507 (Grattan Flood, 64). Pygott was born *c.* 1485. These facts alone put the date forward to Henry VIII's reign, quite apart from the circumstance that the king's compositions are headed: 'the Kynge H.viij'. The whole tone of the MS and of Henry's own songs points to a date early in the reign, perhaps *c.* 1515. This aspect of the MS is briefly discussed in the Introduction, p. 4, above, and at greater length in the Introduction to *MCH8*.

Chappell, in 'An Unpublished Collection', 385, made the happy suggestion about the history of the MS that it got down to Benenden in Kent because Sir Henry Guildford, Controller of the Household, had his seat there. It need not necessarily have been taken down 'for the King to sing from'; Guildford, who was intimately connected with court entertainments early in the reign, may well have been the noble customer who commissioned the MS.

About 1770 it was owned by Stephen Fuller (his name occurs on f.3v); thereafter by Archibald, Earl of Eglinton, and the Lamb family of

Beauport Park, Essex. It was not known to the eighteenth-century historians, nor to Chappell when he compiled his *Popular Music of the Olden Time* (2 vols [1853–9]). Chappell's article of 1867 (with four facsimiles) remains the fullest printed account of the MS to date. More recent descriptions are: Trefusis (with transcriptions of Henry VIII's compositions – omitting, however, H78, 80, 81, 94, 98); Flügel (transcriptions of the words only, with many inaccuracies); PMMS (1891), p. xvi (three musical transcriptions unbelievably bowdlerized); *EEL*, p. 300; Greene, p. 333 (printing the carols); Reese, *MR* 768–.

For the reader's convenience the Anglo-French songs and pieces without words, probably instrumental, are listed below in the order in which they come. The following pages contain, therefore, not only the Literary Text and its commentary but also a complete list of the contents of *Henry VIII's MS*. All the music is printed in *Music at the Court of Henry VIII, q.v.*

H1 B[enedictus]

NOTE: ff.3v–4: [Isaac] (3 voc); no words.

H2 Fortune esperee

NOTE: ff.4v–5: [Busnois] (4 voc); no words.

H3 Alles regretz

NOTE: ff.5v–6: [Hayne van Ghizeghem] (3 voc); no words.

H4 En frolyk weson

NOTE: ff.6v–7: [Barbireau] (3 voc); no words.

H5 La my

NOTE: ff.7v–9: [Isaac] (4 voc); no words.

H6 Fa la sol

NOTE: ff.9v–14: [Cornish] (3 voc); no words. See also *Twenty Songs*, no. 19: a shortened version, attributed to Cornish.

H7 Pastyme with good companye.

NOTE: ff.14v–15: The Kynge H.VIII (3 voc). Strophic setting. Two versions of the same song appear as R12, *q.v.* for text. H7 differs from R12, second version, as follows:
1.2 unto: *H I* untyll, *II* tyl, *III* do tyl | 1.3 so woll: *H* who lust | 1.4 this lyve: *H* thus leve |

1.5 dystaunce: *H* pastaunce | 1.9 To: *H* For | 2.1 woll have nedes: *H* must have sum | 2.4 fan-
tyses: *H* fansys | 2.9 passe-the-day: *H* myrth and play | 3.2 and vyce: *H* vices | 3.3 or: *H* and |
3.10 Y shall: *H* Thus schall I

OTHER SOURCES: (*a*) RA58, f.56, 'pastyme': anon (lute): (*b*) Panmure MS 11, f.10: anon
(1 voc). References to the song are made in: (i) Latimer's *Sermons* (Parker Society, 1844),
pp. 120, 125; (ii) *L&P*, iii, pt 1, no. 1188: Pace to Wolsey, quoting Royal Almoner's sermon; (iii) *Complaint*, p. lxxxii, song 49; (iv) Maitland MS (Quarto), f.31, ed. W. A.
Craigie (STS, 1927), p. 63: a moralized version.

GLOSS: see R12

H8 Adew mes amours et mon desyre ie vous depraunce depart amant et
    sy ie vous a fayt de plesure sy na passaunce commandamant.
        Pardon a moy tres humblemaunt ie le demand Ja my mon cure a
    seruys loyalmant elas ie bien perdieu ma payne.

NOTE: ff.15v–17: Cornish (4 voc)
TEXT: 4: *II adds* elas ie bien perdieu ma payn

H9 Adew madam et ma mastres. Adew mon solas et mon Joy. Adieu
    iusque vous reuoye. Adieu vous diz per graunt tristesse.

NOTE: ff.17v–18 The Kynge H.viij (4 voc). Same music as Song 326 (see p. 258).
TEXT: 1 mon Joy: *II, III, IV* ma Joy | 2 iusque: *II omits* | Adieu vous diz: *II omits* | per:
IV omits

H10 Helas madam cel que ie me tant soffre que soie voutre humble
    seruant voutre vmble seruant ie ray a tousiours e tant que ie
    viueray altre naimeray que vous que [?] e tant que naimeray que
    vous.

NOTE: ff.18v–19: The Kynge H.viij (4 voc)
TEXT: 1 cel: *II* cell; *III, IV* celle | soffre: *II* soffrer (?); *III, IV* soffres | 2 ie ray: *II* que seray,
III que ie seray, *IV* ie seray | a tousiours . . .: *IV* a vous tousiours tant que viueray aultre |
e tant: *III omits* | *second* ie: *III omits* | 3 naimeray: *II* noimay | *second* que: *III, IV omit* | naimeray:
II viueray | *last 4 words: III* vous autre que vous, *IV* viueray altre que vous

H11 Instrumental piece

NOTE: ff.19v–20: anon (4 voc).

Appendix A

H12
> Alas, what shall I do for love?
> For love, alasse, what shall I do,
> Syth now so kynd
> I do yow fynde
> To kepe yow me unto?
> Alasse!

NOTE: ff.20v–21: The Kynge H.viij (4 voc). Through-set; but the words of further strophic verses may be missing.

H13 Hey now now

NOTE: f.21v: Kempe (3 voc). Round; no further words. Cf. H19.

H14
> Alone I leffe, alone,
> And sore I sygh for one.

NOTE: f.22: Doctor Cooper (3 voc). Round. A carol using these two lines for burden is found in PRO Excheq. Misc. 23/1/1 (see Saltmarsh, p. 14, facsimile; p. 21, transcription by Dent), c. 1530. Another carol using the same two lines is Kele, p. 17 (Greene, no. 164); no music. For other references to a popular song of this title, see: (i) tune named to Caius College MS 383, p. 41 (Greene, no. 418); (ii) *A balade in commendation of our Lady* in Thynne's *Chaucer* (1532), f.374–, last verse but one (f.375v, col. i) (I thank P. J. Frankis for this reference). See also Songs 30–4.

TEXT: given three times in the one notated part.

H15
> O my hart and O my hart!
> My hart it is so sore,
> Sens I must nedys from my love depart
> And know no cause wherefore.

NOTE: ff.22v–23: The Kyng H.viij (3 voc). Through-set; but the words of further strophic verses may be missing. For the opening 'tag', cf. Songs 13–14.

H16
> Adew, adew, my hartis lust!
> Adew, my joy and my solace!
> Wyth dowbyl sorow complayn I must
> Untyl I dye, alas, alas!

NOTE: ff.23v–24: Cornysch: (3 voc). Through-set; but the words of further strophic verses may be missing. The words only are in Ashmole MS 176, f.100 (see App. C, no. 14), reading *sorowes* for *sorow* (line 3).

H17
Aboffe all thynge
Now lete us synge
Both day and nyght,
Adew mornyng,
A bud is spryngynge
Of the red rose and the whyght.

NOTE: f.24v: Faredynge: (3 voc). Round. The song possibly celebrates Henry VIII's first-born son, 1511. See *MCH8*, introd.
GLOSS: 4 mornyng: *mourning*
TEXT: *continues in the music with a jumble of repeated lines.*

H18
Downbery down!
Now am I exild my lady fro
And no cause gevyn therto:
Wherfor to her I me complayn, hey now!
Trustyng that dysdayn
Sone shal be slayne
And never more to remayne.

NOTE: f.25: Wylliam Daggere (3 voc). Round. Another version is in RA58, f.4v; see *MCH8*, no. 18, note.
GLOSS: 5 dysdayn: *seems to replace the earlier* daunger *in this period, as a 'technical term' of courtly love.*

H19 Hey now now
NOTE: f.25v: T. Faredyng (3 voc). Round; no further words. Cf. H13.

H20
In May, that lusty sesoun
To geder the flours down
By the medows grene;
The byrdys sang on every syde
So meryly, it joyed my hart
They toyned so clene;
The nyghtyngale sang on hie
Joyfully, so merely,
Among the thornys kene.

NOTE: f.26: T. Faredyng (3 voc). Round. Perhaps a song for a courtly 'Maying'; see *MCH8*, introduction.
GLOSS: 1 lusty: *pleasant* | 2 geder: *gather* | 6 toyned: *sang in musical tones*
TEXT: 4 syde: *perhaps originally part, for the rhyme.*

Appendix A

NOTE: ff.26v–27: Flude (4 voc). Puzzle-canon.

H22   Whoso that wyll hymselff applye
                        To passe the tyme of youth joly,
                        Avaunce hym to the companye
                        Of lusty bloddys and chevalry.

NOTE: ff.27v–28: Rysbye (4 voc). Through-set; further verses missing? Perhaps a tournament song; see *MCH8*, introduction.

GLOSS: 3 avaunce hym: *let him advance himself* | 4 bloddys: *'bloods', gallants* | chevalry: *knights*

H23   The tyme of youthe is to be spent;   [1
                        But vice in it shuld be forfent.

                        Pastymes ther be I nought treulye   [2
                        Whych one may use, and vice denye;

                        And they be plesant to God and man,   [3
                        Those shuld we covit wyn who can;

                        As feaťys of armys, and suche other   [4
                        Wherby actyvenesse oon may utter.

                        Comparysons in them may lawfully be sett,   [5
                        For therby corage is suerly owt fett:

                        Vertue it is then youth for to spend   [6
                        In goode dysporttys whych it dothe fend.

NOTE: ff.28v–29: The kyng H.viii (3 voc). Strophic.

GLOSS: 1.2 forfent: *forbidden* | 2.1 nought: *know it* | 3.1 And: *if* | 3.2 we covit wyn: *we should desire when we can* | 4.2 actyvenesse . . . : *one may display an active nature* | 5.1 Comparysons: *rivalries* | 5.2 corage: *spirit* | 6.2 fend: *defend*

TEXT: 1.1: *III* for to be spent

H24   The thowghtes within my brest,
                        They greve me passyng sore,
                        That I cannot be prest
                        To serve you evermore.

NOTE: ff.29v–30: The Kynge H.viij (3 voc). Through-set; verses missing?

GLOSS: 1.3 prest: *at hand and ready*

TEXT: 4 serve: *I ser*

My love sche morneth [1
For me, for me,
My love sche morneth for me.
Alas, pour hart,
Sen we depart
Morne ye no more for me.

In lovys daunce [2
Syth that oure chaunce
Of absence nedes must be,
My love, I say,
Your love do way
And morne no more for me.

It is no boote [3
To me hart roote
But anguysch and pete,
Wherfore, swete hart,
Your mynde revert
And morne no more for me.

O her kyndnesse, [4
O her gentylnes!
What sayd sche then to me?
The Gode above
Her schuld not move
But styll to morne for me.

Alas, thought I, [5
What remedy?
Venus, to blame are ye.
Now of sum grace
Let se purchase
To helpe my love and me.

Her for to say [6
I tooke this way,
I dyspraysed her beawte;
Yet for all that
Stynt wold sche not,
So trew of love was sche.

Appendix A

At last sche wept;   [7
I to her lept
And sett her on my knee:
The terys ran down
Halff in a swone,
It rewyd my hart to se.

When I sawe this   [8
I dyd her kysse;
Therwyth revyved sche,
And her smalle waste
Ful fast unlast
And sayd sche morned for me.

Then as I ought   [9
I me bethought
And prayd her to be ble,
To take comfort
Of my report
And morne no more for me.

I schall not fayll,   [10
But suere retaylle
From all other that be,
In well and wo
My hart to go
With her that morneth for me.

Thus here an ende;   [11
Goode Lorde, deffend
All lovers that trew be,
And in especyall
From jebardyse all
My love that mornyth for me.

NOTE: ff.30v–31: Cornysh (3 voc). Canonic piece: the two lower voices sing a two-part round; the upper voice is independent. Cf. *Twenty Songs*, no. 14, 'And I mankynd have not in mynd My love that mornyth for me': Gwynneth (4 voc; bass only survives), moralized version, entitled in the index to the book 'My love mourneth'; it has no apparent musical connection with H25. Another moralized version is in *GGB*, p. 140; no music. See also: (i) a couplet 'My love she mornes for me', Cambridge, Trinity College, MS 1157 (see Wilson, *Lost Literature*, 182); (ii) the fragment, PRO Excheq. 163/22/2/57; (iii) the burden of a carol in Harl. MS 1317, f.94v (Greene, no. 462), 'Wep no more for me, swet hart', which has exactly the same metre as H25 and ends 'morne for me'; no music.

GLOSS: 1.5 depart: *are separating from each other* | 2.5 do way: *have done with* | 3.2 me: *my* |
3.5 revert: *turn away, withdraw* | 5.5 purchase: *attempt – i.e. let us see some aid from you* | 6.1 say:
assay | 6.5 stynt: *leave off loving* | 8.5 unlast: *unlaced* | 9.3 ble: *happy* | 9.5 my report: *news of me* |
10.2 retaylle: *refrain?* | 10.4 well: *weal* | 11.5 jebardyse: *jeopardy, peril*

TEXT: 3.1: *MS* It is boote

H26   *Iste tenor ascendit . . .*

NOTE: ff.31v–32: Flude (4 voc). Puzzle-canon.

H27
    A the syghes that cum from my hart   [1
        They greve me passyng sore;
    Sen ye must nedes from me depart,
    Farewell, my joy, for evermore.

    Oft to me her godely swet face   [2
        Was wont to cast an nye;
    And now absence to be in place
    Alas, for wo I dye, I dye.

    I was wont her to behold,   [3
        And take in armys twayne;
    And now with syghs manyfold,
    Farewell, my joe, and welcom payne.

    And I thynk I se her yet,   [4
        As wol to God I cowld,
    Ther myght no joys compare with it
    Unto my hart as now she shuld.

NOTE: ff.32v–33: W. Cornysshe (3 voc). Strophic setting. Another version is RA58, f.1:
anon (tenor only); words pr. Flügel, 258.
GLOSS: 2.2 nye *eye* | 2.3 in place: *instead* | 3.4 joe: *joy*
TEXT: 1.3 Sen: *II, III*, sens | 4.1 And I thynk: *MS* and thynk

H28
    With sorowfull syghs and grevos payne
        Thus ever to endure;
    Alas, pour hart, tyl that we mete agayne,
    Joy shall I never ye may be sure.

NOTE: ff.33v–34: T Fardynge (3 voc). Through-set; verses missing? A poem of similar
metre occurs in BM Add. MS 17942 (pr. Muir, 'Devonshire MS', no. 8), 'Wyth sorowful
syghes and wondes smart | My hart ys persed sodaynly'.

Appendix A

H29

Iff I had wytt for to endyght [1
Of my lady, both fayre and fre,
Of her godnes than wold I wryght;
Shall no man know her name for me.

I love her well with hart and mynd; [2
She ys right trew, I do it se.
My hart to have she doth me bynd;
Shall no mane know her name for me.

She doth not waver as the wynde, [3
Nor for no new me chaunge doth she,
But allway trew I do her fynd;
Shall no man know her name for me.

Yf I to her than war unkynd, [4
Pytte it war that I shuld be,
For she to me ys allway kynd;
Shall no man [know her name for me].

Lernyng it war for women all [5
Unto ther lovers trew for to be;
Promyse I mak that know non shall
Whill I leve her name for me.

My hart she hath and ever shall [6
To by deth departed we be;
Happe what wyll happ, fall what shall,
Shall no man [know her name for me].

NOTE: ff.34v-35: anon (3 voc). Strophic setting. Another version is in RA58, f.5v: anon (tenor only). See also Add. MS 18752, f.58v (ed. E. B. Reed, no. 3): words only; and 'Yf I had space now for to write', listed as Song 122, q.v.

GLOSS: 5.1: *i.e. It would be, if known, a lesson to all women* | 6.2 To: *until* | departed: *separated*

TEXT: 1.3 godnes: *II* godens (?) | 4.2 be: *MS* se | 6.2 by: *MS omits*

H30

Alac, alac, what shall I do,
For care is cast into my hart,
And trew love lokked therto?

NOTE: f.35v: The Kyng H.viij (3 voc). Through-set; verses missing? The possible connection between this song and H31 is discussed in *MCH8*, no. 30, note.

396

Hey nony nony nony nony no,
Hey nony nony nony nony no!

This other day   [1
I hard a may
Ryght peteusly complayne;
She sayd allway
Withowt denay
Her hart was full of payne.

Sshe said, alas,   [2
Withowt trespas
Her dere hart was untrew;
'In every place
I wot he hace
Forsake me for a new.

Seth he untrew   [3
Hath chosen a new
And thynkes with her to rest,
And will not rew,
And I so trew,
Wherfore my hart will brest.

And now I may   [4
In no maner a way
Optayne that I do sew,
So ever and ay
Withowt denay,
Myne owne swet hart, adew.

Adew, derlyng,   [5
Adew, swettyng,
Adew, all my welfare!
Adew, all thyng
To god perteynyng,
Cryst kepe yow frome all care.

Adew, full swete,   [6
Adew, ryght mete
To be a lady's pere!'
With terys wete

And yës replete
She said, 'Adew my dere!'

Adew, farewell,   [7
Adew la bell,
Adew, bothe frend and foo!
I cannott tell
Wher I shall dwell,
My hart it grevyth me so.'

She had nott said   [8
But at-abrayde
Her dere hart was full nere
And saide, 'Goode mayde,
Be not dysmayd,
My love, my derlyng dere.'

In armys he hent   [9
That lady gent;
In voydyng care and mone
That day thay spent
To ther intent
In wyldernes alone.

NOTE: f.36: anon (3 voc). Carol with music for the burden only; the verses were perhaps sung to a well-known tune (see pp. 127–8). Cf. H33, H50. The words of the burden must have been common as a refrain: see, for example, the interlude fragment in Add. MS 15233 (ed. Halliwell, p. 55), which contains the direction 'Here they syng "Hey nony nonye"'.

GLOSS: 1.2 may: *maid* | 2.2 trespas *i.e. on her part* | 2.5 hace: *has* | 3.1–6 Seth ... Wherfore ...: *Since he has chosen ..., for that reason my heart ...* | 5.5 god: *good, i.e. my content* | 6.5 yës replete: *eyes full of tears* | 7.2 la bell: *presumably term of endearment (but why feminine?)* | 8.2 at-abrayde: *suddenly* | 9.1 hent: *took* | 9.2 gent: *pretty* | 9.6 wyldernes: *i.e. the country*

TEXT: B: nonnys *variously dispersed among the voices* | 5.6 frome all: *MS* forme | 9.4 that day: *MS* they day

H32   *A dorio tenor ...*

NOTE: ff.36v–37: Dunstable (3 voc). Puzzle-canon. The only composition by Dunstable (d. 1453) to be found in an early Tudor song-book.

H33   Grene growith the holy,
              So doth the ive,
              Thow wynter blastys blow never so hye,
              Grene growth the holy.

As the holy grouth grene .... [1
  And never chaungyth hew,
So I am, ever hath bene,
  Unto my lady trew.

As the holy grouth grene .... [2
  With ive all alone
When flowerys cannot be sene,
And grenewode levys be gone.

Now unto my lady .... [3
  Promyse to her I make,
Frome all other only
  To her I me betake.

Adew, myne owne lady, ... [4
  Adew, my specyall,
Who hath my hart trewly,
  Be suere, and ever shall.

NOTE: ff.37v–38: The Kyng H.viij (3 voc). Carol with music for the burden only; the verses may have been sung to a well-known tune. Cf. H31, H50.

TEXT: B1 growith: *II* growth | 2.1 As: *MS* A

H34   Whoso that wyll all feattes optayne, ... [1
In love he must be withowt dysdayne,

For love enforcyth all nobyle kynd, ... [2
And dysdayne dyscorages all gentyl mynd.

Wherfor to love and be not loved .... [3
Is wors then deth? Let it be proved!

Love encoragith and makyth on bold; .... [4
Dysdayne abattyth and makith hym colde.

Love ys gevyn to God and man; .... [5
To woman also, I thynk, the same.

But dysdayne ys vice and shuld be refused; .... [6
Yet never the lesse it ys to moch used.

Grett pyte it ware, love for to compell .... [7
With dysdayne bothe falce and subtell.

Appendix A

NOTE: f.39: The Kynge H.viij (3 voc). Strophic setting? Only one line of the words is under-laid to the music. See *MCH8*, no. 34, note, for further comment.

GLOSS: I.I: *i.e. Whosoever will show himself fully valorous* | 2.1: *i.e. strengthens every noble nature* | 2.2 dyscorages: *takes the spirit out of* | 3.2 proved: *tried* | 4.1 on: *one* | 4.2 abattyth: *abateth* | 7.1 compell: *constrain (?)*

TEXT: 2.1 kynd: *MS* kyndes (?) | 2.2 mynd: *MS* myndes (?)

H35   Blow thi horne, hunter, and blow thi horne on hye!
Ther ys a do in yonder wode; in faith, she woll not dy:
Now blow thi horne, hunter, and blow thi horne, joly
    hunter!

Sore this dere strykyn ys,   [1
    And yet she bledes no whytt;
She lay so fayre, I cowde nott mys;
    Lord, I was glad of it!

As I stod under a bank   [2
    The dere shoffe on the mede;
I stroke her so that downe she sanke,
    But yet she was not dede.

There she gothe! Se ye nott,   [3
    How she gothe over the playne?
And yf ye lust to have a shott,
    I warrant her barrayne.

He to go and I to go,   [4
    But he ran fast afore;
I bad hym shott and strik the do,
    For I myght shott no mere.

To the covert bothe thay went,   [5
    For I fownd wher she lay;
And arrow in her hanch she hent;
    For faynte she myght nott bray.

I was wery of the game,   [6
    I went to tavern to drynk;
Now the construccyon of the same –
    What do yow meane or thynk?

Here I leve and mak an end, [7
Now of this hunter's lore;
I thynk his bow ys well unbent,
Hys bolt may fle no more.

NOTE: ff.39v–40: W. Cornysh [in a lighter hand] (3 voc). Apparently a carol with music for the burden only, the verses being sung to a known tune (cf. H31, H33, etc.). The song could, however, be interpreted as a refrain-song, the music of the first verse (i.e. the burden as here printed) being used throughout. Another version is in RA58, f.7v: anon (tenor only). The characteristic *double entendre* of the 'forester' songs is explicitly referred to in 6.3–4. For their use in 'disguisings', see pp. 249–50 and *MCH8,* introduction.

GLOSS: 2.2 shoffe: *'shoved', pushed her way forward* | 3.4 barrayne: *not pregnant, i.e. good eating* | 5.4 faynte: *faintness* | 6.3 construccyon: *i.e. the other meaning of the poem* | 6.4 meane: *imagine, have in mind*

TEXT: B3 now: *III* wow

H36 *De tous bien plane*

NOTE: ff.40v–41: [Hayne van Ghizeghem] (3 voc). A well-known Continental song.

H37 *Jay pryse amours*

NOTE: ff.41v–42: anon (3 voc). A well-known Continental song.

H38

Adew, corage, adew;
Hope and trust,
I fynde you not trew;
Adew, corage, adew, adew.

NOTE: f.42v: W. Cornyshe (3 voc). Through-set; verses missing?
GLOSS: 1 corage: *desire to love, the amorous spirit*
TEXT: 3 not: *III* no

H39

Trolly lolly loly lo,
Syng troly loly lo!
My love is to the grenewode gone,
Now after wyll I go;
Syng trolly loly lo loly lo!

NOTE: ff.43v–44: William Cornyshe (3 voc). Through-set; probably complete, even though short. The words were a common refrain; see, for example, *Complaint,* p. lxxxiii, no. 64. Perhaps a 'Maying' song; see *MCH8,* introduction.

TEXT: 4 after: *I* ter | 5 Syng: *II* syn, *III* hey | *The* trolly lollys *are variously dispersed.*

H40   I love trewly withowt feynyng;
My love, she is so trew to me.
To love her sure whill I am levyng,
My hart with her ever shall be.

NOTE: ff.44v–45: T. Fardynge [in lighter hand] (3 voc). Through-set; verses missing?
TEXT: 2 is so trew: *II* is trew | 3 love: *II* have | whill: *II, III*, whilles | 4 ever shall: *III* shall ever

H41   Yow and I and Amyas,
    Amyas and yow and I,
To the grenewode must we go, alas!
Yow and I, my lyff, and Amyas.

The knyght knokett at the castell gate;   [1
The lady mervelyd who was therat.

To call the porter he wold not blyn;   [2
The lady said he shuld not com in.

The portres was a lady bryght;   [3
Strangenes that lady hyght.

She asked hym what was his name;   [4
He said, 'Desyre, your man, madame.'

She said, 'Desyre, what do ye here?'   [5
He said, 'Madame, as your prisoner.'

He was cownselled to breffe a byll   [6
And shew my lady hys oune wyll.

Kyndnes said she wold yt bere,   [7
And Pyte said she wold be ther.

Thus how thay dyd we cannot say –   [8
We left them ther and went ower way.

NOTE: ff.45v–46: Cornysh (3 voc). Carol with music for the burden only; the verses may have been sung to a well-known tune (cf. H31, H33, etc.). Perhaps a 'Maying' song, see *MCH8*, introduction. *EEL*, p. 337, gives all the available information about the possible topical significance of the name 'Amyas' – there were several persons of this name in the royal service, including a forester or two. The connection between the 'forester' burden and the 'allegory of love' verses is not clear. The verses read like the 'story' of a disguising.

GLOSS: 2.1 blyn: *leave off* | 3.2 hyght: *was called* | 6.1 breffe a byll: *indite a petition* | 7.1 Kyndnes: *natural affection (with sexual attraction)*

TEXT: B3 we: *II* I

H42   *Ough war der mount*

NOTE: ff.46v–47: anon (4 voc). Foreign song with some concordances.

H43   *La season*

NOTE: ff.47v–48: Compere (3 voc). Foreign song.

H44

If love now reynyd as it hath bene	[1
And war rewardit as it hath sene,	
Nobyll men then wold suer enserch	[2
All ways wherby thay myght it rech;	
Butt envy reynyth with such dysdayne,	[3
And causith lovers owtwardly to refrayne,	
Which puttes them to more and more	[4
Inwardly most grevous and sore:	
The faut in whome I cannot sett;	[5
But let them tell which love doth gett.	
To lovers I put now suer this cace –	[6
Which of ther loves doth get them grace?	
And unto them which doth it know	[7
Better than do I, I thynk it so.	

NOTE: ff.48v–49: The Kynge H.viij (3 voc). The words of this song are given at the end, not underlaid in the usual way; the MS index (f.2v, last entry) gives the title 'If love now reynyd'. The form of the song remains obscure. Cf. H48, another and longer version of the same piece entirely without words.

GLOSS: 1.2 sene: *'since', i.e. in the old days (?)* | 2.1 enserch: *search out* | 3.1 envy: *malice* | 5.1 faut: *fault* | 7.2 I thynk it so: *i.e. I am conscious of speaking to experts*

TEXT: 3.1 dysdayne: *MS* envy (Chappell's emendation in 'Unpublished Collection')

H45   *Gentil prince de renom*

NOTE: ff.49v–50: The Kynge H.viij (4 voc). One voice only of this song is by Henry VIII. See p. 112 and *MCH8*, no. 45, note.

Appendix A

H46 Sy fortune mace bien purchase enuers amors que tant mon detenu
non bien mamour on soit tous mes a puis si me semble il que
rennan obtenu puisque de vous puisque de vous aprouchez Je ne
puis

NOTE: ff.50v–51: anon (3 voc). Untraced. Probably Anglo-French.

TEXT: 1 enuers: *II* euers | 2 non: *III* mom | non . . . mamour: *II omits* | 3 rennan: *II* nay
reyne, *III* ren | *II, III omit one* puisque de vous | aprouchez: *II* apurcher

H47
      Wherto shuld I expresse   [1
      My inward hevynes?
      No myrth can make me fayn
      Tyl that we mete agayne.

      Do way, dere hart, not so.   [2
      Let no thought yow dysmaye!
      Thow ye now parte me fro,
      We shall mete when we may.

      When I remembyr me   [3
      Of your most gentyll mynde,
      It may in no wyse agre
      That I shuld be unkynde.

      The daise delectable,   [4
      The violett wan and blo;
      Ye ar not varyable;
      I love you and no mo.

      I make you fast and sure;   [5
      It ys to me gret payne
      Thus longe to endure,
      Tyll that we mete agayne.

NOTE: ff.51v–52: The Kynge H.viij (3 voc). Strophic setting.

GLOSS: 1.3 fayn: *glad, well-pleased* | 2.1: *this verse seems to begin the Lady's answer to her Lover* |
4.2 wan and blo: *pale and 'blue'*

TEXT: 4.1 delectable: *MS* delectale

H48 [If love now reigned]

NOTE: ff.52v–53: The Kyng H.viij (3 voc). This is a longer version of H44, q.v.; it has
no words or title.

H49   A Robyn, gentyl Robyn,   [1
      Tel me how thy lemman doth,
      And thow shal know of myne.

      My lady is unkynde I wis.   [2
      Alac, why is she so?
      She lovyth another better than me
      And yet she will say no.

      I cannot thynk such doubylnes   [3
      For I fynd women trew;
      In faith my lady lovith me well;
      She will change for no new.

NOTE: ff.53v–54: Cornysh (3 voc). Canonic piece, apparently based on popular song. Wyatt's poem (ed. Muir, no. 55, from Egerton MS 2711) represents, I think, a later handling of the song, using this courtly version as a start; it was perhaps sung to the original tune, not to Cornish's version. See p. 111. The Fool in *Twelfth Night*, iv. 2, sings 'Hey Robin' to Malvolio. A tune 'Jolly Robin', perhaps connected, seems to have been well known from the xiv to the xvi century.

GLOSS: 1.2 lemman: *sweetheart*

TEXT: 1.3 shal: *II* shalt

H50   Whilles lyve or breth is in my brest
      My soverayne lord I shall love best.

      My soverayne lorde for my poure sake [1
       Six coursys at the ryng dyd make,
      Of which four tymes he dyd it take;
       Wherfor my hart I hym beqwest,
      And of all other for to love best
       My soverayne lorde.

      My soverayne lord of pusant pure   [2
       As the chefteyne of a waryowere,
      With spere and swerd at the barryoure
       As hardy with the hardyest,
      He provith hymselfe that I sey best,
       My soverayne lorde.

      My soverayne lorde in every thyng   [3
       Above all other as a kyng,
      In that he doth no comparyng

But of a trewth he worthyest
To have the prayse of all the best;
My soverayne lorde.

My soverayne lorde when that I mete,   [4
His cherfull contenance doth replete
My hart with joe that I be hete
Next God but he and ever prest
With hart and body to love best
My soverayne lorde.

So many vertuse gevyn of grace   [5
Ther is none one-lyve that have;
Beholde his favor and his face,
His personage most godlyest!
A vengeance on them that loveth nott best
My soverayne lorde.

The soverayne lorde that is of all,   [6
My soverayne lorde save principall!
He hath my hart and ever shall.
Of God I ask for hym request,
Off all gode fortunes to send hym best;
My soverayne lorde.

NOTE: ff.54v–55: W. Cornyshe (3 voc). Carol with music for the burden only; the verses
were perhaps sung to a well-known tune. See H33, H35, H41. This song clearly reflects the
'correct' attitude of a woman whose knight is jousting for her at a tournament. Perhaps the
carol was sung on some such occasion. The 'soverayne lord' must, surely, be Henry VIII himself; and the lady, Queen Katherine (see verse 4). Alongside the verses of this carol (f.55) are
two scribbles, *henr henr*. They are too faint and flimsy to make much of, and I have compared
them with Henry's known autograph without being able to reach a conclusion. At the bottom
of the same page the composer's name, *Willm Cornyshe*, is written again in a similar hand and
badly smudged.

GLOSS: 1.2 coursys at the ryng: *in the chivalric pastime 'running at the ring' the rider attempted to
carry off on the point of his lance a metal ring suspended from a post* | 2.1 pure: *normally poure, power* |
2.2: *i.e. a chieftain among warriors* | 2.4 hardy: *daring* | 2.5 that I sey best: *best of those that I saw* |
3.3 doth no comparying: *admits no comparisons* | 4.3 joe: *joy* | hete: *pledged* | 4.4 he: *i.e. him* |
prest: *ready and eager* | 5.2 one-lyve: *alive* | 5.4 godlyest: *goodliest* | 6.1: *i.e. God* | 6.2 principall:
specially

TEXT: 3.4 worthyest: *MS* worthyest is *(spoiling rhyme)* | 6.5 fortunes: *MS* fortues

H51   Thow that men do call it dotage,   [1
                 Who lovyth not wantith corage.

And whosoever may love gete,   [2
Frome Venus sure he must it fett;

Or elles from her which is her hayre;   [3
And she to hym most seme most fayre.

Wyth ee and mynd doth both agre;   [4
There is no bote; ther must it be.

The ee doth loke and represent;   [5
But mynd afformyth with full consent.

Thus am I fyxed withowt gruge,   [6
Myne ey with hart doth me so juge.

Love maynteynyth all noble courage;   [7
Who love dysdaynyth ys all of the village.

Soch lovers though thay take payne   [8
It were pete thay shuld optayne;

For often tymes wher they do sewe   [9
Thay hynder lovers that wolde be trew.

For whoso lovith shuld love butt oone;   [10
Chaunge who so wyll, I wyll be none.

NOTE: ff.55v–56: The Kyng H.viii (3 voc). Strophic setting.
GLOSS: 1.2 corage: *spirit, vitality* | 2.2 fett: *fetch* | 3.1 hayre: *heir* | 4.1 Wyth: *when* | ee: *eye* | 5.2 afformyth: *'affirmeth', confirms* | 7.2: *i.e. uncourtly, bucolic* | 9.1 sewe: *make suit*
TEXT: 1.2 not, *II, III: I* no

H52   Instrumental piece

NOTE: ff.56v–57: The Kynge H.viij (3 voc).

H53   *Paramese tenor*

NOTE: ff.57v–58: Fayrfax (4 voc). Puzzle-canon. A related puzzle, *Mese tenor*, by Fayrfax, survives in the Wells fragment. See App. C, no. 89.

H54   Instrumental piece

NOTE: ff.58v–59: The Kyng H.viij (3 voc).

Appendix A

H55 Instrumental piece

NOTE: ff.59v–60: The Kyng H.viij (3 voc).

H56   Departure is my chef payne;
                            I trust ryght wel of retorn agane.

NOTE: f.60v: The Kyng H.viij (4 voc). A three-part round sung over a ground: the ground has the single word 'Departure' and may possibly have been instrumental. The round may be intended as a musical representation of the words 'retorn agane'.

H57 It is to me a ryght gret joy

NOTE: f.61: The Kyng H.viij (3 voc). Round. There are no other words given in the MS.

H58 Instrumental piece

NOTE: ff.61v–62: The Kyng H.viij (3 voc).

H59 Instrumental piece

NOTE: ff.62v–63: Fareding (3 voc).

H60 Instrumental piece

NOTE: ff.63v–64: Cornyshe (3 voc). Apparently in the Locrian mode, but perhaps a *catholicon*, i.e. a piece designed to be played in more than one mode. See, further, *MCH8*, no. 60, and note.

H61 Instrumental piece

NOTE: ff.64v–65: The Kyng H.viij (3 voc).

H62   I have bene a foster   [1
                   Long and many a day;
                   Foster wyl I be no more
                   No lenger shote I may;
                   Yet have I bene a foster.

                   Hange I wyl my nobyl bow   [2
                   Upon the grenewod bough,
                   For I cannott shote in playne
                   Nor yett in rough;
                   Yet have I [bene a foster.]

408

Every bowe for me ys to bygge;   [3
   Myne arow ny worne ys;
The glew ys slypt frome the nyk;
   When I shuld shoote I myse;
   Yet have [I bene a foster.]

Lady Venus hath commaundyd me   [4
   Owt of her courte to go;
Ryght playnly she shewith me
   That beawtye ys my foo;
   Yet have I b[ene a foster.]

My berd ys so hard, God wote,   [5
   When I shulde maydyns kysse,
Thay stand abak and make it strange;
   Lo, age ys cause of this;
   Yet ha[ve I bene a foster.]

Now will I take to me my bedes   [6
   For and my santes booke,
And pray I wyll for them that may,
   For I may nowght but loke;
   Yet ha[ve I bene a foster.]

NOTE: ff.65v–66: D. Cooper (3 voc). Interpreted as a carol by Greene (no. 465); but the music shows it to be a refrain-song. R1, q.v., starts with the same tune and words but deviates. Concerning 'forester' songs, see H35; also, p. 249 and *MCH8*, introduction.

GLOSS: 2.3 in playne: *open ground* | 2.4 in rough: *on broken ground* | 3.3 nyk: *nick* | 5.3 make it strange: *preserve aloofness* | 6.1 bedes: *prayer-beads* | 6.2 santes booke: *book of saints' lives*

TEXT: 5.5 haue: *the first stroke of the* u *is visible; the page has been clipped?* | 6.1 bedes: *Greene* bed | 6.2 santes: *Greene* sauter | 6.4 I: *MS omits*

H63   Farewell, my joy, and my swete hart!   [1
             Farewell myne owne hart rote –
          Frome yow a whyle must I depart;
             Ther ys none other bote.

          Thowgh you depart now thus me fro,   [2
             And leve me all alone,
          My hart ys yours where ever that I go;
             For yow do I mone.

Appendix A

NOTE: ff.66v–68: D. Cooper (3 voc). Through-set.
GLOSS: 1.4 bote: *help* | 2.1 *the Lady's answer (?)*
TEXT: 1.1 hart: *II* harte, harte | 1.3 must I: *II* I must | 2.2 all: *I omits*

H64

Withowt dyscord
And bothe acorde
Now let us be;
Bothe hartes alone
To set in one
Best semyth me.
For when one sole
Ys in the dole
Of lovys payne,
Then helpe must have
Hymselfe to save
And love to optayne.

Wherfor now we
That lovers be
Let us now pray
Onys love sure
For to procure
Withowt denay.
Wher love so sewith,
Ther no hart rewith
But condyscend;
Yf contrarye,
What remedy?
God yt amen.

NOTE: ff.68v–69: The kynge H.viii (3 voc). Strophic setting.
GLOSS: 1.7 sole: *alone* | 1.10: *i.e. he must have help* | 2.4 Onys: *once – i.e. on some one occasion* | 2.6 denay: *refusal* | 2.9 But condyscend: *meaning obscure* | 2.12 amen: *answer our prayer*
TEXT: 1.10 must: *II* to | 2.12 amen: *Flügel*, amen[d]

H65

I am a joly foster
And have ben many a day,
And foster will I be styll
For shote ryght well I may.

410

Wherfore shuld I hang up my bow   [1
   Upon the grenwod bough?
I cane bend and draw a bow
   And shot well enough:
   I am a joly foster.

Wherfor shuld I hang up myne arrow   [2
   Opon the grenwode lynde?
I have strengh to mak it fle
   And kyll bothe hart and hynd:
   I am [a joly foster.]

Wherfor shuld I hang up my horne   [3
   Upon the grenwod tre?
I can blow the deth of a dere
   As well as any that ever I see:
   I am [a joly foster.]

Wherfor shuld I tye up my hownd   [4
   Unto the grenwod spray?
I can luge and make a sute
   As well as any in May:
   I am [a joly foster.]

NOTE: ff.69v–71: anon (3 voc). Carol, or modified carol? It depends on whether the initial burden is to be repeated entire (for which there is no indication) or has been subordinated and shortened into the refrain (cf. H102–4). Greene, no. 466, note, suggests that this forester song answers H62, q.v.

GLOSS: 2.2 lynde: *tree* | 4.3 luge: *throw something so that it 'lodges'* | sute: *pursuit, chase (of game)*

TEXT: B4: *II omits* I may *the first time of singing* | 1.2 bough: *III* bought | 1.4 enough: *II* enowght, *III* enought

H66   Though sum saith that yough rulyth me,   [1
   I trust in age to tarry;
God and my ryght and my dewtye,
   Frome them shall I never vary:
   Though sum say that yough rulyth me.

I pray you all that aged be,   [2
   How well dyd ye your yough carry?
I thynk sum wars of yche degre;
   Therin a wager lay dar I:
   Though sum sayth [that yough rulyth me.]

Appendix A

Pastymes of yough sumtyme among, [3
  None can sey but necessary;
I hurt no man, I do no wrong;
  I love trew wher I dyd mary:
  Thow sum saith [that yough rulyth me.]

Then sone dyscusse that hens we must; [4
  Pray we to God and Seynt Mary
That all amend; and here an end,
  Thus sayth the kyng, the eighth Harry:
  Though sum [saith that yough rulyth me.]

NOTE: ff.71v–73: [Henry VIII] (3 voc); the song is attributed to the king on the strength of verse 4. Apparently an unusual type of refrain-song; the music for verses 3 and 4 differs from that of 1 and 2, only the refrain remaining constant. Greene classifies as a carol. See *MCH8*, no. 66, note, for a full discussion.

GLOSS: 2.3 wars: *was (pl.)?* | 3.1 sumtyme among: *i.e. to be sometimes engaged in pastimes of youth* | 4.1 dyscusse: *decide (?), pronounce, declare (?)*

TEXT: 1.1 saith: *II* say | 1.2 age to: *III* age for to | 1.4 shall I: *II* shall | 1.5 say: *III* sayth | 3.4 trew wher: *I* trew when, *III* trewly wher

H67

    Madame d'amours,
    All tymes or ours
    From dole dolours
    Ower Lord yow gy;
    In all socours
    Unto my pours
    To be as yours
    Untyll I dye.

    And make you sure
    No creatur
    Shall me solur
    Nor yet retayne;
    But to endure
    Ye may be sure,
    Whyls lyf endur,
    Loyall and playne.

NOTE: ff.73v–74: anon (4 voc). Strophic setting.

GLOSS: 1.4 gy: *guide* | 1.5 socours: *helps* | 1.6 pours: *powers – i.e. to my utmost* | 2.3 solur: *solace (?); this is the sense required, but the word is not recorded in the* OED

TEXT: *III lacks text entirely after* 1.1 | 1.3 From: *I omits*

H68
> Adew, adew, le company,
> I trust we shall mete oftener.
> Vive le Katerine et noble Henry!
> Vive le prince, le infant rosary!

NOTE: ff.74v–75: anon (4 voc, but bass missing). Concerning the missing part, see *MCH8*, no. 68. Through-set; verses missing? This song must have been written for the season of festivities, January and February 1511, celebrating the birth of Henry's first-born son (he died at six weeks). See, further, p. 249, and *MCH8*, introduction.

H69   Instrumental piece

NOTE: ff.75v–76: anon (3 voc).

H70   Instrumental piece

NOTE: f.76v. anon (3 voc).

H71   Instrumental piece

NOTE: f.77 anon (3 voc).

H72   Instrumental piece

NOTE: ff.77v–78: The Kynge H.viij (3 voc).

H73   Instrumental piece

NOTE: ff.78v–79: The Kynge H.viij (3 voc).

H74
> Deme the best of every dowt
> Tyll the trowth be tryed owt.

NOTE: f.79v.: J. Fluyd (3 voc). Round. This couplet is also found on a bronze jug of Richard II's reign (see Evans, p. 90). It is there preceded by another, beginning: 'He that will not spare . . .' (not listed in *Index MEV*).

TEXT: The words are given three times under the one notated part. | 2 tryed: *first time* try

H75
> Hey troly loly loly!
> My love is lusty, plesant and demure
> That hath my hart in cure;

Hey troly loly loly loly!
　　As the hauke to the lure,
　　So my hart to her I ensure;
Hey troly loly loly!
　　Glad to do her plesure
　　And thus I wyll endure;
Hey troly loly lo!

NOTE: f.80: anon (3 voc). Round.

GLOSS: 6 ensure: *make follow (?) Perhaps confused with* sew, ensew

TEXT: *The verse is interspersed after each couplet with various* hey troly loly los.

H76　Instrumental piece

NOTE: ff.80v–81: The Kynge H.viij (3 voc).

H77　Instrumental piece

NOTE: ff.81v–82: The Kynge H.viij (3 voc).

H78　*Taunder naken*

NOTE: ff.82v–84: The Kynge H.viij (3 voc).Well-known foreign piece, arranged by the king.

H79　　　Whoso that wyll for grace sew,
　　　　　Hys entent must nedys be trew,
　　　　　And love her in hart and dede,
　　　　　Els it war pyte that he shuld spede;
　　　　　　Many oone sayth that love ys yll,
　　　　　　But those be thay which can no skyll:

　　　　　Or else because they may not opteyne,
　　　　　They wold that other shuld yt dysdayne;
　　　　　But love us a thyng gevyn by God;
　　　　　In that therfor can be non odde,
　　　　　　But perfite in dede and betwene two.
　　　　　　Wherfor, then, shuld we yt excho?

NOTE: ff.84v–85: The Kynge H.viij (3 voc). Strophic setting but whether of two verses of six lines or three verses of four lines is not clear. See, further, *MCH8*, no. 79, note.

GLOSS: 1.4 spede: *be successful* | 1.6 can no skyll: *have no ability* | 2.5 syntax? | 2.6 excho: *eschew*

TEXT: 1.6 those; *II* thes

H80 Instrumental piece

NOTE: ff.85v–86: The Kynge H.viij (3 voc).

H81 [E]n vray amoure

NOTE: ff.86v–87: The Kynge H.viij (4 voc). No more words.

H82

Let not us that yong men be
Frome Venus' ways banysht to be;
Thow that age with gret dysdayne
Wold have yough love to refrayn,
    In ther myndes consyder thei must
    How thay dyd in ther most lust.

For yf thay war in lyk case
And wold then have goten grace,
Thay may not now than gaynesay
That which then was most ther joy;
    Wherfor indede the trouth to say
    It ys for yough the metest play.

NOTE: ff.87v–88: anon (4 voc). Strophically set; musically each verse is in *aab* form. Although this song is not attributed to the king it has exactly his literary manner (cf. the self-justifying tone in other songs of chivalric 'doctryne').

GLOSS: 1.6 most lust: *greatest vigour of youth* | 2.3 than: *unemphatic* then

TEXT: 1.5 thei, *III: I, II, IV* thi

H83 Dulcis amica

NOTE: ff.88v–89: [Prioris] (3 voc). Title only.

H84 Instrumental piece

NOTE: f.89v: anon (3 voc).

H85 [Amys souffres]

NOTE: f.90: (3 voc). No words or title.

H86 Round without words

NOTE: f.90v: anon (3 voc).

Appendix A

H87 *Thys songe is iij parts in one*
NOTE: f.91(i): anon (3 voc). Puzzle-canon.

H88 *Duas partes in unum*
NOTE: f.91(ii): anon (2 voc). Puzzle-canon.

H89 Instrumental piece
NOTE: ff.91v–92: anon (3 voc).

H90 Instrumental piece
NOTE: ff.92v–93: anon (4 voc).

H91 Instrumental piece
NOTE: ff.93v–94: anon (4 voc).

H92   Lusti yough shuld us ensue,   [1
Hys mery hart shall sure all rew;
For whatsoever they do hym tell,
It ys not for hym we know yt well.

For they wold have hym hys libertye refrayne   [2
And all mery company for to dysdayne;
But I wyll not so whatsoever thay say,
But follow hys mynd in all that we may.

How shuld yough hymselfe best use   [3
But all dysdaynares for to refuse?
Yough has as chef assurans
Honest myrth with vertus pastance.

For in them consisteth gret honor,   [4
Though that dysdaynars wold therin put error,
For they do sew to get them grace
All only reches to purchase.

With goode order, councell and equite,   [5
Goode Lord, graunt us our mancyon to be!
For withowt ther goode gydaunce
Yough shuld fall in grett myschaunce;

416

For yough ys frayle and prompt to doo,   [6
As well vices as vertuus to ensew;
Wherfor be thes he must be gydyd
And vertuus pastaunce must be theryn usyd.

Now unto God thys prayer we make,   [7
That this rude play may well be take,
And that we may ower fauttes amend,
An blysse opteyne at ower last end. Amen.

NOTE: ff.94v–97: The Kynge H.viij (3/4 voc). Combined strophic and thr ough-setting each pair of verses is set differently. Concerning the apparently monophonic tenor (verses 3–4), see *MCH8*, no. 92, note: the words are complete, although some music is missing.

GLOSS: 1.1 ensue: *imitate example of* | 1.2: *i.e. all 'disdainers' will wish his merry heart altered* | 3.4 pastance: *'passe-temps', pastime* | 4.1 them: *i.e. honest mirth, etc.* | 4.4 *i.e. only as a means of acquiring wealth* | 5.3 ther: *their (i.e. of good order, consultation and fair dealing)* | 6.3 be thes: *by these (i.e. the same again)* | 7.3 fauttes: *faults* | 7.4 An: *and*

TEXT: 3.3 has as: *MS* as as | 5.4 shuld: *II* shull | in *I, II: III* into | 7.3 fauttes (?)

H93   *Now*

NOTE: f.98 (f.97v is blank): anon (3 voc). Round, without further text. The song presumably had words originally, but they have not been copied out.

H94   Instrumental piece

NOTE: ff.98v–99: The Kynge H.viij (4 voc).

H95   [B]elle sur tautes

NOTE: ff.99v–100: [Agricola] (4 voc). Tenor *incipit: Tota pulchra es*.

H96   Englond, be glad! Pluk up thy lusty hart!
Help now thi kyng, thi kyng, and take his part!

Ageynst the Frenchmen in the feld to fyght   [1
In the quarell of the church and in the ryght,
With spers and sheldys on goodly horsys lyght,
Bowys and arows to put them all to flyght:
Help now thi king [and take his part!]

NOTE: ff.100v–102: anon (3 voc). Modified carol: the second half of the initial burden is sung as a refrain to the verse. Further verses missing? The song was probably written for Henry's invasion of France in 1513, when the Chapel Royal accompanied him. See p. 242 and *MCH8*, introduction. H97 must belong to same occasion.

GLOSS: 1.2 quarell: *cause*

TEXT: B1 lusty: *II omits* | B2 and take his part: *given twice in all Voices, II omits first* part 1.4 To put them all to flyght: *twice in I and II* | 1.5 Help now: *III* Now help

H97 Pray we to God that all may gyde
     That for our kyng so to provid,
     To send hym power to hys corage
     He may acheffe this gret viage:
      Now let us syng this rownd all thre;
      Sent George, graunt hym the victory!

NOTE: f.103 (f.102v is blank): anon (3 voc). Round. Presumably written for the same expedition as H96, q.v.

GLOSS: 1.2: *i.e. that He will so provide* | 1.4 acheffe . . .: *succeed in this expedition* | 1.5 rownd: (an earlier use of this musical term than the *OED* records)

H98 Instrumental piece

NOTE: ff.103v–104: The Kynge H.viij (3 voc).

H99 *Fors solemant*

NOTE: ff.104v–105: [Ockeghem] (3 voc).

H100 Instrumental piece

NOTE: ff.105v–106: anon (3 voc).

H101 And I war a maydyn,   [1
      As many one ys,
     For all the golde in England
     I wold not do amysse.

     When I was a wanton wench   [2
      Of twelve yere of age,
     Thes cowrtyers with ther amorus
     They kyndyld my corage.

     When I was come to   [3
      The age of fifteen yere,

Henry VIII's MS

In all this lond, nowther fre nor bond,
Methought I had no pere.

NOTE: ff.106v–107: anon (5 voc). Strophic setting, but seemingly incomplete as to the words. There are three references to a popular song 'And I were a maid' (here probably in Voice III): (i) Harl. MS 1517, f.94v – title only (see Greene, p. 326); (ii) Bodl. MS Eng, poet. e.1, f.45v – carol (Greene, no. 93) with manuscript heading, 'A song in the tune of | and I were a mayd, etc.'; (iii) in the interlude *Thersites* [1560?] the name-character says of a young woman, '"And I were a maid again" now may be here song' (Hazlitt's Dodsley, i. 405).

GLOSS: 2.3 amorus: *amours*

H102

Why shall not I?
Why shall not I to my lady
Why shall not I be trew?
Why shall not I?

My lady hath me in that grace   [1
She takes me as her howne;
Her mynd is in non other place:
Now sith it ys thus known,
    Why shall not I?

My lady sayth of trouth it ys   [2
No love that can be lost;
Alas, alas, what word ys this?
Her to remember mest
    Why shall not I?

NOTE: ff.107v–108: anon (3 voc). Modified carol: the initial burden is not repeated, but the last phrase of it forms a refrain for the verses (cf. H96, H103, H104).

GLOSS: 1.2 howne: *own* | 2.3 this: *i.e. the word 'lost'* | 2.4 mest: *most*

TEXT: 2.1 of trouth: *II* of non trouth | 2.4 remember mest (Flügel): *I* reme est; *II, III* remember est

H103

What remedy, what remedy?
Such is fortune! What remedy?

A thorne hath percyd my hart ryght sore   [1
Which dayly encressith more and more;
Thus withowt comfort I am forlore;
    What remedy, what remedy?
    Such is fortune! What remedy?

Appendix A

Bewayll I may myn adventure   [2
To se the paynes that I endure
Insaciently withowt recure;
    What remedy, what remedy?
    Such is fortune! What remedy?

O my swet hart, whome I love best,   [3
Whos unkyndnes hath me opprest,
For which my hart is lyk to brest,
    What remedy, what remedy?
    Such is fortune! What remedy?

NOTE: ff.108v–110: anon (3 voc). Modified carol (cf. H102). Illuminated capitals for verse 2 only.

GLOSS: 2.3 insaciently: *insatiately?* (*OED* does not record) | 3.3 brest: *burst*

TEXT: B2 *twice in all Voices* | 1.1: r yght: *II* rygh; *III* so | 1.2 dayly, *II, III*: *I* daily | 2.3 withowt, *II, III*; *I* wthowt | 2.4 *first* What: *I repeats*

H104
    Wher be ye
    My love, my love?
    And where be ye gone?
    I am so sad;
    To make me glad
    Yt is but you, my love, alone.

    Yower company   [1
    Makes me so mery
    From care and from all mone;
    But when ye mysse,
    No joy it is
    But you, my love, alone.

    When ye be hens,   [2
    With your absence
    My myrth and joy is gone;
    Me to comfort
    Is no resort
    But you, my love, alone.

    The tyme passyng   [3
    To daunce or syng,
    To swage sumwhat my mone;

Is nothing,
No comforting
But yow, my love, alone.

Thus with my care   [4
With your welfare,
Crist kepe you from your fone;
And God above
Kepe your love
For you have myne alone.

NOTE: ff.110v–112: anon (3 voc). Modified carol (cf. H102)? The special case of this song
is discussed in *MCH8*, no. 104, note, q.v.

GLOSS: 1.4 mysse: *are absent* | 3.3 swage: *assuage* | 4.3 fone: *foes*

TEXT: B6, 1.6, etc., alone: *variously repeated in all Voices* | B4 am so sad: *III* am sad

H105   *Quid petis, o fily?*
Mater dulcissima ba ba.
O pater, O fili?
Michi plausus oscula da da!

The moder full manerly and mekly as a mayd,   [1
Lokyng on her lytill son, so laughyng in lap layd,
So pretyly, so pertly, so passingly well apayd,
Full softly and full soberly unto her swet son she saide:

I mene this by Mary, our Maker's moder of myght,   [2
Full lovely lookyng on our Lord, the lanterne of lyght,
Thus saying to our Saviour; this saw I in my syght;
This reson that I rede you now, I rede it full ryght:

Musyng on her manners, so ny mard was my mayne,   [3
Save it plesyd me so passyngly that past was my payn;
Yet softly to her swete sonne methought I hard her sayn:
Now, gracious God and goode swete babe, yet ons this
    game agayne.

NOTE: ff.112v–116: Pygott (4 voc). Carol with Latin burden and English verses, the verses
being through-set. The English words, in the old-fashioned alliterative manner, seem considerably older than the musical setting; the dog-Latin lines which compose the burden are
found inside the cover of Peterhouse MS 195 (xiv century) without music. This is the only
vernacular religious song in H. It has interesting musical features; see *MCH8*, no. 105, note.

Appendix A

GLOSS: B: *trs: What are you seeking, O son? Sweetest mother, kiss, kiss (?). O father, O son, Give, give me kisses of liking (?)* | 1.3 pertly: *beautifully* | 1.4 *i.e. Mary 'says' the burden* | 2.1 by: *with reference to* | 2.4 reson: *statement, motto (i.e. the burden, again)* | 3.1 mard . . .: *marred was my strength* | 3.4 ons: *once*

TEXT: B1 Quid: *I* Quit | B3: *I* quid petis o fili | 1.4 softly: *IV* softy | 1.4 swet, *I, III, IV: II omits* | 2.3 Thus . . . Saviour: *IV* sayng oure sauyo^r; *II, III silent* | 3.2 past: *II* passyd | 3.3 hard her: *I omits* her. There is a certain amount of repetition and omission to fit the contrapuntal music in both burden and verses.

H106

My thought oppressed, my mynd in trouble,   [1
My body languisshyng, my hart in payn;
My joyes, dystres; my sorows dowble;
My lyffe as one that dye would fayne;
Myn yës for sorow salt ters doth rayne:
Thus do I lyve in gret hevenes
Withowte hope or comfort off redresse.

My hope frome me is clene exiled,   [2
Exilide for ever which is my payne;
My payne with hope hath me begyled;
Begyled am I, and cannot refrayne;
Refrayne I must yet in dysdayne,
In dysdayn I shall my lyfe endure,
Endure, alas, withowt hope of recure.

Oftyme for death forsoth I call   [3
In releasse off my gret smert,
For death ys endar principall
Of all the sorowes within my hart;
A payne it is, hens to depart,
Yet my lyfe is to me so grevus
That deth is plesur and nothyng noyus.

Thus may ye se my wofull chance,   [4
My chance contrarious from all plesure,
From all plesure to gret penance;
Right suere to have no good aventure,
Good aventure in me to have place:
Nay, nay, for why? Ther ys no space.

NOTE: ff.116v–120: anon (3 voc). Through-set: this procedure and the musical style in general are reminiscent of the secular songs in F. The same may be said of the words: see, for instance, the 'rhetorical' linking in verses 2 and 4.

GLOSS: 2.7 recure: *remedy* | 3.3 endar principall: *chief ender* | 3.7 nothyng noyus: *not at all obnoxious* | 4.5 aventure: *fortune, chance*

TEXT: 1.3 dowble, *III*: *I* dowbbe, *II* dowlle | 1.5 doth: *III* do | 3.1 Oftyme: *II, III* Oftymes | 3.2 releasse: *II, III,* relesse | 3.3 endar, *II*: *I* endart, *III* thender | 3.6 is: *I* it | 4.2 my chance: *II* my woful chance | 4.4 right: *II* righ *(twice)*

H107

Sumwhat musyng [1
And more mornyng
In remembryng
Th'unstedfastnes;
This world beyng
Of such walyng
My contraryng,
What may I gesse?

I fere doutles [2
Remedyles
Is now to cese
My wofull chance;
For unkyndnes
Withowtyn les
And no redresse
Me doth avance

With dysplesance [3
To my grevance
And no surance
Of remedy;
Lo, in this trance,
Now in substance
Such is my chance
Willyng to dye.

Methynk trewly [4
Bowndon am I
And that gretly
To be content;
Seyng planly
Fortune doth wry
All contrary
Fro myn entent.

423

Appendix A

My lyf was lent   [5
To an entent;
It is ny spent;
Welcum, fortune.
Yet I ne went
Thus to be shent;
But she it ment,
Such ys her wone!

NOTE: ff.120v–122: [Fayrfax] (3 voc). Through-set. This is the same song as F24, whence the attribution to Fayrfax comes. See F24 for concordances, gloss and notes.

TEXT: 5.5 yet: *I* ye | 5.8 wone: *I* went, *II*, *III* wont.

H108   I love unloved; suche is myn aventure,
                And cannot cesse tyl I sore smart,
                But love my fo, that fervent creature
                Whose unkyndnes hath kyld myn hart;
                From her love nothinge can me revert
                But leve in payne whyls I endure
                And love unloved; such ys myne adventure.

NOTE: ff.122v–124: anon (3 voc). Through-set, with many melismas, in the *Fayrfax MS* style. A poem 'I love unloved I wotte nott what love may be' is in Bodl. Rawl. C.813 (ed. Padelford, no. 25). Alexander Scott's poem 'To love unluvit' is in *The Bannatyne MS* (ed. Ritchie, iv. 17). See also F21, F27, and Wyatt's 'I love lovyd' (ed. Muir, no. 106). These all belong to a rhetorical, rather than a song, tradition. However, it may have been H108 that the Royal Almoner mentioned in a sermon before the king at Newhall, March 1521 (*L&P*, iii, pt 1, no. 1188) – 'I love unlovydde'.

GLOSS: 6 leve: *live (i.e. I must live . . .)*

TEXT: 7 love: *II omits*

H109   Hey troly loly lo!
                Mayde, whether go you?
                I go to the medowe to mylke my cow.
                Than at the medow I wyll you mete
                To gather the flowres both fayer and swete.
                Nay, God forbede! That may not be –
                I wysse my mother then shall us se!

                Now yn this medow fayer and grene   [1
                We may us sport and not be sene;

424

And yf ye wyll, I shall consent;
How sey ye, mayde? Be ye content?

Nay, in good feyth, I wyll not melle with you;
I pray you, sir, lett me go mylke my cow!
Why, wyll ye nott geve me no comfortt,
That now in the feldes we may us sportt?
Nay, God forbede! That may not be;
I wysse my mothyr than shall us se!

Ye be so nyce and so mete of age   [2
That ye gretly move my corage.
Syth I love you, love me agayne;
Let us make one, though we be twayne!

Nay, in good feyth, [etc.]

Ye have my hert; sey what ye wyll.   [3
Wherfore ye muste my mynde fulfyll,
And graunte me here your maydynhed,
Or elles I shall for you be ded.

Nay, in good feyth, [etc.]

Then for this onse I shal you spare,   [4
But the nexte tyme ye must beware
How in the medow ye mylke your cow.
Adew, farewell and kysse me now!

Nay, in good feyth, [etc.]

NOTE: ff.124v–128: anon (3 voc). Modified carol: the verses are through-set and the burden is considerably modified on repetition.

GLOSS: Bii 1 melle: *associate, (b) sexually* | 2.1 nyce: *just right* | mete: *meet* | 2.2 corage: *desire* | 3.2 mynde: *intention*

TEXT: This is the last song in H and is in a different hand; it may be a later addition, but cannot on musical grounds be much later | Bii 4 now: *II, III, omit* | 3.4 I shall for you: *II, III* for you I shall

THE DREXEL FRAGMENTS

In the binding of a set of 17th-century part-books in the New York Public Library, Drexel MSS 4180–5, are several fragments of early Tudor songs and instrumental pieces. They were first noticed by Mr Thurston Dart, who immediately drew my attention to them and generously allows me to make this preliminary report on them. I did not know of the songs when this book went to press and have not, therefore, been able to incorporate them fully into its scheme. They have, however, been squeezed into Appendix B, Index of Selected Songs, where they are numbered according to the provisional numbering adopted below. Of fifteen distinct pieces, four provide concordances with *The Fayrfax MS* [F19, F24, F37, F40]; one, with *Twenty Songs*, 'The bella, the bella'. Two of the *Fayrfax MS* concordances [F19, F24] correspond to the two sides of the single-leaf fragment now in the Fitzwilliam Museum, Cambridge. Other interesting reflections are aroused by the fact that John Heywood's name can be linked indirectly with two of the Drexel songs, nos. 2 and 5.

1   [A blessid Jhesu, hough fortunyd this: F37]

4180: same page as 4: high treble. *Begins:* My mode is changyd in euery wyse n[ature]; i.e. the opening of Voice II of F37, at the same pitch, to the words of the second line of the poem.

2   ['All a green willow': Song 25]

4184, treble. *Begins:* . . . whan I haue plesyd my lady now and than. *Refrain:* for all a grene wyllo ys [my garl]and.

3   . . . [c]rowne of thorne so scharpe & kene throw my heyd

4180: no clef, ? treble. Devotional verse, probably from a poem of Christ's Pleading.

4   . . . for þi sake man to whom yf þᵘ call at a[ny?]

4180: high treble. Poem of Christ's Pleading, perhaps connected with 3. *Refrain:* In a f[orest?] laytt as I was I . . . vt supra finis. (This may be the burden of a modified carol.)

The Drexel Fragments

5 [Jhoone is sick and ill at ease: F40]

4180: the greater part of the treble (Voice I) of F40, burden and verses 1–2. There are slight gaps owing to the clipping of the page. *Begins:* . . . y[ow] please alake good Jone what may . . .

6 . . . [lo]kyng for her trew love long or that yt was day

4185: treble (?) of a love-song, apparently with strophic verses, as two lines of words are underlaid in the second section. The words quoted may form the refrain. Written over by a later hand.

7 . . . love shuld com. On euery syde þe way she pryde

4184: fragments of a strophic song with two verses in a popular metre (cf. H25). The clefs have been clipped off and the pitch of the part cannot be determined; the melodic idioms suggest one of the upper voices. At the bottom of the page is written: Finis.

8 . . . red rosse fayre and sote off sent trew off [c]olowre

4180: alto range. Apparently a ceremonial song. The words refer to 'thes fflowrys the rose and the thystyll' and end, 'cam neuer in scotlond ne in france'. Carol or refrain-song, connected perhaps with the marriage of Princess Margaret to James IV, 1503. Cf. Song 221.

9 Sumwhat musyng . . . in remembryng þe vnstedfastnes: F24, H107

4183: the first half of the top voice (tenor) of this favourite song, almost note for note the same as other versions.

10 [The bella, the bella we maydens: Song 296]

Three separate fragments: (*a*) 4185: alto; *begins* The bella þe bella we maydyns bere þe bella. (*b*) 4184: treble; *begins* Kella þe bella, *with badly clipped line above* How praty and proper (?). (*c*) 4185: treble and alto; *begins* Syster loke þ^t ye be not forlorn. These are all (words and music) parts of the same setting as occurs (bass only) in *Twenty Songs*, no. 6.

11 . . . thus hath mayd my payne

4181: last stave of bass-part of a love-song (?). Followed on same page by 14.

12 [Thus musyng in my mynd, gretly mervelyng: F19]

4183: Voice II of F19 (last twelve bars) followed by Voice III (first twenty bars of second half). The two versions are almost identical.

Appendix A

13 ... to þe nale tryll Card lye down and whele stond styll

4185: medius part of a carol or refrain-song. *Refrain:* Card lye down ... (?). *Verse begins:*
he þᵗ smythth[?] wᵗ a stafe off ⎰oke
                                    ⎱byrch.

14 Instrumental piece

4181: four staves, in bass-clef, of music without words. Preceded on same page by 11. Perhaps related to 15.

15 Instrumental piece

4181: five staves of one voice of an unidentified piece without words. Perhaps related to 14.

APPENDIX B

Index of Selected Songs

This list contains: (i) the songs of R, F and H; (ii) other surviving English songs and fragments of the period *c.* 1400–*c.* 1530, but excluding the polyphonic carols published as *MC*, nos. 1–119; (iii) songs with Latin, French or Anglo-French words, associated in their MSS with English songs; (iv) certain song-titles, moralizations and broadsides without music, which appear to be related to songs in R, F or H, and various others to which reference is made in the course of the book (I have not attempted to collect all known song-titles of the period); (v) a few songs, possibly of the period, found in later sources; (vi) the little-known songs of John Hall's *Court of Vertue,* of the Arundel Castle *Songs & Sonets,* and of the PRO part-book (SP. 1/246). Scottish songs are omitted from the list.

COLUMN 1: gives the first line, title or rubric of the songs in the original spelling of the first source quoted. The songs are arranged, for easy reference, in alphabetical order of their modern spelling. (Thus 'Y', as personal pronoun, will be found with 'I'.) Numbers not in brackets refer to the present list and are chiefly used to associate the first line of the first Verse of songs in carol-form with the appropriate entry under the first line of the Burden. Numbers in square brackets refer to *The Index of Middle English Verse,* ed. Carleton Brown and R. H. Robbins (1943).

COLUMN 2: gives the source (or if more than one, numbered a, b, c) of the song. In the case of songs from R, F and H, the words *et al.* indicate that concordances exist and are listed in the commentary on the Literary Text in Appendix A under the song given. The sources of songs from other MSS and printed books are listed more fully. The abbreviations used refer to Appendix C, List of Sources, where each source is listed and very briefly described, and where modern editions are noted. Square brackets indicate the principal secondary source for a song of which the original copy is lost. The folio or page number gives the place where the composition *begins*; its extent is not here recorded.

COLUMN 3: gives the composer's and/or author's name; these are separated, when both are known, by an oblique stroke. Square brackets indicate an attribution from another source (such attributions are listed

429

only once; subsequent versions appear as 'anon'). In the case of foreign songs in H, the brackets often mean no more than 'derived from, or related to, a composition by', and should not be taken to indicate composership in the full sense.

COLUMN 4: describes each song. Plain numbers refer to actually surviving voice-parts; numbers in brackets, to total number of voice-parts in the complete song (thus, 1(4) means 'one part survives of a four-part song'). R = 'round'; P = 'puzzle-canon'; L&V = 'lute tablature with voice-part'; lute = 'lute tablature only'; w = 'words only'; kbd = 'keyboard-score'; t = title; tabl. = 'a tablature other than for lute'.

COLUMN 5: gives the barest minimum of comment on the song, a note of further sources of information, and an indication of the relation of the various sources to each other. No attempt has been made to compile a complete *later* history of each song; but it is hoped that all significant references to it in the period *c*. 1400–*c*. 1530 have been included. B=Burden; V = verse; *m* = music, musical; *w* = words; *t* = title. Abbreviations refer to entries either in Appendix C, List of Sources, or in Appendix D, Reference List of Books and Articles. Numbers in bold type refer to entries in the present list.

COLUMN 6: gives the page references in the present text. An italic reference is to the full printed literary text of the song.

(1) First line, title or rubric	(2) Source	(3) Composer/ Author	(4) Description	(5) Comment	(6) Page reference
– A (*interjection*), *see* Ah					
1 Aboffe all thynge Now lete us synge	H17	Farthing	3 R		*391*
2 Absens of you causeth me to sygh	R4	anon	3		*340*
3 Adew adew le company	H68	anon	3(4)		4, 19, 142, 249, 329, *413*
4 Adew adew my hartis lust	H16 *et al.*	Cornish	3		4, 14, 107, *390*
5 Adew corage adew	H38	Cornish	3		*401*
6 *Adew madam et ma mastres*	H9	Henry VIII	4	same *m* as **326**.	112, 258, *389*
7 *Adew mes amours et mon desyre*	H8	Cornish	4		101, *389*
8 *A dorio tenor*	H32	Dunstable	3 P	*MB*, viii, no. 34.	*398*

Index of Selected Songs

(1)	(2)	(3)	(4)	(5)	(6)
9 Affraid alas and whi so sodenli [3131]	F32	anon	4		114, 335, 368–
– Ageynst the Frenchmen in the feld to fyght: 86					
10 A blessid Jhesu hough fortunyd this [1]	F37 *et al.*	Davy	3		374–, 426
11 A gentill Jhesu [3845]	F34	Sheryngham	4		9–, 103, 114, 371–
– A man I have yevyn and made: 49					
12 A my dere a my dere Son [3597]	F30 *et al.*	anon	3	ı	366–
13 A a my herte I knowe yow well	F2	anon	2		332–, 352, 390
14 A myn hert remembir the well [13]	F38	Davy	3		375–, 390
– A myn hart remembir the well: 14					
15 Ah my swete swetyng	Hawkins, iii. 29	anon	*w*	source now lost.	
16 A robyn gentyl robyn	H49 *et al.*	Cornish	3		110–, 125, 129, 135, 138, 405
17 A the syghes that cum from my hart	H27 *et al.*	Cornish	3		101, 130, 331, 395
18 Alac alac what shall I do	H30	Henry VIII	3		396
19 Alas alas alas is my chief song [138]	Mellon f.77v	anon [? Frye]	3	*m* related to **20** | see Kenney, 'W. Frye'.	
20 Alas departynge is ground of woo [146]	Ashm191 f.194v	anon	2	*w* cf. Bannatyne f.225 (iii. 284).	
21 Alas for lak of her presens	F22	Fayrfax	3		360

431

(1)	(2)	(3)	(4)	(5)	(6)
22 Alas it is I that wote nott	F14	Turges [? Fayrfax]	3		13, 357
23 Alas what shall I do for love	H12	Henry VIII	4		390
24 A litell god fayth	RA56 f.32	anon	kbd		
25 'All a green willow'	a 15233 f. &r	anon/J. Heywood	w	d: fragment | see *Broadside Index,*	
	b Folger f.19	anon	lute	351; Roxburghe	
	c 15117 f.18	anon	L&V	Ballads, i. 171,	
	d Drexel no. 2	anon	1	and Cutts, 'Willow Song', for Dallis and other sources.	426
26 Al comfortles lo without any ayd	Hall f.109v	anon	1		
27 *Alles regretz vuidez de ma presence*	H3	[Hayne van Ghizeghem]	3		388
– Alle heyle Mary and welle thou be: 275					
28 Al men that wyll walke in Gods devine wayes	Hall f.1	anon	1		
29 All vertuous men	Hall f.172v	anon	4	Hall's only part-song.	
30 Alone alone Here Y am mysylf alone	R14	anon	3		346, 390
31 Alone alone. . . . Here I sytt alone	F29	anon	3		365–, 390
32 Alone alone. . . . In wyldernys	RA58 f.8	anon	1		390
33 Alone alone Mornyng alone	R10	T. B. (B. T.?)	2		197, 342–, 390
34 Alone I leffe alone And sore [266]	H14 *et al.*	Cooper	3 R		47, 128–, 141, 286, 390
– A mayd perles hath borne godys son: 277					
35 [*Amys souffres*]	H85 *et al.*	anon	3		415

432

Index of Selected Songs

	(1)	(2)	(3)	(4)	(5)	(6)
36	And I mankynd have not in mynd	TS no. 14	Gwynneth	1(4)	moralizes H25 | modified carol.	
37	And I war a maydyn	H101 et al.	anon	5		42, 44, 47, 105, 129, 286, 334, 418–
38	And wyll ye serve me so	TS no. 11	anon	1(3)	cf. Wyatt, no. 113, 'And wylt thou leve me thus'.	
39	*Apre de vowse*	a RA58 f.30 b RA56 f.18v	anon anon	1 kbd	a: no *w* underlaid | b: *t* only | cf. 29247 f.6v (lute).	
–	A prety wenche may be plesur: 165					
–	As Y lay on Yoleis: 183					
40	As I lay slepynge	a [Hawkins, iii. 25] b [Rimbault, 47]	anon Farthing	*w* *w*	b: claims *m* from private source.	
41	As Y lay upon a nyght [353]	a Selden f.18 b Bannatyne f.5v	anon anon	2 *w*	*MC*, no. 11A note.	
42	As I out-rode this enderes night	[Sharp, 115]	anon	3	Greene, no. 79B; and see p. 349 | same *m* as 78.	
43	As I walked the wood so wild [1333]	a Folger f.3 b Huntington f.11v	Jackson anon	lute *w*	*t*, Carew, 113; Slo3501 | b: Robbins, *SL*, no. 20.	44, 286
–	As the holy grouth grene: 103					
–	A thorne hath percyd my hart: 348					
44	Ave Maria I say to that blessyd [453]	C5943 f.168	anon	2		
45	Awake synner out of thi slepe	Pembroke	anon	3		106

M.P. – F F

433

Appendix B

(1)	(2)	(3)	(4)	(5)	(6)
46 Ay besherewe yow be my fay	F41	Cornish/ Skelton	3	see *Garland of Laurel*, 1198 (Dyce, i. 409), 'Of manerly maistres Margery Mylke and Ale	To her he wrote many maters of myrthe'.	378–
47 Behold and see how byrds dothe fly	TS no. 21	Stretton	1(4?)	quodlibet, added in manuscript.	
– Beholde he saide my creature: 143					
48 Beholde it is a joyfull thyng	Hall f.101	anon	1		
– Beholde me I pray the with all thi hole reson: 368					
49 Be hit knowyn to all that byn here [4184]	F48	anon	3		383–
– Be it right or wrong these men among: 229					
50 [B]elle sur tautes with *Tota pulcra es*	H95	[Agricola]	4		417
51 *Benedicam Domino*	a 4900 f.60v	Johnson			
	b 30513 f.81v	Johnson			
	c PRO SP f.24v	anon			
52 Benedicite whate dremyd I this nyght	F12	[Fayrfax]	3		41, 99–, 105, 143, 283, 357
53 *B[enedictus]*	H1 et al.	[Isaac]	3		388
54 Be pes ye make me spille my ale	R3	anon	3		339–
55 Bewar my lytyl fynger	TS no. 4	anon	1(3)	modified carol; not in Greene.	

(1)	(2)	(3)	(4)	(5)	(6)
67 Complayne I may wherevyr I go [see 649]	F28	anon	3		365
68 Concordans musical jugyd by the ere	TS no. 16	anon	1(4)		
69 Considering this world, and th' increse	a [Hawkins, iii. 33]	anon	w	b: claims m from private source.	
	b [Rimbault, 44]	R. Pend	w		
	c Ashm48 f.45	anon	w		
70 *Credo in Deum* That ys withowt [662]	C5943 f.168v	anon	2	versifies The Creed.	
70a . . . [c]rowne of thorne so scharpe and kene	Drexel no. 3	anon	1	fragment.	426
71 Colle to me the rysshys grene	a RA58 f.2	anon	1	a: *m* for B only | b: another *m* setting B only | see also Chappell (1893), i. 38 | *t*, Copland; *Complaint*, song 52.	130
	b RA58 f.14v	anon	1		
72 Danger me hath un- skylfuly [670]	C5943 f.166	anon	2		
73 Demyd wrongfully	F6	anon	2		353–
74 Deme the best of every dowt	H74 *et al.*	Lloyd	3 R		108, 413
75 Departure is my chef payne	H56	Henry VIII	4 R		4, 408
76 *De tous bien plane*	H36 *et al.*	[Hayne van Ghizeghem]	3		21, 401
77 Downbery down	H18 *et al.*	Daggere	3 R		130, 391
78 Doune from heaven from heaven so hie	[Sharp, 118]	anon	3	Greene, no. 79B and see p. 349 | same *m* as 42.	

436

Index of Selected Songs

(1)	(2)	(3)	(4)	(5)	(6)
79 *Duas partes in unum*	H88	anon	2 P		416
80 *Dulcis amica*	H83 *et al.*	[Prioris]	3		415
81 *Dum vincella* [*Dont vient cela*]	a RA56 f.19	[Sermisy]	kbd	chanson used as	
	b RA58 f.30v	anon	1	basse-danse | see	
	c 30513 f.16v	anon	kbd	Reese, *MR*, 564.	
82 *Durez ne puis*	Escorial f.7 *et al.*	Dunstable or Bedingham	3	MB, viii, no. 64.	
83 *Ecce quod natura* [see 488, 546]	a Ashm1393 f.69	anon	2		48, 56, 128
	b Eg3307 f.65	anon	2	*MC*, nos 37, 43, 63;	
	c Selden f.27	anon	2	Greene, nos 65–	
	d Ryman f.23	Ryman	w	66.	
84 Enforce yourselfe as Goddis knyght	F47	Turges	3		105, 241–, 351, 383
85 *En frolyk weson*	H4 *et al.*	[Barbireau]	3		4, 388
86 Englond be glad Pluk up thy lusty hart	H96	anon	3		4, 19, 242, 417–, 419
87 [*E*]*n vray amoure*	H81	Henry VIII	4		245, 387, 415
88 *Esperance ky en*	C5943 f.165	anon	2		
89 Fayre and discrete fresche wommanly	R9	anon	3		342
90 *Fa la sol*	H6 *et al.*	[Cornish]	3	the only instrumental concordance between H and *TS*.	101, 388
91 Farewell my joy and my swete hart	H63	Cooper	3		409–
– *Fetys bel chere*: 339					
92 *Fors solemant*	H99 *et al.*	[Ockeghem]	3		4, 418
92a . . . for thi sake man to whom yf thu call	Drexel no. 4	anon	1	fragment.	426
93 Fortune alas is this thy chaunce	PRO SP f.26	anon	1(3)		
94 *Fortune esperee* [*Fortuna desperata*]	H2 *et al.*	[Busnois]	4		388

(1)	(2)	(3)	(4)	(5)	(6)
95 Fortune unkynde	RA56 f.22	anon	kbd	*t* only.	7
96 Free lusti fresch most goodly	Kk f.129	anon	2	fragment.	
97 Frere Gastkyn wo ye be	RA58 f.24v	Raff Drake	1	*triplex pars.*	
98 From stormy wyndis and grevous wethir	F44	Turges	3		242, 351, 380–
– Gabriel of hye degre: 217					
99 *Gentil prince de renom*	H45 *et al.*	Henry VIII	4		21, 112, *403*
100 *Gloria in excelsis*	C5943 f.166v	anon	2	Latin throughout.	
101 Go hert hurt with adversite [925]	Ashm191 f.192	anon	3	*t*, Cely.	284, 332–
102 Grace and vertew	a RA56 f.20v	anon	kbd		
	b RA58 f.31	anon	1		
103 Grene growith the holy	H33	Henry VIII	3		12, 15, 125, 127, 183, 398–, 401–, 406
104 Have I not cause to morne a [las]	a Mus. f.3	anon	1(?)	incomplete.	
	b [Hawkins, iii. 25]	anon	*w*		
105 Heven and erth	RA58 ff.52, 55v.	anon	lute	*cf. Wyatt*, no. 73 | Ward, 'A Handefull', 179, note 101, summarizes.	135
106 *Helas madam*	H10 *et al.*	Henry VIII	4		112, 245, *389*
107 Hay how the mavys on a brere	R19	anon	3		349–
108 Hey nony nony . . . no	H31	anon	3		397–, 401–
109 Hey now now	H13	Kempe	3 R		390
110 Hey now now	H19	Farthing	3 R		391
111 Hey troly loly	H75	anon	3 R		284, *413–*
112 Hey troly loly lo	H109	anon	3		223, 386, *424–*
113 Hope the medcyn against dreadfull	Hall f.6v	anon	1		

Index of Selected Songs

(1)	(2)	(3)	(4)	(5)	(6)
114 How shall Y plece a creature uncerteyne	R20	anon	3	*MC*, no. 16A.	*350*
115 Hoyda hoyda joly rutterkin	F43	Cornish	3	t, quoted Skelton (Dyce, i. 249).	105, 129, *380*
116 *Hunt is up, The*	a Folger, f.12	anon	lute	bcd: 3 different	
	b 15233 f. fr	anon	*w*	moralizations	d:	
	c GGB, 174	anon	*w*	'Rownde', *sig,*	
	d Ripon (2)	anon	tabl.	'Sctotish tune'	*Broadside Index,* 1175–6 &c.	see Chappell (1893), i. 86–88	the later history of this tune is very complicated.	
117 I am a joly foster	H65	anon	3		250, *410–*
118 I am he that hath you dayly servyd	F15	Turges	3		*358*
119 I am the man whom God	Hall f.65	anon	1		
– Iblessyd be Cristes sonde: 305					
120 If care cause men to cry	a RA58 f.52	anon/[Surrey]	lute	see *Tottel*, ii. 313, for many later versions of *w*	Ward, 'A Handefull', 179, note 100, lists versions of *m*.	
	b Stowe f.120	anon	lute		
	c Ashm176 f.97	anon	*w*		
121 If ever man might him avaunt	[Arundel no. 4]	anon/ Wyatt	1	*Wyatt*, no. 183 from *Tottel*.	*136*
122 Yf I had space now for to write	PRO SP f.28	anon	1(?)	cf. **123**.	*396*
123 Iff I had wytt for to endyght	H29 *et al.*	anon	3	cf. **122**.	105, 114, 130, 217, 284, *396*

Appendix B

(1)	(2)	(3)	(4)	(5)	(6)
124 If I shall enterpryse	Hall f.3	anon	1		
125 If love now reynyd	H44, H48	Henry VIII	3		403–
126 If reason did rule	[Hawkins, iii. 36]	anon	*w*	source now lost.	
127 If right be rackt and over run	[Arundel no. 5]	anon	1		
128 Yf thow fle idelnes [1430]	Selden f.33v	anon	4	fragments.	
129 If truth may take no trusty hold	Hall f.102	anon	1		
130 Yf writers words	PRO SP f.17v	anon	1(?)		
131 Yf ye love me kepe my commandements	PRO SP f.19v	anon	1(?)		
132 I had both monie and a frende	a [Hawkins, iii. 38]	anon	*w*	source(s) now lost	b: claims *m*
	b [Rimbault, 42]	J. Heywood	*w*	from private source.	
133 I have bene a foster Long and many	a H62	Cooper	3		128–, 222, 249–, 339, 408–, 411
	b R1	anon	1(?)		128–, 338–, 409
134 I have loved so many a day	5666 f.3v	anon	1	*MC*, no. 3A.	56
135 I hafe set my hert so hye [1311]	Douce f.20	anon	2	cf. TCC R.4.20, f.170v, related *w* | Carleton Brown, *XIV*, p. 229, *XV*, p. 74.	
136 Ie have so longe kepe schepe [1312]	Douce f.21v	anon	2		
137 I hard a maydyn wepe [1318]	a Ryman f.1v	Ryman(?)	1		56
	b Balliol f.230	anon	*w*B	b: Greene, no. 162.	

Index of Selected Songs

Appendix B

(1)	(2)	(3)	(4)	(5)	(6)
149 In wyldernes Ther founde I Besse	R15 et al.	anon	3		346–
150 In wynter's just return a	RA58 f.52	anon	lute	see Tottel, ii. 144;	126
b	Folger f.13	anon	lute	Broadside Index,	
c	[Arundel no. 2]	anon	1	nos 1213, 1249; and Ward, 'A Handefull', 179, note 100.	
151 In women is rest peas and pacience [1593] a	Baldwin f.99v	Taverner	2	a: the only complete setting of a 'punctuation poem' | b: Robbins, SL, no. 112 | cf. 226.	162, 197, 223, 357
b	Hh f.58	anon	w		
152 In youth in age both in welth	TS no. 2	Cooper	1(3)	modified carol.	
153 . . . I pray daily ther paynys	F16	anon	3	incomplete	358
154 I rede that thou be joly and glad [1347] a	Douce 381 f.22v	anon	2		
b	C5943 f.161	anon	2		
155 Is it not suer a dedly payne	PRO SP f.27	anon	1(?)		
156 Is it not tyme that synne and cryme	Hall f.132v, f.177v	anon	1	f.132v contains w; f.177v m.	
157 Iste tenor ascendit	H26	Lloyd	4 P		317, 395
158 It is to me a ryght gret joy	H57	Henry VIII	3 R		408
159 Jay content	PRO SP f.25v	anon	1(?)		
160 Jay pryse amours	H37 et al.	anon	3		21, 401
161 Je ieo hayen vos tote may fiance	C5943 f.164	anon	3		

(1)	(2)	(3)	(4)	(5)	(6)
178 Lyke as the larke within the marlions	Hall f.108v	anon	1	moralizes *Tottel*, i. 126; see *Tottel*, ii. 259.	
178a . . . [lo]kyng for her trew love long or that	Drexel no. 6	anon	1	fragment.	427
179 Love fayne wolde I	F9	anon	2		355–
179a . . . love shuld com. On every syde the way	Drexel no. 7	anon	1		427
– Love is naturall to every wyght: 281					
180 Love wyll I and leve so yt may	a *TS* no. 13	Taverner	3		
	b Mus(2) f.93v		w		
181 Love wolle I withoute eny variaunce	Ashm1393 f.68v	anon	2	*m* unconnected with **182.**	
182 Luf wil I with variance	Ashm191 f.195v	anon	2	*m* unconnected with **181.**	
183 Lolay lolay [352]	C5943 f.169	anon	1	*MC*, no. 1A *m*	Greene, no. 149, gives 3 other sources of *w*.	
184 Lullay my child and wepe no more [3596]	a Epoet f.20	anon	w	a: *MC*, no. 2A	Greene, no. 151.	56
	b 5666 f.2v	anon	1		
	c C5943 f.145	anon	w		
185 Lully lulla thow littell tine child	[Sharp, 116]	anon	3	MS destroyed; see **42, 78**	*The Coventry Carol*, Greene, no. 112.	
186 Lusti yough shuld us ensue	H92	Henry VIII	3		142, 416–
187 *Madame d'amours* All tymes or ours	H67	anon	4		98, 333–, 412

Index of Selected Songs

Appendix B

(1)	(2)	(3)	(4)	(5)	(6)
200 My feerful dreme nevyr forgete can I [3750]	F36 et al.	Banastir	3		373-
201 My friends the things that do	a 30513 f.65v	anon	kbd	c differs from a &	126
	b PRO SP f.22v	anon	1(?)	b | see Tottel, ii. 150.	
	c [Arundel no. 3]	anon	1		
202 My harte constraines my mouth	Hall f.104v	anon	1		
203 Mi hartys lust and all my pleasure	TS no. 17	Fayrfax	1(3)		
204 My herte ys yn grete mournyng	R11	anon	3		343-
205 My herte ys so plungit yn greffe [2245]	Dublin f.92	anon	1		46, 56, 123-
206 Mi harte my mynd and my hole poure	a TS no. 12	Taverner	1(3)		
	b 18752 f.72		w		
– My lady hath me in that grace: 362					
207 My lytell fole ys gon to play	RA58 f.55v	anon	1	refr: Frisca joly.	
208 My litell prety one	a 4900 f.62v	anon	L&V	see Chappell (1893),	
	b 18752 f.76v	anon	w	i. 71.	
209 My love sche morneth For me	H25 et al.	Cornish	3		14-, 29, 53, 124-, 129, 393-
210 My lute awake and prayse the lord	Hall f.76v	anon	w	heading: 'Syng this as, My pen obey &c'; moralizes Wyatt's 'My lute awake' (no. 66).	136
211 My pen obey my wyll awhyle	Hall f.87v	anon	1	moralizes Wyatt's 'My pen take payn' (no. 103).	125, 136
– My soverayne lorde for my poure sake: 355					

Index of Selected Songs

447

Appendix B

	(1)	(2)	(3)	(4)	(5)	(6)
221	Now fayre fayrest off every fayre	RA58 f.17v	anon/ ?Dunbar	1	celebrates marriage of Princess Margaret to James IV of Scotland (1503) | see *Dunbar*, no. 89 and app. C.	427
222	Now has Mary born a flour	5666 f.3	anon	1	*OHM*, ii. 339 (pr. *m*).	56
223	Now helpe Fortune of thy godenesse	R8	anon	3		341
–	Now yn this medow: 112					
224	Now marcy Jesu I wyll amend [2272]	RA58 f.23	anon	1	modified carol.	
225	Now she that I loved	K8k8	anon	1	fragment of printed broadside, *c.* 1520(?).	
226	Nowe the lawe is led be clere conciens [2364]	F10	Davy	1(2)		28–, 107, 162, 197, 356
227	Nowe well and nowe woo Now frend	Glasgow f.21	anon	1		46, 56
228	Now wold I fayne sum myrthis make [2381]	a Ashm191 f.191	anon	2		
		b Ff f.137v	anon	w		
229	*Nutbrown Maid, The*	a Arnold p. 75	anon	w	history: *EEL*, no. 19, note | a: first printed version. b: only contemporary MS version.	46
		b Balliol f.210v	anon	w		
230	O blessed lord how may this be	R6	anon	2		341

M.P. – G G

	(1)	(2)	(3)	(4)	(5)	(6)
243	O Lord two thinges I the require	Hall f.60	anon	1		
244	O man amend defer no tyme	Hall f.81	anon	1		
245	*Omnes una gaudeamus*	a Eg3307 f.68v	anon	2	*MC*, no. 15A │ Latin throughout.	
		b Selden f.11	anon	2		
246	O my desyre what eylyth the	F7	Newark	2		*354‑*
247	O my hart and o my hart	H15	Henry VIII	3		*131, 331, 390*
248	O my lady dure	RA58 f.16v	Parker	2 R		
249	On tabrets to the Lorde	Hall f.58	anon	1		
250	O *potores exquisiti*	Eg3307 f.72v	anon	3	*w*, a drinking song from Carmina Burana │ *m*, an elaborate, iso‑rhythmic song.	*62*
251	O rote of trouth o princess to my pay	F26	Tutor	3		*21, 363*
252	O *rosa bella*	see *MB* viii	Dunstable	3	Italian *w* through‑out │ *MB* viii, no. 54 │ *t*, Cely.	*284, 332*
–	O sisters too How may we do: 185					
253	*Ough warder mount*	H42 *et al.*	anon	4		*142, 279, 403*
–	Owt of your slepe: 219					
254	*Pange lingua gloriosi corporis*	C5943 f.163	anon	3 R	Latin throughout.	
255	*Paramese tenor*	H53	Fayrfax	4 P		*407*
256	*Parit virgo*	5666 f.5v	anon	1	*MC*, no. 73, note │ not in carol‑form, cf. Eg3307, f.72.	*56, 457*
257	Pastyme with good companye	H7, R12 *et al.*	Henry VIII	3		*112, 138, 142‑, 279, 338, 344‑, 388‑*

(1)	(2)	(3)	(4)	(5)	(6)
258 *Pater noster* most of myght [2738]	C5943 f.167v	anon	2		
259 Pepe I see ye I am glad I have	*Kyng Johan*	anon	1	one line of *m* pr. in text with *w*.	258
260 Phillida was a fair maid	a [Arundel no. 7]	anon	1	two tunes | see *Tottel*, ii. 265 | b: 'and in any tune of the psalms in metre'.	127
	b [Arundel no. 8]	anon	1		
261 Petyously constraynd am I	RA58 f.19v	Cooper/ [Skelton]	1	*CBEL*, i. 410 | *Skelton* (ed. Henderson), p. 19.	
262 Pleasure yt is To here iwys	*TS* no. 15	Cornish	1(4)		
263 *Plus por l'en oyr*	C5943	anon	2		
264 Pouer man dumpe (?)	RA58 f.56	anon	lute		
265 Pray we to God	H97	anon	3 R		5, 418
266 Princesse af youth and floree	Escorial f.114v	anon	3	*t*, quoted *Skelton* (Dyce, i. 40) | Bukofzer, 'An early English chanson'.	
267 *Psallimus cantantes*	a Epoet f.40v	anon	1	a: Latin throughout | b: macaronic carol.	45, 47, 56
	b Kele p. 10	anon	*w*		
268 *Puisque mamour*	see *MB* viii	Dunstable	3	*MB*, viii, no. 55.	
269 Rawyshyd was I	a Ashm176	anon	*w*	b: no more words.	
	b Cotton f.56v	anon	lute		
270 *Quam pulcra es*	Baldwin, f.166v	Henry VIII	3	the king's only known sacred composition.	112
271 *Qui creavit celum* lully lully lu	Chester	anon	1		
272 *Quid petis o fily*	H105	Pygott	4		5, 9, 107, 421–

(1)	(2)	(3)	(4)	(5)	(6)
273 Rasyd is my mynde alacke for pety	RA58 f.17	anon	1		
273a . . . red rosse fayre and sote off sent	Drexel no. 8	anon	1		427
— Rutterkyn is com unto oure towne: 115					
274 Saint Bernard saith the chariot	Hall f.86	anon	1		
275 *Salve sancta parens* [182]	Glasgow f.21	anon	1	*MC*, no. 6A.	45, 56
276 Shall I dispaire then sodeynly	PRO SP f.20	anon	1(?)		
277 She may be callid a soverant lady	*TS* no. 5	Ashwell	4	(?) moralization; in modified carol-form.	
— Syne the tyme I knew yow fyrst: 363					
278 Synge we now all and sum	Ryman f.1	Ryman (?)	1	*MC*, no. 7A | Greene, no. 21 gives other versions of *w*.	56
279 *Si quis amat dictis absentum*	C5943 f.163	anon	3 R	Latin throughout.	
— Sith it concludid was in the Trinite: 9					
280 Sith nothyng can be sure	Hall f.97v	anon	1		
281 Smale pathis to the grenewode	F46	anon	3		*382–*
282 'Smythes' pavan and galliard	RA74 f.37	anon	1	no *w* | (?) connected with Wyatt's 'Now all of chaunge' (no. 158) glossed 'To Smithe of Camden'.	124

(1)	(2)	(3)	(4)	(5)	(6)
296 The bella the bella we maydens	a *TS* no. 6	Taverner	1(4)	b: three separate	427
	b Drexel no. 10	anon	1(4)	fragments.	
297 The bitter swete that straynes my yeldid hart	a PRO SP f.29	anon	1(4)	*w* by Jasper Heywood, in *Gorgeous Gallery*.	
	b 30513 f.109	anon	kbd		
– The burne ys this worlde blynde: 66					
298 The dauning day begins to glare	Hall f.161v	anon	1	connected with **313** (?).	
299 The doleful bell that still	[Arundel no. 12]	anon	1		458
300 The farther I go the more behynde [see 3436, 3504]	F1	Newark	2		3, 108, *352*
301 The ferce and wanton colt	PRO SP f.22	anon	1(?)		
302 The hye desire that Y have for to se	R5	anon	2		*341*
303 The hier that the ceder tree	30513 f.1v	Mulliner	4	*w* by Vaux, in *Paradise of Dainty Devises*	at top of page: *t, La belle fyne*.	
– The knyght knokett at the castell gate: 369					
304 The lytyll prety nyghtyngale	RA58 ff.8v, 9v	anon	1	3 versions, only 1 complete/*t* quoted by Wager.	
305 The merthe of alle this londe	Selden f.19	anon	3	carol for Plough Monday: *MC*, no. 12A.	

(1)	(2)	(3)	(4)	(5)	(6)
317 Thys Yol thys Yol the beste red [3662]	C5943 f.162	'Edmundus'	2	*Tenor qd Edmundus.*	
318 Thofe I doo syng my hert dothe wepe	RA58 f.18v	anon	1		
319 Thei Y synge and murthus make [2185]	Caius p. 210	anon	1	*m* for B only | Greene, no. 441; *MC*, no. 9A | *t*, 'le bon l. don' (see **171**).	45
– Though poetts fayne that fortune: 152					
320 Though sum saith that yough rulyth	H66	Henry VIII	3		*411–*
321 Thow that men do call it dotage	H51	Henry VIII	3		*406–*
322 Though that she cannot redresse	RA58 f.3v	anon	1	cf. PRO Excheq. Misc. E/163/22/2, f.57; similar *w*.	130
323 Thow man envired with temptacion	R7	anon	3		*341*
323a . . . Thus hath mayd my payne	Drexel no. 11				*427*
324 Thus Y compleyne my grevous hevynesse [3722]	Ashm191 f.193v	anon	2		
325 Thus musyng in my mynd	F19 *et al.*	Newark	3		*359, 427*
– Tydynges trew ther be cum new: 220					
326 Tyme to pas with goodly sport	*Elements*	anon	3	pr. Rastell, *c.* 1517 | *m* taken from **6**.	258
327 To complayne me alas why shulde I so	F13	[Fayrfax]	3		*357*
– To Calvery he bare his cross: 199					
328 To leve alone comfort ys none	RA58 f.10	Cole	1		

Index of Selected Songs

	(1)	(2)	(3)	(4)	(5)	(6)
344	Welcome fortune	a Ely(?)	Fayrfax	?	a: *refr.*, see *DNB*,	362
		b 18752 f.28	anon	*w*	vi. 1002 | c: mor-	
		c GGB p.222	anon	*w*	alized | cf. **286**	
					[F24], verse 5,	
					line 4.	
345	Wele were hym that wyst [3892]	C5943 f.162v	anon	3	cf. *Index MEV*, 3893.	
346	Westron wynde when wyll thow blow	RA58 f.5	anon	1	Masses were written by Taverner, Tye and Shepherd on this tune.	7, 130, 237
347	What causyth me wofull thoughtis to thynk	F3	Newark	2		*352–*
348	What remedy what remedy	H103	anon	3		*411, 419–*
349	When dreadful swelling seas	[Arundel no. 9]	anon	1		
350	When fortune had me avaunsyd	RA58 f.21v	anon	1		
–	... whan I have plesyd my lady now and than: 25d					
351	When May	PRO SP f.21v	anon	1(?)	*w*: ? = 'When May is in his prime' by Edwards, in *Paradise of Dainty Devises*.	
352	When youth had led me	[Arundel no. 1]	anon/ [Surrey]	1	see *Tottel*, ii. 131.	
353	Wher be ye My love my love	H104	anon	3		*411, 419, 420–*
–	Wherfor shuld I hang up my bow: 117					
354	Wherto shuld I expresse	H47	Henry VIII	3		*18, 404*

Index of Selected Songs

(1)	(2)	(3)	(4)	(5)	(6)
355 Whilles lyve or breth is in my brest	H50	Cornish	3		1-, 127, 234, 241, 398, 405-
- Who is my love But god above: 36					
356 Who list to here this song	PRO SP f.20v	anon	1(?)		
357 Who list to lerne to thrive	PRO SP f.21	anon	1(?)		
358 Who shall have my fayre lady	F42 et al.	anon	3		223, 329, 333, 379,-
359 Whoso that wyll all feattes	H34	Henry VIII	3		218, 399-
360 Whoso that wyll for grace sew	H79	Henry VIII	3		15, 132, 414
361 Whoso that wyll hym-selff applye	H22	Rysbye	4		241, 392
362 Why shall not I	H102	anon	3		411, 419
363 Why soo unkende alas	RA58 f.6	anon	1	Greene, no. 449.	130-
364 With hevy hart I call and cry	PRO SP f.16v	anon	1(?)		
365 Withowt dyscord And bothe acorde	H64	Henry VIII	3		410
- With pety movyd I am constreynyd: 232					
366 With ryth al my herte now Y [4199]	Douce, f.22	anon	1(?)	fragment.	
367 With sorowfull syghs and grevos	H28	Farthing	3		395
368 Woffully araid [497] a	F33	Cornish	4		12, 39, 101, 103-, 107, 114, 335, 369-, 372
b	F35	Browne	3		
- Ye wryng my hand so sore: 55					

459

Appendix B

(1)	(2)	(3)	(4)	(5)	(6)
369 Yow and I and Amyas	H41	Cornish	3		127–, 243, 402–, 406
370 You proud men all	Hall f.83	anon	1		
– Yower company Makes me so mery: 353					
371 Yowre counturfetyng With doubyll	F18	Newark	3		16, 21, 358–
372 Your mamme shalle have . . .	Mus f.4	anon	1(?)	fragment.	

460

List of Sources

The following list serves principally as an index and key to Appendix B, Index of Selected Songs. The sources are therefore listed in alphabetical order according to the abbreviations used in that Appendix. Plain numbers at the beginning of the list refer to Additional Manuscripts in the British Museum. Song numbers refer to the entries in Appendix B but do not necessarily indicate that a *text* of each song referred to occurs in the source under consideration. In the case of songs from R, F and H, further reference to Appendix A will be necessary in order to find the concordances indicated by *et al.* Brief details are given about the more important or interesting English sources; dates refer to the musical entries in MSS. Selected editions, transcriptions, articles, etc., are listed by the author's name or by short title (see Appendix D for fuller information). The reader's attention is not called in every instance to standard works of reference, such as Hughes-Hughes's *Catalogue of MS Music* or Reese's *Music in the Renaissance*. An author's name without a symbol indicating that words or music are printed draws attention to extended discussion or description.

Additional Manuscripts, British Museum:

1. 4900   (late xvi cent.)
          Songs 51, 138, 208
2. 5666   (early xv cent.)
          Latin grammar, household accounts, songs
          Songs 184, 222, 256
3. 15117 (late xvi cent.)
          Songs 25, 231
4. 15233 (mid-xvi cent.)
          Organ-music, English poems, plays. Associated with St Paul's
          Songs 25, 116
          Ref. Brown (pr. *w*); Pfatteicher (pr. *m*)
5. 17492 *The Devonshire MS* (early mid-xvi cent.)
          Poems of Wyatt's circle; no music
          Songs 16, 57, 215
          Ref. Foxwell, *Study*; Mason; Muir, 'Devonshire MS' (pr. *w*); Seaton;
            Wyatt (pr. *w*)

Appendix C

6. 18752   (early mid-xvi cent.)
Treatises, herbals, etiquette, poems, etc.; no music
Songs 123, 197, 198, 206, 208, 344
Ref. E. B. Reed (pr. *w*)

7. 30513   *The Mulliner Book* (mid-xvi cent.)
Music for keyboard and for cittern
Songs 51, 81, 168, 201, 238, 297, 303
Ref. Mulliner Book (pr. *m*); D. Stevens, *Commentary*

8. 35087   (early xvi cent.)
Flemish chansons
Song 94

9. 35290   The *York Miracle Plays*
The songs belong to the Weavers' Play, *The Appearance of Our Lady to St Thomas*
Songs 289, 337, 338
Ref. York Plays (pr. *w&m*); Stevens, 'Music in Drama'

10. Advoc   Edinburgh, National Library, Advoc. 19.3.1 (xv cent.)
Song 314

11. Arnold   Arnold, *Customs of London* (Antwerp, *c.* 1502)
Song 229

12. Arundel   Arundel Castle, *Songs and Sonets* (Tottel's Miscellany) ed. G. F. Nott (1814)
The tunes in this incomplete copy of Nott's 1814 edition of Tottel were taken from 'an early copy' of Surrey's poems once owned by Sir W. W. Wynne.
Songs 63, 121, 127, 138, 150, 201, 215, 260, 299, 349, 352
Ref. Chappell (1859) (pr. Song 138); Hughey; *Tottel* (ed. Rollins) (*w*)

13. Ashm48   Oxford, Bodleian Library, Ashmole 48 (early xvi cent.)
Song 69

14. Ashm176   Oxford, Bodleian Library, Ashmole 176 (late xvi cent.)
Astrological matter in Latin, English poems; no music. The only known late source of the words of early Tudor court-songs
Songs 4, 66, 120, 333
Ref. Wagner (pr. *w*)

15. Ashm191   Oxford, Bodleian Library, Ashmole 191 (mid-xv cent.)
Fragments of different MSS bound up together
Songs 20, 101, 182, 228, 241, 324
Ref. EBM, i (facs.), ii (pr. *m*); Kenney, 'Walter Frye'

16. Ashm1393 Oxford, Bodleian Library, Ashmole 1393 (xv cent.)
Fragments of different MSS bound up together
Songs 83, 181
Ref. EBM, i (facs.), ii (pr. *m*)

17. Baldwin   British Museum, Royal Library RM 24.d.2: *Baldwin's MS* (*c.* 1600)
A singing-man's collection
Songs 151, 270

18. Balliol   Oxford, Balliol College 354: *Richard Hill's MS* (early xvi cent.)

List of Sources

Citizen's commonplace-book and private anthology; no music
Songs 137, 217, 229, 314
Ref. Dyboski (pr. *w*); Flügel (pr. *w*); Mason

19. Bannatyne Edinburgh, National Library, Advoc. 1.1.6: *The Bannatyne MS* (mid-xvi cent.)
The personal anthology of George Bannatyne, 1568
Songs 20, 41, 148, 341
Ref. Bannatyne MS (pr. *w*)

20. C2750 Cambridge, University Library, Additional 2750 (? late xv cent.)
Song 308

21. C2764(1)C Cambridge, University Library, Additional 2764(1)C (xv cent.)
Song 235

22. C5943 Cambridge, University Library, Additional 5943 (early xv cent.)
English, French and Latin songs, astronomical matter, memoranda, poems without music
Songs 44, 70, 72, 88, 100, 154, 161, 172, 183, 184, 191, 254, 258, 263, 279, 317, 332, 345
Ref. Myers (pr. *m*)

23. Caius Cambridge, Gonville and Caius College 383 (mid-xv cent.)
Songs 34, 56, 171, 319

24. *Captain Cox* see Appendix D
Song 60

25. *Carew* see Appendix D
Songs 43, 60

26. *Cely* see Appendix D
Songs 101, 193, 329

27. Chester Bridgewater House, *Ellesmere MS*
Processional of the Nuns of Chester
Song 271
Ref. Henry Bradshaw Soc. vol. xviii (1899) (facs.)

28. *Complaint* see Appendix D
Songs 12, 71, 257, 313

29. Copland see Appendix D
Songs 12, 71

30. Corpus Oxford, Bodleian Library, Corpus Christi College B 4 (early–mid-xvi cent.)
Song 306a

31. Cotton British Museum, Cotton Titus D.xi (first half of xvi cent.)
Ecclesiastical letters. Treatise by Walter Hilton
Songs 64, 269

32. Dallis Dublin, Trinity College, Thomas Dallis' Lute-Book
Song 25

33. Deutero Ravenscroft, *Deuteromelia* (1609)
Song 60

34. Domit.A British Museum, Cotton Domit.A. xviii
Song 306

463

35. Douce Oxford, Bodleian Library, Douce 381 (early xv cent.)
Fragments bound up together; one fragment consists of French and English songs with music
Songs 135, 136, 154, 173, 195, 198, 366
Ref. EBM, i (facs.), ii (pr. *m*)

36. Drexel New York, Public Library, Drexel 4180–5 (early xvii cent.)
(See postscript to Appendix A, on p. 426 above)
Songs 10, 25, 70*a*, 92*a*, 163, 178*a*, 179*a*, 273*a*, 286, 296, 323*a*, 325, 328*a*

37. Dublin Dublin, Trinity College 158 (late xv cent.)
'Prick of Conscience', *medica*, accounts; one song
Song 205

38. Eg3002 British Museum, Egerton 3002 (early xvi cent.)
Miscellaneous papers, rentals; one song
Song 149

39. Eg3307 British Museum, Egerton 3307 (mid-xv cent.)
Carols, music for Holy Week, etc. (The only substantial collection of carols to be discovered since Greene)
Songs 83, 245, 250, 256
Ref. Bukofzer, *Studies;* Harrison; *MC* (pr. *m* with modernized *w*); Schofield

40. Elements *A New Interlude and Mery of the Nature of iiij Elements* (?1539)
Song 326

41. Ely Ely Cathedral Library [now untraceable: see *DNB*, vi. 1002]
Song 344

42. Epoet Oxford, Bodleian Library, Eng.poet.e.1 (mid–late xv cent.)
'Popular' anthology; contains tunes and names of tunes
Songs 37, 184, 217, 220, 232, 267, 314
Ref. EBM (facs. and *m*); Greene (*w*); *MC* (*m*); Robbins, *Secular Lyrics* (*w*)

42*a*. Escorial Madrid, Escorial, Iv.a.24
Song 266
Ref. Bukofzer, 'An early English chanson'

43. F British Museum, Additional 5465: *The Fayrfax MS*
See Appendix A, p. 351, above

44. Ff Cambridge, University Library, Ff.i.6 (late xv cent.)
Song 228
Ref. Robbins, 'Findern MS'

45. Fitz Cambridge, Fitzwilliam Museum, unnumbered MS fragment (early xvi cent.)
Part of a single leaf, written on both sides
Songs 286, 325

46. Folger Washington, Folger Shakespeare Library, 448.16 (second half of xvi cent.)
Lute-music; the play *July and Julian*; recipes and remedies; accounts (1591) of the estate of Giles Lodge. The lute-music is in two hands; the earlier, soon after *c.* 1550
Songs 25, 43, 57, 116, 144, 150

List of Sources

Songs 104, 236, 372

Ref. EBM, i (facs.), ii (pr. *m*)

63. Mus (2)   Oxford, Bodleian Library, MS.e.Mus.88

Song 180

64. Pammelia   Ravenscroft, *Pammelia*

Song 200

65. Panmure   Panmure 11 (early xvii cent.)

Song 257

66. Pembroke   Cambridge, Pembroke College, folder of MS music fragments

Song 45

67. Pepys   Cambridge, Magdalene College, Pepys 1760 (*c.* 1500)

Chansons and motets; belonged to Prince Arthur (?)

Song 80

68. PRO SP   Public Record Office, SP 1/246 (mid-xvi cent.)

Bass-part of a set of part-songs

Songs 51, 93, 122, 130, 131, 155, 159, 166, 190, 201, 238, 240, 276, 288, 297, 301, 336, 341, 342, 351, 356, 357, 364

Ref. Denis Stevens, 'A Part-Book' (indexes *m*)

69. PRO Exch.   Public Record Office, Excheq.Misc.23/1/1 (early xvi cent.)

Song 34

Ref. Saltmarsh (pr. *m*)

70. R   British Museum, Additional 5665: *Ritson's MS*

see Appendix A, p. 338 above

71. RA56   British Museum, Royal, Appendix 56 (early xvi cent.)

Keyboard music, plain-song Magnificats, notational matter

Songs 24, 39, 81, 95, 102, 192

72. RA58   British Museum, Royal, Appendix 58 (first half of xvi cent.)

Songs, instrumental pieces, church-music, keyboard music, lute tablatures

Songs 17, 32, 39, 58, 60, 65, 71, 77, 81, 97, 102, 105, 120, 123, 150, 167, 168, 207, 216, 221, 224, 248, 253 257, 261, 264, 273, 311, 314, 316, 318, 322, 346, 350, 363

Ref. Byler; Dawes (pr. kbd *m*); Flügel (pr. *w*); Greene (pr. carols); Lumsden; Ward, 'Dumps'

73. RA74   British Museum, Royal, Appendix 74 (mid-xvi cent.)

Song 282

74. Ramsden   Huddersfield Corporation, Ramsden Documents, Rental [unnumbered] (*c.* 1560–80)

Song 197

75. Rimbault   see Appendix D: Rimbault, *A Little Book*

Rimbault's 'ancient manuscripts' and 'parchment books' are a little suspect (see Greene, note to no. 434). He never, in his *Little Book*, gives the text of a poem of which another well authenticated version does not exist. His versions are commonly identical transcripts; but so, to a remarkable degree, are the fragments of song-books such as nos 36 and 45 above.

Songs 40, 69, 132, 163, 189, 306

List of Sources

76. Ripon   Ripon Cathedral Library, *incunabulum* (late xv cent.)
The songs are on a blank leaf of Gerson, *De Consolatione Theologie*, 1488;
they can be dated, stylistically, *c.* 1530
Songs 61, 145
Ref. *Yorkshire Archaeological Journal*, xi (1891), 201 (pr. *w*)

77. Ripon (2)   Ripon Cathedral Library, MS XVII.B.69 (early xvii cent.)
Song 116

78. Ryman   Cambridge, University Library, Ee.i.12 (*c.* 1490)
The songs, hymns and carols, many of them translations or paraphrases, of
James Ryman, a Franciscan; a few scribbled tunes
Songs 83, 137, 219, 237, 278
Ref. Greene (pr. carols); *MC* (pr. *m*); Robbins, *Secular Lyrics*; Zupitza
(pr. *w*)

79. Selden   Oxford, Bodleian Library, Selden b.26 (mid-xv cent.)
Carols, polyphonic music for church use, etc.
Songs 41, 83, 128, 219, 245, 291, 305, 339, 343
Ref. Greene (pr. carols); Harrison

80. Sharp   see Appendix D
Songs 42, 78, 185

81. Sibton   Ipswich and East Suffolk Record Office, 50/9/15.7(1) (*c.* 1461)
Account Book of Sibton Abbey
Song 329

82. Slo3501   British Museum, Sloane 3501 (early xvi cent.)
Book on hunting; the list of songs and dances is introduced without head-
ing or explanation; no music.
Songs 43, 57

83. SS   J. Stafford Smith, *Musica Antiqua* (1812)
Song 164

84. Stowe   British Museum, Stowe 389 (*c.* 1558)
Statutes; lute-music 'writtin by one Raphe Bowle to learne to playe on his
Lutte in anno 1558'
Song 120

85. TCC   Cambridge, Trinity College, O.2.53 (xv cent.)
Song 66

86. TS   *XX Songes*, 1530 (*Bassus* only)
The earliest English book of printed songs in mensural notation, formerly
attributed to Wynkyn de Worde. See Nixon's article in *BM Quarterly*,
xvi (1951), 33, occasioned by the discovery in a binding at Westminster
Abbey of a title leaf of the medius part and a leaf with an unknown
printer's colophon, 'Impryntyd in London at the signe of the black
mores . . .' The bass part-book complete and the first leaf of the treble
are in the British Museum.
Songs 36, 38, 47, 55, 60, 62, 68, 90, 152, 165, 180, 194, 203, 206, 209, 262,
277, 284, 296, 334, 335, 358
Ref. Flügel (pr. *w*); Greene; E. B. Reed, *Christmas Carols* (facs.)

Appendix C

87. *Tottel*   see Appendix D
88. Wager   see Appendix D
89. Wells   Wells Cathedral Library, MS fragment (early xvi cent.)
            Discovered, apparently about 1880, as an end-paper in a law-book; subse-
            quently mislaid and rediscovered in 1952. See Dom Anselm Hughes'
            article in *Annual Report of the Friends of Wells Cathedral* (March 1953).
            Songs 255, 286

APPENDIX D

Reference List of Books and Articles

The following list is not designed as a bibliography of the subjects treated in the pages above but as a key to the books and articles referred to by abbreviation in the notes. Items are, therefore, listed in alphabetical order of author's name, short title, or symbol.

ABDY WILLIAMS, C. F. *A Short Historical Account of the Degrees in Music at Oxford and Cambridge*, 1893

ADAMS, J. Q. ed. *Chief Pre-Shakespearean Dramas*, USA, 1924

Antiquarian Repertory, The. ed. F. GROSE and T. ASTLE, new edn, 4 vols, 1807–9

APEL, W. *The Notation of Polyphonic Music, 900–1600*, third corrected edn, USA, 1945

Archiv: Archiv für das Studium der neueren Sprachen

ARNOLD: see Appendix C, no. 11

Babees Book, The. ed. F. J. FURNIVALL, EETS, xxxii, 1868

BAILLIE, HUGH. 'London Churches, their Music and Musicians, 1485–1560.' Unpublished dissertation for Ph.D., Cambridge, 1958

Bannatyne MS, The. ed. W. TOD RITCHIE, STS, 4 vols, 1928–34

BASKERVILL, C. R. *The Elizabethan Jig*, USA, 1929

BOYD, M. C. *Elizabethan Music and Musical Criticism*, USA, 1940

BRANDL, A. *Quellen des weltlichen Dramas in England vor Shakespeare*, Quellen und Forschungen, lxxx, Strassburg, 1898

BRIDGMAN, NANIE. 'L'Activité Musicale à la Cour de Henry VIII', unpublished dissertation, Paris, 1946

Broadside Index: ROLLINS, H. E. *An Analytical Index to the Ballad-Entries in the Registers of the Company of Stationers of London*, repr. from *Studies in Philology*, xxi, 1924

BROWN, A. 'An Edition of the *Play of Wyt and Science* by John Redford, from BM Add. MS 15233 . . .' [also transcribes poems]. Unpublished dissertation for M.A., London, 1949.

BRUSENDORFF, A. *The Chaucer Tradition*, London, 1925

BUKOFZER, M. F. 'English Chanson on the Continent', *M&L*, xix, 1938 [revised title]

    'An unknown Chansonnier of the Fifteenth Century' [Mellon], *MQ*, xxviii, 1942

    Studies in Medieval and Renaissance Music, USA, 1950

BURNEY, C. *A General History of Music*, 4 vols, 1782–9

BUSZIN, W. F. 'Luther on Music', *MQ*, xxxii, 1946

BYLER, A. W. 'Italian Currents in the Popular Music of England in the Sixteenth Century.' Unpublished dissertation for Ph.D., Chicago, 1952

Appendix D

Captain Cox: Captain Cox, His Ballads and Books; or Robert Laneham's Letter, ed. F. J. FURNI-VALL, Ballad Society, 1871

Carew: The Life of Sir Peter Carew, ed. SIR T. PHILLIPS, *Archaeologia*, xxviii, 1840

CARLETON BROWN, *XIII: English Lyrics of the Thirteenth Century*, ed. CARLETON BROWN, 1932

    XIV: Religious Lyrics of the Fourteenth Century, ed. CARLETON BROWN; second edn rev. G. V. SMITHERS, 1952

    XV: Religious Lyrics of the Fifteenth Century, 1939

CARPENTER, NAN C. 'Skelton and Music: Roty Bully Joys', *RES*, n.s. vi, 1955

CAVENDISH, GEORGE. *The Life and Death of Cardinal Wolsey*, ed. R. S. SYLVESTER, EETS, 1959

CBEL: The Cambridge Bibliography of English Literature

Cely: ALISON HANHAM, 'The Musical Studies of a Fifteenth-Century Wool-Merchant', *RES*, n.s. viii, 1957

CHAMBERS, E. K. *The Elizabethan Stage*. 4 vols, 1923

    The Mediaeval Stage, 2 vols, 1903

    Sir Thomas Wyatt, and some collected Studies, 1933

CHAPPELL (1859): WILLIAM CHAPPELL, *Popular Music of the Olden Time*, 2 vols, [1853–9]

    (1893): WILLIAM CHAPPELL, *Old English Popular Music*, rev. ed. H. E. WOOLDRIDGE, 2 vols, 1893

Charles of Orleans: The English Poems of Charles of Orleans, ed. R. STEELE, EETS, 1941

Chaucer: The Works of Geoffrey Chaucer, ed. F. N. ROBINSON, second edn, 1957

'Colkelbie Sow': see *The Bannatyne MS* (ed. RITCHIE), iv. 279

COLLIER, J. P. *The History of English Dramatic Poetry . . . and the Annals of the Stage*, new edn, 3 vols, 1879

Complaint: The Complaynt of Scotland, 1549, ed. J. A. H. MURRAY, EETS, 1872.

Confessio Amantis: The English Works of John Gower, ed. G. C. MACAULAY, 2 vols, EETS, 1900–1

COPLAND, R. *The manner to dance bace dances*, 1521. Repr. Pear Tree Press, 1937. (trs. from MICHEL TOULOUZE. *L'Art et Instruction de bien Dancer* [before 1496]. Ed. for Royal College of Physicians, London, 1936)

Courtier: B. CASTIGLIONE, *The Book of the Courtier*, trs. SIR THOMAS HOBY, ed. D. HENDERSON, 1928

Court of Venus, The. ed. RUSSELL A. FRASER, USA, 1955

COUSSEMAKER, C. E. H. *Scriptorum de musica medii aevi nova series*, 4 vols, 1864–76

CRAIK, T. W. *The Tudor Interlude; stage, costume, and acting*, 1958

CUTTS, J. P. 'A Reconsideration of the *Willow Song*', *JAMS*, x, 1957

DART, T. 'The Cittern and its English Music', *GSJ*, i, 1948

DAUNEY, W. *Ancient Scotish Melodies*, 1838

DAVEY, H. *History of English Music*, 1895

DAWES, F. ed. *Ten Pieces by Hugh Aston and others*, 1951

DENT, E. J. 'Social Aspects of Music in the Middle Ages' in *Oxford History of Music*: Introductory Volume, ed. P. C. BUCK, 1929

DNB: The Dictionary of National Biography, 22 vols, 1908–

Reference List of Books and Articles

Dorne: The Day-Book of John Dorne, ed. C. R. L. FLETCHER, Oxford Historical Society: Collectanea, first series, 1885

Dunbar: The Poems of William Dunbar, ed. W. M. MACKENZIE, 1932

DYBOSKI, R. ed. *Songs, Carols and miscellaneous Poems* [Balliol 354], EETS, 1908

DYCE: *The Poetical Works of John Skelton*, ed. A. DYCE, 2 vols, 1843

DNB: The Dictionary of National Biography

EBM: Early Bodleian Music, ed. J. F. R. and C. STAINER, 2 vols, 1901

EEH: Early English Harmony, ed. H. E. WOOLDRIDGE and H. V. HUGHES, vol. i, 1897; vol. ii, 1913

EEL: Early English Lyrics, ed. E. K. CHAMBERS and F. SIDGWICK, 1907

EETS: The Early English Text Society

EMS: English Madrigal School, ed. E. H. FELLOWES, 36 vols, 1914–24

EVANS, JOAN. *English Art, 1307–1461*, 1949

Excerpta Historica, ed. S. BENTLEY, 1831 [contains the Privy Purse Expenses of Henry VII]

FEHR, B. ed. 'Die Lieder des Fairfax MS', *Archiv*, cvi, 1901
'Die Lieder der Hs. Sloane 2593', *Archiv*, cix, 1902
'Die Lieder der Hs. Add. 5665 [*Ritson's MS*]', *Archiv*, cvi, 1901
'Weitere Beiträge zur englischen Lyrik des 15. und 16. Jahrhunderts' [Sloane 2593, 1212, 3501; Harl. 367, 541, 7578], *Archiv*, cvii, 1901

FELLOWES, E. H. *English Cathedral Music from Edward VI to Edward VII*, 1941

FLÜGEL, E. ed. 'Liedersammlungen des 16. Jahrhunderts, besonders aus der Zeit Heinrich's VIII', *Anglia*, xii, 1889 [*Henry VIII's MS*; Roy. MSS, App. 58; *Twenty Songs*]
'Liedersammlungen des 16. Jahrhunderts', *Anglia*, xxvi, 1903 [Balliol 354]

FOXWELL, A. K. ed. *The Poems of Sir Thomas Wiat*, 2 vols, 1913
A Study of Sir Thomas Wyatt's Poems, 1911

FRASER, RUSSELL A. 'An Amateur Elizabethan Composer', *M&L*, xxxiii, 1952 [John Hall]

Froissart: The Chronicles of Froissart, trs. JOHN BOURCHIER, LORD BERNERS, ed. G. C. MACAULAY, 1895

FROST, M. *English and Scottish Psalm and Hymn Tunes*, 1953

GALPIN, F. W. *Old English Instruments of Music*, 1910

Gawayne and the Green Knight, ed. I. GOLLANCZ, EETS

GAYLEY, C. M. ed. *Representative English Comedies, from the beginnings to Shakespeare*, 1903–36

GGB: A Compendious Book of Godly and Spiritual Songs commonly known as 'The Gude and Godlie Ballatis', ed. A. F. MITCHELL, STS, 1897

GIBBON, J. M. *Melody and the Lyric*, 1930

Governour, The: SIR THOMAS ELYOT, *The Boke named the Governour*, ed. H. H. S. CROFT, 2 vols, 1880

GOWER: see *Confessio Amantis*

GRATTAN FLOOD, W. H. *Early Tudor Composers*, 1925

GREENE, R. L. *The Early English Carols*, 1935

GREGORY SMITH, G. ed. *Elizabethan Critical Essays*, 2 vols, 1904

Grove (5): Grove's Dictionary of Music and Musicians, fifth edn, ed. E. BLOM, 9 vols, 1954

GSJ: Galpin Society Journal

HALLE (ed. ELLIS): EDWARD HALLE, *The Union of the two Noble and Illustre Famelies of Lancastre and York* [ed. SIR HENRY ELLIS], 1809

Appendix D

HALLE (ed. WHIBLEY): EDWARD HALLE, *Henry VIII*, with an introduction by Charles Whibley, 1904

HALLIWELL-PHILLIPPS, J. O. ed. '*Wit and Science* and early Poetical Miscellanies' [Add. 15233], *Shakespeare Society*, 1848

HAM: Historical Anthology of Music, ed. A. T. DAVISON and W. APEL, vol. i, 1947

HAMMOND, E. P. ed. *English Verse between Chaucer and Surrey*, USA, 1927

HARRIS, D. G. T. 'Musical Education in Tudor Times', *PRMA*, lxv, 1938–9

HARRISON, F. LL. *Music in Medieval Britain*, 1958

HAWES: see *Pastime*

HAWKINS, SIR JOHN. *A General History of the Science and Practice of Music*, 5 vols, 1776

HAYES, G. R. *King's Music: An Anthology*, 1937

Hazlitt's Dodsley: *A Select Collection of Old Plays*, ed. R. DODSLEY, rev. W. C. HAZLITT, fourth edn, 15 vols, 1874–6

HDM: Harvard Dictionary of Music, ed. W. APEL, 1946

HENDERSON: see *Skelton*

HILLEBRAND, H. N. 'The early history of the Chapel Royal', *Modern Philology*, xviii, 1921
   The Child Actors: A Chapter in Elizabethan Stage History, USA, 1926

HLQ: Huntington Library Quarterly

HOOKER, R. *The Laws of Ecclesiastical Polity*, 1593–

HORTON DAVIES. *The Worship of the English Puritans*, 1948

HUGHES, P. *The Reformation in England*, 1950–

HUGHES-HUGHES, A. *Catalogue of Manuscript Music in the British Museum*, 1906–9

HUGHEY, RUTH. 'The Harington MS at Arundel Castle and Related Documents', *The Library*, 4th series, xv, 1935

HUIZINGA, J. *The Waning of the Middle Ages*, English edn, 1924
   Homo Ludens: A Study of the Play-Element in Culture, English edn, 1949

HUNT, J. E. ed. *Cranmer's First Litany, 1544, and Merbecke's Book of Common Prayer, 1550*, 1939

Index MEV: The Index of Middle English Verse, ed. CARLETON BROWN and R. H. ROBBINS, USA, 1943

Italian Relation: A Relation, or rather a True Account, of the Island of England, trs. C. A. SNEYD, Camden Society, 1847

JAMES, M. R. and MACAULAY, G. C. edd. 'Fifteenth Century Carols and other Pieces', *MLR*, viii, 1913

JAMS: Journal of the American Musicological Society

KENNEY, SYLVIA W. 'Contrafacta in the Works of Walter Frye', *JAMS*, viii, 1955
   ' "English Discant" and discant in England', *MQ*, xlv, 1959

Kingis Quhair, The: ed. W. MACKAY MACKENZIE, 1939

'King's Book of Payments' [summarized, for early Henry VIII, in *L&P*, ii, pt 2, pp. 1441–80, iii, pt 2, pp. 1533–]

L&P: Calendar of Letters and Papers of the Reign of Henry VIII, ed. J. S. BREWER and others, 21 vols, 1862–1910

L&P:Milan: Calendar of State Papers . . . existing in the archives of Milan, vol. i, ed. A. B. HINDS, 1912

L&P:Spain: Calendar of Letters . . . preserved in the archives of Simancas and elsewhere, vol. v, pt 2, ed. P. DE GAYANGOS and others, 1888

Reference List of Books and Articles

L&P: Venice: Calendar of State Papers . . . existing in the archives . . . of Venice, ed. R. BROWN, 1864–73; final vol. 1940

LAFONTAINE, H. C. ed. *The King's Musick*, 1909

LANG, P. H. *Music in Western Civilization*, USA, 1941

La Tour-Landry: The Book of the Knight of La Tour-Landry, ed. T. WRIGHT, EETS, 1868

LELAND, JOHN. *De Rebus Britannicis Collectanea*, ed. T. HEARNE, second edn, 6 vols, 1770

LEWIS, C. S. *The Allegory of Love*, 1936
> *English Literature in the Sixteenth Century, excluding Drama*, 1954
> 'The Fifteenth-Century Heroic Line', *Essays and Studies*, xxiv, 1939

LHT: Lord High Treasurer's Accounts of Scotland, 1473–1507, ed. T. DICKSON and SIR J. B. PAUL, 11 vols, 1877–1916

Liber Usualis: Missae et Officii pro dominicis et festis cum cantu gregoriano, Paris, 1950

LUMSDEN, D. 'The Sources of English Lute Music (1540–1620)', unpublished dissertation for Ph.D. Cambridge, 1957

Lydgate: The Minor Poems of John Lydgate, ed. H. N. MacCRACKEN, 2 pts, EETS, 1911, 1934

MacCRACKEN, 'Suffolk': H. N. MacCRACKEN, 'An English Friend of Charles of Orléans', *PMLA*, xxvi, 1911

M&L: Music and Letters

MANLY, J. M. *Specimens of the Pre-Shakespearean Drama*, 2 vols, USA, 1897–8, 1900–3

MASON, H. A. *Humanism and Poetry in the Early Tudor Period*, 1959

MBviii: John Dunstable: Complete Works, ed. M. F. BUKOFZER, Musica Britannica, viii, 1953

MBxv: Music of Scotland, 1500–1700, ed. K. ELLIOTT and H. M. SHIRE, Musica Britannica, xv, 1957

MC: Medieval Carols, ed. JOHN STEVENS, Musica Britannica, iv, second edn, 1958

MCH8: Music at the Court of Henry VIII, ed. JOHN STEVENS, Musica Britannica, xviii, 1961

MILLER, C. K. 'A Fifteenth-Century Record of English Choir Repertory, BM Add. MS 5665.' Unpublished dissertation for Ph.D., Yale, 1948

MLN: Modern Language Notes

MLR: Modern Language Review

MOORE, A. K. *The Secular Lyric in Middle English*, USA, 1951

MORE, SIR THOMAS. *Utopia*, trs. RALPH ROBINSON, ed. G. SAMPSON, 1910

MORISON, S. *English Prayer Books*, 1949

MORLEY, THOMAS. *A Plain and Easy Introduction to Practical Music*, ed. R. A. HARMAN, with an introduction by T. DART, 1952

MQ: Musical Quarterly

MUIR, KENNETH. 'Unpublished Poems in the Devonshire MS', *Proceedings of Leeds Philosophical Society*, vi, 1947

Mulliner Book, The. ed. DENIS STEVENS, Musica Britannica, i, 1951

MUMFORD, IVY L. 'Musical Settings to the Poems of Sir Thomas Wyatt,' *M&L*, xxxvii, 1956

M[YERS], L. S. ed. *Music Cantelenas, Songs, etc* [CUL Add. 5943], 1906

NAGEL, W. *Annalen der englischen Hofmusik, 1509–1649*, Leipzig, 1894

NEILSON, W. A. *The Origins and Sources of 'The Court of Love'*, Studies and Notes in Philology and Literature, vi, USA, 1899

Norfolk HHB: Household Books of John Duke of Norfolk, and Thomas Earl of Surrey, ed. J. P. COLLIER, Roxburghe Club, 1844

Appendix D

Northumberland HHB: The Regulations and Establishment of Henry Algernon Percy, 5th Earl of Northumberland at his castles of Wresill and Lekinfield in Yorkshire, ed. T. PERCY, 1770

OED: The Oxford English Dictionary

OHM: The Oxford History of Music. Introductory vol., 1929; vol. ii (second edn), 1932

Ordinances: A Collection of Ordinances and Regulations for the Government of the Royal Household, Society of Antiquaries, 1790

PADELFORD, F. M. ed. 'The Songs in MS Rawlinson C.813', *Anglia,* xxxi, 1908

Pastime of Pleasure: STEPHEN HAWES. *The Pastime of Pleasure,* ed. W. E. MEAD, EETS, 1928

Paston Letters, The, ed. J. GAIRDNER, 6 vols, 1904

PATTISON, BRUCE. *Music and Poetry of the English Renaissance,* 1948

PERL, C. J. 'Augustine and Music', MQ, xli, 1955

PFATTEICHER, C. *John Redford,* Kassel, 1934

PIRRO, A. *Histoire de la Musique de la fin du XIVe siècle à la fin du XVIe,* Paris, 1940

PMLA: Publications of the Modern Language Society of America

PMMS 1891: A Collection of Songs and Madrigals of the 15th Century, ed. H. B. BRIGGS, Plainsong and Medieval Music Society, 1891

PMMS 1893: Madrigals by English Composers of the Close of the 15th Century, ed. H. B. BRIGGS, Plainsong and Medieval Music Society, 1893

PP Elizabeth: Privy Purse Expenses of Elizabeth of York, ed. N. H. NICOLAS, 1830

PP Henry VII: see *Excerpta Historica*

PP Henry VIII: Privy Purse Expenses of Henry VIII, 1529–32, ed. N. H. NICOLAS, 1827

PP Princess Mary: Privy Purse Expenses of Princess Mary, daughter of Henry VIII, ed. F. MADDEN, 1831

PRMA: Proceedings of the Royal Musical Association

PULVER, J. *A Biographical Dictionary of Old English Music,* 1927

PUTTENHAM, GEORGE. *The Arte of English Poesie,* ed. G. D. WILLCOCK and A. WALKER, 1936

RAWDON BROWN. *Four Years at the Court of Henry VIII: A Selection of Despatches written by the Venetian Ambassador,* trs. R. BROWN, 1854

REED, A. W. *Early Tudor Drama,* 1926

REED, E. B. ed. *Christmas Carols Printed in the Sixteenth Century,* Huntington Library Publications, 1932

    'The Sixteenth-century Lyrics in Add. MS 18752', *Anglia,* xxxiii, 1910

Reese, MMA: GUSTAVE REESE. *Music in the Middle Ages,* 1940

Reese, MR: GUSTAVE REESE. *Music in the Renaissance,* 1954

RES: Review of English Studies

'Revels Accounts of Richard Gibson' [summarized in *L&P,* ii, pt 2, pp. 1490 ff. (1510–18); *L&P,* iii, pt 2, pp. 1548 ff. (1519–22)]

REYHER, P. *Les Masques Anglais,* 1909

RHODES, HUGH. *The Boke of Nurture,* ed. F. J. FURNIVALL, Roxburghe Club, 1867

RIMBAULT, E. F. ed. *A Little Book of Songs and Ballads,* 1851

    Old Cheque Book of the Chapel Royal, 1561–1744, Camden Society, 1872

RITSON, J. ed. *Ancient Songs from the Time of Henry the Third to the Revolution,* 1790, 1829, 1877

    A Select Collection of English Songs, 3 vols, 2nd edn, 1813

Reference List of Books and Articles

ROBBINS, R. H. 'Middle English Carols as Processional Hymns,' *Studies in Philology*, lvi, 1959

'On the Medieval Religious Lyric', unpublished dissertation for Ph.D., Cambridge, 1937

ed. *Secular Lyrics of the Fourteenth and Fifteenth Centuries*, 1952

'The Findern Anthology', *PMLA*, lxix, 1954

'The Poems of Humfrey Newton, Esq., 1466–1536', *PMLA*, lxv, 1950

ROBINSON, F. N. ed.: see *Chaucer*

ROPER, WILLIAM. *The lyfe of Sir Thomas Moore, knighte*, ed. E. V. HITCHCOCK, EETS, 1935

ROSSITER, A. P. *English Drama from Early Times to the Elizabethans*, 1950

RUBEL, V. L. *Poetic Diction in the English Renaissance*, USA, 1941

RUSSELL, JOHN. *The Boke of Nurture folowyng Englondis gise*, ed. F. J. FURNIVALL, Roxburghe Club, 1867

SACHS, C. *The History of Musical Instruments*, 1942

SAHLIN, MARGIT. *Étude sur la carole médiévale*. Uppsala, 1940

SALTMARSH, J. 'Two Medieval Love-Songs set to Music', *Antiquaries' Journal*, xv, 1935

Sanuto: I Diarii di Marino Sanuto, 58 vols, 1879–

Sarum Hymnary: Hymnarium Sarisburiense, pars prima, London, 1851

SEATON, ETHEL. '"The Devonshire MS" and its Medieval Fragments', *RES*, n.s. vii, 1956

SHARP, THOMAS. *A Dissertation on the Pageants or Dramatic Mysteries anciently performed at Coventry*, 1825

SKEAT: *The Works of Geoffrey Chaucer*, ed. W. W. SKEAT, 7 vols, 1894–7

Skelton: The Poetical Works of John Skelton, ed. A. DYCE, 2 vols, 1843

The Complete Poems of John Skelton, ed. P. HENDERSON, 1931

STAFFORD SMITH, J. *A Collection of English Songs in Score for 3 and 4 Voices*, 1779

Musica Antiqua, 1812

Starkey: England in the Reign of Henry VIII: Part I, *Starkey's Life and Letters*, ed. S. J. HERRTAGE; Part II, *A Dialogue between Cardinal Pole and Thomas Lupset*, ed. J. M. COWPER, EETS, 1871–

STEVENS, DENIS. 'A Part-Book in the Public Record Office', *Music Survey*, ii, 1950

The Mulliner Book: A Commentary, 1952

STEVENS, JOHN. 'Carols and Court Songs of the Early Tudor Period'. *PRMA*, lxxvii, 1951

'Carol' [up to the Reformation] in *Grove (5)*

'The Elizabethan Madrigal: "Perfect Marriage" or "Uneasy Flirtation"', *Essays and Studies*, ed. B. WILLEY, 1958

'Hall, John', *Musik in Geschichte und Gegenwart*

'Music in Medieval Drama', *PRMA*, lxxxiv, 1958

'Rounds and Canons from an Early Tudor Song-Book', *M&L*, xxxii, 1951

STEVENSON, R. 'John Marbeck's "Noted Booke" of 1550', *MQ*, xxxvii, 1951

STRUTT, J. *The Sports and Pastimes of the People of England*, new ed. W. HONE, 1834

STOW, JOHN. *The Annales of England*, 1592

STS: The Scottish Text Society

Surrey: The Poems of Henry Howard, Earl of Surrey, ed. F. M. PADELFORD, USA, 1920

Surrey HHB: Household Books of John Duke of Norfolk, and Thomas Earl of Surrey, ed. J. P. COLLIER, Roxburghe Club, 1844

TCM: Tudor Church Music

Appendix D

Tottel: Tottel's Miscellany [Songs and Sonets], *1557–87*, ed. H. E. ROLLINS, 2 vols, USA, 1928–9

TOULOUZE: see COPLAND

TREFUSIS, LADY MARY, ed. *Songs, Ballads and Instrumental Pieces composed by King Henry the Eighth*, Roxburghe Club, 1912

UTLEY, F. L. *The Crooked Rib*, USA, 1944

WAGER, W. *The Longer thou livest, the more foole thou art*, 1569 [concerning Moros's speeches, see *Captain Cox*, p. cxxvii]

WAGNER, B. M. 'New Songs of the Reign of Henry VIII', *MLN*, l, 1935

WALLACE, C. W. *The Evolution of the English Drama up to Shakespeare*, Berlin, 1912

WARD, J. 'Music for *A Handefull of Plesant Delites*', *JAMS*, x, 1957
    'The "Dolfull Domps"', *JAMS*, iv, 1951

WELSFORD, E. *The Court Masque*, 1927

WICKHAM, GLYNNE. *Early English Stages, 1300–1660*. Volume I, *1300–1576*, 1959

WITHINGTON, R. *English Pageantry*, 2 vols, 1918–20

WOODFILL, W. L. *Musicians in English Society from Elizabeth to Charles I*, USA, 1953

Wriothesley's Chronicle, 1485–1559, ed. W. D. HAMILTON, Camden Society, 1875

Wyatt: Collected Poems of Sir Thomas Wyatt, ed. K. MUIR, 1949

York Plays. [An edition is forthcoming in the EETS, ed. ARTHUR BROWN]

ZUPITZA, J. ed. 'Die Gedichte des Franziskaners Jakob Ryman' [Cambridge, UL Ee.1.12], *Archiv*, lxxxix, 1892

Index

Index

Index

Index

Horman, William, 67

Hornpipe, 245, 261

Humanism, 67–70, 73–4, 114, 139, 152, 272, 287, 326

Hunnis, William, 309, 323, 325

Hymns, 41, 49, 52, 56–7, 60, 78, 83, 151

Improvisation, 63–4, 109, 121, 130, 138, 211–12, 257–8, 278, 281–2, 285–7, 289, 293, 311, 313

Instruments, musical, 4, 7, 21–2, 30, 59–60, 67–8, 70, 78–9, 82, 84, 109, 111–12, 126, 171, 235–44, 247, 249, 251, 255–7, 265–8, 274–7, 281, 283, 288–9, 292, 296, 298–9, 302, 306–9, 312–15, 318–320, 323–4, 330n., 331

Interludes, 47, 234, 244, 251–3, 252n., 255, 258, 261, 263, 290, 318, 322

Italy; *Italian Relation*; Italian music; etc., 30, 36, 39, 68, 70, 109–10, 133, 138, 147, 280–3, 287, 302, 308

James IV of Scotland, 166–8, 171, 236, 261, 268–9, 275–6, 279

Johan Johan, 258

Kele, Richard, 47

Keyboard instruments, 3, 7, 24, 267, 276, 302, 311–12, 319

Kingis Quhair, The, 164–5

King Johan, 255–6, 258

Kite, John, 121, 288, 319

Langland, William, 7

Latimer, William, 71

Latin, 5, 7, 14, 45–9, 75–7, 82–4, 109, 117–118, 241, 242n., 244, 274, 279, 303, 309, 323

Lee, Sir Antony, 118, 135

Leland, John, 134, 148, 166–8, 295, 317

Liber Niger, 273, 278, 302, 306, 309, 318

Litany, 49, 51–3, 52n., 53, 83

Liturgy, 7, 35, 50, 52n., 55, 76n., 79–80, 83–4, 86–7, 93, 151, 279

Longer Thou Livest, The, 53

Love problems, 162–3

Love-songs and love-poems, 5, 12–16, 18–20, 47, 91, 120, 122–3, 126, 148, 157–9, 161, 194, 205, 209, 211, 215–17, 220, 223, 223n., 224, 236

Lusty Juventus, 253–5

Lute, 7, 24, 27–8, 30, 32, 70, 72, 92, 109, 112, 120–3, 126–7, 130, 133–8, 143, 149, 238, 243, 245, 250–1, 253, 256, 266–9, 272, 274–82, 284, 301–2, 306–8, 311–14

Luther and Lutheranism, 60–4, 75, 77, 86–87, 89–90

Lydgate, John, 8–10, 108, 121, 125, 157, 161–2, 164, 183–4, 206–7, 225–6

Macaronic songs, 47

Machaut, 226

Madrigals, 36–8, 69, 71, 89, 91–2, 100, 103, 107, 109, 114, 136, 143, 283, 292, 334

Magnificence, 253

Malory, Sir Thomas, 187

Mankind, 256

Margaret, Princess, 166–7, 171, 236, 261, 268–9, 276

Marot, Clement, 85

Mary Queen of Scots, 280

Masks, 234, 246–8, 251–3, 260

Mass, The, 5, 37, 52, 62, 64, 75, 80, 83, 96, 129, 237, 279, 297, 310, 312–13

'Mayings' and May-games, 181–2, 184, 186–187, 243–4, 261, 279, 290, 311

Medwall, Thomas, 254, 256, 261

Melisma, 99–101, 104, 114, 215

Memo, Fra Dionisius, 265–6, 302, 307, 311, 319

Merbecke, John, 75, 83, 92, 95, 325

Metrical Psalms, *see* Psalms

Minstrels, 8, 35, 35n., 43, 49, 51, 109, 118–119, 168, 233, 236, 238, 240, 242–3, 245–6, 248–51, 256, 258, 267–8, 281–282, 296, 298–303, 306–8, 312–16, 318, 320, 322, 324, 326

Miracle Plays, 254

Morality Plays, 170, 287

More, Sir Thomas, 65, 68–70, 91–2, 143, 197, 234, 270, 276, 320–1

Index

Index

Index